FOURTH EDITION

PRINCIPLES OF MACROECONOMICS

Karl E. Case

WELLESLEY COLLEGE

Ray C. Fair

YALE UNIVERSITY

Prentice Hall, Inc., Upper Saddle River, New Jersey 07458

Library of Congress Cataloging in Publication Data

Case, Karl E.
    Principles of macroeconomics/Karl E. Case, Ray C. Fair.—
        4th ed.   656 p.   cm.
    Includes bibliographical references and index.
    ISBN 0-13-440843-8
    1. Macroeconomics. I. Fair, Ray C. II. Title.
HB172.5.C375 1995   95-39055
339—dc20   CIP

Editor-in-Chief: *Jim Boyd*
Executive Editor: *Leah Jewell*
Development Managing Editor: *Steven Rigolosi*
Assistant Editor: *Teresa Cohan*
Director of Production & Manufacturing: *Joanne Jay*
Production Liaison: *Anne Graydon*
Design Director: *Patricia Wosczyk*
Interior Design: *BB&K Design*
Cover Design: *Patricia Wosczyk*
Cover Art: *Theo Rudnak*
Manager of Production Services: *Lorraine Patsco*
Technical Art: *Warren Fishbach*
Manufacturing Buyers: *Marie McNamara and Vincent Scelta*
Marketing Manager: *Susan McLaughlin*
Photo Administration and Research: *Melinda Reo* and *Teri Stratford*
Editorial and Production Assistance: *Mary Beth Sanok* and *Renee Pelletier*
Supplements Development House: *O'Donnell & Associates*
Production House: *York Production Services*
Compositor: *York Graphic Services*
Printer: *VonHoffman Press*

Photo credits follow index.

 © 1996, 1994, 1992, 1989
by Prentice-Hall, Inc.
A Division of Simon & Schuster
Upper Saddle River, New Jersey 07458

Printed in the United States of America
10 9 8 7 6 5 4 3 2 1

ISBN 0-13-440843-8

Prentice Hall International (UK) Limited, *London.*
Prentice Hall of Australia Pty. Limited, *Sydney*
Prentice Hall Canada Inc., *Toronto*
Prentice Hall Hispanoamericana, S.A., *Mexico*
Prentice Hall of India Private Limited, *New Delhi*
Prentice Hall of Japan, Inc., *Tokyo*
Simon & Schuster Asia Pte. Ltd., *Singapore*
Editora Prentice Hall do Brasil, Ltda., *Rio de Janeiro*

BRIEF TABLE OF CONTENTS

CONTENTS

GLOBAL COVERAGE

Because the study of economics crosses national boundaries, this book includes international examples in almost every chapter. The following list is a summary of global examples and discussions in the text.

GLOBAL COVERAGE

This textbook contains the five introductory chapters, 15 macroeconomics chapters, and the four international chapters from our hardbound *Principles of Economics* textbook. It has been specially prepared for macroeconomics courses where professors prefer to assign a paperback "split" rather than a single volume containing coverage of both microeconomics and macroeconomics.

So that users of this book and its companion volume, *Principles of Microeconomics,* can fully understand our methodology in preparing the fourth edition, what follows is an adaption of the preface as it appears in our single hardbound volume.

The process of revising a principles of economics text reveals dramatically how rapidly the world changes. When our first edition was published in 1989, the Berlin Wall had not yet fallen, the Cold War still raged, and Iraq had not yet invaded Kuwait. By the time our third edition was published in 1994, the disintegration of the Soviet Union had given way to a new administration in Washington, a jobless recovery from the recession of 1990–1991, a new tax act, and chaos in Eastern Europe. A year and a half later, the jobless recovery turned into an expansion that the Federal Reserve began trying to slow. The Japanese yen and the German mark appreciated beyond anyone's expectations, NAFTA and GATT were ratified, Mexico did a 180-degree turnaround, and the emerging democracies of central Europe began growing while Russia struggled with the privatization process.

Because events have changed the economic landscape so rapidly, we decided to revise *Principles of Macroeconomics* after two years instead of the usual three. All tables and figures have been updated with the most recent data available, and the case studies (with accompanying videos) that end each part are completely new. And while we continue to cover the core of economic theory, we have added new material on important topics that have only recently emerged as major economic issues. These include the Fed's anti-inflationary responses to a growing economy, the potential effects of balanced-budget legislation, several countries' recent problems with currency debasement and volatile exchange rates, the new trade treaties, and the experiences of transitional economies.

In addition, the fourth edition contains more international material than any previous edition. Almost every chapter contains a global application or example. (A complete list of global examples follows the detailed table of contents.) We've also added additional problems to the end of each chapter and included solutions to the even-numbered problems at the end of the text.

To date, more than 100,000 students and professors have used *Principles of Economics* or one of its split volumes. In this new edition, we have made every effort to be responsive to our readers' suggestions while maintaining the book's basic focus and pedagogical organization. To make the book accessible to a wider range of students, we have cut a great deal of extraneous material, simplified several of the more analytical sections, and redrawn many of the more technical graphs using real numbers rather than variable names. And, to make the book more appealing to today's visual learners, we've completely revised the art, photo, and illustration program. The result, we hope, is a principles book that students will keep on their shelves and use throughout college and beyond.

THE PLAN OF *PRINCIPLES OF MACROECONOMICS*

Despite major revisions and new features, the themes of the fourth edition are the same themes of the first three editions. The purpose of this book is to introduce the discipline of economics and to provide a basic understanding of how economies function. This requires a blend of economic theory, institutional material, and real-world applications. We have tried to maintain a reasonable balance between these ingredients in every chapter in this book. Like the first three editions, the fourth edition also attempts to present different theoretical views in an evenhanded way.

As in the third edition, we remain committed to the view that it is a mistake simply to throw aggregate demand and aggregate supply curves at students in the first few chapters of a principles book. To understand the AS and AD curves, one needs to know about the functioning of the goods market and the money market. The logic behind the simple demand curve is simply wrong when applied to the relationship between aggregate demand and the price level. Similarly, the logic behind the simple supply curve is wrong when applied to the relationship between aggregate supply and the price level.

Part of teaching economics is teaching economic reasoning. Our discipline is built around deductive logic. Once we teach students a pattern of logic, we want and expect them to apply it to new circumstances. When they apply the logic of a simple demand curve or simple supply curve to the aggregate demand or aggregate supply curve, the logic does not fit. We believe the best way to teach the reasoning embodied in the aggregate demand and aggregate supply curves without creating serious confusion is to build up to them carefully.

Organization Like the third edition of *Principles of Macroeconomics*, the macroeconomics section of the fourth edition begins with three introductory chapters (6–8) that introduce students to macroeconomic tools, national income accounting, and inflation and unemployment (both in the United States and abroad). These chapters are followed by two chapters that present the basic functioning of the goods market (Chapters 9 and 10) and two chapters that present the basic functioning of the money market (Chapters 11 and 12). It is in these four chapters that students are introduced to the concepts of fiscal and monetary policy. These chapters are followed by a chapter that brings the two markets together. This chapter, Chapter 13, does in essence a very simplified version of *IS/LM* analysis verbally. (The *IS* and *LM* curves are included in an appendix to Chapter 13 for those instructors who are interested in teaching them.)

Given the groundwork that has been laid in Chapter 13, Chapter 14 proceeds directly to derive the aggregate demand curve and then the aggregate supply curve. The two curves are then put together to determine the aggregate price level and to discuss the various theories of inflation.

Following the development of the *AD* and *AS* curves, we turn to a more detailed look at the labor market in Chapter 15 and discuss various theories of unemployment. By the end of Chapter 15, students have put the goods market, the money market, and the labor market together, and they have analyzed inflation, unemployment, and monetary and fiscal policy. Chapter 16 uses the material learned earlier to analyze a number of current macroeconomic issues, including proposed balanced-budget legislation and business cycles in Europe and Asia.

In Chapter 17, we take a closer look at the behavior of households and firms in the macroeconomy, and in Chapter 18 we use the material in Chapter 17 to analyze further macroeconomic issues. Chapters 17 and 18 have been grouped into an optional part that can be skipped without losing the flow of the material. We close the macro section of the book by looking at some current debates in macroeconomics (Chapter 19) and economic growth and productivity (Chapter 20). We then consider international economics in more detail in Chapters 21–24.

Content In preparing the fourth edition, we have maintained two innovations we introduced in the second edition. The first is the treatment of aggregate supply. Clearly, there is strong disagreement among economists and across economics textbooks on the exact nature of the aggregate supply curve. All economists agree that if input prices rise at the same rate as output prices, the aggregate supply curve is vertical; firms have no incentive to change output if their costs and revenues change at the same rate. For the *AS* curve to have a positive slope in the short run, input prices must either be constant or there must be some lag in their adjustment.

Some textbooks assume that input prices are constant when the overall price level changes, essentially treating the aggregate supply curve as if it were the sum of individual market supply curves. This assumption of constant input prices is obviously unrealistic, and in the second edition we changed our description of the short-run *AS* curve to one that assumes some lag in input price adjustment when the overall price level changes. In addition, we clarified and expanded our description of the long-run aggregate supply curve, incorporating the concept of potential GDP.

Second, we continue to distinguish between inflation (a change in the overall price level) and *sustained* inflation (an increase in the overall price level that continues for some period of time). There can be confusion in students' minds as to what inflation is and whether or not it is a purely monetary phenomenon, and we think that this distinction helps to clarify our discussions.

THE PLAN OF *PRINCIPLES OF MICROECONOMICS*

For professors who are teaching microeconomics, a new version of *Principles of Microeconomics* is also available.

Market research and comments from users of the third edition convinced us that the organization of the microeconomic material is pedagogically sound. For this reason, we have not altered the presentation drastically in the fourth edition of *Principles of Microeconomics*.

The organization of the microeconomic material continues to reflect our belief that the best way to understand how market economies operate—and the best way to understand basic economic theory—is to work through the perfectly competitive model first, including discussions of output *and* input markets and the connections between them, before turning to noncompetitive market structures. When students understand how a simple competitive system works, they can start thinking about how the pieces of the economy "fit together." We think this is a better approach to teaching economics than some of the more traditional approaches, which encourage students to think of economics as a series of disconnected alternative market models.

Doing competition first also allows students to see the power of the market system. It is impossible to discuss the things that markets do well until students have seen how a simple system determines the allocation of resources. This is our purpose in Chapters 6–11. Chapter 12 remains a pivotal chapter that links the world of perfect competition with the imperfect world of noncompetitive markets, externalities, imperfect information, and poverty, all of which we discuss in Chapters 13–17. In Chapters 18–20 students use everything they've learned in Chapters 6–17 to take a closer look at some of the fields of applied microeconomics (the economics of taxation, labor economics, and the economics of health-care reform, immigration, and urban problems). Finally, in Chapters 21–24, we examine some topics in international economics. Although we've chosen to place these chapters at the end of the book, professors can integrate them into their course at any time they feel is appropriate.

We do microeconomics first in the combined volume but have crafted the fourth edition so that professors can proceed directly to either microeconomics or macroeconomics after teaching the five introductory chapters.

HIGHLIGHTS OF THE FOURTH EDITION OF *PRINCIPLES OF MACROECONOMICS*

RECENT DATA, EXAMPLES, EVENTS, AND TOPICS

Every chart, table, and graph in the book has been revised with the most recent data available. In addition, we have integrated topics that have generated a great deal of attention over the last few years—the recession of 1990–1991 and the recovery from it; the national debt;

the European Union, NAFTA, and APEC; and the recent experiences of Poland and Russia, to name just a few.

THE BEA'S NEW PROCEDURE

The Bureau of Economic Analysis (BEA) made a major change at the end of 1995 in its presentation of the national income and product accounts. The focus is no longer on constant-dollar magnitudes and on implicit price deflators, but instead on "chain-type annual weights" quantity and price indexes. This change is much more important than the BEA's change in focus a few years ago from GNP to GDP. Fortunately, we knew about this change in time to incorporate it into the book. (The "new" data have in fact been available in Table 7.1 in the *Survey of Current Business* for a few years.) The BEA's new procedure is carefully explained in Chapter 7, and we no longer refer anywhere in the text to real variables being in constant dollars and to implicit price deflators. The real magnitudes in the figures are the chain-type annual weights quantity indexes, and the prices are the chain-type annual weights price indexes. We also focus on growth rates in the discussion in the text, since this is now the focus of the BEA.

INCREASED COVERAGE OF INTERNATIONAL MATERIAL

We have increased our coverage of international material in three ways. First, we have added many new "Global Perspective" boxes throughout the text. These boxes are designed to illustrate economic logic with global examples and to emphasize today's global economy. Second, we introduce imports and exports into the simple goods market model early in macroeconomics. (We do, however, continue to believe that a complete treatment of open market macroeconomics should not be taught until students have mastered the logic of a simple closed macroeconomy. For this reason, we have chosen to place the "open-economy macro" chapter in International Economics, the final section of the book.) Finally, we have integrated international examples directly into the text whenever appropriate. All international examples are listed in a table following the book's detailed table of contents.

OPTIONAL CHAPTERS

We have tried to keep uppermost in our minds that time is always tight in a principles course. For this reason, we have made sure that certain chapters can be skipped without losing the flow of the material. Chapters 17-20 are optional. The chapters in the international section, with the exception of Chapter 22, can be taught at any time that the instructor deems appropriate.

STUDENT LEARNING AIDS

Each chapter begins with a brief overview of what the student has learned in the previous chapter and ends with a brief "look ahead" to the following chapter. To help students study, key terms have been printed in boldface and glossed to the margins. Each chapter ends with a point-by-point summary of the chapter, a list of review terms and concepts (cross-referenced to text page), and a problem set.

Because many believe that economics must be relevant to be interesting, we have created three types of boxes for the fourth edition. *Global Perspective* boxes provide economic examples from around the world. *Application* boxes apply the theory learned in the text to real-world events and situations. *Issues and Controversies* boxes examine many of the economic issues currently under debate.

In addition, we have set the major principles of economics off from the text in such a way as to highlight their importance. These highlights flow logically from the preceding text and into the text that follows. Students tell us that they find these very useful as a way of reviewing the key points in each chapter to prepare for exams.

PROBLEM SETS AND SOLUTIONS

Each chapter and appendix ends with a problem set that asks students to think about what they've learned in the chapter. These problems are not simple memorization questions. Rather, they ask students to perform graphical analysis or to apply economics to a real-world situation or policy decision. Approximately 40% of the problems are new to this edition. More challenging problems are indicated by an asterisk. The solutions to all even-numbered problems appear at the back of the book. The solutions to all odd-numbered problems, as well as additional problem sets, are available in the Instructor's Resource Manual.

CASE STUDIES

The end-of-part case studies introduced in the second edition proved to be quite popular. The fourth edition features seven new case studies on topics ranging from the international cellular telephone industry to the Venezuelan banking crisis. Each case study is accompanied by a video and questions for analytical thinking. The cases are not simply additional problems, and they are not simple extensions of the text material. They are meant to be applications of some of the *ideas* that the part was designed to teach and are designed to foster critical thinking and "thinking like an economist." They might be used as assignments or for class discussion.

THE TEACHING/LEARNING PACKAGE

Each component of the teaching and learning package has been carefully crafted to ensure that the principles of economics course is a rewarding experience for both instructors and students. All of the supplements have been significantly revised for the fourth edition. In addition, several innovative new supplements are available. To see a sample chapter from each of the ancillaries, ask your sales representative for a Case/Fair supplements sampler.

ECONOMICS EXPLORER MULTIMEDIA SOFTWARE/CD-ROM *(New!)*

The Economics Explorer software/CD-ROM—created by Logal Educational Software with the assistance of Steven Tomlinson of the University of Texas at Austin—combines video, animation, and spreadsheets to create the most powerful instructional software available. Logal has taken the basic economic models from the textbook and created a series of dynamic, interactive simulations that bring economics to life and helps students visualize how math, graphs, and economic intuition are connected.

Economics Explorer comes with 24 prepared labs, each one based on a key economics concept: the multiplier effect, profit maximization, market clearing, and so forth. Within each lab, an instructor introduces the concept with a mini-lecture illustrated with animated charts and graphs, manipulable equations, and film clips tying the concept to the "real world." The instructor then shows the student how to use the economic simulation to solve a problem from the textbook. Students can manipulate the model by entering numbers in equations, shifting curves in graphs, or adjusting values in circular flow diagrams.

Once students have learned to use the simulation, they will want to design their own experiments and test their own conjectures. Playing with Explorer, students can test the limits of economic models, input their own data to recreate events from economic history, and (using Explorer's spreadsheet capabilities) record the results and display them in graphs like those from their textbook. By clicking icons, students can move quickly to any point in a lab or, if they want a quick review, to any topic in the series.

Instructors can use the prepared labs or customize their own exercises using Explorer's user-friendly design tools. The accompanying Instructor's Guide also provides tips for integrating Economics Explorer into your course and using Explorer to add power to classroom presentations.

The Explorer is much more than a computerized study guide. It's a fun, flexible program that takes full advantage of computer power to help students with diverse learning styles visualize economics.

STUDY GUIDES

A comprehensive study guide has been prepared by Thomas Beveridge of North Carolina State University. This study aid reinforces the textbook and provides students with additional applications and exercises. Each chapter in the Study Guide corresponds to a chapter in the textbook and contains the following features:

• **Point-by-Point Objectives:** A list of learning goals for the chapter, along with a brief summary of the material, helpful study hints, practice questions with solutions, and page references to the text.

• **Exercises and Problem Sets:** A series of questions that require the use of graphic or numerical analysis to solve economic problems. Also includes problems that present real-world situations and ask students to apply economic theory to their own experiences.

• **Practice Tests:** A series of multiple-choice, short-answer, discussion, and application questions designed to test students' grasp of the material and help them prepare for exams.

• **Solutions:** Complete solutions—not just answers—to all questions in the Study Guide, complete with page references to the text.

In addition, the Study Guide contains an introductory section (by Steven Pitts of Houston Community College)

that guides students through graphing techniques. "Graphing Pitfalls" sections in selected chapters feature additional tips and insights for students as they learn the graphical material in that chapter.

INSTRUCTOR'S RESOURCE MANUAL

An innovative instructor's resource manual, by Patricia Euzent of the University of Central Florida, is available. The Instructor's Resource Manual (IRM) is the key integrative supplement in the teaching and learning package and has been designed with the *teaching* of economics in mind. Each chapter in the instructor's manual corresponds to a chapter in the student text and includes suggestions for integrating all of the elements (both printed and electronic) of the teaching/learning package into the classroom. The manual also includes chapter outlines with key terminology; teaching notes and lecture suggestions that provide ideas for applying theory, reinforcing key concepts, overcoming student misconceptions, initiating classroom discussion, and integrating outside readings and global examples into the lecture; additional problems with solutions; solutions to all odd-numbered problems in the text; and solutions to all the analytical thinking questions that accompany the book's seven case studies.

The IRM includes a new section not in the previous edition. *Extended Applications for Teaching Economics* is a collection of instructors' favorite ideas, exercises, activities, experiments, and games that help economics come alive.

TEST ITEM FILE

The Case/Fair complete test item file is revised, expanded, and comprehensive test bank of approximately 2400 short-answer/essay, multiple-choice, true/false, and problem set questions. The questions are divided into three levels of difficulty—easy, moderate, and difficult—and are page-referenced to the text. Problem sets (a series of questions based on a graph or scenario) can contain all three levels. Also included are challenging questions that require students to undertake several steps of reasoning, or to work backwards from effect to cause. The test item file is available in printed and electronic (word processing) formats.

PRENTICE HALL CUSTOM TEST

The test item file is designed for use with the Prentice Hall Custom Test, a computerized package that allows users to custom design, save, and generate classroom tests. The test program (which runs on DOS-based computers) permits professors to edit and add or delete questions from the test item file, to edit existing graphics and create new graphics, and to export files to various word processing programs, including WordPerfect and Microsoft Word. Graphics capability ensures that all graphs included in the test item file can be printed next to the appropriate questions.

For those with limited access to computers or secretarial support, Prentice Hall's Telephone Testing Service allows professors to order customized tests by calling a toll-free telephone number a few days before the test is to be administered. Additional information about the various forms of testing service can be obtained from your Prentice Hall sales representative.

REAL-WORLD PROBLEM SETS *(New!)*

This new ancillary, prepared by a team of four authors—Tom Beveridge (North Carolina State University), Lori Dickes (University of Central Florida), Ken Parzych (Eastern Connecticut State University), and Dennis Placone (Clemson University)—for *Principles of Macroeconomics,* provides over 1000 all-new questions that focus on analysis and problem solving. Created to provide the instructor with an additional testing resource and available in both printed and electronic formats, the Real-World Problem Sets can be used as quiz/testing tools or as homework problems.

Each problem set is based on current events and/or newspaper or magazine clippings. Students are asked to analyze a scenario or minicase, draw or interpret graphs, and answer questions. Solutions are provided for each problem.

TRANSPARENCY RESOURCE PACKAGE WITH POWERPOINT TRANSPARENCIES

There are more than 300 graphs and charts in the combined *Principles of Economics* text. The Transparency Resource Package, prepared by Kathy Nantz of Fairfield University and Beth Ingram of Iowa State University, includes reproductions of 130 key text graphs on full-color 8 1/2" x 11" acetates for classroom use. Each acetate is accompanied by lecture notes.

Also included is a series of PowerPoint presentations that summarize concepts and theories, emphasize problem solving, provide visual support for lectures, and show the relevance of economics. The

PowerPoint disk also includes additional sets of time-series data (not included in the textbook), drawn from a variety of sources. Lecture notes include a snapshot of each PowerPoint slide, provide lecture suggestions and discussion questions, and help instructors correlate the slides with the text and their classroom presentations.

ABC/PRENTICE HALL VIDEO LIBRARY FOR *PRINCIPLES OF ECONOMICS*

ABC News and Prentice Hall have combined their experience in academic publishing and global reporting to provide a comprehensive video ancillary to the fourth edition. The library contains 30 news clips from the ABC News programs *Nightline, World News Tonight, Business World,* and *This Week with David Brinkley.* Each of the clips has been chosen to illustrate or supplement a specific discussion in the text. All the videos are timely or timeless, and many can be used at different points in the course. The Video Guide provides suggestions on where and how to integrate each video.

VIDEO GUIDE

The integrated *Video Guide* (prepared by Steven Tomlinson of the University of Texas at Austin) includes a summary of each of the video clips in the Video Library. For each video, the Video Guide includes running time, teaching notes, and in-class exercises.

THE NEW YORK TIMES "THEMES OF THE TIMES" PROGRAM

The New York Times and Prentice Hall are sponsoring "Themes of the Times": a program designed to enhance student access to current information of relevance in the classroom.

Through this program, the core subject matter provided in the text is supplemented by a collection of articles from one of the world's most distinguished newspapers, *The New York Times.* These articles demonstrate the vital, ongoing connections between what is learned in the classroom and what is happening in the world around us.

A new edition of the mini-newspaper is available annually and is provided free to students upon adoption. For students and professors who want to enjoy the wealth of information of *The New York Times* daily, a reduced subscription rate is available in deliverable areas. For information, call toll-free: 1-800-631-1222.

PRINCIPLES OF ECONOMICS SOFTWARE AND WORKBOOK

Working with Microsoft Excel for Windows, the *Principles of Economics* software and workbook allow students to solve problems and create and analyze graphs without getting bogged down in calculations. Prepared by Ray Whitman of the University of the District of Columbia, the software/workbook teaches students how to use Excel with an easy-to-use tutorial. Once they've mastered the basics, students then work with a series of problems built around key economic concepts. Many of the problems are based on text or Study Guide problem sets. Students enter and manipulate data, draft and shift graphs, and answer questions regarding what has happened. Solutions to all exercises are provided at the end of each chapter.

ACKNOWLEDGMENTS

We are grateful to many people for help on the fourth edition. As was the case for the third edition, we are most grateful to Steven Rigolosi, Managing Editor of Development for Business and Economics at Prentice Hall, for overseeing the entire project. The quality of the book owes much to his wise guidance. Joe Boyer proofread the entire manuscript in pages. We also owe much to Leah Jewell, Executive Editor for Economics at Prentice Hall, for her help and enthusiasm.

We are greatly indebted to the supplements team for their help in preparing the teaching/learning package that accompanies the text. Specifically, we would like to thank Tom Beveridge, Steven Tomlinson, Ray Whitman, Dereka Rushbrook, Joseph Ricciardi, Pat Euzent, Kathy Nantz, Beth Ingram, Steven Pitts, Chris Colburn, Lori Dickes, Ken Parzych, and Dennis Placone. We'd also like to thank Carrie O'Donnell, Michele Fitzpatrick, and especially Pamela Barter of O'Donnell and Associates for their help in managing the development of the supplements. We have benefited enormously from working with this dedicated team of professionals.

For their much-appreciated input into *Principles of Microeconomics*, we'd like to thank Richard Duboff of Bryn Mawr and Mark Killingsworth of Rutgers University. We are also indebted to Sarah Bay, Elena Ranguelova, Jack Triplett of the BEA, and Susan Skeath.

A great deal of credit also goes to the many "behind-the-scenes" people at Prentice Hall who helped us prepare the fourth edition. We'd like to thank Anne Graydon, our production liaison and Kirsten Kauffman from the production house; Teri Stratford, photo researcher, for her first-class photos; Theo Rudnak for the cover illustration; Lorraine Patsco, John Nestor, and Warren Fischbach for their help in preparing the art for this edition; Mary Beth Sanok, Kristen Kaiser, and Renée Pelletier, editorial assistants, who helped us in innumerable ways; and Susan McLaughlin, marketing manager, for her enthusiasm and verve. Special thanks go to Teresa Cohan, assistant editor, for her dedication in pulling the many components of this project together.

We also owe a debt of gratitude to those who reviewed the third edition and provided us with valuable insight as we prepared the new edition:

- William T. Bogart, Case Western Reserve University
- David Buffum, College of the Holy Cross
- Ronald Crowe, University of Central Florida
- David Culp, Slippery Rock University
- Richard Duboff, Bryn Mawr College
- Ramzi Frangul, Sacred Heart University
- Roy T. Gobin, Loyola University of Chicago
- Mark Killingsworth, Rutgers University
- Gary F. Langer, Roosevelt University
- Gabriel Manrique, Winona State University
- David Merriman, Loyola University of Chicago
- Joanna Moss, San Francisco State University
- John R. Neill, Western Michigan University
- Jan Palmer, Ohio University
- Martin T. Pond, Purdue University
- Susan Porter-Hudak, Northern Illinois University
- Ruth Shen, San Francisco State University
- John Sullivan, Raritan Valley Community College
- Mohammed Zaheer, Manchester Community Technical College

Last, but not least, the following individuals were of immense help in reviewing all or part of this book and the teaching/learning package in various stages of development:

Lew Abernathy, University of North Texas • Jack Adams, University of Maryland • Doulas Agbetsiafa, Indiana University at South Bend • Sam Alapati, Rutgers University • Polly Allen, University of Connecticut • Stuart Allen, University of North Carolina at Greensboro • Jim Angresano, Hampton-Sydney College • Kenneth S. Arakelian, University of Rhode Island • Harvey Arnold, Indian River Community College • Nick Apergis, Fordham University • Kidane

Asmeron, Pennsylvania State University • James Aylesworth, Lakeland Community College • Kari Battaglia, University of North Texas • Daniel K. Benjamin, Clemson University • Bruce Bolnick, Northeastern University • G. E. Breger, University of South Carolina • Dennis Brennan, William Rainey Harper Junior College • Lindsay Caulkins, John Carroll University • Atreya Chakraborty, Boston College • Harold Christensen, Centenary College • Daniel Christiansen, Albion College • Samuel Kim-Liang Chuah, Walla Walla College • David Colander, Middlebury College • Daniel Condon, University of Illinois at Chicago; Moraine Valley Community College • David Cowen, University of Texas at Austin • Michael Donihue, Colby College • Robert Driskill, Ohio State University • Gary Dymski, University of Southern California • Jay Egger, Towson State University • Noel J. J. Farley, Bryn Mawr College • Mosin Farminesh, Temple University • Dan Feaster, Miami University of Ohio • Susan Feiner, Virginia Commonwealth University • Getachew Felleke, Albright College • Lois Fenske, South Puget Sound Community College • William Field, DePauw University • Bill Foeller, State University of New York at Fredonia • Roger Nils Folsom, San Jose State University • Sean Fraley, College of Mount Saint Joseph • N. Galloro, Chabot College • Tom Gausman, Northern Illinois University, DeKalb • Shirley J. Gedeon, University of Vermont • Gary Gigliotti, Rutgers University • Lynn Gillette, Texas A&M University • Sarah L. Glavin, Boston College • Devra Golbe, Hunter College • Roger Goldberg, Ohio Northern University • Douglas Greenley, Moorhead State University • Lisa M. Grobar, California State University at Long Beach • Benjamin Gutierrez, Indiana University at Bloomington • A. R. Gutowsky, California State University at Sacramento • David R. Hakes, University of Missouri at St. Louis • Stephen Happel, Arizona State University • Mitchell Harwitz, State University of New York at Buffalo • David Hoaas, Centenary College • Harry Holzer, Michigan State University • Bobbie Horn, University of Tulsa • John Horowitz, Ball State University • Janet Hunt, University of Georgia • Fred Inaba, Washington State University • Richard Inman, Boston College • Shirley Johnson, Vassar College • Farhoud Kafi, Babson College • R. Kallen, Roosevelt University • Arthur E. Kartman, San Diego State University • Hirshel Kasper, Oberlin College • Bruce Kaufman, Georgia State University • Dominique Khactu, The University of North Dakota • Phillip King, San Francisco State University • Barbara Kneeshaw, Wayne County Community College • Barry Kotlove, Elmira College • David Kraybill, University of Georgia at Athens • Rosung Kwak, University of Texas at Austin • Melissa Lam, Wellesley College • Jim Lee, Fort Hays State University • Judy Lee, Leeward Community College • Gary Lemon, DePauw University • Alan Leonard, Northern Illinois University • George Lieu, Tuskegee University • Stephen E. Lile, Western Kentucky University • Jane Lillydahl, University of Colorado at Boulder • Al Link, University of North Carolina at Greensboro • Robert Litro, U.S. Air Force Academy, Wallingford, CT • Burl F. Long, University of Florida • Gerald Lynch, Purdue University • Karla Lynch, University of North Texas • Michael Magura, University of Toledo • Don Maxwell, Central State University • Nan Maxwell, California State University at Hayward • J. Harold McClure, Jr., Villanova University • Rick McIntyre, University of Rhode Island • K. Mehtaboin, College of St. Rose • Shahruz Mohtadi, Suffolk University • Joe L. Moore, Arkansas Technical University • Robert Moore, Occidental College • Doug Morgan, University of California at Santa Barbara • Norma C. Morgan, Curry College • John Murphy, North Shore Community College, Massachusetts • Veena Nayak, State University of New York at Buffalo • Randy Nelson, Colby College • David Nickerson, University of British Columbia • Rachel Nugent, Pacific Lutheran University • Akorlie A. Nyatepe-Coo, University of Wisconsin at LaCrosse • Norman P. Obst, Michigan State University • William C. O'Connor, Western Montana College • Kent Olson, Oklahoma State University • Carl Parker, Fort Hays State University • Spirog Patton, Neumann College • Tony Pizelo, Spokane Community College • Michael Rendich, Westchester Community College • Lynn Rittenoure, University of Tulsa • David C. Rose, University of Missouri at St. Louis • Richard Rosenberg, Pennsylvania State University • Mark Rush, University of Florida at Gainesville • Dereka Rushbrook, Ripon College • David L. Schaffer, Haverford College • Gary Sellers, University of Akron • Jean Shackleford, Bucknell University • Linda Shaffer, California State University at Fresno • Geoff Shepherd, University of Massachusetts at Amherst • Bih-Hay Sheu, University of Texas at Austin • Alden Shiers, California Polytechnic State University • Sue Skeath, Wellesley College • Paula Smith, Central State University, Oklahoma • John Solow, University of Iowa at Iowa City • Dusan Stojanovic, Washington University, St. Louis • Ernst W. Stromsdorfer, Washington State University • Michael Taussig, Rutgers University • Timothy Taylor, Stanford University • Sister Beth Anne Tercek, SND, Notre Dame College of Ohio • Jack Trierweler, Northern State University • Brian M. Trinque, University of Texas at Austin • Ann Velenchik, Wellesley College • Chris Waller, Indiana University at Bloomington • Walter Wessels, North Carolina State University • Joan Whalen-Ayyappan, DeVry Institute of Technology • Robert Whaples, Wake Forest University • Leonard A. White, University of Arkansas • Abera Zeyege, Ball State University • James Ziliak, Indiana University at Bloomington

We welcome comments about the fourth edition. Please write to us care of Economics Editor, Prentice Hall Higher Education Division, One Lake Street, Upper Saddle River, N.J. 07458.

Karl E. Case

Ray C. Fair

Save a Tree!

Many of the components of the teaching and learning package are available in electronic format. Disk-based supplements conserve paper and allow you to select and print only the material you plan to use. For more information, please ask your Prentice Hall sales representative.

ABOUT THE AUTHORS

Karl E. Case

is the Marion Butler McLean Professor in the History of Ideas and Professor of Economics at Wellesley College. He also lectures on Economics and Tax Policy in the International Tax Program at Harvard Law School and is a Visiting Scholar at the Federal Reserve Bank of Boston. He received his B.A. from Miami University in 1968, spent three years in the army, and received his M.A. and Ph.D. from Harvard University. In 1980 and 1981 he was a Liberal Arts Fellow in Law and Economics at Harvard Law School.

Professor Case's research has been in the areas of public finance, taxation, and housing. He is the author or coauthor of four other books, including *Economics and Tax Policy* and *Property Taxation: The Need for Reform,* as well as numerous articles in professional journals.

For the past 18 years, he has taught at Wellesley, where he was Department Chair from 1982 to 1985. Before coming to Wellesley, he spent two years as Head Tutor (director of undergraduate studies) at Harvard, where he won the Allyn Young Teaching Prize. He has been a member of the AEA's Committee on Economic Education and was Associate Editor of the *Journal of Economic Education*, responsible for the section on innovations in teaching. He teaches at least one section of the principles course every year.

Ray C. Fair

is Professor of Economics at Yale University. He is a member of the Cowles Foundation at Yale and a Fellow of the Econometric Society. He received a B.A. in economics from Fresno State College in 1964 and a Ph.D. in economics from M.I.T. in 1968. He taught at Princeton University from 1968 to 1974 and has been at Yale since 1974.

Professor Fair's research has primarily been in the areas of macroeconomics and econometrics, with particular emphasis on macroeconometric model building. His publications include *Specification, Estimation, and Analysis of Macroeconometric Models* (Harvard Press, 1984) and *Testing Macroeconometric Models* (Harvard Press, 1994).

Professor Fair has taught introductory and intermediate economics at Yale. He has also taught graduate courses in macroeconomic theory and macroeconometrics.

FOURTH EDITION

PRINCIPLES OF MACROECONOMICS

INTRODUCTION

PART ONE

INTRODUCTION TO ECONOMICS

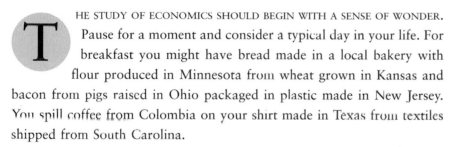

THE SCOPE AND METHOD OF ECONOMICS

THE STUDY OF ECONOMICS SHOULD BEGIN WITH A SENSE OF WONDER. Pause for a moment and consider a typical day in your life. For breakfast you might have bread made in a local bakery with flour produced in Minnesota from wheat grown in Kansas and bacon from pigs raised in Ohio packaged in plastic made in New Jersey. You spill coffee from Colombia on your shirt made in Texas from textiles shipped from South Carolina.

After class you drive with a friend in a Japanese car on an interstate highway system that took 20 years and billions of dollars worth of resources to build. You stop for gasoline refined in Louisiana from Saudi Arabian crude oil brought to the United States on a supertanker that took three years to build at a shipyard in Maine.

At night you call your brother in Mexico City. The call travels over fiber-optic cable to a powerful antenna that sends it to a transponder on one of over 1,000 communications satellites orbiting the earth.

You use or consume tens of thousands of things, both tangible and intangible, every day: buildings, the music of a rock band, the compact disc it is recorded on, telephone services, staples, paper, toothpaste, tweezers, soap, a digital watch, fire protection, antacid tablets, beer, banks, electricity, eggs, insurance, football fields, computers, buses, rugs, subways, health services, sidewalks, and so forth. Somebody made all these things. Somebody decided to organize men and women and materials to produce them and distribute them. Thousands of decisions went into their completion. Somehow they got to you.

One hundred twenty-three million people in the United States—almost half the total population—work at hundreds of thousands of different kinds of jobs producing nearly seven trillion dollars' worth of goods and services every year. Some cannot find work; some choose not to work. Some are rich; others are poor.

The United States imports between $50 billion and $60 billion worth of petroleum and petroleum products each year and exports around $40 billion worth of agricultural products, including food. High-rise office buildings go up in central cities. Condominiums and homes are built in the suburbs. In other places homes are abandoned and boarded up.

Some countries are wealthy. Others are impoverished. Some are growing. Some are stagnating. Some businesses are doing well. Others are going bankrupt.

At any moment in time every society faces constraints imposed by nature and by previous generations. Some societies are handsomely endowed by nature with fertile land, water, sunshine, and natural resources. Others have deserts and few mineral resources. Some societies receive much from previous generations—art, music, technical knowledge, beautiful buildings, and productive factories. Others are left with overgrazed, eroded land, cities leveled by war, or polluted natural environments. *All* societies face limits.

economics *The study of how individuals and societies choose to use the scarce resources that nature and previous generations have provided.*

Economics is the study of how individuals and societies choose to use the scarce resources that nature and previous generations have provided. The key word in this definition is *choose.* Economics is a behavioral science. In large measure it is the study of how people make choices. The choices that people make, when added up, translate into societal choices.

The purpose of this chapter and the next is to elaborate on this definition and to introduce the subject matter of economics. What is produced? How is it produced? Who gets it? Why? Is the result good or bad? Can it be improved?

WHY STUDY ECONOMICS?

There are four main reasons to study economics: to learn a way of thinking, to understand society, to understand global affairs, and to be an informed voter.

TO LEARN A WAY OF THINKING

Probably the most important reason for studying economics is to learn a particular way of thinking. A good way to introduce economics is to review three of its most fundamental concepts: *opportunity cost, marginalism,* and *efficient markets.* If your study of economics is successful, you will find yourself using these concepts every day in making decisions.

■ **Opportunity Cost** What happens in an economy is the outcome of thousands of individual decisions. Households must decide how to divide up their incomes over all the goods and services available in the marketplace. Individuals must decide whether to work or not to work, whether to go to school, and how much to save. Businesses must decide what to produce, how much to produce, how much to charge, and where to locate. It is not surprising that economic analysis focuses on the process of decision making.

Nearly all decisions involve trade-offs. There are advantages and disadvantages, costs and benefits, associated with every action and every choice. A key concept that recurs again and again in analyzing the decision-making process is the notion of *opportunity cost.* The full "cost" of making a specific choice includes what we give up by not making the alternative choice. That which we forgo, or give up, when we make a choice or a decision is called the **opportunity cost** of that decision.

opportunity cost *That which we forgo, or give up, when we make a choice or a decision.*

The concept applies to individuals, businesses, and entire societies. The opportunity cost of going to a movie is the value of the other things you could have done with the same money and time. If you decide to take time off in lieu of working, the opportunity cost of your leisure is the pay that you would have earned had you worked. Part of the cost of a college education is the income you could have earned by working full time instead of going to school. If a firm purchases a new piece of equipment for $3000, it does so because it expects that equipment to generate more profit. There is an opportunity cost, however, since that $3000 could have been deposited in an interest-earning account. To a society, the opportunity cost of using resources for military hardware is the value of the private/civilian goods that could have been produced with the same resources.

The reason that opportunity costs arise is that resources are scarce. *Scarce* simply means *limited*. Consider one of our most important resources—time. There are only 24 hours in a day, and we must live our lives under this constraint. A farmer in rural Brazil must decide whether it is better to stay on the land and continue to farm or to go to the city and look for a job. A hockey player at the University of Vermont must decide whether she will play on the varsity team or spend more time improving her academic work.

■ Marginalism and Sunk Costs A second key concept used in analyzing choices is the notion of *marginalism*. In weighing the costs and benefits of a decision, it is important to weigh only the costs and benefits that are contingent upon the decision. Suppose, for example, that you lived in New Orleans and that you were weighing the costs and benefits of visiting your mother in Iowa. If business required that you travel to Kansas City, the cost of visiting Mom would be only the additional, or *marginal,* time and money cost of getting to Iowa from Kansas City.

Consider the cost of producing this book. Assume that 10,000 copies are produced. The total cost of producing the copies includes the cost of the authors' time in writing the book, the cost of editing, the cost of making the plates for printing, and the cost of the paper and ink. If the total cost were $600,000, then the average cost of one copy would be $60, which is simply $600,000 divided by 10,000.

Although average cost is an important concept, a book publisher must know more than simply the average cost of a book. For example, suppose a second printing is being debated. That is, should another 10,000 copies be produced? In deciding whether to proceed, the costs of writing, editing, making plates, and so forth are irrelevant. Why? Because they have already been incurred—they are *sunk costs.* **Sunk costs** are costs that cannot be avoided, regardless of what is done in the future, because they have already been incurred. All that matters are the costs associated with the additional, or marginal, books to be printed. Technically, *marginal cost* is the cost of producing one more unit of output.

sunk costs *Costs that cannot be avoided, regardless of what is done in the future, because they have already been incurred.*

There are numerous examples in which the concept of marginal cost is useful. For an airplane that is about to take off with empty seats, the marginal cost of an extra passenger is essentially zero; the total cost of the trip is essentially unchanged by the addition of an extra passenger. Thus, setting aside a few seats to be sold at big discounts can be profitable even if the fare for those seats is far below the average cost per seat of making the trip. As long as the airline succeeds in filling seats that would otherwise have been empty, doing so is profitable—marginal revenue is greater than marginal cost.

■ Efficient Markets—No Free Lunch Suppose you are driving on a three-lane highway and you come upon a toll plaza with six toll booths. Three toll booths are straight ahead in the three lanes of traffic, and the three other booths are off to the right. Which lane should you choose? It is usually the case that the wait time is approximately the same no matter what you do. There are usually enough people searching for the shortest line so as to make all the lines about the same length. If one line is much shorter than the others, cars will quickly move into it until the lines are equalized.

As you will see later, the term *profit* in economics has a very precise meaning. Economists, however, often loosely refer to "good deals" or risk-free ventures as *profit opportunities*. Using the term loosely, a profit opportunity exists at the toll booths if one line is shorter than the others. In general, such profit opportunities are rare. At any one time there are many people searching for such opportunities, and as a consequence few exist. At toll booths it is seldom the case that one line is substantially shorter than the others. Markets like this, where any profit opportunities are eliminated almost instantaneously, are said to be **efficient markets.** (We discuss *markets,* the institutions through which buyers and sellers interact and engage in exchange, in detail in Chapter 2.)

efficient market *A market in which profit opportunities are eliminated almost instantaneously.*

The common way of expressing the efficient markets hypothesis is "there's no such thing as a free lunch." How should you react when a stockbroker calls up with a hot tip on the stock market? With skepticism. There are thousands of individuals each day looking for hot tips in the market, and if a particular tip about a stock is valid there will be an immediate rush to buy the stock, which will quickly drive its price up. By the time the tip gets to your broker and then to you, the profit opportunity that arose from the tip (assuming that there was one) likely has disappeared. Similar arguments can be made for bond markets and commodity markets, where there are many experts who take quick advantage of any news that affects prices.

This economists' view that very few profit opportunities exist can, of course, be carried too far. There is a story about two people walking along, one an economist and one not. The noneconomist sees a twenty-dollar bill on the sidewalk and says, "There's a twenty-dollar bill on the sidewalk." The economist replies, "That is not possible. If there were, somebody would already have picked it up."

There are clearly times when profit opportunities exist. Someone has to be first to get the news, and some people have quicker insights than others. Nevertheless, news travels fast, and there are thousands of people with quick insights. The general view that profit opportunities are rare is close to the mark.

The study of economics teaches us a way of thinking and helps us make decisions.

TO UNDERSTAND SOCIETY

Another reason for studying economics is to understand society better. You cannot hope to understand how a society functions without a basic knowledge of its economy, and you cannot understand a society's economy without knowing its economic history. Clearly, past and present economic decisions have an enormous influence on the character of life in a society. The current state of the physical environment, the level of material well-being, and the nature and number of jobs are all products of the economic system.

To get a sense of the ways in which economic decisions have shaped our environment, imagine that you are looking out of a window on the top floor of a high-rise office building in any large city. The workday is about to begin. All around you are other tall glass and steel buildings full of workers. In the distance you see the smoke of factories. Looking down, you see thousands of commuters pouring off trains and buses, and cars backed up on freeway exit ramps. You see trucks carrying goods from one place to another. You also see the face of urban poverty: Just beyond the freeway is a large public housing project and, beyond that, burned-out and boarded-up buildings.

What you see before you is the product of millions of economic decisions made over hundreds of years. People at some point decided to spend time and money building those buildings and factories. Somebody cleared the land, laid the tracks, built the roads, and produced the cars and buses.

Not only have economic decisions shaped the physical environment, they have determined the character of society as well. At no time has the impact of economic change on the character of a society been more evident than in England during the late eighteenth and early nineteenth centuries, a period that we now call the **Industrial Revolution.** Increases in the productivity of agriculture, new manufacturing technologies, and the development of more efficient forms of transportation led to a massive movement of the British population from the countryside to the city. At the beginning of the eighteenth century, approximately two out of three people in Great Britain were engaged in agriculture. By 1812, only one in three remained in agriculture, and by 1900 the figure was fewer than one in ten. People jammed into overcrowded cities and worked long hours in factories. The world had changed completely in two centuries—a period that, in the run of history, was nothing more than the blink of an eye.

It is not surprising that the discipline of economics began to take shape during this period. Social critics and philosophers looked around them and knew that their philosophies must expand to accommodate the changes. Adam Smith's *Wealth of Nations* appeared in 1776. It was followed by the writings of David Ricardo, Karl Marx, Thomas Malthus, and others. Each tried to make sense out of what was happening. Who was building the factories? Why? What determined the level of wages paid to workers or the price of food? What would happen in the future, and what *should* happen? The people who asked these questions were the first economists.

Similar changes continue to affect the character of life today. In 1994 the number of jobs in the United States increased by more than 4 million, but nearly 8 million people who wanted a job could not find one. While the economy was growing, the wages of many workers were falling relative to the cost of living. At the same time, baseball players, many of whom make in excess of a million dollars a year, went on strike. While the Mexican economy has been booming since the United States and Mexico signed a trade treaty in 1993, thousands of Mexicans continue to pour into the United States each week. How does one make sense of all of this? Why do we have unemployment? What forces determine wages? Why is it that baseball players can command such high salaries? What are the ramifications of continued immigration into the United States?

> The study of economics is an essential part of the study of society.

TO UNDERSTAND GLOBAL AFFAIRS

A third reason for studying economics is to understand global affairs. News headlines are filled with economic stories: a potential trade war between the United States and the European Union, the struggle to prevent further collapse of the economies of Eastern Europe and the former Soviet Union, starvation and poverty in Africa.

All countries are part of a world economy, and understanding international relations begins with a basic knowledge of the economic links among countries. For centuries countries have attempted to protect their industries and workers from foreign competition by taxing imports and limiting the number of certain imports. Most economists argue, however, that unrestricted trade is in the long-run interest

MANY ECONOMISTS BELIEVE THAT JAPAN'S RECENT ECONOMIC TROUBLES HAVE WEAKENED ITS ABILITY TO BE A WORLD LEADER. WORRIED ABOUT THEIR FUTURE AND THE PRICES OF THEIR PRODUCTS, JAPANESE FARMERS DEMONSTRATE AGAINST GLOBAL FREE TRADE.

of all countries. Just after World War II many countries signed the General Agreement on Tariffs and Trade (GATT), in which they committed to lowering trade barriers. The process continues today as the Congress debates the most recent version of the GATT. The issue is a passionate one. French farmers, fearing the effects of cheap imports on their livelihood, protested strongly when France committed to signing the new GATT. Labor unions in the United States vowed to defeat any politicians who voted to ratify the North American Free Trade Agreement (NAFTA) with Mexico in 1993 and the new GATT in 1995.

Americans are investing heavily in industries in countries like Indonesia and China. During the 1980s the Japanese bought billions of dollars' worth of U.S. real estate, shares of corporate stocks, and government bonds. During the 1990s the Japanese, suffering economic problems at home, have pulled back, with important consequences for the United States. The end of the apartheid laws that legally separated the races in South Africa has created a new climate for international investment in that country.

The Iraqi invasion of Kuwait in 1990 and the resulting Persian Gulf War in 1991 sent world oil markets on a wild ride and in part led to *recession* (a period of decreasing output and rising unemployment) in the United States. Meanwhile, the countries of Eastern Europe are struggling to create from the ground up economic and social institutions that took centuries to build in the West.

Another important issue in today's world is the widening gap between rich nations and poor nations. In 1995 world population was about 5.7 billion. Of that number, 4.3 billion lived in less-developed countries and 1.4 billion lived in more-developed countries. The 75% of the world's population that lives in the less-developed countries receives less than 20% of the world's income. In dozens of countries, per capita income is only a few hundred dollars a year.

An understanding of economics is essential to an understanding of global affairs.

TO BE AN INFORMED VOTER

A knowledge of economics is essential to be an informed voter. During the last 25 years, the U.S. economy has been on a roller coaster. In 1973–1974, the Organization of Petroleum Exporting Countries (OPEC) succeeded in raising the price of crude oil by 400 percent. Simultaneously, a sequence of events in the world food market drove food prices up by 25 percent. By mid-1974, prices in the United States were rising across the board at a very rapid rate. Partially as a result of government policy to fight runaway inflation, the economy went into a recession in 1975. (An *inflation* is an increase in the overall price level in the economy.) The recession succeeded in slowing price increases, but in the process millions found themselves unemployed.

From 1979 through 1983, it happened all over again. Prices rose rapidly, the government reacted with more policies designed to stop prices from rising, and the United States ended up with an even worse recession in 1982. By the end of that year, 10.8% of the work force was unemployed. Then, in mid-1990—after almost eight years of strong economic performance—the U.S. economy went into another recession. During the third and fourth quarters of 1990 and the first quarter of 1991, gross domestic product (GDP, a measure of the total output of the U.S. economy) fell, and unemployment again increased sharply.

The recession of 1990–1991 was followed by a very slow recovery, which became the key issue in the 1992 presidential election. Exit polls on election day, November 3, 1992, showed that the number one issue on people's minds was the economy. Indeed, the three presidential debates among former President Bush, H. Ross Perot, and President Clinton focused on the candidates' positions on economic issues.

Many of the issues debated during the last election have resurfaced as President Clinton defends his record against opponents' attacks as he heads into the 1996 election. Health-care reform, international trade agreements, economic relations with China and Eastern Europe, and tax policy and deficit reduction remain at the center of the debate. But now Clinton will be judged in part by how well the economy actually performed while he was in office. Although the economy grew in 1993 and 1994, voters expressed their continuing frustration about economic matters by voting against incumbent Democrats in the midterm elections of 1994.

> When we participate in the political process, we are voting on issues that require a basic understanding of economics.

THE SCOPE OF ECONOMICS

Most students taking economics for the first time are surprised by the breadth of what they study. Some think that economics will teach them about the stock market or what to do with their money. Others think that economics deals exclusively with problems like inflation and unemployment. In fact, it deals with all these subjects, but they are pieces of a much larger puzzle.

Economics has deep roots in, and close ties to, social philosophy. An issue of great importance to philosophers, for example, is distributional justice. Why are some people rich and others poor, and whatever the answer, is this fair? A number of nineteenth-century social philosophers wrestled with these questions, and out of their musings economics as a separate discipline was born.

The easiest way to get a feel for the breadth and depth of what you will be studying is to explore briefly the way economics is organized. First of all, there are two major divisions of economics: microeconomics and macroeconomics.

MICROECONOMICS AND MACROECONOMICS

microeconomics *The branch of economics that examines the functioning of individual industries and the behavior of individual decision-making units, that is, business firms and households.*

Microeconomics deals with the functioning of individual industries and the behavior of individual economic decision-making units: business firms and households. Microeconomics explores the decisions that individual businesses and consumers make. Firms' choices about what to produce and how much to charge and households' choices about what and how much to buy help to explain why the economy produces the things it does.

Another big question that microeconomics addresses is who gets the things that are produced. Wealthy households get more output than do poor households, and the forces that determine this distribution of output are the province of microeconomics. Why does poverty exist? Who is poor? Why do some jobs pay more than others?

Think again about all the things you consume in a day, and then think back to that view out over a big city. Somebody decided to build those factories. Somebody decided to construct the roads, build the housing, produce the cars, and smoke the bacon. Why? What is going on in all those buildings? It is easy to see that understanding individual micro decisions is very important to any understanding of society.

macroeconomics *The branch of economics that examines the economic behavior of aggregates—income, employment, output, and so on—on a national scale.*

Macroeconomics looks at the economy as a whole. Instead of trying to understand what determines the output of a single firm or industry or the consumption patterns of a single household or group of households, macroeconomics examines the factors that determine national output, or national product. Microeconomics is concerned with *household* income; macroeconomics deals with *national* income.

While microeconomics focuses on individual product prices and relative prices, macroeconomics looks at the overall price level and how quickly (or slowly) it is rising (or falling). Microeconomics questions how many people will be hired (or fired) this year in a particular industry or in a certain geographical area, and the factors that determine how much labor a firm or industry will hire. Macroeconomics deals with *aggregate* employment and unemployment: how many jobs exist in the economy as a whole, and how many people who are willing to work are not able to find work.

To summarize:

> Microeconomics looks at the individual unit—the household, the firm, the industry. It sees and examines the "trees." Macroeconomics looks at the whole, the aggregate. It sees and analyzes the "forest."

Table 1.1 summarizes these divisions and some of the subjects with which they are concerned.

THE DIVERSITY OF ECONOMICS

Individual economists focus their research and study in many diverse areas. Many of these specialized fields are reflected in the advanced courses offered at most colleges and universities. Some are concerned with economic history or the history of economic thought. Others focus on international economics or growth in less-developed countries. Still others study the economics of cities (urban economics) or the relationship between economics and law. (See the Application box on page 10 titled "The Fields of Economics" for more details.)

Economists also differ in the emphasis they place on theory. Some economists specialize in developing new theories, while others spend their time testing the theories of others. Some economists hope to expand the frontiers of knowledge, while

TABLE 1.1	EXAMPLES OF MICROECONOMIC AND MACROECONOMIC CONCERNS			
DIVISION OF ECONOMICS	PRODUCTION	PRICES	INCOME	EMPLOYMENT
Microeconomics	Production/Output in Individual Industries and Businesses How much steel How much office space How many cars	Price of Individual Goods and Services Price of medical care Price of gasoline Food prices Apartment rents	Distribution of Income and Wealth Wages in the auto industry Minimum wage Executive salaries Poverty	Employment by Individual Businesses and Industries Jobs in the steel industry Number of employees in a firm Number of accountants
Macroeconomics	National Production/Output Total industrial output Gross domestic product Growth of output	Aggregate Price Level Consumer prices Producer prices Rate of inflation	National Income Total wages and salaries Total corporate profits	Employment and Unemployment in the Economy Total number of jobs Unemployment rate

others are more interested in applying what is already known to the formulation of public policies.

As you begin your study of economics, look through your school's course catalog and talk to the faculty about their interests. You will discover that economics encompasses a broad range of inquiry and is linked to many other disciplines.

THE METHOD OF ECONOMICS

Economics asks and attempts to answer two kinds of questions, positive and normative. **Positive economics** attempts to understand behavior and the operation of economic systems *without making judgments* about whether the outcomes are good or bad. It strives to describe what exists and how it works. What determines the wage rate for unskilled workers? What would happen if we abolished the corporate income tax? Who would benefit? Who would lose? The answers to such questions are the subject of positive economics.

In contrast, **normative economics** looks at the outcomes of economic behavior and asks if they are good or bad and whether they can be made better. Normative economics involves judgments and prescriptions for courses of action. Should the government be involved in regulating the price of gasoline? Should the income tax be changed to reduce or increase the burden on upper-income families? Should AT&T have been broken up into a set of smaller companies? Should we protect the automobile industry from foreign competition? Normative economics is often called *policy economics.*

Of course most normative questions involve positive questions. To know whether the government *should* take a particular action, we must know first if it *can* and second what the consequences are likely to be. (For example, if AT&T is broken up, will there be more competition and lower prices?)

Some claim that positive, value-free economic analysis is impossible. They argue that analysts come to problems with biases that cannot help but influence their work. Furthermore, even in choosing what questions to ask or what problems to analyze, economists are influenced by political, ideological, and moral views.

While this argument has some merit, it is nevertheless important to distinguish between analyses that attempt to be positive and those that are intentionally and explicitly normative. Economists who ask explicitly normative questions should be

positive economics *An approach to economics that seeks to understand behavior and the operation of systems without making judgments. It describes what exists and how it works.*

normative economics *An approach to economics that analyzes outcomes of economic behavior, evaluates them as good or bad, and may prescribe courses of action. Also called policy economics.*

A good way to convey the diversity of economics is to describe some of its major fields of study and the issues that economists address.

- **INDUSTRIAL ORGANIZATION** looks carefully at the structure and performance of industries and firms within an economy. How do businesses compete? Who gains and who loses?

- **URBAN AND REGIONAL ECONOMICS** studies the spatial arrangement of economic activity. Why do we have cities? Why are manufacturing firms locating farther and farther from the center of urban areas?

- **ECONOMETRICS** applies statistical techniques and data to economic problems in an effort to test hypotheses and theories. Most schools require economics majors to take at least one course in statistics or econometrics.

- **COMPARATIVE ECONOMIC SYSTEMS** examines the ways alternative economic systems function. What are the advantages and disadvantages of different systems? What is the best way to convert the planned economies of the former Soviet Union to market systems?

- **ECONOMIC DEVELOPMENT** focuses on the problems of poor countries. What can be done to promote development in these nations? Important concerns of development economists include population growth and control, provision for basic needs, and strategies for international trade.

- **LABOR ECONOMICS** deals with the factors that determine wage rates, employment, and unemployment.

How do people decide whether to work, how much to work, and at what kind of job? How have the roles of unions and management changed in recent years?

- **FINANCE** examines the ways in which households and firms actually pay for, or finance, their purchases. It involves the study of capital markets (including the stock and bond markets), futures and options, capital budgeting, and asset valuation.

- **INTERNATIONAL ECONOMICS** studies trade flows among countries and international financial institutions. What are the advantages and disadvantages for a country that allows its citizens to buy and sell freely in world markets? Why is the dollar strong or weak?

- **PUBLIC ECONOMICS** examines the role of government in the economy. What are the economic functions of government, and what should they be? How should the government finance the services that it provides? What kinds of government programs should confront the problems of poverty, unemployment, and pollution?

- **ECONOMIC HISTORY** traces the development of the modern economy. What economic and political events and scientific advances caused the Industrial Revolution that began in eighteenth-century Great Britain? What explains the tremendous growth and progress of post–World War II Japan? What caused the Great Depression of the 1930s?

- **LAW AND ECONOMICS** analyzes the economic function of legal rules

ECONOMICS STUDIES MANY IMPORTANT IS-SUES. IN 1994, MANY CUBAN REFUGEES FLED TO THE UNITED STATES IN HANDMADE RAFTS. WHAT ARE THE IMPLICATIONS OF SUCH MASS MIGRATIONS FOR THE ECONOMIES OF CUBA AND THE UNITED STATES?

and institutions. How does the law change the behavior of individuals and businesses? Do different liability rules make accidents and injuries more, or less, likely? What are the economic costs of crime?

- **THE HISTORY OF ECONOMIC THOUGHT,** which is grounded in philosophy, studies the development of economic ideas and theories over time, from Adam Smith in the eighteenth century to the works of economists such as Thomas Malthus, Karl Marx, and John Maynard Keynes. Because economic theory is constantly developing and changing, studying the history of ideas helps give meaning to modern theory and puts it in perspective.

forced to specify their grounds for judging one outcome superior to another. What does it mean to be better? The criteria for such evaluations must be clearly spelled out and thoroughly understood for conclusions to have meaning.

Positive economics is often divided into descriptive economics and economic theory. **Descriptive economics** is simply the compilation of data that describe phenomena and facts. Examples of such data appear in the *Statistical Abstract of the United States*, a large volume of data published by the Department of Commerce every year that describes many features of the U.S. economy.

Where do all these data come from? The Census Bureau produces an enormous amount of raw data every year, as do the Bureau of Labor Statistics, the Bureau of Economic Analysis, and nongovernment agencies such as the University of Michigan Survey Research Center. One important study now published annually is the *Survey of Consumer Expenditure*, which asks individual households to keep careful records of all their expenditures over a long period of time. Another is the *National Longitudinal Survey of Labor Force Behavior*, conducted over many years by the Center for Human Resource Development at Ohio State University.

Economic theory attempts to generalize about data and interpret them. An **economic theory** is a statement or set of related statements about cause and effect, action and reaction. One of the first theories you will encounter in this text is the *law of demand*, which was most clearly stated by Alfred Marshall in 1890: When the price of a product rises, people tend to buy less of it; when the price of a product falls, they tend to buy more.

The process of observing regular patterns from raw data and drawing generalizations from them is called **inductive reasoning.** In all sciences, theories begin with inductive reasoning and observed regularities. For example, Aristotle believed that the speed at which objects fall toward the earth depends on their size as well as their weight. But in a series of experiments carried out between 1589 and 1591, Galileo was able to show that bodies of very different sizes seemed to fall at approximately the same speed when dropped from the Leaning Tower of Pisa. Over a century later, Galileo's data led Sir Isaac Newton to formulate the theory of gravity, which eventually became the basis of Albert Einstein's work.

Social scientists, including economists, study human behavior. They develop and test theories of how human beings, institutions, and societies behave. The behavior of human beings is by its nature not as regular or predictable as the behavior of electrons, molecules, or planets, but there are patterns, regularities, and tendencies.

Theories do not always arise out of formal numerical data. All of us have been collecting observations of people's behavior and their responses to economic stimuli for most of our lives. We may have observed our parents' reaction to a sudden increase—or decrease—in income or to the loss of a job or the acquisition of a new one. We all have seen people standing in line waiting for a bargain. And, of course, our own actions and reactions are another important source of data.

THEORIES AND MODELS

In many disciplines, including physics, chemistry, meteorology, political science, and economics, theorists build formal models of behavior. A **model** is a formal statement of a theory. It is usually a mathematical statement of a presumed relationship between two or more variables.

A **variable** is a measure that can change from time to time or from observation to observation. Income is a variable—it has different values for different people, and different values for the same person at different times. The rental price of a movie on a videocassette is a variable; it has different values at different stores and at different times. There are countless other examples.

descriptive economics *The compilation of data that describe phenomena and facts.*

economic theory *A statement or set of related statements about cause and effect, action and reaction.*

inductive reasoning *The process of observing regular patterns from raw data and drawing generalizations from them.*

model *A formal statement of a theory. Usually a mathematical statement of a presumed relationship between two or more variables.*

variable *A measure that can change from time to time or from observation to observation.*

Because all models simplify reality by stripping part of it away, they are abstractions. Critics of economics often point to abstraction as a weakness. Most economists, however, see abstraction as a real strength.

The easiest way to see how abstraction can be helpful is to think of a map. A map is a representation of reality that is simplified and abstract. A city or state appears on a piece of paper as a series of lines and colors. The amount of reality that the map maker can strip away before the map loses something essential depends on what the map is going to be used for. If I want to drive from St. Louis to Phoenix, I need to know only the major interstate highways and roads. I lose absolutely nothing and gain clarity by cutting out the local streets and roads. If, on the other hand, I need to get around in Phoenix, I may need to see every street and alley.

Most maps are two-dimensional representations of a three-dimensional world; they show where roads and highways go but do not show hills and valleys along the way. Trail maps for hikers, however, have "contour lines" that represent changes in elevation. When you are in a car, changes in elevation matter very little; they would make a map needlessly complex and much more difficult to read. But if you are on foot carrying a 60-pound pack, a knowledge of elevation is crucial.

Like maps, economic models are abstractions that strip away detail to expose only those aspects of behavior that are important to the question being asked. The principle that irrelevant detail should be cut away is called the principle of **Ockham's razor** after the fourteenth-century philosopher William of Ockham.

But be careful. Although abstraction is a powerful tool for exposing and analyzing specific aspects of behavior, it is possible to oversimplify. Economic models often strip away a good deal of social and political reality to get at underlying concepts. When an economic theory is used to help formulate actual government or institutional policy, political and social reality must often be reintroduced if the policy is to have a chance of working.

The key here is that the appropriate amount of simplification and abstraction depends upon the use to which the model will be put. To return to the map example: You don't want to walk around San Francisco with a map made for drivers—there are too many very steep hills!

■ **All Else Equal: *Ceteris Paribus*** It is almost always true that whatever you want to explain with a model depends on more than one factor. Suppose, for example, that you want to explain the total number of miles driven by automobile owners in the United States. The number of miles driven will change from year to year or month to month; it is a variable. The issue, if we want to understand and explain changes that occur, is what factors cause those changes.

Obviously, many things might have an impact on total miles driven. First, more or fewer people may be driving. This, in turn, can be affected by changes in the driving age, by population growth, or by changes in state laws. Other factors might include the price of gasoline, the household's income, the number and age of children in the household, the distance from home to work, the location of shopping facilities, and the availability and quality of public transport. When any of these variables change, the members of the household may drive more or less. If changes in any of these variables affect large numbers of households across the country, the total number of miles driven will change.

Very often we need to isolate or separate out these effects. For example, suppose that we want to know the impact on driving of a higher tax on gasoline. This change would raise the price of gasoline at the pump, but would not (at least in the short run) affect income, workplace location, number of children, and so forth.

To isolate the impact of one single factor, we use the device of ***ceteris paribus,*** or **all else equal.** We ask: What is the impact of a change in gasoline price on driv-

Ockham's razor *The principle that irrelevant detail should be cut away.*

ceteris paribus *Literally, "all else equal." Used to analyze the relationship between two variables while the values of other variables are held unchanged.*

ing behavior, *ceteris paribus*, or assuming that nothing else changes? If gasoline prices rise by 10%, how much less driving will there be, assuming no simultaneous change in anything else—that is, assuming that income, number of children, population, laws, and so on all remain constant?

> Using the device of *ceteris paribus* is one part of the process of abstraction. In formulating economic theory, the concept helps us simplify reality in order to focus on the relationships that we are interested in.

■ **Expressing Models in Words, Graphs, and Equations** Consider the following statements: "Lower airline ticket prices cause people to fly more frequently." "Higher interest rates slow the rate of home sales." "When firms produce more output, employment increases." "Higher gasoline prices cause people to drive less and to buy more fuel-efficient cars." "When the U.S. dollar falls in value against the value of foreign currencies, firms that export products produced in the United States find their sales increasing."

Each of these statements expresses a relationship between two variables that can be quantified. In each case there is a stimulus and a response, a cause and an effect. Quantitative relationships can be expressed in a variety of ways. Sometimes words are sufficient to express the essence of a theory, but often it is necessary to be more specific about the nature of a relationship or about the magnitude of a response. The most common method of expressing the quantitative relationship between two variables is *graphing* that relationship on a two-dimensional plane. In fact, we will use graphical analysis extensively in Chapter 2 and beyond. Because it is essential that you be familiar with the basics of graphing, a careful review of graphing techniques is presented in the appendix to this chapter.

Quantitative relationships between variables can also be presented through *equations*. For example, suppose we discovered that over time, U.S. households collectively spend, or consume, 90% of their income and save 10% of their income. We could then write:

$$C = .90Y \text{ and } S = .10Y$$

where C is consumption spending, Y is income, and S is saving. Writing explicit algebraic expressions like these helps us understand the nature of the underlying process of decision making. Understanding this process is what economics is all about.

■ **Cautions and Pitfalls** In formulating theories and models, it is especially important to avoid two pitfalls: the post hoc fallacy and the fallacy of composition.

The Post Hoc Fallacy Theories often make statements, or sets of statements, about cause and effect. It can be quite tempting to look at two events that happen in sequence and assume that the first caused the second to happen. Clearly, this is not always the case. This common error is called the **post hoc, ergo propter hoc** (or "after this, therefore because of this") fallacy.

There are thousands of examples. The Colorado Rockies have won seven games in a row. Last night, I went to the game and they lost. I must have "jinxed" them. They lost *because* I went to the game.

Stock market analysts indulge in what is perhaps the most striking example of the post hoc fallacy in action. Every day the stock market goes up or down, and every day some analyst on some national news program singles out one or two of the day's events as *the cause* of some change in the market: "Today the Dow Jones industrial average rose five points on heavy trading; analysts say that the increase was due to progress in talks between the United States and Cuba." Research has

post hoc, ergo propter hoc
Literally, "after this (in time), therefore because of this." A common error made in thinking about causation: If Event A happens before Event B happens, it is not necessarily true that A caused B.

shown that daily changes in stock market averages are very largely random. While major news events, like the Iraq buildup of troops along the Kuwait border in October 1994, clearly have a direct influence on certain stock prices (in this case, the price of oil companies' stock), most daily changes cannot be directly linked to specific news stories.

Very closely related to the post hoc fallacy is the often erroneous link between correlation and causation. Two variables are said to be *correlated* if one variable changes when the other variable changes. But correlation does not imply causation. Cities that have high crime rates also have lots of automobiles, so there is a very high degree of correlation between number of cars and crime rates. Can we argue, then, that cars *cause* crime? No. The reason for the correlation here may have nothing to do with cause and effect. Big cities have lots of people, lots of people have lots of cars, and therefore big cities have lots of cars. Big cities also have high crime rates for many reasons—crowding, poverty, anonymity, unequal distribution of wealth, and the ready availability of drugs, to mention only a few. But the presence of cars is not one of them.

This caution must also be viewed in reverse. Sometimes events that seem entirely unconnected actually *are* connected. In 1978 Governor Michael Dukakis of Massachusetts ran for reelection. Still young, attractive, and quite popular most of the time, Dukakis was nevertheless defeated in the Democratic primary that year by a razor-thin margin. The weekend before, the Boston Red Sox, in the thick of the division championship race, had been badly beaten by the New York Yankees in four straight games. Some very respectable political analysts believe that hundreds of thousands of Boston sports fans vented their anger on the incumbent governor the following Tuesday.

The Fallacy of Composition   To conclude that what is true for a part is necessarily true for the whole is to fall into the **fallacy of composition.** Often what holds for an individual does not hold for a group or for society as a whole. Suppose that a large group of cattle ranchers graze their cattle on the same range. To an individual rancher, more cattle and more grazing mean a higher income. But because its capacity is limited, the land can support only so many cattle. If every cattle rancher increased the number of cattle sent out to graze, the land would become overgrazed and barren, and everyone's income would fall. In short:

> Theories that seem to work well when applied to individuals or households often break down when they are applied to the whole.

■ **Testing Theories and Models: Empirical Economics**   In science, a theory is rejected when it fails to explain what is observed or when another theory better explains what is observed. Prior to the sixteenth century almost everyone believed that the earth was the center of the universe and that the sun and stars rotated around it. The astronomer Ptolemy (A.D. 127–151) built a model that explained and predicted the movements of the heavenly bodies in a geocentric (earth-centered) universe. Early in the sixteenth century, however, the Polish astronomer Nicholas Copernicus found himself dissatisfied with the Ptolemaic model and proposed an alternative theory or model, placing the sun at the center of the known universe and relegating the earth to the status of one planet among many. The battle between the competing models was waged, at least in part, with data based on observations—actual measurements of the movements of the planets. The new model ultimately predicted much better than the old, and in time it came to be accepted.

In the seventeenth century, building on the works of Copernicus and others, Sir Isaac Newton constructed yet another body of theory that seemed to predict plan-

fallacy of composition *The belief that what is true for a part is necessarily true for the whole.*

etary motion with still more accuracy. Newtonian physics became the accepted body of theory, relied on for almost 300 years. Then Albert Einstein did his work. The theory of relativity replaced Newtonian physics because it predicted even better. Relativity was able to explain some things that earlier theories could not.

Economic theories are also confronted with new and often conflicting data from time to time. The collection and use of data to test economic theories is called **empirical economics.**

Numerous large data sets are available to facilitate economic research. For example, economists studying the labor market can now test behavioral theories against the actual working experiences of thousands of randomly selected people who have been surveyed continuously since the 1960s by economists at Ohio State University. Macroeconomists continuously monitoring and studying the behavior of the national economy pass thousands of items of data, collected by both government agencies and private companies, back and forth on diskettes and over telephone lines. Housing market analysts analyze data tapes containing observations recorded in connection with millions of home sales.

All scientific research needs to isolate and measure the responsiveness of one variable to a change in another variable *ceteris paribus*. Physical scientists, such as physicists and geologists, can often impose the condition of *ceteris paribus* by conducting controlled experiments. They can, for example, measure the effect of one chemical on another while literally holding all else constant in an environment that they control completely. Social scientists, who study people, rarely have this luxury.

While controlled experiments are difficult in economics and other social sciences, they are not impossible. Researchers can isolate and measure the effect of one variable on another. There are a number of ways to do this. One way is to observe the behavior of groups of similar people under different circumstances. For example, suppose you wanted to estimate the effect of the tax rate reductions enacted by Congress in 1986 on the amount that households save, an important tax policy issue. Of course, you could look at household saving before and after the change. But who's to say that what you observe is not due to increases in income that occurred at the same time? To isolate the tax effect, you could look at a set of households whose income did not change. Sophisticated computer programs are now allowing economists to isolate variables more easily than ever before.

ECONOMIC POLICY

Economic theory helps us understand how the world works, but the formulation of *economic policy* requires a second step. We must have objectives. What do we want to change? Why? What is good and what is bad about the way the system is operating? Can we make it better?

Such questions force us to be specific about the grounds for judging one outcome superior to another. What does it mean to be better? Four criteria are frequently applied in making these judgments:

Criteria for Judging Economic Outcomes:	1. Efficiency 2. Equity 3. Growth 4. Stability

■ **Efficiency**   In physics "efficiency" refers to the ratio of useful energy delivered by a system to the energy supplied to it. An efficient automobile engine, for example, is one that uses up a small amount of fuel per mile for a given level of power.

efficiency *In economics, allocative efficiency. An efficient economy is one that produces what people want and does so at the least possible cost.*

In economics, **efficiency** means *allocative efficiency*. An efficient economy is one that produces what people want and does so at the least possible cost. If the system allocates resources to the production of things that nobody wants, it is inefficient. If all members of a particular society were vegetarian and somehow half of all that society's resources were used to produce meat, the result would be inefficient. It is inefficient when steel beams lie in the rain and rust because somebody fouled up a shipping schedule. If a firm could produce its product using 25% less labor and energy without sacrificing quality, it too is inefficient.

The clearest example of an efficient change is a voluntary exchange. If you and I each want something that the other has and we agree to exchange, we are both better off, and no one loses. When a company reorganizes its production or adopts a new technology that enables it to produce more of its product with fewer resources, without sacrificing quality, it has made an efficient change. At least potentially, the resources saved could be used to produce more of something.

Inefficiencies can arise in numerous ways. Sometimes they are caused by government regulations or tax laws that distort otherwise sound economic decisions. Suppose that land in Ohio is best suited for corn production and that land in Kansas is best suited for wheat production. Clearly, a law that requires Kansas to produce only corn and Ohio to produce only wheat would be inefficient. If firms that cause environmental damage are in no way held accountable for their actions, the incentive to minimize those damages is lost, and the result is inefficient.

Since most changes that can be made in an economy will leave some people better off and others worse off, we must have a way of comparing the gains and losses that may result from any given change. Most often we simply compare their sizes in dollar terms. A change is efficient if the value of the resulting gains exceeds the value of the resulting losses. In this case the winners can potentially compensate the losers and still be better off.

equity *Fairness.*

■ **Equity** While efficiency has a fairly precise definition that can be applied with some degree of rigor, **equity** ("fairness") lies in the eye of the beholder. Few people agree on what is fair and what is unfair. To many, fairness implies a more equal distribution of income and wealth. Fairness may imply alleviating poverty, but the extent to which poverty should be reduced is the subject of enormous disagreement. For thousands of years philosophers have wrestled with the principles of justice that should guide social decisions. They will probably wrestle with such questions for thousands of years to come.

Despite the impossibility of defining equity or fairness universally, public policy makers judge the fairness of economic outcomes all the time. Rent control laws were passed because some legislators thought that landlords treated low-income tenants unfairly. Certainly most social welfare programs are created in the name of equity.

■ **Growth** As the result of technological change, the building of machinery, and the acquisition of knowledge, societies learn to produce new things and to produce old things better. In the early days of the U.S. economy, it took nearly half the population to produce the required food supply. Today about 2.5% of the country's population is engaged in agriculture.

economic growth *An increase in the total output of an economy.*

When we devise new and better ways of producing the things we use now and develop new products and services, the total amount of production in the economy increases. **Economic growth** is an increase in the total output of an economy. If output grows faster than the population, output per capita rises and standards of living increase. Presumably, when an economy grows there is more of what people want. Rural and agrarian societies become modern industrial societies as a result of economic growth and rising per capita output.

Some policies discourage economic growth and others encourage it. Tax laws, for example, can be designed to encourage the development and application of new production techniques. Research and development in some societies are subsidized by the government. Building roads, highways, bridges, and transport systems in developing countries may speed up the process of economic growth. If businesses and wealthy people invest their wealth outside their country rather than in its own industries, growth in their home country may be slowed.

■ **Stability** Economic **stability** refers to the condition in which national output is steady or growing, with low inflation and full employment of resources. An economy may at times be unstable. During the 1950s and 1960s, the U.S. economy experienced a long period of relatively steady growth, stable prices, and low unemployment. Between 1951 and 1969, consumer prices never rose more than 5% in a single year, and in only two years did the number of unemployed exceed 6% of the labor force. The decades of the 1970s and 1980s, however, were unstable. The United States experienced two periods of rapid price inflation (over 10%) and two periods of severe unemployment. In 1982, for example, 12 million people (10.8% of the work force) were looking for work. The beginning of the 1990s was another period of instability, with a recession occurring in 1990—1991. In 1994 the economy was growing at a large enough rate that fears of inflation began to arise. In response, the Federal Reserve System (the U.S. central bank) acted to raise interest rates with a goal of slowing the country's growth rate. The causes of instability and the ways in which governments have attempted to stabilize the economy are the subject matter of macroeconomics.

stability *A condition in which output is steady or growing, with low inflation and full employment of resources.*

AN INVITATION

This chapter is meant to prepare you for what is to come. The first part of the chapter invited you into an exciting discipline that deals with important issues and questions. You cannot begin to understand how a society functions without knowing something about its economic history and its economic system.

The second part of the chapter introduced the method of reasoning that economics requires and some of the tools that economics uses. We believe that learning to think in this very powerful way will help you better understand the world.

As you proceed, it is important that you keep track of what you've learned in earlier chapters. This book has a plan; it proceeds step by step, each section building on the last. It would be a good idea to read through each chapter's table of contents and flip through each chapter before you read it to be sure you understand where it fits in the big picture.

SUMMARY

1. *Economics* is the study of how individuals and societies choose to use the scarce resources that nature and previous generations have provided.

WHY STUDY ECONOMICS?

2. There are many reasons to study economics, including (a) to learn a way of thinking, (b) to understand society, (c) to understand global affairs, and (d) to be an informed voter.

3. That which we forgo when we make a choice or a decision is the *opportunity cost* of that decision.

THE SCOPE OF ECONOMICS

4. *Microeconomics* deals with the functioning of individual markets and industries and with the behavior of individual decision-making units: firms and households.

5. *Macroeconomics* looks at the economy as a whole. It deals with the economic behavior of aggregates—national output, national income, the overall price level, and the general rate of inflation.

6. Economics is a broad and diverse discipline with many special fields of inquiry. These include economic history, international economics, and urban economics.

THE METHOD OF ECONOMICS

7. Economics asks and attempts to answer two kinds of questions: positive and normative. *Positive economics* attempts to understand behavior and the operation of economies without making judgments about whether the outcomes are good or bad. *Normative economics* looks at the results or outcomes of economic behavior and asks if they are good or bad and whether they can be improved.

8. Positive economics is often divided into two parts. *Descriptive economics* involves the compilation of data that accurately describe economic facts and events. *Economic theory* attempts to generalize and explain what is observed. It involves statements of cause and effect—of action and reaction.

9. An economic *model* is a formal statement of an economic theory. Models simplify and abstract from reality.

10. It is often useful to isolate the effects of one variable or another while holding "all else constant." This is the device of *ceteris paribus*.

11. Models and theories can be expressed in many ways. The most common ways are in words, in graphs, and in equations.

12. Because one event happens before another, the second event does not necessarily happen as a result of the first event. To assume that "after" implies "because" is to commit the fallacy of *post hoc, ergo propter hoc*. The belief that what is true for a part is necessarily true for the whole is the *fallacy of composition*.

13. *Empirical economics* involves the collection and use of data to test economic theories. In principle, the best model is the one that yields the most accurate predictions.

14. To make policy, one must be careful to specify criteria for making judgments. Four specific criteria are used most often in economics: *efficiency, equity, growth,* and *stability*.

REVIEW TERMS AND CONCEPTS

ceteris paribus 12
descriptive economics 11
economic growth 16
economic theory 11
economics 2
efficiency 16
efficient market 4
empirical economics 15

equity 16
fallacy of composition 14
inductive reasoning 11
Industrial Revolution 5
macroeconomics 8
microeconomics 8
model 11
normative economics 9

Ockham's razor 12
opportunity cost 3
positive economics 9
post hoc, ergo propter hoc 13
stability 17
sunk costs 3
variable 11

PROBLEM SET

1. One of the scarce resources that constrain our behavior is time. Each of us has only 24 hours in a day. How do you go about allocating your time in a given day among competing alternatives? How do you go about weighing the alternatives? Once you choose a most important use of time, why do you not spend all your time on it? Use the notion of opportunity cost in your answer.

2. Which of the following statements might be made by someone studying *positive* economics? Briefly explain your answer.
   a. The North American Free Trade Agreement (NAFTA) is likely to lead to increased exports of U.S.-made automobiles to Mexico.
   b. NAFTA is likely to make the people of Mexico better off.

c. The Deficit Reduction Act of 1993 raised income tax rates for households with high incomes. This legislation is likely to reduce savings for that group.

d. The higher taxes imposed by the Deficit Reduction Act of 1993 are unfair.

e. Raising revenue by increasing bridge tolls in New York City is unfair because it will impose larger burdens on lower-income households.

f. Increasing the toll on the bridges into New York City by $2.00 is likely to reduce congestion in the city.

3. Describe one of the major economic issues facing the government of your city or your state. (*Hint:* You might look at a local newspaper. Most issues that make it into the paper will have an impact on people's lives.) Who will be affected by the resolution of this issue? What alternative actions have been proposed? Who will be the winners? The losers?

4. Suppose that all of the 10,000 voting-age citizens of Lumpland are required to register to vote every year. Suppose also that the citizens of Lumpland are fully employed and that they each value their time at $10 per hour. In addition, assume that non-voting high-school students in Lumpland are willing to work for $5 per hour. The government has two choices: (1) It can hire 200 students to work at registration locations for 5 hours per day for 10 days, or (2) it can hire 400 students for 5 hours per day for 10 days. If the government hires 200 students, each of the 10,000 citizens will have to wait in line for an hour to register. If the government hires 400 students, there will be no waiting time.

Assume that the cost of paying the students is obtained by taxing each citizen equally. The current government is very conservative and has decided to hold taxes down by hiring only 200 students. Do you agree with this decision? Why or why not? Is it efficient? Is it fair?

5. Suppose that a city is considering building a bridge across a river. The bridge will be paid for out of tax dollars, and the city gets its revenues from a sales tax imposed on things sold in the city. The bridge would provide more direct access for commuters and shoppers and would alleviate the huge traffic jam that occurs every morning at the bridge down the river in another city.

a. Who would gain if the bridge were built? Could those gains be measured? How?

b. Who would be hurt? Could those costs be measured? How?

c. How would you determine if it were efficient to build the bridge?

6. Define *equity*. How would you decide if building the bridge described in question 5 were fair/equitable?

7. For each of the following situations, identify the full cost (opportunity costs) involved:

a. A worker earning an hourly wage of $8.50 decides to cut back to half time in order to attend Houston Community College.

b. Sue decides to drive to Los Angeles from San Francisco to visit her son, who attends UCLA.

c. Tom decides to go to a wild fraternity party and stays out all night before his physics exam.

d. Annie spends $200 on a new dress.

e. The Confab Company spends $1 million to build a new branch plant that will probably be in operation for at least 10 years.

f. Alex's father owns a small grocery store in town. Alex works 40 hours a week in the store but receives no compensation.

Economics is the most quantitative of the social sciences. If you flip through the pages of this or any other economics text, you will see countless tables and graphs. These tables and graphs serve a number of purposes. First, they illustrate important economic relationships. Second, they make difficult problems easier to understand and analyze. Finally, patterns and regularities that may not be discernible in simple lists of numbers can often be seen when those numbers are laid out in a table or on a graph.

A **graph** is a two-dimensional representation of a set of numbers, or data. There are many ways that numbers can be illustrated by a graph.

TIME SERIES GRAPHS

It is often useful to see how a single measure or variable changes over time. One way to present this information is to plot the values of the variable on a graph, with each value corresponding to a different time period. A graph of this kind is called a **time series graph.** On a time series graph, time is measured along the horizontal scale and the variable being graphed is measured along the vertical scale. Figures 1A.1 and 1A.2 are time series graphs that present the total income in the U.S. economy for each year between 1975 and 1994.* These graphs are based

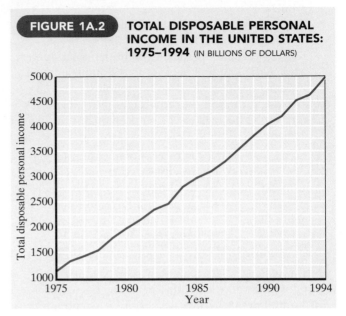

FIGURE 1A.2   TOTAL DISPOSABLE PERSONAL INCOME IN THE UNITED STATES: 1975–1994 (IN BILLIONS OF DOLLARS)

Source: *Economic Report of the President,* 1995, p. 307.

on the data found in Table 1A.1. By displaying these data graphically, we can see clearly that (1) total personal disposable income has been increasing steadily since 1975, and (2) during certain periods, disposable income was increasing at a faster rate than during other periods.

Graphs must be read very carefully. For example, look at Figure 1A.2, which plots the same data that are plotted in Figure 1A.1. Because the values on the vertical axis in Figure 1A.2 start at $1,000 billion rather than at zero, and because the vertical scales are different, you may be led to believe that income is growing much more rapidly in Figure 1A.2 than in Figure 1A.1. This is not true, of course. The same variable is plotted in both graphs.

GRAPHING TWO VARIABLES ON A CARTESIAN COORDINATE SYSTEM

More important than simple graphs of one variable are graphs that contain information on two variables at the same time. The most common method of graphing two variables is the **Cartesian coordinate system.** This system is constructed by simply drawing two perpendicular lines: a horizontal line, or **X axis,** and a vertical line, or **Y axis.** The axes contain measurement scales that intersect at 0

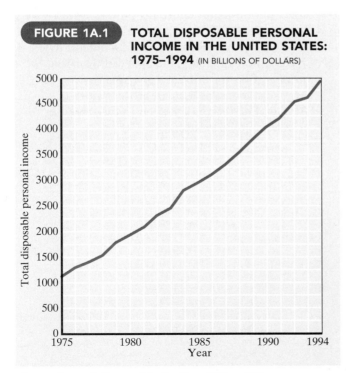

FIGURE 1A.1   TOTAL DISPOSABLE PERSONAL INCOME IN THE UNITED STATES: 1975–1994 (IN BILLIONS OF DOLLARS)

Source: *Economic Report of the President,* 1995, p. 307.

*The measure of income presented in Table 1A.1 and in Figures 1A.1 and 1A.2 is disposable income in billions of dollars. It is an approximation of the total personal income received by all households in the United States added together minus the taxes that they pay.

TABLE 1A.1	TOTAL DISPOSABLE PERSONAL INCOME IN THE UNITED STATES, 1975–1994 (IN BILLIONS OF DOLLARS)

YEAR	TOTAL DISPOSABLE PERSONAL INCOME
1975	1150.9
1976	1264.0
1977	1391.3
1978	1567.8
1979	1753.0
1980	1952.9
1981	2174.5
1982	2319.6
1983	2493.7
1984	2759.5
1985	2943.0
1986	3131.5
1987	3289.5
1988	3548.2
1989	3787.0
1990	4050.5
1991	4236.6
1992	4505.8
1993	4688.7
1994	4959.3

Source: *Economic Report of the President*, 1995, p. 307.

(zero). This point is called the **origin.** On the vertical scale, positive numbers lie above the horizontal axis (that is, above the origin) and negative numbers lie below it. On the horizontal scale, positive numbers lie to the right of the vertical axis (to the right of the origin) and negative numbers lie to the left of it. The point at which the graph intersects the Y axis is called the **Y-intercept.**

When two variables are plotted on a single graph, each point represents a *pair* of numbers. The first number is measured on the X axis and the second number is measured on the Y axis. For example, the following points (X, Y) are plotted on the set of axes drawn in Figure 1A.3: (4, 2), (2, –1), (–3, 4), (–3, –2). Most, but not all, of the graphs in this book are plots of two variables where both values are positive numbers (such as [4, 2] in Figure 1A.3). On these graphs, only the upper right-hand quadrant of the coordinate system (i.e., the quadrant in which all X and Y values are positive) will be drawn.

PLOTTING INCOME AND CONSUMPTION DATA FOR HOUSEHOLDS

Table 1A.2 presents some data that were collected by the Bureau of Labor Statistics (BLS). In a survey of 5,000

FIGURE 1A.3	A CARTESIAN COORDINATE SYSTEM

A Cartesian coordinate system is constructed by drawing two perpendicular lines: a vertical axis (the Y axis) and a horizontal axis (the X axis). Each axis is a measuring scale.

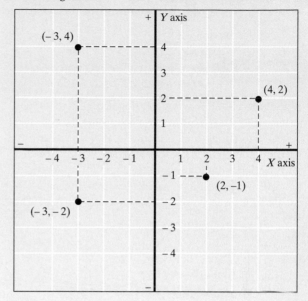

households, each household was asked to keep careful track of all its expenditures. The table shows average income and average spending for those households that were surveyed, ranked by income. For example the average income for the top fifth (20%) of the households was $76,660, and their average spending was $55,411.

TABLE 1A.2	CONSUMPTION EXPENDITURES AND INCOME, 1990*

	AVERAGE INCOME	AVERAGE CONSUMPTION EXPENDITURES
Bottom fifth	$ 5,637	$12,908
2nd fifth	14,115	17,924
3rd fifth	24,500	24,673
4th fifth	38,376	34,247
Top fifth	76,660	55,411

Source: *Statistical Abstract of the United States*, 1992, p. 442.

Income and consumption data are for consumer units. Consumer units are defined as (1) all members of a particular household related by blood, marriage, adoption, or other legal arrangements, (2) a person living alone or sharing a household with others, but who is financially independent, or (3) two or more persons living together who pool their incomes.

Figure 1A.4 presents the numbers from Table 1A.2 graphically using the Cartesian coordinate system. Along the horizontal scale, the X axis, we measure average income. Along the vertical scale, the Y axis, we measure average consumption spending. Each of the five pairs of numbers from the table is represented by a point on the graph. Since all numbers are positive numbers, we need to show only the upper right quadrant of the coordinate system.

FIGURE 1A.4   HOUSEHOLD CONSUMPTION AND INCOME

A graph is a simple two-dimensional geometric representation of data. This graph displays the data from Table 1A.2. Along the horizontal scale (X axis), we measure household income. Along the vertical scale (Y axis), we measure household consumption. *Note:* At point A, consumption equals $12,908 and income equals $5,637; at point B, consumption equals $17,924 and income equals $14,115.

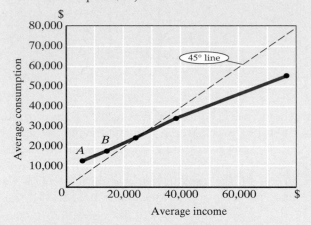

Source: *Statistical Abstract of the United States*, 1992, p. 442.

To help you read this graph, we have drawn a dotted line connecting all the points where consumption and income would be equal. *This 45° line does not represent any data.* Rather, it represents the line along which all variables on the X axis correspond exactly to the variables on the Y axis (for example, [1, 1], [2, 2], [3.7, 3.7], etc.). The heavy blue line traces out the data; the dotted line is only to help you read the graph.

There are several things to look for when reading a graph. The first thing you should notice is whether the line slopes upward or downward as you move from left to right. The blue line in Figure 1A.4 slopes upward, indicating that there seems to be a **positive relationship** between income and spending: The higher a household's income, the more a household tends to consume. If we had graphed the percentage of each group receiving welfare payments along the Y axis, the line would presumably slope downward, indicating that welfare payments are lower at higher income levels. The income level/welfare payment relationship is thus a **negative** one.

SLOPE

The **slope** of a line or curve is a measure that indicates whether the relationship between the variables is positive or negative and how much of a response there is in Y (the variable on the vertical axis) when X (the variable on the horizontal axis) changes. The slope of a line between two points is the change in the quantity being measured on the Y axis divided by the change in the quantity being measured on the X axis. We will normally use Δ (the Greek letter delta) to refer to a change in a variable. In Figure 1A.5, the slope of the line between points A and B is ΔY divided by ΔX. Sometimes

FIGURE 1A.5   A CURVE WITH A POSITIVE SLOPE (a) AND A CURVE WITH A NEGATIVE SLOPE (b)

A *positive* slope indicates that increases in X are associated with increases in Y and that decreases in X are associated with decreases in Y. A *negative* slope indicates the opposite—when X increases, Y decreases and when X decreases, Y increases.

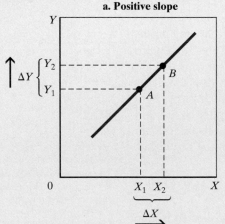
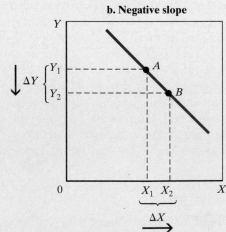

it's easy to remember slope as "the rise over the run," indicating the vertical change over the horizontal change.

To be precise, ΔX between two points on a graph is simply X_2 minus X_1, where X_2 is the X value for the second point and X_1 is the X value for the first point. Similarly, ΔY is defined as Y_2 minus Y_1, where Y_2 is the Y value for the second point and Y_1 is the Y value for the first point. Slope is equal to

$$\frac{\Delta Y}{\Delta X} = \frac{Y_2 - Y_1}{X_2 - X_1}.$$

As we move from A to B in Figure 1A.5a, both X and Y increase; the slope is thus a positive number. On the other hand, as we move from A to B in Figure 1A.5b, X increases [$(X_2 - X_1)$ is a positive number], but Y decreases [$(Y_2 - Y_1)$ is a negative number]. The slope in Figure 1A.5b is thus a negative number, since a negative number divided by a positive number gives a negative quotient.

To calculate the numerical value of the slope between points A and B in Figure 1A.4, we need to calculate ΔY and ΔX. Since consumption is measured on the Y axis, ΔY is 5,016 [$(Y_2 - Y_1) = (17,924 - 12,908)$]. Since income is measured along the X axis, ΔX is 8,478 [$(X_2 - X_1) = (14,115 - 5,637)$]. The slope between A and B is $\Delta Y/\Delta X = 5,016/8,478 = +.592$.

Another interesting thing to note about the data graphed in Figure 1A.4 is that all the points lie roughly along a straight line. (If you look very closely, however, you can see that the slope declines as one moves from left to right; the line becomes slightly less steep.) A straight line has a constant slope. That is, if you pick any two points along it and calculate the slope, you will always get the same number. A horizontal line has a zero slope (ΔY is zero); a vertical line has an "infinite" slope, since ΔY is too big to be measured.

Unlike the slope of a straight line, the slope of a *curve* is continually changing. Consider, for example, the curves in Figure 1A.6. Figure 1A.6a shows a curve with a positive slope that decreases as you move from left to right. The easiest way to think about the concept of increasing or decreasing slope is to imagine what it is like walking up a hill from left to right. If the hill is steep (as it is in the first part of Figure 1A.6a), you are moving a lot in the Y direction for each step you take in the X direction. If the hill is less steep (as it is further along in Figure 1A.6a), you are moving less in the Y direction for every step you take in the X direction. Thus, when the hill is steep, slope ($\Delta Y/\Delta X$) is a larger number than it is when the hill is flatter. The curve in Figure 1A.6b has a positive slope, but its slope *increases* as you move from left to right.

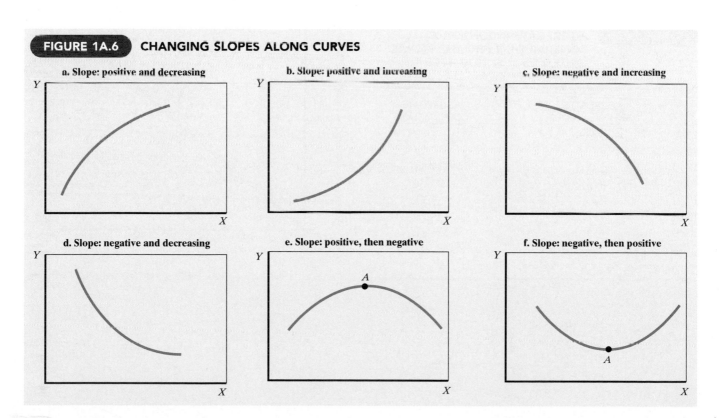

FIGURE 1A.6 **CHANGING SLOPES ALONG CURVES**

a. Slope: positive and decreasing

b. Slope: positive and increasing

c. Slope: negative and increasing

d. Slope: negative and decreasing

e. Slope: positive, then negative

f. Slope: negative, then positive

The same analogy holds for curves that have a negative slope. Figure 1A.6c shows a curve with a negative slope that increases (in absolute value)* as you move from left to right. This time think about skiing down a hill. At first, the descent in Figure 1A.6c is gradual (low slope), but as you proceed down the hill (to the right), you descend more quickly (high slope). Figure 1A.6d shows a curve with a negative slope that *decreases* in absolute value as you move from left to right.

In Figure 1A.6e, the slope goes from positive to negative as X increases. In 1A.6f, the slope goes from negative to positive. At point A in both, the slope is zero. (Remember, slope is defined as $\Delta Y/\Delta X$. At point A, Y is not changing [$\Delta Y = 0$]. Therefore slope at point A is zero.)

SOME PRECAUTIONS

When you read a graph, it is important to think carefully about what the points in the space defined by the axes represent. Table 1A.3 and Figure 1A.7 present a graph of consumption and income that is very different from the one in Table 1A.2 and Figure 1A.4. First, each point in Figure 1A.7 represents a different year; in Figure

1A.4, each point represented a different group of households at the *same* point in time (1990). Second, the points in Figure 1A.7 represent *aggregate* consumption and income for the whole nation measured in *billions* of dollars; in Figure 1A.4, the points represented average *household* income and consumption measured in dollars.

It is interesting to compare these two graphs. All points on the aggregate consumption curve in Figure 1A.7 lie below the 45-degree line, which means that aggregate consumption is always less than aggregate income. On the other hand, the graph of average household income and consumption in Figure 1A.4 crosses the 45-degree line, implying that for some households consumption is larger than income.

---

*The absolute value *of a number is its value disregarding its sign, that is, disregarding whether it is positive or negative: –7 is bigger in absolute value than –4; –9 is bigger in absolute value than + 8.*

TABLE 1A.3	AGGREGATE INCOME AND CONSUMPTION FOR THE ENTIRE UNITED STATES, 1930–1990 (IN BILLIONS OF DOLLARS)	
	AGGREGATE NATIONAL INCOME	AGGREGATE CONSUMPTION
1930	73.8	69.9
1940	79.6	71.0
1950	239.8	192.1
1960	425.7	332.4
1970	833.5	646.5
1980	2198.2	1748.1
1990	4491.0	3761.2

Source: *Economic Report of the President*, 1995, pp. 292, 302.

FIGURE 1A.7   NATIONAL INCOME AND CONSUMPTION

It is important to think carefully about what is represented by points in the space defined by the axes of a graph. In this graph, we have income graphed with consumption, as was the case in Figure 1A.4, but here each observation point is national income and aggregate consumption in *different years*, measured in billions of dollars.

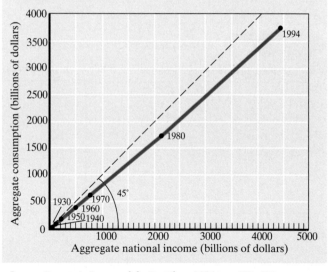

Source: *Economic Report of the President*, 1995, pp. 292, 302.

1. A *graph* is a two-dimensional representation of a set of numbers, or data. A *time series graph* illustrates how a single variable changes over time.

2. The most common method of graphing two variables on one graph is the *Cartesian coordinate system,* which includes an X (horizontal) *axis* and a Y (vertical) *axis.* The points at which the two axes intersect is called the *origin.* The point at which a graph intersects the Y axis is called the *Y-intercept.*

3. The *slope* of a line or curve indicates whether the relationship between the two variables graphed on a Cartesian coordinate system is positive or negative and how much of a response there is in Y (the variable on the vertical axis) when X (the variable on the horizontal axis) changes. The slope of a line between two points is the change in the quantity being measured on the Y axis divided by the change in the quantity being measured on the X axis.

REVIEW TERMS AND CONCEPTS

Cartesian coordinate system A common method of graphing two variables that makes use of two perpendicular lines against which the variables are plotted. 20

graph A two-dimensional representation of a set of numbers, or data. 20

negative relationship A relationship between two variables, X and Y, in which a decrease in X is associated with an increase in Y, and an increase in X is associated with a decrease in Y. 22

origin On a Cartesian coordinate system, the point at which the horizontal and vertical axes intersect. 20

positive relationship A relationship between two variables, X and Y, in which a decrease in X is associated with a decrease in Y, and an increase in X is associated with an increase in Y. 22

slope A measurement that indicates whether the relationship between variables is positive or negative and how much of a response there is in Y (the variable on the vertical axis) when X (the variable on the horizontal axis) changes. 22

times series graph A graph illustrating how a variable changes over time. 20

X axis On a Cartesian coordinate system, the horizontal line against which a variable is plotted. 20

Y axis On a Cartesian coordinate system, the vertical line against which a variable is plotted. 20

Y-intercept The point at which a graph intersects the Y axis. 21

1. Graph each of the following sets of numbers. Draw a line through the points and calculate the slope of each line.

1		2		3		4		5		6	
X	Y	X	Y	X	Y	X	Y	X	Y	X	Y
1	5	1	25	0	0	0	40	0	0	0.1	100
2	10	2	20	10	10	10	30	10	10	0.2	75
3	15	3	15	20	20	20	20	20	20	0.3	50
4	20	4	10	30	30	30	10	30	10	0.4	25
5	25	5	5	40	40	40	0	40	0	0.5	0

2. For each of the following equations graph the line and calculate its slope.
   a. $P = 10 - 2q_D$ (Put q_D on the X axis)
   b. $P = 100 - 4q_D$ (Put q_D on the X axis)
   c. $P = 50 + 6q_S$ (Put q_S on the X axis)
   d. $I = 10,000 - 500r$ (Put I on the X axis)

3. For each of the graphs in Figure 1 below, say whether the curve has a positive or negative slope. Give an intuitive explanation for the slope of each curve.

FIGURE 1

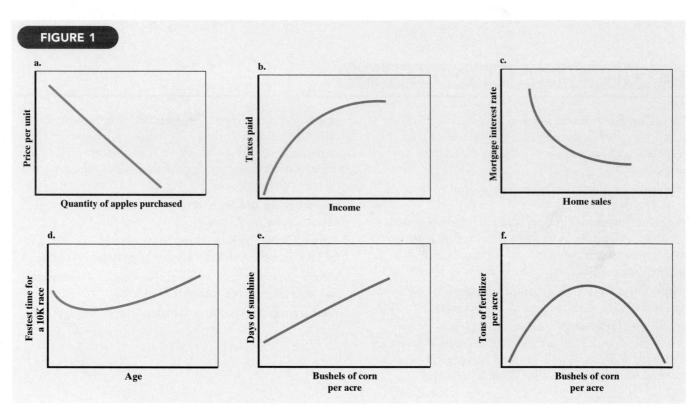

THE ECONOMIC PROBLEM: SCARCITY AND CHOICE

CHAPTER 1 BEGAN WITH A BROAD DEFINITION OF ECONOMICS. AS you saw there, every society has some system or mechanism that transforms what nature and previous generations provide into useful form. Economics is the study of that process and its outcomes. Economists attempt to answer the questions: What gets produced? How is it produced? Who gets it? Why? Is it good or bad? Can it be improved?

This chapter explores these questions further. In a sense, this entire chapter *is* the definition of economics. It lays out the central problems addressed by the discipline and provides the framework that will guide you through the rest of the book.

Human wants are unlimited, but resources are not. Limited, or scarce, resources force individuals and societies to choose. The central function of any economy, no matter how simple or how complex, is to transform resources into useful form in accordance with those choices. The process by which this transformation takes place is called **production.**

The term **resources** is very broad. Some resources are the product of nature: land, wildlife, minerals, timber, energy, even the rain and the wind. At any given time, the resources, or **inputs,** available to a society also include those things that have been produced by previous generations, such as buildings and equipment. Things that are produced and then used to produce other valuable goods or services later on are called *capital resources,* or simply **capital.** Buildings, machinery, equipment, tables, roads, bridges, desks, and so forth are part of the nation's capital stock. *Human resources*—labor, skills, and knowledge—are also an important part of a nation's resources.

production *The process by which resources are transformed into useful forms.*

resources or **inputs** *Anything provided by nature or previous generations that can be used directly or indirectly to satisfy human wants.*

capital *Things that have already been produced that are in turn used to produce other goods and services.*

producers *Those people or groups of people, whether private or public, who transform resources into usable products.*

outputs *Usable products.*

Producers are those who take resources and transform them into usable products, or **outputs.** Private manufacturing firms purchase resources and produce products for the market. Governments do so as well. National defense, the justice system, police and fire protection, and sewer services all are examples of outputs produced by the government, which is sometimes called the *public sector.*

Individual households often produce products for themselves. A household that owns its own home is in essence using land and a structure (capital) to produce "housing services" that it consumes itself. The Chicago Symphony Orchestra is no less a producer than General Motors. An orchestra takes capital resources—a building, musical instruments, lighting fixtures, musical scores, and so on—and combines them with land and highly skilled labor to produce performances.

SCARCITY, CHOICE, AND OPPORTUNITY COST

In the second half of this chapter, we discuss the global economic landscape. But before you can understand the different types of economic systems, it is important to understand the basic economic concepts of scarcity, choice, and opportunity cost.

THE THREE BASIC QUESTIONS

three basic questions *The questions that all societies must answer: (1) What will be produced? (2) How will it be produced? (3) Who will get what is produced?*

All societies must answer **three basic questions:**

1. What will be produced?
2. How will it be produced?
3. Who will get what is produced?

Stated a slightly different way, the economic system must determine the *allocation of scarce resources* among producers, the *mix of output,* and the *distribution of that output* (Figure 2.1).

■ **Scarcity and Choice in a One-Person Economy** The simplest economy is one in which a single person lives alone on an island where no one has ever been before. Consider Bill, the survivor of a plane crash, who finds himself cast ashore in such a place. Here, individual and society are one; there is no distinction between social and private. *Nonetheless, nearly all of the basic decisions that characterize complex economies must be made.* That is, although Bill himself will get whatever he produces, he still must decide how to allocate the resources of the island, what to produce, and how and when to produce it.

FIGURE 2.1

The Three Basic Questions

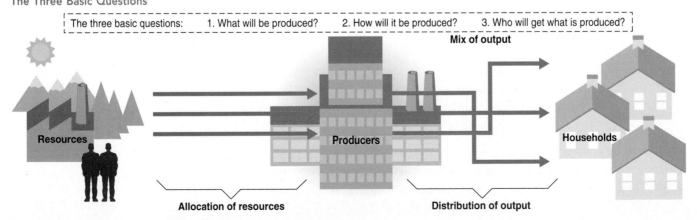

First, Bill must decide *what* he wants to produce. Notice that the word *needs* does not appear here. Needs are absolute requirements, but beyond just enough water, basic nutrition, and shelter to survive, they are very difficult to define. What is an "absolute necessity" for one person may not be for another. In any case, Bill must put his wants in some order of priority and make some choices.

Next he must look at the *possibilities*. What can he do to satisfy his wants, given the limits of the island? In every society, no matter how simple or complex, people are constrained in what they can do. In this society of one, Bill is constrained by time, his physical condition, his knowledge, his skills, and the resources and climate of the island.

Given that resources are limited, or scarce, Bill must decide *how* to use them best to satisfy his hierarchy of wants. Food would probably come close to the top of his list. Should he spend his time simply gathering fruits and berries? Should he hunt for game? Should he clear a field and plant seeds? Clearly, the answers to these questions depend on the character of the island, its climate, its flora and fauna (*are* there any fruits and berries?), the extent of his skills and knowledge (does he know anything about farming?), and his preferences (he may be a vegetarian).

■ **Opportunity Cost**   The concepts of *constrained choice* and *scarcity* are central to the discipline of economics. They can be applied when discussing the behavior of individuals like Bill and when analyzing the behavior of large groups of people in complex societies.

Given the scarcity of time and resources, Bill has less time to gather fruits and berries if he chooses to hunt—he trades more meat for less fruit. There is a trade-off between food and shelter, too. If Bill likes to be comfortable, he may work on building a nice place to live, but that may require giving up the food he might have produced. As we noted in Chapter 1, that which we forgo when we make a choice is the **opportunity cost** of that choice.

opportunity cost *That which we give up, or forgo, when we make a choice or a decision.*

Bill may occasionally decide to rest, to lie on the beach and enjoy the sun. In one sense, that benefit is free—he doesn't have to pay for the privilege. In reality, however, it does have a cost, an opportunity cost. Lying in the sun means using time that otherwise could have been spent doing something else. The true cost of that leisure is the value to Bill of the other things he could have produced, but did not, during the time he spent on the beach.

In the 1960s, the United States decided to put a human being on the moon. To do so required devoting enormous resources to the space program, resources that could have been used to produce other things. The opportunity cost of placing a man on the moon was the total value of all the other things that those resources could have produced. Among other possibilities, taxes might have been lower. That would have meant more income for all of us to spend on goods and services. Those same resources could also have been used for medical research, to improve education, to repair roads and bridges, to aid the poor, or to support the arts.

In making everyday decisions it is often helpful to think about opportunity costs. Should I go to the dorm party or not? First, it costs $4 to get in. When I pay out money for anything, I give up the other things that I could have bought with that money. Second, it costs two or three hours. Clearly, time is a valuable commodity for a college student. I have exams next week and I need to study. I could go to a movie instead of the party. I could go to another party. I could sleep. Just as Bill must weigh the value of sunning on the beach against more food or better housing, so I must weigh the value of the fun I may have at the dorm party against everything else I might otherwise do with the time and money.

■ Scarcity and Choice in an Economy of Two or More Now suppose that another survivor of the crash, Colleen, appears on the island. Now that Bill is not alone things are more complex, and some new decisions must be made. Bill's and Colleen's preferences about what things to produce are likely to be different. They will probably not have the same knowledge or skills. Perhaps Colleen is very good at tracking animals, while Bill has a knack for building things. How should they split the work that needs to be done? Once things are produced, they must decide how to divide them. How should their products be distributed?

The mechanism for answering these fundamental questions is clear when Bill is alone on the island. The "central plan" is his; he simply decides what he wants and what to do about it. The minute someone else appears, however, a number of decision-making arrangements immediately become possible. One or the other may take charge, in which case that person will decide for both of them. The two may agree to cooperate, with each having an equal say, and come up with a joint plan. Or they may agree to split the planning, as well as the production duties. Finally, they may go off to live alone at opposite ends of the island. Even if they live apart, however, they may take advantage of each other's presence by specializing and trading.

> Modern industrial societies must answer exactly the same questions that Colleen and Bill must answer, but the mechanics of larger economies are naturally more complex. Instead of two people living together, the United States has over 260 million. Still decisions must be made about what to produce, how to produce it, and who gets it.

theory of comparative advantage *Ricardo's theory that specialization and free trade will benefit all trading parties, even those that may be absolutely more efficient producers.*

■ Specialization, Exchange, and Comparative Advantage The idea that members of society benefit by specializing in what they do best has a long history and is one of the most important and powerful ideas in all of economics. David Ricardo, a major nineteenth-century British economist, formalized the point precisely. According to Ricardo's **theory of comparative advantage**, specialization and free trade will benefit all trading parties, even when some are "absolutely" more efficient producers than others. Ricardo's basic point applies just as much to Colleen and Bill as it does to different nations.

To keep things simple, suppose that Colleen and Bill have only two tasks to accomplish each week: gathering food to eat and cutting logs to be used in constructing a house. If Colleen could cut more logs than Bill in one day, and Bill could gather more nuts and berries than Colleen could, specialization would clearly lead to more total production. Both Bill and Colleen would benefit if Colleen only cuts logs and Bill only gathers nuts and berries. But suppose that Bill is slow and somewhat clumsy in his nut-gathering and that Colleen is better at both cutting logs *and* gathering food. Ricardo's point is that it still pays for them to specialize and exchange.

Suppose that Colleen can cut 10 logs per day and that Bill can cut only 5. Also suppose that Colleen can gather 10 bushels of food per day and that Bill can gather only 8 (see table embedded in Figure 2.2). Assume also that Bill and Colleen value bushels of food and logs equally. How then can the two gain from specialization and exchange? Think of opportunity costs. When Colleen gives up a day of food production to work on the house, she cuts 10 logs and sacrifices 10 bushels of food. The opportunity cost of 10 logs is thus 10 bushels of food if Colleen switches from food to logs. But because Bill can cut only 5 logs in a day, he has to work for 2 days to cut 10 logs. In 2 days, Bill could have produced 16 bushels of food (2 days × 8 bushels per day). The opportunity cost of 10 logs is thus 16 bushels of food if Bill switches from food to logs.

FIGURE 2.2
Comparative Advantage and
Opportunity Costs

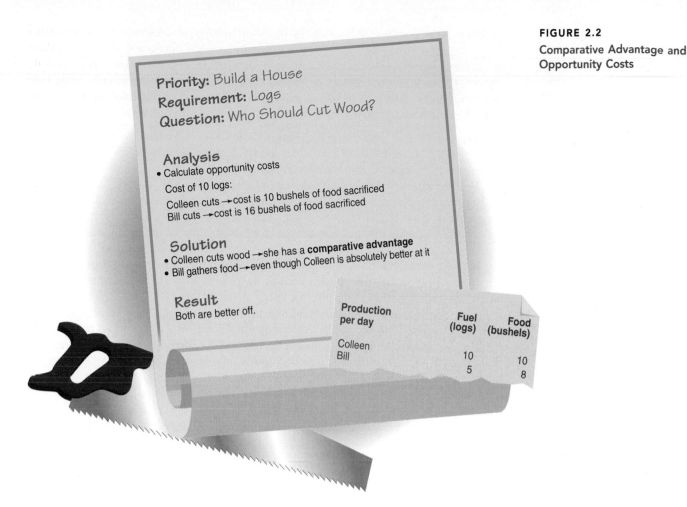

Priority: Build a House
Requirement: Logs
Question: Who Should Cut Wood?

Analysis
• Calculate opportunity costs
  Cost of 10 logs:
  Colleen cuts → cost is 10 bushels of food sacrificed
  Bill cuts → cost is 16 bushels of food sacrificed

Solution
• Colleen cuts wood → she has a **comparative advantage**
• Bill gathers food → even though Colleen is absolutely better at it

Result
Both are better off.

Production per day	Fuel (logs)	Food (bushels)
Colleen	10	10
Bill	5	8

As Figure 2.2 makes clear, even though Colleen is *absolutely* more efficient at food production than Bill, she should specialize in logs and let Bill specialize in food. This way, the maximum number of logs and bushels are produced. A person or a country is said to have a comparative advantage in producing a good or service if it is *relatively* more efficient than a trading partner at doing so. Colleen is relatively more efficient at log production because the opportunity cost of switching from food to logs is lower for her than it is for Bill.

Looking at the same problem from the standpoint of food production leads to exactly the same conclusion. If Colleen were to switch from cutting logs to gathering food, she would sacrifice 10 logs to produce only 10 bushels of food. But if Bill were to switch from cutting logs to gathering food, he would sacrifice 10 logs to produce a full 16 bushels! Even though Colleen has an *absolute advantage* in both cutting logs and producing food, Bill has a *comparative advantage* producing food because for the same sacrifice of logs, Bill produces much more food.

The theory of comparative advantage shows that trade and specialization work to raise productivity. But specialization may also lead to the development of skills that enhance productivity even further. By specializing in log cutting, Colleen will get even stronger shoulders. By spending more time at gathering food, Bill will refine his food-finding skills. The same applies to countries that engage in international trade. A country that specializes in producing textiles will refine its skills in textile making, while a country that specializes in growing corn will increase its corn-growing skills.

The degree of specialization in modern industrial societies is breathtaking. Once again let your mind wander over the range of products and services available or under development today. As knowledge expands, specialization becomes a necessity. This is true not only for scientists and doctors but also in every career from tree surgeon to divorce lawyers. Understanding specialization and trade will help you to explain much of what goes on in today's global economy.

■ **Weighing Present and Expected Future Costs and Benefits** Very often we find ourselves weighing benefits available today against benefits available tomorrow. Here too the notion of opportunity cost is helpful.

While alone on the island, Bill had to choose between cultivating a field and just gathering wild nuts and berries. Gathering nuts and berries provides food now; gathering seeds and clearing a field for planting will yield food tomorrow, if all goes well. Using today's time to farm may well be worth the effort if doing so will yield more food than Bill would otherwise have in the future. By planting, Bill is trading present value for future values. Working to gather seeds and clear a field has an opportunity cost—the present leisure he might consume and the value of the berries he might gather if he did not work the field.

The simplest example of trading present for future benefits is the act of saving. When I put income aside today for use in the future, I give up some things that I could have had today in exchange for something tomorrow. The saver must weigh the value of what that income can buy today against what it might be expected to buy later. Since nothing is certain, some judgment about future events and expected values must be made. What are interest rates likely to be? What will my income be in ten years? How long am I likely to live?

We trade off present and future benefits in small ways all the time. If you decide to study rather than go to the dorm party, you are trading present fun for the expected future benefits of higher grades. If you decide to go outside on a very cold day and run five miles, you are trading discomfort in the present for being in better shape later on.

■ **Capital Goods and Consumer Goods** A society trades present for expected future benefits when it devotes a portion of its resources to research and development or to investment in capital. As we said earlier in this chapter, *capital* in its broadest definition is anything that is produced that will be used to produce other valuable goods or services over time.

Building capital means trading present benefits for future ones. Bill and Colleen might trade gathering berries or lying in the sun for cutting logs to build a nicer house in the future. In a modern society, resources used to produce capital goods could have been used to produce **consumer goods**—that is, goods for present consumption. Heavy industrial machinery does not directly satisfy the wants of anyone, but producing it requires resources that could instead have gone into producing things that do satisfy wants directly—food, clothing, toys, or golf clubs.

consumer goods *Goods produced for present consumption.*

Capital is everywhere. A road is capital. Once built, we can drive on it or transport goods and services over it for many years to come. The benefits of producing it will be realized over many years. A house is also capital. When it is built, the builder presumes that it will provide shelter and valuable services for a long time. Before a new manufacturing firm can start up, it must put some capital in place. The buildings, equipment, and inventories that it owns are its capital. As it contributes to the production process, this capital yields valuable services through time.

In Chapter 1 we talked about the enormous amount of capital—buildings, roads, factories, housing, cars, trucks, telephone lines, and so forth—that you might see from a window high in a skyscraper. Much of it was put in place by previous generations, yet it continues to provide valuable services today; it is part of this generation's endowment of resources. In order to build every building, every road, every factory, every house, every car or truck, society must forgo using resources to produce consumer goods today. To get an education, I pay tuition and put off joining the work force for a while.

Capital need not be tangible. When you spend time and resources developing skills or getting an education, you are investing in human capital—your own human capital—that will continue to exist and yield benefits to you for years to come. A computer program produced by a software company may come on a tangible disk that costs 75¢ to make, but its true intangible value comes from the ideas embodied in the program itself, which will drive computers to do valuable tasks over time. It too is capital.

The process of using resources to produce new capital is called **investment.** (In everyday language, the term *investment* is often used to refer to the act of buying a share of stock or a bond, as in "I invested in some Treasury bonds." In economics, however, investment always refers to the creation of capital: the purchase or putting in place of buildings, equipment, roads, houses, and the like.) A wise investment in capital is one that yields future benefits that are more valuable than the present cost. When you spend money for a house, for example, presumably you value its future benefits. That is, you expect to gain more from living in it than you would from the things you could buy today with the same money.

Capital is able to generate future benefits in excess of cost by increasing the productivity of labor. A person who has to dig a hole can dig a bigger hole with a shovel than without a shovel. A computer can do in several seconds what it took hundreds of bookkeepers hours to do 15 years ago. This increased productivity makes it less costly to produce products.

> Because resources are scarce, the opportunity cost of every investment in capital is forgone present consumption.

THE PRODUCTION POSSIBILITY FRONTIER

A simple graphical device called the **production possibility frontier (ppf)** illustrates the principle of constrained choice and scarcity. The ppf is a graph that shows all the combinations of goods and services that can be produced if all of society's resources are used efficiently. Figure 2.3 on the next page shows a ppf for a hypothetical economy.

On the Y axis we measure the quantity of capital goods produced, and on the X axis, the quantity of consumption goods. All points below and to the left of the curve (the shaded area) represent combinations of capital and consumption goods that are possible for the society given the resources available and existing technology. Points above and to the right of the curve, such as point G, represent combinations that cannot be reached. If an economy were to end up at point A on the graph, it would be producing no consumption goods at all; all resources would be used for the production of capital. If an economy were to end up at point B, it would be devoting all of its resources to the production of consumer goods and none of its resources to the formation of capital.

While all economies produce some of each kind of good, different economies emphasize different things. About 16% of gross output in the United States in 1993 was new capital. In Japan, capital accounted for about 30% of gross output in 1993, while in Uruguay the figure was 14 percent. Japan is closer to point A on its ppf, Uruguay closer to B, and the United States is somewhere in between.

Points that are actually on the production possibility frontier can be thought of as points of both full resource employment and production efficiency. (Recall from Chapter 1 that an efficient economy is one that produces the things that

investment *The process of using resources to produce new capital.*

production possibility frontier (ppf) *A graph that shows all the combinations of goods and services that can be produced if all of society's resources are used efficiently.*

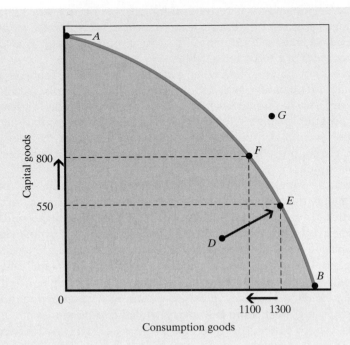

...lity Frontier

...ossibility
...a number
...cepts. One of
...nt is *oppor-*
...opportunity
...g more capi-
tal goods is that fewer consumption goods can be produced. Moving from *E* to *F*,
the number of capital goods
increases from 550 to 800. To
produce more capital goods,
resources must be transferred
from the production of consumer goods. Moving from *E*
to *F*, the number of consumer
goods decreases from 1300 to
1100.

people want at least cost. *Production efficiency* is a state in which a given mix of
outputs is produced at least cost.) Resources are not going unused, and there is no
waste. Points that lie within the shaded area, but that are not on the frontier, represent either unemployment of resources or production inefficiency. An economy producing at point *D* in Figure 2.3 can produce more capital goods and more consumption goods, for example, by moving to point *E*. This is possible only if resources
were initially not fully employed or if resources were not being used efficiently.

■ **Unemployment**   During the Great Depression of the 1930s, the U.S. economy experienced prolonged unemployment. Millions of workers who were willing to work
found themselves without jobs. In 1933, 25% of the civilian labor force was unemployed. This figure stayed above 14% until 1940, when increased defense spending by the United States created millions of jobs. In 1975, 1982, and again in 1992,
the economy experienced high levels of unemployment. In June of 1975, the unemployment rate went over 9% for the first time since the 1930s. In December of 1982,
when the unemployment rate hit 10.8%, nearly 12 million were out looking for
work. In June of 1992, the number of unemployed rose to just under 10 million.

In addition to the hardship that falls on the unemployed themselves, unemployment of labor means unemployment of capital. During the downturn of 1982,
industrial plants were running at less than 69% of their total capacity. That meant
that a considerable fraction of the nation's industrial capital was sitting idle and,
in effect, being wasted. Clearly, when there is unemployment we are not producing all that we can.

Periods of unemployment correspond to points inside the production possibility frontier, points like *D* in Figure 2.3. Moving onto the frontier from a point like
D means moving up and to the right, achieving full employment of resources and
increasing production of both capital goods and consumer goods.

■ **Inefficiency**   Production inefficiency is one way an economy can fail to be efficient. An economy is also inefficient when it is producing at the wrong point on
the ppf—that is, when it is producing a combination of goods and services that
does not match the wants of its people.

Certainly, a badly managed economy will not produce up to potential and will be inside the ppf. Suppose, for example, that the land and climate in Ohio are best suited for corn production and that the land and climate in Kansas are best suited for wheat production. If Congress passes a law forcing farmers in Ohio to plant 50% of their acreage in wheat and farmers in Kansas to plant 50% in corn, neither corn nor wheat production will be up to potential. The economy will be at a point like *A* in Figure 2.4—inside the production possibility frontier. Allowing each state to specialize in producing the crop that it produces best increases the production of both corn and wheat and moves the economy to a point like *B* in Figure 2.4.

In extreme cases, a wrong output mix is obvious. Suppose, for example, that a society uses all of its resources to produce beef efficiently, but that everyone in the society is a vegetarian. The result is a total waste of resources (assuming that the society cannot trade beef for vegetables with another society).

A wrong mix of output can be less obvious, however. Beef production is a highly competitive industry in the United States. Hundreds of thousands of farmers sell millions of cattle each year to hundreds of meat packing firms. Most grocery stores have plentiful stocks at reasonable prices because there are many suppliers competing for business.

Suppose that the government were to grant the sole right to produce beef (that is, a *monopoly*) to a single company. Even if all resources remained fully and efficiently employed, the monopoly would push the economy to a less desirable point on the ppf—that is, a point at which beef is underproduced and other goods are overproduced, a point such as *D* instead of *C* in Figure 2.5 on page 36. This is because without competition monopolists will restrict output and raise their prices. In the absence of the monopoly, the society can move back to point *C*, which more closely matches the preferences of its people.

■ **Negative Slope and Opportunity Cost** As we've seen, points that lie on the production possibility frontier represent points of full resource employment and production efficiency. But society can choose only one point on the curve. Because a society's choices are constrained by available resources and existing technology, when those resources are fully and efficiently employed it can produce more capital goods only by reducing production of consumption goods. The opportunity cost of the additional capital is the forgone production of consumption goods.

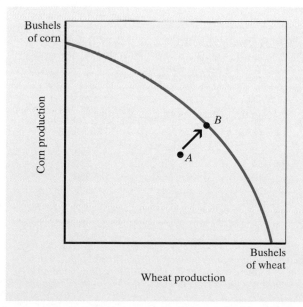

FIGURE 2.4

Inefficiency from Misallocation of Land in Farming

Society can end up inside its production possibility frontier at a point like *A* by using its resources inefficiently. If, for example, Ohio's climate and soil were best suited for corn production and those of Kansas were best suited for wheat production, a law that forces Kansas farmers to produce corn and Ohio farmers to produce wheat would result in less of both. In such a case, society might be at point *A* rather than point *B*.

FIGURE 2.5

Inefficient Mix of Output Resulting from a Monopoly

Even if resources are combined efficiently in production, the result is inefficient if the economy is not producing the combination of goods and services that people want. This can occur if a monopoly controls an industry.

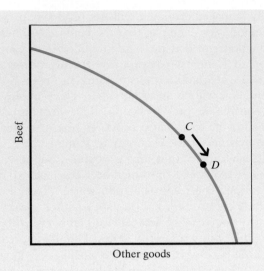

The fact that scarcity exists is illustrated by the negative slope of the production possibility frontier. In moving from point E to point F in Figure 2.3, capital production *increases* by $800 - 550 = 250$ units (a positive change), but that increase in capital can be achieved only by shifting resources out of the production of consumption goods. Thus, in moving from point E to point F in Figure 2.3, consumption good production *decreases* by $1300 - 1100 = 200$ units of the consumption good (a negative change). The slope of the curve, the ratio of the change in capital goods to the change in consumption goods, is negative.[1]

■ **The Law of Increasing Opportunity Costs** We have noted that the slope of the ppf indicates the trade-off that a society faces between two goods that it produces. We can learn something further about the shape of the frontier and the terms of this trade-off. Let us look at the trade-off between corn and wheat production in Ohio and Kansas. In a recent year Ohio and Kansas together produced 510 million bushels of corn and 380 million bushels of wheat. Table 2.1 presents these two numbers plus some hypothetical combinations of corn and wheat production that might exist for Ohio and Kansas together. Figure 2.6 graphs the data from Table 2.1.

TABLE 2.1	PRODUCTION POSSIBILITY SCHEDULE FOR TOTAL CORN AND WHEAT PRODUCTION IN OHIO AND KANSAS	
POINT ON PPF	TOTAL CORN PRODUCTION (MILLIONS OF BUSHELS PER YEAR)	TOTAL WHEAT PRODUCTION (MILLIONS OF BUSHELS PER YEAR)
A	700	100
B	650	200
C	510	380
D	400	500
E	300	550

---

[1]*The value of the slope of a society's production possibility frontier is called the* marginal rate of transformation (MRT). *In Figure 2.3, the MRT between point E and point F is simply the ratio of the change in capital goods (a positive number) to the change in consumption goods (a negative number).*

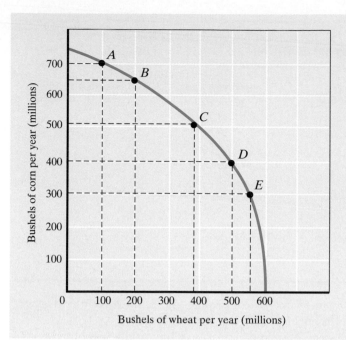

FIGURE 2.6

Corn and Wheat Production in Ohio and Kansas

The ppf illustrates that the opportunity cost of corn production increases as we shift resources from wheat production to corn production. Moving from *E* to *D*, we get an additional 100 million bushels of corn at a cost of 50 million bushels of wheat. Moving from *B* to *A*, we get only 50 million bushels of corn at a cost of 100 million bushels of wheat. The cost *per bushel* of corn—measured in lost or forgone wheat—has increased four times.

Suppose that the demand for corn dramatically increases. If this happens, farmers would probably shift some of their acreage from wheat production to corn production. Such a shift is represented by a move from point *C* (where corn = 510, and wheat = 380) up and to the left along the ppf toward points *A* and *B* in Figure 2.6. As this happens, it becomes more and more difficult to produce additional corn. The best land for corn production was presumably in corn, and the best land for wheat production in wheat. As we try to produce more and more corn, the land is less and less well suited to that crop. And as we take more and more land out of wheat production, we will be taking increasingly better wheat-producing land. All of this is to say that the opportunity cost of more corn, measured in terms of wheat, increases.

Moving from *E* to *D*, we can get 100 million bushels of corn (400 − 300) by sacrificing only 50 million bushels of wheat (550 − 500)—that is, we get two bushels of corn for every bushel of wheat.[2] However, when we are already taxing the ability of the land to produce corn, it becomes more difficult to produce more corn, and the opportunity cost goes up. Moving from *B* to *A*, we can get only 50 million bushels of corn (700 − 650) by sacrificing 100 million bushels of wheat (200 − 100). For every bushel of wheat, we now get only half a bushel of corn. On the other hand, if the demand for *wheat* were to increase substantially and we were to move down and to the right along the production possibility frontier, it would become increasingly difficult to produce wheat, and the opportunity cost of wheat, in terms of corn, would rise.

It is important to remember that the ppf represents choices available within the constraints imposed by the current state of agricultural technology. In the long run, technology may improve, and when that happens we have *growth*.

■ **Economic Growth** **Economic growth** is characterized by an increase in the total output of an economy. It occurs when a society acquires new resources or when society learns to produce more with existing resources. New resources may mean a larger labor force or an increased capital stock. The production and use of new machinery and equipment (capital) increases the productivity of workers. Improved

economic growth *An increase in the total output of an economy. It occurs when a society acquires new resources or when it learns to produce more using existing resources.*

_____

[2]*This implies that the marginal rate of transformation is* −2 *between* D *and* E. *Change in corn =* + 100; *change in wheat =* −50. MRT = +100/ −50 = −2.

TABLE 2.2

INCREASING PRODUCTIVITY IN CORN AND WHEAT PRODUCTION IN THE UNITED STATES, 1935–1992

	CORN		WHEAT	
	YIELD PER ACRE (BUSHELS)	LABOR HOURS PER 100 BUSHELS	YIELD PER ACRE (BUSHELS)	LABOR HOURS PER 100 BUSHELS
1935–1939	26.1	108	13.2	67
1945–1949	36.1	53	16.9	34
1955–1959	48.7	20	22.3	17
1965–1969	78.5	7	27.5	11
1975–1979	95.3	4	31.3	9
1981–1985	107.2	3	36.9	7
1985–1990	112.8	NA*	38.0	NA*
1992	131.4	NA*	39.4	NA*

Sources: U.S. Department of Agriculture, Economic Research Service, Agricultural Statistics, 1992; Statistical Abstract of the United States, 1994.
*Data not available.

productivity also comes from technological change and *innovation,* the discovery and application of new, efficient techniques of production.

The last 30 years have seen dramatic increases in the productivity of U.S. agriculture. Based on data compiled by the Department of Agriculture, Table 2.2 shows that yield per acre in corn production has increased fivefold since the late 1930s, while the labor required to produce it has dropped dramatically. Productivity in wheat production has also increased, at only a slightly less remarkable rate: Output per acre has almost tripled, while labor requirements are down nearly 90 percent.

FIGURE 2.7

Economic Growth Shifts the ppf Up and to the Right

Productivity increases have enhanced the ability of the United States to produce both corn and wheat. As Table 2.2 shows, productivity increases were more dramatic for corn than for wheat. The shifts in the ppf were thus not parallel.

Note: The ppf also shifts if the amount of land or labor in corn and wheat production changes. Although we emphasize productivity increases here, the actual shifts between years were in part due to land and labor changes.

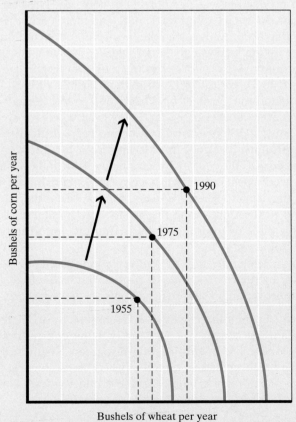

These increases are the result of more efficient farming techniques, more and better capital (tractors, combines, and other equipment), and advances in scientific knowledge and technological change (hybrid seeds, fertilizers, and so forth). As you can see in Figure 2.7, increases such as these shift the ppf up and to the right.

Sources of Growth and the Dilemma of the Poor Countries Economic growth arises from many sources, the two most important of which, over the years, have been the accumulation of capital and technological advances. For poor countries, capital is essential; they must build the communication networks and transportation systems necessary to develop industries that function efficiently. They also need capital goods to develop their agricultural sectors.

Recall that capital goods are produced only at a sacrifice of consumption goods. The same can be said for technological advances. Technological advances come from research and development that uses resources, and thus they too must be paid for. The resources used to produce capital goods—to build a road, a tractor, or a manufacturing plant—*and* to develop new technologies could have been used to produce consumption goods.

When a large part of a country's population is very poor, taking resources out of the production of consumption goods such as food and clothing is very difficult. In addition, in some countries those wealthy enough to invest in domestic industries may choose instead to invest abroad because of political turmoil at home. As a result, it often falls to the governments of poor countries to generate revenues for capital production and research out of tax collections.

All these factors have contributed to the growing gap between poor and rich nations. Figure 2.8 graphs the result, using production possibility frontiers. On the

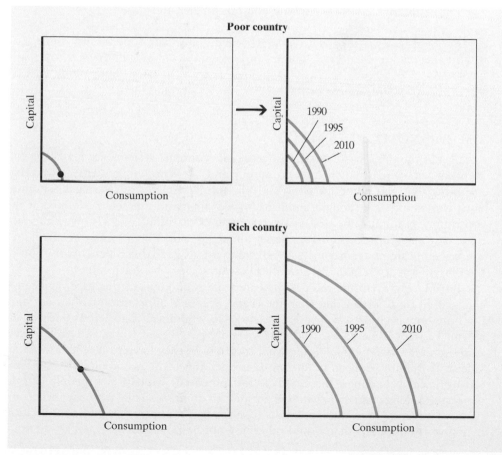

FIGURE 2.8

Capital Goods and Growth in Poor and Rich Countries

Rich countries find it easier to devote resources to the production of capital than poor countries do. But the more resources that flow into capital production, the faster the rate of economic growth. Thus the gap between poor and rich countries has grown over time.

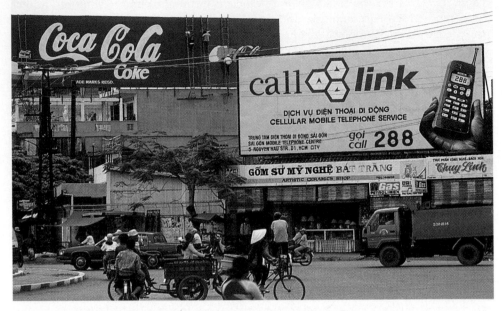

ONE OF THE ROUTES TO ECONOMIC GROWTH IS INVESTMENT IN CAPITAL. DESPITE LOW PER CAPITA INCOME, HANOI (VIETNAM) IS ORDERING CELLULAR PHONES BY THE THOUSANDS, AS WELL AS MORE THAN 300,000 FIBER-OPTIC PHONE LINES PER YEAR.

left, the rich country devotes a larger portion of its production to capital, while the poor country produces mostly consumption goods. On the right, you see the result: The ppf of the rich country shifts up and out farther and faster.

> Although it exists only as an abstraction, the production possibility frontier illustrates a number of very important concepts that we shall use throughout the rest of this book: scarcity, unemployment, inefficiency, opportunity cost, the law of increasing opportunity cost, and economic growth.

THE ECONOMIC PROBLEM

Recall that the three basic questions facing all economic systems are (1) What will be produced? (2) How will it be produced? and (3) Who will get it?

When Bill was alone on the island, the mechanism for answering these questions was simple: He thought about his own wants and preferences, looked at the constraints and limits imposed by the resources of the island and his own skills and time, and made his decisions. As he set about his work, he allocated available resources quite simply, more or less by dividing up his available time. Distribution of the output was irrelevant. Because Bill was the society, he got it all.

Introducing even one more person into the economy—in this case, Colleen—changed all that. With Colleen on the island, resource allocation involves deciding not only how each person spends time but also who does what. Labor must be allocated to the various tasks. And now there are two sets of wants and preferences. And even after two people decide what to produce, they have to decide how to divide it. If Bill and Colleen go off on their own and form two completely separate self-sufficient economies, there will be lost potential. Clearly, two people can do many more things together than one person can do alone. They may use their comparative advantages in different skills to specialize. Cooperation and coordination may give rise to gains that would otherwise not be possible.

When a society consists of millions of people, the problem of coordination and cooperation becomes enormous, but so does the potential for gain. In large, complex economies, specialization can go wild, with people working in jobs as different in their detail as an impressionist painting is from a blank page. The range of products available in a modern industrial society is beyond anything that could have been imagined a hundred years ago, and so is the range of jobs.

The amount of coordination and cooperation in a modern industrial society is almost impossible to imagine. Yet something seems to drive economic systems, if sometimes clumsily and inefficiently, toward producing the things that people want. Given scarce resources, how, exactly, do large, complex societies go about answering the three basic economic questions? This is the **economic problem,** and this is what this text is about.

economic problem *Given scarce resources, how exactly do large, complex societies go about answering the three basic economic questions?*

ECONOMIC SYSTEMS

Now that you understand the economic problem, we can explore how different economic systems go about answering the three basic questions.

COMMAND ECONOMIES

In some modern societies government plays a big role in answering the basic economic questions. In pure **command economies,** a central authority or agency generally draws up a plan that establishes what will be produced and when, sets production goals, and makes rules for distribution. Planners in command economies use complex computer programs to determine the materials, labor, and energy inputs required to produce a variety of output targets. The final output targets are then set with an eye toward the same constraint that the single manager of a one-person economy faces—limited resources. Centrally determined income policies then establish how much compensation workers and managers receive for their labors.

command economy *An economy in which a central authority or agency draws up a plan that establishes what will be produced and when, sets production goals, and makes rules for distribution.*

Even in pure planned economies, people do exercise some choice. Commodities are sold at prices set by the government, and to the extent that they are able to pay those prices people are free to buy what is available. Sometimes more is demanded than is produced; sometimes goods are left on the shelves. These signals are used in the next plan to adjust output targets.

It is an understatement to say that the planned economies have not fared well over the last decade. In fact, the planned economies of Eastern Europe and the former Soviet Union—including the Russian Republic—have completely collapsed. (Another former command economy, that of Poland, is doing better. For more details, see the Global Perspective box on page 42 titled "Poland and the Russian Republic: An Update.") China remains committed to many of the principles of a planned economy, but reforms have moved it sharply away from pure central planning.

LAISSEZ-FAIRE ECONOMIES: THE FREE MARKET

At the opposite end of the spectrum from the command economy is the **laissez-faire economy.** The term *laissez faire,* which, translated literally from French, means "allow [them] to do," implies a complete lack of government involvement in the economy. In this type of economy, individual people and firms pursue their own self-interest without any central direction or regulation; the sum total of millions of individual decisions ultimately determines all basic economic outcomes. The central institution through which a laissez-faire system answers the basic questions is the **market,** a term that is used in economics to signify an institution through which buyers and sellers interact and engage in exchange.

laissez-faire economy *Literally from the French: "allow [them] to do." An economy in which individual people and firms pursue their own self-interests without any central direction or regulation.*

market *The institution through which buyers and sellers interact and engage in exchange.*

In the late 1980s the command economies of Eastern Europe collapsed like a string of dominoes. The process began when the Berlin Wall, which had separated the Communist East from the capitalist West for nearly 30 years, was torn down in November 1989. Finally, in 1991, the once mighty Soviet Union disintegrated, ending 75 years of communism and nearly half a century of Cold War with the West.

What lies ahead for the economies of the newly independent countries of the former Soviet Union and for the economies of the other Eastern European nations? One fear is that complete economic collapse will lead to chaos and ethnic warfare, and the events of 1993 and 1994 in Bosnia and Serbia attest to this danger. There is, however, one country where the transition from central planning and government control to the free market showed some early signs of working: Poland.

> *An economic success story is taking shape in Poland, three years after the country became the first in Eastern Europe to risk the rigors of "shock therapy" . . . . [rapid decontrol of prices and privatization of government enterprises]. . . .*
>
> *Industrial production, which declined a precipitous 39 percent in 1990 and 1991, is on the rise, and Poland is on track this year to become the first among former Communist nations to record annual economic growth. . . .*
>
> *Polish policy makers were supported in 1990 by an overwhelming public consensus for radical change, and have been encouraged since*

PEOPLE WHO VISIT PLANNED ECONOMIES FREQUENTLY COMMENT ON THE LACK OF VARIETY IN CONSUMER GOODS. THIS PROBLEM HAS SUBSTANTIALLY DECREASED IN POLAND, WHICH BEGAN ITS TRANSITION TO A FREE-MARKET ECONOMY IN THE EARLY 1990S.

> *then to stay the course by an explosion of pent-up entrepreneurial spirit and by a relatively productive agricultural sector that was already largely in private hands. . . .*
>
> *"I think they've made it," said Jeffrey Sachs, the Harvard economist who helped shape Poland's economic program. . . . "They have definitely turned the corner. The panic is over. The reforms are secure."*

While Russia has moved much more slowly, and the political turmoil there was even greater than in Poland, reform was on track by the summer of 1994 and Russia's huge economy was beginning to show signs of life:

> *This August [1994], there is an eerie stability. Monthly inflation is down to 6 percent compared with 26 percent a year ago. Salaries are worth more with the ruble stronger, and con-*

> *sumer spending is up. There is consensus on economic policy under Prime Minister Viktor S. Chernomyrdin, who has adopted the tight-money policies he criticized in January . . . .*
>
> *On a trip this week down the Volga River, talking to ordinary Russians, Mr. Yeltsin had a new announcement: "I see that in many regions the economic slide has stopped."*

Sources: Stephen Engelberg, "21 Months of 'Shock Therapy' Resuscitates Polish Economy," *The New York Times,* December 17, 1992, p. 1; Steven Erlanger, "End of Russia's Economic Slide Brings Eerie Calm," *The New York Times,* August 22, 1994, p. 1.

The interactions between buyers and sellers in any market range from simple to complex. Early explorers of the North American Midwest who wished to exchange with Native Americans did so simply by bringing their goods to a central place and trading them. Today, a jewelry maker in Maine may sell gold necklaces to a buyer through the Home Shopping Network that shows the product on television—customers call in orders and pay with a credit card. Ultimately, funds are transferred through a complicated chain of financial transactions. The result is that a buyer in Oakland, California, buys a necklace from an unseen jewelry producer in Maine.

In short:

> Some markets are simple and others are complex, but they all involve buyers and sellers engaging in exchange. The behavior of buyers and sellers in a laissez-faire economy determines what gets produced, how it is produced, and who gets it.

The following chapters explore market systems in great depth. A quick preview is worthwhile here, however.

■ **Consumer Sovereignty** In a free, unregulated market, goods and services are produced and sold only if the supplier can make a profit. In simple terms, making a profit means selling goods or services for more than it costs to produce them. Clearly, you can't make a profit unless someone wants the product that you are selling. This logic leads to the notion of **consumer sovereignty:** The mix of output found in any free market system is dictated ultimately by the tastes and preferences of consumers who "vote" by buying or not buying. Businesses rise and fall in response to consumer demands; no central directive or plan is necessary.

In a free market economy, producers may be small or large. One person who hand paints eggshells may start to sell them as a business; a woman who has been showing her poodle may start handling other people's dogs in the show ring. On a larger scale, a group of furniture designers may put together a large portfolio of sketches, several million dollars, and start a bigger business. At the extreme are huge corporations like IBM, Mitsubishi, and Exxon, each of which sells tens of billions of dollars' worth of products every year.

consumer sovereignty *The idea that consumers ultimately dictate what will be produced (or not produced) by choosing what to purchase (and what not to purchase).*

■ **Individual Production Decisions: Free Enterprise** Under a free market system, individual producers must also figure out how to organize and coordinate the actual production of their products or services. The owner of a small shoe repair shop must buy the equipment and tools that she needs, hang signs, and set prices by herself. In a big corporation, so many people are involved in planning the production process that in many ways corporate planning resembles the planning in a command economy. Whether the firms are large or small, however, production decisions in a market economy are made by separate private organizations acting in what they perceive to be their own interests.

Individuals seeking profits also start new businesses. Since new businesses require capital investment before they can begin operation, starting a new business involves risk. Every day new businesses are born and others fail. A well-run business that produces a product for which demand exists will succeed; a poorly run business or one that produces a product for which little demand exists is likely to fail. It is through *free enterprise* that new products and new production techniques find their way into use.

Proponents of free market systems argue that free enterprise leads to more efficient production and better response to diverse and changing consumer preferences. If a producer produces inefficiently, competitors will come along, fight for the business, and eventually take it away. Thus in a free market economy, competition forces producers to use efficient techniques of production. It is competition, then, that ultimately dictates how outputs are produced.

■ **Distribution of Output**   In a free market system, the distribution of output—who gets what—is also determined in a decentralized way. The amount that any one household gets depends on its income and wealth. *Income* is the amount that a household earns each year. It comes in a number of forms: wages, salaries, interest, and the like. *Wealth* is the amount that households have accumulated out of past income through saving or inheritance.

To the extent that income comes from working for a wage, it is at least in part determined by individual choice. You will work for the wages available in the market only if these wages (and the things they can buy) are sufficient to compensate you for what you give up by working. Your leisure certainly has a value also. You may discover that you can increase your income by getting more education or training. You *can't* increase your income, however, if you acquire a skill that no one wants.

Although your income determines how much of society's output you can buy and consume, not all income comes from working. Individuals may also earn income by owning all or part of a business for which they do not work. Those who risk their wealth by buying shares in companies or by lending it out to be used for business investments earn a return on their wealth. Returns may come directly, as profit, or indirectly, as interest or dividends on stock. (We discuss these options in detail in Chapter 3.) In a free market economy, people make independent decisions about what to do with their wealth.

In sum:

> In a free market system, the basic economic questions are answered without the help of a central government plan or directives. This is what the "free" in free market means—the system is left to operate on its own, with no outside interference. Individuals pursuing their own self-interest will go into business and produce the products and services that people want; others will decide whether to acquire skills or not, whether to work or not, and whether to buy, sell, invest, or save the income that they earn.

price *The amount that a product sells for per unit. It reflects what society is willing to pay.*

■ **Price Theory**   The basic coordinating mechanism in a free market system is price. A **price** is the amount that a product sells for per unit, and it reflects what society is willing to pay. Prices of inputs—labor, land, capital—determine how much it costs to produce a product. Prices of various kinds of labor, or *wage rates*, determine the rewards for working in different jobs and professions. Many of the independent decisions made in a market economy involve the weighing of prices and costs, so it is not surprising that much of economic theory focuses on the factors that influence and determine prices. This is why microeconomic theory is often simply called *price theory*.

MIXED SYSTEMS, MARKETS, AND GOVERNMENTS

The differences between command economies and laissez-faire economies in their pure forms are enormous. But in fact these pure forms do not exist in the world; all real systems are in some sense "mixed." That is, individual enterprise exists and independent choice is exercised even in economies in which the government plays the major role.

Conversely, no market economies exist without government involvement and government regulation. The United States has basically a free market economy, but government purchases accounted for about 18% of its total production in 1994. The government directly employs about 15% of all workers, and taxes are about a third of the total income of the economy. The government also redistributes income by means of taxation and social welfare expenditures, and it regulates many economic activities.

One of the major themes in this book, and indeed in economics, is the tension between the advantages of free, unregulated markets and the need for government involvement in the economy. Advocates of free markets argue that such markets work best when left to themselves. They produce only what people want; without buyers, sellers go out of business. Competition forces firms to adopt efficient production techniques. Wage differentials lead people to acquire needed skills. Competition also leads to innovation in both production techniques and products. The result is quality and variety. But market systems have problems too.

> Even staunch defenders of the free enterprise system recognize that market systems are not perfect. First, they do not always produce what people want at lowest cost—there are inefficiencies. Second, rewards (income) may be unevenly distributed, and some groups may be left out. Third, periods of unemployment and inflation recur with some regularity.

Many people point to these problems as reasons for government involvement. Indeed, for some problems government involvement may be the only solution. But government decisions are made by people who presumably, like the rest of us, act in their own self-interest. While governments may indeed be called upon to improve the functioning of the economy, there is no guarantee that they will do so. Just as markets may fail to produce an allocation of resources that is perfectly efficient and fair, governments may fail to improve matters.

■ **Inefficiencies** Free markets may not produce all the goods that people want and are willing to pay for. There are some goods and services whose benefits are social, or collective, such as national defense, open park areas, a justice system, and police protection. These are called **public** or **social goods**. The fact that the benefits of such goods are collective presents the private market with a problem: Once a public good is produced, everyone gets to enjoy its benefits, whether they have paid for it or not. If police protection lowers a city's crime rate, all citizens of that city are safer.

public, or social, goods *Goods and services whose benefits are social, or collective.*

How, then, can a private business firm make a profit "selling" such a service to individual consumers? In most cases, it cannot. A private firm selling an automobile won't give it to you unless you pay for it. A producer of a public good doesn't have that option. Thus, if there is a public good that citizens decide they want, they must collectively arrange for its production. Traditionally, societies have funded public goods through governments, which are granted taxing authority.

Government intervention may also be necessary because private decision makers in search of profits can make bad decisions from society's point of view. The market system provides an incentive to produce a product if, and only if, people are willing to pay more for it than the cost of the resources needed to produce it. This works to society's advantage as long as the resource costs reflect the *full* cost to society of producing the product. For example, if the environment is damaged during the production process and producers do not factor in these costs, profit-producing activities may not balance out to society's advantage. Governments involve themselves in free markets to make sure that decision makers consider all the benefits and costs of their decisions. That is why we have the Environmental Protection Agency and similar agencies.

Markets work best when they are competitive. Competition forces producers to choose the most efficient methods of production. Inefficient producers are driven out of business by the forces of competition. Competition also leads to innovation and new products. Sometimes, however, powerful firms in free markets can gain control of their markets and block competition. A firm that gains control of a market may stifle innovation, charge higher prices than necessary, and cause a general misallocation of resources. Since the turn of the century, noncompetitive behavior has been illegal in the United States.

■ **Redistribution of Income** Governments may also get involved in a basically free market system because the final distribution of income (and thus of output) is considered inequitable. Free market systems are based on the principle of individual self-interest and enterprise: Our rewards are supposed to be commensurate with how well we compete. But some people are not well equipped to compete—some are physically unable to work; some are mentally unable to hold a job. Whatever the cause, thousands of people find that they cannot get along economically. Sometimes this is their fault, and sometimes it is not. In all cases, however, society must decide what, if anything, to do about it.

Every government redistributes income to a certain extent. In the United States, welfare, unemployment compensation, and a host of other programs have been designed to assist people who are poor or are temporarily without work.

Income redistribution is a subject of endless debate. Some claim that taxes on the rich and programs for the poor destroy the incentives that the market provides for hard work, enterprise, and risk taking. Others argue that because many of the poor, particularly children, are in the position they are in through no fault of their own, cuts in income redistribution programs are cruel and unfair.

■ **Stabilization** Macroeconomics explores the causes and consequences of unemployment and price inflation. In market economies, the level of unemployment is not planned, and prices are set freely by the forces of supply and demand. But governments may, through taxing and spending policies and by regulating the banking system, exert a stabilizing influence over prices and over the general level of output and employment. Like income redistribution, the desirability and the character of government involvement in the macroeconomy are hotly debated.

LOOKING AHEAD

This chapter has described the economic problem in broad terms. We have outlined the questions that all economic systems must answer. We also discussed very broadly the two kinds of economic systems and some of the advantages and disadvantages of each. In the next chapter we turn from the general to the specific. There we discuss in some detail the institutions of U.S. capitalism: how the private sector is organized, what the government actually does, and how the international sector operates. Chapters 4 and 5 then begin the task of analyzing the way market systems work.

SUMMARY

1. Every society has some system or mechanism for transforming what nature and previous generations have provided into useful form. Economics is the study of that process and its outcomes.

2. *Producers* are those who take resources and transform them into usable products, or *outputs*. Private firms, households, and governments all produce something.

SCARCITY, CHOICE, AND OPPORTUNITY COST

3. All societies must answer *three basic questions:* What will be produced? How will it be produced? Who will get what is produced? These three questions make up the *economic problem.*

4. One person alone on an island must make the same basic decisions that complex societies make. When society consists of more than one person, questions of distribution, cooperation, and specialization arise.

5. Because resources are scarce relative to human wants in all societies, using resources to produce one good or service implies *not* using them to produce something else. This concept of *opportunity cost* is central to an understanding of economics.

6. Using resources to produce *capital* that will in turn produce benefits in the future implies *not* using those resources to produce consumer goods in the present.

7. Even if one individual or nation is absolutely more efficient at producing goods than another, all parties will gain if they specialize in producing goods in which they have a *comparative advantage.*

8. A *production possibility frontier* (ppf) is a graph that shows all the combinations of goods and services that can be produced if all of society's re sources are used efficiently. The production possibility frontier illustrates a number of important economic concepts: scarcity, unemployment, inefficiency, increasing opportunity cost, and economic growth.

9. *Economic growth* occurs when society produces more, either by acquiring more resources or by learning to produce more with existing resources. Improved productivity may come from additional capital, or from the discovery and application of new, more efficient, techniques of production.

ECONOMIC SYSTEMS

10. In some modern societies, government plays a big role in answering the three basic questions. In pure *command economies,* a central authority generally draws up a plan that determines what will be produced, how it will be produced, and who will get it.

11. A *laissez-faire economy* is one in which individuals independently pursuing their own self-interest, without any central direction or regulation, ultimately determine all basic economic outcomes.

12. A *market* is an institution through which buyers and sellers interact and engage in exchange. Some markets involve simple face-to-face exchange; others involve a complex series of transactions, often over great distance or electronically.

13. There are no purely planned economies and no pure laissez-faire economies; all economies are mixed. Individual enterprise, independent choice, and relatively free markets exist in centrally planned economies, and there is significant government involvement in market economies such as that of the United States.

14. One of the great debates in economics revolves around the tension between the advantages of free, unregulated markets and the need for government involvement in the economy. Free markets produce what people want, and competition forces firms to adopt efficient production techniques. The need for government intervention arises because free markets are characterized by inefficiencies and an unequal distribution of income and experience regular periods of inflation and unemployment.

REVIEW TERMS AND CONCEPTS

capital 27
command economy 41
comparative advantage 30
consumer goods 32
consumer sovereignty 43
economic growth 37
economic problem 41

investment 33
laissez-faire economy 41
market 41
opportunity cost 29
outputs 28
price 44
producers 28

production 27
production possibility frontier (ppf) 33
public, or social goods 45
resources or Inputs 27
three basic questions 28

1. Kristen and Anna live in the beach town of Santa Monica. They own a small business in which they make wristbands and potholders and sell them to people on the beach. Kristen can make 15 wristbands per hour, but only 3 potholders. Anna is a bit slower and can make only 12 wristbands or 2 potholders in an hour.

| | OUTPUT PER HOUR | |
	KRISTEN	ANNA
Wristbands	15	12
Potholders	3	2

a. For Kristen, what is the opportunity cost of a potholder? For Anna? Who has a comparative advantage in the production of potholders? Explain.

b. Who has a comparative advantage in the production of wristbands? Explain.

c. Assume that Kristen works 20 hours per week in the business. If Kristen were in business on her own, graph the possible combinations of potholders and wristbands that she could produce in a week. Do the same for Anna.

d. If Kristen devoted half of her time (10 out of 20 hours) to wristbands and half of her time to potholders, how many of each would she produce in a week? If Anna did the same thing, how many of each would she produce? How many wristbands and potholders would be produced in total?

e. Suppose that Anna spent all 20 hours of her time on wristbands and Kristen spent 17 hours on potholders and 3 hours on wristbands. How many of each would be produced?

f. Suppose that Kristen and Anna can sell all their wristbands for $1 each and all their potholders for $5.50 each. If each of them worked 20 hours per week, how should they split their time between wristbands and potholders? What is their maximum joint revenue?

2. Define *capital*. What distinguishes land from capital? Is a tree capital?

3. "Studying economics instead of going to town and partying is like building a boat instead of lying on the beach." Explain this statement carefully using the concepts of capital and opportunity cost.

4. Suppose that a simple society has an economy with only one resource, labor. Labor can be used to produce only two commodities—X, a necessity good (food), and Y, a luxury good (music and merriment). Suppose that the labor force consists of 100 workers. One laborer can produce either 5 units of necessity per month (by hunting and gathering) or 10 units of luxury per month (by writing songs, playing the guitar, dancing, and so on).

a. On a graph, draw the economy's production possibility frontier. Where does the ppf intersect the Y axis? Where does it intersect the X axis? What meaning do those points have?

b. Suppose the economy ended up producing at a point *inside* the ppf. Give at least two reasons why this could occur. What could be done to move the economy to a point *on* the ppf?

c. Suppose you succeeded in lifting your economy to a point on its ppf. What point would you choose? How might your small society decide the point at which it wanted to be?

d. Once you have chosen a point on the ppf, you still need to decide how your society's product will be divided up. If you were a dictator, how would you decide? What would happen if you left product distribution to the free market?

5. One of the justifications for government involvement in a free market economy is that the market system is unlikely to produce "public goods" in sufficient quantity.

a. Define a *public good*.

b. Why does the private market have a difficult time allocating resources to the production of public goods?

c. Give five examples of goods provided by federal, state, or local governments that may yield public benefits.

d. Assume that the production of public good X requires a certain amount of land, labor, and capital that the government will have to procure. How would you measure the full costs of this good's provision? (*Hint:* recall opportunity costs.)

e. If you were a benevolent dictator, how would you go about determining if the production of a particular public good were worth it? How would you measure its benefits?

6. What progress has been made during the last year in Eastern Europe? Which countries are growing? Which are in decline? What factors seem to have contributed to the differences in success across countries?

THE STRUCTURE OF THE U.S. ECONOMY: THE PRIVATE, PUBLIC, AND INTERNATIONAL SECTORS

THE PREVIOUS CHAPTER DESCRIBED THE ECONOMIC PROBLEM. ALL societies are endowed by nature and by previous generations with scarce resources. A process called "production" combines and transforms these resources into goods and services that are demanded by the members of society.

At the end of Chapter 2, we briefly described the economic systems that exist in the world today. This chapter describes the basic institutional structure of the U.S. economy in more detail. Because most production is undertaken by private individuals and organizations, we first look at the private sector. The **private sector** is made up of independently owned firms that exist to make a profit, nonprofit organizations, and individual households. It includes Chrysler Corporation, Occidental College, the Catholic Church, soybean farms in Iowa, the corner drugstore, and the babysitter down the street. The private sector is defined by independent ownership and control. In essence, it includes all the decision-making units within the economy that are not part of the government.

Next, we turn to a discussion of the public sector. The **public sector** is the government and its agencies at all levels—federal, state, and local. Government employees—tax assessors, public school teachers, post office workers, colonels in the army, Supreme Court justices, and the President—

private sector *Includes all independently owned profit-making firms, nonprofit organizations, and households; all the decision-making units in the economy that are not part of the government.*

public sector *Includes all agencies at all levels of government—federal, state, and local.*

work in the public sector. Just as the Ford Motor Company uses land, labor, and capital to produce automobiles, the public sector uses land, labor, and capital to produce goods and services such as police and fire protection, education, and national defense. The public sector in the United States also produces some things that are simultaneously produced by the private sector. The post office provides overnight express-mail service that competes directly with similar services provided by private firms such as FedEx and United Parcel Service. The University of Michigan, part of the public sector, directly competes for "buyers" of its "product" with private sector schools such as Northwestern University and Colorado College.

international sector *From any one country's perspective, the economies of the rest of the world.*

Finally, we provide a brief introduction to the **international sector** and discuss the importance of imports and exports to the U.S. economy. From any one country's perspective, the international sector consists of the economies of the rest of the world. The U.S. economy has, over the last several decades, become increasingly influenced by events abroad. The exodus of refugees from Cuba, the elimination of farm subsidies in France, the end of a recession in Japan, and other global events all have important implications for the functioning of the U.S. economy. In a very real sense there is only one economy: the world economy.

Recall the distinction drawn in Chapter 1 between descriptive economics and economic theory, and then notice what this chapter is not. We do not analyze behavior in this chapter. Here we describe institutions only as they exist. We also try very hard to avoid any normative distinctions. We do not talk about proper or improper roles of government in the economy, for example, or the things that governments might do to make the economy more efficient or fair.

In Chapter 4, we begin to analyze behavior. Before we begin the analysis in Chapter 4, however, it is important to have some sense of the institutional landscape. One purpose for studying economics is to understand the world and what people actually do. This chapter provides some important facts that describe the realities of the U.S. economy.

THE PRIVATE SECTOR: BUSINESS AND INDUSTRIAL ORGANIZATION IN THE UNITED STATES

How is business organized in the United States? Let us see first how the law permits *individual firms* to be organized. Then we can talk about the different ways that *industries* are structured. An individual firm's behavior depends on both its own legal structure and its relationship to other firms in its industry.

THE LEGAL ORGANIZATION OF FIRMS

Most private sector activity takes place within business firms that exist to make a profit. Some other private sector organizations that exist for reasons other than profit—clubs, cooperatives, and nonprofit organizations, for example—do produce goods or services. Because these organizations represent a small fraction of private sector activity, however, we focus here on profit-making firms.

> A business set up to make profits may be organized in one of three basic legal forms: (1) a proprietorship, (2) a partnership, or (3) a corporation. A single business may pass through more than one of these forms of organization during its development.

proprietorship *A form of business organization in which a person simply sets up to provide goods or services at a profit. In a proprietorship, the proprietor (or owner) is the firm. The assets and liabilities of the firm are the owner's assets and liabilities.*

■ **The Proprietorship** The least complex and most common form a business can take is the simple **proprietorship.** There is no legal process involved in starting a proprietorship. You simply start operating. You must, however, keep records of revenues and costs and pay personal income taxes on your profit.

A professor who does consulting on the side, for example, receives fees and has costs (computer expenses, research materials, and so forth). This consulting business is a proprietorship, even though the proprietor is the only employee and the business is very limited. A large restaurant that employs hundreds of people may also be a proprietorship if it is owned by a single person. Many doctors and lawyers in private practice report their incomes and expenses as proprietors.

In a proprietorship, one person owns the firm. In a sense, that person *is* the firm. If the firm owes money, the proprietor owes the money; if the firm earns a profit, the proprietor earns a profit. There is no limit to the proprietor's responsibility; if the business gets into financial trouble, the proprietor alone is liable. That is, if a business does poorly or ends up in debt, those debts are the proprietor's personal responsibility. There is no wall of protection between a proprietor and her business, as we will see there is between corporations and their owners.

The Internal Revenue Service estimates that there are over 14.7 million proprietorships in the United States. That is one for every 13 adults in the country. Most of these proprietorships are small; while they make up over 70% of all businesses, they account for only 6% of total sales (Table 3.1).

■ **The Partnership** A **partnership** is a proprietorship with more than one proprietor. When two or more people agree to share the responsibility for a business, they form a partnership. While no formal legal process is required to start this kind of business, most partnerships are based on agreements, signed by all the partners, that detail who pays what part of the costs and how profits shall be divided. Because profits from partnerships are taxable, accurate records of receipts and expenditures must be kept and each party's profits must be reported to the IRS.

In a partnership, as in a proprietorship, there is no limit to the liability of the owners (that is, the partners) for the firm's debts. But with a partnership it can be worse because each partner is both jointly and separately liable for all the debts of the partnership. If you own one third of a partnership that goes out of business with a debt of $300,000, you owe your creditors $100,000, and so does each of your partners. But if your partners skip town, you owe the entire $300,000.

Just under 8% of all firms in the United States are partnerships, and they account for only 4.4% of total sales (see again Table 3.1).

■ **The Corporation** A **corporation** is a formally established legal entity that exists separately from those who establish it and those who own it. To establish a corporation, a corporate charter must be obtained from a state government. In most states this is quite easily accomplished. A lawyer simply fills out the appropriate paperwork and files it with the right state agency, along with certain fees. When a

partnership *A form of business organization in which there is more than one proprietor. The owners are responsible jointly and separately for the firm's obligations.*

corporation *A form of business organization resting on a legal charter that establishes the corporation as an entity separate from its owners. Owners hold shares and are liable for the firm's debts only up to the limit of their investment, or share, in the firm.*

TABLE 3.1	NUMBER OF FIRMS AND SALES BY TYPE OF BUSINESS, 1990			
	NUMBER OF FIRMS (THOUSANDS)	PERCENT OF TOTAL FIRMS	TOTAL SALES ($ BILLIONS)	PERCENT OF TOTAL SALES
Proprietorships	14,783	73.7	731	6.0
Partnerships	1,554	7.8	541	4.4
Corporations	3,717	18.5	10,914	89.6
Total	20,054	100.0	12,186	100.0

Source: Statistical Abstract of the United States, 1994, p. 539.

share of stock *A certificate of partial ownership of a corporation that entitles the holder to a portion of the corporation's profits.*

net income *The profits of a firm.*

dividends *The portion of a corporation's profits that the firm pays out each period to shareholders. Also called* distributed profits.

retained earnings *The profits that a corporation keeps, usually for the purchase of capital assets. Also called* undistributed profits.

corporation is formed, **shares of stock** (certificates of partial ownership) are issued and either sold or assigned. A corporation is owned by its shareholders, who are in a sense partners in the firm's success or failure. Each share of stock entitles the holder to a portion of the corporation's profits. Shareholders differ from simple partners, however, in two important ways: First, the liability of shareholders is limited to the amount they paid for the stock. If the company goes out of business or bankrupt, the shareholders may lose what they have invested, but no more than that. They are *not* liable for the debts of the corporation beyond the amount they invested. Second, the federal government and all but four states levy special taxes on corporations. These government bodies do not levy special taxes on proprietors and partners.

The federal corporate income tax is a tax on the **net income**, or profits, of corporations. The tax is 15% of net income on the first $50,000, but it rises to 25% for taxable income between $50,000 and $75,000 and to 34% after income exceeds $75,000. (In 1993, as part of President Clinton's deficit reduction package, the top rate was raised to 35% on taxable net income over $10 million.) Actually, 99% of all corporate net income is taxed at the 34% rate.[1] In essence, this means that tax is paid twice on corporate net income: once by the corporation when it pays tax on its profits, and again by the shareholders when they pay personal income tax on their **dividends**—that is, the share of profits they receive from the corporation.

The special privilege granted to corporations limiting their liability is often called a *franchise*. Some view the corporate tax as a payment to the government in exchange for this grant of limited liability status. In New York State, the state corporation tax is actually called the franchise tax.

Corporate net income is usually divided into three pieces. Some of it is paid to federal and state governments in the form of taxes. Some of it is paid out to shareholders as dividends (sometimes called *distributed profits*). And some of it usually stays within the corporation to be used for the purchase of capital assets. This part of corporate profits is called **retained earnings**, or *undistributed profits*.

In 1994, corporations in the United States earned total profits at an annual rate of $524.5 billion. Out of this, $202.5 billion in taxes were paid, leaving $322.0 billion in after-tax profits. Of this amount, $205.2 billion was paid out to shareholders and the rest, $116.8 billion, was retained. In percentage terms, taxes accounted for 38.6%, while shareholders directly received 39.1% of total profits (Table 3.2). Turning again to Table 3.1, in 1990 there were 3.7 million corporations, just under 20% of all firms. But these 3.7 million firms accounted for about 90% of total sales.

TABLE 3.2	THE DISTRIBUTION OF CORPORATE PROFITS IN 1994	
	BILLIONS OF DOLLARS	PERCENT OF BEFORE-TAX PROFIT
Profits before tax	524.5	100.0
Minus profits tax liability	−202.5	−38.6
Profits after tax	322.0	61.4
Minus dividends paid	−205.2	−39.1
Undistributed profits	116.8	22.3

Source: U.S. Department of Commerce, Bureau of Economic Analysis.

---

[1]*Statistical Abstract of the United States, 1994, and authors' estimate.*

Many corporations are very large. Each year *Fortune* magazine publishes a list of the 500 largest industrial corporations in the United States. Topping the *Fortune* 500 in 1994 was General Motors. GM's total sales in 1993 were nearly $134 billion. The company employed over 710,800 people that year!

The internal organization of a firm, whether it is a proprietorship, a partnership, or a corporation, affects its behavior and the behavior of potential investors. For example, because they are protected by a corporation's limited liability status, potential investors may be more likely to back high-risk but potentially high-payoff corporate ventures.

While a firm's internal structure is important, it is less important to an understanding of a firm's behavior than is the organization of the industry or the market in which the firm competes. For example, whether it is a proprietorship or a corporation, a firm with little or no competition is likely to behave differently from a firm facing stiff competition from many rivals. With this in mind, we now expand our focus from the individual firm to the industry.

THE ORGANIZATION OF INDUSTRIES

The term **industry** is used loosely to refer to groups of firms that produce similar products. Industries can be defined narrowly or broadly, depending on the issue being discussed. For example, a company that produces and packages cheese is a part of the cheese industry, the dairy products industry, the food products industry, and the agricultural products industry.[2]

Whether we define industries broadly or narrowly, how firms within any industry behave depends on how that industry is organized. When we speak of **market organization** we refer to the way an industry is structured: how many firms there are in an industry, whether products are virtually the same or differentiated, whether or not firms in the industry can control prices or wages, whether or not competing firms can freely enter and leave the industry, and so forth. The kind of industry—or *market*—in which a firm operates determines, in large part, how it will behave.

In the discussion that follows, we analyze industries as if their structures fit their definitions precisely. In reality, however, industries are not always easy to categorize. Some industries have some characteristics generally associated with one form of organization and other characteristics associated with a different form of organization. Nonetheless, these categories provide a useful and convenient framework for thinking about the organization of industries in the U.S. economy.

■ **Perfect Competition** At one end of the market-organization spectrum is the competitive industry in which many relatively small firms produce nearly identical products. **Perfect competition** is a very precisely defined form of industry structure. (The word *perfect* here does not refer to virtue. It simply means "total," or "complete.") In a perfectly competitive industry, no single firm has any control over prices. That is, no single firm is large enough to affect the market price of its product or the prices of the inputs that it buys. This crucial observation follows from two characteristics of competitive industries. First, a competitive industry is composed of many firms, each small relative to the size of the industry. Second, every firm in a perfectly competitive industry produces exactly the same product; the output of one firm cannot be distinguished from the output of the others. Products in a perfectly competitive industry are said to be **homogeneous.**

These characteristics limit the decisions open to competitive firms and simplify the analysis of competitive behavior. Because all firms in a perfectly competitive in-

industry *All the firms that produce a similar product. The boundaries of a "product" can be drawn very widely ("agricultural products"), less widely ("dairy products"), or very narrowly ("cheese"). The term* industry *can be used interchangeably with the term* market.

market organization *The way an industry is structured. Structure is defined by how many firms there are in an industry, whether products are differentiated or are virtually the same, whether or not firms in the industry can control prices or wages, and whether or not competing firms can enter and leave the industry freely.*

perfect competition *An industry structure (or market organization) in which there are many firms, each small relative to the industry, producing virtually identical products and in which no firm is large enough to have any control over prices. In perfectly competitive industries, new competitors can freely enter and exit the market.*

homogeneous products *Undifferentiated outputs: products that are identical to, or indistinguishable from, one another.*

---

[2]*The U.S. Department of Commerce has devised a code system, the Standard Industrial Classification (S.I.C.) System, which defines industries at various levels of detail.*

dustry produce virtually identical products, and because each firm is small relative to the market, perfectly competitive firms have no control over the prices at which they sell their output. Taking prices as a given, then, each firm can decide only how much output to produce and how to produce it.

Consider agriculture, the classic example of a perfectly competitive industry. A wheat farmer in South Dakota has absolutely no control over the price of wheat. Prices are determined not by the individual farmers but rather by the interaction of many suppliers and many demanders. The only decisions left to the wheat farmer are how much wheat to plant and when and how to produce the crop.

Another mark of perfectly competitive industries is ease of entry. *Ease of entry* means that new firms can easily enter a market and compete for profits. No barriers exist to prevent new firms from competing. New firms can, and do, frequently enter such industries in search of profits, while others go out of business when they suffer losses. For example, anyone who has been to Seattle, Washington recently, knows the importance of coffee. Several years ago, a firm called Starbucks opened a series of gourmet coffee shops in the city. Within a short while, business was booming, and Starbucks was making enormous profits. The success of Starbucks attracted competition, and hundreds of new firms entered the market during the 1990s. Entry was easy: After all, to sell coffee all you need is a place to do business, a coffee maker, perhaps an espresso machine, and some effort. Today, Seattle's landscape is filled with coffee and espresso signs; even McDonald's sells gourmet coffee there. Starbucks has expanded nationwide, and it is likely to attract competition wherever it goes because entry into the market is easy.

When a firm *exits* an industry, it simply stops producing a product. Sometimes an exiting firm goes out of business altogether. During the last ten years, for example, thousands of small farmers have gone out of business, sold off their assets, paid what bills they could, and disappeared.

To summarize:

> Perfectly competitive industries are made up of many firms, each small relative to the size of the total market. In these industries, individual firms do not distinguish or differentiate their products from those of their competitors. Product prices are determined by market forces and are virtually unaffected by decisions of any single firm. Entry into and exit from the market are relatively easy.

■ **Monopoly**   At the other end of the spectrum is **monopoly,** a market or industry in which only one firm produces a product for which there are no close substitutes.

When there is only one firm in a market, that firm sets the price of its product. This does not mean, however, that monopolies can set any price they please. Even monopolies face the constraint of the market. Even if a firm produces a good that everyone likes, the firm gains nothing if it charges a price so high that no one buys it. The price a monopolist chooses determines the quantity it will be able to sell: It will sell more at lower prices and less at higher prices. Thus, even a monopolist is subject to discipline imposed by the market.

For a monopoly to remain a monopoly, it must find some way to keep other firms from entering its market and competing for profits. Often governments erect such **barriers to entry.** Sometimes they grant an exclusive license to one producer. In Taiwan, for example, the national government licensed only one company to produce beer and prohibited beer imports until 1987. In the United States, public utilities—electric power and gas companies, for example, most of which are privately owned—have traditionally been shielded by the government from competition. For many years the American Telephone and Telegraph Company was essentially the exclusive producer of telephone services, both local and long distance. However, dramatic changes in the telecommunications industry in the last few years, including the breakup of AT&T by the courts in 1983, have made that market much more competitive.

Sometimes monopolies are specific to a particular time and location. Professional sports teams sign exclusive vendor agreements for games. Most often, for example, a single vendor will be responsible for food and beverage sales at a pro football game. Since most stadiums do not permit you to bring food and beverages into a game, the vendor is providing a service for which there is no close substitute, and entry is blocked. Have you ever noticed the price of food and drinks at a pro ballgame?

In sum:

> A monopoly is a one-firm industry that produces a product for which there are no close substitutes. Such a firm can set price, but its pricing behavior is constrained by its market: It can sell a product only if people are willing to buy it. A monopolist is protected from competition by barriers to entry.

■ **Monopolistic Competition**   Somewhere between monopoly and competition, but much closer to competition, is a very common hybrid market organization called **monopolistic competition.** In a monopolistically competitive industry, many firms compete for essentially the same customers, but each firm produces a slightly different product. If these firms can *differentiate* their products successfully, they establish a *brand loyalty* that allows them to enjoy the benefits of a monopoly.

monopoly *An industry structure (or market organization) in which there is only one large firm that produces a product for which there are no close substitutes. Monopolists can set prices but are subject to market discipline. For a monopoly to continue to exist, something must prevent potential competitors from entering the industry and competing for profits.*

barrier to entry *Something that prevents new firms from entering and competing in an industry.*

monopolistic competition *An industry structure (or market organization) in which many firms compete, producing similar but slightly differentiated products. There are close substitutes for the product of any given firm. Monopolistic competitors have some control over price. Price and quality competition follow from product differentiation. Entry and exit are relatively easy, and success invites new competitors.*

ISSUES AND CONTROVERSIES

THE CHANGING MIX OF JOBS IN THE UNITED STATES

As the following excerpt from a recent article from *The New York Times* points out, you shouldn't believe everything you hear about the current job situation in the United States:

The notion that Americans are working more for less pay is firmly embedded in public rhetoric. And it is practically gospel that the growing American economy cannot deliver the higher pay that American workers want.

No doubt many Americans are losing ground economically. But in fact most of the 5.5 million jobs the economy has added in the last two and a half years are in occupations that pay more, not less, than the average, which is now about $15.50 an hour.

This year alone [1994], 72 percent of the 2.5 million new jobs have been for managers, from the chief executive to the branch sales manager, and for professionals, from surgeons and nurses to software programmers, accountants and high school teachers. And despite its reputation for low wages, the service sector is adding most of the higher-wage jobs.

As a result, average hourly pay for all employees . . . is slowly rising, government data show, not falling as so many politicians and commentators have been saying. Average hourly compensation, which in-

THE FASTEST GROWING SECTOR OF THE U.S. ECONOMY OVER THE PAST TWO DECADES HAS BEEN THE SERVICE SECTOR. TRADITIONAL MANUFACTURING AND ASSEMBLY-LINE JOBS (LEFT) ARE INCREASINGLY BE-ING REPLACED BY JOBS IN SERVICE-PRODUCING INDUSTRIES LIKE SOFTWARE DEVELOPMENT, TRAVEL, AND RESTAURANTS (RIGHT). THIS TRANSITION IS NOT NECESSARILY BAD FOR THE ECONOMY; RECENT DATA SHOW THAT MOST OF THE 5.5 MILLION JOBS ADDED TO THE ECONOMY IN 1993 AND 1994 PAY MORE THAN THE HOURLY AVERAGE.

cludes health benefits, paid vacations, pensions and other benefits, is also rising. . . .

Indeed, average hourly pay has risen 2.5 percent in the early 1990's, about as much as it did throughout the entire 1980's. . . .

The source of much of the improvement is the service sector, which is supposed to have been producing only low-wage jobs like hamburger flipping and baby-sitting.

Service companies—from McDonald's to J. P. Morgan—

have dominated job creation in the economic expansion of the last three years, just as they did during the Reagan Administration years. But in an information-age economy that values skills, experience and education ever more highly, these companies have not been hiring just fast-food cooks, nurse's aides or cleaners.

Source: Sylvia Nasar, "Statistics Reveal Bulk of New Jobs Pay Over Average," *The New York Times*, October 17, 1994, p. A1.

Government in the United States operates on three different levels—federal, state, and local. Each of these levels has assumed a different set of functions and responsibilities over the years, and although there is some overlap, each level derives its main revenues from different sources. How big is this public sector? What does it spend its money on, and where does it get its money?

THE SIZE OF THE PUBLIC SECTOR

An economy's **gross domestic product,** or **GDP,** is the total value of all goods and services produced in the economy in a given period of time, say, a year. The concept of GDP is used extensively in macroeconomics. Here it is enough to say that GDP is used as a measure of a nation's total annual "output." As you can see from Figure 3.2, public expenditure at all levels, as a percentage of GDP, increased from 18.4% in 1940 to 33.5% in 1994. The federal portion of total expenditures increased more rapidly, more than doubling since 1940, while the state and local share grew only from 8.4% of GDP to 10.7% in the same period.[4]

Government spending can be broken into three major categories: purchases of goods and services, transfer payments to households, and interest payments. **Purchases of goods and services** make up that portion of national output that government actually uses, or "consumes," directly. They include the airplanes purchased from McDonnell Douglas by the air force, the new Senate office building (in the year that it was built), and the paper, books, and pens produced by private companies that are used by government employees. This category also includes the wages and salaries paid for the services of government employees.

Table 3.5 on the next page shows that government nondefense purchases of goods and services have stayed at roughly the same percentage of GDP (a little over 13%) since 1970. Government defense purchases of goods and services have generally decreased as a percentage of GDP since 1960.

gross domestic product (GDP) *The total value of all goods and services produced by a national economy within a given time period.*

government purchases of goods and services *A category of government spending that includes the portion of national output that the government uses, or "consumes," directly—ships for the navy, memo pads for the FBI, salaries for government employees.*

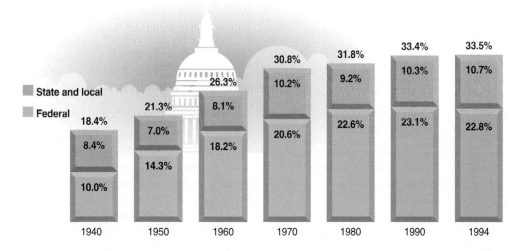

State and local
Federal

18.4%
8.4%
10.0%
1940

21.3%
7.0%
14.3%
1950

26.3%
8.1%
18.2%
1960

30.8%
10.2%
20.6%
1970

31.8%
9.2%
22.6%
1980

33.4%
10.3%
23.1%
1990

33.5%
10.7%
22.8%
1994

FIGURE 3.2

Total Government Expenditure as a Percentage of GDP, 1940–1994

Total government expenditures grew from 18.4% of GDP in 1940 to 33.5% in 1994. While the share of state and local governments grew less than two percentage points, the federal share more than doubled.

Source: Economic Report of the President, 1991, 1993, and updates. Grants to states and localities included in federal.

[4]*Federal grants to state and local governments are included as a federal expenditure rather than a state and local expenditure because they are paid for out of federal tax revenues. Federal grants in 1994 amounted to $197.6 billion. Including this figure with state and local expenditures would push state and local expenditures to 13.6% of GDP in 1994.*

TABLE 3.5	THE SIZE OF THE PUBLIC SECTOR, 1940–1994

GOVERNMENT EXPENDITURE AS A PERCENTAGE OF GDP

	1940	1950	1960	1970	1980	1990	1994
Total	18.4	21.3	26.3	30.8	31.8	33.4	33.5
Purchases of goods and services, nondefense	11.9	8.5	10.6	13.4	13.5	13.2	13.1
Purchases of goods and services, defense	2.2	5.0	8.8	7.6	5.3	5.7	4.3
Transfer payments	2.7	6.2	5.7	8.3	11.7	12.3	14.2
Interest payments (net)	1.2	1.5	1.3	1.2	1.2	2.2	2.0

GOVERNMENT EMPLOYMENT AS A PERCENTAGE OF TOTAL EMPLOYMENT (EXCLUDING MILITARY) IN THE ECONOMY

	1950	1960	1970	1980	1990	1994
Total	13.3	15.4	17.7	18.0	16.6	16.8
Federal	4.2	4.2	3.8	3.2	2.8	2.5
State and local	9.1	11.2	13.9	14.8	13.8	14.3

Sources: *Economic Report of the President, 1991, 1993,* and updates.

government transfer payments
Cash payments made by the government directly to households for which no current services are received. They include social security benefits, unemployment compensation, and welfare payments.

government interest payments
Cash payments made by the government to those who own government bonds.

Transfer payments are cash payments made directly to households—social security benefits, unemployment compensation payments, welfare payments, and so forth. The government receives no current services in return for these payments. **Interest payments** are also cash payments, but they are paid to those who own government bonds. Taken together, transfer payments and interest payments account for nearly the entire increase in government expenditure between 1960 and 1994.

The increase in the size of the social security system accounts for much of the increase in transfer payments. Social security is a self-financing system in which benefits are paid out of taxes contributed by workers and their employers. Some have argued that because workers who have contributed will ultimately be entitled to benefits, the system should be separated from other federal receipts and expenditures for accounting purposes, but this has not been done so far.

As Table 3.5 shows, interest payments in 1990 almost doubled as a percentage of GDP over the 1980 level. This is because of the huge deficits run up during the early 1980s. When the government spends more than it taxes, it must borrow. It does so by issuing bonds, and it must pay interest on the bonds. The figure dropped in 1994 because interest rates fell.

Another way to look at the relative size of the public sector is to look at government employment as a percentage of total employment (see again Table 3.5). In 1994 federal government civilian employment was only 2.5% of total employment. In addition, federal civilian employment as a percentage of total employment in the United States has fallen steadily since 1950. State and local government employment grew steadily as a fraction of total employment in the economy through 1980. Since 1980, however, it has dropped back to about the 1970 level. Total government employment in 1994 was 16.8% of total employment in the economy, down from 18.0% in 1980.

How big is the public sector in the United States relative to the public sectors in other countries? Good statistics on employment and spending are not easy to find, but Figure 3.3 presents some international comparisons based on taxes collected. (Taxes support the public sector's activities, and tax data are easy to find.) The figure shows total national and local taxes as a percentage of gross domestic product (GDP).

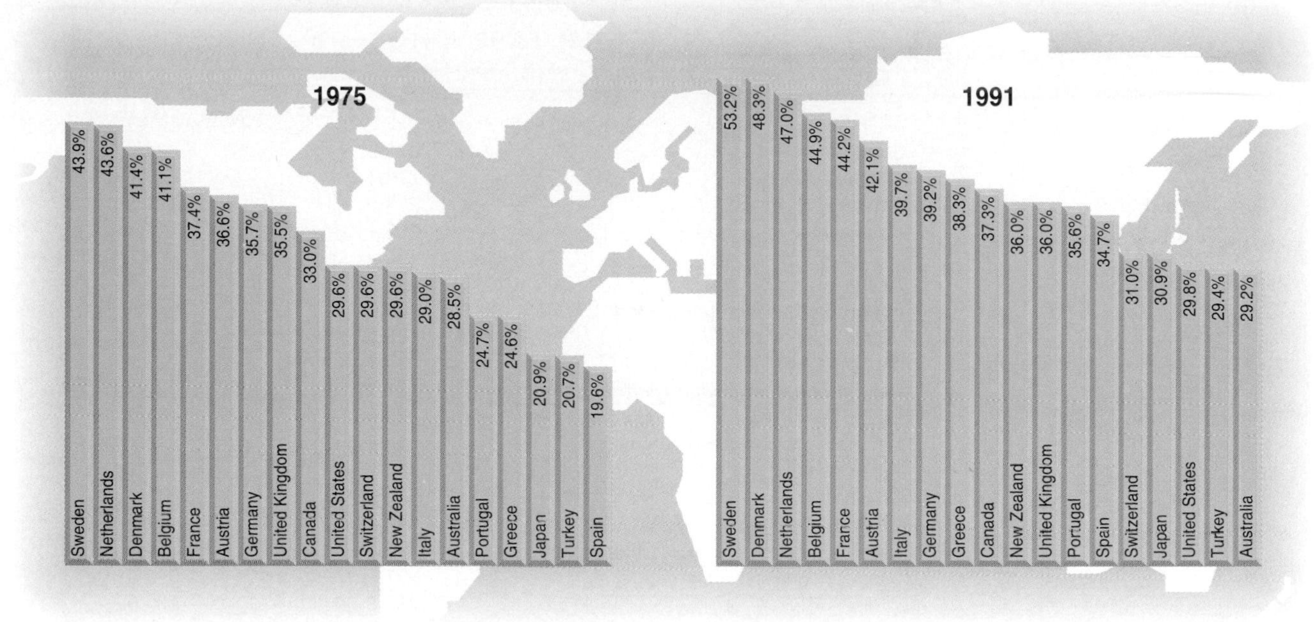

FIGURE 3.3

Taxes as a Percentage of Gross Domestic Product, 1975 and 1991

Source: *Statistical Abstract of the United States,* 1994, p. 867.

In 1975, U.S. federal, state, and local taxes amounted to 29.6% of GDP. This placed the United States in a tie for tenth place among the 19 countries in the comparison. Between 1975 and 1991, taxes as a percentage of GDP increased in all 19 countries. The smallest increase was registered in the United States, where taxes as a percentage of GDP remained virtually constant. As of 1991, only Turkey and Australia among the group of more developed countries had lower taxes as a percentage of GDP than the United States.

GOVERNMENT EXPENDITURES

The detailed breakdown of the federal budget for fiscal year 1994 in Table 3.6 on page 64 shows that the top six categories account for over 86% of the total. National defense and social security alone account for about 40% of federal spending. Table 3.7 compares the same categories for 1984 and 1994. With the end of the Cold War, expenditures for national defense have been shrinking sharply. Expenditures for Medicare and health have been growing rapidly. The crisis in health-care costs that is such an important issue today is evident in these numbers. Medicare and health-care expenditures taken together rose from 10.3% of the budget in 1984 to 17.3% of the budget in 1994.

Table 3.8 on page 65 shows state and local government spending by category in 1992. In that year, 33.6% of all state and local spending went for education, mostly public elementary and secondary education, although all states spend money on higher education as well. Since 1975, education and highways have contracted as a portion of the total budget, while interest on debt, public welfare, and health and hospitals have assumed a significantly larger share.

TABLE 3.6	FEDERAL EXPENDITURES BY FUNCTION 1994	
	BILLIONS OF DOLLARS	**PERCENTAGE OF TOTAL**
Social security	320.5	21.6
National defense	279.8	18.9
Income security	214.6	14.5
Net interest	203.4	13.7
Medicare	143.6	9.7
Health	112.3	7.6
Education, training, employment	50.8	3.4
Veterans benefits	38.1	2.6
Transportation	37.6	2.5
Natural resources environment	22.3	1.5
International affairs	19.0	1.3
Science, space, and technology	17.3	1.2
Agriculture	16.9	1.1
Administration of justice	16.5	1.1
General governments	14.3	1.0
Community and regional development	9.3	0.6
Miscellaneous and offsetting receipts	−37.4	−2.5
Total	1483.8	100.0

Source: *Statistical Abstract of the United States, 1994*, pp. 334–335.

SOURCES OF GOVERNMENT REVENUE

A breakdown of the sources of federal tax revenues appears in Table 3.9. The biggest single source of revenue for the federal government is the *individual income tax,* which accounted for 48.4% of total revenues in 1980. That figure dropped to 40.8% in 1992, but rose again in 1994 to 44.8% as a result of the tax increase enacted in 1993. Federal income tax is withheld from most people's pay each week by their employers, who send it to the Internal Revenue Service. Self-employed people are responsible for sending in their own estimated taxes four times each year. Each year we must add up our total income, subtract the items that we are allowed to exclude or deduct, and figure out the total tax that we should have paid for the previous year. If we owe more than we paid, we must send the difference to the IRS by April 15. If we paid more than we owe, we get a refund.

Social insurance taxes are levied at a flat rate on wages and salaries up to a maximum amount. Because these taxes are figured as a percentage of wages and

social insurance, or **payroll, taxes** *Taxes levied at a flat rate on wages and salaries. Proceeds support various government-administrated social-benefit programs, including the social security system and the unemployment benefits system.*

TABLE 3.7	FEDERAL EXPENDITURES BY FUNCTION: PERCENTAGE SHARES OF TOTAL COMPARED FOR 1984 AND 1994		
	1984	**1994**	**CHANGE IN SHARE**
National defense	26.7	18.9	−7.8
Social security	20.9	21.6	+0.7
Income security	13.2	14.5	+1.3
Net interest	13.0	13.7	+0.7
Medicare	6.7	9.7	+3.0
Health	3.6	7.6	+4.0
All other	15.9	14.0	−1.9
Total	100.0	100.0	

Source: *Statistical Abstract of the United States, 1994*, p. 332.

TABLE 3.8	STATE AND LOCAL EXPENDITURES BY FUNCTION		
	BILLIONS OF DOLLARS, 1992	PERCENTAGE OF TOTAL, 1992	PERCENTAGE OF TOTAL, 1975
Education	326.8	33.6	38.2
Public welfare	154.2	15.9	11.8
Health and hospitals	88.1	9.1	8.2
Highways	66.5	6.8	9.8
Interest on debt	55.2	5.7	3.8
Police and fire	48.9	5.0	5.2
General administration	18.1	1.9	3.8
Other*	214.2	22.0	19.2
Total	972.0	100.0	100.0

*Includes parks, sanitation, and housing, among other areas.

Source: *Statistical Abstract of the United States, 1994*, p. 302.

salaries and are levied on both employers and employees, they are also known as **payroll taxes.** The payroll tax is levied at a flat rate of 7.65% on employees and another 7.65% on employers. Self-employed persons pay between 12.8% and 14.2% depending on their income.

Social insurance taxes go into one of several trust funds that pay social security cash and health benefits to retirees, the disabled, and the survivors of workers who paid into the system. Payroll taxes also fund the unemployment compensation system.

Payroll taxes now account for a much larger portion of federal revenues than they have in the past. In 1994, they brought in 37.6% of total federal revenues, up from 31.3% fourteen years earlier. In 1965, they brought in only 19% of total revenues. The tax rate has been increased steadily because of worries about the future solvency of the system. A huge number of people will reach retirement age soon after the year 2000. At the same time, the labor force will be smaller. Because the tax rate required to support the increasing number of elderly then would be intolerable, the rate was sharply increased during the 1970s. It continues to increase now, in order to generate a surplus in the social security trust funds that should prevent the system's collapse in the future.

Corporate income taxes are levied on the net income of corporations only, not on the profits of other forms of business organization (proprietorships or partnerships), which are taxed directly as ordinary personal income to the owners. While payroll taxes have been increasing as a share of total tax revenues, corporate income taxes have had their ups and downs. In 1960, they accounted for nearly 25% of federal revenues. Table 3.9 shows that they accounted for 12.8% in 1980 and only 10.6% in 1994. Big cuts came in 1981 when Congress enacted the Economic

corporate income taxes *Taxes levied on the net incomes of corporations.*

TABLE 3.9	FEDERAL RECEIPTS BY SOURCE, 1980 AND 1994			
	1980		1994	
	BILLIONS OF DOLLARS	PERCENT	BILLIONS OF DOLLARS	PERCENT
Individual income taxes	244.1	48.4	549.9	44.8
Corporate income taxes	64.6	12.8	130.7	10.6
Social insurance taxes	157.8	31.3	461.9	37.6
Excise taxes	24.3	4.8	54.5	4.4
Gift and estate taxes	6.4	1.3	12.7	1.0
Customs duties	7.2	1.4	19.2	1.6
Total	504.4	100.0	1229.0	100.0

Sources: *Statistical Abstract of the United States, 1994*, p. 331.

Recovery Tax Act, designed to stimulate business investment. The Tax Reform Act of 1986 sharply reduced personal income taxes and partly offset the lost revenues by increasing the corporation tax.

Excise taxes make up only about 4.4% of the federal total. These are taxes on specific commodities like cigarettes, alcoholic beverages, gasoline, tires and tubes, and telephone service.

The sources of state and local revenues in 1994 appear in Table 3.10. Sales taxes, levied primarily by states, account for 24.0% of the total. Property taxes, which account for 20.2% of the total, are levied primarily by local governments (such as counties, cities, and towns) on the estimated, or "assessed," value of commercial, industrial, and residential property. Personal income taxes account for 18.7% of state and local revenues, while social insurance taxes account for 7.5% and corporate taxes account for 3.8 percent. Of total state and local revenue, 20.9% comes in the form of federal grants.

THE INTERNATIONAL SECTOR: IMPORTS AND EXPORTS IN THE UNITED STATES

One of the great economic lessons of the 1970s and 1980s was that all economies, regardless of their size, depend to some extent on other economies and are affected by events outside their borders. Ask anyone in Iowa about the impact of foreign trade on farm prices and therefore on the well-being of U.S. farmers. Or ask steelworkers in Pittsburgh and Youngstown about the effect of cheap German and Japanese steel on the economies of those towns. One of the biggest issues in the 1992 presidential election campaign was the North American Free Trade Agreement (NAFTA), which was signed by President Bush in December 1992, and approved by the Congress in 1993. The purpose of NAFTA is to reduce trade barriers between the United States, Canada, and Mexico. In 1995, the Congress ratified the General Agreement on Tariffs and Trade (GATT), also designed to reduce trade barriers, after extended and often bitter debate.

The United States economy is by no means "closed." Thousands of transactions between the United States and virtually every country in the world take place daily. In 1994 the United States sold $47.1 billion in agricultural products to the rest of the world and bought about $51.2 billion in petroleum products from other countries. Overall, the United States imported $816.9 billion worth of goods and services in 1994, 12.1% of its GDP.

The growth of the international sector of the U.S. economy is a relatively recent phenomenon. Prior to 1970, imports and exports of goods and services ac-

TABLE 3.10	STATE AND LOCAL TAX RECEIPTS, 1994	
	BILLIONS OF DOLLARS	PERCENT OF TOTAL TAXES
Sales taxes	226.2	24.0
Property taxes	190.8	20.2
Personal income taxes	176.5	18.7
Social insurance taxes	70.9	7.5
Corporate taxes	35.4	3.8
Federal grants	197.6	20.9
Other	46.0	4.9
Total	943.4	100.0

Sources: U.S. Department of Commerce, Bureau of Economic Analysis.

counted for a relatively small and stable fraction of U.S. GDP. Table 3.11 shows imports and exports for selected years since 1929. In all but a few years between 1929 and 1970, imports accounted for only 4% to 6% of GDP. During the Depression and immediately following World War II, the figure dropped below 4%, but never rose above 6 percent.

Beginning in 1970, however, the volume of international trade increased significantly. Imports and exports doubled as a percentage of GDP by the end of the 1970s. Imports reached more than 11% by 1980. Exports dropped to 7.6% in 1985 and 1986, but rebounded to 10% by 1990. Imports have held fairly steady at around 11 to 12% of GDP since 1987.

■ **The Composition of U.S. Trade**   Table 3.12 on the next page lists the types of merchandise imported and exported in 1994. Perhaps the most surprising thing about this merchandise is its tremendous diversity.

The largest category—about 40% of U.S. exports and a little over a quarter of its imports—is capital goods except automotive, a very broad category that includes many specialized and diverse products. The second most important category of U.S. exports is industrial supplies and materials—$115.9 billion in 1994. In third and fourth places are consumer goods except automotive and automobiles.

Prior to 1970, imports of petroleum and petroleum products never amounted to more than $3 billion annually and were never more than 10% of total imports. The rapid increase in oil prices in 1973–1974 changed all this. Table 3.13 chroni-

TABLE 3.11	U.S. IMPORTS AND EXPORTS OF GOODS AND SERVICES, 1929–1994			
	EXPORTS OF GOODS AND SERVICES		IMPORTS OF GOODS AND SERVICES	
	BILLIONS OF DOLLARS	PERCENTAGE OF GDP	BILLIONS OF DOLLARS	PERCENTAGE OF GDP
1929	7.1	6.8	5.9	5.7
1933	2.4	4.3	2.1	3.8
1945	7.4	3.5	7.9	3.7
1955	21.1	5.5	18.1	4.5
1960	25.3	5.0	22.8	4.5
1965	35.4	5.3	31.5	4.7
1970	57.0	5.8	55.8	5.7
1974	124.3	8.9	127.5	9.1
1976	148.9	8.8	151.1	9.0
1978	186.1	8.6	212.3	9.8
1980	279.2	10.6	293.9	11.1
1981	303.0	10.2	317.7	10.7
1982	282.6	9.0	303.2	9.7
1983	276.7	8.3	328.1	9.9
1984	302.4	8.2	405.1	11.0
1985	302.1	7.6	417.6	10.5
1986	319.2	7.6	451.7	10.7
1987	364.0	8.2	507.1	11.4
1988	444.2	9.2	552.2	11.5
1989	508.0	9.7	587.7	11.2
1990	557.1	10.0	628.5	11.3
1991	601.1	10.5	620.9	10.8
1992	638.1	10.6	668.4	11.1
1993	659.1	10.4	724.3	11.4
1994	718.7	10.7	816.9	12.1

Source: U.S. Department of Commerce, Bureau of Economic Analysis.

TABLE 3.12   MAJOR CATEGORIES OF MERCHANDISE IMPORTS AND EXPORTS BY THE UNITED STATES, 1994

EXPORTS	BILLIONS OF DOLLARS	PERCENTAGE OF TOTAL
Agricultural products	47.1	9.2
Nonagricultural products	465.0	90.8
Total	512.1	100.0
Food, feeds, and beverages	42.0	8.2
Industrial supplies and materials	115.9	22.6
Capital goods except automotive (machinery, aircraft, etc.)	205.6	40.1
Automobiles, vehicles, parts, and engines	57.6	11.2
Consumer goods except automotive	60.0	11.7
All other	31.0	6.1
Total	512.1	100.0

IMPORTS	BILLIONS OF DOLLARS	PERCENTAGE OF TOTAL
Petroleum and petroleum products	51.2	7.6
Nonpetroleum products	626.0	92.4
Total	677.2	100.0
Food, feeds, and beverages	31.0	4.6
Industrial supplies and materials	156.7	23.1
Capital goods except automotive (machinery, aircraft, etc.)	184.7	27.3
Automobiles, vehicles, parts, and engines	118.7	17.5
Consumer goods except automotive	146.3	21.6
All other	39.8	5.9
Total	677.6	100.0

Sources: U.S. Department of Commerce, Bureau of Economic Analysis.

TABLE 3.13   U.S. IMPORTS OF CRUDE PETROLEUM, 1970–1993

	BILLIONS OF DOLLARS	PERCENTAGE OF GENERAL IMPORTS
1970	2.8	7.0
1974	24.3	23.7
1975	24.8	25.2
1978	39.1	22.4
1979	56.0	26.7
1980	77.6	31.7
1981	75.6	29.0
1982	59.4	24.3
1983	52.3	20.3
1984	55.9	17.2
1985	49.6	14.4
1986	34.1	9.2
1987	41.5	10.2
1988	38.8	8.8
1989	49.1	10.4
1990	60.5	12.2
1991	50.1	10.3
1992	50.4	9.5
1993	49.7	8.6

Source: *Statistical Abstract of the United States, 1994,* p. 818.

cles the rise and fall of crude petroleum as a major import. By 1980 crude oil accounted for nearly a third of total imports. But in the early 1980s the United States began to cut its consumption of petroleum. By 1988, petroleum and natural gas accounted for only 8.8% of total imports. With the 1990 invasion of Kuwait, oil prices rose and the dollar volume of imports jumped back to over 12% of the total. After the Persian Gulf War, prices again fell and the figure dropped back to 8.6% in 1993.

Two other important categories of imports that have received a great deal of attention because of their impact on major U.S. industries are automobiles and iron and steel. In 1994 imports of automobiles and parts totaled $118.7 billion.

FROM INSTITUTIONS TO THEORY

This chapter has sketched the institutional structure of the U.S. economy. As we turn to economic theory, both positive and normative, you should reflect on the basic realities of economic life in the United States presented here. Why is the service sector expanding and the manufacturing sector contracting? Why is the public sector as large as it is? What economic functions does it perform? What determines the level of imports and exports? What effects do cheap foreign products have on the U.S. economy?

One of the most important questions in economics concerns the relative merits of public sector involvement in the economy. Should the government be involved in the economy, or should the market be left to its own devices? Before we can confront these and other important issues, we need to establish a theoretical framework. Our study of the economy and its operation begins in Chapter 4 with the behavior of suppliers and demanders in private markets.

SUMMARY

1. The *private sector* is made up of privately owned firms that exist to make a profit, nonprofit organizations, and individual households. The *public sector* is the government and its agencies at all levels—federal, state, and local. The *international sector* is the global economy. From any one country's perspective; the international sector consists of the economies of the rest of the world.

THE PRIVATE SECTOR: BUSINESS AND INDUSTRIAL ORGANIZATION IN THE UNITED STATES

2. A *proprietorship* is a firm with a single owner. A *partnership* has two or more owners. Proprietors and partners are fully liable for all the debts of the business. A *corporation* is a formally established legal entity that limits the liability of its owners. The owners are not responsible for the debts of the firm beyond what they invest.

3. The term *industry* is used loosely to refer to groups of firms that produce similar products. Industries can be broadly or narrowly defined. A company that produces cheese belongs to the cheese industry,

the dairy industry, the food products industry, and the agricultural products industry.

4. In *perfect competition,* no single firm has any control over prices. This follows from two characteristics of this industry structure: (1) Perfectly competitive industries are composed of many firms, each small relative to the size of the industry, and (2) each firm in a perfectly competitive industry produces exactly the same product—that is, products are *homogeneous.*

5. A *monopoly* is a *market organization,* or industry structure, in which there is only one firm producing a product for which there are no close substitutes. To remain a monopoly in a profitable industry, a firm must be able to block the entry of competing firms.

6. *Monopolistic competition* is an industry structure in which many firms compete, but in which each firm produces a slightly different product. Although each firm's product is unique, however, there are many close substitutes. Entry and exit into monopolistically competitive industries are relatively easy.

7. An *oligopoly* is an industry with a small number of firms. In general, entry of new firms into an oligopolistic industry is difficult but possible.

THE PUBLIC SECTOR: TAXES AND GOVERNMENT SPENDING IN THE UNITED STATES

8. Public expenditures at all levels increased from 18.4% of GDP in 1940 to 33.5% in 1994. The federal portion of total expenditures grew more rapidly than the state and local portions, more than doubling since 1940.

9. Other measures of the size of the public sector have not increased as rapidly. Government employment increased slightly from 15.4% of total employment in 1960 to 16.8% in 1994.

10. National defense and social security account for over 40% of federal spending. The top four categories of state and local spending are education, public welfare, health and hospitals, and highways.

11. Individual income taxes and social insurance taxes together accounted for about 80% of federal revenues in 1994. Over the last quarter century, social insurance taxes have increased dramatically as a portion of total federal revenues. Sales taxes and property taxes accounted for about 44% of state and local revenues in 1994.

THE INTERNATIONAL SECTOR: IMPORTS AND EXPORTS IN THE UNITED STATES

12. Thousands of transactions between the United States and virtually every other country in the world take place daily. This has led to the increased importance of the international sector in the United States economy. In 1994, the United States imported $816.9 billion worth of goods and services, 12.1% of its GDP.

REVIEW TERMS AND CONCEPTS

barrier to entry 55

corporate income taxes 65

corporation 51

dividends 52

excise taxes 66

government interest payments 62

government purchases of goods and services 61

government transfer payments 62

gross domestic product (GDP) 61

homogeneous products 53

industry 53

international sector 50

market organization 53

monopolistic competition 55

monopoly 55

net income 52

oligopoly 56

partnership 51

perfect competition 53

private sector 49

proprietorship 50

public sector 49

retained earnings 52

share of stock 52

social insurance, or payroll, taxes 64

PROBLEM SET

1. Health care continues to be a major issue in the 1990s. Look up the latest figures on health-care expenditures as a percentage of GDP. What share of total government expenditure (federal, state, and local) is devoted to health care?

2. a. How many separate governments are there in the United States? (You can find the number in *The Statistical Abstract of the United States* and other publications.) What percentage of the total number are "local" governments?

   b. What are the five biggest functions of local government?

   c. What is the logic for assigning these functions to local government as opposed to state or federal government?

3. Do a short research project on one of the following large government programs. What does the program accomplish or hope to accomplish? What is the basic logic for government involvement? How much was spent on the program in 1995 compared to 1980?
   a. Medicare
   b. Medicaid
   c. Social security
   d. State colleges and universities
   e. Student financial aid
   f. Aid to Families with Dependent Children (AFDC)
   g. Food stamps
   h. Interstate highways

4. The Congress debated the GATT in 1994 and approved it in 1995. What groups in the United States were opposed to its passage? Why? What are the basic arguments in favor of the GATT?

5. The latest data on the federal budget and on international trade in this chapter are for 1994. What events during 1995 had an impact on federal receipts and expenditures? On the volume of imports and exports?

6. The chapter contains conflicting evidence on whether the public sector has expanded relative to the rest of the economy in the last 10 to 20 years. What figures might be quoted in support of this proposition? Do they tell the whole story? Discuss.

7. What are the differences between a proprietorship and a corporation? If you were going to start a small business, which form of organization would you choose? What are the advantages and disadvantages of the two forms of organization?

8. "Most firms are corporations, but they account for a relatively small portion of total output in the United States." Do you agree or disagree with this statement? Explain your answer.

9. In 1994 shareholders directly received only 39.1% of total corporate profits. What happened to the rest?

10. Perfectly competitive industries are made up of large numbers of firms, each small relative to the size of the industry and each producing homogeneous products. What does this imply about an individual firm's ability to influence price? Explain your answer.

11. How is a monopolistically competitive industry like a monopoly? In what ways is it like a perfectly competitive industry?

12. How is it possible for government spending to increase as a percentage of GDP while taxes and government employment are both decreasing?

13. Why is the federal government spending much more on interest payments now than it was a decade ago? Explain.

DEMAND, SUPPLY, AND MARKET EQUILIBRIUM

C HAPTERS 1 AND 2 INTRODUCED THE DISCIPLINE, METHODOLOGY, and subject matter of economics. Chapter 3 described the institutional landscape of the U.S. economy—its private, public, and international sectors. We now begin the task of analyzing how a market economy actually works. This chapter and the next present an overview of the way individual markets work. They introduce some of the concepts needed to understand both microeconomics and macroeconomics.

As we proceed to define terms and make assumptions, it is important to keep in mind what we are doing. In Chapter 1 we were very careful to explain what economic theory attempts to do. Theories are abstract representations of reality, like a map that represents a city. We believe that the models presented here will help you understand the workings of the economy just as a map helps you get where you want to go in a city. But just as a map presents one view of the world, so too does any given theory of the economy. Alternatives exist to the theory that we present. We believe, however, that the basic model presented here, while sometimes abstract, is useful in gaining an understanding of how the economy works.

In the simple island society discussed in Chapter 2, the economic problem was solved directly. Colleen and Bill allocated their time and used the resources of the island to satisfy their wants. Bill might be a farmer, Colleen a hunter and carpenter. He might be a civil engineer, she a doctor. Exchange occurred, but complex markets were not necessary.

In societies of many people, however, production must satisfy wide-ranging tastes and preferences. Producers therefore specialize. Farmers produce more food than they can eat in order to sell it to buy manufactured goods. Physicians are paid for specialized services, as are attorneys, construction workers, and editors. When there is specialization, there must be exchange, and exchange takes place in markets.

This chapter begins to explore the basic forces at work in market systems. The purpose of our discussion is to explain how the individual decisions of households and firms together, without any central planning or direction, answer the three basic questions: What will be produced, how will it be produced, and who will get what is produced? We begin with some definitions.

FIRMS AND HOUSEHOLDS: THE BASIC DECISION-MAKING UNITS

Throughout this book, we discuss and analyze the behavior of two fundamental decision-making units: *firms*—the primary producing units in an economy—and *households*—the consuming units in an economy. Both are made up of people performing different functions and playing different roles. In essence, then, what we are developing is a theory of human behavior.

A **firm** exists when a person or a group of people decides to produce a product or products by transforming *inputs* (that is, resources in the broadest sense) into *outputs* (the products that are sold in the market). Some firms produce goods; others produce services. Some are large, some are small, and some are in between. But all firms exist to transform resources into things that people want. The Colorado Symphony Orchestra takes labor, land, a building, musically talented people, electricity, and other inputs and combines them to produce concerts. The production process can be extremely complicated. The first flutist in the orchestra, for example, uses training, talent, previous performance experience, a score, an instrument, the conductor's interpretation, and her own feelings about the music to produce just one contribution to an overall performance.

Most firms exist to make a profit for their owners, but some do not. Columbia University, for example, fits the description of a firm: It takes inputs in the form of labor, land, skills, books, and buildings and produces a service that we call education. Although it sells that service for a price, it does not exist to make a profit, but rather to provide education of the highest quality possible.

Still, most firms exist to make a profit. They engage in production because they can sell their product for more than it costs to produce it. The analysis of firm behavior that follows rests on the assumption that *firms make decisions in order to maximize profits*.

An **entrepreneur** is one who organizes, manages, and assumes the risks of a firm. It is the entrepreneur who takes a new idea or a new product and turns it into a successful business. All firms have implicit in them some element of entrepreneurship. When a new firm is created—whether a proprietorship, a partnership, or a corporation—someone must organize the new firm, arrange financing, hire employees, and take risks. That person is an entrepreneur. Sometimes existing companies introduce new products, and sometimes new firms develop or improve on an old idea, but

firm *An organization that transforms resources (inputs) into products (outputs). Firms are the primary producing units in a market economy.*

THE COLORADO SYMPHONY ORCHESTRA IS A FIRM. IT COMBINES INPUTS (LAND, LABOR, A CONCERT HALL, MUSICALLY TALENTED PEOPLE, AND ELECTRICITY) AND USES THEM TO PRODUCE OUTPUTS (MUSICAL PERFORMANCES).

entrepreneur *A person who organizes, manages, and assumes the risks of a firm, taking a new idea or a new product and turning it into a successful business.*

at the root of it all is entrepreneurship, which some see as the core of the free enterprise system.

At the root of the debate about the potential of free enterprise in formerly socialist Eastern Europe is the question of entrepreneurship. Does an entrepreneurial spirit exist in that part of the world? If not, can it be developed? Without it the free enterprise system breaks down.

The consuming units in an economy are **households.** A household may consist of any number of people: a single person living alone, a married couple with four children, or 15 unrelated people sharing a house. Household decisions are presumably based on the individual tastes and preferences of the consuming unit. The household buys what it wants and can afford. In a large, heterogeneous, and open society such as the United States, wildly different tastes find expression in the marketplace. A six-block walk in any direction on any street in Manhattan or a drive from the Chicago Loop south into rural Illinois should be enough to convince anyone that it is difficult to generalize about what people like and do not like.

Even though households have wide-ranging preferences, they also have some things in common. All—even the very rich—have ultimately limited incomes, and all must pay in some way for the things they consume. While households may have some control over their incomes—they can work more or less—they are also constrained by the availability of jobs, current wages, their own abilities, and their accumulated and inherited wealth (or lack thereof).

INPUT MARKETS AND OUTPUT MARKETS: THE CIRCULAR FLOW

Households and firms interact in two basic kinds of markets: product, or output, markets and input, or factor, markets. Goods and services that are intended for use by households are exchanged in **product** or **output markets.** In output markets, competing firms *supply* and households *demand.*

To produce goods and services, firms must buy resources in **input** or **factor markets.** Firms buy inputs from households, which supply these inputs. When a firm decides how much to produce (supply) in output markets, it must simultaneously decide how much of each input it needs to produce the desired level of output. To produce automobiles, Chrysler Corporation must use many inputs, including tires, steel, complicated machinery, and many different kinds of skilled labor.

Figure 4.1 shows the *circular flow* of economic activity through a simple market economy. Note that the flow reflects the direction in which goods and services flow through input and output markets. For example, goods and services flow from firms to households through output markets. Labor services flow from households to firms through input markets. Payment (most often in money form) for goods and services flows in the opposite direction. Payment for goods and services flows from households to firms, and payment for labor services flows from firms to households.

In input markets, households *supply* resources. Most households earn their incomes by working—they supply their labor in the **labor market** to firms that demand labor and pay workers for their time and skills. Households may also loan their accumulated or inherited savings to firms for interest or exchange those savings for claims to future profits, as when a household buys shares of stock in a corporation. In the **capital market,** households supply the funds that firms use to buy capital goods. In exchange, these households receive interest or claims to future profits. Households may also supply land or other real property in exchange for rent in the **land market.**

households *The consuming units in an economy.*

product or **output markets** *The markets in which goods and services are exchanged.*

input or **factor markets** *The markets in which the resources used to produce products are exchanged.*

labor market *The input/factor market in which households supply work for wages to firms that demand labor.*

capital market *The input/factor market in which households supply their savings, for interest or for claims to future profits, to firms that demand funds in order to buy capital goods.*

land market *The input/factor market in which households supply land or other real property in exchange for rent.*

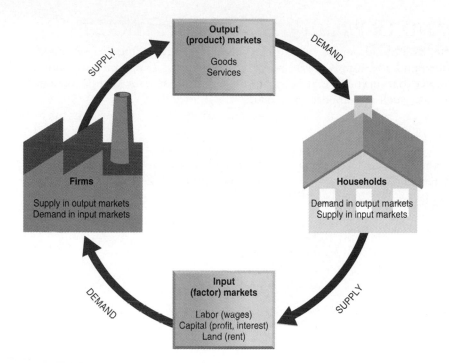

FIGURE 4.1

The Circular Flow of Economic Activity

Diagrams like this one show the circular flow of economic activity, hence the name *circular flow diagram*. Here, goods and services flow clockwise: Labor services supplied by households flow to firms, and goods and services produced by firms flow to households. Money (not pictured here) flows in the opposite (counterclockwise) direction: Payment for goods and services flows from households to firms, and payment for labor services flows from firms to households.

Inputs into the production process are also called **factors of production.** Land, labor, and capital are the three key factors of production. Throughout this text, we use the terms *input* and *factor of production* interchangeably. Thus, input markets and factor markets mean the same thing.

Early economics texts included entrepreneurship as a type of input, just like land, labor, and capital. Treating entrepreneurship as a separate factor of production has fallen out of favor, however, partially because it is unmeasurable. Most economists today implicitly assume that it is in plentiful supply. That is, if profit opportunities exist, it is likely that entrepreneurs will crop up to take advantage of them. This assumption has turned out to be a good predictor of actual economic behavior and performance.

The supply of inputs and their prices ultimately determine households' income. The amount of income a household earns thus depends on the decisions it makes concerning what types of inputs it chooses to supply. Whether to stay in school, how much and what kind of training to get, whether to start a business, how many hours to work, whether to work at all, and how to invest savings are all household decisions that affect income.

As you can see, then:

> Input and output markets are connected through the behavior of both firms and households. Firms determine the quantities and character of outputs produced and the types of quantities of inputs demanded. Households determine the types and quantities of products demanded and the quantities and types of inputs supplies.[1]

Color Guide

Note that in Figure 4.1 households are depicted in *blue* and firms are depicted in *red*. From now on all diagrams relating to the behavior of households will be blue or shades of blue, and all diagrams relating to the behavior of firms will be in red or shades of red.

factors of production *The inputs into the production process. Land, labor, and capital are the three key factors of production.*

---

[1]*Our description of markets begins with the behavior of firms and households. Modern orthodox economic theory essentially combines two distinct but closely related theories of behavior. The "theory of household behavior," or "consumer behavior," has its roots in the works of nineteenth-century utilitarians such as Jeremy Bentham, William Jevons, Carl Menger, Leon Walras, Vilfredo Pareto, and F. Y. Edgeworth. The "theory of the firm" developed out of the earlier classical political economy of Adam Smith, David Ricardo, and Thomas Malthus. In 1890 Alfred Marshall published the first of many editions of his* Principles of Economics. *That volume pulled together the main themes of both the classical economists and the utilitarians into what is now called "neoclassical economics." While there have been many changes over the years, the basic structure of the model that we build can be found in Marshall's work.*

DEMAND IN PRODUCT/OUTPUT MARKETS

In real life, households make many decisions at the same time. To see how the forces of demand and supply work, however, let us focus first on the amount of a single product that an individual household decides to consume within some given period of time, such as a month or a year.

> A household's decision about what quantity of a particular output, or product, to demand depends upon a number of factors:
>
> - The *price of the product* in question.
> - The *income available* to the household.
> - The household's *amount of accumulated wealth*.
> - The *prices of other products* available to the household.
> - The household's *tastes and preferences*.
> - The household's *expectations* about future income, wealth, and prices.

quantity demanded *The amount (number of units) of a product that a household would buy in a given period if it could buy all it wanted at the current market price.*

Quantity demanded is the amount (number of units) of a product that a household would buy in a given period *if it could buy all it wanted at the current market price.*

Of course, the amount of a product that households finally purchase depends on the amount of product actually available in the market. But the quantity demanded at any moment may exceed or fall short of the quantity supplied. These differences between the quantity demanded and the quantity supplied are very important. The phrase *if it could buy all it wanted* is critical to the definition of quantity demanded because it allows for the possibility that quantity supplied and quantity demanded are unequal.

Our analysis of demand and supply is leading up to a theory of how market prices are determined. Prices are determined by interaction between demanders and suppliers. To understand this interaction, we first need to know how product prices influence the behavior of suppliers and demanders *separately*. We therefore begin our discussion of output markets by focusing exclusively on this relationship.

■ **Changes in Quantity Demanded versus Changes in Demand** The most important relationship in individual markets is that between market price and quantity demanded. For this reason, we need to begin our discussion by analyzing the likely response of households to changes in price using the device of *ceteris paribus,* or "all else equal." That is, we will attempt to derive a relationship between the quantity demanded of a good per time period and the price of that good, holding income, wealth, other prices, tastes, and expectations constant.

It is very important to distinguish between price changes, which affect the quantity of a good demanded, and changes in other factors (such as income), which change the entire relationship between price and quantity. For example, if a family begins earning a higher income, it might buy more of a good at every possible price. To be sure that we distinguish between changes in price and other changes that affect demand, we will throughout the rest of the text be very precise about terminology. Specifically:

Changes in the price of a product affect the *quantity demanded* per period. Changes in any other factor, such as income or preferences, affect *demand*. Thus we say that an increase in the price of Coca-Cola is likely to cause a decrease in the *quantity of Coca-Cola demanded*. Similarly, we say that an increase in income is likely to cause an increase in the *demand* for most goods.

PRICE AND QUANTITY DEMANDED: THE LAW OF DEMAND

A **demand schedule** shows the quantities of a product that a household would be willing to buy at different prices. Table 4.1 presents a hypothetical demand schedule for Anna, a student who went off to college to study economics while her boyfriend went to art school. If telephone calls were free (a price of zero), Anna would call her boyfriend every day, or 30 times a month. At a price of $.50 per call, she makes 25 calls a month. When the price hits $3.50, she cuts back to seven calls a month. This same information presented graphically is called a **demand curve**. Anna's demand curve is presented in Figure 4.2.[2]

You will note in Figure 4.2 that *quantity* is measured along the horizontal axis, and *price* is measured along the vertical axis. This is the convention we follow throughout this book.

■ **Demand Curves Slope Downward** The data in Table 4.1 show that at lower prices, Anna calls her boyfriend more frequently; at higher prices, she calls less

TABLE 4.1

ANNA'S DEMAND SCHEDULE FOR TELEPHONE CALLS

PRICE (PER CALL)	QUANTITY DEMANDED (CALLS PER MONTH)
$ 0	30
.50	25
3.50	7
7.00	3
10.00	1
15.00	0

demand schedule *A table showing how much of a given product a household would be willing to buy at different prices.*

demand curve *A graph illustrating how much of a given product a household would be willing to buy at different prices.*

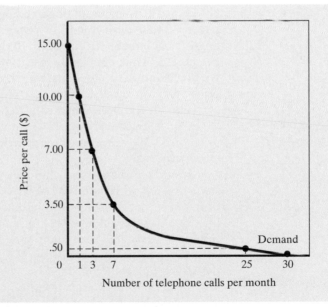

FIGURE 4.2

Anna's Demand Curve

The relationship between price and quantity demanded presented graphically is called a *demand curve*. Demand curves have a negative slope, indicating that lower prices cause quantity demanded to increase. Note that Anna's demand curve is blue; demand in product markets is determined by household choice.

[2]*Drawing a smooth curve, as we do in Figure 4.2, suggests that Anna can make a quarter of a phone call or half of a phone call. For example, according to the graph, at a price of $12 per call, Anna would make half a call and at $8 per call, about a call and a half. While fractional purchases are for goods that are divisible, such as phone calls—you might talk for one minute instead of two minutes—and products sold by weight, they are impossible for large purchases, such as automobiles. We use the term* lumpy *to describe goods that cannot be divided. You would not draw a smooth, downward sloping curve of a household's demand for automobiles, for example, because there might be only one (or at most two) points, and any points in between would be meaningless. Whenever we draw a smooth demand curve, we are assuming divisibility.*

frequently. There is thus a *negative, or inverse, relationship between quantity demanded and price.* When price rises, quantity demanded falls, and when price falls, quantity demanded rises. Thus demand curves always slope downward. This negative relationship between price and quantity demanded is often referred to as the **law of demand**, a term first used by economist Alfred Marshall in his 1890 textbook.

law of demand *The negative relationship between price and quantity demanded: As price rises, quantity demanded decreases. As price falls, quantity demanded increases.*

Some people are put off by the abstractness of demand curves. Of course, we don't actually draw our own demand curves for products. When we want to make a purchase, we usually face only a single price, and how much we would buy at other prices is irrelevant. But demand curves help analysts understand the kind of behavior that households are *likely* to exhibit if they are actually faced with a higher or lower price. We know, for example, that if the price of a good rises enough, the quantity demanded must ultimately drop to zero. The demand curve is thus a tool that helps us explain economic behavior and predict reactions to possible price changes.

Marshall's definition of a social "law" captures the idea:

> The term "law" means nothing more than a general proposition or statement of tendencies, more or less certain, more or less definite . . . a *social law* is a statement of social tendencies; that is, that a certain course of action may be expected from the members of a social group under certain conditions.[3]

It seems reasonable to expect that consumers will demand more of a product at a lower price and less of it at a higher price. Households must divide their incomes over a wide range of goods and services. If the price of a pound of beef rises while income and the prices of all other products remain the same, the household must sacrifice more of something else in order to buy each pound of beef. If I spend $4.50 for a pound of prime beef, I am sacrificing the other things that I might have bought with that $4.50. If the price of prime beef were to jump to $7 per pound, while chicken breasts remained at $1.99 (remember *ceteris paribus*— we are holding all else constant), I would have to give up more chicken and/or other items in order to buy that pound of beef. So I would probably eat more chicken and less beef. Anna calls her boyfriend three times when phone calls cost $7 each. A fourth call would mean sacrificing $7 worth of other purchases. At a price of $3.50, however, the opportunity cost of each call is lower, and she calls more frequently.

Another explanation behind the fact that demand curves are very likely to slope downward rests on the notion of *utility.* Economists use utility as a measure of happiness or satisfaction. Presumably we consume goods and services because they give us utility. But as we consume more of a product within a given period of time, it is likely that each additional unit consumed will yield successively less satisfaction. The utility I gain from a second ice cream cone is likely to be less than the utility I gained from the first; the third is worth even less, and so forth. This *law of diminishing marginal utility* is an important concept in economics. If each successive unit of a good is worth less to me, I am not going to be willing to pay as much for it. It is thus reasonable to expect a downward slope in the demand curve for that good.

The idea of diminishing marginal utility also helps to explain Anna's behavior. The demand curve is a way of representing what she is willing to pay per phone call. At a price of $7, she calls her boyfriend three times per month. A fourth call,

---

[3]*Alfred Marshall,* Principles of Economics, *8th ed. (New York: Macmillan, 1948), p. 33. (The first edition was published in 1890.)*

however, is worth less than the third—that is, the fourth call is worth less than $7 to her, so she stops at three. If the price were only $3.50, however, she would keep right on calling. But even at $3.50, she would stop at seven calls per month. This behavior reveals that the eighth call has less value to Anna than the seventh.

Thinking about the ways that people are affected by price changes also helps us see what is behind the law of demand. Consider this example: Luis lives and works in Mexico City. His elderly mother lives in Santiago, Chile. Last year, the airlines servicing South America got into a price war, and the price of flying between Mexico City and Santiago dropped from 2,000 pesos to 1,000 pesos. How might Luis's behavior change?

First, he is better off. Last year he flew home to Chile three times at a total cost of 6,000 pesos. This year he can fly to Chile the same number of times, buy exactly the same combination of other goods and services that he bought last year, and have 3,000 pesos left over! Because he is better off—his income can buy more—he may fly home more frequently. Second, the opportunity cost of flying home has changed. Before the price war Luis had to sacrifice 2,000 pesos worth of other goods and services each time he flew to Chile. After the price war he must sacrifice only 1,000 pesos worth of other goods and services for each trip. The trade-off has changed. Both of these effects are likely to lead to a higher quantity demanded in response to the lower price.[4]

In sum:

It is reasonable to expect quantity demanded to fall when price rises, *ceteris paribus,* and to expect quantity demanded to rise when price falls, *ceteris paribus.* Demand curves have a negative slope.

■ **Other Properties of Demand Curves**   Two additional things are notable about Anna's demand curve. First, it intersects the *Y*, or price, axis. This means that there is a price above which no calls will be made. In this case, Anna simply stops calling when the price reaches $15 per call.

As long as households have limited incomes and wealth, all demand curves will intersect the price axis. For any commodity, there is always a price above which a household will not, or cannot, pay. Even if the good or service is very important, all households are ultimately "constrained," or limited, by income and wealth.

Second, Anna's demand curve intersects the *X,* or quantity, axis. Even at a zero price, there is a limit to the number of phone calls Anna will make. If telephone calls were free, she would call 30 times a month, but not more.

That demand curves intersect the quantity axis is a matter of common sense. Demands for most goods are limited, if only by time, even at a zero price.

OTHER DETERMINANTS OF HOUSEHOLD DEMAND

Of the many factors likely to influence a household's demand for a specific product, we have considered only the price of the product itself. Other determining factors include household income and wealth, the prices of other goods and services, tastes and preferences, and expectations.

---

[4]*These separate effects are called the "income" and "substitution" effects of the price change. They will be formally defined and discussed in later chapters.*

income *The sum of all a household's wages, salaries, profits, interest payments, rents, and other forms of earnings in a given period of time. It is a flow measure.*

wealth or **net worth** *The total value of what a household owns minus what it owes. It is a stock measure.*

normal goods *Goods for which demand goes up when income is higher and for which demand goes down when income is lower.*

inferior goods *Goods for which demand falls when income rises.*

substitutes *Goods that can serve as replacements for one another; when the price of one increases, demand for the other goes up.*

■ **Income and Wealth** Before we proceed, we need to define two terms that are often confused, *income* and *wealth*. A household's **income** is the sum of all the wages, salaries, profits, interest payments, rents, and other forms of earnings received by the household *in a given period of time*. Income is thus a *flow* measure: We must specify a time period for it—income *per month* or *per year*. You can spend or consume more or less than your income in any given period. If you consume less than the amount of your income, you save. To consume more than your income in a period, you must either borrow or draw on savings accumulated from previous periods.

Wealth is the total value of what a household owns less what it owes. Another word for wealth is **net worth**—the amount a household would have left if it sold off all its possessions and paid off all its debts. Wealth is a *stock* measure: It is measured at a given moment, or point, in time. If, in a given period, you spend less than your income, you save; the amount that you save is added to your wealth. Saving is the flow that affects the stock of wealth. When you spend more than your income, you *dissave*—you reduce your wealth.

Clearly, households with higher incomes and higher accumulated savings or inherited wealth can afford to buy more things. In general, then, we would expect higher demand at higher levels of income/wealth and lower demand at lower levels of income/wealth. Goods for which demand goes up when income is higher and for which demand goes down when income is lower are called **normal goods.** Movie tickets, restaurant meals, telephone calls, and shirts are all normal goods.

But generalization in economics can be hazardous. Sometimes demand for a good falls when household income rises. Consider, for example, the various qualities of meat available. When a household's income rises, it is likely to buy higher quality meats—its demand for filet mignon is likely to rise—but its demand for lower quality meats—chuck steak, for example—is likely to fall. Transportation is another example. At higher incomes, people can afford to fly. People who can afford to fly are less likely to take the bus long distances. Thus higher income may reduce the number of times someone takes a bus. Goods for which demand falls when income rises are called **inferior goods.**

■ **Prices of Other Goods and Services** No consumer decides in isolation on the amount of any one commodity to buy. Rather, each decision is part of a larger set of decisions that are made simultaneously. Obviously, households must apportion their incomes over many different goods and services. As a result, the price of any one good can and does affect the demand for other goods.

This is most obviously the case when goods are substitutes for each other. To return to our lonesome first-year student: If the price of a telephone call rises to $10, Anna will call her boyfriend only once a month (see Table 4.1). But of course she can get in touch with him in other ways. Presumably she substitutes some other, less costly, form of communication, such as writing more letters.

Consider another example: There is currently much discussion about the relative merits of cars produced in the United States and cars produced in Japan. Recently, U.S. consumers have faced a sharp rise in the price of Japanese cars. As a result, we would expect to see consumers substitute U.S.-made cars for Japanese-made cars. The demand for U.S. cars should rise and the quantity of Japanese cars demanded should fall.

When an *increase* in the price of one good causes demand for another good to *increase* (a positive relationship), we say that the goods are **substitutes.** A *fall* in the price of a good causes a *decline* in demand for its substitutes. Substitutes are goods that can serve as replacements for one another.

To be substitutes, two products need not be identical. Identical products are called **perfect substitutes.** Japanese cars are not identical to American cars. Nonetheless, all have four wheels, are capable of carrying people, and run on gasoline. Thus, significant changes in the price of one country's cars can be expected to influence demand for the other country's cars. Compact discs are substitutes for records and tapes, restaurant meals are substitutes for meals eaten at home, and flying from New York to Washington is a substitute for taking the train.

Often, two products "go together"—that is, they complement each other. Our lonesome letter writer, for example, will find her demand for stamps and stationery rising as she writes more letters. Bacon and eggs are **complementary goods,** as are cars and gasoline, and cameras and film. During a price war among the airlines in the summer of 1994 when travel became less expensive, the demand for taxi service to and from airports and for luggage increased across the country. When two goods are complements, a *decrease* in the price of one results in *increase* in demand for the other, and vice versa.

Because any one good may have many potential substitutes and complements at the same time, a single price change may affect a household's demands for many goods simultaneously; the demand for some of these products may rise while the demand for others may fall. For example, one of the newest technologies for personal computers is the CD-ROM. Massive amounts of data can now be stored digitally on compact disks that can be read by personal computers with a CD-ROM drive. When these drives first came on the market they were quite expensive, selling for several hundreds of dollars each. Now they are much less expensive, and most new computers have them built in. As a result, the demand for the CD-ROM disks (complementary goods) is soaring. Apple now includes an encyclopedia and ten years of *Time* magazine on CDs in one of its special student packages. As more and more students adopt the CD technology and the price of CDs and CD hardware falls, fewer people will be buying encyclopedias printed on paper (substitute goods).

■ **Tastes and Preferences** Income, wealth, and the prices of things available are the three factors that determine the combinations of things that a household is *able to* buy. You know that you cannot afford to rent an apartment at $1,200 per month if your monthly income is only $400. But within these constraints, you are more or less free to choose what to buy. Your final choice depends on your individual tastes and preferences.

Changes in preferences can and do manifest themselves in market behavior. As the medical consequences of smoking have become more and more clear, for example, more and more people have stopped smoking. As a result, the demand for cigarettes has dropped significantly. Fifteen years ago the major big-city marathons drew only a few hundred runners. Now tens of thousands enter and run. The demand for running shoes, running suits, stopwatches, and other running items has greatly increased.

Within the constraints of prices and incomes, it is preference that shapes the demand curve. But it is difficult to generalize about tastes and preferences. First of all, they are volatile: Five years ago, more people smoked cigarettes and fewer people had VCRs. Second, they are idiosyncratic: Some people like to talk on the telephone, while others prefer the written word; some people prefer dogs, while others are crazy about cats; some people like chicken wings, while others prefer legs. The diversity of individual demands is almost infinite.

■ **Expectations** What you decide to buy today certainly depends on today's prices and your current income and wealth. But you also have expectations about what

perfect substitutes *Identical products.*

complements, complementary goods *Goods that "go together"; a decrease in the price of one results in an increase in demand for the other, and vice versa.*

your position will be in the future. You may have expectations about future changes in prices, too, and these may affect your decisions today.

Examples of the ways expectations affect demand abound. When people buy a house or a car, they often must borrow part of the purchase price and pay it back over a number of years. In deciding what kind of house or car to buy, they presumably must think about their income today, as well as what their income is likely to be in the future.

As another example, consider a student in his final year of medical school living on a scholarship of $10,000. Compare him with another person earning $5 an hour at a full-time job, with no expectation of a significant change in income in the future. The two have virtually identical incomes. But even if they had the same tastes, the medical student is likely to demand different things, simply because he expects a major increase in income later on.

Increasingly, economic theory has come to recognize the importance of expectations. We will devote a good deal of time to discussing how expectations affect more than just demand. For the time being, however, it is important to understand that demand depends on more than just *current* incomes, prices, and tastes.

SHIFT OF DEMAND VERSUS MOVEMENT ALONG A DEMAND CURVE

Recall that a demand curve shows the relationship between quantity demanded and the price of a good. Such demand curves are derived while holding income, tastes, and other prices constant. If this condition of *ceteris paribus* were relaxed, we would have to derive an entirely new relationship between price and quantity.

Let us return once again to Anna (Table 4.1 and Figure 4.2). Suppose that when we derived the demand schedule in Table 4.1, Anna had a part-time job that paid $200 per month. Now suppose that her parents inherit some money and begin sending her an additional $200 per month. Assuming that she keeps her job, Anna's income is now $400 per month.[5]

With her higher income, Anna would probably call her boyfriend more frequently, regardless of the price of a call. Table 4.2 and Figure 4.3 present Anna's original-income schedule (D_1) and increased-income demand schedule (D_2). At $.50 per call, the frequency of her calls (or the quantity she demands) increases from 25

TABLE 4.2	SHIFT OF ANNA'S DEMAND SCHEDULE DUE TO INCREASE IN INCOME	
PRICE (PER CALL)	SCHEDULE D₁ QUANTITY DEMANDED (CALLS PER MONTH AT AN INCOME OF $200 PER MONTH)	SCHEDULE D₂ QUANTITY DEMANDED (CALLS PER MONTH AT AN INCOME OF $400 PER MONTH)
$ 0	30	35
.50	25	33
3.50	7	18
7.00	3	12
10.00	1	7
15.00	0	2
20.00	0	0

[5]*The income from home may affect the amount of time Anna spends working. In the extreme, she may quit her job and her income will remain at $200. In essence, she would be spending the entire $200 on leisure. Here we assume that she keeps the job and that her income is higher. The point is that since labor supply decisions affect income, they are closely tied to output demand decisions. In a sense, the two decisions are made simultaneously.*

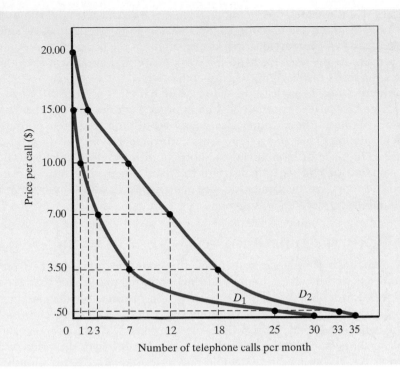

FIGURE 4.3
Shift of a Demand Curve
Following a Rise in Income
When the price of a good
changes, we move *along* the
demand curve for that good.
When any other factor that
influences demand changes
(income, tastes, etc.), the relationship between price and
quantity is different; there is a
shift of the demand curve, in
this case from D_1 to D_2.

to 33 calls per month; at $3.50 per call, frequency increases from 7 to 18 calls per month; at $10 per call, frequency increases from one to seven calls per month. (Note in Figure 4.3 that even if calls are free, Anna's income matters; at zero price, her demand increases. With a higher income, she may visit her boyfriend more, for example, and more visits might mean more phone calls to organize and plan.)

The conditions that were in place at the time the original demand curve was derived have now changed. In other words, a factor that affects Anna's demand for telephone calls (in this case, her income) has changed, and there is now a new relationship between price and quantity demanded. Such a change is referred to as a **shift of the demand curve.**

It is very important to distinguish between a change in quantity demanded—that is, some movement *along* a demand curve—and a shift of demand. Demand schedules and demand curves show the relationship between the price of a good or service and the quantity demanded per period, *ceteris paribus.* If price changes, quantity demanded will change—this is a **movement along the demand curve.** When any of the other factors that influence demand change, however, a new relationship between price and quantity demanded is established—this is a *shift of the demand curve.* The result, then, is a *new* demand curve. Changes in income, preferences, or prices of other goods cause the demand curve to shift:

shift of a demand curve *The change that takes place in a demand curve when a new relationship between quantity demanded of a good and the price of that good is brought about by a change in the original conditions.*

movement along a demand curve *What happens when a change in price causes quantity demanded to change.*

Change in *price* of a good or service

    leads to

       → Change in *quantity demanded* (*Movement along* the demand curve).

Change in *income, preferences,* or *prices of other goods or services*

    leads to

       → Change in *demand* (*Shift of* demand curve).

Figure 4.4 illustrates this point. In Figure 4.4a, an increase in household income causes demand for hamburger (an inferior good) to decline, or shift to the left from D_1 to D_2. (Because quantity is measured on the horizontal axis, a decrease means a move to the left.) Demand for steak (a normal good), on the other hand, increases, or shifts to the right, when income rises.

In Figure 4.4b, an increase in the price of hamburger from $1.49 to $2.49 a pound causes a household to buy less hamburger each month. In other words, the higher price causes the *quantity demanded* to decline from ten pounds to five pounds per month. This change represents a movement *along* the demand curve for hamburger. In place of hamburger, the household buys more chicken. The household's demand for chicken (a substitute for hamburger) rises—the demand curve shifts to the right. At the same time, the demand for catsup (a good that complements hamburger) declines—its demand curve shifts to the left.

FROM HOUSEHOLD DEMAND TO MARKET DEMAND

market demand *The sum of all the quantities of a good or service demanded per period by all the households buying in the market for that good or service.*

Market demand is simply the sum of all the quantities of a good or service demanded per period by all the households buying in the market for that good or service. Figure 4.5 on page 86 shows the derivation of a market demand curve from three individual demand curves. (Although this market demand curve is derived from the behavior of only three people, most markets have thousands or even millions of demanders.) As the table in Figure 4.5 shows, when the price of a pound of coffee is $3.50, both A and C would purchase four pounds per month, while B would buy none; at that price, presumably, B drinks tea. Market demand at $3.50 would thus be a total of four plus four, or eight pounds. At a price of $1.50 per pound, however, A would purchase eight pounds per month, B three pounds, and C nine pounds. Thus, at $1.50 per pound, market demand would be eight plus three plus nine, or twenty pounds of coffee per month.

The total quantity demanded in the marketplace at a given price, then, is simply the sum of all the quantities demanded by all the individual households shopping in the market *at that price*. A market demand curve shows the total amount of a product that would be sold at each price if households could buy all they wanted at that price. As Figure 4.5 shows, the market demand curve is the sum of all the individual demand curves—that is, the sum of all the individual quantities demanded at each price. The market demand curve thus takes its shape and position from the shapes, positions, and number of individual demand curves. If more people decide to shop in a market, more demand curves must be added, and the market demand curve will shift to the right. Market demand curves may also shift as a result of preference changes, income changes, or changes in the number of demanders.

As a general rule throughout this book, capital letters refer to the entire market and lowercase letters refer to individual households or firms. Thus, in Figure 4.5, Q refers to total quantity demanded in the market, while q refers to the quantity demanded by individual households.

SUPPLY IN PRODUCT/OUTPUT MARKETS

In addition to dealing with households' demands for outputs, economic theory also deals with the behavior of business firms, which supply in output markets and demand in input markets (see again Figure 4.1). Firms engage in production, and we assume that they do so for profit. Successful firms make profits because they are able to sell their products for more than it costs to produce them.

profit *The difference between revenues and costs.*

Supply decisions can thus be expected to depend on profit potential. Because **profit** is the simple difference between revenues and costs, supply is likely to react

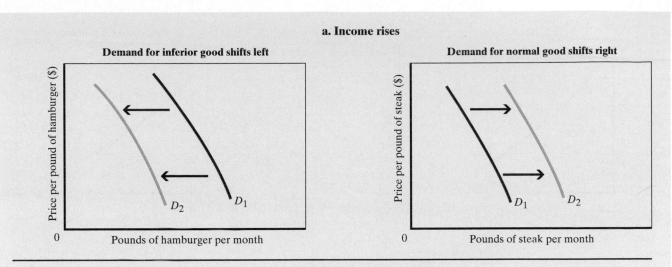

a. Income rises

Demand for inferior good shifts left

Price per pound of hamburger ($)

D_2 D_1

0   Pounds of hamburger per month

Demand for normal good shifts right

Price per pound of steak ($)

D_1 D_2

0   Pounds of steak per month

b. Price of hamburger rises

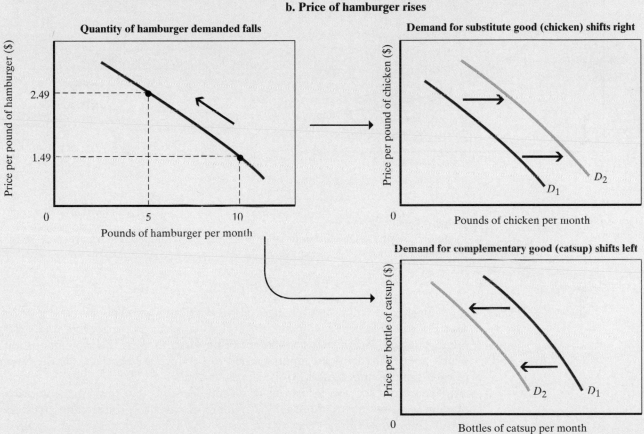

Quantity of hamburger demanded falls

Price per pound of hamburger ($)

2.49

1.49

0   5   10

Pounds of hamburger per month

Demand for substitute good (chicken) shifts right

Price per pound of chicken ($)

D_1 D_2

0   Pounds of chicken per month

Demand for complementary good (catsup) shifts left

Price per bottle of catsup ($)

D_2 D_1

0   Bottles of catsup per month

FIGURE 4.4

Shifts versus Movement along a Demand Curve

a. When income increases, the demand for inferior goods *shifts to the left* and the demand for normal goods *shifts to the right*. **b.** If the price of hamburger rises, the quantity of hamburger demanded declines—this is a movement along the demand curve. The same price would shift the demand for chicken (a substitute for hamburger) to the right and the demand for catsup (a complement to hamburger) to the left.

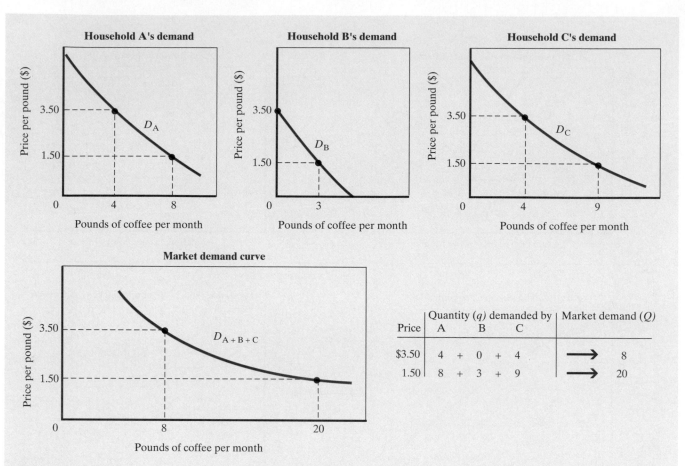

FIGURE 4.5

Deriving Market Demand from Individual Demand Curves

Total demand in the marketplace is simply the sum of the demands of all the households shopping in a particular market. It is the sum of all the individual demand curves—that is, the sum of all the individual quantities demanded at each price.

to changes in revenues and changes in production costs. The amount of revenue that a firm earns depends on the price of its product in the market and on how much it sells. Costs of production depend on many factors, the most important of which are (1) the kinds of inputs needed to produce the product, (2) the amount of each input required, and (3) the prices of inputs.

The supply decision is just one of several decisions that firms make in order to maximize profit. There are usually a number of ways to produce any given product. A golf course can be built by hundreds of workers with shovels and grass seed or by a few workers with heavy earth-moving equipment and sod blankets. Hamburgers can be individually fried by a short-order cook or grilled by the hundreds on a mechanized moving grill. Firms must choose the production technique most appropriate to their products and projected levels of production. The best method of production is the one that minimizes cost, thus maximizing profit.

Which production technique is best, in turn, depends on the prices of inputs. Where labor is cheap and machinery is expensive and difficult to transport, firms are likely to choose production techniques that use a great deal of labor. Where machines are available and labor is scarce or expensive, they are likely to choose more capital-intensive methods. Obviously, the technique ultimately chosen determines input requirements. Thus, by choosing an output supply target and the most appropriate technology, firms determine which inputs to demand.

To summarize:

> Assuming that its objective is to maximize profits, a firm's decision about what quantity of output, or product, to supply depends on
> 1. The price of the good or service
> 2. The cost of producing the product, which in turn depends on
>   ■ The price of required inputs (labor, capital, and land), and
>   ■ The technologies that can be used to produce the product
> 3. The prices of related products

With the caution that no decision exists in a vacuum, let us begin our examination of firm behavior by focusing on the output supply decision and the relationship between quantity supplied and output price, *ceteris paribus*.

PRICE AND QUANTITY SUPPLIED: THE LAW OF SUPPLY

Quantity supplied is the amount of a particular product that a firm would be willing and able to offer for sale at a particular price during a given time period. A **supply schedule** shows how much of a product a firm will supply at alternative prices. Table 4.3 itemizes the quantities of soybeans that an individual farmer such as Clarence Brown might supply at various prices. If the market paid $1.50 or less a bushel for soybeans, Brown would not supply any soybeans. For one thing, it costs more than $1.50 to produce a bushel of soybeans; for another, Brown can use his land more profitably to produce something else. At $1.75 per bushel, however, at least some soybean production takes place on Brown's farm, and a price increase from $1.75 to $2.25 per bushel causes the quantity supplied by Brown to increase from 10,000 to 20,000 bushels per year. The higher price may justify shifting land from wheat to soybean production or putting previously fallow land into soybeans. Or it may lead to more intensive farming of land already in soybeans, using expensive fertilizer or equipment that was not cost-justified at the lower price.

Generalizing from Farmer Brown's experience, we can reasonably expect an increase in market price to lead to an increase in quantity supplied. In other words, there is a positive relationship between the quantity of a good supplied and price. This statement sums up the **law of supply.**

The information in a supply schedule presented graphically is called a **supply curve.** Supply curves slope upward. The upward, or positive, slope of Brown's curve in Figure 4.6 on page 88, for example, reflects this positive relationship between price and quantity supplied.

Note in Brown's supply schedule, however, that when price rises above $4 to $5, quantity supplied no longer increases. Often an individual firm's ability to respond to an increase in price is constrained by its existing scale of operations, or capacity, in the short run. For example, Brown's ability to produce more soybeans depends on the size of his farm, the fertility of his soil, and the types of equipment he has. The fact that output stays constant at 45,000 bushels per year suggests that he is running up against the limits imposed by the size of his farm and his existing technology.

In the longer run, however, Brown may acquire more land, or technology may change, allowing for more soybean production. The terms *short run* and *long run* have very precise meanings in economics; we will discuss them in detail later. Here it is important only to understand that time plays a critical role in supply decisions.

TABLE 4.3

CLARENCE BROWN'S SUPPLY SCHEDULE FOR SOYBEANS

PRICE (PER BUSHEL)	QUANTITY SUPPLIED (BUSHELS PER YEAR)
$1.50	0
1.75	10,000
2.25	20,000
3.00	30,000
4.00	45,000
5.00	45,000

quantity supplied *The amount of a particular product that a firm would be willing and able to offer for sale at a particular price during a given time period.*

supply schedule *A table showing how much of a product firms will supply at different prices.*

law of supply *The positive relationship between price and quantity of a good supplied: An increase in market price will lead to an increase in quantity supplied, and a decrease in market price will lead to a decrease in quantity supplied.*

supply curve *A graph illustrating how much of a product a firm will supply at different prices.*

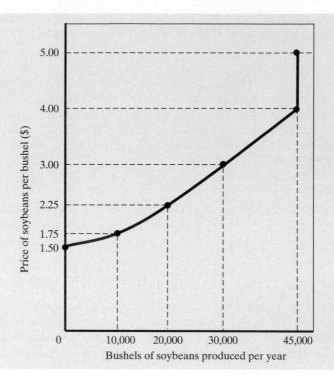

FIGURE 4.6

Clarence Brown's Individual Supply Curve

A producer will supply more when the price of output is higher. The slope of a supply curve is positive. Note that the supply curve is red. Supply is determined by choices made by firms.

When prices change, firms' immediate response may be different from what they are able to do after a month or a year. Short-run and long-run supply curves are often different.

OTHER DETERMINANTS OF FIRM SUPPLY

Of the factors listed above that are likely to affect the quantity of output supplied by a given firm, we have thus far discussed only the price of output. Other factors that affect supply include the cost of producing the product and the prices of related products.

■ **The Cost of Production**   Regardless of the price that a firm can command for its product, price must exceed the cost of producing the output for the firm to make a profit. Thus, the supply decision is likely to change in response to changes in the cost of production. Cost of production depends on a number of factors, including the available technologies and the price of the inputs (labor, land, capital, energy, and so forth) that the firm needs.

Technological change can have an enormous impact on the cost of production over time. Consider agriculture. The introduction of fertilizers, the development of complex farm machinery, and the use of bioengineering to increase the yield of individual crops all have powerfully affected the cost of producing agricultural commodities. Farm productivity in the United States has been increasing dramatically for decades. Yield per acre of corn production has increased fivefold since the late 1930s, and the amount of labor required to produce 100 bushels of corn has fallen from 108 hours in the late 1930s to 20 hours in the late 1950s to less than 3 hours today.

When a technological advance lowers the cost of production, output is likely to increase. When yield per acre increases, individual farmers can and do produce more. The output of the Ford Motor Company increased substantially after the introduction of assembly line techniques. The production of electronic calculators, and later personal computers, boomed with the development of inexpensive techniques to produce microprocessors.

Cost of production is also affected directly by the price of the factors of production. During 1994 timber prices in the United States rose dramatically. As a result, the cost of building new homes jumped significantly and the supply of new homes dropped. Also, during the summer of 1994 a strike in the Nigerian oil fields caused the world price of oil to increase from around $14 a barrel to around $22. As a result, cab drivers faced higher gasoline prices, airlines faced higher fuel costs, and manufacturing firms faced higher heating bills. The result: Cab drivers probably spent less time driving around looking for fares, airlines cut a few low-profit routes, and some manufacturing plants stopped running extra shifts. The moral of this story: Increases in input prices raise costs of production and are likely to reduce supply.

■ **The Prices of Related Products** Firms often react to changes in the prices of related products. For example, if land can be used for either corn or soybean production, an increase in soybean prices may cause individual farmers to shift acreage out of corn production and into soybeans. Thus, an increase in soybean prices actually affects the amount of corn supplied.

Similarly, if beef prices rise, producers may respond by raising more cattle. But leather comes from cowhide. Thus, an increase in beef prices may actually increase the supply of leather.

SHIFT OF SUPPLY VERSUS MOVEMENT ALONG A SUPPLY CURVE

A supply curve shows the relationship between the quantity of a good or service supplied by a firm and the price that good or service brings in the market. Higher prices are likely to lead to an increase in quantity supplied, *ceteris paribus*. Remember: The supply curve is derived holding everything constant except price. When the price of a product changes *ceteris paribus,* a change in the quantity supplied follows—that is, a *movement along* the supply curve takes place. But, as you have seen, supply decisions are also influenced by factors other than price. New relationships between price and quantity supplied come about when factors other than price change, and the result is a *shift* of the supply curve. When factors other than price cause supply curves to shift, we say that there has been a *change in supply.*

Recall that the cost of production depends upon the price of inputs and the technologies of production available. Now suppose that a major breakthrough in the production of soybeans has occurred: Genetic engineering has produced a superstrain of disease- and pest-resistant seed. Such a technological change would enable individual farmers to supply more soybeans at *any* market price. Table 4.4 and

TABLE 4.4	SHIFT OF SUPPLY SCHEDULE FOR SOYBEANS FOLLOWING DEVELOPMENT OF A NEW DISEASE-RESISTANT SEED STRAIN	
	SCHEDULE S_1	SCHEDULE S_2
PRICE (PER BUSHEL)	QUANTITY SUPPLIED (BUSHELS PER YEAR USING OLD SEED)	QUANTITY SUPPLIED (BUSHELS PER YEAR USING NEW SEED)
$1.50	0	5,000
1.75	10,000	23,000
2.25	20,000	33,000
3.00	30,000	40,000
4.00	45,000	54,000
5.00	45,000	54,000

When the price of a product changes, we move *along* the supply curve for that product; the quantity supplied rises or falls. When any other factor affecting supply changes, the supply curve *shifts*.

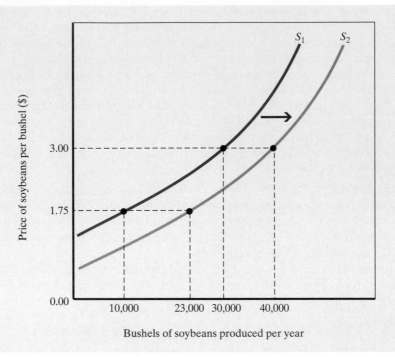

Figure 4.7 describe this change. At $3 a bushel, farmers would have produced 30,000 bushels from the old seed (schedule S_1 in Table 4.4); with the lower cost of production and higher yield resulting from the new seed, they produce 40,000 bushels (schedule S_2 in Table 4.4). At $1.75 per bushel, they would have produced 10,000 bushels from the old seed; but with the lower costs and higher yields, output rises to 23,000 bushels.

Increases in input prices may also cause supply curves to shift. We have already mentioned the increase in oil prices that occurred in 1994. Since fertilizers are made in part from petrochemicals and in part from tractors that run on gasoline, Farmer Brown would have faced higher costs in 1994 than he did in 1993. Such increases in production cost shift the supply curve to the left—that is, less is produced at any given market price. If Brown's soybean supply curve shifted far enough to the left, it would intersect the price axis at a higher point, meaning that it would take a higher market price to induce Brown to produce any soybeans at all.

As with demand, it is very important to distinguish between *movements along* supply curves (changes in quantity supplied) and *shifts in* supply curves (changes in supply):

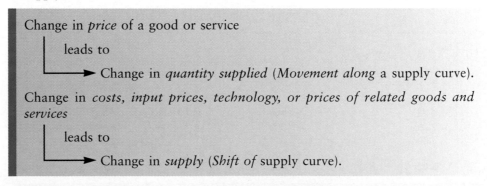

FROM INDIVIDUAL FIRM SUPPLY TO MARKET SUPPLY

Market supply is determined in the same fashion as market demand. It is simply the sum of all that is supplied each period by all producers of a single product. Figure 4.8 derives a market supply curve from the supply curves of three individual firms. (In a market with more firms, total market supply would be the sum of the amounts produced by each of the firms in that market.) As the table in Figure 4.8 shows, at a price of $3 farm A supplies 30,000 bushels of soybeans, farm B supplies 10,000 bushels, and farm C supplies 25,000 bushels. At this price, the total amount supplied in the market is 30,000 plus 10,000 plus 25,000, or 65,000 bushels. At a price of $1.75, however, the total amount supplied is only 25,000 bushels (10,000 plus 5,000 plus 10,000). The market supply curve is thus the simple addition of the individual supply curves of all the firms in a particular market—that is, the sum of all the individual quantities supplied at each price.

market supply *The sum of all that is supplied each period by all producers of a single product.*

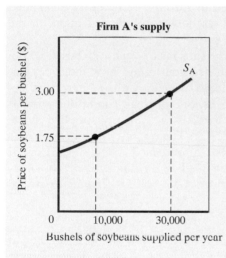
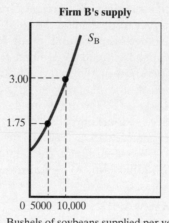
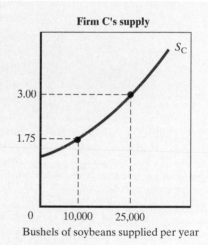

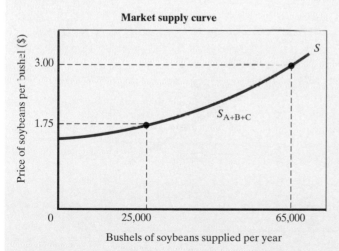

Price	Quantity (*q*) supplied by			Market supply (*Q*)
	A	B	C	
$3.00	30,000 +	10,000 +	25,000	→ 65,000
1.75	10,000 +	5,000 +	10,000	→ 25,000

FIGURE 4.8

Deriving Market Supply from Individual Firm Supply Curves

Total supply in the marketplace is the sum of all the amounts supplied by all the firms selling in the market; it is the sum of all the individual quantities supplied at each price.

The position and shape of the market supply curve depends on the positions and shapes of the individual firms' supply curves from which it is derived. But it also depends on the number of firms that produce in that market. If firms that produce for a particular market are earning high profits, other firms may be tempted to go into that business. When the technology to produce computers for home use became available, literally hundreds of new firms got into the act. The popularity and profitability of professional football has three times led to the formation of new leagues. When new firms enter an industry, the supply curve shifts to the right. When firms go out of business, or "exit" the market, the supply curve shifts to the left.

MARKET EQUILIBRIUM

So far we have identified a number of factors that influence the amount that households demand and firms supply in product (output) markets. The discussion has emphasized the role of market price as a determinant both of quantity demanded and quantity supplied. We are now ready to see how supply and demand in the market interact to determine the final market price.

We have been very careful in our discussions thus far to separate household decisions about how much to demand from firm decisions about how much to supply. The operation of the market, however, clearly depends on the interaction between suppliers and demanders. At any moment, one of three conditions prevails in every market: (1) The quantity demanded exceeds the quantity supplied at the current price, a situation called *excess demand;* (2) The quantity supplied exceeds the quantity demanded at the current price, a situation called *excess supply;* or (3) the quantity supplied equals the quantity demanded at the current price, a situation called **equilibrium.** At equilibrium, no tendency for price to change exists.

EXCESS DEMAND

Excess demand exists when quantity demanded is greater than quantity supplied at the current price. Figure 4.9, which plots both a supply curve and a demand curve

equilibrium *The condition that exists when quantity supplied and quantity demanded are equal. At equilibrium, there is no tendency for price to change.*

excess demand *The condition that exists when quantity demanded exceeds quantity supplied at the current price.*

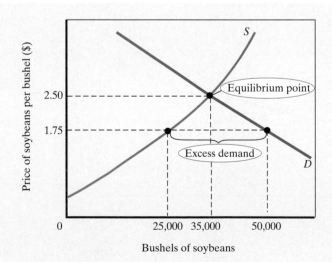

FIGURE 4.9

Excess Demand

At a price of $1.75 per bushel, quantity demanded exceeds quantity supplied. When *excess demand* arises, there is a tendency for price to rise. As price rises from $1.75 to $2.50, quantity demanded falls from 50,000 to 35,000 and quantity supplied rises from 25,000 to 35,000. When quantity demanded equals quantity supplied, excess demand is eliminated and the market is in equilibrium. Here, the equilibrium price is $2.50, and the equilibrium quantity is 35,000 bushels.

on the same graph, illustrates such a situation. As you can see, market demand at $1.75 per bushel (50,000 bushels) exceeds the amount that farmers are currently supplying (25,000 bushels).

When excess demand occurs in an unregulated market, there is a tendency for price to rise as demanders compete against each other for the limited supply. The adjustment mechanisms may differ, but the outcome is always the same. For example, consider the mechanism of an auction. In an auction, items are sold directly to the highest bidder. When the auctioneer starts the bidding at a low price, many people bid for the item. At first there is excess demand: Quantity demanded exceeds quantity supplied. As would-be buyers offer higher and higher prices, bidders drop out, until the one who offers the most ends up with the item being auctioned. Price rises until quantity demanded and quantity supplied are equal.

At a price of $1.75 (see Figure 4.9 again), farmers produce soybeans at a rate of 25,000 bushels per year, but at that price the demand is for 50,000 bushels. Most farm products are sold to local dealers who in turn sell large quantities in major market centers, where bidding would push prices up if quantity demanded exceeded quantity supplied. As price rises above $1.75, two things happen: (1) The quantity demanded falls as buyers drop out of the market and perhaps choose a substitute, and (2) the quantity supplied increases as farmers find themselves receiving a higher price for their product and shift additional acres into soybean production.[6]

This process continues until the excess demand is eliminated. In Figure 4.9, this occurs at $2.50, where quantity demanded has fallen from 50,000 to 35,000 bushels per year and quantity supplied has increased from 25,000 to 35,000 bushels per year. When quantity demanded and quantity supplied are equal and there is no further bidding, the process has achieved an equilibrium, a situation in which *there is no natural tendency for further adjustment*. Graphically, the point of equilibrium is the point at which the supply curve and the demand curve intersect.

The process through which excess demand leads to higher prices is different in different markets. Consider the market for houses in the hypothetical town of Boomville with a population of 25,000 people, most of whom live in single-family homes. Normally about 75 homes are sold in the Boomville market each year. But last year, a major business opened a plant in town, creating 1,500 new jobs that pay good wages. This attracted new residents to the area, and real estate agents now have more buyers than there are properties for sale. Quantity demanded now exceeds quantity supplied. In other words, there is excess demand.

Auctions are not unheard of in the housing market, but they are rare. This market usually works more subtly, but the outcome is the same. Properties are sold very quickly and housing prices begin to rise. Boomville sellers soon learn that there are more buyers than usual, and they begin to "hold out" for higher offers. As prices for houses in Boomville rise, quantity demanded eventually drops off and quantity supplied increases. Quantity supplied increases in at least two ways: (1) Encouraged by the high prices, builders begin constructing new houses, and (2) some people, attracted by the higher prices their homes will fetch, put their houses

---

[6]*Once farmers have produced in any given season, they cannot change their minds and produce more, of course. When we derived Clarence Brown's supply schedule in Table 4.3, we imagined him reacting to prices that existed at the time he decided how much land to plant in soybeans. In Figure 4.9, the upward slope shows that higher prices justify shifting land from other crops. Final price may not be determined until final production figures are in. For our purposes here, however, we have ignored this timing problem. Perhaps the best way to think about it is that demand and supply are flows, or rates, of production—that is, we are talking about the number of bushels produced per production period. Adjustments in the rate of production may take place over a number of production periods.*

on the market. Discouraged by higher prices, however, some potential buyers (demanders) may begin to look for housing in neighboring towns and settle on commuting. Eventually, equilibrium will be reestablished, with the quantity of houses demanded just equal to the quantity of houses supplied.

While the mechanics of price adjustment in the housing market differ from the mechanics of an auction, the outcome is exactly the same:

> When quantity demanded exceeds quantity supplied, price tends to rise. When the price in a market rises, quantity demanded falls and quantity supplied rises until an equilibrium is reached at which quantity demanded and quantity supplied are equal.

This process is called *price rationing*. When excess demand exists, some people will be satisfied and some will not. When the market operates without interference, price increases will distribute what is available to those who are willing and able to pay the most. As long as there is a way for buyers and sellers to interact, those who are willing to pay more will make that fact known somehow. (We discuss the nature of the price system as a rationing device in great detail in Chapter 5.)

EXCESS SUPPLY

excess supply *The condition that exists when quantity supplied exceeds quantity demanded at the current price.*

Excess supply exists when the quantity supplied exceeds the quantity demanded at the current price. As with excess demand, the mechanics of price adjustment in the face of excess supply can differ from market to market. If automobile dealers find themselves with unsold cars in the fall when the new models are coming in, for example, you can expect to see price cuts. Sometimes dealers offer discounts to encourage buyers; sometimes buyers themselves simply offer less than the price initially asked. In any event, products do no one any good sitting in dealers' lots or on warehouse shelves. The auction metaphor introduced earlier can also be applied here: If the initial asking price is too high, no one bids, and the auctioneer tries a lower price. It's almost always true, and 1995 was no exception, that certain items do not sell as well as anticipated during the Christmas holidays. After Christmas most stores have big sales during which they lower the prices of overstocked items. Quantities supplied exceeded quantities demanded at the current prices, so stores cut prices.

Across the state from Boomville is Bustville, where last year a drug manufacturer shut down its operations and 1,500 people found themselves out of work. With no other prospects for work, many residents decided to pack up and move. They put their houses up for sale, but there were few buyers. The result was an excess supply of houses: The quantity of houses supplied exceeded the quantity demanded at the current prices.

As houses sit unsold on the market for months, sellers start to cut their asking prices. Potential buyers begin offering considerably less than sellers are asking. As prices fall, two things are likely to happen. First, the low housing prices may attract new buyers. People who might have bought in a neighboring town see that there are housing bargains to be had in Bustville, and quantity demanded rises in response to price decline. Second, some of those who put their houses on the market may be discouraged by the lower prices and decide to stay in Bustville. Developers are certainly not likely to be building new housing in town. Lower prices thus lead to a decline in quantity supplied as potential sellers pull their houses from the market. This was exactly the situation in New England and California in the early 1990s.

Figure 4.10 illustrates another excess supply situation. At a price of $3 per bushel, farmers are supplying soybeans at a rate of 40,000 bushels per year, but buyers demand only 22,000. With 18,000 (40,000 minus 22,000) bushels of soybeans going unsold, the market price falls. As price falls from $3 to $2.50, quantity supplied decreases from 40,000 bushels per year to 35,000. The lower price causes quantity demanded to rise from 22,000 to 35,000. At $2.50, quantity demanded and quantity supplied are equal. For the data shown here, then, $2.50 and 35,000 bushels are the equilibrium price and quantity.

Early in 1994, crude oil production worldwide exceeded the quantity demanded, and prices fell significantly as competing producer countries tried to maintain their share of world markets. Although the mechanism by which price is adjusted is different for automobiles, housing, soybeans, and crude oil, the outcome is the same:

> When quantity supplied exceeds quantity demanded at the current price, the price tends to fall. When price falls, quantity supplied is likely to decrease and quantity demanded is likely to increase until an equilibrium price is reached where quantity supplied and quantity demanded are equal.

CHANGES IN EQUILIBRIUM

When supply and demand curves shift, the equilibrium price and quantity change. The following example will help to illustrate this point.

South America is a major producer of coffee beans. A cold snap there can reduce the coffee harvest enough to affect the world price of coffee beans. In the summer of 1994, a major freeze hit Brazil and Colombia and drove up the price of coffee on world markets to a record $2.40 per pound.

Figure 4.11 on the next page illustrates how the freeze pushed up coffee prices. Initially, the market was in equilibrium at a price of $1.20. At that price, the quantity demanded was equal to quantity supplied (13.2 billion pounds). At a price of $1.20 and a quantity of 13.2 billion pounds, the demand curve (labeled D) intersected the initial supply curve (labeled S_1). (Remember that equilibrium exists when quantity demanded equals quantity supplied—the point at which the supply and demand curves intersect.)

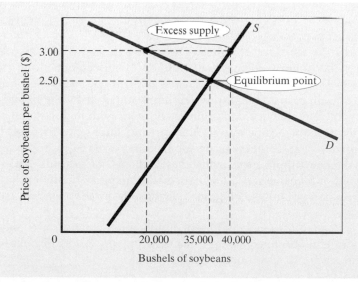

FIGURE 4.10

Excess Supply

At a price of $3, quantity supplied exceeds quantity demanded by 18,000 bushels. This excess supply will cause price to fall.

FIGURE 4.11

The Coffee Market: A Shift of Supply and Subsequent Price Adjustment

Before the freeze, the coffee market was in equilibrium at a price of $1.20. At that price, quantity demanded equaled quantity supplied. The freeze shifted the supply curve to the left (from S_1 to S_2), increasing equilibrium price to $2.40.

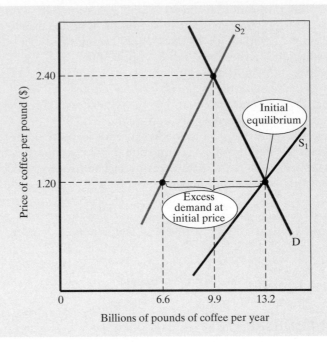

The freeze caused a decrease in the supply of coffee beans. That is, it caused the supply curve to shift to the left. In Figure 4.11, the new supply curve (the supply curve that shows the relationship between price and quantity supplied after the freeze) is labeled S_2.

At the initial equilibrium price, $1.20, there is now an excess demand for coffee. If the price were to remain at $1.20, quantity demanded would not change; it would remain at 13.2 billion pounds. But at that price, quantity supplied would drop to 6.6 billion pounds. At a price of $1.20, quantity demanded is greater than quantity supplied.

When excess demand exists in a market, price can be expected to rise, and rise it did. As the figure shows, price rose to a new equilibrium at $2.40. At $2.40, quantity demanded is again equal to quantity supplied, this time at 9.9 billion pounds—the point at which the new supply curve (S_2) intersects the demand curve.

Notice that as the price of coffee rose from $1.20 to $2.40, two things happened. First, the quantity demanded declined (a movement along the demand curve) as people shifted to substitutes such as tea and hot cocoa. Second, the quantity supplied began to rise, but within the limits imposed by the damage from the freeze. (It might also be that some countries or areas with high costs of production, previously unprofitable, came into production and shipped to the world market at the higher price.) That is, the quantity supplied increased in response to the higher price *along* the new supply curve, which lies to the left of the old supply curve. The final result was a higher price ($2.40), a smaller quantity finally exchanged in the market (9.9 billion pounds), and coffee bought only by those willing to pay $2.40 per pound.

Figure 4.12 presents ten examples of supply and demand shifts and the resulting changes in equilibrium price and quantity. Be sure to go through each graph carefully and ensure that you understand each.

A. DEMAND SHIFTS

1. Increase in income: X is a normal good
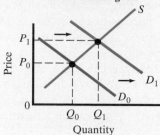

2. Increase in income: X is an inferior good
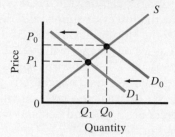

3. Decrease in income: X is a normal good
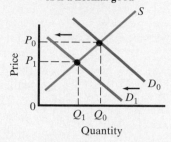

4. Decrease in income: X is an inferior good
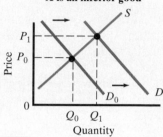

5. Increase in the price of a substitute for X
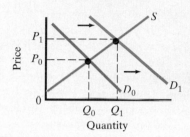

6. Increase in the price of a complement for X
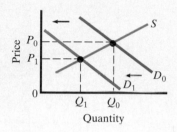

7. Decrease in the price of a substitute for X
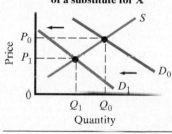

8. Decrease in the price of a complement for X
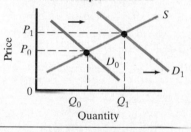

B. SUPPLY SHIFTS

9. Increase in the cost of production of X
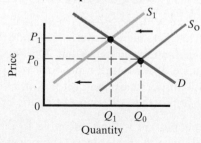

10. Decrease in the cost of production of X
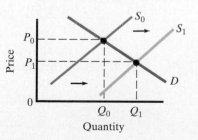

FIGURE 4.12

Examples of Supply and Demand Shifts for Product X

DEMAND AND SUPPLY IN PRODUCT MARKETS: A REVIEW

As you continue your study of economics, you will discover that it is a discipline full of controversy and debate. There is, however, little disagreement about the basic way that the forces of supply and demand operate in free markets. If you hear that a freeze in Florida has destroyed a good portion of the citrus crop, you can bet that the price of oranges will rise.[7] If you read that the weather in the Midwest has been good and a record corn crop is expected, you can bet that corn prices will fall. When fishermen in Massachusetts go on strike and stop bringing in the daily catch, you can bet that the price of fish will go up. (For additional examples of how the forces of supply and demand work, see the Application box titled "Supply and Demand in the News.")

Here are some important points to remember about the mechanics of supply and demand in product markets:

1. A demand curve shows how much of a product a household would buy if it could buy all it wanted at the given price. A supply curve shows how much of a product a firm would supply if it could sell all it wanted at the given price.
2. Quantity demanded and quantity supplied are always per time period—that is, per day, per month, or per year.
3. The demand for a good is determined by household income and wealth, the prices of other goods and services, tastes and preferences, and expectations.
4. The supply of a good is determined by costs of production and the prices of related products. Costs of production are determined by available technologies of production and input prices.
5. Be careful to distinguish between movements along supply and demand curves and shifts of these curves. When the price of a good changes, the quantity of that good demanded or supplied changes—that is, a movement occurs along the curve. When any other factor changes, the curves shift, or change position.
6. Market equilibrium exists only when quantity supplied equals quantity demanded at the current price.

LOOKING AHEAD: MARKETS AND THE ALLOCATION OF RESOURCES

You can already begin to see how markets answer the basic economic questions of what is produced, how it is produced, and who gets what is produced. A firm will produce what is profitable to produce. If it can sell a product at a price that is sufficient to leave a profit after production costs are paid, it will in all likelihood produce that product. Resources will flow in the direction of profit opportunities.

■ Demand curves reflect what people are willing and able to pay for products; they are influenced by incomes, wealth, preferences, the prices of other goods,

---

[7]*In economics you have to think twice, however, even about a "safe" bet. If you bet that the price of frozen orange juice will rise after a freeze, you will lose your money. It turns out that much of the crop that is damaged by a freeze can be used, but for only one thing—to make frozen orange juice. Thus, a freeze actually* increases *the supply of frozen juice on the national market. Following the last two hard freezes in Florida, the price of oranges shot up, but the price of orange juice fell sharply!*

The basic forces of supply and demand are at work throughout the world, as the following news articles illustrate. As an exercise, draw and label demand and supply diagrams for each situation.

1. Two consecutive leftward shifts of supply, causing a dramatic increase in prices:

[June 29, 1994] Coffee prices surged more than 25 percent yesterday, the largest one-day rise in more than seven years, as a damaging frost struck much of the coffee-growing areas of Brazil.

"We are going to see this market skyrocket," said Judith Ganes, coffee analyst for Merrill Lynch. "Consumers are likely to feel it at the retail level."

Coffee for July delivery jumped 33.8 cents, to $1.5975 a pound—after peaking earlier at $1.80—its highest price since November 1986.

[July 11, 1994] A second killing frost in key coffee-growing regions of Brazil sent coffee futures soaring 25% to their highest level in eight years. Including the toll from last month's freeze, the damage could wipe out 50% or more of next year's crop.

In hectic trading on New York's Coffee, Sugar and Cocoa Exchange yesterday, coffee for September delivery rose 46.45 cents to $2.3375 a pound, a new contract high.

2. Supply shifts to the right, causing prices to fall:

[September 15, 1994] Farmers across the Midwest have begun bringing in their crops and the harvest shows the result of nearly perfect weather for finishing the corn and beans. A forecast by the United States Department of Agriculture on Monday for a 2.318-billion-bushel soybean harvest may have to be revised upward.

"The yields out here are just tremendous," said Don Roose, an analyst in West Des Moines, Iowa, with U.S. Commodities, Inc. . . .

At the Chicago Board of Trade, wheat for delivery in September fell 8.5 cents, to $3.705 a bushel, and September corn fell 4 cents, to $2.17 a bushel. September oats were 1.75 cents lower at $1.26 a bushel, and September soybeans were 11.5 cents lower at $5.64 a bushel.

3. Excess supply (rising stockpiles) and an expanding supply combine to push prices lower:

[September 15, 1994] Gasoline [prices] tumbled for a fourth day, falling to a five-month low, as stockpiles continue to rise and refiners in the United States keep trying to sell inventories before environmental regulations requiring a different formulation take effect.

Gasoline stockpiles rose 1.8 percent last week, to 209.4 million barrels, the American Petroleum Institute said in its weekly supply report. Traders had expected the report to show that supplies were little changed.

THE U.S. GRAIN HARVEST IN 1994 WAS PARTICULARLY BOUNTIFUL. THE RESULT WAS AN INCREASE IN THE SUPPLY OF GRAIN AND A DECREASE IN PRICES.

Sources: Leonard Sloane, "Coffee Futures Soar 25%, Biggest Daily Rise in 7 Years," *The New York Times,* June 29, 1994; Suzanne McGee, "Second Cold Snap Harms Brazil's Coffee Crop, Sending Prices to Highest Level in Eight Years," *The Wall Street Journal,* July 11, 1994; "Good Harvests in Midwest Depress Commodity Prices," *The New York Times,* September 15, 1994; "Lumber Prices Fall Sharply on Canadian Strike Outlook," *The New York Times,* September 15, 1994; "Cocaine Prices Rice, and Police Efforts May Be Responsible," *The New York Times,* June 14, 1990.

and expectations. Because product prices are determined by the interaction of supply and demand, prices reflect what people are willing to pay. If people's preferences or incomes change, resources will be allocated differently. Consider, for example, an increase in demand—a shift in the market demand curve. Beginning at an equilibrium, households simply begin buying more. At the equilibrium price, quantity demanded becomes greater than quantity supplied. When there is excess demand, prices will rise, and higher prices mean higher profits for firms in the industry. Higher profits, in turn, provide existing firms with an incentive to expand and new firms with an incentive to enter the industry. Thus, the decisions of independent private firms responding to prices and profit opportunities determine *what* will be produced. No central direction is necessary.

Adam Smith saw this self-regulating feature of markets more than 200 years ago:

> Every individual . . . by pursuing his own interest . . . promotes that of society. He is led . . . by an invisible hand to promote an end which was no part of his intention.[8]

The term Smith coined, the *invisible hand,* has passed into common parlance and is still used by economists to refer to the self-regulation of markets.

■ Firms in business to make a profit have a good reason to choose the best available technology—lower costs mean higher profits. Thus, individual firms determine *how* to produce their products, again with no central direction.

■ So far we have barely touched on the question of distribution—*who* gets what is produced? But you can see part of the answer in the simple supply and demand diagrams. When a good is in short supply, price rises. As it does, those who are willing and able to continue buying do so; others stop buying.

The next chapter begins with a more detailed discussion of these topics. How, exactly, is the final allocation of resources (the mix of output and the distribution of output) determined in a market system?

---

[8]*Adam Smith,* The Wealth of Nations, *p. 456.*

SUMMARY

1. In societies with many people, production must satisfy wide-ranging tastes and preferences, and producers must therefore specialize.

FIRMS AND HOUSEHOLDS: THE BASIC DECISION-MAKING UNITS

2. A *firm* exists when a person or a group of people decides to produce a product or products by transforming resources, or *inputs,* into *outputs*—the products that are sold in the market. Firms are the primary producing units in a market economy. We assume firms make decisions to maximize profits.

3. *Households* are the primary consuming units in an economy. All households' incomes are subject to constraints.

INPUT MARKETS AND OUTPUT MARKETS: THE CIRCULAR FLOW

4. Households and firms interact in two basic kinds of markets: *product or output markets* and *input or factor markets.* Goods and services intended for use by households are exchanged in output markets. In output markets, competing firms supply and competing households demand. In input markets, competing firms demand and competing households supply.

5. Ultimately, firms determine the quantities and character of outputs produced, the types and quantities of inputs demanded, and the technologies used in production. Households determine the types and quantities of products demanded and the types and quantities of inputs supplied.

DEMAND IN PRODUCT/OUTPUT MARKETS

6. The quantity demanded of an individual product by an individual household depends on (1) income, (2) wealth, (3) the price of the product, (4) the prices of other products, (5) tastes and preferences, and (6) expectations about the future.

7. Quantity demanded is the amount of a product that an individual household would buy in a given period if it could buy all it wanted at the current price.

8. A *demand schedule* shows the quantities of a product that a household would buy at different prices. The same information presented graphically is called a *demand curve*.

9. The *law of demand* states that there is a negative relationship between price and quantity demanded: As price rises, quantity demanded decreases, and vice versa. Demand curves slope downward.

10. All demand curves eventually intersect the price axis because there is always a price above which a household cannot, or will not, pay. All demand curves also eventually intersect the quantity axis because demand for most goods is limited, if only by time, even at a zero price.

11. When an increase in income causes demand for a good to rise, that good is a *normal good*. When an increase in income causes demand for a good to fall, that good is an *inferior good*.

12. If a rise in the price of good X causes demand for good Y to increase, the goods are *substitutes*. If a rise in the price of X causes demand for Y to fall, the goods are *complements*.

13. Market demand is simply the sum of all the quantities of a good or service demanded per period by all the households buying in the market for that good or service. It is the sum of all the individual quantities demanded at each price.

SUPPLY IN PRODUCT/OUTPUT MARKETS

14. Quantity supplied by a firm depends on (1) the price of the good or service, (2) the cost of producing the product, which includes the prices of required inputs and the technologies that can be used to produce the product, and (3) the prices of related products.

15. Market supply is the sum of all that is supplied each period by all producers of a single product. It is the sum of all the individual quantities supplied at each price.

16. It is very important to distinguish between *movements* along demand and supply curves and *shifts* of demand and supply curves. The demand curve shows the relationship between price and quantity demanded. The supply curve shows the relationship between price and quantity supplied. A change in price is a movement along the curve. Changes in tastes, income, wealth, expectations, or prices of other goods and services cause demand curves to shift; changes in costs, input prices, technology, or prices of related goods and services cause supply curves to shift.

MARKET EQUILIBRIUM

17. When quantity demanded exceeds quantity supplied at the current price, excess demand exists and the price tends to rise. When prices in a market rise, quantity demanded falls and quantity supplied rises until an equilibrium is reached at which quantity supplied and quantity demanded are equal. At equilibrium, there is no further tendency for price to change.

18. When quantity supplied exceeds quantity demanded at the current price, excess supply exists and the price tends to fall. When price falls, quantity supplied decreases and quantity demanded increases until an equilibrium price is reached where quantity supplied and quantity demanded are equal.

REVIEW TERMS AND CONCEPTS

capital market 74

complements, complementary goods 81

demand curve 77

demand schedule 77

entrepreneur 73

equilibrium 92

excess demand 92

excess supply 94

factors of production 75

firm 73

households 74

income 80

inferior goods 80

input or factor markets 74

PROBLEM SET

1. Illustrate the following with supply and demand curves:
   a. Between 1994 and 1995, employment and income in California fell, creating a decline in the demand for housing and lowering home prices.
   b. In 1994, the U.S. dollar fell in value on foreign currency markets. One result was that U.S. exports looked less expensive to foreign buyers. As a result, the demand for U.S.-produced wheat increased.
   c. Before economic reforms were implemented in Poland, the price of meat was held substantially below equilibrium by law. When reforms were implemented, prices rose dramatically, the quantity demanded fell, and the quantity supplied rose.
   d. The government imposes a regulation that sharply decreases the number of trees available for lumber production in the United States to protect two endangered species. Illustrate the effects on the lumber market and on the housing market.

2. Housing prices in Boston and Los Angeles have been on a roller coaster ride. Illustrate each of the following situations with supply and demand curves:
   a. In both cities an increase in income combined with expectations of a strong market shifted demand and caused prices to rise rapidly during the mid- to late 1980s.
   b. By 1990, the construction industry boomed as more and more developers started new residential projects. But those new projects expanded the supply of housing just as demand was shifting as a result of falling incomes and expectations during the 1990–1991 recession.
   c. In late 1994, housing markets in higher-income towns in the Boston area were experiencing price increases at the same time as housing markets in lower-income towns, especially in areas hit hard

by a decline in manufacturing employment, saw housing prices continue to fall. In part this effect was due to "trade-up" buyers selling houses in lower-income areas and buying houses in higher-income areas.
   d. Despite falling incomes, housing markets in lower-income areas in Los Angeles were actually experiencing some price increases in 1994 and 1995 as immigration of lower-income households continued.

3. There has been a great debate among housing policy analysts over the best way to increase the number of housing units available to low-income households. One strategy is to provide people with housing "vouchers," paid for by the government, that can be used to "rent" housing supplied by the private market. A second strategy is to have the government subsidize housing suppliers or simply to build public housing.
   a. Illustrate both supply- and demand-side strategies using supply and demand curves. Which strategy will result in higher rents?
   b. Critics of housing vouchers (the demand-side strategy) argue that because the supply of housing to low-income households is limited and will not respond at all to higher rents, demand vouchers will serve only to drive up rents and make landlords better off. Illustrate their point with supply and demand curves.

4. The following two sets of statements contain common errors. Identify and explain each.
   a. Demand increases. This causes prices to rise. Higher prices cause demand to fall. Therefore prices fall back to their original levels.
   b. The supply of meat in Russia increases. This causes meat prices to fall. Lower prices mean that Russian households spend more on meat.

5. In August of 1993, the Boston Red Sox were battling it out with the Toronto Blue Jays for first place in the American League East. On August 2, the Red Sox played the Blue Jays in Boston. All tickets to the Blue Jays game were sold out a month in advance, and many people who wanted to get tickets could not. The following week the Sox traveled to Ohio to play the Cleveland Indians (a team in last place). The Cleveland game broke records for low attendance. In fact, only 1,600 went to that game in a stadium that seats 80,000! Fenway Park in Boston holds 36,000 people. Cleveland Stadium holds 80,000. Assume for simplicity that tickets to all regular season games are priced at $10.

   a. Draw supply and demand curves for tickets to each of the two games. Draw one graph for each game. (*Hint:* Supply is fixed. It does not change with price.)

   b. Is there a pricing policy that would have filled the ballpark for the Cleveland game?

   c. The price system was not allowed to work to ration the Blue Jays tickets. How do you know? How do you suppose the tickets were rationed?

6. The U.S. government administers two programs that affect the market for cigarettes. Media campaigns and labeling requirements are aimed at making the public aware of the health dangers of cigarettes. At the same time, the Department of Agriculture maintains a program of price supports for tobacco. Under this program, the supported price is above the market equilibrium price, and the government limits the amount of land that can be devoted to tobacco production. Are these two programs at odds with respect to the goal of reducing cigarette consumption? Explain carefully. As a part of your answer, illustrate graphically the effects of both policies on the market for cigarettes.

7. In 1999, a rare disease hits the U.S. cattle herd, causing a 20% decrease in U.S. beef production. As a result chicken prices rise. Illustrate this situation with supply and demand curves (draw diagrams for both markets).

*8. Consider the market for pizza. Suppose that the market demand for pizza is given by the equation $Q_d = 300 - 20P$ and the market supply for pizza is given by the equation $Q_s = 20P - 100$, where Q_d = quantity demanded, Q_s = quantity supplied, P = price (per pizza).

   a. Graph the supply and demand schedules for pizza using $5 through $15 as the value of P.

   b. In equilibrium, how many pizzas would be sold and at what price?

   c. What would happen if suppliers set the price of pizza at $15? Explain the market adjustment process.

   d. Suppose that the price of hamburgers, a substitute for pizza, doubles. Assume that this leads to a doubling of the demand for pizza (that is, at each price consumers demand twice as much pizza as before). Write the equation for the new market demand for pizza.

   e. Find the new equilibrium price and quantity of pizza.

*Note: Problems marked with an asterisk are more challenging

price rationing *The process by which the market system allocates goods and services to consumers when quantity demanded exceeds quantity supplied.*

THE PRICE SYSTEM, SUPPLY, AND DEMAND

E VERY SOCIETY HAS A SYSTEM OF INSTITUTIONS THAT DETERMINES what is produced, how it is produced, and who gets what is produced. Although in some societies these decisions are made centrally, through planning agencies or by government directive, in every society many decisions are made in a decentralized way, through the operation of markets.

Markets exist in all societies, and Chapter 4 provided a bare-bones description of how markets operate. In this chapter, we continue our examination of supply, demand, and the price system.

THE PRICE SYSTEM: RATIONING AND ALLOCATING RESOURCES

The market system, also called the *price system,* performs two important and closely related functions in a society with unregulated markets. First, it provides an automatic mechanism for distributing scarce goods and services. That is, it serves as a **price rationing** device for allocating goods and services to consumers when the quantity demanded exceeds the quantity supplied. Second, the price system ultimately determines both the allocation of resources among producers and the final mix of outputs.

PRICE RATIONING

Consider first the simple process by which the price system eliminates excess demand. Figure 5.1 shows hypothetical supply and demand curves for lobsters caught off the coast of New England.

Lobsters are considered a delicacy. They are served in the finest restaurants, and people cook them at home on special occasions. Maine produces most of the lobster catch in the United States, and anyone who drives up

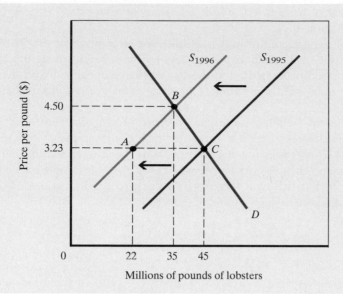

FIGURE 5.1

The Market for Lobsters
Suppose that in 1996, 20,000 square miles of lobstering waters off the coast of Maine are closed. The supply curve shifts to the left. Before the waters are closed, the lobster market is in equilibrium at the price of $3.23 and a quantity of 45 million pounds. The decreased supply of lobster leads to higher prices, and a new equilibrium is reached at $4.50 and 35 million pounds.

the Maine coast cannot avoid the hundreds of restaurants selling lobster rolls, steamed lobster, and baked stuffed lobster.

As Figure 5.1 shows, the equilibrium price of live New England lobsters was $3.23 per pound in 1995. At this price, lobster boats brought in lobsters at a rate of 45 million pounds per year—an amount that was just enough to satisfy demand.

Market equilibrium existed at $3.23 per pound, because at that price quantity demanded was equal to quantity supplied. (Remember that equilibrium occurs at the point where the supply and demand curves intersect. In Figure 5.1, this occurs at point C.)

Now suppose that in 1996 the waters off a section of the Maine coast become contaminated with a poisonous parasite. As a result, the Department of Agriculture is forced to close 20,000 square miles of the most productive lobstering areas. Even though many of the lobster boats shift their trapping activities to other waters, there is a sharp reduction in the quantity of lobster supplied. The supply curve shifts to the left, from S_{1995} to S_{1996}. This shift in the supply curve creates a situation of excess demand at $3.23. At that price, the quantity demanded is 45 million pounds and the quantity supplied is 22 million pounds. Quantity demanded exceeds quantity supplied by 23 million pounds (45 million minus 22 million).

The reduced supply causes the price of lobster to rise sharply. As the price rises, the available supply is "rationed." Who gets it? Those who are willing and able to pay the most.

You can see the market's price rationing function clearly in Figure 5.1. As the price rises from $3.23, the quantity demanded declines along the demand curve, moving from point C (45 million pounds) toward point B (35 million pounds). The higher prices mean that restaurants must charge much more for lobster rolls and stuffed lobsters. As a result, many people simply decide to stop buying lobster or order it less frequently when they dine out. Some restaurants drop it from the menu entirely, and some shoppers at the fish counter turn to lobster substitutes such as swordfish and salmon.

As the price rises, lobster trappers (suppliers) also change their behavior. They stay out longer and put out more traps than they did when the price was $3.23 per pound. Quantity supplied increases from 22 million pounds to 35 million pounds.

This increase in price brings about a movement along the 1996 supply curve from point A to point B.

Finally, a new equilibrium is established at a price of $4.50 per pound and a total output of 35 million pounds. At the new equilibrium, total production is 35 million pounds per year, and the market has determined who gets the lobsters. *The lower total supply is rationed to those who are willing and able to pay the higher price.*

This idea of "willingness to pay" is central to the distribution of available supply, and willingness depends on both desire (preferences) and income/wealth. Willingness to pay does not necessarily mean that only the very rich will continue to buy lobsters when the price increases. Lower-income people may continue to buy some lobster, but they will have to be willing to sacrifice more of other goods in order to do so.

In sum:

> The adjustment of price is the rationing mechanism in free markets. Price rationing means that whenever there is a need to ration a good—that is, when excess demand exists—in a free market, the price of the good will rise until quantity supplied equals quantity demanded—that is, until the market clears.

There is some price that will clear any market you can think of. Consider the market for a famous painting such as van Gogh's *Portrait of Dr. Gachet*. Figure 5.2 illustrates the operation of such a market. At a low price, there would be an enormous excess demand for such an important painting. The price would be bid up until there was only one remaining demander. The demander who gets the painting would be the one who is willing and able to pay the most. Presumably, that price would be very high. In fact, van Gogh's *Portrait of Dr. Gachet* sold for a record $82.5 million in 1990. If the product is in strictly scarce supply, as a single painting is, its price is said to be *demand determined;* that is, its price is determined solely and exclusively by the amount that the highest bidder or highest bidders are willing to pay.

One might interpret the statement that "there is some price that will clear any market" to mean "everything has its price." But that is not exactly what it means. Suppose you own a small silver bracelet that has been in your family for many generations. It is quite possible that you wouldn't sell it for *any* amount of money. Does this mean that the market is not working, or that quantity supplied and quantity demanded are not equal? Not at all. It means simply that *you* are the highest bidder. By turning down all bids, you are setting your own price, revealing that the bracelet is worth more to you than to those who bid on it. To keep the bracelet, you must be willing to forgo what anybody offers for it.

CONSTRAINTS ON THE MARKET AND ALTERNATIVE RATIONING MECHANISMS

On occasion, both governments and private firms decide to use some mechanism other than the market system to ration an item for which there is excess demand at the current price. (This was often the case in the former Soviet Union and other Communist nations like Cuba. See the Global Perspective box on page 108 titled "The Market Comes to Cuba" for more details.) Policies designed to stop price rationing are commonly justified in a number of ways.

The rationale most often used is fairness. It is not "fair" to let landlords charge high rents, not "fair" for oil companies to run up the price of gasoline, not "fair" for insurance companies to charge enormous premiums, and so on. After all, the argument goes, we have no choice but to pay—housing and insurance are neces-

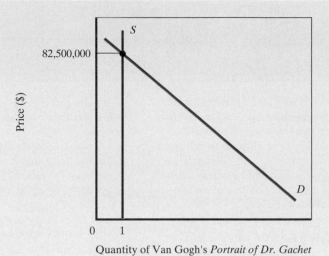

FIGURE 5.2
Market for a Rare Painting
There is some price that will clear any market, even if supply is strictly limited. In an auction for a unique painting, the price (bid) will rise to eliminate excess demand until there is only one bidder willing to purchase the single available painting.

sary, and one needs gasoline to get to work. While it is not precisely true that price rationing allocates goods and services solely on the basis of income and wealth, income and wealth do constrain our wants. Why should all the gasoline or all the tickets to the World Series go just to the rich? it is asked.

Various schemes to keep price from rising to equilibrium are based on several perceptions of injustice, among them (1) that price-gouging is bad, (2) that income is unfairly distributed, and (3) that some items are necessities, and everyone should be able to buy them at a "reasonable" price. Regardless of the rationale, the following examples will make two things clear:

1. Attempts to bypass price rationing in the market and to use alternative rationing devices are much more difficult and costly than they would seem at first glance.
2. Very often, such attempts distribute costs and benefits among households in unintended ways.

■ **Oil, Gasoline, and OPEC** In 1973 and 1974, the Organization of Petroleum Exporting Countries (OPEC) imposed an embargo on shipments of crude oil to the United States. What followed was a drastic reduction in the quantity of gasoline available at local gas pumps.

Had the market system been allowed to operate, refined gasoline prices would have increased dramatically until quantity supplied was equal to quantity demanded. Those who were willing and able to pay a very high price would have been the ones to get the gasoline. But the government decided that rationing gasoline to only those who were willing and able to pay the most was unfair, and Congress imposed a **price ceiling,** or maximum price, of 57¢ per gallon of leaded regular gasoline. That price ceiling was intended to keep gasoline "affordable," but it also perpetuated the excess demand. At the restricted price, quantity demanded remained greater than quantity supplied, and the available gasoline had to be divided up somehow among all potential demanders.

You can see the effects of the price ceiling by looking carefully at Figure 5.3 on page 109. If the price had been set by the interaction of supply and demand, it would have increased to approximately $1.50 per gallon. Instead, Congress made it illegal to sell gasoline for more than 57¢ per gallon. At that price, quantity de-

price ceiling *A maximum price that sellers may charge for a good, usually set by government.*

Price rationing allocates goods and services to those who are willing and able to pay for them. One of the central premises of communism is that price rationing for basic necessities, such as food, is unfair; everyone should be able to afford such items as food and shelter. But regulating prices to "fair" levels below equilibrium means that quantity supplied will be less than quantity demanded.

In addition, preventing the price mechanism from operating requires that some device other than price be used to ration the available goods. Before the collapse of communism in the Soviet Union and Eastern Europe, people waited in long lines at state stores, which could not meet the citizens' demands. The stores were not well stocked in part because farmers could get a much better price for their goods on the illegal black market.

Although Cuba has remained committed to Communist principles, in 1994 the door opened for the first time to market-oriented reforms. Farmers are now allowed to sell some of their products in an open market. The hope is that higher prices will result in greater quantities of agricultural goods supplied:

> SAN NICOLÁS, Cuba—This might have been called a market town when there was still anything much to buy. But as farmers rumbled into it this weekend on loaded-down tractors and their customers came however they could, San Nicolás seemed almost in the midst of a new discovery.
>
> A marketplace of sorts was set up on the long concrete platform that had housed the local "free farmers' market" until 1986, when the ruling Communist Party abolished it and others as a dangerous deviation from the revolutionary course . . . .
>
> [The marketplace was established as] a step to halt the economic free fall that began in 1989 with the collapse of Cuba's trading partners in the Soviet bloc. . . After meeting quotas for the state, farmers will be allowed to sell their surplus produce in public markets at whatever price they can get . . . .
>
> "This is a start," said Elvira Núñez, a slight 73-year-old woman who was delicately packing a few squashes into a shopping bag made from an old sugar sack. "Because people have to eat in order to live."

Source: Tim Golden, "Cubans Get a Taste of Capitalism," The New York Times, September 26, 1994, p. A1.

---

manded exceeded quantity supplied and a state of excess demand existed. Since the price system was not allowed to function, an alternative rationing system had to be found to distribute the available supply of gasoline.

Several devices were tried. The most common of all nonprice rationing systems is **queuing**, a term that simply means waiting in line. During 1974 very long lines began to appear at gas stations, starting as early as 5 A.M. Often people waited for hours to purchase gasoline. Under this system, gasoline went to those who were willing to pay the most, but the sacrifice was measured in hours and aggravation rather than in dollars.[1]

queuing *A nonprice rationing mechanism that uses waiting in line as a means of distributing goods and services.*

---

[1]*You can also show formally that the result is inefficient—that there is a resulting net loss of total value to society. First, there is the cost of waiting in line. Time has a value. With price rationing, no one has to wait in line and the value of that time is saved. Second, there may be additional lost value if the gasoline ends up in the hands of someone who places a lower value on it than someone else who gets no gas. Suppose, for example, that the market price of gasoline if unconstrained would rise to $2, but that the government has it fixed at $1. There will be long lines to get gas. Imagine that to motorist A, ten gallons of gas is worth $35 but that she fails to get it because her time is too valuable to wait in line. To motorist B, ten gallons is worth only $15, but his time is worth much less, so he gets the gas. Clearly, in the end, A could pay B for the gas and both could be better off. If A pays B $30 for the gas, A is $5 better off and B is $15 better off. In addition, A doesn't have to wait in line. Thus, the allocation that results from nonprice rationing involves a net loss of value. Such losses are called dead weight losses.*

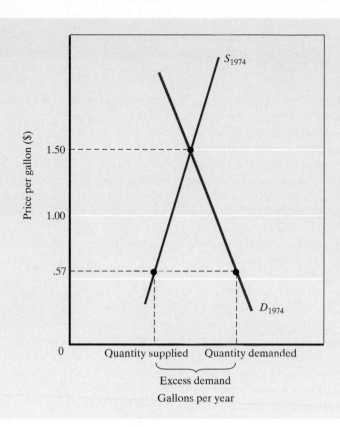

FIGURE 5.3
Excess Demand Created by a Price Ceiling of 57¢ per Gallon of Leaded Gasoline in 1974
In 1974, a ceiling price of 57¢ per gallon of leaded regular gasoline was imposed. If the price had instead been set by the interaction of supply and demand, it would have increased to approximately $1.50 per gallon. At 57¢ per gallon, the quantity demanded exceeded the quantity supplied. Since the price system was not allowed to function, an alternative rationing system had to be found to distribute the available supply of gasoline.

A second nonprice rationing device used during the gasoline crisis was that of **favored customers.** Many gas station owners decided not to sell gasoline to the general public at all but to reserve their scarce supplies for friends and favored customers. Not surprisingly, many customers tried to become "favored" by offering side payments to gas station owners. Owners also charged high prices for service. By doing so, they increased the real price of gasoline but hid it in service overcharges to get around the ceiling.

Yet another method of dividing up available supply is the use of **ration coupons.** It was suggested in both 1974 and 1979 that families be given ration tickets, or coupons, that would entitle them to purchase a certain number of gallons of gasoline each month; that way, everyone would get the same amount, regardless of income. Such a system had been employed in the United States during the 1940s, when wartime price ceilings on meat, sugar, butter, tires, nylon stockings, and many other items were imposed.

When ration coupons are used with no prohibition against trading them, however, the result is almost identical to a system of price rationing. Those who are willing and able to pay the most simply buy up the coupons and use them to purchase gasoline, chocolate, fresh eggs, or anything else that is sold at a restricted price.[2] This means that the price of the restricted good will effectively rise to the market-clearing price. For instance, suppose that you decide not to sell your ration coupon. You are then forgoing what you would have received by selling the coupon. Thus the "real" price of the good you purchase will be higher (if only in opportunity cost) than the restricted price. Even when trading coupons is declared illegal,

favored customers *Those who receive special treatment from dealers during crises.*

ration coupons *Tickets or coupons that entitle individual persons to purchase a certain amount of a given product per month.*

---

[2]*Of course, if you are assigned a number of tickets, and you sell them, you are better off than you would be with price rationing. Ration tickets thus serve as a way of redistributing income.*

black market *A market in which illegal trading takes place at market-determined prices.*

it is virtually impossible to stop black markets from developing. In a **black market,** illegal trading takes place at market-determined prices. (For more details on the black market, see the Issues and Controversies box titled "Tickets? Supply Meets Demand on the Sidewalk.")

■ **The World Cup, 1994** Another way to understand the rationing function of the price system is to look at the ways in which tickets to popular sporting events and concerts are sold and distributed. One of the most interesting recent examples is the 1994 World Cup soccer tournament.

In the summer of 1994, the World Cup came to the United States. The matches took place in nine cities, including Boston, Washington, Chicago, and Los Angeles. A total of 52 games were played among qualifying teams representing 24 countries. The final game between Italy and Brazil was played on July 17 in the Rose Bowl in Pasadena, California. (Brazil won.)

Regarding supply, a total of 3.6 million tickets were available for the games. Demand for soccer tickets was very high. Soccer is without question the most popular sport in the world, and it is literally true that wars have been fought because of the outcome of matches. With national pride at stake, tens of thousands of people flocked to the United States. In addition, the sport's growing popularity in the United States led to high ticket demand by U.S. residents. Rather than charging market-clearing prices, the event's organizers decided to charge "fair" prices and set the average ticket price at about $58.

This price was below equilibrium, and there was excess demand for the tickets almost from the time that they went on sale. Interestingly, organizers of similar high-interest sporting events (like the Super Bowl, the NBA playoffs, and the World Series) almost always price tickets below the level that would just fill the stadiums. Why? In their words, to do otherwise would be "unfair"; only the "rich" would be able to attend if prices were set too high. As Alan Rothenberg, Chairman of World Cup USA put it: "We definitely could have charged more. . . . Obviously we wanted to price the tickets high enough so we can pay for the event. . . . but at the same time not be unfair to the public."

We have seen, however, that if the price system is not going to be used to allocate the tickets among demanders, another method must be found. One method gives the tickets to certain favored customers. *The Washington Post* (December 25, 1993) reported that 25 to 30% of the seats at RFK Stadium were committed to "corporate sponsors, city officials, members of Congress, and other dignitaries." Another 15% were held for soccer's world governing body, and yet another 15% were held for the "U.S. soccer community"—coaches, officials, and players. The remaining tickets were sold through a mail lottery and, in some cities, by queuing.

The distribution of tickets was not really over until the final match was played. Consider the demand for tickets to the final match that were distributed to fans months earlier. The organizing body did charge more for final game tickets—the price of the cheapest ticket was $180 and the most expensive $475, with the average around $300. But consider the potential demand! As *Worth* magazine (May 1994) put it, "Foreign fans will be waving huge wads of bills near game day." Because the Rose Bowl holds only 91,794 people, by some estimates the equilibrium ticket price was in the vicinity of $3,000!

WHEN SOCCER MANIA HIT THE UNITED STATES IN 1994, THE DEMAND FOR TICKETS FOR THE WORLD CUP FINAL GAMES WAS VERY HIGH. RATHER THAN CHARGING MARKET-CLEARING PRICES FOR TICKETS, THE EVENT'S ORGANIZERS DECIDED TO CHARGE "FAIR" PRICES. AS A RESULT, A LUCRATIVE UNDERGROUND MARKET FOR THE TICKETS DEVELOPED. MANY PEOPLE SHOWED THAT THEY WERE WILLING AND ABLE TO PAY IN EXCESS OF $3000 PER TICKET.

Whenever a limit is placed on price, there is the opportunity for profit. "Scalpers" make their living by obtaining tickets (either by standing in line or by buying them from those willing to sell) and then reselling those tickets to those willing to pay more. In most states, scalping is illegal. The point of restricting prices, whether done by private promoters or the government, is to make the tickets available at affordable prices. Remember, however, that if that price is set below equilibrium, some nonprice rationing mechanism—such as standing in line, a lottery, or favored customers—must be used to distribute the tickets.

Is scalping good or bad for society? The fact that it is illegal might suggest that it is bad. But as the following article from the *New York Times* suggests, most economists do not. Think carefully about the arguments presented. What side are you on?

Ticket scalping has been very good to Kevin Thomas, and he makes no apologies. He sees himself as a classic American entrepreneur: a high-school dropout from the Bronx who taught himself a trade, works seven nights a week, earns $40,000 a year, and at age 26 has $75,000 in savings, all by providing a public service outside New York's theaters and sports arenas.

He has just one complaint. "I've been busted about 30 times in the last year," he said one recent evening, just after making $280 at a Knicks game. "You learn to deal with it—I give the cops a fake name, and I pay the fines when I have to, but I don't think it's fair. I look at scalping like working as a stockbroker, buying low and selling high. If people are willing to pay me the money, what kind of problem is that?"

It is a significant problem to public officials in New York and New Jersey, who are cracking down on street scalpers like Mr. Thomas and on licensed ticket brokers. Undercover officers are enforcing new restrictions on reselling tickets at marked-up prices, and the attorneys general of the two states are pressing well-publicized cases against more than a dozen ticket brokers.

But economists tend to see scalping from Mr. Thomas's perspective. To them, the governments' crusade makes about as much sense as the old campaigns by Communist authorities against "profiteering." Economists argue that the restrictions inconvenience the public, reduce the audience for cultural and sports events, waste the police's time, deprive New York City of tens of millions of dollars of tax revenue, and actually drive up the cost of many tickets.

Source: John Tierney, "Tickets? Supply Meets Demand on the Sidewalk." *New York Times,* December 26, 1992.

Figure 5.4 illustrates the situation. The supply curve is vertical at 91,794 tickets—the fixed number of seats available. As the demand curve shows, some people were willing to pay prices far in excess of $3,000—and many did. The *Los Angeles Times* reported that one man paid $250,000 for a set (unspecified number) of tickets. Even before tickets were issued, an extensive and complicated black market had begun operating. Ticket agents and scalpers ran advertisements in newspapers offering thousands of dollars for good seats in order to resell them at a profit.

Now consider someone who paid $180 for a final game ticket and went to the game. What price did she really pay to go to the game? The answer: A lot more than $180, since she could easily have sold her ticket for 15 times what she paid for it. All of a sudden the opportunity cost of going to the game changed. To attend the final game she had to give up the opportunity to sell her ticket at a great profit. By not selling her ticket, she revealed that going to the game was worth more to her than all the other things that $3,000 or $4,000 could buy.

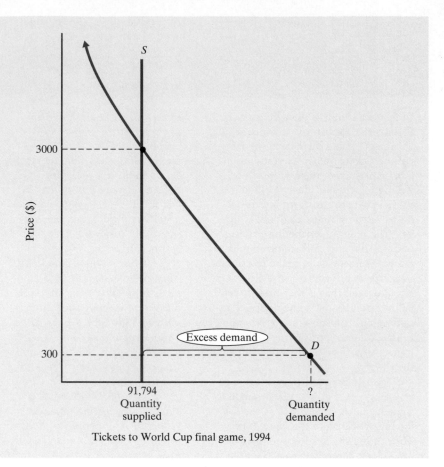

FIGURE 5.4

Supply of and Demand for World Cup Final Game Tickets, Brazil versus Italy, July 17, 1994

World Cup 1994 final game tickets were initially sold for an average face price of about $300. The Rose Bowl in Pasadena holds 91,794 people. Thus, the supply curve is vertical at 91,794 tickets. At $300, the quantity demanded far exceeded the quantity supplied. The result was enormous excess demand.

What, then, can we conclude about alternatives to the price rationing system?

> No matter how good the intentions of private organizations and governments, it is very difficult to prevent the price system from operating and to stop willingness to pay from asserting itself. Every time an alternative is tried, the price system seems to sneak in the back door. With favored customers and black markets, the final distribution may be even more unfair than that which would result from simple price rationing.

PRICES AND THE ALLOCATION OF RESOURCES

Thinking of the market system as a mechanism for allocating scarce goods and services among competing demanders is very revealing. But the market determines much more than just the distribution of final outputs. It also determines what gets produced and how resources are allocated among competing uses.

Consider a change in consumer preferences that leads to an increase in demand for a specific good or service. During the 1970s, for example, people began going to restaurants much more frequently than before. Researchers think that this trend, which continues today, is partially the result of social changes (such as a dramatic rise in the number of two-earner families) and partially the result of rising incomes. The market responded to this change in demand by shifting resources, both capital and labor, into more and better restaurants.

With the increase in demand for restaurant meals, the price of eating out rose, and the restaurant business became more profitable. The higher profits attracted new businesses and provided old restaurants with an incentive to expand. As new capital, seeking profits, flowed into the restaurant business, so too did labor. New restaurants need chefs. Chefs need training, and the higher wages that came with increased demand provided an incentive for them to get it. In response to the increase in demand for training, new cooking schools opened up and existing schools began to offer courses in the culinary arts.

This story could run on and on, but the point is clear:

> Price changes resulting from shifts of demand in output markets cause profits to rise or fall. Profits attract capital; losses lead to disinvestment. Higher wages attract labor and encourage workers to acquire skills. At the core of the system, supply, demand, and prices in input and output markets determine the allocation of resources and the ultimate combinations of things produced.

SUPPLY AND DEMAND ANALYSIS: AN OIL IMPORT FEE

The basic logic of supply and demand is a powerful tool of analysis. As an extended example of the power of this logic, we will consider a recent proposal to impose a tax on imported oil. The idea of raising the federal gasoline tax is hotly debated, with many arguing strongly for such a tax. Many economists, however, believe that a fee on imported crude oil, which is used to produce gasoline, would have better effects on the economy than would a gasoline tax.

Consider the facts. Between 1985 and 1989, the United States increased its dependence on oil imports dramatically. In 1989, total U.S. demand for crude oil was 13.6 million barrels per day. Of that amount, only 7.7 million barrels per day (57%) were supplied by U.S. producers, with the remaining 5.9 million barrels per day (43%) imported. The price of oil on world markets that year averaged about $18. This heavy dependence on foreign oil left the United States vulnerable to the price shock that followed the Iraqi invasion of Kuwait in August 1990. In the months following the invasion, the price of crude oil on world markets shot up to $40 per barrel.

Even before the invasion, many economists and some politicians had recommended a stiff oil import fee (or tax) that would, it was argued, reduce the U.S. dependence on foreign oil by (1) reducing overall consumption and (2) providing an incentive for increased domestic production. An added bonus would be improved air quality from the reduced driving that would be brought about by higher gasoline prices.

Simple supply and demand analysis makes the arguments of the import fee proponents easier to understand. The two diagrams in Figure 5.5 on page 114 show the world market for crude oil and the U.S. market for crude oil in 1989. World production was about 56 million barrels per day in 1989, and the average world price was (as we saw above) about $18. These amounts are shown as the equilibrium price and quantity in Figure 5.5a.

Figure 5.5b shows the U.S. market. Assume that the United States can buy all the oil that it wants at the world price of $18. This means that domestic producers cannot get away with charging any more than $18 per barrel. (Why would anyone pay more than $18 for a barrel of U.S.-produced oil when they can get as much foreign oil as they want for $18 per barrel?) The curve labeled *Supply*US shows the amount that domestic suppliers will produce at each price level. At a price of $18, domestic production is 7.7 million barrels. Stated somewhat differently, U.S. pro-

FIGURE 5.5

The World and U.S. Markets for Crude Oil, 1989

At a world price of $18, domestic production is 7.7 million barrels per day and the total quantity of oil demanded in the United States is 13.6 million barrels per day. The difference is total imports (5.9 million barrels per day). If the government levies a 33% tax on imports, the price of a barrel of oil rises to $24. The quantity demanded falls to 12.2 million barrels per day. At the same time, the quantity supplied by domestic producers increases to 9.0 million barrels per day, and the quantity imported falls to 3.2 million barrels per day.

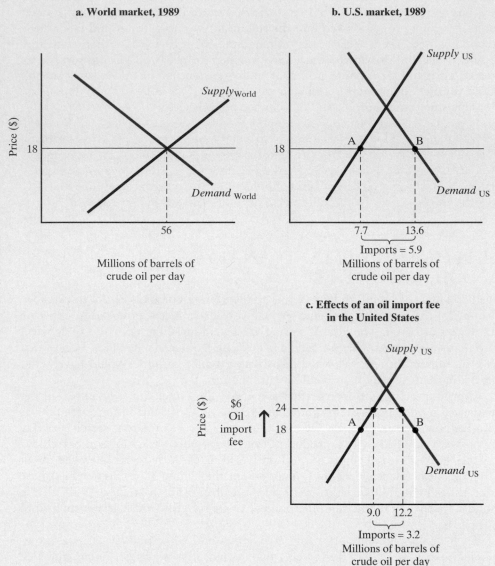

a. World market, 1989

Price ($)

$Supply_{World}$

18

$Demand_{World}$

56

Millions of barrels of
crude oil per day

b. U.S. market, 1989

$Supply_{US}$

18   A   B

$Demand_{US}$

7.7   13.6

Imports = 5.9

Millions of barrels of
crude oil per day

**c. Effects of an oil import fee
in the United States**

Price ($)

$Supply_{US}$

$6
Oil
import
fee

24

18   A   B

$Demand_{US}$

9.0   12.2

Imports = 3.2

Millions of barrels of
crude oil per day

ducers will produce at point *A* on the supply curve. The total quantity of oil demanded in the United States in 1989 was 13.6 million barrels per day. This can also be seen in Figure 5.5b. At a price of $18, the quantity demanded in the United States is point *B* on the demand curve.

The difference between the total quantity demanded (13.6 million barrels per day) and domestic production (7.7 million barrels per day) is total imports (5.9 million barrels per day).

Now suppose that the government levies a tax of 33% on imported oil. Since the import price is $18, a tax of $6 (or .33 × $18) per barrel means that importers of oil in the United States will pay a total of $24 per barrel ($18 + $6). This new higher price means that U.S. producers can also charge up to $24 for a barrel of crude. Note, however, that the tax is paid only on imported oil. Thus the entire $24 paid for domestic crude goes to domestic producers.

Figure 5.5c shows the result of the tax. First, the higher price leads to a reduction in the quantity of oil demanded. The quantity demanded drops to 12.2 million barrels per day. This is a movement *along* the demand curve from point *B* to point *D*. At the same time, the quantity supplied by domestic producers increases to 9.0 million barrels per day. This is a movement *along* the supply curve from point *A* to point *C*. With an increase in domestic quantity supplied and a decrease in domestic quantity demanded, imports decrease to 3.2 million barrels per day (12.2 − 9.0).[3]

The tax also generates revenues for the federal government. The total tax revenue collected is equal to the tax per barrel ($6) times the number of imported barrels. Since the quantity imported is 3.2 million barrels per day, total revenue is $6 × 3.2 million, or $19.2 million *per day*. This amount is equal to about $7 billion per year ($19.2 million per day × 365 days per year).

What does all of this mean? In the final analysis, an oil import fee would (1) increase domestic production and (2) reduce overall consumption. This would in turn help with the problem of air pollution and simultaneously reduce U.S. dependence on foreign oil. In addition, it would help to reduce the U.S. government's budget deficit, which is now running over $200 billion per year.

LOOKING AHEAD

We have now examined the basic forces of supply and demand and discussed the nature of the market/price system and some other important concepts. These basic concepts will serve as building blocks for what comes next. Whether you are studying microeconomics or macroeconomics, you will be studying the function of markets and the behavior of market participants in more detail in the following chapters.

Since the concepts presented in the first five chapters are so important to your understanding of what is to come, this might be a good point for a brief review of Part One.

SUMMARY

THE PRICE SYSTEM: RATIONING AND ALLOCATING RESOURCES

1. In a market economy, the market system (or price system) serves two functions. It determines the allocation of resources among producers and the final mix of outputs. It also distributes goods and services on the basis of willingness and ability to pay. In this sense, it serves as a *price rationing* device.

2. Governments, as well as private firms, sometimes decide not to use the market system to ration an item for which there is an excess demand at current prices. Examples of nonprice rationing systems include *queuing, favored customers,* and *ration coupons.* The most common rationale for policies or practices designed to avoid price rationing is "fairness."

3. Attempts to bypass the market and use alternative nonprice rationing devices are much more difficult and costly than it would seem at first glance. Schemes that open up opportunities for favored customers, black markets, and side payments often end up less "fair" than the free market.

SUPPLY AND DEMAND ANALYSIS: AN OIL IMPORT FEE

4. The basic logic of supply and demand is a powerful tool for analysis. For example, supply and demand analysis shows that an oil import tax will reduce quantity of oil demanded, increase domestic production, and generate revenues for the government.

---

[3]*These figures were not chosen randomly. It is interesting to note that in 1985 the world price of crude oil averaged about $24 a barrel. Domestic production was 9.0 million barrels per day, and domestic consumption was 12.2 million barrels per day, with imports of only 3.2 million. The drop in price between 1985 and 1989 increased imports to 5.9 million, an 84% increase.*

black market 110

favored customers 109

price ceiling 107

price rationing 104

queuing 108

ration coupons 109

PROBLEM SET

1. Illustrate the following with supply and/or demand curves:
   a. A situation of excess labor supply (unemployment) caused by a "minimum wage" law.
   b. The effect of a sharp increase in heating oil prices on the demand for insulation material.

2. The box on page 111 makes the argument that scalping, which is illegal in most states, may in fact serve a useful function. Do you agree or disagree? Write an essay explaining your answer.

3. Illustrate the following with supply and/or demand curves:
   a. The federal government "supports" the price of wheat by paying farmers not to plant wheat on some of their land.
   b. As the economy has begun to recover from the recession of 1990–1991, incomes are rising and expectations about the future are becoming more positive. As a result, home prices in many parts of the country are rising.
   c. The impact of an increase in the price of chicken on the price of hamburger.
   d. In an upcoming election, the voters of Massachusetts will be asked to decide whether to abolish rent control. Under rent control, rents are held by law to levels below equilibrium. If rent control is discontinued, there will be an impact on housing demand and supply.
   e. Incomes rise, shifting the demand for gasoline. Crude oil prices rise, shifting the supply of gasoline. At the new equilibrium, the quantity of gasoline sold is less than it was before. (Crude oil is used to produce gasoline).

4. "The price of blue jeans has risen substantially in recent years. Demand for blue jeans has also been rising. This is hard to explain because the law of demand says that higher prices should lead to lower demand." Do you agree?

5. In an effort to "support" the price of some agricultural goods, the Department of Agriculture pays farmers a subsidy in cash for every acre that they leave *unplanted*. The Agriculture Department argues that the subsidy increases the "cost" of planting and that it will reduce supply and increase the price of competitively produced agricultural goods. Critics argue that because the subsidy is a payment to farmers, it will reduce costs and lead to lower prices. Which argument is correct? Explain.

SUPPLY AND DEMAND IN THE U.S. PAPER INDUSTRY

CASE STUDY

At first glance, the paper industry seems to be a simple one: Mills process pulp into paper, which has a broad variety of end uses including packaging, newsprint, and office paper. But the demand for paper fluctuates widely, making events in the industry hard to predict. As the economy moves into boom periods or contractions, the demand for paper follows, and may surge or drop with little warning. The economic recovery of 1994 that followed a two-year decrease in economic activity was tipped over the edge by faster-than-expected growth in Europe and Asia: European and Asian growth led to more spending, which contributed to rapid jumps in the demand for the corrugated boxes used in shipping. The increase in overseas demand meant not only new markets for paper but also less competition for U.S. producers.

After spending the first half of the 1990s in a slump, with increasing inventories and prices at 50-year lows, the paper industry saw its prices increase dramatically and profits rise over 100% in 1994, with similar increases in 1995 (Figure 1). Mills that had been temporarily closed in 1993 were running at full capacity by the end of 1994. Although some renewed contracts included price hikes of up to 30%, some manufacturers were choosing to phase in price increases gradually, for fear of alienating long-term customers.

The price of pulp, the basic raw material used to make paper, had risen along with the price of final paper, almost doubling to over $700 a ton by the beginning of 1995. Some industry observers expected federal restrictions on timber harvesting in the Northwest to create excess demand in the industry, further increasing prices, but increased production in Canada and the South

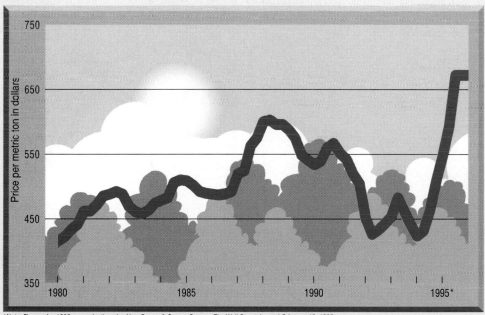

FIGURE 1
The Price of Paper, 1980–1995

*Note: Figures for 1995 are projections by Alex. Brown & Sons. Source: *The Wall Street Journal*, February 15, 1995.

117

(where paper companies have large tree farms) has compensated for the cutbacks. Over time, however, paper companies—pressured by environmental activists and environmentally aware consumers—will continue to look for alternatives to trees as a source of pulp. One favorite is the kenaf plant, a relative of cotton and okra, which yields over three times more fiber per acre than typical tree plantations, and which can be processed into pulp using 90% less chemicals.

Despite the increased demand, the supply of final paper products was still constrained by mill capacity. The 65 North American mills in the newsprint industry were running at maximum production levels in 1995. Even if all these firms' profits were used for investment in new mills, the three-year period needed to construct a new mill would keep supply fixed in the short run, adding to the increase in paper companies' profits.

Questions for Analytical Thinking

1. Recycled materials are used in the production of corrugated boxes (30%) and newsprint (40%). What impact would you expect the increase in pulp prices to have on the market for waste paper (that is, used paper that can be recycled)?

2. New U.S. regulations led to lower federal timber harvests in 1994. Some paper companies grow most of their own timber; others rely on purchases in the open market. How might each of these companies be affected by laws that decrease the supply of timber?

3. Newsprint paper typically accounts for 20% of a newspaper's annual budget. Given greatly increased newsprint prices, what sort of changes in operations might be expected at a typical newspaper? How might the composition of the news change? (Consider local, national, and international news; advertising; public service announcements; crossword puzzles; etc.)

4. How would the length of time needed to construct a new news-print mill be likely to affect the volatility of prices in the industry?

5. Would you expect the elasticity of demand for paper products to be high or low? What about the demand for pulp? Would either of these be likely to change in the long run?

Sources: Patrick Reilly, "Soaring Newsprint Prices Sting Readers," *The Wall Street Journal,* February 25, 1995; "This Paper Recovery Is No Pulp Fiction," *Business Week,* January 9, 1995; "Suddenly, Paper Is on a Burn," *Business Week,* November 21, 1994.

THE PAPER INDUSTRY RELIES ON A STEADY FLOW OF TIMBER, WHICH IS OFTEN HARVESTED AND THEN FLOATED DOWN-RIVER TO A PAPER MILL. AT THE MILL, THE LOGS ARE TURNED INTO PULP, WHICH IS IN TURN CONVERTED INTO PAPER. DUE TO MAJOR INCREASES IN DEMAND, THE LOGGING AND PAPER INDUSTRIES ARE HAVING A HARD TIME KEEPING UP. THE RESULT HAS BEEN A STEADY INCREASE IN THE PRICE OF PAPER; PRICES ARE EXPECTED TO CONTINUE RISING UNTIL JUST AFTER THE YEAR 2000.

MACROECONOMICS

PART TWO

CONCEPTS AND PROBLEMS IN MACROECONOMICS

INTRODUCTION TO MACROECONOMICS

We NOW BEGIN OUR STUDY OF MACROECONOMICS. WE TOUCHED on the differences between microeconomics and macroeconomics in Chapter 1. **Microeconomics** is the branch of economics that examines the functioning of individual industries and the behavior of individual decision-making units, typically business firms and households. With a few simple assumptions about how these units behave (firms maximize profits, households maximize satisfaction, or utility), we can derive useful conclusions about how markets work, how resources are allocated, and so forth.

Macroeconomics takes a different perspective. Instead of focusing on the factors that influence the production of particular products and the behavior of individual industries, macroeconomics focuses on the determinants of total national output. Macroeconomics studies not household income but *national* income, not individual prices but the *overall* price level. It does not analyze the demand for labor in the automobile industry but rather total employment in the economy.

Both microeconomics and macroeconomics are concerned with the decisions of households and firms. Microeconomics deals with individual decisions, while macroeconomics deals with the sum of these individual decisions. The word *aggregate* is used in macroeconomics to refer to sums. When we speak of **aggregate behavior,** we mean the behavior of all households and firms taken together. We also

microeconomics *The branch of economics that deals with the functioning of individual industries and the behavior of individual decision-making units—business firms and households.*

macroeconomics *The branch of economics that deals with the economy as a whole. Macroeconomics focuses on the determinants of total national income, deals with aggregates such as aggregate consumption and investment, and looks at the overall level of prices rather than individual prices.*

aggregate behavior *The behavior of all households and firms taken together.*

sticky prices *Prices that do not always adjust rapidly to maintain equality between quantity supplied and quantity demanded.*

microeconomic foundations of macroeconomics *The underlying microeconomic principles behind macroeconomic analysis.*

Great Depression *The period of severe economic contraction and high unemployment that began in 1929 and continued throughout the 1930s.*

speak of aggregate consumption and aggregate investment, which refer to total consumption and total investment in the economy.

Since microeconomists and macroeconomists look at the economy from different perspectives, you might expect that they will reach somewhat different conclusions about the way the economy behaves. This is true to some extent. Microeconomists generally conclude that markets work well. They see prices as flexible, adjusting to maintain equality between quantity supplied and quantity demanded. Macroeconomists, however, observe that important prices in the economy—for example, the wage rate (or price of labor)—often seem "sticky." **Sticky prices** are prices that do not always adjust rapidly to maintain equality between quantity supplied and quantity demanded. Microeconomists do not expect to see the quantity of apples supplied exceeding the quantity of apples demanded, because the price of apples is not sticky. But macroeconomists—who analyze aggregate behavior—examine periods of high unemployment, where the quantity of labor supplied appears to exceed the quantity of labor demanded. At such times, it appears that wage rates do not adjust fast enough to equate the quantity of labor supplied and the quantity of labor demanded.

Until fairly recently, macroeconomists tended to be relatively uninterested in reconciling their analyses with the postulates and conclusions of microeconomic theory. The new trend among macroeconomists, however, is to try to make macroeconomic analysis consistent with microeconomic postulates—that is, with the idea that firms and households make their decisions along the lines suggested by microeconomic theory. If prices do not appear to adjust to equate the quantity supplied and the quantity demanded, for example, macroeconomists now look for solid microeconomic reasons why this is the case.

The task of reconciling macroeconomics and microeconomics is an extremely difficult one. Much less agreement about the way things work is apparent in macroeconomics than in microeconomics. But in recent years, this chaos has partly (but only partly) subsided, largely as a result of the increasing use of microeconomic principles to help explain macroeconomic events. One of the aims of this book is to explain the **microeconomic foundations of macroeconomics.**

THE ROOTS OF MACROECONOMICS

THE GREAT DEPRESSION

Economic events of the 1930s, the decade of the **Great Depression,** spurred a great deal of thinking about macroeconomic issues. The 1920s had been generally prosperous years for the U.S. economy. Virtually everyone who wanted a job could get one, incomes rose substantially, and prices were stable. Beginning in late 1929, however, things took a sudden turn for the worse. In 1929, 1.5 million people were unemployed. By 1933, that number had increased to 13 million out of a labor force of 51 million. In 1929, the United States produced $103 billion worth of new goods and services; by 1933, production had fallen to $55 billion, a drop of nearly 50 percent. In October of 1929, when stock prices collapsed on Wall Street, billions of dollars of personal wealth were lost. Unemployment remained above 14% of the labor force until 1940.

The 1930s saw enormous suffering across the United States and around the world as the Depression spread to Europe and beyond. In the United States, the number of suicides increased nearly 30%, and millions of families were pushed into poverty.

■ **Classical Models**   Before the Great Depression, economists generally applied microeconomic models, sometimes referred to as "classical models," to economy-wide problems. (In fact, the word "macroeconomics" was not even invented until after World War II.) For example, classical supply and demand analysis assumed that an excess supply of labor would drive down wages to a new equilibrium level; as a result, unemployment would not persist.

In other words, classical economists believed that *recessions* (downturns in the economy) were self-correcting. As output falls and the demand for labor shifts to the left, the argument went, the wage rate will decline, thereby raising the quantity of labor demanded by firms who would want to hire more workers at the new lower wage rate. (Graph this movement along the new demand curve yourself.)

In fact, however, during the Great Depression unemployment levels remained very high for nearly ten years. In large measure, the failure of simple classical models[1] to explain the prolonged existence of high unemployment provided the impetus for the development of macroeconomics. Thus, it is not surprising that the application of what we now call macroeconomics was born in the 1930s.

■ **The Keynesian Revolution**   One of the most important works in the history of economics, *The General Theory of Employment, Interest and Money,* by John Maynard Keynes, was published in 1936. Building on what was already understood about markets and their behavior, Keynes set out to construct a theory that would explain the confusing economic events of his time.

Much of macroeconomics has deep roots in Keynes's work. According to Keynes, it is not prices and wages that determine the level of employment, as classical models had suggested, but rather the level of aggregate demand for goods and services. Keynes also believed that governments could intervene in the economy and affect the level of output and employment. The government's role during periods when private demand is low, Keynes argued, is to stimulate aggregate demand and, by so doing, to lift the economy out of recession. (For more on Keynes, see the Application box on pages 122 123 titled "The Great Depression and John Maynard Keynes.")

RECENT MACROECONOMIC HISTORY

After World War II, and especially in the 1950s, Keynes's views began to gain increasing influence over both professional economists and government policy makers. Governments came to believe that they could intervene in their economies to attain specific employment and output goals, and they began to use their powers to tax and spend, as well as their ability to affect interest rates and the money supply, for the explicit purpose of controlling the economy's ups and downs. This view of government policy became firmly established in the United States with the passage of the Employment Act of 1946. This act established the President's Council of Economic Advisors, a group of economists who advise the President on economic issues. It also committed the federal government to intervening in the economy to prevent large declines in output and employment.

■ **Fine Tuning in the 1960s**   The notion that the government could, and should, act to stabilize the macroeconomy reached the height of its popularity in the 1960s. During these years, Walter Heller, the chairman of the Council of Economic Advisors under both President Kennedy and President Johnson, coined the phrase

---

[1]*Classical models are also sometimes known as "market clearing" models because they emphasize that prices and wages adjust to ensure that markets always clear—that is, that the quantity supplied is equal to the quantity demanded.*

THE GREAT DEPRESSION AND JOHN MAYNARD KEYNES

Much of the framework of modern macroeconomics comes from the works of John Maynard Keynes, whose *General Theory of Employment, Interest and Money* was published in 1936. The following excerpt by Robert L. Heilbroner provides some insights into Keynes's life and work.

> By 1933 the nation was virtually prostrate. On street corners, in homes, in Hoovervilles (communities of makeshift shacks), 14 million unemployed sat, haunting the land . . . .
>
> It was the unemployment that was hardest to bear. The jobless millions were like an embolism in the nation's vital circulation; and while their indisputable existence argued more forcibly than any text that something was wrong with the system, the economists wrung their hands and racked their brains . . . . but could offer neither diagnosis nor remedy. Unemployment—this kind of unemployment—was simply not listed among the possible ills of the system: it was absurd, impossible, unreasonable, and paradoxical. But it was there.
>
> It would seem logical that the man who would seek to solve this impossible paradox of

JOHN MAYNARD KENYES.

> not enough production existing side by side with men fruitlessly seeking work would be a Left-winger, an economist with strong sympathies for the proletariat, an angry man. Nothing could be further from the fact. The man who tackled it was almost a dilettante with nothing like a chip on his shoulder. The simple truth was that his talents inclined in every direction. He had, for example, written a most recondite book on mathe-

> matical probability, a book that Bertrand Russell had declared "impossible to praise too highly"; then he had gone on to match his skill in abstruse logic with a flair for making money—he accumulated a fortune of £500,000 by way of the most treacherous of all roads to riches: dealing in international currencies and commodities. More impressive yet, he had written his mathematics treatise on the side, as it were, while engaged in Government service, and he piled up his private wealth by applying himself for only half an hour a day while still abed.
>
> But this is only a sample of his many-sidedness. He was an economist, of course—a Cambridge don with all the dignity and erudition that go with such an appointment . . . . He managed to be simultaneously the darling of the Bloomsbury set, the cluster of Britain's most avant-garde intellectual brilliants, and also the chairman of a life insurance company, a niche in life rarely noted for its intellectual abandon. He was a pillar of stability in delicate matters of international diplomacy, but his official cor-

fine tuning *The phrase coined by Walter Heller to refer to the government's role in regulating inflation and unemployment.*

fine tuning to refer to the government's role in regulating inflation and unemployment. During the 1960s, many economists believed that the government could use the tools available to it to manipulate unemployment and inflation levels fairly precisely.

■ **Disillusionment Since the 1970s** Since 1970, the U.S. economy has been through a series of dramatic fluctuations in employment, output, and inflation. In

rectness did not prevent him from acquiring a knowledge of other European politicians that included their . . . neuroses and financial prejudices . . . . He ran a theater, and he came to be a Director of the Bank of England. He knew Roosevelt and Churchill and also Bernard Shaw and Pablo Picasso. . . .

His name was John Maynard Keynes, an old British name (pronounced to rhyme with "rains") that could be traced back to one William de Cahagnes and 1066. Keynes was a traditionalist; he liked to think that greatness ran in families, and it is true that his own father was John Neville Keynes, an illustrious enough economist in his own right. But it took more than the ordinary gifts of heritage to account for the son; it was as if the talents that would have sufficed half a dozen men were by happy accident crowded into one person.

By a coincidence he was born in 1883, in the very year that Karl Marx passed away. But the two economists who thus touched each other in time, although each was to exert the profoundest influence

AS PEOPLE LOST THEIR HOMES OR WERE EVICTED FROM THEIR APARTMENTS DURING THE GREAT DEPRESSION, COMMUNITIES OF MAKESHIFT SHACKS SPRANG UP ACROSS THE UNITED STATES. THE "HOOVERVILLE" PICTURED HERE WAS PHOTOGRAPHED IN DUBUQUE, IOWA IN 1940.

on the philosophy of the capitalist system, could hardly have differed from one another more. Marx was bitter, at bay, heavy and disappointed; as we know, he was the draftsman of Capitalism Doomed. Keynes loved life and sailed through it *buoyant, at ease, and consummately successful to become the architect of Capitalism Viable.*

Source: Robert L. Heilbroner, *The Worldly Philosophers* (New York: Simon & Schuster, 1961). Reprinted by permission.

1974–1975 and again in 1980–1982, the United States experienced severe recessions. While not as catastrophic as the Great Depression of the 1930s, these recessions left millions without jobs and resulted in billions of dollars of lost output and income. In 1974–1975 and again in 1979–1981, the United States experienced very high rates of inflation. The U.S. economy also experienced a moderate recession in 1990–1991 and very slow growth for about two years after the recession. (We discuss these events in more detail in later chapters.)

stagflation *Occurs when the overall price level rises rapidly (inflation) during periods of recession or high and persistent unemployment (stagnation).*

Moreover, the 1970s witnessed the birth of a new phenomenon called **stagflation** (stagnation + inflation). Stagflation occurs when the overall price level rises rapidly (inflation) during periods of recession or high and persistent unemployment (stagnation). Until the 1970s, rapidly rising prices had been observed only in periods when the economy was prospering and unemployment was low (or at least declining). The problem of stagflation proved to be a vexing one, both for macroeconomic theorists and for policy makers concerned with the health of the economy.

It was clear by 1975 that the macroeconomy was considerably more difficult to control than either Heller's words or textbook theory had led economists to believe. The events of the 1970s and afterward have had an important influence on macroeconomic theory. Much of the faith in the simple Keynesian model and the "conventional wisdom" of the 1960s has been lost. New ways of understanding the behavior of the macroeconomy have been proposed, but as yet there is no consensus as to which explanation is best. It is precisely this flux in macroeconomics, the sense that the discipline is wide open and that many of the most important issues have yet to be resolved, that makes it so exciting to study.

MACROECONOMIC CONCERNS

Having established the aggregate focus of macroeconomics, we can now turn to some of the major questions and problems with which the discipline is concerned. Many of these questions do not have agreed-upon answers, and all the questions will require more exploration before we can hope to answer them. Our object here is to give you a sense of what the coming chapters are about.

There is no standard list of the crucial topics in macroeconomics, but we can easily identify four major concerns of the discipline (not necessarily in order of importance):

- First, macroeconomics is concerned with the *aggregate price level.* Increases in the overall price level (inflation) are, of course, of great concern to policy makers and to citizens at large, as well as to economists.

- Second, macroeconomics is concerned with *aggregate output* (the quantity of goods and services being produced in the economy), particularly when the economy does not seem to be producing as much as it is capable of producing.

- The third concern, which is closely related to the second, is *total employment.* An economy may not be producing as much as it is capable of producing because it is not employing all the people who want jobs (unemployment).

- Fourth and finally, the *rest of the world* and its *relationship to the domestic economy* must be considered. The U.S. economy, for example has a profound impact on the economies of the rest of the world, and developments in other countries have important effects on the United States as well.

Each of these issues is of great concern to the government, which would like to have low inflation, high output and employment, and a prosperous world economy. In fact, several of these goals were embodied in the Employment Act of 1946. How effective the government can be in achieving these goals is a matter of considerable debate, but the goals themselves are clear. (The effectiveness of government policies is the subject of later chapters.)

One troublesome fact should be kept in mind throughout all our discussions:

Almost all macroeconomic events are interrelated, and making progress on one front often means making conditions worse on another front.

For example, some economists believe that the only way to cure inflation is to put the economy into a recession (thereby increasing unemployment and lowering output). Not all the good things we want may be compatible with each other, and thus macroeconomics is rife with trade-offs. One of the main aims of the following chapters is to explore and explain the nature of these trade-offs. But now let us return to the key concerns of macroeconomics for a more detailed examination.

INFLATION

Inflation is an increase in the overall price level. The reduction of inflation has long been a goal of government policy. Especially problematic are **hyperinflations,** or periods of very rapid increases in the overall price level.

> **inflation** *An increase in the overall price level.*

> **hyperinflation** *A period of very rapid increases in the overall price level.*

Most Americans are unaware of what life is like under very high inflation. In some countries, however, people are accustomed to prices rising by the day, by the hour, or even by the minute. During the hyperinflation in Bolivia in 1984 and 1985, for example, the price of one egg rose from 3,000 pesos to 10,000 pesos in one week. In 1985, three bottles of aspirin sold for the same price as a luxury car had sold for in 1982. At the same time, the problem of handling money became quite burdensome. Banks stopped counting deposits—a $500 deposit was equivalent to about 32 million pesos, and it just did not make sense to count a huge mail sack full of bills. Bolivia's currency, printed in West Germany and England, was the country's third biggest import in 1984, surpassed only by wheat and mining equipment.

The almost unbelievable rise in prices in Bolivia is really only a small part of the story, however. When inflation approaches the stratospheric rates of 2000% per year, the economy, and indeed the whole organization, of a country begin to break down. Workers may go on strike to demand wage increases in line with the high inflation rate, firms find it almost impossible to secure credit, and the economy grinds to a halt. Fortunately, dramatic hyperinflations usually end very abruptly. In the course of only a few months, Bolivia went from having the highest inflation rate in the world to having one of the lowest inflation rates in the Western Hemisphere.

Luckily, hyperinflations are quite rare. Nonetheless, economists have devoted much effort to identifying the costs and consequences of even moderate inflation. Who gains from inflation, and who loses? What costs does inflation impose on society, and how severe are they? What causes inflation, and what is the best way of stopping it? We will focus on some of these questions in Chapters 8 and 14. It will be obvious throughout the following chapters that inflation is a major issue in macroeconomics.

AGGREGATE OUTPUT AND THE BUSINESS CYCLE

Rather than moving along on a perfectly even keel at all times, economies tend to experience short-term ups and downs in their performance. The technical name for these ups and downs is the **business cycle.** The main measure of how an economy is doing is **aggregate output,** the total quantity of goods and services produced in

> **business cycle** *The cycle of short-term ups and downs in the economy.*

> **aggregate output** *The total quantity of goods and services produced in an economy in a given period.*

the economy in a given period. Clearly, when less is produced (in other words, when aggregate output decreases), there are fewer goods and services to go around, and the standard of living declines. When firms cut back on production, they also lay off workers, thus increasing the rate of unemployment.

Recessions are periods of time during which aggregate output declines. It has become conventional to classify an economic downturn as a "recession" when aggregate output declines for two consecutive quarters. A prolonged and deep recession is called a **depression,** although economists do not agree on when a recession becomes a depression. Since the beginning of the twentieth century, the U.S. economy has experienced one depression (during the 1930s), three severe recessions (1946, 1974–1975, and 1980–1982), and a number of less severe, shorter recessions (1954, 1958, 1970, and 1990–1991). Other countries have also experienced recessions throughout the twentieth century, some roughly coinciding with U.S. recessions and some not. In 1994, while the U.S. recovery was well underway, Japan was still in a recession.

Devising explanations for and predicting the business cycle is one of the main concerns of macroeconomics. The key questions are: Why does the economy fluctuate so much, and why at times does it not seem to respond to the simple forces of supply and demand?

UNEMPLOYMENT

You cannot listen to the news or read a newspaper without noticing that data on the unemployment rate are released each month. The **unemployment rate**—that is, the percentage of the labor force that is unemployed—is a key indicator of the economy's health. Because the unemployment rate is usually closely related to the economy's aggregate output, announcements of each month's new figure are followed with great interest by economists, politicians, and policy makers.

Although macroeconomists are interested in learning why the unemployment rate has risen or fallen in a given period, they also try to answer a more basic question: Why is there any unemployment at all? Of course, we do not expect to see zero unemployment. At any given time, some firms may go bankrupt due to competition from rival firms, bad management, or just bad luck. Employees of such firms typically are not able to find new jobs as soon as they have lost their old ones, and while they are looking for work, they will be counted as unemployed. Also, workers entering the labor market for the first time may require a few weeks, or even months, to find a job.

If we base our analysis on supply and demand, as we have in all our discussions so far, we would expect conditions to change in response to the existence of unemployed workers. Specifically, when there is unemployment beyond some minimum amount, there is an excess supply of workers—at the going wage rates, there are people who want to work who cannot find work. In microeconomic theory, the response to excess supply is a decrease in the price of the commodity in question and therefore an increase in the quantity demanded, a reduction in the quantity supplied, and the restoration of equilibrium. With the quantity supplied equal to the quantity demanded, the market clears.

The existence of unemployment seems to imply that the aggregate labor market is not in equilibrium—that something prevents the quantity supplied and the quantity demanded from equating. But why do labor markets not clear when so many other markets do? Or is it that labor markets are clearing and the unemployment data are reflecting something different? The implications of the unemployment data are a major puzzle in macroeconomics and a major focus of Chapters 8 and 15.

recession *A period during which aggregate output declines. Conventionally, a period in which aggregate output declines for two consecutive quarters.*

depression *A prolonged and deep recession.*

unemployment rate *The percent-age of the labor force that is unemployed.*

GLOBAL ISSUES

Finally, economic conditions in the rest of the world have important effects on the U.S. economy. If the value of the dollar falls relative to the Japanese yen, are unemployment or inflation levels in the United States affected? What happens to the United States if Germany expands its money supply? How does an increase in oil prices affect the global economy?

Clearly, a complete analysis of the economy must take into account the effects of the events in the United States on the rest of the world and the effects of the events in the rest of the world on the United States. These issues are addressed throughout the chapters that follow. Chapter 22 provides a more detailed look at macroeconomics in an open economy.

THE ROLE OF GOVERNMENT IN THE MACROECONOMY

A major part of our discussion of macroeconomics concerns the potential role of government in influencing the economy. Here we mention briefly four kinds of policy that the government has used to influence the macroeconomy:

Government policies for influencing the macroeconomy:	1. fiscal policy 2. monetary policy 3. incomes policies 4. supply-side policies

THE BERLIN WALL, WHICH HAD SEPARATED THE TWO HALVES OF BERLIN SINCE 1961, WAS DISMANTLED IN NOVEMBER 1989. SINCE THEN, THE REUNIFIED GERMANY HAS FACED NUMEROUS ECONOMIC CHALLENGES. MACROECONOMICS STUDIES NOT ONLY WHAT HAS HAPPENED IN GERMANY SINCE 1989, BUT ALSO HOW ECONOMIC EVENTS IN GERMANY AFFECT THE REST OF THE WORLD.

■ **Fiscal Policy** One of the major ways in which the federal government affects the economy is through its tax and expenditure decisions, or **fiscal policy.** The federal government collects taxes from households and firms and spends these funds on various items ranging from missiles to parks to social security payments to interstate highways. Both the magnitude and composition of these taxes and expenditures have a major effect on the economy.

One of Keynes's main ideas in the 1930s was that fiscal policy could and should be used to stabilize the level of output and employment in the economy. More specifically, Keynes believed that the government should cut taxes and/or raise spending—so-called *expansionary fiscal policies*—to get the economy out of a slump. Conversely, he held that the government should raise taxes and/or cut spending—so-called *contractionary fiscal policies*—to bring the economy out of an inflation.

fiscal policy *Government policies regarding taxes and expenditures.*

■ **Monetary Policy** Taxes and spending are not the only variables that the government controls. Through the Federal Reserve, the nation's central bank,[2] the government can determine the quantity of money in the economy. The effects and proper role of **monetary policy** are among the most hotly debated subjects in macroeconomics. Most economists agree that the quantity of money supplied affects the overall price level, interest rates and exchange rates, the unemployment

monetary policy *The tools used by the Federal Reserve to control the money supply.*

---

[2] *The Federal Reserve is a quasi-independent agency, and it does not always do what the President or Congress wants it to do. Nevertheless, because it is part of the government rather than part of the private sector, we consider it in this section.*

rate, and the level of output. The main controversies arise regarding how monetary policy manifests itself and exactly how large its effects are.

incomes policies *Direct attempts by the government to control prices and wages.*

■ **Incomes Policies** Although monetary and fiscal policies are the two major tools that the government uses to control the U.S. economy, other instruments are also available. **Incomes policies** are direct attempts by government to control prices and wages. They generally take the form of regulations specifying the maximum amount by which prices or wages are permitted to rise. Sometimes, voluntary guidelines are used instead of rigid controls—the government may simply plead with firms and labor unions to show restraint in their price- and wage-setting behavior. The effectiveness of wage and price controls is a point of some controversy, although such controls are generally viewed with disfavor in the United States because they are believed to prevent the price system from functioning as an efficient allocator of resources.

supply-side policies *Government policies that focus on aggregate supply and increasing production rather than stimulating aggregate demand.*

■ **Supply-Side Policies** Some economists have advocated **supply-side policies** for managing the economy. Advocates of supply-side economics reject the Keynesian notion that the government should act to stimulate aggregate demand; they focus instead on aggregate supply and on increasing production. In practice, the main instrument of supply-side policy has been the tax system. (In this sense, supply-side policy is just a special case of fiscal policy.) Personal taxes were reduced in 1981 and again in 1986. The goal was to increase the labor supply by increasing the incentive to work and to increase the supply of capital by increasing the incentive to save. In addition, the 1981 tax cuts sharply reduced business taxes and provided extra tax incentives to stimulate investment. Proponents of these policies argued that stimulating the supply of labor and capital and increasing investment was the best way to increase the supply of goods and services. We discuss the pros and cons of supply-side policies in Chapter 19.

THE COMPONENTS OF THE MACROECONOMY

Macroeconomics focuses on four groups in the economy: *households* and *firms* (the private sector), the *government* (the public sector), and the *rest of the world* (the international sector). We provided data on each of these sectors in Chapter 3. These four groups interact in a variety of ways, many of which involve either the receipt or payment of income.

THE CIRCULAR FLOW DIAGRAM

circular flow *A diagram showing the income received and payments made by each sector of the economy.*

A useful way of seeing the economic interactions among the four groups in the economy is to examine a **circular flow** diagram, which shows the income received and payments made by each sector. A simple circular flow diagram is pictured in Figure 6.1.

Let's walk through the circular flow step by step. Households work for firms and the government, and they receive wages for their work. Hence our diagram shows a flow of wages *into* the household sector as payment for those services. Households also receive interest on corporate and government bonds and dividends from firms. Many households receive other payments from the government, such as social security benefits, veterans' benefits, and welfare payments. Economists call these kinds of payments from the government (for which the recipients do not supply goods, services, or labor) **transfer payments.** Together, these receipts make up the total income received by the households.

transfer payments *Cash payments made by the government to people who do not supply goods, services, or labor in exchange for these payments. They include social security benefits, veterans' benefits, and welfare payments.*

Households spend by buying goods and services from firms and by paying taxes to the government. These items make up the total amount paid out by the

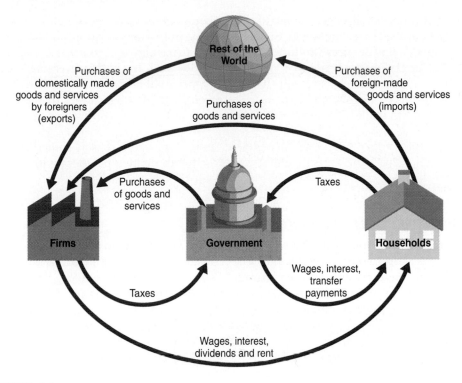

FIGURE 6.1

The Circular Flow of Payments

Households receive income from firms and the government, purchase goods and services from firms, and pay taxes to the government. They also purchase foreign-made goods and services (imports). Firms receive payments from households and the government for goods and services; they pay wages, dividends, interest, and rents to households, and taxes to the government. The government receives taxes from both firms and households, pays both firms and households for goods and services—including wages to government workers—and pays interest and transfers to households. Finally, people in other countries purchase goods and services produced domestically (exports). *Note:* Though not shown in this diagram, firms and governments also purchase imports.

households. The difference between the total receipts and the total payments of the households is the amount that the households save or dissave.[3] If households receive more than they spend, they *save* during the period. If they receive less than they spend, they *dissave*. A household can dissave by using up some of its previous savings or by borrowing. In the circular flow diagram, household spending is shown as a flow *out* of the household sector.

Firms sell goods and services to households and the government. These sales earn revenue, which shows up in the circular flow diagram as a flow of funds *into* the firm sector. Firms pay wages, interest, and dividends to households, and they pay taxes to the government. These payments are shown as flowing *out* of the firm sector.

The government collects taxes from households and firms. The government also makes payments. It buys goods and services from firms, pays wages and interest to households, and makes transfer payments to households. If the government's revenue is less than its payments, the government is dissaving.

---

[3]*Saving by households is sometimes termed a "leakage" from the circular flow because it withdraws income, or current purchasing power, from the system.*

Finally, households spend some of their income on *imports*—goods and services produced in the rest of the world. Similarly, people in foreign countries purchase *exports*—goods and services produced by domestic firms and sold to other countries.

One of the major lessons of the circular flow diagram is that everyone's expenditure is someone else's receipt. If you buy a personal computer from IBM, you make a payment to IBM and IBM receives revenue. If IBM pays taxes to the government, it has made a payment and the government has received revenue. In short:

> Everyone's expenditures go somewhere. It is impossible to sell something without there being a buyer, and it is impossible to make a payment without there being a recipient. Every transaction must have two sides.

THE THREE MARKET ARENAS

Another way of looking at the ways households, firms, the government, and the rest of the world relate to each other is to consider the markets in which they interact. The three broadly defined market arenas in which households, firms, the government, and the rest of the world interact, as depicted in Figure 6.2, are:

The three market arenas:	1. goods-and-services market
	2. labor market
	3. money (financial) market

■ **Goods-and-Services Market** Households and the government purchase goods and services from firms in the *goods-and-services market*. In this market, firms also purchase goods and services from each other. For example, Levi Strauss buys denim from other firms to make its blue jeans. In addition, firms buy capital goods from other firms. If General Motors needs new robots on its assembly lines, it will probably buy them from another firm rather than make them itself.

Firms *supply* to the goods-and-services market. Households, the government, and firms *demand* from this market. Finally, the rest of the world both buys from and sells to the goods-and-services market. As we mentioned in Chapter 3, the United States now imports hundreds of billions of dollars' worth of automobiles, VCRs, oil, and other goods. At the same time, the United States exports hundreds of billions of dollars worth of computers, airplanes, and agricultural goods.

FIGURE 6.2
The Three Basic Markets
Households, firms, the government, and the rest of the world all interact in the goods-and-services, labor, and money markets.

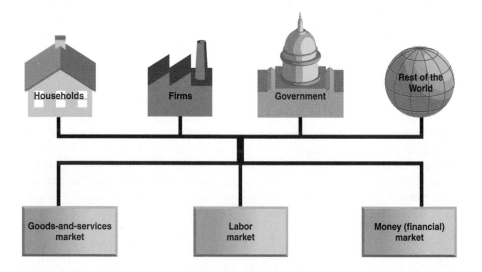

■ **Labor Market** Interaction in the *labor market* takes place when firms and the government purchase labor from households. In this market, households *supply* labor, and firms and the government *demand* labor. In the U.S. economy, firms are the largest demanders of labor, although the government is also a substantial employer. The total supply of labor in the economy depends on the sum of decisions made by households. Individuals must decide whether to enter the labor force (whether to look for a job at all) and how many hours to work.

Labor is also supplied to and demanded from the rest of the world. In recent years, the labor market has become an international market. For example, vegetable and fruit farmers in California would find it very difficult to bring their product to market if it were not for the labor of migrant farm workers from Mexico. For years, Turkey has provided Germany with "guest workers" who are willing to take low-paying jobs that more prosperous German workers avoid. Even the United States exports some labor. When Iraq invaded Kuwait in 1990, thousands of U.S. citizens working in Kuwait (for foreign as well as U.S. firms) were trapped and held hostage for a few months. Recent data show that the percentage of graduates of U.S. colleges and professional schools seeking jobs abroad has jumped sharply.

■ **Money Market** In the *money market*—sometimes called the *financial market*—households purchase stocks and bonds from firms. Households *supply* funds to this market in the expectation of earning extra income in the form of dividends on stocks and interest on bonds. Households also *demand* (borrow) funds from this market to finance various purchases. Firms borrow to build new facilities in the hope of earning more in the future. The government borrows by issuing bonds. The rest of the world both borrows from and lends to the money market; every morning you can now hear reports on the radio about the Japanese and British stock markets. Much of the borrowing and lending of households, firms, the government, and the international sector is coordinated by financial institutions—commercial banks, savings and loan associations, insurance companies, and the like. These institutions take deposits from one group and lend them to others.

When a firm, a household, or the government borrows to finance a purchase, it has an obligation to pay that loan back, usually at some specified time in the future. Most loans also involve payment of interest as a fee for the use of the borrowed funds. When a loan is made, the borrower nearly always signs a "promise to repay," or *promissory note,* and gives it to the lender. When the federal government borrows, it issues "promises" called **Treasury bonds, notes,** or **bills** in exchange for money. Corporations issue **corporate bonds.** A corporate bond might state, for example, "General Electric Corporation agrees to pay $5,000 to the holder of this bond on January 1, 1998, and interest thereon at 8.3% annually until that time."

Instead of issuing bonds to raise funds, firms can also issue shares of stock. A **share of stock** is a financial instrument that gives the holder a share in the firm's ownership and therefore the right to share in the firm's profits. If the firm does well, the value of the stock increases, and the stockholder receives a *capital gain*[4] on the initial purchase. In addition, the stock may pay **dividends**—that is, the firm may choose to return some of its profits directly to its stockholders, rather than retaining them internally to buy capital. If, however, the firm does poorly, so does the stockholder. The capital value of the stock may fall, and dividends may not be paid.

Treasury bonds, notes, and **bills** *Promissory notes issued by the federal government when it borrows money.*

corporate bonds *Promissory notes issued by corporations when they borrow money.*

shares of stock *Financial instruments that give to the holder a share in the firm's ownership and therefore the right to share in the firm's profits.*

dividends *The portion of a corporation's profits that the firm pays out each period to its shareholders.*

---

[4]*A capital gain occurs whenever the value of an asset increases. If you bought a stock for $1,000 and it is now worth $1,500, you have earned a capital gain of $500. A capital gain is "realized" when you sell the asset. Until you sell, the capital gain is accrued but not realized.*

It is important to realize that stocks and bonds are simply contracts, or agreements, between parties. I agree to loan you a certain amount, and you agree to repay me this amount plus something extra at some future date. Or I agree to buy part ownership in your firm, and you agree to give me a share of the firm's future profits.

One of the critical variables in the money market is the *interest rate*. Although we sometimes talk as if there were only one interest rate, there is never just one interest rate at any given time. Rather, the interest rate on a given loan reflects the length of the loan and the perceived risk to the lender. A business that is just getting started, for example, will have to pay a higher rate than will General Motors. A 30-year mortgage has a different interest rate than a 90-day loan. Nevertheless, interest rates tend to move up and down together, and their movement reflects general conditions in the financial market. (We discuss the complexities of interest rates in later chapters.)

THE METHODOLOGY OF MACROECONOMICS

Macroeconomists build models based on theories, and they test their models using data. In this sense, the methodology of macroeconomics is similar to the methodology of microeconomics.

CONNECTIONS TO MICROECONOMICS

How do macroeconomists try to explain aggregate behavior? One approach assumes that the same factors that affect individual behavior also affect aggregate behavior. For example, we know from microeconomics that an individual's wage rate should affect that person's consumption habits and the amount of labor he or she is willing to supply. If we were to apply this microeconomic hypothesis to the aggregate data, we would say that the average wage rate in the economy should affect total consumption and total labor supply (which, in fact, seems to be true).

The reason for looking to microeconomics for help in explaining macroeconomic events is quite simple:

> Macroeconomic behavior is the sum of all the microeconomic decisions made by individual households and firms. If the movements of macroeconomic aggregates, such as total output or total employment, reflect decisions being made by individual firms and households, we cannot possibly understand the former without some knowledge of the factors that influence the latter.

Consider the problem of unemployment. The unemployment rate is the number of people unemployed as a fraction of the labor force. To be classified as "in the labor force," a person must either have a job or be seeking one actively. To understand aggregate unemployment, then, we need to understand individual household behavior in the labor market. Why do people choose to enter the labor force? Under what circumstances will they drop out? Why does unemployment exist even when the economy seems to be doing very well? A knowledge of microeconomic behavior is the logical starting point for macroeconomic analysis.

AGGREGATE DEMAND AND AGGREGATE SUPPLY

aggregate demand *The total demand for goods and services in an economy.*

A major theme as we work our way through the next few chapters is the behavior of aggregate demand and aggregate supply. **Aggregate demand** is the total demand for goods and services in an economy. **Aggregate supply** is the total supply of goods and services in an economy.

Figure 6.3 shows *aggregate demand* and *aggregate supply* curves. Measured on the horizontal axis is aggregate output. Measured on the vertical axis is the *overall price level*, not the price of a particular good or service. (This is a very important point—be sure to keep it in mind.) The economy is in equilibrium at the point at which these curves intersect.

As you will discover, aggregate demand and supply curves are much more complicated than the simple demand and supply curves that we described in Chapters 4 and 5. The simple logic of supply, demand, and equilibrium in individual markets does not explain what is depicted in Figure 6.3. Indeed, it will take us the entire next chapter just to describe what is meant by "aggregate output" and the "overall price level." Furthermore, although we will look to the behavior of households and firms in individual markets for clues about how to analyze aggregate behavior, there are important differences when we move from the individual to the aggregate level.

Consider, for example, *demand,* one of the most important concepts in economics. When the price of a specific good increases, perhaps the most important determinant of consumer response is the availability of other goods that can be substituted for the good whose price has increased. Part of the reason that an increase in the price of airline tickets causes a decline in the quantity of airline tickets demanded is that a higher price relative to other goods means that the opportunity cost of buying a ticket is higher: The sacrifice required in terms of other goods and services has increased. But when the overall price level changes, there may be no changes at all in relative prices. When analyzing the behavior of aggregate demand, the availability of substitutes is irrelevant.

Microeconomics teaches us that, *ceteris paribus,* the quantity demanded of a good falls when its price rises and rises when its price falls. (This is the microeconomic law of demand.) In other words, individual demand curves and market demand curves slope downward to the right. The reason that the *aggregate* demand curve in Figure 6.3 slopes downward to the right is much more complex, however. As we will see later, the downward slope of the aggregate demand curve is related to what goes on in the money (financial) market.

aggregate supply *The total supply of goods and services in an economy.*

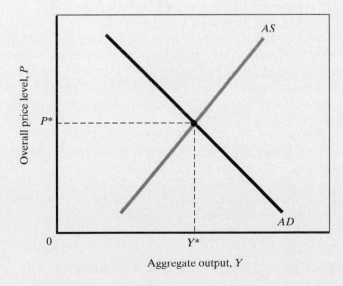

FIGURE 6.3

The Aggregate Demand and Aggregate Supply Curves

A major theme in macroeconomics is the behavior of aggregate demand and aggregate supply. The logic behind the aggregate demand and aggregate supply curves is much more complex than the logic underlying the simple demand and supply curves described in Chapters 4 and 5.

The aggregate supply curve is also very different from the supply curve of an individual firm or market. A firm's supply curve is derived under the assumption that all its input prices are fixed. In other words, the firm's input prices are assumed to remain unchanged as the price of the firm's output changes. When we derived Clarence Brown's soybean supply schedule in Chapter 4, for example, we took his input prices as fixed. A change in an input price leads to a shift in Brown's supply curve, not a movement along it. If we are examining changes in the overall price level, however, *all* prices are changing (including input prices), so the aggregate supply curve cannot be based on the assumption of fixed input prices. We will see later that the aggregate supply curve is a source of much controversy in macroeconomics.

Because of the complexity of the aggregate demand and aggregate supply curves, we will need to build our analysis piece by piece. In Chapter 7, we discuss the methods of measuring economic activity and aggregate output. In Chapter 8, we describe the key macroeconomic problems of business cycles, inflation, and unemployment. Chapters 9 through 14 present the material we need to understand the equilibrium levels of aggregate output and the overall price level. In these chapters, we discuss the behavior of households, firms, and the government in both the goods-and-services market and the money market. Chapter 15 brings the labor market into the picture. Later chapters elaborate on this material and discuss a number of important macroeconomic policy issues.

THE U.S. ECONOMY IN THE TWENTIETH CENTURY: TRENDS AND CYCLES

As we said earlier in this chapter, most macroeconomic variables go through ups and downs over time, and the economy as a whole experiences periods of prosperity and periods of recession. The general trend of the U.S. economy in the twentieth century, however, has been toward prosperity. One measure of an economy's prosperity is the amount of goods and services that it produces during a year, or its gross domestic product (GDP). (GDP is the subject of the next chapter.) An economy is said to grow from one year to another if GDP is larger in the second year than in the first. Between 1900 and 1994, the U.S. economy grew at an average rate of 3% per year. In other words, during those years the economy was on average 3% richer each year than it had been the year before.

It is important to remember that we are discussing the average growth rate here. The economy did not actually grow by 3% every year. In some years, growth was less than 3%, and in some years growth was actually negative (that is, GDP fell). In other years, the growth rate was greater than 3 percent. It is thus important to distinguish between *long-term, or secular, trends* in economic performance and *short-term, or cyclical, variations*.

Consider, for instance, the world's climate. Measurements have revealed that the earth's average temperature has been slowly but steadily rising for the past 18,000 years (a long-term secular trend). This does not mean, however, that every day, week, month, and year since 16,000 B.C. has been slightly warmer than the one before. There are seasonal fluctuations in climate as well as day-to-day variations, and there are even centuries-long cooling and warming periods within this 18,000-year span.

EXPANSION AND CONTRACTION: THE BUSINESS CYCLE

Macroeconomics is concerned both with long-run trends—Why has the U.S. economy done so well over the past 100 years while Great Britain's has done rather poorly?—and with short-run fluctuations in economic performance—Why did the world experience a severe recession in the early 1980s? Most of this part of the text focuses on short-run fluctuations, because they are somewhat better understood. As we mentioned earlier in this chapter, these short-term ups and downs in the economy are known as the *business cycle*. A typical business cycle is illustrated in Figure 6.4.

Because the U.S. economy on average grows over time, the business cycle in Figure 6.4 shows an overall positive trend—the *peak* (that is, the highest point) of a new business cycle is higher than the peak of the previous cycle. The period from a *trough*, or bottom of the cycle, to a peak is called an **expansion** or a **boom.** During an expansion, output and employment are growing. The period from a peak to a trough is called a **contraction, recession,** or **slump.** During a recession, output and employment are falling.

In judging whether an economy is expanding or contracting, it is important to note the difference between the level of economic activity and its rate of change. If, for example, the economy has just left a trough (point *A* in Figure 6.4), it will be growing (rate of change is positive), but its level of output will still be low. Conversely, if the economy has just started to decline from a peak (point *B* in Figure 6.4), it will be contracting (rate of change is negative), but its level of output will still be high.

The business cycle in Figure 6.4 is symmetric, which means that the length of an expansion is the same as the length of a contraction. All business cycles are not symmetric, however. It is possible, for example, for the expansion phase to be longer than the contraction phase. When contraction comes, it may be fast and sharp, while expansion may be slow and gradual. Moreover, the economy is not nearly as regular as the business cycle in Figure 6.4 indicates. While there are ups and downs in the economy, they tend to be fairly erratic.

What do actual business cycles in the United States look like? You can see the answer to this question in Figure 6.5, where the percentage deviation of U.S. GDP around its trend is plotted for the 1900–1994 period. Although many business cycles have occurred in the last nine decades, each business cycle has been unique. The economy is not so simple that it has regular cycles.

The periods of the Great Depression and World War II are clearly the low and high points of Figure 6.5, although other large contractions and expansions have

expansion or **boom** *The period in the business cycle from a trough up to a peak, during which output and employment rise.*

contraction, recession, or **slump** *The period in the business cycle from a peak down to a trough, during which output and employment fall.*

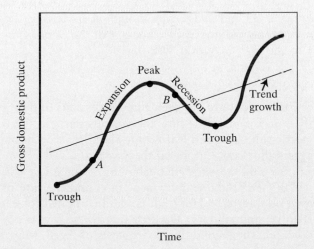

FIGURE 6.4

A Typical Business Cycle

In this business cycle, the economy is expanding as it moves through point *A* from the trough to the peak. When the economy moves from a peak down to a trough, through point *B*, the economy is in recession.

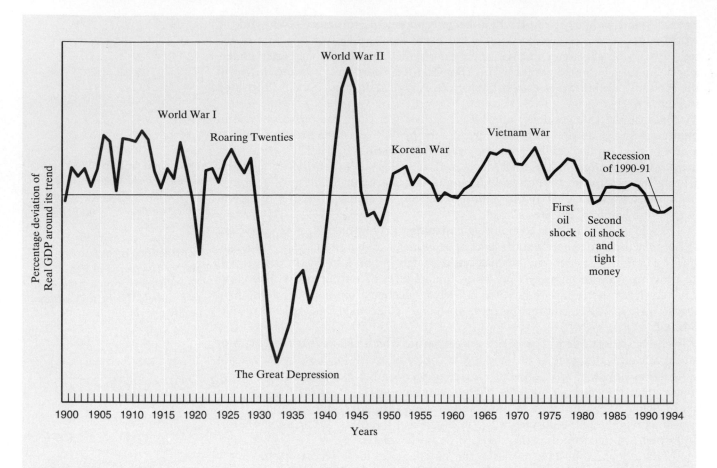

FIGURE 6.5

Percentage Deviation of Real GDP around Its Trend, 1900–1994

taken place. In particular, the expansion in the 1960s is noteworthy, as are the recessions at the beginning of the 1980s and 1990s. Some of the cycles have been long in duration, and some have been very short. Note also that GDP actually increased between 1933 and 1937, even though at its peak in 1937 GDP was still quite low. The economy did not really come out of the Depression until the defense buildup prior to the start of World War II.

THE U.S. ECONOMY SINCE 1970

Since 1970, the U.S. economy has seen three recessions and large fluctuations in the rate of inflation. By analyzing how the various parts of the economy behaved during these hectic times, we can learn a lot about macroeconomic behavior. The following chapters thus concentrate on these years.

Figures 6.6, 6.7 and 6.8 show the behavior of three key variables during the period since 1970: GDP, the unemployment rate, and the rate of inflation. These graphs are based on quarterly data (that is, data compiled for each quarter of the year) rather than on annual data. The first quarter of a year consists of January, February, and March; the second quarter consists of April, May, and June; and so on. The Roman numerals I, II, III, and IV denote the four quarters. (For example, "1972 III" refers to the third quarter, or summer, of 1972.)

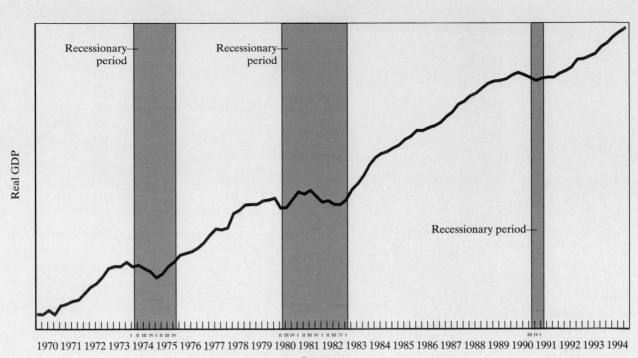

FIGURE 6.6

Real GDP, 1970 I–1994 IV

Real GDP in the United States since 1970 has risen overall, but there have been three recessionary periods: 1974 I–1975 IV, 1980 II–1983 I, and 1990 III–1991 I.

Figure 6.6 plots GDP for the period 1970 I–1994 IV. In the following chapters we will look at three recessionary periods within this period: 1974 I–1975 IV, 1980 II–1983 I, and 1990 III–1991 I. These periods make useful reference points when we examine how other variables behave during the three periods.[5]

One of the main concerns of macroeconomics is unemployment, as we said earlier. Unemployment generally rises during recessions and falls during expansions. This can be seen clearly in Figure 6.7 on page 138, which plots the unemployment rate for the period 1970 I–1994 IV. Note that unemployment rose in all three recessions. In the 1974–1975 recession, the unemployment rate reached a maximum of about 9% in the second quarter of 1975. During the 1980–1982 recession, it reached a maximum of about 11% in the fourth quarter of 1982. The unemployment rate continued to rise after the 1990–1991 recession and reached a peak of about 8% in 1992 III.

Macroeconomics is also concerned with the inflation rate. A measure of the overall price level is the GDP price index, an economy-wide price index. (The construction of the GDP price index is discussed in the next chapter. It is an index of

---

[5]As Figure 6.6 shows, GDP rose in the middle of 1981 before falling again in the last quarter of 1981. Given this fact, one possibility would be to treat the 1980 II–1983 I period as if it included two separate recessionary periods: 1980 II–1981 I and 1981 IV–1983 I. Because the expansion in 1981 was so short-lived, however, we have chosen not to separate the period into two parts.

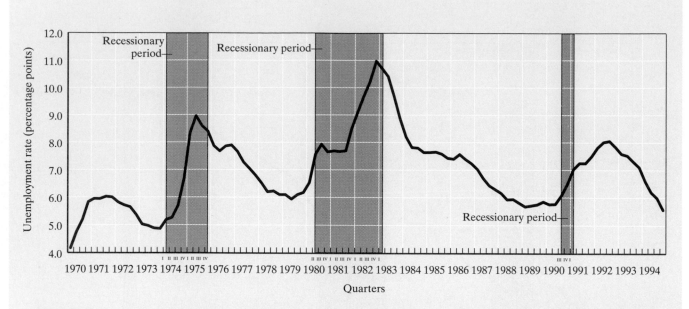

FIGURE 6.7

Unemployment Rate, 1970 I–1994 IV

The U.S. unemployment rate since 1970 shows wide variations. The three recessionary reference periods show increases in the unemployment rate.

prices of all domestically produced goods in the economy.) The percentage change in the GDP price index provides one measure of the overall rate of inflation. Figure 6.8 plots the percentage change in the GDP price index for the 1970 I –1994 IV period.[6] For reference purposes, we have picked two periods within this time as showing particularly high inflation: 1973 IV–1975 IV and 1979 I–1981 IV. In the first period, the inflation rate peaked at 10.9% in the first quarter of 1975. In the second period, it peaked at 9.9% in the fourth quarter of 1980. Since 1983, the rate of inflation has been quite low by the standards of the 1970s. In the fourth quarter of 1994 it was only 2.8 percent.

One of the main concerns of macroeconomics is to explain the behavior of and the connections among variables such as GDP, the unemployment rate, and the GDP price index. When you can understand the movements shown in Figures 6.6, 6.7, and 6.8, you will have come a long way in understanding how the economy works.

---

[6]*The percentage change in Figure 6.8 is the percentage change over four quarters. For example, the value for 1970 I is the percentage change from 1969 I, the value for 1970 II is the percentage change from 1969 II, and so on.*

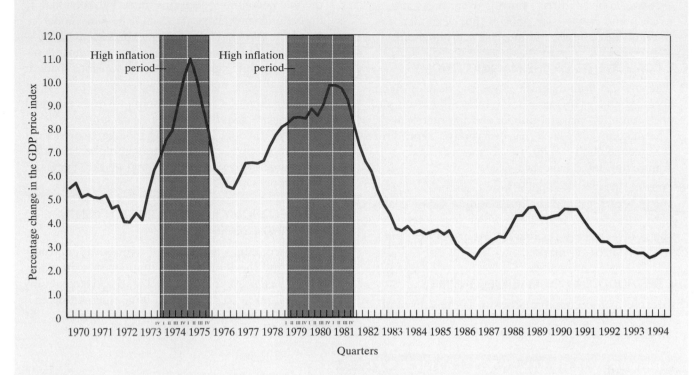

FIGURE 6.8

Percentage Change in the GDP Price Index (four-quarter average), 1970 I–1994 IV

The percentage change in the GDP price index measures the overall rate of inflation. Since 1970, inflation has been high in two periods: 1973 IV–1975 IV and 1979 I–1981 IV. Inflation since 1983 has been moderate.

SUMMARY

1. *Microeconomics* is the branch of economics that examines the functioning of individual industries and the behavior of individual decision-making units. *Macroeconomics* is concerned with the sum, or aggregate, of these individual decisions—the consumption of *all* households in the economy, the amount of labor supplied and demanded by *all* individuals and firms, the total amount of *all* goods and services produced.

THE ROOTS OF MACROECONOMICS

2. Macroeconomics was born out of the effort to explain the *Great Depression* of the 1930s. Since that time, the discipline has evolved, concerning itself with new issues as the problems facing the economy have changed. Through the late 1960s, it was believed that the government could "fine tune" the economy to keep it running on an even keel at all times. The poor economic performance of the 1970s, however, showed that *fine tuning* does not always work.

MACROECONOMIC CONCERNS

3. The four topics of primary concern to macroeconomists are increases in the overall price level, or *inflation;* the level of aggregate output in the economy; the level of aggregate employment and the rate of unemployment; and the interrelationships of the world's economies.

THE ROLE OF GOVERNMENT IN THE MACROECONOMY

4. Among the tools that governments have available to them for influencing the macroeconomy are *fiscal policy* (decisions on taxes and government spending); *monetary policy* (control of the money supply);

incomes policies (direct controls over wages and prices); and *supply-side policies* (policies that focus on aggregate supply and increasing production).

THE COMPONENTS OF THE MACROECONOMY

5. The *circular flow* diagram shows the flow of income received and payments made by the three sectors of the economy—private, public, and international. The diagram illustrates that everybody's expenditure is someone else's receipt. In other words, every transaction must have two sides.

6. Another way of looking at how households, firms, the government, and the international sector relate is to consider the markets in which they interact: the goods-and-services market, labor market, and money (financial) market.

THE METHODOLOGY OF MACROECONOMICS

7. Because macroeconomic behavior is the sum of all the microeconomic decisions made by individual households and firms, we cannot possibly understand the former without some knowledge of the factors that influence the latter. The movements of macroeconomic aggregates reflect decisions made by individual firms and households.

8. A major theme in macroeconomics is the behavior of *aggregate demand* and *aggregate supply*. However, the logic underlying the aggregate demand and supply curves is much more complex than the logic underlying simple individual market demand and supply curves.

THE U.S. ECONOMY IN THE TWENTIETH CENTURY: TRENDS AND CYCLES

9. Macroeconomics is concerned with both long-run trends and the short-run fluctuations that are part of the *business cycle*. Since 1970, the U.S. economy has seen three *recessions* and large fluctuations in the rate of *inflation*.

REVIEW TERMS AND CONCEPTS

aggregate behavior 120
aggregate demand 132
aggregate output 125
aggregate supply 133
business cycle 125
circular flow 128
contraction, recession, or **slump** 135
corporate bonds 131
depression 126
dividends 131

expansion or **boom** 135
fine tuning 122
fiscal policy 127
Great Depression 120
hyperinflation 125
incomes policy 128
inflation 125
macroeconomics 119
microeconomic foundations of macroeconomics 120
microeconomics 119

monetary policy 127
recession 126
shares of stock 131
stagflation 124
sticky prices 120
supply-side policy 128
transfer payments 128
Treasury bonds, notes, or **bills** 131
unemployment rate 126

PROBLEM SET

1. The economy was the number one issue during the 1992 presidential campaign. Most people believed that the economy was in recession. However, a careful look at the data shows that GDP stopped falling and began growing in the spring of 1991. In other words, the recession ended a full year and a half before the election. What was it about the economy that led the public to perceive things as so bad? In what ways do members of society actually benefit during a "recovery" from recession? (*Hint:* Think about the labor market.)

2. During 1995, the U.S. economy continued to recover from the recession of the early 1990s. However, different regions of the economy were growing at very different rates. The recession hit hardest in California and the Northeast, and the recovery was late in coming in those regions. California and Connecticut had very slow job growth right through 1994.

Describe the economy of your state. What is the most recently reported unemployment rate? How has the number of payroll jobs changed over the last three months? The last year? How does your state's performance compare to the U.S. economy's performance over the last year? What explanations have been offered in the press? How accurate are these?

3. Explain briefly how macroeconomics is different from microeconomics. How can macroeconomists use microeconomic theory to guide them in their work, and why might they wish to do so?

4. In 1994, a company paid its blue-collar employees $7.50 per hour but its white-collar employees only $5 per hour. It gave all employees a $1 raise in 1995, so that blue-collar employees were making $8.50 and white-collar employees $6 per hour. Yet the average wage paid to all employees in the company actually declined between 1994 and 1995. How is this possible? How does this question have anything to do with macroeconomics?

5. During 1993, when the economy was growing very slowly, President Clinton recommended a series of spending cuts and tax increases designed to reduce the deficit. These were passed by Congress in the Omnibus Budget Reconciliation Act of 1993. Some who opposed the bill argues that the United States was pursuing a "contractionary fiscal policy" at precisely the wrong time. Explain their logic.

6. Many of the expansionary periods during the twentieth century have occurred during wars. Why do you think this is true?

7. In the 1940s, one could buy a can of soda for 5¢, eat dinner at a restaurant for less than a dollar, and purchase a house for $10,000. From this statement, it follows that consumers today are worse off than consumers in the 1940s. Comment.

*8. During 1994 and 1995, the Federal Reserve became increasingly concerned with inflation. As the economy grew at a more and more rapid rate, the Fed acted to raise interest rates sharply. For example, the interest rate that home buyers had to pay on 30-year fixed-rate mortgages jumped from 7% to over 9%. This policy was designed to slow the rate of spending growth in the economy. How might higher interest rates be expected to slow the rate of spending growth? Give some examples.

national income and product accounts *Data collected and published by the government describing the various components of national income and output in the economy.*

Measuring National Output and National Income

Macroeconomics relies heavily on data, much of it collected by the government. To study the economy, we need data on total output, total income, total consumption, and the like. One of the main sources of these data are the **national income and product accounts,** which describe the various components of national income in the economy.

The national income and product accounts do more than just convey data about the performance of the economy. They also provide an important conceptual framework that macroeconomists use to think about how the various pieces of the economy fit together. When an economist thinks about the macroeconomy, the categories and vocabulary he or she uses come from the national income and product accounts.

The national income and product accounts can be compared to the mechanical or wiring diagrams for an automobile engine. The diagrams by themselves do not explain how an engine works, but they do identify and name the key parts of an engine and show how they are connected. Trying to understand the macroeconomy without having an understanding of national income accounting is like trying to fix an engine without a mechanical diagram and with no names for the engine parts.

GROSS DOMESTIC PRODUCT

The key concept in the national income and product accounts is **gross domestic product,** or **GDP.**

> GDP is the total market value of a country's output. More specifically, it is the market value of all final goods and services produced within a given period of time by factors of production located within a country.

U.S. GDP for 1994—in other words, the value of all the output produced by factors of production in the United States in 1994—was $6738.4 billion.

gross domestic product (GDP) *The total market value of all final goods and services produced within a given period by factors of production located within a country.*

FINAL GOODS AND SERVICES

The phrase *goods and services produced* in the definition of GDP refers to **final goods and services.** Many goods are **intermediate goods;** that is, they are produced by one firm for use in further processing by another firm. Tires sold to automobile manufacturers, for example, are intermediate goods. The value of intermediate goods is not counted in GDP.

Why aren't intermediate goods counted in GDP? Suppose that in producing a car GM pays $100 to Goodyear for tires. GM uses these tires (among other components) to assemble a car, which it then sells for $12,000. The value of the car (including its tires) is $12,000, not $12,000 + $100. In other words, the final price of the car already reflects the value of all its components. To count in GDP both the value of the tires sold to the automobile manufacturers and the value of the automobiles sold to the consumers would result in double counting.

Double counting can also be avoided by counting only the value added to a product by each firm in its production process. The **value added** during some stage of production is the difference between the value of goods as they leave that stage of production and the cost of the goods as they entered that stage. Value added is illustrated in Table 7.1. The four stages of the production of a gallon of gasoline are (1) oil drilling, (2) refining, (3) shipping, and (4) retail sale. In the first stage of production, value added is simply the value of sales. In the second stage, the refiner purchases the oil from the driller, refines it into gasoline, and sells it to the shipper. The refiner pays the driller $0.50 per gallon and charges the shipper $0.65. The value added by the refiner is thus $0.15 per gallon. The shipper then sells the gasoline to retailers for $0.80. The value added in the third stage of production is thus $0.15. Finally, the retailer sells the gasoline to consumers for $1.00. The value added at the fourth stage is $0.20, and the total value added in the production process is $1.00, the same as the value of sales at the retail level. Adding the total values of sales at each stage of production ($0.50 + $0.65 + $0.80 + $1.00 = $2.95) would significantly overestimate the value of the gallon of gasoline.

final goods and services *Goods and services produced for final use.*

intermediate goods *Goods that are produced by one firm for use in further processing by another firm.*

value added *The difference between the value of goods as they leave a stage of production and the cost of the goods as they entered that stage.*

TABLE 7.1	VALUE ADDED IN THE PRODUCTION OF A GALLON OF GASOLINE (HYPOTHETICAL NUMBERS)	
STAGE OF PRODUCTION	VALUE OF SALES	VALUE ADDED
(1) Oil drilling	$0.50	$0.50
(2) Refining	0.65	0.15
(3) Shipping	0.80	0.15
(4) Retail sale	1.00	0.20
Total value added		$1.00

As Table 7.2 shows, government purchases accounted for $1175.3 billion, or 17.4% of U.S. GDP in 1994. Federal government spending in 1994 accounted for 6.5% of GDP, and state and local government spending accounted for 11.0 percent.

net exports (EX − IM) *The difference between exports (sales to foreigners of U.S.-produced goods and services) and imports (U.S. purchases of goods and services from abroad). The figure can be positive or negative.*

■ **Net Exports (EX − IM)** The value of **net exports (EX − IM)** is the difference between *exports* (sales to foreigners of U.S.-produced goods and services) and *imports* (U.S. purchases of goods and services from abroad). This figure can be positive or negative. In 1994, the United States exported less than it imported; the level of net exports was thus negative (−$98.2 billion). Before 1976, the United States had generally been a net exporter. That is, exports exceeded imports, so the net export figure was positive.

The reason for including net exports in the definition of GDP is fairly simple. First, consumption, investment, and government spending (C, I, and G) include expenditures on goods produced both domestically and by foreigners. Therefore, C + I + G overstates domestic production because it contains expenditures on foreign-produced goods—that is, imports. Thus, imports (IM) have to be subtracted out of GDP to obtain the correct figure. At the same time, C + I + G understates domestic production because some of what a nation produces is sold abroad and is therefore not included in C, I, or G. Thus, exports (EX) have to be added in. For example, if a U.S. firm produces computers and sells them in Germany, the computers are clearly part of U.S. production and should thus be counted as part of U.S. GDP.

THE INCOME APPROACH

Table 7.3 presents the income approach to calculating GDP, which looks at GDP in terms of who receives it as income rather than in terms of who purchases it.

The income approach to GDP breaks down GDP into four components: national income, depreciation, indirect taxes minus subsidies, and net factor payments to the rest of the world:

GDP = National income + Depreciation + (Indirect taxes − Subsidies) + Net factor payments to the rest of the world.

TABLE 7.3	COMPONENTS OF GDP, 1994: THE INCOME APPROACH		
		BILLIONS OF DOLLARS	PERCENTAGE OF GDP
Gross Domestic Product		6738.4	100.0
National Income		5458.4	81.0
Compensation of employees		4004.6	59.4
Proprietors' income		473.7	7.0
Corporate profits		542.7	8.1
Net interest		409.7	6.1
Rental income		27.7	0.4
Depreciation		715.3	10.6
Indirect Taxes Minus Subsidies		553.1	8.2
Net Factor Payments to the Rest of the World		11.5	0.2

Source: See Table 7.2.

We examine each of these components in the sections that follow. As you proceed, keep in mind the cardinal rule that total expenditures always equal total income.

■ National Income **National income** is the total income earned by factors of production owned by a country's citizens. Table 7.3 shows that national income is the sum of five items: (1) compensation of employees, (2) proprietors' income, (3) corporate profits, (4) net interest, and (5) rental income. **Compensation of employees,** which is the largest of the five items by far, includes wages and salaries paid to households by firms and by the government, as well as various supplements to wages and salaries such as contributions that employers make to social insurance and private pension funds. **Proprietors' income** is the income of unincorporated businesses, and **corporate profits** are the income of corporate businesses. **Net interest** is the interest paid by business. (Interest paid by households and by the government is not counted in GDP because it is not assumed to flow from the production of goods and services.) Finally, **rental income,** a very minor item, is the income received by property owners in the form of rent.

■ Depreciation Recall from our discussion of net versus gross investment that when capital assets wear out or become obsolete, they decline in value. The measure of that decrease in value is called depreciation. This depreciation is a part of GDP in the income approach.

It may seem odd that we must *add* depreciation to national income when we calculate GDP by the income approach. But remember that we want a measure of *all* income, including income that results from the replacement of existing plant and equipment. Because national income does not include depreciation,[4] to get to total income (gross domestic product) we need to add depreciation. In 1994, depreciation accounted for $715.3 billion, or 10.6% of U.S. GDP.

■ Indirect Taxes Minus Subsidies The next income component in Table 7.3 is indirect taxes minus subsidies. In calculating final sales on the expenditures side, **indirect taxes**—sales taxes, customs duties, and license fees, for example—are included. These taxes must thus be accounted for on the income side.

A simple example will help to clarify this point. Suppose that the sales tax is 7% and that a firm sells 100,000 jellybeans for $100 plus tax. The total sales price is thus $107, and this is the value of output recorded in the expenditure approach to calculating GDP. Of this $107, $7 goes to pay the tax to the government, some goes to pay wages to the workers in the jellybean factory, and some goes to pay interest. The rest is the firm's profits plus depreciation.

To have the income and expenditure sides match, the sales tax must be recorded on the income side. If it were not included as part of income, then the basic rule that everyone's expenditure is someone else's income would be violated. Indirect taxes are an expenditure of the households or firms who buy things, but they are not income of firms that sell the products. (Thinking along these lines, indirect taxes can be considered income of the government.) We must thus add indirect taxes on the income side to make things balance.

Subsidies are payments made by the government for which it receives no goods or services in return. These subsidies are subtracted from national income to get GDP. (Remember that in the definition of GDP above is indirect taxes *minus* subsidies). For example, farmers receive substantial subsidies from the

---

national income *The total income earned by the factors of production owned by a country's citizens.*

compensation of employees *Includes wages, salaries, and various supplements—employer contri-butions to social insurance and pension funds, for example—paid to households by firms and by the government.*

proprietors' income *The income of unincorporated businesses.*

corporate profits *The income of corporate businesses.*

net interest *The interest paid by business.*

rental income *The income received by property owners in the form of rent.*

indirect taxes *Taxes like sales taxes, customs duties, and license fees.*

subsidies *Payments made by the government for which it receives no goods or services in return.*

---

[4]*The reason national income does not include depreciation is that depreciation has been subtracted from corporations' total revenue in computing the value of corporate profits, and the value of corporate profits is what is used in computing national income.*

government. Subsidy payments to farmers are income to farm proprietors and are thus part of national income, but they do not come from the sale of agricultural products and thus are not part of GDP. To balance the expenditure side with the income side, these subsidies must be subtracted on the income side.

■ **Net Factor Payments to the Rest of the World**   The last component in Table 7.3 is **net factor payments to the rest of the world,** which equals the payments of factor income (that is, income to the factors of production) to the rest of the world *minus* the receipts of factor income from the rest of the world. This item is added for the following reason. National income is defined as the income of factors of production *owned* by the country. GDP, however, is output produced by factors of production located *within* the country. In other words, national income includes some income that should not be counted in GDP—namely, the income a country's citizens earn abroad—and this income must be subtracted. In addition, national income does not include some income that is counted in GDP—namely, the foreigners' income in the country whose GDP we are calculating—and this income must be added. Table 7.3 shows that the value of net factor payments to the rest of the world was positive in 1994 ($11.5 billion). This means that U.S. payments of factor income to the rest of the world exceeded U.S. receipts of factor income from the rest of the world in 1994.

As you can see in Table 7.3, U.S. GDP as calculated by the income approach was $6738.4 billion in 1994—the same amount that we calculated by using the expenditure approach.

> **net factor payments to the rest of the world** *Payments of factor income to the rest of the world minus the receipt of factor income from the rest of the world.*

FROM GDP TO PERSONAL INCOME

Although GDP is the most important item in national income accounting, some other concepts are also useful to know. Some of these are presented in Table 7.4.

TABLE 7.4 GDP, GNP, NATIONAL INCOME, PERSONAL INCOME, AND DISPOSABLE PERSONAL INCOME, 1994	DOLLARS (BILLIONS)
GDP	6738.4
Plus: Receipts of factor income from the rest of the world	+167.1
Less: Payments of factor income to the rest of the world	−178.6
Equals: **GNP**	6726.9
Less: Depreciation	−715.3
Equals: **Net national product (NNP)**	6011.5
Less: Indirect taxes minus subsidies	−553.1
Equals: **National income**	5458.4
Less: Corporate profits minus dividends	−348.4
Less: Social insurance payments	−626.0
Plus: Personal interest income received from the government and consumers	+254.3
Plus: Transfer payments to persons	+963.4
Equals: **Personal income**	5701.7
Less: Personal taxes	−742.1
Equals: **Disposable personal income**	4959.6

Source: See Table 7.2.

The first part of Table 7.4 shows how GNP is calculated from GDP. Remember that a country's GDP is total production by factors of production located within that country, while its GNP is total production by factors of production owned by that country. If we take U.S. GDP, add to it factor income earned by U.S. citizens from the rest of the world (receipts of factor income from the rest of the world), and subtract from it factor income earned in the United States by foreigners (payments of factor income to the rest of the world), we get GNP.

From GNP, we can calculate net national product (NNP). Recall that the expenditure approach to GDP includes gross investment as one of the components of GDP (and of GNP). Gross domestic product does not, therefore, account for the fact that some of the nation's capital stock is used up in the process of producing the nation's product. **Net national product (NNP)** is gross national product minus depreciation. In a sense, it is a nation's total product minus (or "net of") what is required to maintain the value of its capital stock. Because GDP does not take into account any depreciation of the capital stock that may have occurred, NNP is sometimes a better measure of how the economy is doing than is GDP.

To calculate national income, we subtract indirect taxes minus subsidies from NNP (i.e., we subtract indirect business taxes and add subsidies). We subtract indirect taxes because they are included in NNP but do not represent payments to factors of production and are thus not part of national income. We add subsidies because they are payments to factors of production but are not included in NNP.

Personal income is the total income of households. To calculate personal income from national income, two items are subtracted: (1) corporate profits minus dividends, and (2) social insurance payments. Both of these items need some explanation. First, some corporate profits are paid to households in the form of dividends, and dividends are clearly part of personal income. The profits that remain after dividends are paid—corporate profits minus dividends —are not paid to households as income. Therefore, corporate profits minus dividends must be subtracted from national income when computing personal income. Second, social insurance payments are payments made to the government, some by firms and some by employees. Because these payments are not received by households, they too must be subtracted from national income when computing personal income.

In addition, two items must be added to national income to calculate personal income: (1) personal interest income received from the government and consumers, and (2) transfer payments to persons. As we have pointed out, interest payments made by the government and consumers (households) are not counted in GDP and thus are not reflected in national income figures.[5] But these payments are income received by households, so they must be added to national income when computing personal income.[6] Similarly, transfer payments to persons are not counted in GDP because they do not represent the production of any goods or

net national product (NNP) *Gross national product minus depreciation; a nation's total product minus what is required to maintain the value of its capital stock.*

personal income *The total income of households. Equals (national income) minus (corporate profits minus dividends) minus (social insurance payments) plus (interest income received from the government and households) plus (transfer payments to households). The income received by households after paying social insurance taxes but before paying personal income taxes.*

---

[5]*The reason that interest payments on government bonds are not included in national income, while interest payments on bonds of private firms are, is that government debt is assumed to be the result of activities, such as past wars, that do not add to current production. In contrast, it is presumed that firms sell bonds to finance investment that does add to current production. Similarly, interest payments by households are not included in national income because they are not considered to add to current production.*
[6]*Note that households can both pay and receive interest. As a group, households receive more interest than they pay.*

TABLE 7.5

DISPOSABLE PERSONAL INCOME AND PERSONAL SAVING, 1994

	DOLLARS (BILLIONS)
Disposable personal income	4959.6
Less:	
Personal consumption expenditures	−4628.4
Interest paid by consumers to business	−117.6
Personal transfer payments to foreigners	−10.5
Equals: **Personal saving**	203.1
Personal saving as a percentage of disposable personal income:	4.1%

Source: See Table 7.2.

services. But social security checks and other cash benefits are obviously income received by households, and they must therefore also be added to national income when computing personal income.

Personal income is the income received by households before paying personal income taxes but after paying social insurance contributions. The amount of income that households have to spend or save is called **disposable personal income,** or **after-tax income.** It is equal to personal income minus personal taxes.

disposable personal income or **after tax income** *Personal income minus personal income taxes. The amount that households have to spend or save.*

Because disposable personal income is the amount of income that households can spend or save, it is an important income concept. As Table 7.5 shows, there are three categories of spending: (1) personal consumption expenditures, (2) interest paid by consumers to business, and (3) personal transfer payments to foreigners. The amount of disposable personal income that is left after total personal spending is **personal saving.** For example, if your monthly disposable income is $500 and you spend $450 of it, you have $50 left over at the end of the month. Your personal saving is thus $50 for the month. Your personal saving level can be negative: If you earn $500 and spend $600 during the month, you have *dissaved* $100. In order to spend $100 more than you earn, of course, you will either have to borrow the $100 from someone, take the $100 from your savings account, or sell an asset that you own.

personal saving *The amount of disposable income that is left after total personal spending in a given period.*

The **personal saving rate** is the percentage of disposable personal income that is saved, and it is an important indicator of household behavior. A low saving rate means that households are spending a large amount of their income. A high saving rate means that households are cautious in their spending behavior. As Table 7.5 shows, the U.S. personal saving rate in 1994 was 4.1 percent. Saving rates tend to rise during recessionary periods, when consumers become anxious about their future, and fall during boom times, as pent-up spending demand gets released.

personal saving rate *The percentage of disposable personal income that is saved. If the personal saving rate is low, households are spending a large amount relative to their incomes; if it is high, households are spending cautiously.*

This completes our discussion of the various components of gross domestic product, gross national product, net national product, national income, and personal income. We now turn to another key concept, the distinction between nominal and real GDP. In the process, we will also discuss the aggregate price level and how it is measured.

NOMINAL VERSUS REAL GDP

current dollars *The current prices that one pays for goods and services.*

So far, we have looked at GDP measured in **current dollars,** or the current prices that one pays for things. When a variable is measured in current dollars, it is said to be described in *nominal terms.* **Nominal GDP** is thus GDP measured in current dollars—that is, with all components of GDP valued at their current prices.

nominal GDP *Gross domestic product measured in current dollars.*

In many applications of macroeconomics, nominal GDP is not a very desirable measure of production. Why is this so? Assume that there is only one good—say, pizza—produced in the economy. Suppose that in both years 1 and 2, 100 units (slices) of pizza were produced. Production thus remained the same for year 1 and year 2. But suppose that the price of pizza increased from $1.00 per slice in year 1 to $1.10 per slice in year 2. Nominal GDP in year 1 is thus $100 (100 units × $1.00 per unit), and nominal GDP in year 2 is $110 (100 units × $1.10 per unit). Nominal GDP has thus increased by $10, even though no more slices of pizza were produced. If we use nominal GDP to measure growth, we can be misled into thinking that production has grown when all that has really happened is a rise in the price level.

If there were only one good in the economy—again say, pizza—it would be easy to measure production and compare one year's value to another. We would just add up all the pizza slices produced each year. In the example in the previous paragraph, production is 100 in both years. If the number of slices had increased to 105 in year 2, we would simply say that production increased by five slices between year 1 and year 2, which is a 5% increase. But, of course, there is more than one good in the economy, so we must consider this case.

At the end of 1995, the Bureau of Economic Analysis (BEA) of the U.S. Department of Commerce—which produces the national income and product accounts—made a major change in the procedure that it uses to adjust nominal GDP for price changes. The new procedure has some important advantages over the older one, as we will see. To the extent that this change leads to improved measures of GDP, it can have significant and positive effects on policy decisions. The decisions of both monetary policy makers and fiscal policy makers are influenced by GDP growth, and improved measures of growth should lead to better decisions.

As you read the following discussion, keep in mind that the job of adjusting nominal GDP to account for price changes is not an easy one. Even in an economy of just apples and oranges, it would not be obvious how one could add up apples and oranges to get an overall measure of output. The BEA's task is to add up thousands of goods, each of whose price is changing over time.

Underlying our discussion is the concept of an **index.** To compute an index for a single variable, we first assign a given value to the index—usually 1 or 100—in a specified year, called the **base year.** Then from this base year the index changes by the same percentage as the variable itself changes. For example, if the variable is employment, the base year is 1987, and a value of 100 is assigned to the base year, the employment index would be 100 in 1987. If employment then grew by 3.5% in 1988, the employment index in 1988 would be 103.5. If instead employment had fallen by 1.0% in 1988, the employment index in 1988 would be 99.0.

index *A measure of a variable or group of variables.*

base year *In computing an index, the year in which the index is assigned a specified value—usually 1 or 100. In computing a fixed-weight index, the year chosen for the weights.*

An index, however, need not pertain to just one variable. Suppose that we had values on the quantities of apples and oranges produced and on their prices for a number of years. Suppose also that we are not interested in the individual quantities and prices of apples and oranges, but rather in the total quantity of fruit and in the overall price of fruit ("fruit" is taken here to be just apples and oranges). We cannot, as the saying goes, just add up apples and oranges, but we *can* construct fruit indexes. We can construct a fruit *quantity* index to measure the total quantity of fruit, and a fruit *price* index to measure the overall price of fruit. Both quantity and price indexes are explained in detail in the pages that follow: They can be constructed for any number of goods. If *all* goods and services in the economy are included, the quantity index is a quantity index for GDP and the price index is a GDP price index. A quantity index for GDP is an index of the total quantity of all goods and services produced in the economy. It is a measure of total "real" production, or "real" GDP.

weight *The importance attached to an item within a group of items.*

In computing indexes, we will use the concept of a **weight.** We will use price weights for quantity-index calculations and quantity weights for price-index calculations. What is a weight? It is easiest to define the term by way of an example. Suppose that in your economics course there is a final exam and two other tests. If the final exam counts for one half of the grade and the other two tests for one fourth each, the "weights" are simply one half, one fourth, and one fourth. If instead the final exam counts for 80% of the grade and the other two tests for 10% each, the weights are .8, .1, and .1. The more important an item is in a group, the larger its weight.

CALCULATING REAL GDP

All of the main issues involved in adjusting nominal GDP for price changes can be discussed using a simple three-good economy and two years. Table 7.6 presents all the data that we will need. The table presents price and quantity data for two years and three goods. The goods are labeled *A, B,* and *C,* and the years are labeled 1 and 2. *P* denotes price, and *Q* denotes quantity.

The first thing to note from Table 7.6 is that *nominal output*—output in current dollars—in year 1 for good *A* is the price of good *A* in year 1 ($.50) times the number of units of good *A* produced in year 1 (6), which is $3.00. Similarly, nominal output in year 1 is $7 \times \$.30 = \$2.10$ for good *B* and $10 \times \$.70 = \$7.00$ for good *C.* The sum of these three amounts, $12.10 in column 5, is nominal GDP in year 1 in this simple economy. Nominal GDP in year 2—calculated by using year 2's quantities and year 2's prices—is $19.20 (column 8). Nominal GDP has thus risen from $12.10 in year 1 to $19.20 in year 2, an increase of 58.7 percent.[7]

You can see from the table that the price of each good changed between year 1 and year 2—the price of good *A* fell (from $.50 to $.40) and the prices of goods *B* and *C* rose (*B* from $.30 to $1.00; *C* from $.70 to $.90). Some of the change in nominal GDP between years 1 and 2 is thus due to price changes and not production changes. How much can we attribute to price changes and how much to production changes? This is where things get tricky. The BEA's old procedure was to pick a base year and use the prices in that base year as weights to calculate a GDP quantity index for all years. This is called a **fixed-weight procedure** because the weights that are used, which are the prices, are the same for all years—namely, the prices that prevailed in the base year. It will be useful to consider carefully how

fixed-weight procedure *A procedure for computing an index that uses weights from a given base year.*

TABLE 7.6					A THREE-GOOD ECONOMY			
	(1)	(2)	(3)	(4)	(5) GDP IN YEAR 1 IN YEAR 1 PRICES $P_1 \times Q_1$	(6) GDP IN YEAR 2 IN YEAR 1 PRICES $P_1 \times Q_2$	(7) GDP IN YEAR 1 IN YEAR 2 PRICES $P_2 \times Q_1$	(8) GDP IN YEAR 2 IN YEAR 2 PRICES $P_2 \times Q_2$
	PRODUCTION		PRICE PER UNIT					
	YEAR 1 Q_1	YEAR 2 Q_2	YEAR 1 P_1	YEAR 2 P_2				
Good *A*	6	11	$.50	$.40	$3.00	$5.50	$2.40	$4.40
Good *B*	7	4	$.30	$1.00	$2.10	$1.20	$7.00	$4.00
Good *C*	10	12	$.70	$.90	$7.00	$8.40	$9.00	$10.80
Total					$12.10	$15.10	$18.40	$19.20

[7]*The percentage change is calculated as [(19.20 − 12.10)/12.10] × 100 = .587 × 100 = 58.7 percent.*

fixed-weight quantity indexes are constructed before considering the BEA's new procedure for constructing a GDP quantity index.

■ **Computing Quantity Indexes Using Fixed Price Weights** To construct a quantity index, we must first identify the specific quantities that we are concerned with—here the quantities of goods *A, B,* and *C* in Table 7.6. Assume that we want to construct an index of the quantities of these three goods. One method is to give all the goods an equal weight and just add up their individual quantities to get a quantity index of all goods. But this method assumes that all goods are of equal importance—clearly an unrealistic assumption. If one of the goods were boxes of salt and one were cars, we would *not* want to weight these two goods the same. If the economy produced ten boxes of salt and ten cars in year 1 and eight boxes of salt and 12 cars in year 2, we would not want to say that the total production of the economy was the same in the two years (20 units).

To take account of the relative importance of various goods in the construction of a quantity index, we need to look at the prices of the goods. Table 7.7 shows how to construct a fixed-weight quantity index for goods *A, B,* and *C,* first using prices in year 1 and then using prices in year 2. To summarize these calculations: If we take year 1 as the base year, Table 7.7 shows that the quantity index is 100.00 in year 1 and 124.79 in year 2. This is an increase in the quantity index of 24.79% from year 1 to year 2. If we take year 2 as the base year, the quantity

---

TABLE 7.7 **CONSTRUCTING A FIXED-WEIGHT QUANTITY INDEX** (PRICES AND QUANTITIES FROM TABLE 7.6)

BASE YEAR = YEAR 1

First: Calculate bundle quantities for both years, using prices for year 1

	GOOD A	GOOD B	GOOD C	
Year 1 { Prices in year 1	$.50	$.30	$.70	
Quantities in year 1	× 6	× 7	×10	Bundle
	$3.00 +	$2.10 +	$7.00 =	$12.10 quantity in year 1
Year 2 { Prices in year 1	$.50	$.30	$.70	
Quantities in year 2	×11	× 4	×12	Bundle
	$5.50 +	$1.20 +	$8.40 =	$15.10 quantity in year 2

Second: Determine quantity indexes for both years

$$\text{Quantity index in year 1} = \frac{\text{bundle quantity in year 1}}{\text{bundle quantity in base year}} \times 100 =$$

$$\frac{\$12.10}{\$12.10} \times 100 = 100.00$$

$$\text{Quantity index in year 2} = \frac{\text{bundle quantity in year 2}}{\text{bundle quantity in base year}} \times 100 =$$

$$\frac{\$15.10}{\$12.10} \times 100 = 124.79$$

Third: Determine the percentage change in the quantity index from year 1 to year 2

$$\text{Percentage change} = \left(\frac{\text{Year 2 index} - \text{Year 1 index}}{\text{Year 1 index}}\right) \times 100 =$$

$$\left(\frac{124.79 - 100.00}{100.00}\right) \times 100 = 24.79$$

The quantity index has increased 24.79% from year 1 to year 2.

BASE YEAR = YEAR 2

First: Calculate bundle quantities for both years, using prices for year 2

	GOOD A	GOOD B	GOOD C	
Year 1 { Prices in year 2	$.40	$1.00	$.90	
Quantities in year 1	× 6	× 7	×10	Bundle
	$2.40 +	$7.00 +	$9.00 =	$18.40 quantity in year 1
Year 2 { Prices in year 2	$.40	$1.00	$.90	
Quantities in year 2	×11	× 4	×12	Bundle
	$4.40 +	$4.00 +	$10.80 =	$19.20 quantity in year 2

Second: Determine quantity indexes for both years

$$\text{Quantity index in year 1} = \frac{\text{bundle quantity in year 1}}{\text{bundle quantity in base year}} \times 100 =$$

$$\frac{\$18.40}{\$18.40} \times 100 = 100.00$$

$$\text{Quantity index in year 2} = \frac{\text{bundle quantity in year 2}}{\text{bundle quantity in base year}} \times 100 =$$

$$\frac{\$19.20}{\$18.40} \times 100 = 104.35$$

Third: Determine the percentage change in the quantity index from year 1 to year 2

$$\text{Percentage change} = \left(\frac{\text{Year 2 index} - \text{Year 1 index}}{\text{Year 1 index}}\right) \times 100 =$$

$$\left(\frac{104.35 - 100.00}{100.00}\right) \times 100 = 4.35$$

The quantity index has increased 4.35% from year 1 to year 2.

index is 100.00 in year 1 and 104.35 in year 2. This is an increase in the quantity index of 4.35% from year 1 to year 2.

This example shows that quantity-index calculations can be sensitive to the choice of the base year. Using year 1 as the base year, the quantity index increases by 24.79% from year 1 to year 2; but using year 2 as the base year, the quantity index increases by only 4.35 percent.

■ **The Problems of Fixed Price Weights** In general, there are a number of problems with using fixed price weights to construct quantity indexes. For example, 1987 price weights, which were the last price weights the BEA used before it changed procedures, are not likely to be very accurate for, say, the 1950s. Many structural changes have taken place in the U.S. economy in the last 30 to 40 years, and it seems unlikely that 1987 prices are good weights to use for the 1950s.

Another problem is that the use of fixed price weights does not account for the responses in the economy to supply shifts. Say, for example, that bad weather leads to a lower production of oranges in year 2. In a simple supply and demand diagram for oranges, this corresponds to a shift of the supply curve to the left, which leads to an increase in the price of oranges and a decrease in the quantity demanded. As consumers move up the demand curve, they are substituting away from oranges. Conversely, if technical advances in year 2 result in cheaper ways of producing computers, the result is a shift of the computer supply curve to the right, which leads to a decrease in the price of computers and an increase in the quantity demanded. Consumers are substituting towards computers. (You should be able to draw supply-and-demand diagrams for both these cases.) Table 7.6 shows this tendency. The quantity of good *A* rose between years 1 and 2 and the price decreased (the computer case), whereas the quantity of good *B* fell and the price increased (the orange case). The computer supply curve has in fact been shifting to the right over time, due primarily to technical advances. The result has been large decreases in the price of computers and large increases in the quantity demanded.

To see why these responses pose a problem for the use of fixed price weights, consider the calculations in Table 7.7 again. Because the price of good *A* was higher in year 1, the increase in production of good *A* is weighted more if we use year 1 as the base year than it would be if we used year 2 as the base year. Also, because the price of good *B* was lower in year 1, the decrease in production of good *B* is weighted less if we use year 1 as the base year. These effects make the overall change in GDP larger if we use year 1 price weights than if we use year 2 price weights to calculate the GDP quantity index. Using year 1 price weights ignores the kinds of substitution responses discussed in the previous paragraph and thus leads to what many people feel are too-large estimates of GDP changes. In the past, the BEA tended to move the base year forward about every five years, resulting in the past estimates of GDP growth being revised downward. It is undesirable to have past growth estimates change simply because of the change to a new base year. (The last change in the base year was from 1982 to 1987.)

■ **The New Procedure** So what did the BEA do to improve its GDP estimates? It made two important changes.[8] To explain these changes, we will continue to use the three-good, two-year example in Table 7.6.

The first change was to split the difference between the use of the two possible base years. What does "splitting the difference" mean? Remember from Table 7.7 that the quantity index increased from year 1 to year 2 by 24.79% using year

[8]For a detailed discussion of the new procedure, see Allan H. Young, "Alternative Measures of Change in Real Output and Prices," Survey of Current Business, April 1992, 32-48, and Jack E. Triplett, "Economic Theory and BEA's Alternative Quantity and Price Indexes," Survey of Current Business, April 1992, 49-52. The authors are indebted to Jack Triplett of the BEA for helpful discussions on this material.

1 prices, but only by 4.35% using year 2 prices. One way to split the difference would be to take the simple average of these two numbers, which is 14.57 percent. What the BEA in fact did was to take what is called the *geometric* average, which for the current example is 14.11 percent.[9] The calculation of the new quantity index is presented in Table 7.8. The two averages (14.57% and 14.11%) are clearly quite close, and the use of either average would give similar results. The main point here is not that the geometric average was used, but that the first change was to split the difference using some average. Note that this procedure requires the use of two "base" years.

The second change was to use years 1 and 2 as the base years when computing the percentage change in the quantity index between years 1 and 2, then use years 2 and 3 as the base years when computing the percentage change in the quantity index between years 2 and 3, and so on. The two base years thus change as the calculations move through time. Once the percentage changes for a sequence of years are computed, they are "chained" together. In Table 7.8 the GDP quantity index is 100.00 in year 1 and 114.11 in year 2. Now say that between years 2 and 3 the percentage change in the quantity index is computed to be 6.50% (using years 2 and 3 as the base years and computing the geometric average as discussed above). The index for year 3 would then be a 6.50% change from 114.11, which gives an index for year 3 of 121.53 (114.11 × 1.065). Then the percentage change between years 3 and 4 for the index would be computed, and so on. The BEA calls the quantity index of GDP computed in this way the *chain-type annual weights quantity index of GDP*, which we will simply call **real GDP**.[10]

Once the GDP quantity index (which we are calling real GDP) has been created, it is easy to interpret. For example, if the value of the index is 100.00 in year 1 and 114.11 in year 2, we can say that real GDP increased by 14.11% from year 1 to year 2. If the value of the index is 121.53 in year 3, which is a 6.50% increase

real GDP *A measure of GDP that removes the effects of price changes from changes in nominal GDP.*

| TABLE 7.8 | COMPUTING A QUANTITY INDEX UNDER THE BEA'S NEW PROCEDURE |

First: Take the square root of the product of the two quantity indexes:

	QUANTITY INDEX BASE YEAR 1 (FROM TABLE 7.7)	×	QUANTITY INDEX BASE YEAR 2 (FROM TABLE 7.7)	=	PRODUCT	SQUARE ROOT OF THE PRODUCT IS THE NEW QUANTITY INDEX
Year 1	100.00	×	100.00	=	10,000.00	100.00
Year 2	124.79	×	104.35	=	13,021.84	114.11

Second: Determine the percentage change in the new quantity index from year 1 to year 2:

$$\text{Percentage change in quantity index} = \left(\frac{\text{Year 2 quantity index} - \text{Year 1 quantity index}}{\text{Year 1 quantity index}} \right) \times 100 = \frac{114.11 - 100.00}{100.00} \times 100 = 14.11$$

The quantity index has increased 14.11% from year 1 to year 2.

[9]*The geometric average of two numbers x and y is the square root of the product x × y. In the current example (see Table 22.7) x is 124.79 and y is 104.35. The square root of 124.59 × 104.35 is 114.11, which gives us 14.11 percent.*

[10]*The GDP data are in fact computed quarterly rather than just annually, and some modifications of the above discussion would be needed to handle the quarterly case. However, the basic points are the same, and it is unnecessary here to give the quarterly details.*

It should also be noted that the first change made by the BEA could have been done without the second change. One could, for example, use years 1 and 8 as base years in computing the percentage changes for each pair of years between 1 and 8. For example, the percentage change between years 1 and 2 would be based on price weights for years 1 and 8 and the quantity values for years 1 and 2. The BEA does in fact produce indexes like this, called benchmark-years weights indexes, *but the main focus is on the chain-type annual weights indexes.*

from 114.11, we can say that real GDP increased by 6.50% from year 2 to year 3. We can also say that real GDP increased by 21.53% over the two-year period—year 1 to year 3.

Clearly, the route to calculating real GDP is quite involved. If you were asked to define real GDP in a short phrase, you would be hard pressed to do so. Real GDP is a measure of output that attempts to adjust for price changes to allow comparisons of production across years, but you should be aware that this adjustment is quite complex. To define "real GDP," you must explain the steps that are used to construct the percentage changes from year to year.

It should also be stressed that there is no one "right" way of computing real GDP. The economy consists of many goods, each with its own price, and there is no exact way of adding together the production of different goods. What we *can* say is that the BEA's new procedure for computing real GDP avoids the problems associated with the use of fixed weights, and its seems clearly to be an improvement over the old procedure.

THE GDP PRICE INDEX

We now switch gears from quantity indexes to price indexes. One of economic policy makers' main goals is to keep changes in the overall price level small. For this reason policy makers need not only good measures of how real output is changing but also good measures of how the overall price level is changing. A measure of real output is real GDP, as discussed above. Is there also a measure of the overall price level? The answer is yes, but again it will take some discussion to get to it. Fortunately, we can continue to use Table 7.6 to discuss how price indexes are computed. The same issues that arose when we calculated quantity indexes also arise when we calculate price indexes.

Consider the price data in Table 7.6. The price of good *A* fell from $.50 in year 1 to $.40 in year 2; the price of good *B* rose from $.30 to $1.00; and the price of good *C* rose from $.70 to $.90. If we were interested only in how individual prices change, this is all the information we would need. But if we are interested in how the overall price level changes, we need to construct an index of all prices. The question of what weights to use arises here just as it did when we calculated quantity indexes. In calculating quantity indexes, the weights were prices, but in calculating price indexes, the weights are now quantities. Again, similar base-year issues arise.

■ **Computing Price Indexes Using Fixed Quantity Weights** Many of the price indexes that the government publishes are constructed using fixed weights. For this reason, it is useful to consider how fixed-weight price indexes are constructed before we consider the BEA's new procedure for constructing the GDP price index.

To construct a price index, we must first identify the specific set of prices that we are concerned with—here the prices of goods *A, B,* and *C* in Table 7.6. Assume that we want to construct an index of the prices of these three goods. One method is to give all goods an equal weight and just take the simple average of the individual prices to get a price index of all the goods. But this method assumes that all goods are of equal importance. If we were interested in constructing a price index that measures the cost of living, we would not want to assign equal weight to rent and pepper. Most of us spend a tiny fraction of our income on pepper, and even if the price of pepper were to quadruple, the change would have little impact on the cost of living. But many people spend a sizable portion of their income on rent, so a doubling of rents would have a major impact on the cost of living.

To take into account the relative importance of various goods, we need to look at the quantities produced of each good. Table 7.9 shows how to construct a fixed-weight price index for goods *A, B,* and *C,* first using quantities in year 1 and then using quantities in year 2. To summarize these calculations: If we take year 1 as the base year, Table 7.9 shows that the price index is 100.00 in year 1 and 152.07 in year 2. This is a 52.07% increase in the price index from year 1 to year 2. If we take year 2 as the base year, the price index is 100.00 in year 1 and 127.15 in year 2. This is a 27.15% increase in the price index from year 1 to year 2.

This example shows that price-index calculations can be sensitive to the choice of the base year. The percentage change in the price index from year 1 to year 2 is higher if we use year 1 as the base year (52.07%) than if we use year 2 (27.15 percent). This is because year 1 quantity weights do not take into account the economy's substitution toward good *A*, whose price dropped, and away from good *B*, whose price rose. Fixed-weight price index calculations suffer from the same problems we saw when we calculated a fixed-weight quantity index.

■ **The New Procedure**   Although the government still publishes fixed-weight price indexes (some of which we discuss in the next chapter), the BEA no longer uses a fixed-weight procedure to calculate price indexes for the national income and product accounts. The BEA made two changes from its prior fixed-weight procedure of computing a price index, just as it made two changes from its prior fixed-weight procedure of computing a quantity index. The first change was to split the difference using geometric averages. Table 7.10 shows how the new price index is calculated. As the table shows, the percentage change in the new index from year 1

TABLE 7.9	**CONSTRUCTING A FIXED-WEIGHT PRICE INDEX** (PRICES AND QUANTITIES FROM TABLE 7.6)

BASE YEAR = YEAR 1

First: Calculate bundle prices for both years, using quantities for year 1

		GOOD A	GOOD B	GOOD C	
Year 1	Prices in year 1	$.50	$.30	$.70	Bundle
	Quantities in year 1	× 6	× 7	×10	price in year 1
		$3.00 +	$2.10 +	$7.00 =	$12.10

Year 2	Prices in year 2	$.40	$1.00	$.90	Bundle
	Quantities in year 1	×6	× 7	×10	price in year 2
		$2.40 +	$7.00 +	$9.00 =	$18.40

Second: Determine price indexes for both years

Price index in year 1 = $\dfrac{\text{bundle price in year 1}}{\text{bundle price in base year}} \times 100 =$

$\dfrac{\$12.10}{\$12.10} \times 100 = 100.00$

Price index in year 2 = $\dfrac{\text{bundle price in year 2}}{\text{bundle price in base year}} \times 100 =$

$\dfrac{\$18.40}{\$12.10} \times 100 = 152.07$

Third: Determine the percentage change in the price index from year 1 to year 2

Percentage change = $\left(\dfrac{\text{Year 2 index} - \text{Year 1 index}}{\text{Year 1 index}}\right) \times 100 =$

$\left(\dfrac{152.07 - 100.00}{100.00}\right) \times 100 = 52.07$

The price index has increased 52.07% from year 1 to year 2.

BASE YEAR = YEAR 2

First: Calculate bundle prices for both years, using quantities for year 2

		GOOD A	GOOD B	GOOD C	
Year 1	Prices in year 1	$.50	$.30	$.70	Bundle
	Quantities in year 2	× 11	× 4	×2	price in year 1
		$5.50 +	$1.20 +	$8.40 =	$15.10

Year 2	Prices in year 2	$.40	$1.00	$.90	Bundle
	Quantities in year 2	×11	× 4	×12	price in year 2
		$4.40 +	$4.00 +	$10.80 =	$19.20

Second: Determine price indexes for both years

Price index in year 1 = $\dfrac{\text{bundle price in year 1}}{\text{bundle price in base year}} \times 100 =$

$\dfrac{\$15.10}{\$15.10} \times 100 = 100.00$

Price index in year 2 = $\dfrac{\text{bundle price in year 2}}{\text{bundle price in base year}} \times 100 =$

$\dfrac{\$19.20}{\$15.10} \times 100 = 127.15$

Third: Determine the percentage change in the price index from year 1 to year 2

Percentage change = $\left(\dfrac{\text{Year 2 index} - \text{Year 1 index}}{\text{Year 1 index}}\right) \times 100 =$

$\left(\dfrac{127.15 - 100.00}{100.00}\right) \times 100 = 27.15$

The price index has increased 27.15% from year 1 to year 2.

to year 2 is 39.05 percent. The second change is that the percentage changes in the price index are now chained together in the same way that the percentage changes in the quantity index are chained together. The BEA calls the price index of GDP computed in this way the *chain-type annual weights GDP price index,* which we will simply call the **GDP price index.**

GDP price index *A price index for GDP.*

Once the GDP price index has been created, it is easy to interpret. For example, if the value of the index is 100.00 in year 1 and 139.05 in year 2, we can say that the percentage change in the price index from year 1 to year 2 was 39.05 percent. If the index is 146.00 in year 3 (a 5.00% increase from year 2), we can say that the percentage change in the price index from year 2 to year 3 is 5.00 percent. We can also say that the percentage change in the price index over the two-year period—year 1 to year 3—was 46.00 percent.

As with the concept of real GDP, you have been led through a somewhat involved route to understanding what the GDP price index is and how it is calculated. In a loose sense, the GDP price index is a quantity-weighted average of the prices of all the goods in the economy, but you should be aware why this definition is loose: To define the GDP price index precisely, you must explain the steps that are used to construct the percentage changes from year to year.

As with real GDP, there is no one "right" way of computing a GDP price index, or any price index for that matter. In fact, as noted above, the government publishes many price indexes. Most of these indexes are based on the use of fixed quantity weights in a given base year. They thus do no take account of the substitution away from goods whose prices are increasing and toward goods whose prices are decreasing or increasing less rapidly. The GDP price index thus differs from most other price indexes because it does not use fixed weights. It is also a price index for all the goods and services produced in the economy. Other price indexes cover fewer goods and services.

CONSTANT DOLLARS AND THE ADDING-UP PROBLEM

In our discussion so far we have focused only on indexes and made no mention of dollars. Can anything "real" be measured in dollars? Under the BEA's old, fixed-weight procedure, it was possible to measure real variables in "constant" dollars. Because you will undoubtedly see older references to variables measured in constant dollars, it will be useful to explain how the BEA used the fixed-weight procedure to measure variables in constant dollars.

constant dollars *Dollars in a given base year. Used under the BEA's old procedure for computing real GDP.*

Column 6 of Table 7.6 shows that GDP in year 2 using year 1 prices is $15.10. In this case GDP is said to be in "year 1 dollars," or **constant dollars**— that is, dollars in a given base year. "Real GDP" here is GDP quoted in constant

| **TABLE 7.10** | | COMPUTING A PRICE INDEX UNDER THE BEA'S NEW PROCEDURE | | | |

First: Take the square root of the product of the two price indexes:

	PRICE INDEX BASE YEAR 1 (FROM TABLE 7.9)	×	PRICE INDEX BASE YEAR 2 (FROM TABLE 7.9)	=	PRODUCT	SQUARE ROOT OF THE PRODUCT IS THE NEW PRICE INDEX
Year 1	100.00	×	100.00	=	10,000.00	100.00
Year 2	152.07	×	127.15	=	19,335.70	139.05

Second: Determine the percentage change in the new price index from year 1 to year 2:

$$\text{Percentage change in price index} = \left(\frac{\text{Year 2 price index} - \text{Year 1 price index}}{\text{Year 1 price index}}\right) \times 100 = \frac{139.05 - 100.00}{100.00} \times 100 = 39.05$$

The price index has increased 39.05% from year 1 to year 2.

dollars, and it is measured without computing quantity indexes. However, we can measure GDP in constant dollars only by using fixed price weights (in this case, year 1 prices). Under the BEA's new procedure, in which the price weights are not fixed, there is no equivalent of column 6 in Table 7.6, and we cannot talk about constant dollars. In other words, the use of constant dollars is tied to the use of fixed price weights. This is why the BEA's new procedure features quantity indexes rather than variables in constant dollars. The last base year the BEA used before it switched procedures was 1987, and constant dollars in this case were 1987 dollars. All real variables were said to be in "1987 dollars."

Do any problems arise under the new procedure because constant dollars can no longer be used? There is one, which concerns the components of GDP. We know from earlier in this chapter that nominal GDP is the sum of nominal consumption, nominal investment, nominal government spending, and nominal net exports. Does this sum also hold for the real concepts? The answer is yes for the variables denominated in constant dollars under the old procedure, but no using the new procedure. Under the old procedure, the BEA could simply present each component in constant dollars and then add all the components together to get GDP in constant dollars. Under the new procedure, the BEA presents quantity indexes for the components, and quantity indexes cannot be added together.

Fortunately, this "adding-up problem" under the new procedure is not as serious as it might at first sound. Consider doing the following. First, take the price index for GDP for a given year computed the new way and divide the nominal value of GDP in that year by this price index.[11] Call the resulting value "real" GDP. Now do the same for each of the components of GDP—dividing the price index for each component computed the new way into the component's nominal value. Call the resulting value of each of the components the "real" value of the component. Finally, add up the "real" values of all the components: $SUM =$ "real" $C +$ "real" $I +$ "real" $G +$ "real" $(EX - IM)$.

It turns out in practice that the difference between the sum of the "real" values of the components, SUM, and the "real" value of GDP is fairly small as a percentage of GDP, and it changes in a fairly smooth way over time. For many practical purposes one can assume that the difference is small enough to be ignored, which is what we will do in the following chapters. In other words, we will assume that the GDP equation (GDP $= C + I + G + [EX - IM]$) holds in real terms. None of our analysis is affected by the fact that the difference is not exactly zero.

LIMITATIONS OF THE GDP CONCEPT

We generally think of increases in GDP as good. Indeed, increasing GDP (or preventing its decrease) is usually considered one of the chief goals of the government's macroeconomic policy. Because some serious problems arise when we try to use GDP as a measure of happiness or well-being, however, we now point out some of the limitations of the GDP concept as a measure of welfare.

GDP AND SOCIAL WELFARE

A decrease in crime clearly increases social welfare, but crime levels are not measured in GDP. If crime levels went down, society as a whole would be better off, but a decrease in crime is not an increase in output, and thus it is not reflected in GDP. Neither is an increase in leisure time. Yet, to the extent that households desire extra leisure time (rather than having it forced on them by a lack of jobs in the economy), an increase in leisure is also an increase in social welfare. Furthermore, some increases in social welfare are associated with a *decrease* in GDP. An increase

---

[11] *If the price index is 100 in the base year (rather than 1), it is divided by 100 first before being divided into nominal GDP.*

in leisure during a time of full employment, for example, leads to a decrease in GDP because less time is spent on producing output.

In addition, most nonmarket and domestic activities, such as housework and child care, are not counted in GDP even though they amount to real production. However, if I decide to send my children to day care or hire someone to clean my house or to drive my car for me, GDP increases. The salaries of day-care staff, cleaning people, and chauffeurs are counted in GDP, but the time I spend doing the same things is not counted. In other words, a mere change of institutional arrangements, even though no more output is being produced, can show up as a change in GDP.

Furthermore, GDP seldom reflects losses or social ills. GDP accounting rules do not adjust for production that pollutes the environment. The more production there is, the larger is GDP, regardless of how much pollution results in the process.

GDP also has nothing to say about the distribution of output among individuals in a society. It does not distinguish, for example, between the case in which most output goes to a few people and the case in which output is evenly divided among all people. One cannot use GDP to measure the effects of redistributive policies (which take income from some people and give income to others). Such policies have no direct impact on GDP. GDP is also neutral about the kinds of goods that an economy produces. Symphony performances, handguns, cigarettes, professional football games, Bibles, soda pop, milk, economics textbooks, and comic books all get counted, regardless of the different values that society might attach to them.

In spite of these limitations, GDP is still a highly useful measure of economic activity and well-being. If you doubt this assertion, answer this simple question: Would you rather live in the United States of 200 years ago, when rivers were less polluted and crime rates were probably lower, or in the United States of today? Most people would say that they prefer the present. Even with all the "negatives," GDP per person and the average standard of living are dramatically higher today than they were 200 years ago.

THE UNDERGROUND ECONOMY

Many transactions in the economy are simply missed in the calculation of GDP, even though in principle they should be counted. Most illegal transactions are missed unless they are "laundered" back into legitimate business. Income that is earned but not reported as income for tax purposes is usually missed, although some adjustments are made in the GDP calculations to take misreported income into account. The part of the economy that should be counted in GDP but is not is sometimes called the **underground economy.**

Tax evasion is usually thought to be the major incentive for people to participate in the underground economy. A number of studies have attempted to estimate the size of the U.S. underground economy, with estimates ranging from 5% to 30% of GDP.[12] While these figures may seem quite dramatic, the estimated size of the U.S. underground economy is comparable to the size of the underground economy in most European countries and is probably much smaller than the size of the underground economy in the Eastern European countries. Estimates of Italy's underground economy range from 10% to 35% of Italian GDP. At the lower end of the scale, estimates for Switzerland range from 3% to 5%.

---

underground economy *The part of the economy in which transactions take place and in which income is generated that is unreported and therefore not counted in GDP.*

TABLE 7.11	
PER CAPITA GNP FOR SELECTED COUNTRIES, 1993	
COUNTRY	**U.S. DOLLARS**
Switzerland	36,410
Japan	31,450
Denmark	26,510
Norway	26,340
Sweden	24,830
United States	24,750
Germany	23,560
Austria	23,120
France	22,360
Canada	20,670
Finland	18,970
United Kingdom	17,970
Australia	17,510
Israel	13,760
Spain	13,650
Portugal	7,890
Greece	7,390
Mexico	3,750
Chile	3,070
Botswana	2,590
Turkey	2,120
Jamaica	1,390
Jordan	1,190
Philippines	830
Bolivia	770
Indonesia	730
Egypt	660
Mali	300
Mozambique	80

Source: The World Bank Atlas, 1995.

---

[12]*See, for example, Edgar L. Feige, "Defining and Estimating Underground and Informal Economies: The New Industrial Economic Approach,"* World Development *19(7) (1990); and "The Underground Economy in the United States,"* Occasional Paper No. 2, U.S. Department of Labor, September 1992.

Why should we care about the underground economy? To the extent that GDP reflects only a part of economic activity rather than being a complete measure of what the economy produces, it is obviously misleading. Unemployment rates, for example, may be lower than officially measured if people work in the underground economy without reporting this fact to the government. Also, if the size of the underground economy varies between countries—as it certainly does—we can be misled when we compare GDP between countries. For example, Italy's GDP would be much higher if we considered its underground sector as part of the economy, while Switzerland's GDP would change very little.

PER CAPITA GDP/GNP

GDP and GNP are sometimes measured in per capita terms. **Per capita GDP or GNP** is simply a country's GDP or GNP divided by its population. It is a better measure of well-being for the average person than is total GDP or GNP. Table 7.11 lists the per capita GNP of various countries for 1993. Switzerland is the country with the highest per capita GNP, followed next by Japan, Denmark, and Norway. These four countries plus four other European countries, Canada, and the United States had per capita GNP values over $20,000 in 1993.

In some countries, the only way to purchase consumer goods may be the underground market. Here, Russian consumers buy appliances from the back of a truck.

per capita GDP or **GNP** *A country's GDP or GNP divided by its population.*

LOOKING AHEAD

This chapter has introduced you to many of the key variables that macroeconomists are interested in, including GDP and its various components. There is, however, much more to be learned regarding the main data that macroeconomists use. In the next chapter we discuss the data on employment, unemployment, and the labor force, and in Chapters 11 and 12 we discuss the data on money and interest rates. Finally, in Chapter 22 we discuss in more detail the data on the relationship between the United States and the rest of the world.

SUMMARY

1. One of the main sources of data on the key variables in the macroeconomy are the national income and product accounts. These accounts provide an important conceptual framework that macroeconomists use to think about how the various pieces of the economy fit together.

GROSS DOMESTIC PRODUCT

2. *Gross domestic product (GDP)* is the key concept in national income accounting. GDP is the total market value of all final goods and services produced within a given period by factors of production located within a country. GDP excludes intermediate goods, because to include goods both when they are purchased as inputs and when they are sold as final products would be double counting and thus an overstatement of the value of production.

3. GDP excludes all transactions in which money or goods change hands but in which no new goods and services are produced. GDP includes the income of foreigners working in the United States and the profits that foreign companies earn in the United States. GDP excludes the income of U.S. citizens working abroad and profits earned by U.S. companies in foreign countries.

4. *Gross national product (GNP)* is the market value of all final goods and services produced during a given period by factors of production owned by a country's citizens.

CALCULATING GDP

5. The *expenditure approach* to computing GDP adds up the amount spent on all final goods and services during a given period. The four main categories of expenditures are *personal consumption expenditures (C), gross private domestic investment (I), government purchases of goods and services (G),* and *net exports (EX − IM)*. The sum of these four equals GDP.

6. The three main components of personal consumption expenditures (C) are *durable goods, nondurable goods,* and *services*.

7. *Gross private domestic investment (I)* is the total investment made by the private sector in a given period of time. There are three kinds of investment: *nonresidential investment, residential investment,* and *changes in business inventories*. Gross investment does not take *depreciation*—the decrease in the value of assets—into account. *Net investment* is equal to gross investment minus depreciation.

8. Government purchases of goods and services (G) include expenditures by state, federal, and local governments for final goods and labor. The value of *net exports (EX − IM)* equals the differences between exports (sales to foreigners of U.S.-produced goods and services) and imports (U.S. purchases of goods and services from abroad).

9. Because every payment (expenditure) by a buyer is at the same time a receipt (income) for the seller, GDP can also be computed in terms of who receives it as income. This is the *income approach* to calculating gross domestic product. The GDP equation using the income approach is GDP = National income + Depreciation + (Indirect taxes − Subsidies) + Net factor payments to the rest of the world.

FROM GDP TO PERSONAL INCOME

10. GNP minus depreciation is known as *net national product* (NNP). *National income* is the total amount earned by the factors of production in the economy; it is equal to NNP less indirect taxes minus subsidies. *Personal income* is the total income of households. *Disposable personal income* is what households have to spend or save after paying their taxes. The *personal saving rate* is the percentage of disposable personal income that is saved rather than spent.

NOMINAL VERSUS REAL GDP

11. GDP that is measured in current dollars (the current prices that one pays for goods) is called *nominal GDP*. If we use nominal GDP to measure growth, we can be misled into thinking that production has grown when all that has really happened is a rise in the price level, or inflation. A better measure of production is *real GDP*, which is nominal GDP adjusted for prices changes.

12. The GDP price index is a measure of the overall price level.

LIMITATIONS OF THE GDP CONCEPT

13. We generally think of increases in GDP as good, but some problems arise when we try to use GDP as a measure of happiness or well-being. The peculiarities of GDP accounting mean that institutional changes can change the value of GDP even if real production has not changed. GDP ignores most social ills, such as pollution. Furthermore, GDP tells us nothing about what kinds of goods are being produced or how income is distributed across the population. GDP also ignores many transactions of the underground economy.

14. *Per capita GDP or GNP* is a country's GDP or GNP divided by its population. Per capita GDP or GNP is a better measure of well-being for the average person than is total GDP or GNP.

REVIEW TERMS AND CONCEPTS

base year 155

change in business inventories 147

compensation of employees 151

constant dollars 162

corporate profits 151

current dollars 154

depreciation 149

disposable personal income, or after-tax, income 154

durable goods 147

expenditure approach 145

Equations:

Expenditure approach to GDP: $GDP = C + I + G + (EX - IM)$

$GDP = $ Final sales $+$ GDP $-$ Change in business inventories

Net investment $=$ Capital end of period $-$ Capital beginning of period

Income approach to GDP: GDP $=$ National income $+$ Depreciation $+$ (Indirect taxes $-$ Subsidies) $+$ Net factor payments to the rest of the world

PROBLEM SET

1. From the table (below and right), calculate the following:
   a. Gross private investment
   b. Net exports
   c. Gross domestic product
   d. Gross national product
   e. Net national product
   f. National income
   g. Personal income
   h. Disposable income

Transfer payments	15
Subsidies	5
Social insurance payments	35
Depreciation	50
Receipts of factor income from the rest of the world	4
Government purchases	75
Imports	50
Payments of factor income to the rest of the world	5
Personal interest income from government and households	35
Indirect taxes	20

Exports	60
Net private domestic investment	100
Personal taxes	60
Corporate profits	45
Personal consumption expenditures	250
Dividends	4

2. How do we know that calculating GDP by the expenditure approach yields the same answer as calculating GDP by the income approach?

3. Why do we bother to construct real GDP if we already know nominal GDP?

4. Consider the following data for the country of Fruitopia:

	Production (in number of units)		Price per unit (in units of currency)	
	1994	1995	1994	1995
Apples	10	20	10	10
Oranges	5	8	10	12
Peaches	20	15	5	10

For parts a through f set all indexes for 1994 at 100.

    a. Construct values of the fixed-weight quantity index for 1994 and 1995, using 1994 as the base year. What is the percentage change in this quantity index?

    b. Construct values of the fixed-weight quantity index for 1994 and 1995, using 1995 as the base year. What is the percentage change in this quantity index?

    c. Construct values of the fixed-weight price index for 1994 and 1995, using 1994 as the base year. What is the percentage change in this price index?

    d. Construct values of the fixed-weight price index for 1994 and 1995, using 1995 as the base year. What is the percentage change in this price index?

    e. Construct values of the quantity index for 1994 and 1995, using the BEA's new procedure. What is the percentage change in this new quantity index from 1994 to 1995?

    f. Construct values of the price index for 1994 and 1995, using the BEA's new procedure. What is the percentage change in this new price index from 1994 to 1995?

    g. What are some of the problems of fixed-weight indexes? How do the questions in parts a-f of this problem demonstrate them? How does the BEA's approach to quantity and price indexes attempt to solve these problems?

5. Explain what double counting is and discuss why GDP is not equal to total sales.

6. Consider the economy of Junk Food City:

	Production (in number of units)			Price per unit (in units of currency)		
	1994	1995	1996	1994	1995	1996
Cookies	200	300	250	1	1.5	2.5
Chips	200	300	400	1	2	2

For both parts a and b set indexes equal to 100 in 1994.

    a. Calculate the BEA's new quantity index for Junk Food City for each year. What is the percentage change in this index between 1994 and 1995? Between 1995 and 1996? Between 1994 and 1996?

    b. Calculate the BEA's new price index for each year. What is the percentage change in the index between 1994 and 1995? Between 1995 and 1996? Between 1994 and 1996?

7. Which of the following transactions would not be counted in GDP? Explain your answers.

    a. General Motors issues new shares of stock to finance the construction of a plant.

    b. General Motors builds a new plant.

    c. Company A successfully launches a hostile takeover of Company B, in which it purchases all the assets of Company B.

    d. Your grandmother wins $10 million in the state lottery.

    e. You buy a new copy of this textbook.

    f. You rent your copy of this textbook to your roommate for a semester.

    g. The government pays out social security.

    h. A public utility installs new antipollution equipment in its smokestacks.

    i. Luigi's Pizza buys 30 pounds of mozzarella cheese, holds it in inventory for one month, and then uses it to make pizza, which it sells.

    j. You spend the entire weekend cleaning your apartment.

    k. A drug dealer sells $500 worth of illegal drugs.

8. If you buy a new car, the entire purchase is counted as consumption in the year in which you make the transaction. Explain briefly why this is in one sense an "error" in national income accounting. (*Hint:* How is the purchase of a car different from the purchase of a pizza?) How might you correct this error?

9. Explain why imports are subtracted in the expenditure approach to calculating GDP.

10. GDP calculations do not directly include the economic costs of environmental damage (for example, global warming, acid rain). Do you think these costs should be included in GDP? Why or why not? How could GDP be amended to include environmental damage costs?

MACROECONOMIC PROBLEMS: UNEMPLOYMENT AND INFLATION

SOMETIME DURING 1990, TOTAL EMPLOYMENT IN THE UNITED STATES stopped growing and began to decline. In May of that year, total employment hit 119.9 million. By October, more than 500,000 people had lost their jobs, and by March 1991, more than 1.5 million people had lost their jobs. At the same time, after nearly eight years of steady growth, real output declined in the third and fourth quarters of 1990 and the first quarter of 1991. For many, this recession was a curiosity, something to read about in the newspaper. After all, about 118.5 million out of 120 million workers still had their jobs. But for the workers who lost their jobs, the pain was real:

> Standing in the unemployment line today, a cross section of Americans from a beautician to a film editor to a sales manager to a corporate vice president, voiced a shared sense of insecurity about the future as jobs disappear and companies close. They said their hunt for work had taken on new urgency as they watched the economy worsen and opportunities dry up. Gathered at an unemployment office in west Los Angeles, they listened with a very personal concern to the news that the unemployment rate in California had climbed today to its highest point in four years.
>
> "The hardest thing is to see how panicked people are," said Bill Williams, a part owner of a small marketing company in Huntington Beach that recently went out of business. "Right now I don't have a dime. I'm worried about buying things like sugar. I'm close to losing my home."[1]

---

[1]Seth Mydans, "For Jobless, Era of Plenty Fades to Fear," The New York Times, *December 8, 1990, p. 1.*

By 1995, the recession of 1990–1991 was far behind. Millions of jobs had been created as the economy expanded, at first slowly in 1991 and 1992, but at an increasingly rapid rate in 1993 and 1994. By late 1994, employment had reached over 122 million and the number of unemployed had dropped by 2.2 million. As unemployment dropped, the nation's attention shifted to another problem: inflation. Business sections of the nation's leading newspapers began to focus on prices:

> With unemployment falling most places and every region of the American economy growing, manufacturers are beginning to raise prices, the Federal Reserve said in a report released today. . . . Federal Reserve officials have been worried that rapid economic growth could lead to shortages of materials and skilled workers, pushing up prices and inflation.[2]

Fifteen years earlier, the United States had wrestled with high inflation. Prices *increased* an average of 11.3% in 1979 and 13.5% in 1980. As President Jimmy Carter noted in a report to Congress in January 1980:

> It is my strong conviction that inflation remains the nation's number one economic problem. Energy and housing prices are still moving up rapidly, adding directly to inflation and continuing to threaten a new price-wage spiral in the rest of the economy. Our immediate objective must be to prevent the spread of double-digit price increases from oil to the rest of economy. . . . Halting the spread of inflation is not enough, however. We must take steps to reduce it.[3]

These "twin evils" of unemployment and inflation are two of the chief concerns of macroeconomists. In this chapter we explore these concerns in more detail, describing the periodic ups and downs in the economy that we call the business cycle. Later chapters focus on the likely causes of business cycles and some of the things that government may do to prevent or minimize the damage they create. First, however, we need to know a little bit more about what the business cycle is. What are recessions and depressions? Who is hurt by them? What are the consequences of inflation? Who benefits and who loses when the price level rises rapidly? Why should policy makers in Washington be concerned about the business cycle?

RECESSIONS, DEPRESSIONS, AND UNEMPLOYMENT

recession *Roughly, a period in which real GDP declines for at least two consecutive quarters. Marked by falling output and rising unemployment.*

Recall that a **recession** is roughly a period in which real GDP declines for at least two consecutive quarters. Also recall that real GDP is a measure of the actual output of goods and services in the economy during a given period of time. Thus, when real GDP falls, less is being produced. When less output is produced, fewer inputs are used, employment declines, the unemployment rate rises, and a smaller percentage of the capital stock at our disposal is utilized (that is, more plants and equipment are running at less than full capacity). When real output falls, real income declines.

depression *A prolonged and deep recession. The precise definitions of prolonged and deep are debatable.*

A **depression** is a prolonged and deep recession, although there is much disagreement over how severe and how prolonged a recession must be in order to be called a depression. Nearly everyone agrees that the U.S. economy experienced a depression between 1929 and the late 1930s. The most severe recession since the 1930s took place between 1980 and 1982.

In Figure 6.6, we divided the period since 1970 into three "recessionary" periods, 1974–1975, 1980–1982, and 1990–1991. Table 8.1 summarizes some of the differences between the recession of 1980–1982 and the early part of the Great Depression. Between 1929 and 1933, real GDP declined by almost 30 percent. In

---

[2]Keith Bradsher, *"Fed Report Said to Point to Rate Rise,"* The New York Times, *November 3, 1994, p. D1.*
[3]*Jimmy Carter,* Economic Report of the President, *transmitted to Congress, January 1980.*

TABLE 8.1	REAL GDP AND UNEMPLOYMENT RATES, 1929–1933 AND 1980–1982

THE EARLY PART OF THE GREAT DEPRESSION, 1929–1933

	PERCENTAGE CHANGE IN REAL GDP	UNEMPLOYMENT RATE	NUMBER OF UNEMPLOYED (MILLIONS)
1929		3.2	1.5
1930	−9.4	8.9	4.3
1931	−8.6	16.3	8.0
1932	−13.4	24.1	12.1
1933	−2.1	25.2	12.8

Note: Percentage fall in real GDP between 1929 and 1933 was 29.8 percent.

THE RECESSION OF 1980–1982

	PERCENTAGE CHANGE IN REAL GDP	UNEMPLOYMENT RATE	NUMBER OF UNEMPLOYED (MILLIONS)	CAPACITY UTILIZATION (PERCENTAGE)
1979		5.8	6.1	85.2
1980	−0.2	7.1	7.6	80.9
1981	2.5	7.6	8.3	79.9
1982	−2.3	9.7	10.7	72.1

Note: Percentage change in real GDP between 1979 and 1982 was 0.0 percent.

Sources: Historical Statistics of the United States and U.S. Department of Commerce, Bureau of Economic Analysis.

other words, in 1933 the United States produced 30% less than it had in 1929. While only 3.2% of the labor force was unemployed in 1929, 25.2% was unemployed in 1933. By contrast, during the recession of 1980–1982, the growth rate of real GDP on average was just zero. The unemployment rate rose from 5.8% in 1979 to 9.7% in 1982. *Capacity utilization rates,* which show the percentage of factory capacity being used in production, are not available for the 1930s, so we have no point of comparison. However, Table 8.1 does show that capacity utilization fell from 85.2% in 1979 to 72.1% in 1982. Clearly, although the recession in the early 1980s was severe, it did not come close to the severity of the Great Depression.

DEFINING AND MEASURING UNEMPLOYMENT

The most frequently discussed symptom of a recession is unemployment. In September of 1982, the United States' unemployment rate was over 10% for the first time since the 1930s. But although unemployment is widely discussed, most people are unaware of what unemployment statistics mean or how they are derived.

The unemployment statistics released to the press on the first Friday of each month are based on a survey of households conducted by the Bureau of Labor Statistics (BLS), a branch of the Department of Labor. Each month the BLS draws a sample of 65,000 households and completes interviews with all but about 2,500 of them. Each interviewed household answers questions regarding the work activity of household members 16 years of age or older during the calendar week that contains the twelfth of the month. (The survey is conducted in the week that follows the week that contains the twelfth of the month.)

employed *Any person 16 years old or older (1) who works for pay, either for someone else or in his or her own business for one or more hours per week, (2) who works without pay for 15 or more hours per week in a family enterprise, or (3) who has a job but has been temporarily absent, with or without pay.*

unemployed *A person 16 years old or older who is not working, is available for work, and has made specific efforts to find work during the previous four weeks.*

not in the labor force *People who are not looking for work, either because they do not want a job or because they have given up looking.*

labor force *The number of people employed plus the number of unemployed.*

unemployment rate *The ratio of the number of people unemployed to the total number of people in the labor force.*

If a household member 16 years of age or older worked one hour or more as a paid employee, either for someone else or in his or her own business or farm, that person is classified as **employed.** A household member is also considered employed if he or she worked 15 hours or more without pay in a family enterprise. Finally, a household member is counted as employed if he or she held a job from which he or she was temporarily absent due to illness, bad weather, vacation, labor-management disputes, or personal reasons, whether that person was paid or not.

Those who are not employed fall into one of two categories: (1) unemployed or (2) not in the labor force. To be considered **unemployed,** a person must be available for work and have made specific efforts to find work during the previous four weeks. Persons who are not looking for work, either because they do not want a job or because they have given up looking, are classified as **not in the labor force.** People not in the labor force include full-time students, retirees, individuals in institutions, and those staying home to take care of children or elderly parents.

The total **labor force** in the economy is the number of people employed plus the number of unemployed:

$$\text{Labor force} = \text{Employed} + \text{Unemployed}$$

The total population 16 years of age or older is equal to the number of people in the labor force plus the number not in the labor force:

$$\text{Population} = \text{Labor force} + \text{Not in labor force}$$

With these numbers, several ratios can be calculated. The **unemployment rate** is the ratio of the number of people unemployed to the total number of people in the labor force:

$$\text{Unemployment rate} = \frac{\text{Unemployed}}{\text{Employed} + \text{Unemployed}}$$

In January 1995, the labor force contained 133.9 million people, 126.4 million of whom were employed and 7.5 million of whom were looking for work. The unemployment rate was thus 5.6 percent:

$$\frac{7.5}{126.4 + 7.5} = 5.6\%$$

The ratio of the labor force to the population 16 years old or over is called the **labor-force participation rate:**

labor-force participation rate *The ratio of the labor force to the total population 16 years old or older*

$$\text{Labor-force participation rate} = \frac{\text{Labor force}}{\text{Population}}$$

Table 8.2 shows the relationship among these numbers for selected years since 1953. The year 1982 has been added to show the effects of the recession. Although the unemployment rate has gone up and down, the labor-force participation rate has grown steadily since 1953. Most of this increase is due to the growth in the participation rate of women between the ages of 25 and 54.

Looking at column 3 in Table 8.2, you can see how many new workers the U.S. economy has managed to absorb in recent years. The number of employed workers increased by nearly 38 million between 1953 and 1982 and by nearly 24 million between 1982 and 1994.

TABLE 8.2		EMPLOYED, UNEMPLOYED, AND THE LABOR FORCE, 1953–1994				
	(1) POPULATION 16 YEARS OLD OR OVER (MILLIONS)	(2) LABOR FORCE (MILLIONS)	(3) EMPLOYED (MILLIONS)	(4) UNEMPLOYED (MILLIONS)	(5) LABOR-FORCE PARTICIPATION RATE	(6) UNEMPLOYMENT RATE
1953	109.3	65.2	63.4	1.8	59.7	2.8
1960	119.1	71.5	67.6	3.9	60.0	5.5
1970	139.2	84.9	80.8	4.1	61.0	4.8
1980	169.3	108.5	100.9	7.6	64.1	7.0
1982	173.9	111.9	101.2	10.7	64.3	9.6
1994	198.6	132.8	124.8	8.0	66.9	6.0

Source: U.S. Department of Labor, Bureau of Labor Statistics.

COMPONENTS OF THE UNEMPLOYMENT RATE

Because the unemployment rate is a single number, it can convey only a limited amount of information. To understand the level of unemployment better, we must look at unemployment rates across groups of people, regions, and industries.

■ **Unemployment Rates for Different Demographic Groups**   Marked differences in rates of unemployment exist across demographic groups. Table 8.3 shows the unemployment rate for November 1982—the worst month of the recession in 1982— and for January 1995, broken down by race, sex, and age. In November 1982, when the overall unemployment rate hit 10.8%, the rate for whites stood at 9.2%, while the rate for blacks stood at more than twice that level—19.5 percent.

During the recession in 1982, men fared worse than women. In November 1982, 9.5% of all white men, but only 8.9% of all white women, were unemployed. For blacks, 21% of black men and 17.9% of black women were unemployed. Teenagers between 16 and 19 years of age fared worst. Black men between 16 and 19 experienced an unemployment rate of 54.9% in 1982. The figure was nearly as high (46.9%) for black women in the same age bracket.

While the rates were much lower for all groups in January 1995, the pattern was similar. The highest unemployment rates were for black teenagers—34.0% for black men and 37.1% for black women. Among both blacks and whites 20 years and over, the January 1995 unemployment rate for women was slightly lower than the rate for men.

The main point of Table 8.3 is that an unemployment rate of 5.6% does not mean that every group in society has a 5.6% unemployment rate. In fact,

There are large differences in unemployment rates across demographic groups.

■ **Unemployment Rates in States and Regions**   Unemployment rates vary by geographical location. For a variety of reasons, not all states and regions have the same level of unemployment. For one thing, states and regions have different combinations of industries, which do not all grow and decline at the same time and at the same rate. For another, the labor force is not completely mobile—that is, workers often cannot or do not want to pack up and move to take advantage of job opportunities in other parts of the country.

The last 20 years have seen remarkable changes in the relative prosperity of regions. None have been quite as dramatic as the changing fortunes of the Northeast

TABLE 8.3			
UNEMPLOYMENT RATES BY DEMOGRAPHIC GROUP, 1982 AND 1995			
		NOV. 1982	JAN. 1995
TOTAL		10.8	5.6
WHITE		9.2	4.9
Men	20+ Yrs.	9.5	4.4
	16–19 Yrs.	24.1	15.0
Women	20+ Yrs.	8.9	4.3
	16–19 Yrs.	19.5	13.1
BLACK		19.5	10.2
Men	20+ Yrs.	21.0	9.2
	16–19 Yrs.	54.9	34.0
Women	20+ Yrs.	17.9	8.5
	16–19 Yrs.	46.9	37.1

Source: U.S. Department of Labor, Bureau of Labor Statistics.

TABLE 8.4

REGIONAL DIFFERENCES IN UNEMPLOYMENT, 1975, 1982, AND 1991

	1975	1982	1991
U.S. avg.	8.5	9.7	6.7
Cal.	9.9	9.9	7.5
Fla.	10.7	8.2	7.3
Ill.	7.1	11.3	7.1
Mass.	11.2	7.9	9.0
Mich.	12.5	15.5	9.2
N.J.	10.2	9.0	6.6
N.Y.	9.5	8.6	7.2
N.C.	8.6	9.0	5.8
Ohio	9.1	12.5	6.4
Tex.	5.6	6.9	6.6

Sources: Statistical Abstract of the United States, various editions.

and the oil-rich Southwest. During the early 1970s, the Northeast (and New England in particular) was hit by a serious decline in its industrial base. Textile mills, leather goods plants, and furniture factories closed up in the face of foreign competition or moved south to states with lower wages. During the recession of 1975, Massachusetts and Michigan had very high unemployment rates (11.2% and 12.5% respectively). Riding the crest of rising oil prices, Texas had one of the lowest unemployment rates at that time (5.6%) (Table 8.4).

During the recession of 1982, Texas continued to do well, and the fortunes of Massachusetts took a sharp turn for the better. In fact, the unemployment rate in Massachusetts went from nearly three points above the national average during the 1975 recession to nearly two points below the national average during the 1982 recession.

By 1987, things had changed dramatically. Although not shown in Table 8.4, Massachusetts had one of the lowest unemployment rates in the country in 1987 (an amazing 2.8%) and Texas (at 8.5%) had one of the highest. In Massachusetts, high-technology firms such as Wang Laboratories and Digital Equipment, two firms that employed a total of over 100,000 people, had grown dramatically. In contrast, the fall in crude oil prices from over $30 per barrel to under $15 per barrel in the early 1980s forced the oil-based economy of Texas into a deep and prolonged recession. Then, in 1991, Massachusetts experienced yet another reversal of fortune, with an unemployment rate of 9 percent.

The economy of Michigan is heavily tied to the fortunes of the automobile industry. During the recession of 1982, Michigan had the highest unemployment rate in the country at 15.5%. Not only did the automobile industry suffer from the decline in the U.S. economy, it also faced stiff foreign competition, primarily from Japan. Michigan also suffered in 1991, with an unemployment rate of 9.2 percent.

The important point here is that:

> The unemployment rate does not tell the whole story. A low national rate of unemployment does not mean that the entire nation is growing and producing at the same rate.

■ **Unemployment Rates in Different Industries** Unemployment rates also differ from industry to industry. Table 8.5 shows that in January 1995 workers in the construction industry experienced unemployment rates over twice the national average. The three lowest unemployment rates were for finance (2.9%), government (3.2%), and durable goods manufacturing (4.2%).

■ **Discouraged-Worker Effects** Remember that people who decide to stop looking for work are classified as having dropped out of the labor force rather than as being unemployed. During recessions people often become so discouraged about ever finding a job that they stop looking. This actually lowers the unemployment rate, because those no longer looking for work are no longer counted as unemployed.

discouraged-worker effect *The decline in the measured unemployment rate that results when people who want to work but cannot find jobs grow discouraged and stop looking, thus dropping out of the ranks of the unemployed and the labor force.*

A simple example can demonstrate how this **discouraged-worker effect** lowers the unemployment rate. Suppose that there are 10 million unemployed out of a labor force of 100 million. This would mean an unemployment rate of 10/100 = .10, or 10 percent. If 1 million of these 10 million unemployed people simply stop looking for work and drop out of the labor force, there would be 9 million unemployed out of a labor force of 99 million. The unemployment rate would then drop to 9/99 = .091, or 9.1 percent.

The Bureau of Labor Statistics survey provides some evidence on the size of the discouraged-worker effect. Respondents who indicate that they have stopped searching for work are asked why they have done so. If the respondent cites inability to find employment as the sole reason for not searching, that person might reasonably be classified as a discouraged worker.

The number of discouraged workers seems to hover around 1% of the labor force in normal times. During the 1980–1982 recession, the number of discouraged workers increased steadily to a peak of 1.5 percent. By the end of the first quarter of 1991, the recession of 1990–1991 had produced 997,000 discouraged workers.[4] Some economists argue that adding the number of discouraged workers to the number who are now classified as unemployed gives a better picture of the unemployment situation.

■ **The Duration of Unemployment** The unemployment rate measures unemployment at a given point in time. It tells us nothing about how long the average unemployed worker is out of work.

Table 8.6 shows that during recessionary periods, not only are there more workers unemployed, but the average duration of unemployment rises. In fact, between 1979 and 1983, the average duration of unemployment rose from 10.8 weeks to 20 weeks. The slow growth following the 1990–1991 recession resulted in an increase in duration of unemployment to 17.9 weeks in 1992 and to 18.8 weeks in 1994.

THE COSTS OF UNEMPLOYMENT

In the Employment Act of 1946, the Congress of the United States declared that it was the

> continuing policy and responsibility of the federal government to use all practicable means. . . . to promote maximum employment, production, and purchasing power.

In 1978, Congress passed the Full Employment and Balanced Growth Act, commonly referred to as the *Humphrey-Hawkins Act,* which formally established a specific unemployment target of 4 percent.

Why should full employment be a policy objective of the federal government? What costs does unemployment impose on society?

■ **Some Unemployment Is Inevitable** Before we discuss the costs of unemployment, it must be noted that some unemployment is simply part of the natural workings of the labor market. Remember that to be classified as unemployed, a person must be looking for a job. Every year, thousands of people enter the labor force for the first time. Some have dropped out of high school, some are high school or college graduates, and still others are finishing graduate programs. At the same time, new firms are starting up and others are expanding and creating new jobs, while other firms are contracting or going out of business. In April 1991, for example, the Defense Department announced the closing of 31 major military installations. As a result of these closings, tens of thousands of civilian workers were forced to find other work, and businesses near those bases contracted. In short, the economy is dynamic: People grow and acquire skills and the structure of the job market is continuously changing.

At any given moment, then, there is a set of job seekers and a set of jobs that must be matched with one another. It is important that the right people end up in the right jobs. The right job for a person will depend on that person's particular skills, his or her preferences regarding work environment (large firm or small, formal or informal), where he or she lives, and his or her willingness to commute. At the same time, firms want workers that can meet the requirements of the job and grow with the company.

[4]The New York Times, *April 6, 1991, p. 1.*

TABLE 8.5
UNEMPLOYMENT IN DIFFERENT INDUSTRIES, 1995

	JANUARY 1995
Mining	5.1
Construction	11.7
Manufacturing	4.7
Durable goods	4.2
Nondurable goods	5.4
Transportation and public utilities	4.7
Wholesale and retail trade	6.6
Finance	2.9
Services	5.2
Agriculture	10.7
Government	3.2
National average	5.6

Source: Bureau of Labor Statistics, *Monthly Labor Review* (June 1995).

TABLE 8.6
AVERAGE DURATION OF UNEMPLOYMENT, 1979–1994

	WEEKS
1979	10.8
1980	11.9
1981	13.7
1982	15.6
1983	20.0
1984	18.2
1985	15.6
1986	14.8
1987	13.7
1988	13.5
1989	11.9
1990	12.1
1991	13.8
1992	17.9
1993	18.1
1994	18.8

Sources: Statistical Abstract of the United States, and Bureau of Labor Statistics, *Monthly Labor Review* (June 1995).

Remember from the previous chapter that a fixed-weight price index like the CPI does not account for consumers' substitution away from high-priced goods. Therefore,

> Changes in the CPI somewhat overstate changes in the cost of living.

producer price indexes (PPIs)
Measures of prices that producers receive for products at all stages in the production process.

Other popular price indexes are **producer price indexes (PPIs)**, once called *wholesale price indexes.* These are indexes of prices that producers receive for products at all stages in the production process, not just the final stage. The indexes are calculated separately for various stages in the production process. The three main categories are *finished goods, intermediate materials,* and *crude materials,* although there are subcategories within each of these categories.

One advantage of some of the producer price indexes is that they detect price increases early in the production process. Because their movements sometimes foreshadow future changes in consumer prices, they are sometimes considered to be leading indicators of future consumer prices.

THE COSTS OF INFLATION

If you asked most people why inflation is "bad," they would tell you that it lowers the overall standard of living by making goods and services more expensive. That is, it cuts into people's purchasing power. People are fond of recalling the days when a bottle of Coca-Cola cost a dime and a hamburger cost a quarter. Just think what we could buy today if prices had not changed!

What people usually do not think about is what their incomes were in the "good old days." The fact that the cost of a Coke has increased from 10¢ to 50¢

TABLE 8.9			THE CPI, 1950–1994			
PERCENTAGE CHANGES IN THE CPI				**CPI**		
1950	1.3	1972	3.2	1950	24.1	1972	41.8
1951	7.9	1973	6.2	1951	26.0	1973	44.4
1952	1.9	1974	11.0	1952	26.5	1974	49.3
1953	0.8	1975	9.1	1953	26.7	1975	53.8
1954	0.7	1976	5.8	1954	26.9	1976	56.9
1955	−0.4	1977	6.5	1955	26.8	1977	60.6
1956	1.5	1978	7.6	1956	27.2	1978	65.2
1957	3.3	1979	11.3	1957	28.1	1979	72.6
1958	2.8	1980	13.5	1958	28.9	1980	82.4
1959	0.7	1981	10.3	1959	29.1	1981	90.9
1960	1.7	1982	6.2	1960	29.6	1982	96.5
1961	1.0	1983	3.2	1961	29.9	1983	99.6
1962	1.0	1984	4.3	1962	30.2	1984	103.9
1963	1.3	1985	3.6	1963	30.6	1985	107.6
1964	1.3	1986	2.0	1964	31.0	1986	109.7
1965	1.6	1987	3.6	1965	31.5	1987	113.7
1966	2.9	1988	4.1	1966	32.4	1988	118.4
1967	3.1	1989	4.7	1967	33.4	1989	124.0
1968	4.2	1990	5.4	1968	34.8	1990	130.7
1969	5.5	1991	4.3	1969	36.7	1991	136.3
1970	5.7	1992	3.0	1970	38.8	1992	140.4
1971	4.4	1993	3.0	1971	40.5	1993	144.6
		1994	2.6			1994	148.3

Sources: Economic Report of the President, 1995, and updates.

does not mean anything in real terms if people who once earned $5000 now earn $25,000. Why? The reason is simple:

> People's income comes from wages and salaries, profits, interest and rent, and income from these sources increases during inflations as well. The wage rate is the price of labor, rent is the price of land, and so forth. During inflations, most prices—including input prices—tend to rise together, and input prices determine both the incomes of workers and the incomes of owners of capital and land.

■ Inflation Changes the Distribution of Income

Whether you gain or lose during a period of inflation depends on whether your income rises faster or slower than the prices of the things you buy. The group most often mentioned when the impact of inflation is discussed is the group of people living on fixed incomes. Clearly, if your income is fixed and prices rise, your ability to purchase goods and services falls proportionately. But who are the fixed-income earners?

Most people think of the elderly. Indeed, many retired workers living on private pensions receive monthly checks that will never increase. Many pension plans, however, pay benefits that are *indexed* to inflation. That is, the benefits these plans provide automatically increase when the general price level rises. If prices rise 10%, for example, benefits also rise 10 percent. The biggest source of income for the elderly is social security. These benefits are fully indexed; when prices rise (that is, when the CPI rises) by 5%, social security benefits also increase by 5 percent.

The poor have not fared so well. Welfare benefits, which are not indexed, have not kept pace with the price level over the last two decades. Indeed, benefits to families with dependent children under the AFDC program declined 33% in real terms between 1970 and 1988. In five states—Idaho, Illinois, Kentucky, New Jersey, and Texas—the average benefits fell by more than 50% in real terms.[9]

■ Effects on Debtors and Creditors

It is also commonly believed that debtors benefit at the expense of creditors during an inflation. Certainly, if I loan you $100 to be paid back in a year, and prices increase 10% in the meantime, I get back 10% less in real terms than what I loaned you.

But suppose that we had both anticipated that prices would rise 10 percent. Of course, I would have taken this into consideration in the deal that I made with you. That is, I would charge you an interest rate high enough to cover the decrease in value due to the anticipated inflation. If, for example, we agree on a 15% interest rate, then you must pay me $115 at the end of a year. The difference between the interest rate on a loan and the inflation rate is referred to as the **real interest rate.** In our deal, I will earn a real interest rate of 5 percent. By charging a 15% interest rate, I have taken into account the anticipated 10% inflation rate. In this sense, I am not hurt by the inflation—I keep pace with inflation and earn a profit on my money, too—despite the fact that I am a creditor.

On the other hand, an unanticipated inflation—that is, an inflation that takes people by surprise—can hurt creditors. If the actual inflation rate during the period of my loan to you turns out to be 20%, then I as a creditor will be hurt. I charged you 15% interest, expecting to get a 5% real rate of return, when I needed to charge you 25% to get the same 5% real rate of return. Because inflation turned out to be higher than expected, I got a negative real return of 5 percent. Thus, we can say that:

In the 1940s, a bottle of Coca-Cola cost .5 cents. In many places today, a can of Coke costs 60 cents. However, this is not a relative price increase if the overall price level has risen by a factor of 12 during this period, which is roughly what has happened.

real interest rate *The difference between the interest rate on a loan and the inflation rate.*

---

[9]Alicia H. Munnell, "The Current Status of Our Social Welfare System," Federal Reserve Bank of Boston, monograph (1987).

> Inflation that is higher than expected benefits debtors and inflation that is lower than expected benefits creditors.

■ **Administrative Costs and Inefficiencies**   There are, of course, costs associated even with anticipated inflation. One obvious cost is the administrative cost associated with simply keeping up. During the rapid inflation in Israel in the early 1980s, a telephone hotline was set up to give the hourly price index! Store owners have to recalculate and re-post prices frequently, and this takes time that could be used more efficiently.

More frequent banking transactions may be required of people as well. For example, interest rates tend to rise with anticipated inflation. When interest rates are high, the opportunity costs of holding cash outside of banks is high. People therefore hold less cash and need to stop at the bank more often. (We discuss this phenomenon in more detail in the next part of this book.) In addition, if people are not fully informed, or if they do not understand what is happening to prices in general, they may make mistakes in their business dealings. These mistakes can lead to a misallocation of resources.

■ **Increased Risk and Slower Economic Growth**   When unanticipated inflation occurs regularly, the degree of risk associated with investments in the economy increases. Increases in uncertainty may make investors reluctant to invest in capital and to make long-term commitments. To the extent that the level of investment falls, the prospects for long-term economic growth are lessened.

INFLATION: PUBLIC ENEMY NUMBER ONE?

Economists have debated the seriousness of the costs of inflation for decades. Some, like Alan Blinder, claim that "inflation, like every teenager, is grossly misunderstood, and this gross misunderstanding blows the political importance of inflation out of all proportion to its economic importance."[10] Others, like Phillip Cagan and Robert Lipsey, argue that "it was once thought that the economy would in time make all the necessary adjustments [to inflation], but many of them are proving to be very difficult. . . . for financial institutions and markets, the effects of inflation have been extremely unsettling."[11]

No matter what the real economic cost of inflation, it seems clear that people don't like it. It makes us uneasy and unhappy. In 1974, President Ford verbalized some of this discomfort when he said that "our inflation, our public enemy number one, will unless whipped destroy our country, our homes, our liberties, our property, and finally our national pride, as surely as any well-armed wartime enemy."[12] In this belief, our elected leaders have vigorously pursued policies designed to stop inflation. This brings us around to where we started. If, as we suggested earlier, the recessions of 1975 and 1982 were the price we had to pay to stop inflation, stopping inflation is indeed costly.

GLOBAL UNEMPLOYMENT RATES AND INFLATION

Unemployment and inflation are not just concerns of the United States. Other countries at times experience high unemployment or high inflation (or both). The

---

[10]*Alan Blinder,* Hard Heads, Soft Hearts: Tough-Minded Economics for a Just Society *(Reading, Mass.: Addison-Wesley, 1987).*
[11]*Phillip Cagan and Robert Lipsey, "The Financial Effects of Inflation," National Bureau of Economic Research (Cambridge, Mass.: General Series #103, 1978), pp. 67–68.*
[12]*U.S. President,* Weekly Compilation of Presidential Documents, *vol. 10, no. 41, p 1247. Cited in Blinder,* Hard Heads.

Great Depression of the 1930s was a worldwide phenomenon, and most countries experienced high rates of inflation in the 1970s after the OPEC oil price increases. Most European countries experienced high unemployment rates in the 1980s. In 1984, for example, the unemployment rate was 11.8% in the United Kingdom, 9.5% in France, 7.9% in West Germany, 10.1% in Italy, and 19.8% in Spain. Today, unemployment remains high in these countries; all of them experienced at least one year of over 10% unemployment between 1993 and 1995, and during this period the unemployment rate in Spain averaged over 20 percent. The inflation rates in these countries were high as the 1980s began, but by 1984 inflation had come down. Between 1980 and 1984 the inflation rate fell from 19.4% to 4.5% in the United Kingdom, from 11.4% to 7.4% in France, from 5.0% to 2.1% in West Germany, from 20.1% to 11.7% in Italy, and from 15.4% to 11.6% in Spain.

Japan, in contrast, has had modest inflation and low unemployment rates. Between 1980 and 1993, the unemployment rate in Japan never rose above 2.9 percent.[13] The Japanese inflation rate was 4.5% in 1980 and 3.9% in 1981, but between 1982 and 1993 it was never higher than 2.3 percent.

Unemployment and inflation in the Western industrialized countries are mild compared to the problems that developing countries face. The United Nations estimates that in 1991 there were over a half billion unemployed or underemployed people in the developing world, close to 30% of its labor force.[14] This is about the size of the entire industrialized world's labor force. Double-digit rates of inflation, occasionally at fantastically high levels, are frequently observed in developing countries. Table 8.10 gives some examples.

During certain times of macroeconomic crisis, unemployment and inflation rates can reach eye-popping levels. The Great Depression is an extreme example of how bad unemployment can get. The classic case of hyperinflation, or inflation that has gotten out of control, is Germany after World War I. Between January 1922 and November 1923, the German price level rose by 10 billion percent! People were carrying cash around in wheelbarrows. The economies of Eastern Europe have struggled with both double-digit inflation and unemployment in making the transition from centrally planned to free-market economies. Their situation has been improving, though. The unemployment rate has been coming down, and so has inflation. Ukraine, for instance, brought its inflation rate down from 670% per year in November 1994 to 80% per year by May 1995.

TABLE 8.10

INFLATION IN DEVELOPING COUNTRIES

COUNTRY	PERIOD	AVERAGE ANNUAL INFLATION RATE (%)
Jamaica	1960–85	11
Costa Rica	1960–86	12
Colombia	1950–85	14
Mexico	1948–85	14
Zaire	1950–84	20
Bolivia	1958–83	20
Israel	1953–82	21
Peru	1960–84	26
Brazil	1963–84	42
Argentina	1963–81	54

Source: Ball, Lawrence, et al., "The New Keynesian Economics and the Output-Inflation Trade-off," Brookings Papers on Economic Activity, *1988, #1, pp. 1–65*

LOOKING AHEAD

This ends our introduction to the basic concepts and problems of macroeconomics. The first chapter of this part introduced the field, the second discussed the measurement of national product and national income, and this chapter discussed two of the macroeconomy's major problems—unemployment and inflation—in detail.

Thus far, however, we have said nothing about what *determines* the level of national output, the number of employed and unemployed workers, and the rate of inflation in an economy. The following chapters provide you with the background in macroeconomic theory you need to understand *how* the macroeconomy functions. With this knowledge, you will also be able to understand how the government can influence the economy through its taxing, spending, and monetary policies.

---

[13]*The unemployment rate may, however, be underestimated in Japan's official statistics. For example, unofficial estimates place Japan's unemployment rate as high as 8.9% in 1994. See "One in Ten?", The* Economist, *July 1, 1995, pp. 25–27.*
[14]*United Nations Population Fund,* Population and the Environment: Challenges Ahead (New York: UNFPA, 1991). *These numbers should be taken with caution, since the data may miss many people who work in the informal sectors of these economies.*

RECESSIONS, DEPRESSIONS, AND UNEMPLOYMENT

1. A *recession* is a period in which real GDP declines for at least two consecutive quarters. When less output is produced, employment declines, the unemployment rate rises, and a smaller percentage of the capital stock is used. When real output falls, real income declines.

2. A *depression* is a prolonged and deep recession, although there is disagreement over how severe and how prolonged a recession must be in order to be called a depression.

3. The *unemployment rate* is the ratio of the number of unemployed people to the number of people in the labor force. To be considered unemployed and in the labor force, a person must be looking for work.

4. Marked differences in rates of unemployment exist across demographic groups, regions, and industries. Blacks, for example, experience much higher unemployment rates than whites.

5. When a person decides to stop looking for work, that person is considered to have dropped out of the labor force and is no longer classified as unemployed. People who stop looking because they are discouraged about ever finding a job are sometimes called *discouraged workers*.

6. Some unemployment is inevitable. Because new workers are continually entering the labor force, because industries and firms are continuously expanding and contracting, and because people switch jobs, there is a constant process of job search as workers and firms try to match the best people to the available jobs. This unemployment is both natural and beneficial for the economy.

7. The unemployment that occurs because of short-run job/skill matching problems is called *frictional unemployment*. The unemployment that occurs because of longer-run structural changes in the economy is called *structural unemployment*. The *natural rate of unemployment* is the sum of the frictional rate and the structural rate. The increase in unemployment that occurs during recessions and depressions is called *cyclical unemployment*.

8. The major costs associated with recessions and unemployment are decreased real output, the damage done to the people who are unemployed, and lost output in the future. Benefits of recessions are that they may help to reduce inflation, increase efficiency, and improve a nation's balance of payments.

INFLATION

9. An *inflation* is an increase in the overall price level. It happens when many prices increase simultaneously. Inflation is measured by calculating the average increase in the prices of a large number of goods during some period of time. A *deflation* is a decrease in the overall price level. A *sustained inflation* is an increase in the overall price level that continues over a significant period of time.

10. A number of different indexes are used to measure the overall price level. Among them are the *GDP price index, consumer price index (CPI),* and *producer price indexes (PPIs)*.

11. Whether a person gains or loses during a period of inflation depends on whether his or her income rises faster or slower than the prices of the things he or she buys. The elderly are more insulated from inflation than most people think, because social security benefits and many pensions are indexed to inflation. Welfare benefits, which are not indexed to inflation, have not kept pace with inflation since 1970.

12. Inflation that is higher than expected benefits debtors, and inflation that is lower than expected benefits creditors.

GLOBAL UNEMPLOYMENT RATES AND INFLATION

13. Unemployment rates and rates of inflation differ markedly across time and countries and can reach quite high levels at times.

consumer price index (CPI) 181
cyclical unemployment 177
deflation 180
depression 170
discouraged-worker effect 175
employed 172
frictional unemployment 177
inflation 180
labor force 172
labor-force participation rate 172
natural rate of unemployment 177

not in the labor force 172
producer price indexes (PPIs) 182
real interest rate 184
recession 170

structural unemployment 177
sustained inflation 181
unemployed 172
unemployment rate 172

Equations:

1. Labor force = Employed + Unemployed

2. Population = Labor force + Not in labor force

3. Unemployment rate = $\dfrac{\text{Unemployed}}{\text{Employed} + \text{Unemployed}}$

4. Labor-force participation rate = $\dfrac{\text{Labor force}}{\text{Population}}$

PROBLEM SET

1. Between May and June of 1994, total employment in the U.S. economy fell from 122,872,000 to 122,430,000-a decline of 442,000. At the same time, the number of *unemployed* dropped by 85,000, from 7,902,000 to 7,817,000, and the unemployment rate fell a bit from 6.042% to 6.001 percent.

   a. How can unemployment fall when the number employed is also falling?

   b. From these numbers, calculate approximately how large the labor force was in May and in June.

2. In August, 1995, economists were saying that the U.S. economy was close to full employment even though the unemployment rate was above 5 percent. How can they make this assertion?

3. Using the data in Table 8.2, calculate the changes in the unemployment rate and the labor-force participation rate that would occur if one million unemployed persons dropped out of the labor force in 1994.

4. "When an inefficient firm or a firm producing a product that people no longer want goes out of business, people are unemployed, but that's part of the normal process of economic growth and development; the unemployment is part of the natural rate and need not concern policy makers." Discuss this statement and its relevance to the economy today.

5. What is the unemployment rate in your state today? What was it in 1970, 1975, and 1982? How has your state done relative to the national average? Do you know, or can you determine, why?

6. Suppose that all wages, salaries, welfare benefits, and other sources of income were indexed to inflation. Would inflation still be considered a problem? Why or why not?

7. a. What do the CPI and the PPI measure? Why do we need all these price indexes? (Think about what purpose you would use each one for.)

   b. Consider an economy with two goods, gum and lemon drops. Suppose that, between year 1 and year 2, there is a downward shift in the supply schedule for gum and an upward shift in the supply schedule for lemon drops. Explain why the CPI for this two-good economy would overstate the increase in the cost of living.

8. Consider the following statements:

   a. "More people are employed in Tappania now than at any time in the past 50 years."

   b. "The unemployment rate in Tappania is higher now than it has been in 50 years."

Can both of these statements be true at the same time? Explain.

THE CPI AND ECONOMIC POLICY

THE U.S. CENSUS, WHICH IS CONDUCTED EVERY TEN YEARS BY THE U.S. CENSUS BUREAU, IS AN IMPORTANT SOURCE OF ECONOMIC DATA FOR THE UNITED STATES. ANOTHER IMPORTANT SOURCE FOR ECONOMIC DATA IS THE BUREAU OF LABOR STATISTICS, WHICH IS RESPONSIBLE FOR ISSUING MONTHLY PRICE AND EMPLOYMENT DATA.

To determine whether or not you can buy more with your income today than you could with your income a decade ago, you must use a price index, such as the CPI, to adjust for changes in the overall price level. However, there are certain problems inherent in using the CPI for this purpose.

Why? The CPI does not fully capture technological advance and improvements in product quality, and so it tends to overestimate in-flation. For example, the cars we purchase today are more fuel efficient and require lower maintenance than those we purchased five years ago, just as today's computers are much more powerful than those manufactured in the early 1990s. The CPI does not fully account for these advances.

Other price indexes suffer from similar difficulties. For example, the PPI (producer price index) has a tendency to overstate price movements.

It is not adjusted completely for the dramatic changes in the power and speed of communications equipment and incorporates no price index for software, despite the fact that software is a large non-labor expense for many companies.

These may seem like small issues, but they have important effects on the creation and conduct of economic policy. If changes in price indexes like the CPI and PPI overstate the actual rate of inflation and if policy makers are not completely aware of this, they may follow policies that are too restrictive. They may base their decisions on the (mistaken) view that inflation is higher than it really is.

In addition, social security payments, military pensions, and federal employee pay increases are all indexed to the CPI. For this reason, a 1% overstatement of the CPI can cost the government many billions of dollars per year. Federal Reserve Chairman Alan Greenspan has argued that CPI changes may overestimate inflation by between .5 and 1.5 percent per year.

The public sector is not the only sector that is adversely affected by an inflated CPI. Many private wage contracts are tied to the CPI. This means that when the CPI increases, workers' wages are adjusted upward automatically. If the CPI overstates inflation, then private businesses end up paying their employees more than they otherwise would.

Questions for Analytical Thinking

1. Who are the winners and who are the losers when the CPI is overstated? When it is understated?

2. If you were living on social security payments, would you prefer the CPI to be overstated or understated? Would your views change if you were responsible for reducing the U.S. government debt?

3. How might inaccuracies or omissions in government data contribute to cyclical behavior in the economy through their effects on business and policy decisions?

4. Is your family better off now than it was five years ago? How do you know, and how would you measure your well-being now versus five years ago?

Additional readings: Bell, Carolyn Shaw, "Measuring Inflation," *Boston Globe,* February 14, 1995; U.S. Bureau of the Census, *Income and Poverty Report,* 1994; "The Good Statistics Guide: Which Country Boasts the Best (or the Least Bad) Statistics?", *The Economist,* September 11, 1993; Economic Policy Institute, *The State of Working America* (Armonk, NY: Sharpe, 1993); Mandel, Michael, "The Real Truth About the Economy," *Business Week,* November 7, 1994; Richter, Paul, "Average American Better Off than Ever," *Los Angeles Times,* February 2, 1995; Thomas, Rich, and Michael Meyer, "Do the Numbers Lie?", *Newsweek,* February 13, 1995.

9

PART THREE

MACROECONOMIC PRINCIPLES AND POLICY

AGGREGATE EXPENDITURE AND EQUILIBRIUM OUTPUT

WE NOW BEGIN OUR DISCUSSION OF MACROECONOMIC THEORY. We know how to calculate national income, but what factors *determine* national income? We know how to define and measure inflation and unemployment, but what circumstances *cause* inflation and unemployment? And what, if anything, can government do to reduce unemployment, inflation, and other macroeconomic maladies?

Analyzing the various components of the macroeconomy is a complex undertaking. The level of national income and the overall price level—two of the chief concerns of macroeconomists—are influenced by events in three broadly defined "markets": goods-and-services markets, financial (money) markets, and labor markets. We will explore each of these markets, as well as the links between them and the corresponding markets in the rest of the world, in more detail in the chapters that follow.

■ **Macroeconomic Markets** Figure 9.1 presents the plan of the next seven chapters of this book, which form the core of macroeconomic theory. In Chapters 9 and 10, we describe the market for goods and services, often called simply the *goods market*. In Chapter 9, we explain several basic concepts and show how the equilibrium level of national income is determined in a very simple economy with no government and no imports or exports. In Chapter 10, we provide a more complete picture of the economy by adding government purchases, taxes, and net exports to the analysis.

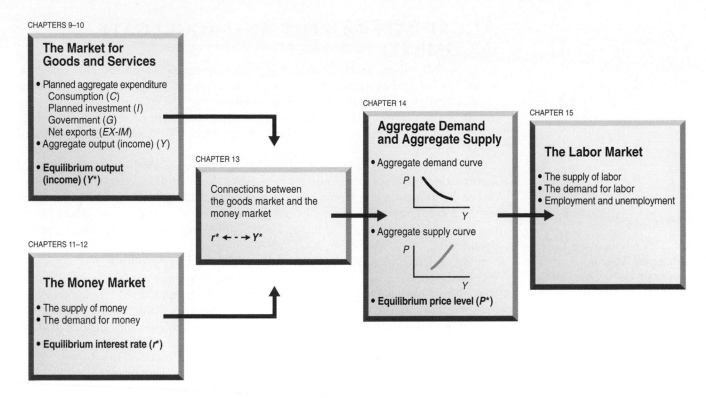

The Market for Goods and Services

- Planned aggregate expenditure
  Consumption (*C*)
  Planned investment (*I*)
  Government (*G*)
  Net exports (*EX-IM*)
- Aggregate output (income) (*Y*)

- **Equilibrium output (income) (*Y**)**

CHAPTER 13

Connections between the goods market and the money market

$r^* \leftarrow - \rightarrow Y^*$

CHAPTERS 11–12

The Money Market

- The supply of money
- The demand for money

- **Equilibrium interest rate (*r**)**

CHAPTER 14

Aggregate Demand and Aggregate Supply

- Aggregate demand curve

- Aggregate supply curve

- **Equilibrium price level (*P**)**

CHAPTER 15

The Labor Market

- The supply of labor
- The demand for labor
- Employment and unemployment

FIGURE 9.1
Understanding Markets in the Macroeconomy

In Chapters 11 and 12, we focus on the *money market*. Chapter 11 introduces the money market and the banking system and discusses the way the U.S. central bank (the Federal Reserve) controls the money supply. Chapter 12 analyzes the demand for money and the way interest rates are determined. Chapter 13 then examines the relationship between the goods market and the money market. Chapter 14 explores the aggregate demand and supply curves first mentioned in Chapter 6. Chapter 14 also analyzes how the overall price level is determined, as well as the relationship between national income and the price level. Finally, Chapter 15 discusses the supply of and demand for labor and the functioning of the *labor market* in the macroeconomy. This material is essential to an understanding of employment and unemployment.[1]

Before we begin our discussion of aggregate output and aggregate income, we need to stress that production, consumption, and the other activities that we will be discussing in this and the following chapters are ongoing activities. Nonetheless, it is helpful to think about these activities as if they took place in a series of *production periods*. During each period, some output is produced, income is generated, and spending takes place. At the end of each period we can examine the results. Was everything that was produced in the economy sold? What percentage of income was spent? What percentage was saved? Is output (income) likely to rise or fall in the next period? The answers to these questions help us to keep track of the economy's performance.

---

[1]*Throughout Chapters 9–15, we provide examples and policy applications relevant to our discussion in each chapter. In Chapter 16, we use everything we know about the three broadly defined markets to analyze such macroeconomic topics as stabilization policy and the federal budget deficit.*

AGGREGATE OUTPUT AND AGGREGATE INCOME (Y)

Each period, firms produce some aggregate quantity of goods and services, which we refer to as *aggregate output* (Y). In Chapter 7, we introduced the concept of real gross domestic product as a measure of the quantity of output produced in the economy, Y. Output includes the production of services, consumer goods, and investment goods. It is important to think of these as components of "real" output.

We have already seen that GDP (Y) can be calculated either in terms of income or in terms of expenditures. Because every dollar of expenditure is received by someone as income, we can compute total GDP (Y) either by adding up the total amount spent on all final goods during a period *or* by adding up all the income—wages, rents, interest, and profits—received by all the factors of production.

We will use the variable Y to refer to both **aggregate output** and **aggregate income** because, in fact, they are the same thing seen from two different points of view. When output increases, additional income is generated. More workers may be hired and paid; workers may put in, and be paid for, more hours; and owners may earn more profits. When output is cut, income falls, workers may be laid off or work fewer hours (and be paid less), and profits may fall. In sum:

aggregate output *The total quantity of goods and services produced (or supplied) in an economy in a given period.*

aggregate income *The total income received by all factors of production in a given period.*

> In any given period, there is an exact equality between aggregate output (production) and aggregate income. You should be reminded of this fact whenever you encounter the combined term **aggregate output (income).**

aggregate output (income) (Y) *A combined term used to remind you of the exact equality between aggregate output and aggregate income.*

Aggregate output can also be looked on as the aggregate quantity supplied, because it is the amount that firms are supplying (producing) during the period. In the discussions that follow, we use the phrase *aggregate output* (*income*), rather than *aggregate quantity supplied,* but keep in mind that the two are equivalent. Also remember that "aggregate output" means "real GDP."

■ **Think in Real Terms** It is essential from the outset that you think in "real terms." For example, when we talk about output (Y), we mean real output, not nominal output. Although we discussed in Chapter 7 that the calculation of real GDP is complicated, you can ignore these complications in the following analysis, for the reasons we saw in Chapter 7. You can also ignore the fact that the GDP identity does not hold in real terms. To help make things easier to read, we will frequently use dollar values for Y, but do not confuse Y with nominal output. The main point is to think of Y as being in real terms—the quantities of goods and services produced, not the dollars circulating in the economy.

INCOME, CONSUMPTION, AND SAVING (Y, C, AND S)

Each period (weeks, months, years, etc.), households receive some aggregate amount of income (Y). In a simple world with no government, no taxes, and no imports, a household can do two, and only two, things with its income: It can buy domestically produced goods and services—that is, it can *consume*—or it can save. The part of its income that a household does not consume in a given period is called **saving** (Figure 9.2). Thus, total household saving in the economy (represented by the letter S) is by definition equal to income minus consumption (represented by the letter C):

saving (S) *The part of its income that a household does not consume in a given period. Distinguished from savings, which is the current stock of accumulated saving.*

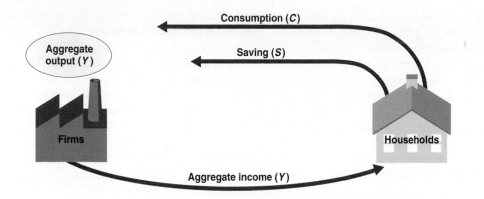

FIGURE 9.2
Saving ≡ Aggregate
Income − Consumption

All income is either spent on
consumption or saved in an
economy in which there is no
government. Thus, $S \equiv Y - C$.

$$Saving \equiv Income - Consumption$$
$$S \equiv Y - C$$

The triple equal sign simply means that this equation is an **identity**, or something that is true at all times. You will encounter several important identities in this chapter; be sure to commit them to memory.

identity *Something that is true at all times.*

It is very important to remember that saving does *not* refer to the total savings that have been accumulated over time. Saving (without the final *s*) refers to the portion of a *single period's* income that is not spent in that period. Saving (*S*) is the amount that is added to (or subtracted from) *accumulated savings* in any given period. *Saving* is a flow variable; *savings* is a stock variable. (Review Chapter 4 if you are unsure of the difference between stock and flow variables.)

EXPLAINING SPENDING BEHAVIOR

At this point, we have said absolutely nothing about behavior. We have not described the consumption and saving behavior of households, nor have we speculated about how much aggregate output firms will decide to produce in a given period. Rather, we have only a framework and a set of definitions to work with.

But macroeconomics, you will recall, is the study of behavior. To understand the functioning of the macroeconomy, we must understand the behavior of households and firms. In our simple economy in which there is no government, there are two types of spending behavior: spending by households, or *consumption*, and spending by firms, or *investment*.

■ **Household Consumption and Saving** How do households decide how much to consume? In any given period, the amount of aggregate consumption in the economy depends on a number of factors, including:

Some Determinants of Aggregate Consumption:	
	1. Household income
	2. Household wealth
	3. Interest rates
	4. Households' expectations about the future

That these factors work together to determine the spending and saving behavior of households, both individually and in the aggregate, should not be surprising.

Households with higher income and higher wealth are likely to spend more than households with less income and less wealth. Lower interest rates reduce the cost of borrowing, so lower interest rates are likely to stimulate spending. (The reverse is true for higher interest rates, which increase the cost of borrowing and are likely to decrease spending.) Finally, positive expectations about the future are likely to increase current spending, while uncertainty about the future is likely to decrease current spending. In 1990, for example, households began consuming less partly because of their uncertainty about the outcome of the Persian Gulf conflict.

While all these factors are important, we will concentrate for now on the relationship between income and consumption.[2] In *The General Theory*, Keynes argued that the amount of consumption undertaken by a household is directly related to its income:

> The higher someone's income is, the higher his or her consumption is likely to be. Thus, people with more income tend to consume more than people with less income.

consumption function *The relationship between consumption and income.*

The relationship between consumption and income is called a **consumption function.** Figure 9.3 shows a hypothetical consumption function for an individual household. The curve is labeled $c(y)$, which is read "c as a function of y," or "consumption as a function of income." There are several things you should notice about the curve. First, it has a positive slope. In other words, as y increases, so does c. Second, the curve intersects the c axis above zero. This means that even at an income of zero, consumption is positive. Even if a household found itself with a zero income, it still must consume to survive. It would borrow or live off its savings, but its consumption could not be zero.

Keep in mind that Figure 9.3 shows the relationship between consumption and income for an individual household. But also remember that macroeconomics is concerned with aggregate consumption. Specifically, macroeconomists want to

FIGURE 9.3

A Consumption Function for a Household

A consumption function for an individual household shows the level of consumption at each level of household income.

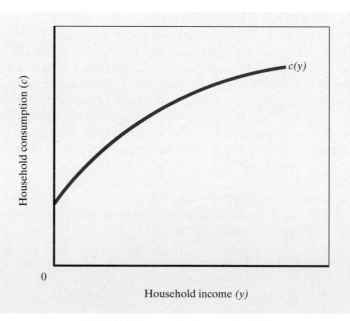

_____

[2]*The assumption that consumption is dependent solely on income is, of course, overly simplistic. Nonetheless, many important insights about how the economy works can be obtained through this simplification. In Chapter 17, we relax this assumption and consider the behavior of households and firms in the macroeconomy in more detail.*

know how *aggregate* consumption (the total consumption of all households) is likely to respond to changes in *aggregate* income. If all individual households increase their consumption as income increases, and we assume that they do, it is reasonable to assume that a positive relationship exists between aggregate consumption (C) and aggregate income (Y).

For the sake of simplicity, let us assume that points of aggregate consumption, when plotted against aggregate income, lie along a straight line, as in Figure 9.4. Because the aggregate consumption function is a straight line, we can write the following equation to describe it:

$$C = a + bY$$

Y, as you know, represents aggregate output (income). C stands for aggregate consumption. The letter *a* is the point at which the consumption function intersects the C axis; it is a constant. The letter *b* is the slope of the line. Note that the slope of the line in this case is $\Delta C/\Delta Y$ (since consumption [C] is measured on the vertical axis, and income [Y] is measured on the horizontal axis).[3] Every time that income increases (say by ΔY), consumption increases by *b* times ΔY. Thus, $\Delta C = b \times \Delta Y$ and $\Delta C/\Delta Y = b$.

Suppose, for example, that the slope of the line in Figure 9.4 were .75 (that is, $b = .75$). In this case, an increase in income (ΔY) of $100 would increase consumption by $b\Delta Y = .75 \times \$100$, or $75.

The **marginal propensity to consume (MPC)** is the fraction of a change in income that is consumed. In the consumption function above, *b* is the MPC. An MPC of .75 simply means that consumption changes by three quarters (.75) of the change in income. The slope of the consumption function is thus the MPC:

marginal propensity to consume (MPC) *That fraction of a change in income that is consumed, or spent.*

Marginal propensity to consume ≡ Slope of consumption function $= \dfrac{\Delta C}{\Delta Y}$

There are only two places income can go: consumption or saving. Thus, if $0.75 of a $1.00 increase in income goes to consumption, the remaining $0.25

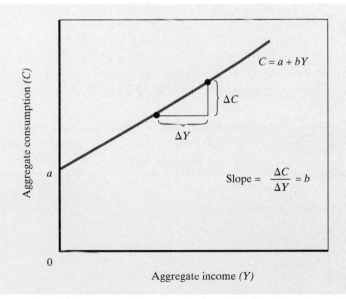

FIGURE 9.4

An Aggregate Consumption Function

The consumption function shows the level of consumption at every level of income. The upward slope indicates that higher levels of income lead to higher levels of consumption spending.

[3]The Greek letter Δ (delta) means "change in." For example, ΔY (read "delta Y") means the "change in income." If income (Y) in 1995 is $100 and income in 1996 is $110, then ΔY for this period is $110 - \$100 = \$10$. For a review of the concept of slope, see the Appendix to Chapter 1.

must go to saving. Likewise, if income decreases by $1.00, consumption will decrease by $0.75 and saving will decrease by $0.25. The **marginal propensity to save** (**MPS**) is the fraction of a change in income that is saved: $\Delta S/\Delta Y$, where ΔS is the change in saving. Because everything not consumed is saved, the *MPC* and the *MPS* must add up to one:

$$MPC + MPS \equiv 1$$

Because the *MPC* and the *MPS* are such important concepts, it may help to review their definitions one more time:

The marginal propensity to consume (*MPC*) is the fraction of an increase in income that is consumed (or the fraction of a decrease in income that comes out of consumption). The marginal propensity to save (*MPS*) is the fraction of an increase in income that is saved (or the fraction of a decrease in income that comes out of saving).

Since C is aggregate consumption and Y is aggregate income, it follows that the *MPC* is *society's* marginal propensity to consume out of national income and that the *MPS* is *society's* marginal propensity to save out of national income.

■ **Numerical Example** The numerical examples used in the rest of this chapter are based on the following consumption function:

$$C = \underbrace{100}_{a} + \underbrace{.75Y}_{b}$$

This equation is simply an extension of the generic $C = a + bY$ consumption function we have been discussing. At a national income of zero, consumption is $100 billion ($a$). As income rises, so does consumption. We will assume that for every $100 billion increase in income (ΔY), consumption rises by $75 billion ($\Delta C$). This means that the slope of the consumption function (b) is equal to $\Delta C/\Delta Y$, or $75 billion/$100 billion = .75. The marginal propensity to consume out of national income is therefore .75; the marginal propensity to save is .25. Some numbers derived from this consumption function appear in Table 9.1 and are graphed in Figure 9.5.

Now consider saving. We already know that $Y \equiv C + S$. That is, income equals consumption plus saving. Therefore, once we know how much consumption will result from a given level of income, we also know how much saving there will be.

TABLE 9.1	**CONSUMPTION SCHEDULE DERIVED FROM THE EQUATION $C = 100 + .75Y$**
AGGREGATE INCOME, Y (BILLIONS OF DOLLARS)	**AGGREGATE CONSUMPTION, C (BILLIONS OF DOLLARS)**
0	100
80	160
100	175
200	250
400	400
600	550
800	700
1000	850

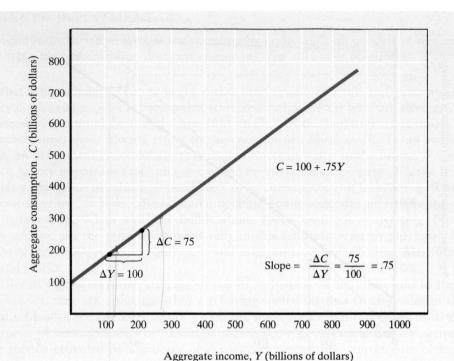

In this simple consumption function, consumption is $100 billion at an income of zero. As income rises, so does consumption. For every $100 billion increase in income, consumption rises by $75 billion. The slope of the line is .75.

Recall that saving is everything that is not consumed:

$$S \equiv Y - C$$

From the numbers in Table 9.1, we can easily derive the saving schedule in Table 9.2. At an income of $200 billion, consumption is $250 billion; saving is thus a negative $50 billion ($S \equiv Y - C = 200 billion $-$ $250 billion $= -$50 billion). At an aggregate income of $400 billion, consumption is exactly $400 billion, and saving is zero. At $800 billion in income, saving is a positive $100 billion.

These numbers are graphed as a saving function in Figure 9.6 on page 196. The 45° line, which appears as a solid black line in the top part of Figure 9.6, provides

TABLE 9.2	DERIVING A SAVING SCHEDULE FROM A CONSUMPTION SCHEDULE		
Y AGGREGATE INCOME (BILLIONS OF DOLLARS)	−	C AGGREGATE CONSUMPTION (BILLIONS OF DOLLARS)	≡	S AGGREGATE SAVING (BILLIONS OF DOLLARS)
0		100		−100
80		160		−80
100		175		−75
200		250		−50
400		400		0
600		550		50
800		700		100
1000		850		150

THE SAVING/INVESTMENT APPROACH TO EQUILIBRIUM

We have already noted that aggregate income must either be saved or spent. By definition, then, $Y \equiv C + S$—which, you remember, is an identity. The equilibrium condition is $Y = C + I$, but this is not an identity because it does not hold when we are out of equilibrium.[5] Substituting $C + S$ for Y, the equilibrium condition, we can write:

> Saving/investment approach to equilibrium: $C + S = C + I$
> Since we can subtract C from both sides of this equation, we are left with $S = I$. Thus, only when planned investment equals saving will there be equilibrium.

This saving/investment approach to equilibrium stands to reason intuitively if we recall two things: (1) Output and income are equal, and (2) saving is income that is not spent. Because it is not spent, saving is like a leakage out of the spending stream. Only if that leakage is counterbalanced by some other component of planned spending can the resulting planned aggregate expenditure equal aggregate output. This other component is planned investment (I).

This counterbalancing effect can be seen clearly in Figure 9.9. Aggregate income flows into the households, and consumption and saving flow out. The diagram shows saving flowing from households into the financial market. Firms use this saving to finance investment projects. If the planned investment of firms equals the saving of households, then planned aggregate expenditure ($AE \equiv C + I$) equals aggregate output (income) (Y), and there is equilibrium. In this case, the *leakage* out of the spending stream—saving—is matched by an equal *injection* of planned investment spending into the spending stream. For this reason, the saving/investment approach to equilibrium is also called the *leakages/ injections approach* to equilibrium.

FIGURE 9.9

Planned Aggregate Expenditure and Aggregate Output (Income)

Saving is a leakage out of the spending stream. If planned investment is exactly equal to saving, then planned aggregate expenditure is exactly equal to aggregate output, and there is equilibrium.

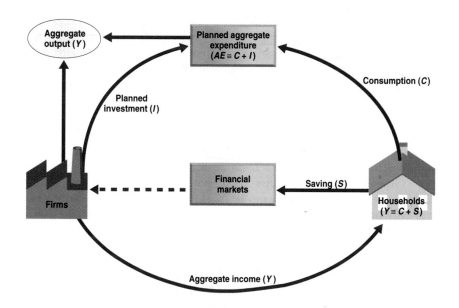

---

[5]*It would be an identity if* I *included unplanned inventory accumulations—in other words, if* I *were actual investment rather than planned investment.*

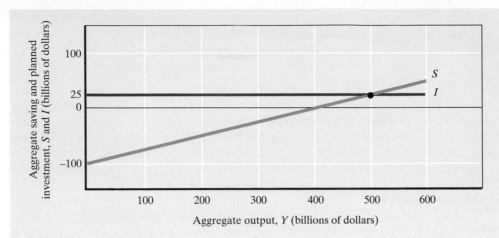

FIGURE 9.10

The $S = I$ Approach to Equilibrium

Aggregate output will be equal to planned aggregate expenditure only when saving equals planned investment ($S = I$). Saving and planned investment are equal at $Y = 500$.

Figure 9.10 reproduces the saving schedule derived in Figure 9.6 and the horizontal investment function from Figure 9.7. Notice that $S = I$ at one, and only one, level of aggregate output, $Y = 500$. At $Y = 500$, $C = 475$ and $I = 25$. In other words, $Y = C + I$, and therefore equilibrium exists.

ADJUSTMENT TO EQUILIBRIUM

We have now defined equilibrium and learned how to find it, but we have said nothing about how firms might react to *disequilibrium*. Now let us consider the actions that firms might take when planned aggregate expenditure exceeds aggregate output (income).

We already know that the only way firms can sell more than they produce is by selling some inventory. This means that when planned aggregate expenditure exceeds aggregate output, unplanned inventory reductions have occurred. It seems reasonable to assume that firms will respond to unplanned inventory reductions by increasing output. If firms increase output, then income must also increase (since output and income are simply two ways of measuring the same thing). As General Motors builds more cars, for example, it hires more workers (or pays its existing work force for working more hours), buys more steel, uses more electricity, and so on. These purchases by GM represent income for the producers of labor, steel, electricity, and so on. Therefore, if GM (and all other firms) try to keep their inventories intact by increasing production, they will generate more income in the economy as a whole. This in turn will lead to more consumption. Remember, when income rises, consumption also rises.

The adjustment process will continue as long as output (income) is below planned aggregate expenditure. Thus, if firms react to unplanned inventory reductions by increasing output, an economy with planned spending greater than output will adjust to equilibrium, with Y higher than before. Similarly, if planned spending is less than output, there will be unplanned increases in inventories. In this case, firms will respond by reducing output. As output falls, income falls, consumption falls, and so forth, until equilibrium is restored, with Y lower than before.

As Figure 9.8 shows, at any level of output above $Y = 500$, such as $Y = 800$, output will fall until it reaches equilibrium at $Y = 500$, and at any level of output below $Y = 500$, such as $Y = 200$, output will rise until it reaches equilibrium at $Y = 500$.[6]

THE MULTIPLIER

Now that we know how the equilibrium value of income is determined, we need to ask: How does the equilibrium level of output change when planned investment changes? In other words, if there is a sudden change in planned investment, how will output respond, if it responds at all? As we will see, the change in equilibrium output is *greater* than the initial change in planned investment. Output changes by a multiple of the change in planned investment. Not surprisingly, this multiple is called the **multiplier.**

multiplier *The ratio of the change in the equilibrium level of output to a change in some autonomous variable.*

autonomous variable *A variable that is assumed not to depend on the state of the economy—that is, when it is taken as given.*

More formally, the multiplier is defined as the ratio of the change in the equilibrium level of output to a change in some autonomous variable. A variable is **autonomous** when it is assumed not to depend on the state of the economy—that is, when it is taken as given. For the purposes of this chapter, we consider planned investment to be autonomous. This simplifies our analysis and provides a strong foundation for our later discussions.

With planned investment taken as given, we can now ask the question of how much the equilibrium level of output changes when planned investment changes. Remember that we are not trying here to explain *why* planned investment changes; we are simply asking how much the equilibrium level of output changes when (for whatever reason) planned investment changes. (Beginning in Chapter 13, we will no longer take planned investment as given and will explain how planned investment is determined.)

Consider, as an example, a sustained increase in planned investment of $25 billion—that is, suppose that I increases from $25 billion to $50 billion and stays at $50 billion. If equilibrium existed at $I = $25 billion, an increase in planned investment of $25 billion will cause a disequilibrium, with planned aggregate expenditure greater than aggregate output by $25 billion. Firms immediately see unplanned reductions in their inventories, and, as a result, they begin to increase output.

For the sake of illustration, let us say that the increase in planned investment comes from an anticipated increase in travel that leads airlines to purchase more airplanes, car rental companies to increase purchases of automobiles, and bus companies to purchase more buses. (These are, of course, capital goods.) The firms experiencing unplanned inventory declines will therefore be automobile manufacturers, bus producers, and aircraft producers—General Motors, Ford, McDonnell Douglas, Boeing, and so forth. In response to declining inventories of planes, buses, and cars, these firms will increase output.

Now suppose that these firms raise output by the full $25 billion increase in planned investment. Does this restore equilibrium? No, because when output goes up, people earn more income and a part of that income will be spent. This increases planned aggregate expenditure even further. In other words, an increase in I also leads indirectly to an increase in C. To produce more airplanes, Boeing has to hire more workers or ask its existing employees to work more hours. It also must buy

---

[6]*In discussing simple supply and demand equilibrium in Chapters 4 and 5, we saw that when quantity supplied exceeds quantity demanded, the price falls and the quantity supplied declines. Similarly, when quantity demanded exceeds quantity supplied, the price rises and the quantity supplied increases. In the analysis here we are ignoring potential changes in prices or in the price level and focusing on changes in the level of real output (income). Later, after we have introduced money and the price level into the analysis, prices will be very important. At this stage, however, only aggregate output (income) (Y) adjusts when aggregate expenditure exceeds aggregate output (with inventory falling) or when aggregate output exceeds aggregate expenditure (with inventory rising).*

more engines from General Electric, more tires from Goodyear, and so forth. Owners of these firms will earn more profits, produce more, hire more workers, and pay out more in wages and salaries.

This added income does not just vanish into thin air. It is paid to households that spend some of it and save the rest. The added production thus leads to added income, which leads to added consumption spending.

Therefore, if planned investment (I) goes up by $25 billion initially *and is sustained at this higher level,* an increase of output of $25 billion will *not* restore equilibrium, because it generates even more consumption spending (C). People buy more consumer goods. There are unplanned reductions of inventories of basic consumption items—washing machines, food, clothing, and so forth—and this prompts other firms to increase output. Thus, the cycle starts all over again.[7]

Clearly, then, output and income can rise by significantly more than the initial increase in planned investment. The question is: By how much? In other words, How large is the multiplier? This question is answered graphically in Figure 9.11 on page 206. Assume that the economy is in equilibrium at point A, where equilibrium output is 500. The increase in I of 25 shifts the $AE \equiv C + I$ curve up by 25, because I is higher by 25 at every level of income. The new equilibrium occurs at point B, where the equilibrium level of output is 600. Like point A, point B is on the 45° line and is thus an equilibrium value. Output (Y) has thus increased by 100 (600 − 500), or four times the initial increase in planned investment of 25, between point A and point B. The multiplier in this example is therefore 4. At point B, aggregate spending is also higher by 100. If 25 of this additional 100 is investment (I), as we know it is, the remaining amount—75—is added consumption (C). From point A to point B then, $\Delta Y = 100$, $\Delta I = 25$, and $\Delta C = 75$.

Why doesn't the multiplier process go on forever? Because only a fraction of the increase in income is consumed in each round. Successive increases in income become smaller and smaller in each round of the multiplier process until equilibrium is restored.

The size of the multiplier depends on the slope of the planned aggregate expenditure line. The steeper the slope of this line, the greater the change in output for a given change in investment. When planned investment is fixed, as it is in our example, the slope of the $AE \equiv C + I$ line is just the marginal propensity to consume ($\Delta C/\Delta Y$). The greater the MPC, the greater the multiplier. This should not be surprising. A large MPC means that consumption increases a lot when income increases. The more consumption changes, the more output has to change to achieve equilibrium.

---

[7]*Figure 9.9 can help you understand the multiplier effect more clearly. Note in the figure how an increase in planned investment makes its way through the circular flow. Initially, aggregate output is at equilibrium with Y = C + I. That is, every period, aggregate output is produced by firms, and every period, planned aggregate expenditure is just sufficient to take all those goods and services off the market.*

Now note what happens when planned investment spending increases and is sustained at a higher level. Firms experience unplanned declines in inventories and they increase output; more real output is produced in subsequent periods. But the added output means more income; thus we see added income flowing to households. This, in turn, means more spending. Households spend some portion of their added income (equal to the added income times the MPC) on consumer goods.

The higher consumption spending means that even if firms responded fully to the increase in investment spending in the first round, the economy is still out of equilibrium. Follow the added spending back over to firms in Figure 9.9 and you can see that with higher consumption, planned aggregate expenditure will be greater. Firms again see an unplanned decline in inventories and they respond by increasing the output of consumer goods. This sets off yet another round of income and expenditure increases: Output rises, and income rises as a result, thus increasing consumption. Higher consumption leads to yet another disequilibrium, inventories fall, and output (income) rises again.

FIGURE 9.11

The Multiplier as Seen in the Planned Aggregate Expenditure Diagram

At point *A*, the economy is in equilibrium at *Y* = 500. When *I* increases by 25, planned aggregate expenditure is initially greater than aggregate output. As output rises in response, additional consumption is generated, pushing equilibrium output up by a multiple of the initial increase in *I*. The new equilibrium is found at point *B*, where *Y* = 600. Equilibrium output has thus increased by 100 (600 – 500), or *four times* the amount of the increase in planned investment.

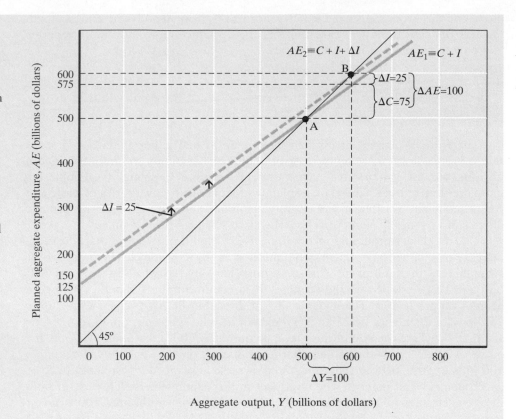

■ **The Multiplier Equation** Is there a way to determine the size of the multiplier without using graphic analysis? The answer is yes.

Consider the following. Assume, as we did above, that the market is in equilibrium at an income level of *Y* = 500. Now suppose that planned investment (*I*), and thus planned aggregate expenditure (*AE*), increases and remains higher by, $25 billion. Planned aggregate expenditure is thus greater than output, there is an unplanned inventory reduction, and firms respond by increasing output (income) (*Y*). This leads to a second round of increases, and so on.

What will restore equilibrium? Look back at Figure 9.10 and recall that planned aggregate expenditure (*AE* ≡ *C* + *I*) is not equal to aggregate output (*Y*) unless *S* = *I*; the leakage of saving must exactly match the injection of planned investment spending for the economy to be in equilibrium. Recall also that we assumed that planned investment jumps to a new higher level and stays there; it is a *sustained* increase of $25 billion in planned investment spending. As income rises, consumption rises and so does saving. Our *S* = *I* approach to equilibrium thus leads us to conclude that:

> Equilibrium will be restored only when saving has increased by exactly the amount of the initial increase in *I*.

Otherwise, *I* will continue to be greater than *S*, and *C* + *I* will continue to be greater than *Y*. (The *S* = *I* approach to equilibrium leads to an interesting paradox in the macroeconomy. For more details, see the Issues and Controversies box titled "The Paradox of Thrift.")

An interesting paradox can arise when households attempt to increase their saving. What happens if households become concerned about the future and want to save more today to be prepared for hard times tomorrow? If households increase their planned saving, the saving schedule in the Figure 1 shifts upward, from S to S'. The plan to save more is, of course, a plan to consume less, and the resulting drop in spending leads to a drop in income. Income drops by a multiple of the initial shift in the saving schedule. Before the increase in saving, equilibrium exists at point A, where $S = I$ and $Y = \$500$ billion. Increased saving shifts the equilibrium to point B, the point at which $S' = I$. New equilibrium output is thus $300 billion—a $200 billion decrease ($\Delta Y$) from the initial equilibrium.

Thus, by consuming less, households have actually *caused* the hard times about which they were apprehensive. What is worse, the new equilibrium finds saving at the same level as it was before consumption dropped ($25 billion). In their attempt to save more, households have caused a contraction in output, and thus in income. They end up consuming less, but they have not saved any more.

It should be clear why saving at the new equilibrium is equal to saving at the old equilibrium. Equilibrium requires that saving equal planned investment, and since planned investment is unchanged, saving must remain unchanged for

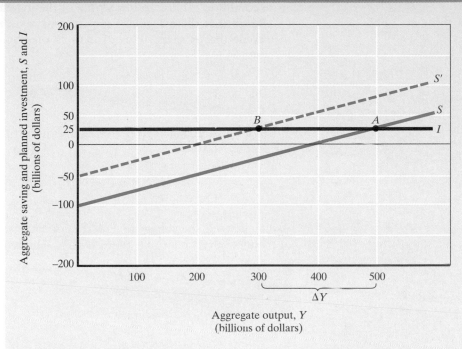

FIGURE 1

The Paradox of Thrift

An increase in planned saving from S to S' causes equilibrium output to decrease from $500 billion to $300 billion. The decreased consumption that accompanies increased saving leads to a contraction of the economy and thus to a reduction of income. But at the new equilibrium, saving is the same as it was at the initial equilibrium. Thus, increased efforts to save have caused a drop in income but no overall change in saving.

equilibrium to exist. This paradox shows that the interactions among sectors in the economy can be of crucial importance.

The **paradox of thrift** is "paradoxical" because it contradicts the widely held belief that "a penny saved is a penny earned." This may be true for an individual, but when society as a whole saves more, the result is a drop in income but no increased saving.

Does the paradox of thrift always hold? Recall our assumption that planned investment is fixed. Let

us drop this assumption for a moment. If the extra saving that households want to do to ward off hard times is channeled into additional investment through financial markets, there is a shift up in the I schedule. The paradox could then be averted. If investment increases, a new equilibrium can be achieved at a higher level of saving and income. This result, however, depends critically on the existence of a channel through which additional household saving finances additional investment.

It is possible to figure how much Y must increase in response to the additional planned investment before equilibrium will be restored. Y will rise, pulling S up with it until the change in saving is exactly equal to the change in planned investment—that is, until S is again equal to I at its new higher level. Since added saving is a *fraction* of added income (the *MPS*), the increase in *income* required to restore equilibrium must be *a multiple* of the increase in planned investment.

Recall that the marginal propensity to save (*MPS*) is the fraction of a change in income that is saved. It is defined as the change in S (ΔS) over the change in income (ΔY):

$$MPS \equiv \frac{\Delta S}{\Delta Y}$$

Since ΔS must be equal to ΔI for equilibrium to be restored, we can substitute ΔI for ΔS and solve:

$$MPS = \frac{\Delta I}{\Delta Y}. \text{ Therefore, } \Delta Y = \Delta I \times \frac{1}{MPS}.$$

As you can see, the change in equilibrium income (ΔY) is equal to the initial change in planned investment (ΔI) times $1/MPS$. The multiplier is thus $1/MPS$:

$$\text{Multiplier} \equiv \frac{1}{MPS}$$

Because $MPS + MPC \equiv 1$, $MPS \equiv 1 - MPC$. It therefore follows that the multiplier is also equal to:

$$\text{Multiplier} \equiv \frac{1}{1 - MPC}$$

In our example, the *MPC* is .75, so the *MPS* must equal $1 - .75$, or .25. Thus, the multiplier is 1 divided by .25, or 4. The change in the equilibrium level of Y is thus $4 \times \$25$ billion, or $\$100$ billion.[8] It is also important to note that the same analysis holds when planned investment falls. If planned investment falls by a certain amount and is sustained at this lower level, output will fall by a multiple of the reduction in I. As the initial shock is felt and firms cut output, they lay people off. The result: Income, and subsequently consumption, falls.

■ **The Size of the Multiplier in the Real World**   In considering the size of the multiplier, it is important to realize that the multiplier we derived in this chapter is based on a *very* simplified picture of the economy. First, we have assumed that planned investment is fixed and does not respond to changes in the economy. Second, we have thus far ignored the role of government, financial markets, and the rest of the world in the macroeconomy. For these reasons, it would be a mistake to move on from this chapter thinking that national income can be increased by $\$100$ billion simply by increasing planned investment spending by $\$25$ billion.

As we relax these assumptions in the following chapters, you will see that most of what we add to make our analysis more realistic has the effect of *reducing* the size of the multiplier. For example:

---

[8]*The multiplier can also be derived algebraically, as the appendix to this chapter demonstrates.*

1. The appendix to Chapter 10 shows that when tax payments depend on income (as they do in the real world), the size of the multiplier is reduced. As the economy expands, tax payments increase and act as a drag on the economy. The multiplier effect is thus smaller.

2. As you will see in Chapter 13, planned investment (I) is not fixed; rather, it depends on the interest rate in the economy. This too has the effect of reducing the size of the multiplier.

3. Thus far we have not discussed how the overall price level is determined in the economy. When we do so in Chapter 14, we will see that part of an expansion of the economy is likely to take the form of an increase in the price level rather than an increase in output. When this happens, the size of the multiplier is reduced.

4. We introduce the role of imports and exports in Chapter 10 and treat them fully in Chapter 22. In these chapters, you will see that the multiplier effect on domestic production will be reduced if some domestic spending leaks into foreign markets.

These juicy tidbits give you something to look forward to as you proceed through the rest of this book. For now, however, it is enough to point out that:

> In reality, the size of the multiplier is about 1.4. That is, a sustained increase in autonomous spending of $10 billion into the U.S. economy can be expected to raise real GDP over time by about $14 billion.

This is a far cry from the value of 4.0 that we used in this chapter.

■ The Multiplier In Action: Recovering From The Great Depression

The Great Depression began in 1930 and lasted nearly a decade. Real output in 1938 was lower than real output in 1929, and the unemployment rate never fell below 14% of the labor force between 1930 and 1940. How is it possible that the economy got "stuck" at such a low level of income and a high level of unemployment? The essentially Keynesian model that we have analyzed in this chapter can help us to answer this question.

If firms do not wish to undertake much investment (I is low) or if consumers decide to increase their saving and cut back on consumption, then planned spending will be low. Firms do not want to produce more because, with many workers unemployed, households do not have the income to buy the extra output that firms might produce. And households, who would purchase more if they had more income, cannot find jobs that would enable them to earn additional income. The economy is thus caught in a vicious cycle.

How might such a cycle be broken? One possibility is for planned aggregate expenditure to increase, thereby increasing aggregate output via the multiplier effect. This increase in AE may occur naturally, or it may be caused by a change in government policy.

In the late 1930s, for example, the economy experienced a surge of both residential and nonresidential investment. Between 1935 and 1940, total investment spending (in real terms) increased 64% and residential investment more than doubled. There can be no doubt that this increased investment had a multiplier effect. In just five years, employment in the construction industry increased by more than 400,000, employment in manufacturing industries jumped by more than 1 million, and total employment grew by more than 5 million. As more workers were employed, more income was generated, and some of this added income was spent on consumption goods. Inventories declined and firms began to expand output.

The multiplier story is not a complicated one. When the real output of an economy grows, real income also grows. Firms expand production, hire workers, and pay out wages and profits. In turn, households devote one part of their higher incomes to saving and the rest to consumption.

During 1994 and 1995, both the United States and China were experiencing a period of rising GDP. The experiences of a consumer products company in China and the automobile industry in the United States illustrate how an expansion can effect the behavior of individual firms.

CHINA

As China's economy has grown rapidly in the 1990s, demand for consumer products has increased, and so have output and employment at Unilever, a company that produces consumer products like soaps (Lux) and skin cream (Pond's):

> Starting with a handful of people in China a decade ago, Unilever has enjoyed one of the fastest growth rates of any foreign company in China. The 700 people it employed two years ago have reached 2,500 today, of whom only 80 are expatriates.
>
> The local employees range from production workers to more than [80] recent university graduates who . . . are being drawn rapidly into the multinational's management

As China's economy has grown, so has the demand for consumer products like Unilever's Lux soap. As a result of this increase, Unilever has increased output and employment.

> training programmes in China and abroad.
>
> The group expects its Chinese sales to rise from $200 [million] a year to $1.5 [billion] in 1999.[1]

UNITED STATES

Nowhere has the effect of a growing economy been seen more clearly than in the U.S. automobile and truck industry:

> DETROIT—Drawn by the fresh curves of some 1995 vehicles and the reduced prices on 1994 models, customers continued to flock to new car dealerships in October [1994], buying 8.9 percent more cars and light trucks than were sold during the brisk period a year ago, the auto makers reported today.
>
> During October, the first month of the 1995 model year, sales of cars rose 2.9 percent, to 738,221, while sales of light trucks—pickups, minivans and sport utility vehicles—rose 18.8 percent, to 525,285.

Sources: 1. Roderick Oram, "Wait and You'll Be Too Late," *Financial Times,* November 7, 1994, p. iv. 2. James Bennet, "Big Three Set Records for Trucks as Vehicle Sales Jump 8.9%," *The New York Times,* November 4, 1994, p. D1.

Between 1935 and 1940, real output (income) increased by more than one third and the unemployment rate dropped from 20.3% to 14.6 percent.

But 14.6% is still a very high rate of unemployment; the Depression was not yet over. Between 1940 and 1943, however, the Depression ended, with the unemployment rate dropping to 1.9% in 1943. This recovery was triggered by the mobilization for World War II and the significant increase in government purchases of goods and services, which rose from $14 billion in 1940 to $88.6 billion in 1943. In the next chapter, we will explore this *government spending multiplier,* and you'll see how the government can help stimulate the economy by increasing its spending.

The multiplier is a perfectly general concept that applies in all economies, not just that of the United States. For more on the multiplier effect in China, see the Global Perspective box titled "The Multiplier around the World in 1994."

LOOKING AHEAD: THE GOVERNMENT AND INTERNATIONAL SECTORS

In this chapter, we have taken the first important step in understanding how the economy works. We have described the behavior of two sectors (household and firm) and have discussed how equilibrium is achieved in the market for goods and services. In the next chapter, we will relax some of the assumptions we have made and take into account the roles of government spending and net exports in the economy. This will give us a more realistic picture of how our complex economy works.

SUMMARY

AGGREGATE OUTPUT AND AGGREGATE INCOME (Y)

1. Each period, firms produce an aggregate quantity of goods and services called *aggregate output* (Y). Because every dollar of expenditure is received by someone as income, aggregate output and aggregate income are the same thing.

2. The total amount of aggregate consumption that takes place in any given period of time depends on factors such as household income, household wealth, interest rates, and households' expectations about the future.

3. In an economy in which there are no imports or exports and no government, households can do only two things with their income: They can either spend on consumption or they can save. The letter C is used to refer to aggregate consumption by households. The letter S is used to refer to aggregate saving by households. By definition, saving equals income minus consumption: $S \equiv Y - C$.

4. The higher someone's income is, the higher his or her consumption is likely to be. This also holds true for the economy as a whole: There is a positive relationship between aggregate consumption (C) and aggregate income (Y).

5. The *marginal propensity to consume* (MPC) is the fraction of a change in income that is consumed, or spent. The *marginal propensity to save* (MPS) is the fraction of a change in income that is saved.

Because all income must be either saved or spent, $MPS + MPC \equiv 1$.

6. The primary form of spending that firms engage in is investment. Strictly speaking, *investment* refers to the purchase by firms of new buildings and equipment and additions to inventories, all of which add to firms' capital stock.

7. *Actual investment* can differ from planned investment because changes in firms' inventories are part of actual investment and inventory changes are not under the complete control of firms. Inventory changes are partly determined by how much households decide to buy. The letter I is used to refer to planned investment only.

EQUILIBRIUM AGGREGATE OUTPUT (INCOME)

8. In an economy with no government, no imports, and no exports, *planned aggregate expenditure* (AE) equals consumption plus planned investment: $AE \equiv C + I$. *Equilibrium* in the goods market is achieved when planned aggregate expenditure equals aggregate output: $C + I = Y$. This holds if, and only if, planned investment and actual investment are equal.

9 Because aggregate income must be saved or spent, the equilibrium condition $Y = C + I$ can be rewritten as $C + S = C + I$, or $S = I$. Thus, only when planned investment equals saving will there be equilibrium. This approach to equilibrium is called

the *saving/investment approach* to equilibrium or the *leakages/injections approach* to equilibrium.

10. When aggregate expenditure exceeds aggregate output (*income*), there is an unplanned fall in inventories. Firms will therefore increase output. This increased output leads to increased income and even more consumption. This process will continue as long as output (income) is below planned aggregate expenditure. If firms react to unplanned inventory reductions by increasing output, an economy with planned spending greater than output will adjust to equilibrium, with Y higher than before.

11. Equilibrium output changes by a multiple of the change in planned investment or any other au-

tonomous variable. The multiplier is equal to $1/MPS$.

12. When households increase their planned saving, income decreases and saving does not change. Saving does not increase because in equilibrium saving must equal planned investment and planned investment is fixed. If planned investment also increased, this *paradox of thrift* could be averted and a new equilibrium could be achieved at a higher level of saving and income. This result, however, depends critically on the existence of a channel through which additional household saving finances additional investment.

REVIEW TERMS AND CONCEPTS

actual investment 198

aggregate income 190

aggregate output 190

aggregate output (income) (Y) 190

autonomous variable 204

change in inventory 197

consumption function 192

desired, or **planned, investment (I)** 198

equilibrium 199

identity 191

investment 197

marginal propensity to consume (MPC) 193

marginal propensity to save (MPS) 194

multiplier 204

Equations:

1. $S \equiv Y - C$

2. $MPC \equiv$ slope of consumption function $\equiv \dfrac{\Delta C}{\Delta Y}$

3. $MPC + MPS \equiv 1$

4. $AE \equiv C + I$

5. Equilibrium condition: $Y = AE$ or $Y = C + I$

6. Saving/investment approach to equilibrium: $S = I$

7. Multiplier $\equiv \dfrac{1}{MPS} \equiv \dfrac{1}{1 - MPC}$

paradox of thrift 207

planned aggregate expenditure (AE) 198

saving (S) 190

PROBLEM SET

1. Explain the multiplier intuitively. Why is it that an increase in planned investment of $100 raises equilibrium output by more than $100? Why is the effect on equilibrium output finite? How do we know that the multiplier is $1/MPS$?

2. Explain how planned investment can differ from actual investment.

3. The following is the consumption schedule for the Republic of Nurd in 1994:

Y	50	60	70	80	90	100	110	120	130	140	150
C	52	62	71.5	80.5	89	97	104	110	115	119	122.5

a. Construct a graph of the consumption function. (Assume that within each income range the slope of the consumption function is constant.)

b. Compute the marginal propensity to consume over each income range. What is the geometrical meaning of the *MPC?* Explain why.

c. Compute and graph the saving schedule (saving as a function of income, *Y*) for Nurd. Also compute the marginal propensity to save over each income range.

d. Suppose that planned investment spending (*I*) is constant at $10. What is the equilibrium level of

Nurd's gross domestic product (*Y*)? Graph the equilibrium level of income/output (*Y*) in two ways.

e. Suppose that planned investment (*I*) on Nurd increases to $18 and remains at that level. What will Nurd's new equilibrium level of income/output (*Y*) be? Compute and show this equilibrium point graphically.

4. You are given the following data regarding Freedonia, a legendary country:

(1) Consumption function: $C = 200 + 0.8Y$

(2) Investment function: $I = 100$

(3) $AE \equiv C + I$

(4) $AE = Y$

a. What is the marginal propensity to consume in Freedonia? The marginal propensity to save?

b. Graph equations (3) and (4) and solve for equilibrium income.

c. Suppose equation (2) were changed to
(2′) $I = 110$.
What is the new equilibrium level of income? By how much does the $10 increase in planned investment change equilibrium income? What is the value of the multiplier?

d. Calculate the saving function for Freedonia. Plot this saving function on a graph with equation (2). Explain why the equilibrium income in this graph must be the same as in part b.

5. If I decide to save an extra dollar, my saving goes up by that amount. But if everyone decides to save an extra dollar, income falls and saving does not rise. Explain.

6. You learned earlier that expenditures and income should always be equal. In this chapter, you've learned that *AE* and aggregate output (income) can be different. Is there an inconsistency here?

DERIVING THE MULTIPLIER ALGEBRAICALLY

In addition to deriving the multiplier using the simple substitution we used in the chapter, we can also derive the formula for the multiplier by using simple algebra.

Recall that our consumption function is

$$C = a + bY$$

where *b* is the marginal propensity to consume. In equilibrium,

$$Y = C + I$$

All we have to do now is solve these two equations for *Y* in terms of *I*. Substituting the first equation into the second, we get

$$Y = \underbrace{a + bY}_{C} + I$$

This equation can be rearranged to yield

$$Y - bY = a + I$$
$$Y(1 - b) = a + I$$

We can then solve for *Y* in terms of *I* by dividing through by $(1 - b)$:

$$Y = (a + I) \left(\frac{1}{1 - b}\right)$$

Now look carefully at this expression and think about increasing *I* by some amount, ΔI, with *a* held constant. If *I* increases by ΔI, income will increase by

$$\Delta Y = \Delta I \times \frac{1}{1 - b}$$

Since $b \equiv MPC$, the expression becomes

$$\Delta Y = \Delta I \times \frac{1}{1 - MPC}$$

The multiplier is thus

$$\frac{1}{1 - MPC}$$

Finally, since $MPS + MPC \equiv 1$, *MPS* is equal to $1 - MPC$, making the alternative expression for the multiplier $1/MPS$, just as we saw in the chapter.

10

THE GOVERNMENT AND FISCAL POLICY

F EW AREAS IN EITHER MACROECONOMICS OR MICROECONOMICS arouse as much controversy as the question of the proper role of government in the economy. In microeconomics, the active presence of government in regulating competition, providing roads and education, and redistributing income is much applauded by those who believe that a free market simply does not work well if left to its own devices. Opponents of government intervention argue that it is the government, rather than the market, that performs badly. These critics point to bureaucracy and inefficiency that they argue could be eliminated or reduced if the government played a smaller role in the economy. Many believe that the Republican sweep of the midterm elections in November 1994 was a mandate for less government.

In macroeconomics, the debate over what the government can and should do has a similar flavor, although the issues are somewhat different. At one end of the spectrum are the Keynesians and their intellectual descendants, who believe that the macroeconomy is likely to fluctuate too much if left on its own and that the government should play an important role in smoothing out fluctuations in the business cycle. These ideas can be traced back to Keynes's analysis in *The General Theory*, which suggests that governments can use their taxing and spending powers to increase aggregate expenditure (and thereby stimulate aggregate output) in times of recessions or depressions. At the other end of the spectrum are those who claim that government spending is at best incapable of stabilizing the economy and at worst destabilizing and harmful.

Perhaps the one thing most people can agree on is that, like it or not, governments are important actors in the economies of virtually all countries. On these grounds alone, it is worth our while to analyze the way in which the government influences the functioning of the macroeconomy.

While the government has a wide variety of powers—including regulating firms' entry into and exit from an industry, setting standards for product quality, setting minimum wage levels, and regulating the disclosure of information—in macroeconomics we study a government with general, but more limited, powers. Specifically, government can affect the macroeconomy through two specific policy channels: fiscal policy and monetary policy. **Fiscal policy,** the focus of this chapter, refers to the government's spending and taxing behavior—in other words, its budget policy.[1] Fiscal policy is generally divided into three categories: (1) policies regarding government purchases of goods and labor, (2) policies regarding taxes, and (3) policies regarding transfer payments (such as unemployment compensation, social security benefits, welfare payments, and veterans' benefits) to households. **Monetary policy,** the focus of the next two chapters, refers to the behavior of the nation's central bank, the Federal Reserve, regarding the nation's money supply.

fiscal policy *The government's spending and taxing policies.*

monetary policy *The behavior of the Federal Reserve regarding the nation's money supply.*

GOVERNMENT PARTICIPATION IN THE ECONOMY

Given the scope and power of local, state, and federal governments in the U.S. economy, it should be stressed that there are some matters over which these governments exert great control and some matters that are beyond their control. There is an important distinction between variables that a government controls directly and variables that are a consequence of government decisions *combined with the state of the economy.*

For example, tax rates are controlled by the government. By law, Congress has the authority to levy taxes: It decides who and what should be taxed and at what rate. Tax *revenue,* on the other hand, is not subject to complete control by the government. Revenue from the personal income tax system depends both on personal tax rates (which Congress sets) *and* on the income of the household sector (which depends on many factors that are not under direct government control, such as how much households decide to work). Revenue from the corporate profits tax depends both on corporate profits tax rates and on the size of corporate profits. The government controls corporate tax rates but not the size of corporate profits.

Government spending also depends both on government decisions and on the state of the economy. For example, one of the most important transfer programs in the United States is the unemployment insurance program, which pays benefits to people who are unemployed. When the economy goes into a recession, the number of unemployed workers increases and so does the level of government unemployment insurance payments.

Because taxes and expenditures often go up or down in response to changes in the economy rather than as the result of conscious decisions by policy makers, we will occasionally use the term **discretionary fiscal policy** to refer to changes in taxes or spending that are the result of conscious changes in government policy.

discretionary fiscal policy *Changes in taxes or spending that are the result of conscious changes in government policy.*

---

[1]*The word* fiscal *comes from the root* fisc, *which refers to the "treasury" of a government.*

GOVERNMENT PURCHASES (G), NET TAXES (T), AND DISPOSABLE INCOME (Y_d)

In the previous chapter, we explored the equilibrium level of national output for a simple economy with no government and no imports and exports. The purpose of that chapter was to provide you with a general idea of how the macroeconomy operates.

Clearly, though, it is much more realistic to consider an economy in which government is an active participant. After all, there are no countries in the world without a government. We therefore begin our discussion of fiscal policy by adding the government sector into the simple economy described in the previous chapter.

To keep things simple, we will combine two major government activities—the collection of taxes and the payment of transfer payments—into a category we will call **net taxes (T)**. Specifically, net taxes are equal to the tax payments made to the government by firms and households minus transfer payments made to households by the government. The other variable we will consider is government purchases of goods and services (G).

Our earlier discussions of household consumption did not take taxes into account. We simply assumed that all the income generated in the economy was either spent or saved by households. However, when we take into account the role of government in the economy, as Figure 10.1 does, we see that as income (Y) flows toward households, the government takes income from households in the form of net taxes (T). The income that ultimately gets to households is called **disposable, or after-tax, income (Y_d)**:

$$\text{Disposable income} = \text{Total income} - \text{Net taxes} \quad Y_d \equiv Y - T$$

net taxes (T) *Taxes paid by firms and households to the government minus transfer payments made to households by the government.*

disposable, or **after-tax, income (Y_d)** *Total income minus net taxes: $Y - T$.*

FIGURE 10.1

Adding Net Taxes (T) and Government Purchases (G) to the Circular Flow of Income

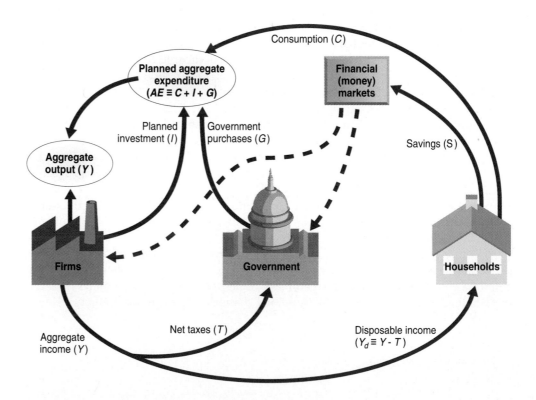

Y_d excludes taxes paid by households and includes transfer payments made to households by the government. Note that for now we are assuming that T does not depend on Y—that is, net taxes do not depend on income. This assumption is relaxed in Appendix B to this chapter. Taxes that do not depend on income are sometimes called *lump-sum taxes*.

As Figure 10.1 also shows, the disposable income (Y_d) of households must end up either as consumption (C) or saving (S). Thus, it follows that

$$Y_d \equiv C + S$$

Remember that the triple equal sign means that this equation is an identity, or something that is always true.

Because disposable income is simply aggregate income (Y) minus net taxes (T), we can write another identity:

$$Y - T \equiv C + S$$

Adding T to both sides, we get:

$$Y \equiv C + S + T$$

This identity simply says that aggregate income gets cut into three pieces. Government takes a slice (net taxes, T), and then households divide the rest between consumption and saving (C and S).

Because governments spend money on goods and services, we also need to expand our definition of planned aggregate expenditure. Planned aggregate expenditure (AE) is equal to the sum of consumption spending by households (C), planned investment by business firms (I), *and* government purchases of goods and services (G):

$$AE \equiv C + I + G$$

A government's **budget deficit** is the difference between what it spends (G) and what it collects in taxes (T) in a given period:

$$\text{Budget deficit} \equiv G - T$$

budget deficit *The difference between what a government spends and what it collects in taxes in a given period: $G - T$.*

If G exceeds T, the government must borrow from the public to finance the deficit. It does so by selling Treasury bonds and bills (more on this later). In this case, a part of household saving (S) goes to the government. Observe from the dotted lines in Figure 10.1 that some S goes to firms to finance investment projects and some goes to the government to finance its deficit.[2]

■ **Adding Taxes to the Consumption Function**   In the last chapter, we examined the consumption behavior of households and noted that aggregate consumption (C) depends on aggregate income (Y): In general, the higher aggregate income is, the higher is aggregate consumption. For the sake of illustration, we used a specific linear consumption function:

$$C = a + bY$$

where a is the amount of consumption that would take place if national income were zero and b is the marginal propensity to consume.

---

[2]*Although it is almost unheard of these days, governments do sometimes run budget surpluses. A surplus occurs when net taxes are greater than government purchases of goods and services. A surplus is simply a negative deficit.*

We need to modify this consumption function slightly now that we have added government to the economy. With taxes now a part of the picture, it makes sense to assume that disposable income (Y_d), rather than before-tax income (Y), determines consumption behavior. If you earn a million dollars, but have to pay $950,000 in taxes, you have no more disposable income than someone who earns only $50,000 but pays no taxes. In terms of what you have available for spending on current consumption, what matters is your disposable income, not your before-tax income.

It is very easy to modify our aggregate consumption function to incorporate disposable income rather than before-tax income. Instead of $C = a + bY$, we can simply write

$$C = a + bY_d$$

$$\text{or}$$

$$C = a + b (Y - T)$$

Our new consumption function now has consumption depending on disposable income rather than on before-tax income.

■ **Investment**   What about investment? The government can have an important effect on investment behavior through its tax treatment of depreciation and its other tax policies. Investment may also vary with economic conditions and interest rates, as we will see a little later. For our present purposes, however, we shall continue to assume that planned investment (I) is fixed.

EQUILIBRIUM OUTPUT: $Y = C + I + G$

We know from the previous chapter that equilibrium occurs where $Y = AE$—that is, where aggregate output equals planned aggregate expenditure. Remember that planned aggregate expenditure in an economy with a government is $AE \equiv C + I + G$. We can thus write the equilibrium condition as:

> Equilibrium condition: $Y = C + I + G$

The equilibrium analysis we presented in the previous chapter holds here also. If output (Y) exceeds planned aggregate expenditure $(C + I + G)$, there will be an unplanned increase in inventories. In other words, actual investment will exceed planned investment. Conversely, if $C + I + G$ exceeds Y, there will be an unplanned decrease in inventories.

Let us work through a numerical example to illustrate the government's effect on the macroeconomy and the equilibrium condition. First, our specific consumption function, which was $C = 100 + .75Y$ before we introduced the government sector, now becomes

$$C = 100 + .75Y_d$$

$$\text{or}$$

$$C = 100 + .75 (Y - T)$$

Second, we assume that the government is currently purchasing $100 billion of goods and services and collecting net taxes (T) of $100 billion.[3] In other words, the

---

[3]*As we pointed out earlier, the government does not have complete control over tax revenues and transfer payments. We ignore this problem here, however, and set tax revenues minus transfers at a fixed amount. Things will become more realistic later in this chapter and in Appendix B.*

TABLE 10.1 — FINDING EQUILIBRIUM FOR $I = 100$, $G = 100$, AND $T = 100$
(ALL FIGURES IN BILLIONS OF DOLLARS)

(1) OUTPUT (INCOME) Y	(2) NET TAXES T	(3) DISPOSABLE INCOME $Y_d \equiv Y - T$	(4) CONSUMPTION SPENDING $(C = 100 + .75\,Y_d)$	(5) PLANNED SAVING S $(Y_d - C)$	(6) PLANNED INVESTMENT SPENDING I	(7) GOVERNMENT PURCHASES G	(8) UNPLANNED AGGREGATE EXPENDITURE $C + I + G$	(9) ADJUST- INVENTORY CHANGE $Y - (C + I + G)$	(10) MENT TO DISEQUILI- BRIUM
300	100	200	250	-50	100	100	450	-150	Output ↑
500	100	400	400	0	100	100	600	-100	Output ↑
700	100	600	550	50	100	100	750	-50	Output ↑
900	100	800	700	100	100	100	900	0	Equilibrium
1100	100	1000	850	150	100	100	1050	+ 50	Output ↓
1300	100	1200	1000	200	100	100	1200	+ 100	Output ↓
1500	100	1400	1150	250	100	100	1350	+ 150	Output ↓

government is running a balanced budget, financing all of its spending with taxes. Third, we assume that planned investment (I) is $100 billion.

Table 10.1 calculates planned aggregate expenditure at several levels of disposable income. For example, at $Y = 500$, disposable income is $Y - T$, or 400. Therefore, $C = 100 + .75(400) = 400$. Assuming that I is fixed at $100 billion, and assuming that G is fixed at $100 billion, planned aggregate expenditure is 600 ($C + I + G = 400 + 100 + 100$). Since output ($Y$) is only 500, planned spending is greater than output by 100. As a result, there is an unplanned inventory decrease of 100, giving firms an incentive to raise output. Thus, output of $500 billion is below equilibrium.

If $Y = 1300$, however, then $Y_d = 1200$, $C = 1000$, and planned aggregate expenditure is 1200. Here, planned spending is *less* than output, there will be an unplanned inventory increase of 100, and firms will have an incentive to cut back output. Thus, output of $1300 billion is above equilibrium. Only when output is 900 are output and planned aggregate expenditure equal, and only at $Y = 900$ does equilibrium exist.

In Figure 10.2 on page 220, we derive the same equilibrium level of output graphically. First, the consumption function must be drawn, taking into account the net taxes of 100. The old function was $C = 100 + .75Y$. The new function is $C = 100 + .75(Y - T)$ or $C = 100 + .75 (Y - 100)$. This can be rewritten as $C = 100 + .75Y - 75$, or $C = 25 + .75Y$. The marginal propensity to consume has not changed—we assume that it remains .75. Thus, for example, consumption at an income of zero is $25 billion ($C = 25 + .75Y = 25 + .75(0) = 25$). Note that the consumption function in Figure 10.2 plots the points in columns 1 and 4 of Table 10.1.

Planned aggregate expenditure, you will recall, is arrived at by adding planned investment to consumption. But now, in addition to 100 in investment, we have government purchases of 100. Thus, because I and G are constant at 100 each at all levels of income, we add $I + G = 200$ to consumption at every level of income. The result is the new AE curve. This curve is just a plot of the points in columns 1 and 8 of Table 10.1. The 45° line helps us find the equilibrium level of real output, which, as we already know, is 900. If you examine any level of output above or below 900, you will find disequilibrium. Look, for example, at $Y = 500$ on the graph. At this level, planned aggregate expenditure is 600, but output is only 500. Inventories will fall below what was planned, and firms will have an incentive to increase output.

■ **The Leakages/Injections Approach to Equilibrium** As we did in the last chapter, we can also examine equilibrium using the leakages/injections approach. Look again

FIGURE 10.2

Since *G* and *I* are both fixed at $100 billion, the aggregate expenditure function is the new consumption function displaced upward by *I* + *G* = 200. Equilibrium occurs at *Y* = *C* + *I* + *G* = $900 billion.

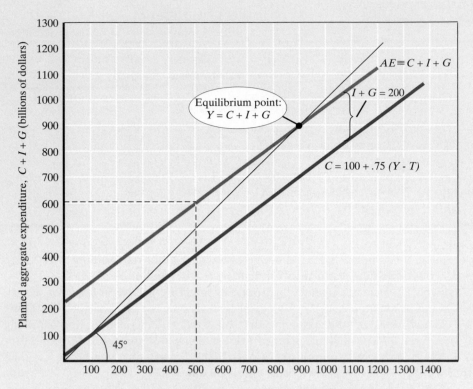

at the circular flow of income in Figure 10.1. The government takes out net taxes (*T*) from the flow of income—a leakage—and households save (*S*) some of their income—also a leakage from the flow of income. The planned spending injections are government purchases (*G*) and planned investment (*I*). If leakages (*S* + *G*) equal planned injections (*I* + *G*), there is equilibrium:

Leakages/injections approach to equilibrium: $S + T = I + G$

This equilibrium condition is easy to derive. We know that in equilibrium, aggregate output (income) (*Y*) equals planned aggregate expenditure (*AE*). By definition, *AE* equals *C* + *I* + *G*, and by definition *Y* equals *C* + *S* + *T*. Therefore, at equilibrium

$$C + S + T = C + I + G$$

Subtracting *C* from both sides leaves

$$S + T = I + G$$

Note that equilibrium does *not* require that *G* = *T* (a balanced government budget) or that *S* = *I*. It is only necessary that the sum of *S* and *T* equals the sum of *I* and *G*.

Column 5 of Table 10.1 calculates aggregate saving by subtracting consumption from disposal income at every level of disposable income ($S \equiv Y_d - C$). Since *I* and *G* are fixed, *I* + *G* equals 200 at every level of income. The table shows that *S* + *T* equals 200 only at *Y* = 900. Thus, the equilibrium level of output (income) is 900, the same answer we arrived at through numerical and graphical analysis.

FISCAL POLICY AT WORK: THE MULTIPLIER EFFECTS

You can see from Figure 10.2 that if the government were able to change the levels of either G or T, it would be able to change the equilibrium level of output (income). At this point, we are assuming that the government does control G and T.

THE GOVERNMENT SPENDING MULTIPLIER

Let's begin our analysis of fiscal policy's effects on the macroeconomy with a simple story. Suppose that you are the chief economic adviser to the President and that the economy is sitting at the equilibrium output pictured in Figure 10.2. Output and income are being produced at a rate of $900 billion per year, and the government is currently buying $100 billion worth of goods and services each year and is financing them with $100 billion in taxes. The budget is balanced. In addition, the private sector is investing (producing capital goods) at a rate of $100 billion per year.

At this point, the President calls you into the Oval Office and says, "Unemployment is too high. We need to lower unemployment by increasing output and income." After some careful research, you determine that an acceptable unemployment rate could be achieved only if aggregate output increases to $1100 billion.

The question you now need to answer is: How can the government use taxing and spending policy—fiscal policy—to increase the equilibrium level of national output? Suppose that the President has let it be known that taxes must remain at present levels—the Congress just passed a major tax reform package—so adjusting T is out of the question for several years. That leaves you with G. Your only option is thus to increase government spending while holding taxes constant.

To increase spending without raising taxes (which provides the government with revenue to spend), the government must borrow. When G is bigger than T, the government runs a deficit, and the difference between G and T must be borrowed. For the moment we will ignore the possible effect of the deficit and focus only on the effect of a higher G with T constant.

Meanwhile, the President is awaiting your answer. How much of an increase in spending would be required to generate a $200 billion increase in the equilibrium level of output, pushing it from $900 billion up to $1100 billion and reducing unemployment to the President's acceptable level?

You might be tempted to say that since we need to increase income by 200 (1100 − 900), we should increase government spending by the same amount.[4] But consider what would happen if we do. The increased government spending will throw the economy out of equilibrium. Since G is a component of aggregate spending, planned aggregate expenditure will increase by 200. Planned spending will be greater than output, inventories will be lower than planned, and firms will have an incentive to increase output. Suppose output rises by the desired 200. You might be tempted to think, "Well, we increased spending by 200 and output by 200, so equilibrium is restored."

As we know, however, there is more to the story than this. The moment that output rises, the economy is generating more income. After all, this was the desired effect: the creation of more employment. Some of the newly employed workers become consumers and some of their income gets spent. With higher consumption spending, planned spending will be greater than output, inventories will be lower than planned, and firms will raise output, and thus income, again. This time firms are responding to the new consumption spending. Already, total income is over 1100.

---

[4]*For the rest of this discussion, we will assume but not state that figures are in billions of dollars.*

This story should sound familiar. It is the multiplier in action. Although this time it is government spending (G) that is changed rather than planned investment (I), the effect is the same as the multiplier effect we described in the previous chapter. An increase in government spending has exactly the same impact on the equilibrium level of output and income as an increase in planned investment. A dollar of extra spending from either G or I is identical with respect to its impact on equilibrium output. Thus, the equation for the government spending multiplier is the same as the equation for the multiplier for a change in planned investment.[5]

$$\text{Government spending multiplier} \equiv \frac{1}{MPS}$$

government spending multiplier *The ratio of the change in the equilibrium level of output to a change in government spending.*

Formally, the **government spending multiplier** is defined as the ratio of the change in the equilibrium level of output to a change in government spending. This is the same definition we used in the previous chapter, but now the autonomous variable is government spending rather than planned investment.

Remember that we were thinking of increasing government spending (G) by 200. We can use the multiplier analysis to see what the new equilibrium level of Y would be for an increase in G of 200. The multiplier in our example is 4. (Since b—the MPC—is .75, the MPS must be 1 − .75, or .25. And 1/.25 = 4). Thus, Y will increase by 800 (4 × 200). Since the initial level of Y was 900, the new equilibrium level of Y is 900 + 800 = 1700 when G is increased by 200.

The level of 1700 is much larger than the level of 1100 that we calculated as necessary to lower unemployment to the desired level. Let us back up, then. If we want Y to increase by 200 and if the multiplier is 4, we need G to increase by only 200/4 = 50. In other words, if G changes by 50, the equilibrium level of Y will change by 200, and the new value of Y will be 1100 (900 + 200), as desired.

Looking at Table 10.2, we can check our answer to be sure that it is an equilibrium. Look first at the old equilibrium of 900. When government purchases (G) were equal to 100, aggregate output (income) was equal to planned aggregate expenditure (AE ≡ C + I + G) at Y = 900. But now G has increased to 150. Thus, at Y = 900, (C + I + G) is greater than Y, there's an unplanned fall in inventories and output will rise. The question is: By how much? The multiplier told us that equi-

TABLE 10.2			FINDING EQUILIBRIUM AFTER A $50 BILLION GOVERNMENT SPENDING INCREASE (ALL FIGURES IN BILLIONS OF DOLLARS; G HAS INCREASED FROM 100 IN TABLE 10.1 TO 150 HERE)							
(1)	(2)	(3)	(4)	(5)	(6) PLANNED	(7)	(8) PLANNED	(9) UNPLANNED	(10) ADJUST-
OUTPUT (INCOME)	NET TAXES	DISPOSABLE INCOME	CONSUMPTION SPENDING	SAVING S	INVESTMENT SPENDING	GOVERNMENT PURCHASES	AGGREGATE EXPENDITURE	INVENTORY CHANGE	MENT TO DISEQUILI-
Y	T	$Y_d \equiv Y - T$	$(C = 100 + .75\ Y_d)$	$(Y_d - C)$	I	G	C + I + G	Y − (C + I + G)	BRIUM
300	100	200	250	−50	100	150	500	−200	Output ↑
500	100	400	400	0	100	150	650	−150	Output ↑
700	100	600	550	50	100	150	800	−100	Output ↑
900	100	800	700	100	100	150	950	−50	Output ↑
1100	100	1000	850	150	100	150	1100	0	Equilibrium
1300	100	1200	1000	200	100	150	1250	+50	Output ↓

---

[5]*We derive the government spending multiplier algebraically in Appendix A to this chapter.*

librium income would rise by four times the change in G, which was 50. Thus, Y should rise by $4 \times 50 = 200$, from 900 to 1100 before equilibrium is restored. Let's check. If $Y = 1100$, then consumption is $C = 100 + .75 \ Y_d = 100 + .75(1000) = 850$. Since I equals 100 and G now equals 100 (the original level of G) + 50 (the additional G brought about by the fiscal policy change) = 150, then $C + I + G = 850 + 100 + 150 = 1100$. Thus, $Y = AE$, and the economy is in equilibrium.

The graphic solution to the President's problem is presented in Figure 10.3. An increase in G of 50 shifts the planned aggregate expenditure function up by 50. As you can see, the new equilibrium income occurs where the new AE line (AE_2) crosses the 45° line, which is at $Y = 1100$.

THE TAX MULTIPLIER

Remember that fiscal policy involves policies regarding government spending *and* policies regarding taxation. What effect does a change in tax policy have on the economy? To shed some light on this question, imagine the following situation. You are still chief economic adviser to the President, but now the President instructs you to devise a plan to reduce unemployment to an acceptable level *without* increasing the level of government spending. In your plan, instead of increasing government spending (G), you decide to cut taxes and maintain the current level of spending. A tax cut increases disposable income, which is likely to lead to added consumption spending. (Remember our general rule that increased income leads to increased consumption.) Would the impact of a decrease in taxes on aggregate output (income) be the same as it would be for an increase in G?

Clearly, a decrease in taxes would increase income. The government spends no less than it did before the tax cut, and households find they have a larger after-tax,

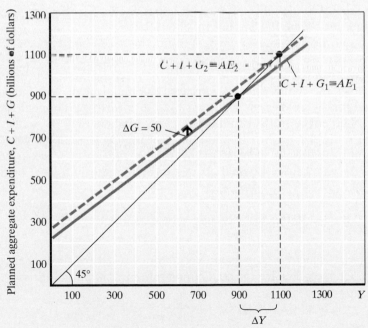

FIGURE 10.3

The Government Spending Multiplier

Increasing government spending by $50 billion shifts the AE function up by 50. As Y rises in response, additional consumption is generated. Overall, the equilibrium level of Y increases by 200, from 900 to 1100.

or disposable, income than they had before. This leads to an increase in consumption. Thus, planned aggregate expenditure will increase, which will lead to inventories being lower than planned, which will lead to a rise in output. When output rises, more workers will be employed and more income will be generated, causing a second-round increase in consumption, and so on. Thus, income will increase by a multiple of the decrease in taxes. But there is a wrinkle:

> The multiplier for a change in taxes is *not the same* as the multiplier for a change in government spending.

tax multiplier *The ratio of change in the equilibrium level of output to a change in taxes.*

Why does the **tax multiplier**—that is, the ratio of change in the equilibrium level of output to a change in taxes—differ from the spending multiplier? To answer this question, it is helpful to compare the ways in which a tax cut and a spending increase work their way through the economy.

Look back at Figure 10.1. When the government increases its spending, there is an immediate and direct impact on the economy's *total* spending. Because G is a component of planned aggregate expenditure, an increase in G leads to a dollar-for-dollar increase in planned aggregate expenditure. When taxes are cut, however, there is no direct impact on spending. Taxes enter the picture only because they have an effect on the household's disposable income, and households' disposable income influences their consumption (which is part of total spending). As Figure 10.1 shows, the tax cut flows through households before affecting aggregate expenditure.

Let's assume that the government decides to cut taxes by $1. By how much would spending increase? We already know the answer to this question. The marginal propensity to consume tells us how much consumption spending changes when disposable income changes. In the example we have been using throughout this chapter, the marginal propensity to consume out of disposable income is .75. This means that if households' after-tax incomes rise by $1, they will increase their consumption not by the full $1, but by only $0.75.[6]

To summarize: When government spending increases by $1, planned aggregate expenditure increases initially by the full amount of the rise in G, or $1. When taxes are cut, however, the initial increase in planned aggregate expenditure is only the MPC times the change in taxes. Because the initial increase in planned aggregate expenditure is smaller for a tax cut than it is for a government spending increase, the final effect on the equilibrium level of income will be smaller.

To figure the size of the tax multiplier, we use the same logic we used to derive the multiplier for an increase in investment and an increase in government purchases. As you know, the final change in the equilibrium level of output (income) (Y) is:

$$\Delta Y = (\text{initial increase in aggregate expenditure}) \times \left(\frac{1}{MPS}\right)$$

Since the initial change in aggregate expenditure caused by a tax change of ΔT is $(-\Delta T \times MPC)$, we can solve for the tax multiplier by simple substitution:

$$\Delta Y = (-\Delta T \times MPC) \times \left(\frac{1}{MPS}\right) = -\Delta T \times \left(\frac{MPC}{MPS}\right)$$

---

[6]*What happens to the other $.25? Remember that whatever households do not consume is, by definition, saved. The missing $.25 thus gets allocated to saving.*

Because a tax cut will cause an *increase* in consumption expenditures and output and a tax increase will cause a *reduction* in consumption expenditures and output, the tax multiplier is a negative multiplier:

$$\text{Tax multiplier} \equiv -\left(\frac{MPC}{MPS}\right)$$

We derive the tax multiplier algebraically in Appendix A to this chapter.

If the *MPC* is .75, as it is in our example, the multiplier is $-.75/.25 = -3$. Under these conditions, a tax cut of $100 billion will increase the equilibrium level of output by $-\$100 \times -\$3 = \$300$ billion. This is very different than the effect of our government spending multiplier of 4. Under these same conditions, a $100 billion increase in *G* will increase the equilibrium level of output by $400 billion ($100 billion × 4).

THE BALANCED-BUDGET MULTIPLIER

We have now discussed (1) changing government spending with no change in taxes, and (2) changing taxes with no change in government spending. But what happens if government spending and taxes are increased by the same amount? That is, what if the government decides to pay for its extra spending by increasing taxes by the same amount? Such a move would not change the government's budget deficit, since the increase in expenditures would be exactly matched by an increase in tax income.

You might think in this case that equal increases in government spending and taxes have no effect on equilibrium income. After all, the extra government spending is just equal to the extra amount of tax revenues collected by the government. But careful thought should convince you that this is not so. Take, for example, a government spending increase of $40 billion. We know from the analysis above that an increase in *G* of $40 billion, with taxes (*T*) held constant, should increase the equilibrium level of income by $40 billion × the government spending multiplier. The multiplier is $1/MPS$ or $1/.25 = 4$. Thus, the equilibrium level of income should rise by $160 billion ($40 billion × 4).

Now let us suppose that instead of keeping tax revenues constant, we finance the $40 billion increase in government spending with an equal increase in taxes, so as to maintain a balanced budget. What happens to aggregate spending as a result of both the rise in *G* and the rise in *T*? There are two initial effects. First, government spending rises by $40 billion. This effect is direct, immediate, and positive. But now the government also collects $40 billion more in taxes. The tax increase has a *negative* impact on overall spending in the economy, but it does not fully offset the increase in government spending.

The final impact of a tax increase on aggregate expenditure depends on how households respond to it. The only thing we know about household behavior so far is that households spend 75% of their added income and save 25 percent. We know that when disposable income falls, both consumption and saving are reduced. A tax *increase* of $40 billion reduces disposable income by $40 billion, and that means consumption falls by $40 billion × *MPC*. Since $MPC = .75$, consumption falls by $30 billion ($40 billion × .75).

The net result in the beginning is thus that government spending rises by $40 billion and consumption spending falls by $30 billion. This means that aggregate expenditure increases by $10 billion right after the simultaneous balanced-budget increases in *G* and *T*.

balanced-budget multiplier
The ratio of change in the equilibrium level of output to a change in government spending where the change in government spending is balanced by a change in taxes so as not to create any deficit. The balanced-budget multiplier is equal to one: The change in Y resulting from the change in G and the equal change in T is exactly the same size as the initial change in G or T itself.

So we know that a balanced-budget increase in G and T will raise output. But the question is: By how much? How large is this **balanced-budget multiplier**? The answer may surprise you:

> Balanced-budget multiplier $\equiv 1$

Let us combine what we know about the tax multiplier and the government spending multiplier to explain why this is so. To find the final effect of a simultaneous increase in government spending and increase in net taxes, we need to add the multiplier effects of the two. The government spending multiplier is $1/MPS$. The tax multiplier is $-MPC/MPS$. The sum of the two is $(1/MPS) + (-MPC/MPS) \equiv (1 - MPC)/MPS$. Because $MPC + MPS \equiv 1$, then $1 - MPC \equiv MPS$. This means that $(1 - MPC)/MPS \equiv MPS/MPS \equiv 1$.[7]

Now let us work through our numerical example. Using the government spending multiplier, we discovered that a \$40 billion increase in G would *raise* output at equilibrium by \$160 billion (\$40 billion $\times$ the government spending multiplier of 4). Using the tax multiplier, we know that a \$40 billion tax hike will *reduce* the equilibrium level of output by \$120 billion (\$40 billion $\times$ the tax multiplier of -3). The net effect is thus \$160 billion minus \$120 billion, or \$40 billion. It should be clear, then, that the effect on equilibrium Y is equal to the balanced increase in G and T. In other words, the net increase in the equilibrium level of Y resulting from the change in G and the change in T is exactly the size of the initial change in G or T itself.

If the President wanted to raise Y by \$200 billion without increasing the deficit, a simultaneous increase in G and T of \$200 billion would do the trick. To see that this is so, look at the numbers in Table 10.3. Back in Table 10.1, we discovered an equilibrium level of output of \$900. With both G and T up by \$200, the new equilibrium is \$1100—higher by \$200 billion. At no other level of Y do we find $(C + I + G) = Y$. In sum:

> An increase in government spending has a direct initial effect on planned aggregate expenditure; a tax increase does not. The initial effect of the tax increase is that households cut consumption by the MPC times the change in taxes. This change in consumption is less than the change in taxes, because the MPC is less than one. The positive stimulus from the government spending increase is thus greater than the negative stimulus from the tax increase. The net effect is that the balanced-budget multiplier is one.

Table 10.4 summarizes everything that we have said about fiscal policy multipliers. If any of these effects are still unclear to you, go back and review the relevant discussions in this chapter.

■ **A Warning** Although we have now added the role of government to our discussion, the story we have told about the multiplier is still incomplete and oversimplified. As noted at the end of the previous chapter, adding more realism to our story has the effect of reducing the size of the multiplier.

One example of this is the case in which taxes depend on income, which is the case in the "real world." For the sake of simplicity, we have been treating net taxes (T) as a lump-sum, fixed amount. Appendix B to this chapter shows that the size of the multiplier is reduced when we make the more realistic assumption that taxes depend on income. We continue to add more realism to our analysis

---

[7]*We also derive the balanced-budget multiplier in Appendix A to this chapter.*

TABLE 10.3 — FINDING EQUILIBRIUM AFTER A $200-BILLION BALANCED-BUDGET INCREASE IN G AND T

(ALL FIGURES IN BILLIONS OF DOLLARS; BOTH G AND T HAVE INCREASED FROM 100 IN TABLE 10.1 TO 300 HERE.)

(1) OUTPUT (INCOME) Y	(2) NET TAXES T	(3) DISPOSABLE INCOME $Y_d \equiv Y - T$	(4) CONSUMPTION SPENDING $(C = 100 + .75\,Y_d)$	(5) PLANNED INVESTMENT SPENDING I	(6) GOVERNMENT PURCHASES G	(7) PLANNED AGGREGATE EXPENDITURE $C + I + G$	(8) UNPLANNED INVENTORY CHANGE $Y - (C + I + G)$	(9) ADJUSTMENT TO DISEQUILIBRIUM
500	300	200	250	100	300	650	−150	Output ↑
700	300	400	400	100	300	800	−100	Output ↑
900	300	600	550	100	300	950	−50	Output ↑
1100	300	800	700	100	300	1100	0	Equilibrium
1300	300	1000	850	100	300	1250	+50	Output ↓
1500	300	1200	1000	100	300	1400	+100	Output ↓

in the next section and in the chapters that follow. (See also the Application box on page 228 titled "Fiscal Policy during the Recessions of 1974–1975, 1980–1982, and 1990–1991" for a discussion of the government's use of fiscal policy during the last three recessions.)

ADDING THE INTERNATIONAL SECTOR

In Chapter 6, we noted that the U.S. economy does not operate in a vacuum. Rather, it influences and is influenced by the rest of the world. Up until this point, though, we have not taken into account the role of imports and exports in the macroeconomy.

Opening the economy to foreign trade adds a fourth component to planned aggregate expenditure—exports of goods and services, which we denote as EX. Exports are foreign purchases of goods and services produced in the United States. Opening the economy to the rest of the world also means that U.S. consumers and businesses have greater choice because they can decide to buy foreign-produced goods and services (imports, or IM) in addition to domestically produced goods and services.

We can therefore think of imports (IM) as a leakage from the circular flow and exports (EX) as an injection into the circular flow. (Review Figure 6.1.) With

TABLE 10.4 — SUMMARY OF FISCAL POLICY MULTIPLIERS

	POLICY STIMULUS	MULTIPLIER	FINAL IMPACT ON EQUILIBRIUM Y
Government-spending multiplier	Increase or decrease in the level of government purchases: ΔG	$\dfrac{1}{MPS}$	$\Delta G \cdot \dfrac{1}{MPS}$
Tax multiplier	Increase or decrease in the level of net taxes: ΔT	$\dfrac{-MPC}{MPS}$	$\Delta T \cdot \dfrac{-MPC}{MPS}$
Balanced-budget multiplier	Simultaneous balanced-budget increase or decrease in the level of government purchases and net taxes: $\Delta G = \Delta T$	1	ΔG

As we've seen throughout this chapter, the government can stimulate a sluggish economy by increasing government expenditures (G) and cutting taxes (T). Such policies have the effect of increasing aggregate expenditure (demand) and increasing equilibrium output (income). For this reason, you might expect the government to increase G and/or cut T whenever the economy is in a recession.

In fact, the government has taken very different actions to deal with the three recessions that the U.S. economy has experienced since 1970. The last time that the President and Congress consciously used fiscal policy to fight a recession was in 1975, during the administration of President Gerald Ford. The following passage from the *Economic Report of the President, 1976* suggests that the policy succeeded in accomplishing its goals:

During the first part of 1975 the economy moved rapidly through the final stages of the most severe recession of the postwar period. Real gross national product (GNP) fell at an annual rate of 9.2 percent in the first quarter and then began to increase. . . .

Economic policy shifted early in the year to counter the decline in output. The President proposed a $16-billion tax reduction in the State of the Union message in January and the Congress enacted a $21-billion net reduction in March. Because of these tax cuts, and associated one-time social security

AS THE ECONOMY ENTERS A RECESSION, NATIONAL OUTPUT DECREASES AND HOUSEHOLDS HAVE LESS INCOME. WITH LOWER INCOMES, PEOPLE SPEND LESS AND SOME FIRMS MAY GO OUT OF BUSINESS.

payments, real disposable personal income rose sharply in the second quarter. . . .

GNP rose sharply in the second half of the year; and by the end of the year the initial phase of a recovery was clearly evident. . . .

The idea of using fiscal policy to stimulate aggregate expenditure and increase output during a recession was explicitly rejected by President Reagan in the 1980s. Instead, the Reagan administration favored policies designed to stimulate the supply side (rather than the demand side) of the market. These *supply-side policies* (which we discuss in more detail in Chapter 19) focused on cutting taxes (a fiscal policy tool) to increase incentives to work, save, and invest. Reagan believed that the added labor supply and investment brought about by the lower taxes would lead to an expansion of the supply of goods and services, which, in turn, would reduce inflation and unemployment.

President Reagan's policy worked, at least partially for reasons he did not intend. There is no question that the major supply-side tax cuts enacted in 1981 with President Reagan's blessing had the effect of stimulating aggregate *demand* (spending). This outcome makes perfect sense if you remember the theory we've developed so far: Lower taxes mean higher disposable income, and higher disposable income means more consumption and ultimately greater output.

This trend against using fiscal policy to stimulate the economy continued into the 1990s. Just as the recession of 1990–1991 was beginning, Congress and President Bush passed the Omnibus Budget Reconciliation Act, which *cut* federal expenditures and *increased* taxes in an effort to reduce the federal deficit. Clearly, this policy did not serve to stimulate the economy, which remained sluggish until the end of 1992.

imports and exports accounted for, the equilibrium condition for the economy becomes:

> Open-economy equilibrium position: $Y = C + I + G + (EX - IM)$

The expression $(EX - IM)$ is referred to as **net exports.**

Increases or decreases in net exports can throw the economy out of equilibrium and cause national income to change. For example, a large decrease in exports, *ceteris paribus,* would mean a drop in spending on domestically produced goods and services. The result would be an unplanned rise in inventories and a fall in output. Furthermore, if some domestic spending leaks into foreign markets (imports), the multiplier effect on domestic production will be reduced.

We discuss the international sector and its effects on the macroeconomy in much more detail in Chapter 22. For now, though, we continue to use the equation $Y = C + I + G$ as the basis of our analysis. Doing so allows us to keep our discussions clear and concise. Keep in mind, though, that the international sector is an important player in the macroeconomy.

net exports *An economy's total exports* (EX) *minus its total imports* (IM).

THE FEDERAL BUDGET

Because fiscal policy is the manipulation of items in the federal budget, we need to consider those aspects of the budget that are most relevant to our study of macroeconomics. The **federal budget** is an enormously complicated document, running to thousands of pages each year. It lists in great detail all the things the government plans to spend money on and all the sources of government revenues for the coming year. It is the product of a complex interplay of social, political, and economic forces.

In fact, "the budget" is really three different budgets. First, it is a *political document* that dispenses favors to certain groups or regions (the elderly benefit from social security, farmers from agricultural price supports, students from federal loan programs, and so on) and places burdens (taxes) on others. Second, it is a *reflection of certain goals* the government wants to achieve. For example, in addition to assisting farmers, agricultural price supports are meant to preserve the "family farm." Tax breaks for corporations engaging in research and development of new products are meant to encourage such research. Finally, the budget may be an *embodiment of some beliefs about how (if at all) the government should manage the macroeconomy.* The macroeconomic aspects of the budget are thus only a part of a more complicated story, a story that may at times be of more concern to political scientists than to economists.

federal budget *The budget of the federal government.*

AN OVERVIEW OF THE BUDGET

A highly condensed version of the federal budget is shown in Table 10.5 on page 230. (Some of this reviews material from Chapter 3, but here we highlight the budget components of particular importance to macroeconomics.) In 1994, the government had total receipts of $1379.0 billion, largely from personal income taxes ($565.6 billion) and contributions for social insurance ($555.1 billion).[8] Receipts from corporate taxes accounted for $167.1 billion, or only 12.1% of total receipts. Not everyone is aware of the fact that corporate taxes as a percentage of government receipts are quite small relative to personal taxes and social security taxes.

---

[8]*Contributions for social insurance are employer and employee social security taxes.*

TABLE 10.5	FEDERAL GOVERNMENT RECEIPTS AND EXPENDITURES, 1994 (BILLIONS OF DOLLARS)	
	AMOUNT	PERCENTAGE OF TOTAL
Receipts		
Personal taxes	565.6	41.0
Corporate taxes	167.1	12.1
Indirect business taxes	91.2	6.6
Contributions for social insurance	555.1	40.3
Total	1379.0	100.0
Expenditures		
Purchases of goods and services: defense	292.3	19.0
nondefense	145.0	9.4
Transfer payments	682.5	44.4
Grants-in-aid to state and local governments	197.6	12.8
Net interest payments	191.5	12.5
Net subsidies of government enterprises	29.2	1.9
Total	1538.1	100.0
Surplus (+) or deficit (−) (Receipts − Expenditures)	−159.1	

Source: U.S. Department of Commerce, Bureau of Economic Analysis.

The federal government also made $1538.1 billion in expenditures in 1994. Of this amount, $682.5 billion represented transfer payments (social security, military retirement benefits, and unemployment compensation).[9] Defense spending ($292.3 billion) was the next largest component of government expenditures, followed by grants-in-aid to state and local governments ($197.6 billion) and interest on the federal debt ($191.5 billion).

THE FEDERAL BUDGET DEFICIT AND THE FEDERAL DEBT

Table 10.5 makes it clear that the federal government spent substantially more than it took in during 1994. The result was a deficit of $159.1 billion in 1994.

The 1994 deficit, though high, was nothing new. In fact, the federal deficit has been quite high since the early 1980s. You can see this in Figure 10.4, where the federal deficit as a percentage of GDP is plotted for the 1970 I–1994 IV period. As the figure clearly shows, the deficit has been positive throughout the entire period. In no quarter within this 100-quarter period were revenues greater than expenditures. The deficit has varied from a low of 0.2% of GDP in 1970 I to highs of 6.5% in 1975 II and 5.7% in 1982 IV. The deficit as a percentage of GDP fell in the late 1980s, but it rose sharply in 1991 and 1992.

How did such large deficits come about? There are several reasons. First, government purchases as a percentage of GDP have generally risen since 1980. This increase primarily reflects the defense buildup of the Reagan years. Second, interest payments as a percentage of GDP have risen substantially since 1980. Third, personal income tax rates have fallen since 1981 as a result of the Economic Recovery Tax Act of 1981. With defense spending and interest payments rising rapidly and personal tax rates falling, it is not surprising that the deficit rose sub-

---

[9]*Remember that there is an important difference between transfer payments and government purchases of goods and services. Much of the government budget goes for things that an economist would classify as transfers (payments that are grants or gifts) rather than purchases of goods and services. It is only the latter that are included in our variable G. Transfers are counted as part of net taxes.*

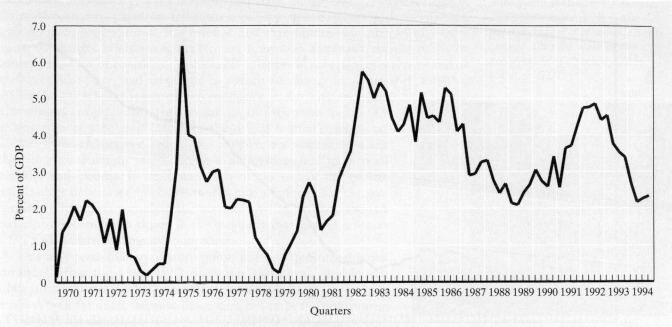

FIGURE 10.4

The Federal Government Deficit as a Percentage of GDP, 1970 I–1994 IV

While the federal deficit was positive over the entire 1970–1994 period, the deficits in the 1980s were particularly large by historical standards.

stantially during the 1980s. The government has simply been spending a lot more than it has been collecting in taxes.

When the government runs a deficit, it must borrow to finance it. To borrow, the federal government sells government securities to the public. It issues pieces of paper promising to pay a certain amount, with interest, in the future. In return, it receives funds from the buyers of the paper and uses these funds to pay its bills. This borrowing increases the **federal debt,** the total amount owed by the federal government. The federal debt is the total of all accumulated deficits minus surpluses over time.

federal debt *The total amount owed by the federal government.*

Given the large deficits that the federal government has run up since the early 1980s, it should not be surprising that the federal debt has risen sharply from the early 1980s on. You can see this in Figure 10.5 on page 232, where the federal debt as a percentage of GDP is plotted for the 1970 I–1994 IV period. The debt has risen rapidly since 1982—from 19.7% of GDP in 1982 I to 46.2% in 1994 IV.

THE ECONOMY'S INFLUENCE ON THE DEFICIT

The economic consequences of the government debt are dicussed in detail in Chapter 16. We conclude this chapter with a discussion of the way the economy affects the deficit.

■ **Tax Revenues Depend on the State of the Economy**   As we said earlier, some parts of the government's budget depend on the state of the economy, over which the government has no direct control. Take, for example, the revenue side of the budget. The government passes laws that set tax rates and tax brackets. These are clearly variables that the government does control. Tax revenue, on the other hand, depends on taxable income, and income depends on the state of the economy, which the government does *not* control. The government can set a personal income

structural deficit *The deficit that remains at full employment.*

cyclical deficit *The deficit that occurs because of a downturn in the business cycle.*

TABLE 10.6

GOVERNMENT DEFICITS AND DEBT AS A PERCENTAGE OF NOMINAL GDP, 1994, FOR SELECTED COUNTRIES

	DEFICIT	DEBT
Canada	5.3	64.2
France	5.8	40.3
Germany	2.5	38.4
Italy	9.2	112.9
Japan	3.0	7.8
United Kingdom	6.9	37.7
United States	2.0	56.0

Source: International Monetary Fund, *World Economic Outlook,* May 1995.

billion. Also suppose that if there were full employment, the deficit would fall to $75 billion. The $75 billion deficit that would remain even with full employment would be due to the structure of tax and spending programs rather than to the state of the economy. This deficit—the deficit that remains at full employment—is sometimes called the **structural deficit.** The structural deficit is the deficit of the full-employment budget. The $175 billion ($250 billion − $75 billion) part of the deficit that is caused by the fact the economy is in a slump is known as the **cyclical deficit.** The existence of the cyclical deficit depends on where the economy is in the business cycle, and it ceases to exist when full employment is reached. By definition, the cyclical deficit of the full-employment budget is zero.

DEBT AND DEFICITS IN THE REST OF THE WORLD

The United States is not the only country in the world that has a problem with budget deficits. Table 10.6 shows the deficit and debt in 1994 as a percent of GDP for six countries plus the United States. The table shows that Italy's government ran a deficit equal to 9.2% of its GDP in 1994 and had an outstanding debt equal to 112.9% of its GDP that year. The United States had the lowest deficit as a percentage of GDP in 1994, followed by Germany and Japan. Japan's government debt was only 7.8% of its GDP, but the values for the other countries were much higher. Canada was the next highest after Italy, with a debt equal to 64.2% of GDP in 1994.

THE MONEY MARKET AND MONETARY POLICY: A PREVIEW

We have now seen how households, firms, and the government interact in the goods market, how equilibrium output (income) is determined, and how the government uses fiscal policy to influence the economy. (We've also provided a brief introduction to the international sector's influence on aggregate expenditure and equilibrium output.) Our next task, which we undertake in the following two chapters, is to analyze the money market and monetary policy—the government's other major tool for influencing the economy.

SUMMARY

1. The government can affect the macroeconomy through two specific policy channels. *Fiscal policy* refers to the government's taxing and spending behavior. *Discretionary fiscal policy* refers to changes in taxes or spending that are the result of conscious changes in government policy. *Monetary policy* refers to the behavior of the Federal Reserve regarding the nation's money supply.

GOVERNMENT PARTICIPATION IN THE ECONOMY

2. The government does not have complete control over tax revenues and certain expenditures, which are partially dictated by the state of the economy.

3. As a participant in the economy, the government makes purchases of goods and services (G), collects taxes, and makes transfer payments to households.

Net taxes (T) is equal to the tax payments made to the government by firms and households minus transfer payments made to households by the government.

4. *Disposable,* or *after-tax, income* (Y_d) is equal to the amount of income received by households after taxes: $Y_d \equiv Y - T$. After-tax income determines households' consumption behavior.

5. The *budget deficit* is equal to the difference between what the government spends and what it collects in taxes: $G - T$. When G exceeds T, the government must borrow from the public to finance its deficit.

6. In an economy in which a government is a participant, planned aggregate expenditure equals consumption spending by households (C) plus planned investment spending by firms (I) plus government spending on goods and services (G): $AE \equiv C + I +$

G. Because the condition $Y = AE$ is necessary for the economy to be in equilibrium, it follows that $Y = C + I + G$ is the macroeconomic equilibrium condition. The economy is also in equilibrium when leakages out of the system equal injections into the system. This occurs when savings and net taxes (the leakages) equal planned investment and government purchases (the injections): $S + T = I + G$.

FISCAL POLICY AT WORK: THE MULTIPLIER EFFECTS

7. Fiscal policy has a multiplier effect on the economy. A change in government spending gives rise to a multiplier equal to $1/MPS$. A change in taxation brings about a multiplier equal to $-MPC/MPS$. A simultaneous equal increase or decrease in government spending and taxes has a multiplier effect of one.

ADDING THE INTERNATIONAL SECTOR

8. Opening the economy to foreign trade adds two additional components to the equilibrium condition: exports (EX) and imports (IM). Exports are an injection into the circular flow; imports are a leakage from the circular flow. Thus the equilibrium condition for the economy becomes $Y = C + I + G + (EX - IM)$ when the international sector is taken into account. The expression ($EX - IM$) is referred to as *net exports*.

THE FEDERAL BUDGET

9. The federal deficit has been quite large in recent years. Reasons for the deficit include the defense buildup of the Reagan years, the high amount of interest paid on already-existing debt, and cuts in personal tax rates. With defense spending and interest payments rising rapidly and personal income tax rates falling, the government has simply been spending more than it has been collecting in taxes.

10. *Automatic stabilizers* are revenue and expenditure items in the federal budget that automatically change with the state of the economy and thus tend to stabilize GDP. For example, during expansions the government automatically takes in more revenue, because people are making more money that is taxed. Higher income and tax brackets also mean fewer transfer payments.

11. *Fiscal drag* is the negative effect on the economy that occurs when average tax rates increase because taxpayers have moved into higher income brackets during an expansion. These higher taxes reduce disposable income and slow down the expansion. Since 1982, tax brackets have been indexed to inflation, and this has reduced the fiscal drag built into the tax system.

12. The *full-employment budget* is an economist's construction of what the federal budget would be if the economy were producing at a full-employment level of output. The *structural deficit* is the federal deficit that remains even at full employment. *Cyclical deficits* occur when there is a downturn in the business cycle.

REVIEW TERMS AND CONCEPTS

automatic stabilizers 233
balanced-budget multiplier 226
budget deficit 217
cyclical deficit 234
discretionary fiscal policy 215
disposable, or **after-tax, income (Y_d)** 216
federal budget 229
federal debt 231
fiscal drag 233
fiscal policy 215
full-employment budget 233
government spending multiplier 222
monetary policy 215

net exports (EX − IM) 229
net taxes (T) 216

structural deficit 234
tax multiplier 224

Equations:

1. Disposable income $\quad Y_d \equiv Y - T$

2. $AE \equiv C + I + G$

3. Government budget deficit $\equiv G - T$

4. Equilibrium in an economy with government: $Y = C + I + G$

5. Leakages/injections approach to equilibrium in an economy with government: $S + T = I + G$

6. Government spending multiplier $= \dfrac{1}{MPS}$

7. Tax multiplier $\equiv -\dfrac{MPC}{MPS}$

8. Balanced-budget multiplier $\equiv 1$

9. Open-economy equilibrium position: $Y = C + I + G + (EX - IM)$

1. Define *saving* and *investment*. Data for the simple closed economy of Newt show that in 1995 saving exceeded investment and the government is running a balanced budget. What is likely to happen? What would happen if the government were instead running a deficit and saving were equal to investment?

2. Crack economists in the economy of Yuk estimate the following:

Real output/income	1000 billion Yuks
Government purchases	200 billion Yuks
Total net taxes	200 billion Yuks
Investment spending (planned)	100 billion Yuks

Assume that Yukkers consume 75% of their disposable incomes and that they save 25 percent.

   a. You are asked by the business editor of the *Yuk Gazette* to predict the events of the next few months. Using the data above, can you make a forecast? (Assume that investment is constant.)

   b. If no changes were made, at what level of GDP (Y) would the economy of Yuk settle?

   c. Some local conservatives blame Yuk's problems on the size of the government sector. They suggest cutting government purchases by 25 billion Yuks. What effect would such cuts have on the economy? (Be specific.)

3. "A $1 increase in government spending will raise equilibrium income by more than a $1 tax cut, yet both have the same impact on the budget deficit. So if we care about the budget deficit, the best way to stimulate the economy is through increases in spending, not cuts in taxes." Comment.

4. Assume that in 1996, the following situation prevails in the Republic of Nurd:

$Y = \$200$	$G = \$0$
$C = \$160$	$T = \$0$
$S = \$40$	
I (planned) $= \$30$	

Assume that households consume 80% of their income, that they save 20% of their income, that $MPC = .8$, and $MPS = .2$. That is, $C = .8Y_d$ and $S = .2Y_d$.

   a. Is the economy of Nurd in equilibrium? What is Nurd's equilibrium level of income? What is likely to happen in the coming months if the government takes no action?

   b. If $200 is the "full employment" level of Y, what fiscal policy might the government follow if its goal is full employment?

   c. If the full-employment level of Y is $250, what fiscal policy might the government follow?

   d. Suppose that $Y = \$200$, $C = \$160$, $S = \$40$, and $I = \$40$. Is Nurd's economy in equilibrium?

   e. Starting with the situation in d., suppose that the government starts spending $30 each year with no taxation and continues to spend $30 every period. If I remains constant, what will happen to the equilibrium level of Nurd's domestic product (Y)? What will the new levels of C and S be?

   f. Starting with the situation in d., suppose that the government starts taxing the population $30 each year without spending anything and continues to tax at that rate every period. If I remains constant, what will happen to the equilibrium level of Nurd's domestic product (Y)? What will be the new levels of C and S? How does your answer to f. differ from your answer to e? Why?

5. Suppose that all tax collections are fixed (rather than dependent on income), and that all spending and transfer programs are also fixed (in the sense that they do not depend on the state of the economy, as, for example, unemployment benefits now do). If this were the case, would there be any automatic stabilizers in the government budget? Would there be any distinction between the full-employment deficit and the actual budget deficit? Explain.

6. Answer the following questions:

   a. $MPS = .4$. What is the government spending multiplier?

   b. $MPC = .9$. What is the government spending multiplier?

   c. $MPS = .5$. What is the government spending multiplier?

   d. $MPC = .75$. What is the tax multiplier?

   e. $MPS = .1$. What is the tax multiplier?

   f. If the government spending multiplier is 6, what is the tax multiplier?

   g. If the tax multiplier is -2, what is the government spending multiplier?

   h. If government purchases and taxes are both increased by $100 billion simultaneously, what will the effect be on equilibrium output (income)?

7. What is the relationship between the government budget deficit and the government debt? Suppose that the United States managed to balance its budget in fiscal year 1995. Would there be any effect on the size of the debt?

DERIVING THE FISCAL POLICY MULTIPLIERS

THE GOVERNMENT SPENDING AND TAX MULTIPLIERS

In the chapter, we noted that the government spending multiplier is equal to 1/MPS. (This is the same as the investment multiplier.) We can also show that the government spending multiplier is the same as the investment multiplier by using our hypothetical consumption function:

$$C = a + b \, (Y - T)$$

where b is the marginal propensity to consume. As you know, the equilibrium condition is

$$Y = C + I + G$$

Substituting for C, we get

$$Y = a + b(Y - T) + I + G$$

$$Y = a + bY - bT + I + G$$

This equation can be rearranged to yield

$$Y - bY = a + I + G - bT$$

$$Y(1 - b) = a + I + G - bT$$

We can then solve for Y by dividing through by $(1 - b)$:

$$Y = \frac{1}{(1 - b)}(a + I + G - bT)$$

We see from this last equation that if G increases by one with the other determinants of Y (a, I, and T) remaining constant, Y increases by $1/(1 - b)$. Thus, the multiplier is, as before, simply $1/(1 - b)$, where b is the marginal propensity to consume. And, of course, $1 - b$ equals the marginal propensity to save, so the government spending multiplier is 1/MPS.

We can also derive the tax multiplier. The last equation above says that when T increases by \$1, holding a, I, and G constant, income decreases by $b/(1 - b)$ dollars. The tax multiplier is thus $-b/(1 - b)$, or $-MPC/(1 - MPC) = -MPC/MPS$. (Remember that we add the negative sign to the tax multiplier because the tax multiplier is a *negative* multiplier.)

THE BALANCED-BUDGET MULTIPLIER

It is quite easy to show formally that the balanced-budget multiplier is equal to one. As you know, when taxes and government spending are simultaneously increased by the same amount, there are two effects on planned aggregate expenditure: one positive and one negative. The initial impact of a balanced-budget increase in government spending and taxes on aggregate expenditure would be the *increase* in government purchases (ΔG) minus the *decrease* in consumption (ΔC) caused by the tax increase. The decrease in consumption brought about by the tax increase is equal to $\Delta C = \Delta T(MPC)$.

Increase in spending:	ΔG
$-$*Decrease in spending:*	$\Delta C = \Delta T(MPC)$
$=$ *Net increase in spending*	$\Delta G - \Delta T(MPC)$

In a balanced-budget increase, $\Delta G = \Delta T$, so we can substitute:

Net initial increase in spending:

$$\Delta G - \Delta G(MPC) = \Delta G(1 - MPC).$$

Since $MPS = (1 - MPC)$, the initial increase in spending is

$$\Delta G(MPS).$$

We can now apply the expenditure multiplier $\left(\frac{1}{MPS}\right)$ to this net initial increase in spending:

$$\Delta Y = \Delta G(MPS)\left(\frac{1}{MPS}\right) = \Delta G$$

Thus, the final total increase in the equilibrium level of Y is just equal to the initial balanced increase in G and T. In other words, the balanced-budget multiplier is one.

THE CASE IN WHICH TAX REVENUES DEPEND ON INCOME

In this chapter, we used the simplifying assumption that the government collects taxes in a lump sum. This made our discussion of the multiplier effects somewhat easier to follow. But now suppose that the government collects taxes not solely as a lump sum that is paid regardless of income, but also partly in the form of a proportional levy against income. As we noted earlier, this is clearly a more realistic assumption. Typically, tax collections are either based on income (as with the personal income tax) or they closely follow the ups and downs in the economy (as with sales taxes). Thus, instead of setting taxes equal to some fixed amount, let us say that tax revenues depend on income. If we call the amount of net taxes collected T, we can write: $T = T_0 + tY$.

This equation contains two parts. First, we note that net taxes (T) will be equal to an amount T_0 if income (Y) is zero. Second, the tax rate (t) indicates how much net taxes change as income changes. Suppose that T_0 is equal to -200 and t is 1/3. The resulting tax function is $T = -200 + 1/3Y$, which is graphed in Figure 10A.1. Note that when income is zero, the government collects "negative net taxes," which simply means that it makes transfer payments of 200. As income rises, tax collections increase because every extra dollar of income generates $.33 in extra revenues for the government.

How do we incorporate this new tax function into our discussion? It is actually quite simple. All we need to do is replace the old value of T (in the example in the chapter, T was set equal to 100) with the new value, $-200 + 1/3Y$. Look first at the consumption equation. Consumption (C) still depends on disposable income, as it did before. Also, disposable income is still $Y - T$, or income minus taxes. Instead of disposable income equaling $Y - 100$, however, the new equation for disposable income is

$$Y_d \equiv Y - T$$

$$Y_d \equiv Y - (-200 + 1/3Y)$$

$$Y_d \equiv Y + 200 - 1/3Y$$

Since consumption still depends on after-tax income, exactly as it did before, we have

$$C = 100 + .75Y_d$$

$$C = 100 + .75 (Y + 200 - 1/3Y)$$

Nothing else needs to be changed. We solve for equilibrium income exactly as before, by setting planned

FIGURE 10A.1 THE TAX FUNCTION.

This graph shows net taxes (taxes minus transfer payments) as a function of aggregate income.

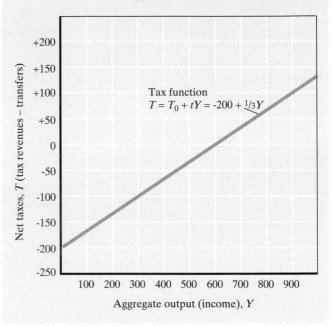

aggregate expenditure equal to aggregate output. Recall that planned aggregate expenditure is $C + I + G$, and aggregate output is Y. If we assume, as before, that $I = 100$ and $G = 100$, the equilibrium is

$$Y = C + I + G$$

$$Y = \underbrace{100 + .75 (Y + 200 - 1/3Y)}_{C} + \underbrace{100}_{I} + \underbrace{100}_{G}.$$

This equation may look difficult to solve, but it is not. It simplifies to

$$Y = 100 + .75Y + 150 - .25Y + 100 + 100$$

$$Y = 450 + .5Y$$

$$.5Y = 450$$

This means that $Y = 450/.5 = 900$. The new equilibrium level of income is thus 900.

It is useful to consider the graphic analysis of this equation as shown in Figure 10A.2. The most important thing you should note from Figure 10A.2 is that when we make taxes a function of income (instead of merely a lump-sum amount), the AE function becomes *flatter*

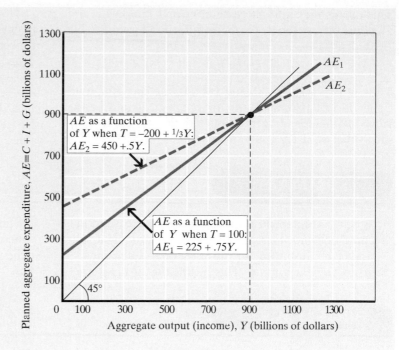

FIGURE 10A.2 DIFFERENT TAX SYSTEMS

When taxes are strictly lump sum ($T = 100$) and do not depend on income, the aggregate expenditure function is steeper than when taxes depend on income.

[In figure:]

AE as a function of Y when $T = -200 + \frac{1}{3}Y$: $AE_2 = 450 + .5Y$.

AE as a function of Y when $T = 100$: $AE_1 = 225 + .75Y$.

than it was before. Why is this so? When tax collections do not depend on income, an increase in income of $1 means that disposable income also increases by a dollar. Because taxes are a constant amount, adding more income does not raise the amount of taxes paid. Disposable income therefore changes dollar-for-dollar with any change in income.

When taxes depend on income, however, a $1 increase in income does not increase disposable income by a full dollar, because some of the additional dollar must go to pay extra taxes. In fact, under the modified tax function of Figure 10A.2, an extra dollar of income will increase disposable income by only $.67, because $.33 of the extra dollar goes to the government in the form of taxes.

No matter how taxes are calculated, the marginal propensity to consume out of disposable (or after-tax) income is the same—each extra dollar of disposable income will increase consumption spending by $.75. But a $1 change in before-tax income does not have the same effect on disposable income in each case. Suppose we were to increase income by $1. With the lump-sum tax function, disposable income would rise by $1, and consumption would increase by $MPC \times Y_d$, or $.75. When taxes depend on income, disposable income would rise by only $.67 from the $1 increase in income, and consumption would rise by only the MPC times the change in disposable income, or $.75 \times .67 = $.50.

Clearly, if a $1 increase in income raises expenditure by $.75 in one case, and by only $.50 in the other, the second aggregate expenditure function must be flatter than the first.

THE GOVERNMENT SPENDING AND TAX MULTIPLIERS ALGEBRAICALLY

All of this means that if taxes are a function of income, the three multipliers (investment, government spending, and tax) are less than they would be if taxes were a lump-sum amount. Using the same linear consumption function we used in the last two chapters, we can derive the multiplier:

$$C = a + b\,(Y - T)$$
$$C = a + b\,(Y - T_0 - tY)$$
$$C = a + bY - bT_0 - btY$$

We know that $Y = C + I + G$. Through substitution we get:

$$Y = \underbrace{a + bY - bT_0 - btY}_{C} + I + G$$

Solving for Y:

$$Y = \frac{1}{(1) - b + bt}\,(a + I + G - bT_0)$$

This means that a $1 increase in G or I (holding a and T_0 constant) will increase the equilibrium level of Y by:

$$\frac{1}{1 - b + bt}$$

Thus, if $b = MPC = .75$ and $t = .20$, the spending multiplier is 2.5. (Compare this to 4, which would be the value of the spending multiplier if taxes were a lump sum—that is, if $t = 0$.)

Holding a, I, and G constant, a fixed or lump-sum tax cut (a cut in T_0) will increase the equilibrium level of income by:

$$\frac{b}{1 - b + bt}$$

Thus, if $b = MPC = .75$ and $t = .20$, the tax multiplier is -1.875. (Compare this to -3, which would be the value of the tax multiplier if taxes were a lump sum.)

SUMMARY

1. When taxes depend on income, a $1 increase in income does not increase disposable income by a full dollar, because some of the additional dollar must go to pay extra taxes. This means that if taxes are a function of income, the three multipliers (investment, government spending, and tax) are less than they would be if taxes were a lump-sum amount.

PROBLEM SET

1. You are given the following model for the economy of a country:
   (1) Consumption function: $C = 85 + 0.5Y_d$
   (2) Investment function: $I = 85$
   (3) Government spending: $G = 60$
   (4) Net taxes: $T = -40 + 0.25Y$
   (5) Disposable income: $Y_d \equiv Y - T$
   (6) Equilibrium: $Y = C + I + G$.

Solve for equilibrium income. *(Hint:* Be very careful in doing the calculations. They are not difficult, but it is easy to make careless mistakes that produce dramatically wrong results.) How much does the government collect in net taxes when the economy is in equilibrium? What is the government's budget deficit or surplus?

THE MONEY SUPPLY AND THE FEDERAL RESERVE SYSTEM

I N THE LAST TWO CHAPTERS, WE EXPLORED HOW CONSUMERS, FIRMS, and the government interact in the goods market. We now turn to a discussion of the money market. This chapter and the next show how money markets work in the macroeconomy. We begin with an overview of what money is and the role it plays in the U.S. economy. We then discuss the forces that determine the supply of money and show how banks create money. Finally, we discuss the workings of the nation's central bank, the Federal Reserve, and the tools it has at its disposal to control the money supply.

It is interesting to note that microeconomics has little to say about money. Microeconomic theories and models are concerned primarily with *real* quantities (apples, oranges, hours of labor) and *relative* prices (the price of apples relative to the price of oranges, the price of labor relative to the prices of other goods). Most of the key ideas in microeconomics simply do not require that one know anything about money. As we shall see, this is not the case in macroeconomics.

AN OVERVIEW OF MONEY

You often hear people say things like "He makes a lot of money" (in other words, "He has a high income") or "She's worth a lot of money" (meaning "She is very wealthy"). It is true that your employer uses money to pay you your income, and your wealth may be accumulated in the form of money. But *money is not income, and money is not wealth.*

As a way of understanding that money and income are not the same thing, think of a $20 bill. That single bill may pass through a thousand hands in a year, and it may never be used to pay anyone a salary. Suppose, for example, that I get a crisp, new $20 bill from an automatic teller machine, and I spend it on dinner. The restaurant puts that $20 bill in a bank in the next day's deposit. The bank gives it to a woman cashing a check the following day; she spends it at a baseball game that night. The bill has been through many hands and it has yet to be part of anyone's income.

WHAT IS MONEY?

We will soon get to a formal definition of money, but it is important that you start out with the right basic idea:

> Money is anything that is generally accepted as a medium of exchange.

Most people take the ability to obtain and use money for granted. When the whole monetary system works well, as it generally does in the United States, the basic mechanics of the system are virtually invisible. People simply take it for granted that they can walk into any store, restaurant, boutique, or gas station and buy whatever they want, as long as they have enough green pieces of paper in their pockets.

Indeed, the idea that you can buy things with money is so natural and obvious that it seems almost absurd to mention it. But stop and ask yourself the following questions: "How is it that a shop owner is willing to part with a steak and a loaf of bread that I can eat in exchange for some pieces of paper that are intrinsically worthless?" And why, on the other hand, are there times and places where it takes a shopping cart full of money to purchase a dozen eggs? The answers to these questions lie in what money is: a means of payment, a store of value, and a unit of account.

■ **A Means of Payment, or Medium of Exchange** Money is vital to the working of a market economy. You can see why if you imagine what life would be like without it. The alternative to a monetary economy is **barter,** a process by which people exchange goods and services for other goods and services directly instead of exchanging via the medium of money.

How does a barter system work? Suppose you wake up in the morning and decide you want bacon, eggs, and orange juice for breakfast. Instead of going to the store and buying these things with money, you would have to find someone who has these items and is willing to trade them. You would also have to have something the bacon seller, the orange juice purveyor, and the egg vendor want. Having lots of pencils to trade will do you no good if the bacon, orange juice, and egg sellers do not want pencils.

A barter system requires a *double coincidence of wants* for trade to take place. That is, to effect a trade, I not only have to find someone who has what I want, but that person must also want what I have. Where the range of goods traded is small, as it is in relatively unsophisticated economies, it is not difficult to find someone to trade with, and barter is often used. In a complex society with many goods, however, barter exchanges involve an intolerable amount of effort. Imagine trying to find people who offer for sale all the things you buy in a typical trip to the grocery store, and who are willing to accept goods that you have to offer in exchange for their goods.

Some agreed-upon **medium of exchange** (or, as it is sometimes called, **means of payment**) neatly eliminates the double-coincidence-of-wants problem. Under a

barter *The direct exchange of goods and services for other goods and services.*

medium of exchange, or **means of payment** *What sellers generally accept and buyers generally use to pay for goods and services.*

monetary system, money is exchanged for goods or services when people buy things; goods or services are exchanged for money when people sell things. No one ever has to trade goods for other goods directly. The importance of money as a lubricant in the functioning of a market economy can hardly be overstated.

■ **A Store of Value** Economists have identified other roles for money aside from its primary function as a medium of exchange. Money also serves as a **store of value**—that is, as an asset that can be used to transport purchasing power from one time period to another. If you raise chickens and at the end of the month sell them for more than the amount you want to consume immediately, you may decide to keep some of your earnings in the form of money that you will hold until the time you want to spend it.

store of value *An asset that can be used to transport purchasing power from one time period to another.*

There are many other stores of value besides money. You could have decided to hold your "surplus" earnings by buying such things as antique paintings, baseball cards, or diamonds, which you could sell later when you want to spend your earnings. Money has several important advantages over these other stores of value, however. First, it comes in convenient denominations and is easily portable. You don't have to worry about making change for a Renoir to buy a gallon of gasoline. Second, because money is also a means of payment, it is easily exchanged for goods at all times. (A Renoir, of course, is not easily exchanged for other goods.) These two factors comprise the **liquidity property of money.** Money is easily spent, flowing out of your hands like liquid. Renoirs and ancient Aztec statues are neither convenient nor portable and are not readily accepted as a means of payment.

liquidity property of money *The property of money that makes it a good medium of exchange as well as a store of value: It is portable and readily accepted and thus easily exchanged for goods.*

The main disadvantage of using money as a store of value is that the value of money actually falls when the prices of goods and services rise. If, for example, the price of potato chips rises from $1 per bag to $2 per bag, the value of a dollar bill, in terms of potato chips, falls from one bag to half a bag. When this happens, it may be better to use potato chips (or perhaps antiques or real estate) as a store of value.

■ **A Unit of Account** Finally, money also serves as a **unit of account**—that is, as a consistent way of quoting prices. All prices are quoted in monetary units. A textbook is quoted as costing $45, not 140 bananas or 4 videotapes, and a banana is quoted as costing 25¢, not 1.4 apples or 16 pages of a textbook.

unit of account *A standard unit that provides a consistent way of quoting prices.*

Obviously, a standard unit of account is extremely useful when quoting prices. This function of money may have escaped your notice—after all, what else would people quote prices in except money?

COMMODITY AND FIAT MONIES

Introductory economics textbooks are full of stories about the various items that have been used as money by various cultures—candy bars, cigarettes (in World War II prisoner-of-war camps), huge wheels of carved stone (on the island of Yap in the South Pacific), cowrie shells (in West Africa), beads (among North American Indians), cattle (in southern Africa), small green scraps of paper (in contemporary North America). The list goes on and on. These various kinds of money are generally divided into two groups, commodity monies and fiat money.

Commodity monies are those items used as money that also have an intrinsic value in some other use. For example, prisoners of war made purchases with cigarettes, quoted prices in terms of cigarettes, and held their wealth in the form of accumulated cigarettes. Of course, cigarettes could also be smoked—they had an alternative use apart from serving as money. Gold represents another form of

commodity monies *Items used as money that also have intrinsic value in some other use.*

SOME OF YAP'S STONE MONEY WHEELS ARE SO LARGE THAT THEY ARE NEVER MOVED.

fiat, or **token, money** *Items designated as money that are intrinsically worthless.*

legal tender *Money that a government has required to be accepted in settlement of debts.*

currency debasement *The decrease in the value of money that occurs when its supply is increased rapidly.*

commodity money. For hundreds of years gold could be used directly to buy things, but it also had other uses, ranging from jewelry to dental fillings.

By contrast, money in the United States today is mostly fiat money. **Fiat money,** sometimes called **token money,** is money that is intrinsically worthless. The actual value of a one-, ten-, or fifty-dollar bill is basically zero; what other uses are there for a small piece of paper with some green ink on it?

Why would anyone agree to use worthless scraps of paper as money instead of something that has at least some value, such as gold, cigarettes, or cattle? If you think the answer is "Because the paper money is backed by gold or silver," you are wrong. True, there was a time when dollar bills were convertible directly into gold. The government backed each dollar bill in circulation by holding a certain amount of gold in its vaults. If the price of gold were $35 per ounce, for example, the government agreed to sell one ounce of gold for 35 dollar bills. But dollar bills are no longer backed by any commodity—gold, silver, or anything else. They are exchangeable only for dimes, nickels, pennies, other dollars, and so on.

In essence, the public accepts paper money as a means of payment and a store of value simply because the government has taken steps to ensure that its money is accepted. The government declares its paper money to be **legal tender.** That is, the government declares that its money must be accepted in settlement of debts. It does this by fiat (hence the term *fiat money*). It passes laws defining certain pieces of paper printed in certain inks on certain plates to be legal tender, and that is that. Printed on every Federal Reserve note in the United States is the phrase, "This note is legal tender for all debts, public and private." Often, the government can get a start on gaining acceptance for its paper money by requiring that it be used to pay taxes. (Note that you cannot use chickens, baseball cards, or Renoir paintings to pay your taxes, only checks or currency.)

Aside from declaring its currency legal tender, the government usually does one other thing to ensure that paper money will be accepted: It promises the public that it will not print paper money so fast that it loses its value. The practice of expanding the supply of currency so rapidly that it loses much of its value has been a problem throughout history and is known as **currency debasement.** Debasement of the currency has been a special problem of governments that lack the strength to take the politically unpopular step of raising taxes. Printing money to be used on government expenditures of goods and services can serve as a substitute for tax increases, and weak governments have often relied on the printing press to finance their expenditures. A recent example of this is Brazil, where the inflation rate hit a record of 1,759% in 1990. We will discuss the links between money and inflation at great length in later chapters.

MEASURING THE SUPPLY OF MONEY IN THE UNITED STATES

We now turn to a more detailed look at the various kinds of money in the United States. Recall that money possesses the following properties: It is used to buy things (a means of payment); it is used as a means of holding wealth (a store of value); and it is used to quote prices (a unit of account). Unfortunately, these characteristics apply to a broad range of assets in the U.S. economy. As we will see, it is not at all clear where we should draw the line and say, "Up to this is money, beyond this is something else."

To solve the problem of multiple monies, economists have given different names to different measures of money. The two most common measures of money are transactions money, also called *M*1, and broad money, also called *M*2.

■ M1: Transactions Money   What should be counted as money? Clearly, coins and dollar bills, as well as higher denominations of currency, must be counted as money—they fit all the requirements. But what about checking accounts? Checks too can be used to buy things and can serve as a store of value. In fact, bankers call checking accounts *demand deposits,* because depositors have the right to go to the bank and cash in (demand) their entire checking account balances at any time. Thus, your checking account balance is virtually equivalent to bills in your wallet, and it should be included as part of the amount of money you hold.

If we take the value of all currency (including coins) held outside of bank vaults and add to it the value of all demand deposits, travelers checks, and other checkable deposits, we have defined **M1,** or **transactions money.** As its name suggests, this is the money that can be directly used for transactions—to buy things:

> $M1 \equiv$ Currency held outside banks + Demand deposits + Travelers checks + Other checkable deposits

M1, or **transactions money** *Money that can be directly used for transactions.*

A *checkable deposit* is any deposit account with a bank or other financial institution on which a check can be written. Checkable deposits include demand deposits (discussed above); *negotiable order of withdrawal (NOW) accounts,* which are like checking accounts that pay interest; and *automatic-transfer savings (ATS) accounts,* which automatically transfer funds from savings to checking (or vice versa) when the balance on one of those accounts reaches a predetermined level.

M1 on July 17, 1995, was $1141.5 billion. Notice that M1 is a stock measure. That is, it is measured at a point in time. It is the total amount of coins and currency outside of banks and the total dollar amount in checking accounts *on a specific day.* Until now, we have considered supply as a flow—a variable with a time dimension: the quantity of wheat supplied *per year,* the quantity of automobiles supplied to the market *per year,* and so forth. Remember, however, that M1 is a stock variable.

Cash remains an important part of the U.S. economy, but some people believe that it is becoming a thing of the past. For more details, see the Issues and Controversies box on page 246 titled "Is Cash Becoming Obsolete?"

■ M2: Broad Money   Although M1 is the most widely used measure of the money supply, there are others with which you should be familiar. Should savings accounts be considered money, for example? Many of these accounts cannot be used for transactions directly, but it is easy to convert them into cash or to transfer funds from a savings account into a checking account. And what about money market accounts (which allow only a few checks per month but pay market-determined interest rates) and money market mutual funds (which sell shares and use the proceeds to purchase a variety of short-term securities)? These can be used to write checks and make purchases, although such purchases are generally limited to sums over a certain amount.

If we add these **near monies,** close substitutes for transactions money, to M1, we arrive at **M2,** sometimes called **broad money** because it includes various not-quite-money monies such as savings accounts, money market accounts, and other near monies.

near monies *Close substitutes for transactions money, such as savings accounts and money market accounts.*

> $M2 \equiv$ M1 + Savings accounts + Money market accounts + Other near monies

M2, or **broad money** *M1 plus savings accounts, money market accounts, and other near monies.*

On July 17, 1995, M2 was $3705.8 billion, considerably larger than the total M1 of $1141.5 billion. The main advantage of looking at M2 instead of M1 is that

When we think of money, the first thing that comes to mind is cash. Coins and currency remain the means of payment used for many transactions. But new technology is becoming available that could make cash obsolete. The following article appeared in *The New York Times* in late 1994:

The relentless march of technology into the smallest details of everyday life may be reaching the final frontier: the advent of the electronic penny.

Banks, credit card companies and even the governments of some countries are racing to introduce *"electronic purses," wallet-size cards embedded with rechargeable microchips that store sums of money for people to use instead of cash for everything from buying fast food to paying highway tolls.*

With 80 percent of the 360 billion transactions in the United States each year paid for with cash, and 90 percent of that 80 percent involving amounts of less than $20, the theoretical appeal of the electronic purse, or stored-value card, seems clear. . . .

"What consumers want is convenience, and if you look at cash, it's really quite inconvenient," said Donald J. Gleason, president of the Smart Card Enterprise unit of Electronic Payment Services, known as E.P.S., which runs the MAC cash machine network. "And for merchants, cash is a nightmare. It is expensive to handle, count and deposit, and they have slippage, which is their way of saying theft."*

Source: Saul Hansell, "An End to the 'Nightmare' of Cash?" *The New York Times*, September 6, 1994, p. D1.

M2 is sometimes more stable. For instance, when banks introduced new forms of interest-bearing checking accounts in the early 1980s, M1 shot up dramatically as people switched their funds from savings accounts to checking accounts. M2 remained fairly constant during this period, however, because the fall in savings account deposits and the rise in checking account balances were both part of M2 and thus canceled each other out.

■ **Beyond M2** As we noted earlier, a wide variety of financial instruments bear some resemblance to money, and some economists have advocated including almost all of them as part of the money supply. In recent years, for example, credit cards have come to be used extensively in exchange. Everyone who has a credit card has a credit limit—you can charge only a certain amount on your card before you have to pay it off. Usually we pay our credit card bills with a check. One of the very broad definitions of money includes the amount of available credit on credit cards (your charge limit minus what you have charged but not paid) as part of the money supply.

There are no hard and fast rules for deciding what is money and what is not money. This poses problems for economists and for those in charge of economic policy. However, *for our purposes here, "money" will always refer to transactions money, or M1*. For the sake of simplicity, we will say that M1 is the sum of two *general* categories: currency in circulation and deposits. Keep in mind, however, that M1 has *four* specific components: currency held outside banks, demand deposits, travelers checks, and other checkable deposits.

THE PRIVATE BANKING SYSTEM

Most of the money in the United States today is "bank money" of one sort or another. *M*1 is made up largely of checking account balances rather than currency, and currency makes up an even smaller part of *M*2 and other broader definitions of money. Thus, any understanding of money requires some knowledge of the structure of the private banking system.

Banks and other financial intermediaries borrow from individuals or firms with excess funds and lend to those who need funds. For example, commercial banks receive funds in various forms, including deposits in checking and savings accounts. They take these funds and loan them out in the form of car loans, mortgages, commercial loans, and so forth. Banks and banklike institutions are called **financial intermediaries** because they "mediate," or act as a link between people who have funds to lend and those who need to borrow.

FREEDOM NATIONAL BANK IN NEW YORK CITY CLOSED ITS DOORS IN NOVEMBER, 1990. AFTER SUFFERING FROM BAD INVESTMENTS AND HARD TIMES IN THE 1980S, THE BANKING INDUSTRY IS BEGINNING TO REBOUND.

The main types of financial intermediaries are commercial banks, followed by savings and loan associations, life insurance companies, and pension funds. Since about 1970, the legal distinctions between the different types of financial intermediaries have narrowed considerably. It used to be the case, for example, that checking accounts could be held only in commercial banks and that commercial banks could not pay interest on checking accounts. Savings and loan associations were prohibited from offering certain kinds of deposits and were restricted primarily to making loans for mortgages.

financial intermediaries *Banks and other institutions that act as a link between those who have money to lend and those who want to borrow money.*

The Depository Institutions Deregulation and Monetary Control Act, enacted by Congress in 1980, eliminated many of the previous restrictions on the behavior of financial institutions. Many types of institutions now offer checking accounts, and interest is paid on many types of checking accounts. Savings and loan associations now make loans for many things besides home mortgages. The Sears Financial Network is one of a number of financial service firms offering, under one roof, a wide variety of services that used to be offered by separate providers such as banks, brokerage houses, insurance companies, and financial planners.

HOW BANKS CREATE MONEY

So far we have described the general way that money works and the way the supply of money is measured in the United States. But how much money is there available at a given time? Who supplies it, and how does it get supplied? The time has now come to analyze these questions in detail. In particular, we want to explore a process that many find mysterious: the way that banks *create money*.

A HISTORICAL PERSPECTIVE: GOLDSMITHS

A useful way of understanding how banks create money is to consider the origins of the modern banking system. In the fifteenth and sixteenth centuries, citizens of many lands used gold as money, particularly for large transactions. Because gold is both inconvenient to carry around and susceptible to theft, people began to place their gold with goldsmiths for safekeeping. Upon receiving the gold, a goldsmith would issue a receipt to the depositor, charging him a small fee for looking after his gold. After a time, these receipts themselves, rather than the gold that they represented, began to be traded for goods. The receipts thus became a form of paper money, making it unnecessary to go to the goldsmith to withdraw gold each time a transaction took place.

At this point, all the receipts issued by goldsmiths were backed 100% by gold. If a goldsmith had 100 ounces of gold in his safe, he would issue receipts for only 100 ounces of gold, and no more. Goldsmiths thus functioned as mere warehouses where people stored gold for safekeeping. The goldsmiths found, however, that people did not come often to withdraw gold. Why should they, when paper receipts that could easily be converted to gold were "as good as gold"? (In fact, receipts were better than gold—more portable, safer from theft, and so on.) As a result, goldsmiths had a large stock of gold continuously on hand.

Since they had what amounted to "extra" gold sitting around, goldsmiths gradually realized that they could lend out some of this gold to would-be borrowers without any fear of running out of gold. Why would they do this? Quite simply, because it was to their advantage to do so—instead of just keeping their gold idly in their vaults, they earned interest on the loans they made. Something subtle, but dramatic, happened at this point. The goldsmiths changed from mere depositories for gold into banklike institutions that had the power to create money. This transformation occurred as soon as goldsmiths began making loans. Without adding any more real gold to the system, the goldsmiths increased the amount of money in circulation by creating additional claims to gold (that is, receipts, which entitled the bearer to receive a certain number of ounces of gold on demand).[1] There were thus more claims than there were ounces of gold.

A more detailed example may help to clarify this point. Suppose you go to a goldsmith who is functioning only as a depository, or warehouse, and ask for a loan to buy a plot of land that costs 20 ounces of gold. Also suppose that the goldsmith has 100 ounces of gold on deposit in his safe and receipts for exactly 100 ounces of gold out to the various people who deposited the gold. If the goldsmith decides he is tired of being a mere goldsmith and wants to become a real bank, he will loan you some gold. You don't want the gold itself, of course; rather, you want a slip of paper that represents 20 ounces of gold. The goldsmith in essence "creates" money for you by simply giving you a receipt for 20 ounces of gold (even though his entire supply of gold already belongs to various other people).[2] When he does so, there will be receipts for 120 ounces of gold in circulation instead of the 100 ounces' worth of receipts before your loan, and the supply of money will have increased.

People often think that the creation of money is mysterious, perhaps even magical. In fact, far from being mystical, the creation of money is simply an accounting procedure, among the most mundane of human endeavors. You may also harbor a suspicion that the whole process is fundamentally unsound, or somehow dubious. After all, the banking system began when someone issued claims for gold that already belonged to someone else. Here you may be on slightly firmer ground.

---

[1] *Remember, these receipts circulated as money, and people used them to make transactions without feeling the need to cash them in—that is, to exchange them for gold itself.*
[2] *In return for lending you the receipt for 20 ounces of gold, the goldsmith expects to get an IOU promising to repay the amount (in gold itself or with a receipt from another goldsmith) with interest after a certain period of time.*

Goldsmiths-turned-bankers did face certain problems. Once they started making loans, their receipts outstanding (claims on gold) were greater than the amount of gold they had in their vaults at any given moment. If the owners of the 120 ounces' worth of gold receipts all presented their receipts and demanded their gold at the same time, the goldsmith would find himself in trouble. With only 100 ounces of gold on hand, there would be no way to give off everyone his or her gold at once.

In normal times, people would be quite happy to hold receipts instead of real gold, and this problem would never arise. If, however, people began to worry about the goldsmith's financial safety, they might begin to have doubts about whether their receipts really were as good as gold. Knowing that there were more receipts outstanding than there were ounces of gold in the goldsmith's vault, people might start to demand gold for receipts.

This situation leads to a paradox. It makes perfect sense to hold paper receipts (instead of gold) if you know you can always get gold for your paper. In normal times, goldsmiths could feel perfectly safe in loaning out more gold than they actually had in their possession. But once you (and everyone else) start to doubt the safety of the goldsmith, then you (and everyone else) would be foolish not to demand your gold back from the vault.

A **run** on a goldsmith (or in our day, a **run on a bank**) occurs when many people present their claims at the same time. These runs tend to feed on themselves. If I see you going to the goldsmith to withdraw your gold, I may become nervous and decide to withdraw my gold as well. In fact, it is the *fear* of a run that usually causes the run to take place. Runs on a bank can be triggered by a variety of causes: rumors that an institution may have made loans to dubious borrowers who cannot repay them, wars, failures of other institutions that have borrowed money from the bank, and so on. As you will see later in this chapter, today's bankers differ from goldsmiths, in that today's banks are subject to a "required reserve ratio." Goldsmiths had no legal reserve requirements, although the amount that they loaned out was subject to the restriction imposed on them by their fear of running out of gold.

run on a bank *Occurs when many of those who have claims on a bank (deposits) present them at the same time.*

THE MODERN BANKING SYSTEM

To understand how the modern banking system works, you need to have a passing familiarity with some basic principles of accounting. Once you are comfortable with the way banks keep their books, the whole process of money creation will seem quite logical.

■ **A Brief Review of Accounting** Central to accounting practices is the statement that "the books always balance." In practice, this means that if we take a snapshot of a firm—any firm, including a bank—at a particular moment in time, then by definition:

$$\text{Assets} - \text{Liabilities} \equiv \text{Capital (or Net Worth), or}$$
$$\text{Assets} \equiv \text{Liabilities} + \text{Capital.}$$

Assets are things that a firm owns that are worth something. For a bank, these assets include the bank building, its furniture, its holdings of government securities, cash in its vaults, bonds, stocks, and so forth. Most important among a bank's assets, for our purposes at least, are its *loans*. When a bank makes a loan, the borrower gives the bank an *IOU*, a promise to repay a certain sum of money on or by a certain date. This promise is an asset of the bank because it is worth something. The bank could (and sometimes does) sell the IOU to another bank for cash.

Other bank assets include cash on hand (sometimes called *vault cash*) and deposits with the United States' central bank—the **Federal Reserve Bank (the Fed).** As we will see later in this chapter, federal banking regulations require that banks keep a certain portion of their deposits on hand as vault cash or on deposit with the Fed.

A firm's *liabilities* are simply its debts—what it owes. Stated another way, a bank's liabilities are the promises to pay, or IOUs, that it has issued. A bank's most important liabilities are its deposits. *Deposits* are debts owed to the depositors, because when you deposit money in your account, you are in essence making a loan to the bank.

The basic rule of accounting says that if we add up a firm's assets and then subtract the total amount it owes to all those who have lent it funds, the difference is the firm's net worth. *Net worth* represents the value of the firm to its stockholders or owners. How much would you pay for a firm that owns $200,000 of diamonds and had borrowed $150,000 from a bank to pay for them? Clearly, the firm is worth $50,000—the difference between what it owns and what it owes. If the price of diamonds were to fall, bringing their value down to only $150,000, the firm would be worth nothing at all.

We can keep track of a bank's financial position using a simplified balance sheet called a T account. By convention, the bank's assets are listed on the left-hand side of the T account, its liabilities and net worth on the right-hand side. By definition, the balance sheet always balances, so that the sum of the item(s) on the left side of the T account is exactly equal to the sum of the item(s) on the right side of the T account.

The T account of a hypothetical bank is shown in Figure 11.1. The bank has $110 million in *assets,* of which $20 million are **reserves,** the deposits that the bank has made at the Fed and its cash on hand (coins and currency). Reserves are an asset to the bank because the bank can go to the Fed and get cash for them, just the way you can go to the bank and get cash for the amount in your savings account. Our bank's other asset is its loans, worth $90 million.

Why do banks hold reserves/deposits at the Fed? There are many reasons, but perhaps the most important is the legal requirement that they hold a certain percentage of their deposit liabilities as reserves. The percentage of its deposits that a bank must keep as reserves is known as the **required reserve ratio.** If the reserve ratio is 20%, then a bank with deposits of $100 million must hold $20 million as reserves, either as cash or as deposits at the Fed. To simplify matters, we will assume that banks hold all of their reserves in the form of deposits at the Fed.

On the liabilities side of the T account, the bank has taken deposits of $100 million, so it owes this amount to its depositors. This means that the bank has a

Federal Reserve System (the Fed) *The central bank of the United States.*

reserves *The deposits that a bank has at the Federal Reserve bank plus its cash on hand.*

required reserve ratio *The percentage of its total deposits that a bank must keep as reserves at the Federal Reserve.*

FIGURE 11.1

T Account for a Typical Bank (millions of dollars)

The balance sheet of a bank must always balance, so that the sum of assets (reserves and loans) equals the sum of liabilities (deposits and net worth).

Assets		Liabilities	
Reserves	20	100	Deposits
Loans	90	10	Net worth
Total	110	110	Total

net worth of $10 million to its owners ($110 million in assets − $100 million in liabilities = $10 million net worth). The net worth of the bank is what "balances" the balance sheet.

A rule worth remembering is as follows:

> When some item on a bank's balance sheet changes, there must be at least one other change somewhere else to maintain balance.

For example, if a bank's reserves increase by $1, then one of the following must also be true: (1) its other assets (say, loans) decrease by $1; (2) its liabilities (deposits) increase by $1; or (3) its net worth increases by $1. Various fractional combinations of these are also possible.

■ **The Creation of Money** Like the goldsmiths, today's bankers seek to earn income by lending money out at a higher interest rate than they pay depositors for use of their money.

In modern times, the chances of a run on a bank are fairly small; and, even if there is a run, the central bank protects the private banks in various ways. Therefore:

> Banks usually make loans up to the point where they can no longer do so because of the reserve requirement restriction.

A bank's required amount of reserves is equal to the required reserve ratio times the total deposits in the bank. If, for example, a bank has deposits of $100 and the required ratio is 20%, the required amount of reserves is $20. The difference between a bank's actual reserves and its required reserves is its **excess reserves**:

> Excess reserves = Actual reserves − Required reserves

If banks make loans up to the point where they can no longer do so because of the reserve requirement restriction, this means that banks make loans up to the point where their excess reserves are zero.

To see why this is so, note that when a bank has excess reserves, it has credit available, and it can make loans. Actually, a bank can make loans *only* if it has excess reserves. When a bank makes a loan, it simply creates a demand deposit for the borrower. This creation of a demand deposit causes the bank's excess reserves to fall because the extra deposits created by the loan use up some of the excess reserves the bank has on hand. An example will help to clarify this.

Assume for simplicity that there is only one private bank in the country, that the required reserve ratio is 20%, and that the bank starts off with nothing, as shown in Panel 1 of Figure 11.2. Now suppose that dollar bills are in circulation and that someone deposits 100 of them in the bank. The bank deposits the $100 with the central bank, so it now has $100 in reserves, as shown in Panel 2. The bank now has assets (reserves) of $100 and liabilities (deposits) of $100. If the required reserve ratio is 20%, the bank has excess reserves of $80.

How much can the bank lend and still meet the reserve requirement? For the moment, let's suppose that anyone who gets a loan keeps the entire proceeds in the bank or pays them to someone else who does. Nothing is withdrawn as cash. In this case, the bank can lend $400 and still meet the reserve requirement, as you can see in Panel 3 of Figure 11.2. With $80 of excess reserves, the bank can have up to $400 of additional deposits. The $100 in reserves plus $400 in loans (which are made as deposits) equal $500 in deposits. With $500 in deposits and a required

excess reserves *The difference between a bank's actual reserves and its required reserves.*

FIGURE 11.2
Balance Sheets of a Bank in a Single-Bank Economy

Panel 1

Assets	Liabilities
Reserves 0	0 Deposits

Panel 2

Assets	Liabilities
Reserves 100	100 Deposits

Panel 3

Assets	Liabilities
Reserves 100 Loans 400	500 Deposits

reserve ratio of 20%, the bank must have reserves of $100 (20% of $500)—and it does. The bank can lend no more than $400 because if it were to do so, its reserve requirement would exceed $100. When a bank has no excess reserves and thus can make no more loans, it is said to be *loaned up*.

Remember, the money supply (*M*1) equals cash in circulation plus deposits. Before the initial deposit, the money supply was $100 ($100 cash and no deposits). After the deposit and the loans, the money supply is $500 (no cash outside of bank vaults and $500 in deposits). It is clear, then, that when cash is converted into deposits, the supply of money can change.

The bank whose T accounts are presented in Figure 11.2 is allowed to make loans of $400 based on the assumption that loans that are made *stay in the bank* in the form of deposits. Now suppose that I borrow from the bank to buy a personal computer, and I write a check to the computer store. If the store also deposits its money in the bank, my check merely results in a reduction in my account balance and an increase to the store's account balance within the bank. No cash has left the bank. As long as the system is closed in this way—remember that we have so far assumed that there is only one bank—the bank knows that it will never be called upon to release any of its $100 in reserves. It can thus expand its loans up to the point where its total deposits are $500.

In practice, of course, there are many banks in the country, a situation that is depicted in Figure 11.3. As long as the banking system as a whole is closed, it is still possible for an initial deposit of $100 to result in an expansion of the money supply to $500, but more steps are involved when there is more than one bank.

An example will help to explain why this is so. Assume that Mary makes an initial deposit of $100 in Bank 1, and that the bank deposits the entire $100 with the Fed. (See Panel 1 of Figure 11.3.) Also assume that all loans that a bank makes are withdrawn from the bank as the individual borrowers write checks to pay for

	Panel 1		Panel 2		Panel 3	
	Assets	Liabilities	Assets	Liabilities	Assets	Liabilities
Bank 1	Reserves 100	100 Deposits	Reserves 100 Loans 80	180 Deposits	Reserves 20 Loans 80	100 Deposits
Bank 2	Reserves 80	80 Deposits	Reserves 80 Loans 64	144 Deposits	Reserves 16 Loans 64	80 Deposits
Bank 3	Reserves 64	64 Deposits	Reserves 64 Loans 51.20	115.20 Deposits	Reserves 12.80 Loans 51.20	64 Deposits

Summary:	Deposits
Bank 1	100
Bank 2	80
Bank 3	64
Bank 4	51.20
⋮	⋮
Total	500.00

FIGURE 11.3
The Creation of Money: Balance Sheets of Three Banks

merchandise. After Mary's deposit, Bank 1 can make a loan of up to $80 to its customer Bill, because it needs to keep only $20 of its $100 deposit as reserves. (We are assuming a 20% required reserve ratio.) In other words, Bank 1 has $80 in excess reserves.

Bank 1's balance sheet at the moment of the loan to Bill appears in Panel 2 of Fig 11.3. Bank 1 now has loans of $80. It has credited Bill's account with the $80, so its total deposits are $180 ($80 in loans plus $100 in reserves). Bill then writes a check for $80 for a set of shock absorbers for his car. Bill wrote his check to Sam's Car Shop, and Sam deposits Bill's check in his bank, Bank 2. When the check clears, Bank 1 transfers $80 in reserves to Bank 2. Bank 1's balance sheet now looks like that in Panel 3 of Fig 11.3. Its assets include reserves of $20 and loans of $80; its liabilities are $100 in deposits. Both sides of the T account balance: The bank's reserves are 20% of its deposits, as required by law, and it is fully loaned up.

Now look at Bank 2. Since Bank 1 has transferred $80 in reserves to Bank 2, it now has $80 in deposits and $80 in reserves. (See Panel 1, Bank 2.) Since its reserve requirement is also 20%, it has excess reserves of $64 on which it can make loans.

Now assume that Bank 2 loans the $64 to Kate to pay for a textbook and that Kate writes a check for $64 payable to the Manhattan College Bookstore. The final position of Bank 2, after it honors Kate's $64 check by transferring $64 in reserves to the bookstore's bank, is reserves of $16, loans of $64, and deposits of $80 (Panel 3, Bank 2).

The Manhattan College Bookstore deposits Kate's check in its bank account with Bank 3. Bank 3 now has excess reserves, because it has added $64 to its reserves. With a reserve ratio of 20%, Bank 3 can loan out $51.20 (80% of $64, leaving 20% in required reserves to back the $64 deposit).

As the process is repeated over and over, the total amount of deposits created is $500, the sum of the deposits in each of the banks. Because the banking system can be looked upon as one big bank, the outcome here for many banks is the same as the outcome in Figure 11.2 for one bank.[3]

■ **The Money Multiplier** In practice, the banking system is not completely closed—some leakage out of the system does take place. Still, the important point here is that:

> An increase in bank reserves leads to a greater than one-for-one increase in the money supply. Economists call the relationship between the final change in deposits and the change in reserves that caused this change the **money multiplier.** Stated somewhat differently, the money multiplier is the multiple by which deposits can increase for every dollar increase in reserves.

money multiplier *The multiple by which deposits can increase for every dollar increase in reserves; equal to one divided by the required reserve ratio.*

Do not confuse the money multiplier with the spending multipliers we discussed in the last two chapters. They are not the same thing.

In the example we just examined, reserves increased by $100 when the $100 in cash was deposited in a bank, and the amount of deposits increased by $500 ($100 from the initial deposit, $400 from the loans made by the various banks from their excess reserves). The money multiplier in this case is thus $500/$100 = 5. Mathematically, the money multiplier can be defined as:

$$\text{Money multiplier} \equiv \frac{1}{\text{Required reserve ratio}}$$

[3]*If banks create money when they make loans, does repaying a loan "destroy" money? The answer is yes.*

In the United States, the required reserve ratio varies, depending on the size of the bank and the type of deposit. For large banks and for checking deposits, the ratio is currently 10%, which makes the potential money multiplier 1/.10 = 10.0. This means that an increase in reserves of $1 could cause an increase in deposits of $10.00 if there were no leakage out of the system.

■ **The Fed and the Money Supply** We have now seen how the private banking system creates money by making loans. However, private banks are not free to create money at will. Their ability to create money is controlled by the volume of reserves in the system, which is in turn controlled by the Federal Reserve. The Federal Reserve, therefore, has the ultimate control over the money supply. We examine the structure and function of the Federal Reserve in the sections that follow.

THE FEDERAL RESERVE SYSTEM

Founded in 1913 by an act of Congress (to which major reforms were added in the 1930s), the Federal Reserve is the central bank of the United States. The Fed is a complicated institution with many responsibilities, including the regulation and supervision of over 8,000 commercial banks. The organization of the Federal Reserve System is presented in Figure 11.4.

The *Board of Governors* is the most important group within the Federal Reserve System. The board consists of seven members, each appointed for 14 years by the President of the United States. The *chair* of the Federal Reserve, who is appointed by the President and whose term runs for four years, usually dominates the entire Federal Reserve System and is sometimes said to be the second most powerful person in the United States. The Fed is an independent agency in that it does not take orders from the President or from Congress.

The United States is divided into 12 Federal Reserve districts, each of which has its own Federal Reserve bank. These districts are indicated on the map in Figure 11.4. The district banks are like branch offices of the Federal Reserve in that they carry out the rules, regulations, and functions of the central system in their districts and report to the Board of Governors on local economic conditions.

U.S. monetary policy, that is, the behavior of the Federal Reserve regarding the money supply, is formally set by the **Federal Open Market Committee (FOMC).** The FOMC consists of the seven members of the Federal Reserve System's Board of Governors, the president of the New York Federal Reserve Bank, and, on a rotating basis, four of the presidents of the 11 other district banks. The FOMC sets goals regarding the money supply and interest rates, and it directs the **Open Market Desk** in the New York Federal Reserve Bank to buy and/or sell government securities. (We discuss the specifics of open market operations at length later in this chapter.)

FUNCTIONS OF THE FED

As noted above, the Fed is the central bank of the United States. (A brief discussion of the central banks of other countries, and the challenges they faced in 1995, is found in this chapter's Global Perspective box, on page 256.) Central banks are sometimes known as "bankers' banks" because only banks (and occasionally foreign governments) can have accounts in them. As a private citizen, you cannot go to the nearest branch of the Fed and open a checking account or apply to borrow money.

Although from a macroeconomic point of view the Fed's crucial role is to control the money supply, the Fed also performs several important functions for banks. These functions include clearing interbank payments, regulating the banking

Federal Open Market Committee (FOMC) *A group composed of the seven members of the Fed's Board of Governors, the president of the New York Federal Reserve Bank, and four of the other eleven district bank presidents on a rotating basis; it sets goals regarding the money supply and interest rates and directs the operation of the Open Market Desk in New York.*

Open Market Desk *The office in the New York Federal Reserve Bank from which government securities are bought and sold by the Fed.*

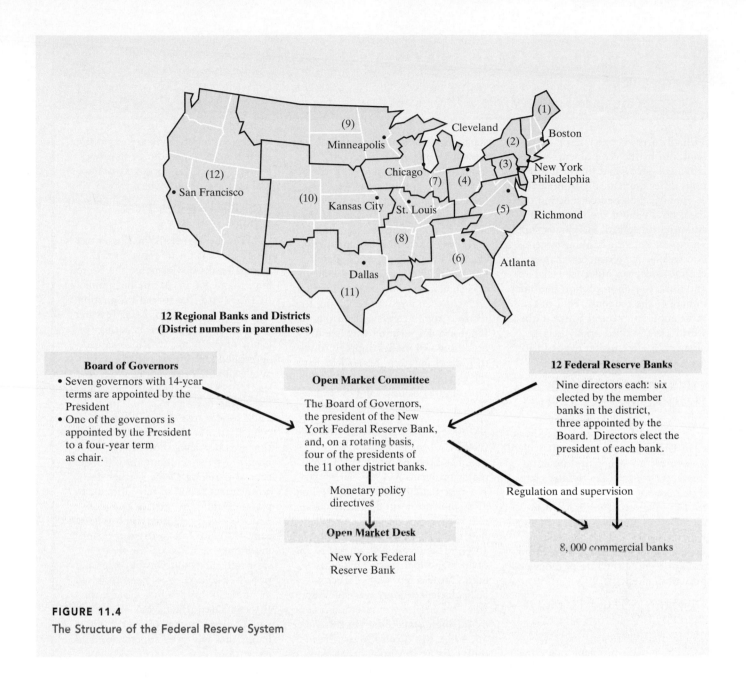

FIGURE 11.4
The Structure of the Federal Reserve System

system, and assisting banks that are in a difficult financial position. The Fed is also responsible for managing exchange rates and the nation's foreign exchange reserves.[4] In addition, it is often involved in intercountry negotiations on international economic issues. In the early 1980s, for example, then Chair Paul Volcker played a major role in negotiations with foreign governments on issues relating to the serious debt problems of developing countries. More recently, Chair Alan Greenspan has been involved in discussions with European central bankers regarding the monetary problems of reuniting East and West Germany and "opening up" Eastern Europe.

---

[4]Foreign exchange reserves *are holdings of the currencies of other countries (for example, French francs) by the U.S. government. We discuss exchange rates and foreign exchange markets at length in Chapter 22.*

Virtually every country has a central bank run by the government. While banking systems and financial institutions differ dramatically from country to country, the essential function of the central bank is the same in all countries: to control the money supply and to regulate the banking system. As you will see in subsequent chapters, central banks can influence behavior and thus have an impact on the functioning of the economy. Four of the most important central banks in the world are described briefly below, along with a discussion of the major problem that each faced in 1995.

THE UNITED STATES: THE FEDERAL RESERVE SYSTEM (NICKNAME: "THE FED")

The Fed Chairman in 1995 was Alan Greenspan. Greenspan is widely known for his strong anti-inflation views. As you will see in later chapters, excess monetary expansion can lead to inflation. The threat of increasing inflation was the Fed's number one worry as the U.S. economy moved into 1995. Thus, the Fed policy was to hold the rate of money growth in check.

GERMANY: THE DEUTSCHE BUNDESBANK (NICKNAME: "THE BUBBA")

The biggest problem facing Germany in recent years has been the economic effects of reunification. The German monetary problem was enormous. The East German currency had to be exchanged for new West German deutsche marks without creating wild inflationary swings. This was accomplished in an amazingly orderly way, and inflation remained in check. In early 1995, Bundesbank President Tietmeyer's major concern was similar to Alan Greenspan's. The German economy was beginning to recover from a recession and the Bundesbank's position was one of holding down money supply growth to prevent inflation. Many felt that the expansion in Germany was about nine months behind the U.S. expansion.

JAPAN: THE BANK OF JAPAN (NICKNAME: "BOJ")

The Bank of Japan faced two major problems in 1995. First, the Japanese banking system was feeling great pressure from defaulted real estate loans and land values that had fallen sharply between 1992 and 1994. (This problem is similar to the savings and loan crisis the United States faced a few years earlier.) Second, the economy was stuck in what has been a very deep recession by Japanese standards. On December 16, 1994, Mr. Yasuro Matsushita took over as Governor of the Bank of Japan. He is likely to continue the policy of modest monetary expansion to help bring Japan out of its slow growth period. Inflation was not a real concern of the Bank in 1995.

RUSSIA: THE CENTRAL BANK OF RUSSIA

The Central Bank of Russia has problems that dwarf those of the central banks of Germany, the United States, and Japan. At the beginning of 1995, after the forced resignation of Viktor Gerashenko, Mrs. Tatyana Paramonova took over as acting Chair of the Bank, which remained embroiled in political controversy. While the list of economic woes in the New Russia was long, near the top of the list was hyperinflation. In 1992, prices rose about 2000 percent. By the beginning of 1995, inflation was *down* to about 15% per month. As the economy moved from central planning to the market, the government found it very difficult to maintain military salaries and to finance a collapsing industrial structure. Ultimately, it resorted to printing money to make up for the shortfall; the result was hyperinflation. In addition to its need to break its addiction to printing money, the Russian Central Bank has a new private banking system of over 2,000 banks that will need supervision and regulation.

■ **Clearing Interbank Payments** Suppose you write a $100 check, drawn on your bank, the First Bank of Fresno (FBF), to pay for some tulip bulbs from Crockett Importers of Miami, Florida. Since Crockett Importers does not bank at FBF, but rather at Banco de Miami, how does your money get from your bank to the bank in Florida?

The answer is simple: The Fed does it. Both FBF and Banco de Miami have accounts at the Federal Reserve. When Crockett Importers receives your check and deposits it at the Banco de Miami, the bank submits the check to the Federal Reserve, asking it to collect the funds from FBF. The Fed then presents the check to FBF and is instructed to debit FBF's account for the $100 and to credit the account of Banco de Miami. Since accounts at the Fed count as reserves, FBF loses $100 in reserves and Banco de Miami gains $100 in reserves. In essence, the two banks have traded ownerships of their deposits at the Federal Reserve. Note that the *total* volume of reserves has not changed, however, and neither has the money supply.

This function of clearing interbank payments allows banks to shift money around virtually instantaneously. All they need to do is wire the Fed and request a transfer, and the funds move at the speed of electricity from one computer account to another.

■ **Other Duties of the Fed**　Besides facilitating the transfer of funds between banks, the Fed performs several other important duties. It is responsible for many of the regulations governing banking practices and standards. For example, the Federal Reserve has the authority to control mergers between banks, and it is responsible for examining banks to ensure that they are financially sound and that they conform to a host of government accounting regulations. And, as we saw earlier, the Fed also sets reserve requirements for all financial institutions.

One of the most important responsibilities of the Fed is to act as the **lender of last resort** for the banking system. As our discussion of goldsmiths suggested, banks are subject to the possibility of runs on their deposits. In the United States, most deposits of less than $100,000 are insured by the Federal Deposit Insurance Corporation (FDIC). The existence of deposit insurance makes panics less likely. Because depositors know they can always get their hands on their money, even if the bank fails, they are less likely to withdraw their deposits. Not all deposits are insured, however, and the possibility of bank panics remains real. Thus, the Federal Reserve stands ready to provide funds to a troubled bank that cannot find any other sources of funds.

The Fed is the ideal lender of last resort for two reasons. First, providing funds to a bank that is in dire straits is risky and not likely to be very profitable, and it is hard to find private banks or other private institutions that are willing to perform this function. The Fed, by contrast, is a nonprofit institution whose function is to serve the overall welfare of the public. Thus, the Fed would certainly be interested in preventing catastrophic banking panics such as those that occurred in the late 1920s and the 1930s.

Second, the Fed has an essentially unlimited supply of funds with which to bail out banks that are facing the possibility of runs. The reason, as we shall see, is that the Fed can simply create reserves at will. A promise by the Fed that it will support a bank is thus a very convincing one. Unlike any other lender, the Fed can never run out of money. Therefore, the explicit or implicit support of the Fed should be enough to assure depositors that they are in no danger of losing their funds.

lender of last resort *One of the functions of the Fed: It provides funds to troubled banks that cannot find any other sources of funds.*

THE FED'S BALANCE SHEET

Although it is a special bank, the Federal Reserve is in some ways very similar to an ordinary commercial bank. Like an ordinary bank, the Fed has a balance sheet that records its asset and liability position at any moment in time. The balance sheet for the Federal Reserve is presented in Table 11.1 on page 258.

As the asset side of the balance sheet shows, the Fed owns about $11 billion of gold. *Do not think that this gold has anything to do with the supply of money.* Most of the gold was acquired during the 1930s, when it was purchased from the U.S. Treasury Department. Since 1934, the dollar has not been backed by (that is, it is not convertible into) gold. You cannot take a dollar bill to the Fed and ask to receive gold for it; all you can get for your old dollar bill is a new dollar bill.[5] Although it is unrelated to the money supply, the Fed's gold nevertheless counts as an asset on its balance sheet, because it is something of value that the Fed owns.

The balance sheet also mentions an asset called "loans to banks." These loans are an asset of the Federal Reserve in just the same way that a private commercial bank's loans are among its assets. The Fed sometimes makes loans to commercial banks that are short of reserves.[6] The $84 million in Table 11.1 represents these kinds of loans.

The largest of the Fed's assets by far consist of government securities: about $369 billion worth at the end of March 1995. Government securities are obligations of the federal government, such as Treasury bills and government bonds, which the Fed has purchased over the years. The way in which these bonds are acquired has important implications for the Fed's control of the money supply. (We return to this topic after our survey of the Fed's balance sheet.)

The bulk of the Fed's liabilities are Federal Reserve notes. The dollar bill you carry in your pocket when you go to the store to buy a quart of milk is clearly an asset from your point of view—it is something you own that has value. But since every financial asset is by definition a liability of some other agent in the economy, whose liability is that dollar bill? Quite simply: That dollar bill, and bills of all other denominations in the economy, are a liability—an IOU—of the Federal Reserve. They are, of course, rather strange IOUs, because all they can be redeemed for are other IOUs of exactly the same type. They are, nonetheless, classified as liabilities of the Fed.

The Fed's balance sheet also shows that, like an ordinary commercial bank, the Fed has accepted deposits. These deposits are recorded as liabilities. The bulk of the Fed's deposits come from commercial banks. Remember that commercial banks are required to keep a certain share of their own deposits as deposits at the Fed. Since a bank's deposits at the Fed (its reserves) are an asset from the bank's point of view, those same reserves must be a liability from the Fed's point of view.

TABLE 11.1		ASSETS AND LIABILITIES OF THE FEDERAL RESERVE SYSTEM, MARCH 31, 1995 (millions of dollars)	
ASSETS		**LIABILITIES**	
Gold	$11,053	$379,191	Federal Reserve notes (outstanding)
Loans to banks	84		Deposits:
U.S. government securities	369,300	30,009	Bank reserves (from depository institutions)
		4,543	U.S. Treasury
All other assets	52,071	18,765	All other liabilities and net worth
Total	$432,508	$432,508	Total

Source: *Federal Reserve Bulletin, July 1995.*

---

[5]*The fact that the Fed is not obliged to provide gold for currency means that it can never go bankrupt. When the currency was backed by gold, it would have been possible for the Fed to run out of gold if too many of its depositors came to it at the same time and asked to exchange their deposits for gold. But if depositors come to the Fed and wish to withdraw their deposits today, all they can get are dollar bills. It should also be noted that the dollar was convertible into gold internationally until August 15, 1971.*
[6]*Recall that commercial banks are required to keep a set percentage of their deposit liabilities on deposit at the Fed. If a bank suddenly finds itself short of reserves, one of its alternatives is to borrow the reserves it needs from the Fed.*

Table 11.1 also shows that the Fed has accepted a small volume of deposits from the U.S. Treasury. In effect, the Fed acts as the bank for the U.S. government. When the government needs to pay for something it has bought (a new aircraft carrier, for example) it may write out a check to the supplier of the ship drawn on its "checking account" at the Federal Reserve. Similarly, when the government receives revenues from tax collections, fines, or sales of government assets, it may deposit these funds in its account at the Fed.

HOW THE FED CONTROLS THE MONEY SUPPLY

The key to understanding how the Fed controls the supply of money in the U.S. economy is an appreciation of the role of reserves. As we have said, the required reserve ratio establishes a link between the reserves of the commercial banks and the deposits (money) that commercial banks are allowed to create.

The reserve requirement, in essence, determines how much a given bank has available to lend. If, for example, the required reserve ratio is 20%, then each $1 of reserves can support $5 in deposits. A bank that has reserves of $100,000 cannot have more than $500,000 in deposits. If it did, it would fail to meet the required reserve ratio.

If you recall that the *money supply* is equal to the sum of deposits inside banks and the currency in circulation outside of banks, you can see that reserves provide the leverage that the Fed needs to control the money supply:

> If the Fed wants to increase the supply of money, it creates more reserves, thereby freeing banks to create additional deposits by making more loans. If it wants to decrease the money supply, it reduces reserves.

The key question then becomes, of course: How does the Fed control the supply of reserves? There are three major tools available to the Fed for changing the money supply. These are (1) changing the required reserve ratio, (2) changing the discount rate, and (3) open market operations. We shall explore each of these in turn.

THE REQUIRED RESERVE RATIO

The simplest way for the Fed to alter the supply of money is to change the required reserve ratio. An analysis of how this process works is presented in Table 11.2. Let us assume that the initial required reserve ratio is 20 percent.

In Panel 1, a simplified version of the Fed's balance sheet (in billions of dollars) shows that reserves are $100 billion and currency outstanding is another $100 billion. The total value of the Fed's assets is $200 billion, which we assume to be all in the form of government securities. Assuming that there are no excess reserves—that banks stay fully loaned up—the $100 billion in reserves supports $500 billion in deposits at the commercial banks. (Remember that the money multiplier equals 1/required reserve ratio = 1/.20 = 5. Thus, $100 billion in reserves can support $500 billion [$100 billion × 5] in deposits when the required reserve ratio is 20 percent.) The supply of money (M1, or transactions money) is therefore equal to $600 billion: $100 billion in currency and $500 billion in (checking account) deposits at the commercial banks.

Now suppose that the Fed wants to increase the supply of money to $900 billion. If it lowers the required reserve ratio from 20% to 12.5% (as shown in Panel 2 of Table 11.2), then the same $100 billion of reserves could support $800 billion in deposits instead of only $500 billion. In this case, the money multiplier is 1/.125, or 8. At a required reserve ratio of 12.5% then, $100 billion in reserves can sup-

TABLE 11.2   **A DECREASE IN THE REQUIRED RESERVE RATIO FROM 20% TO 12.5% INCREASES THE SUPPLY OF MONEY (ALL FIGURES IN BILLIONS OF DOLLARS)**

PANEL 1: REQUIRED RESERVE RATIO = 20%

FEDERAL RESERVE				COMMERCIAL BANKS			
ASSETS		LIABILITIES		ASSETS		LIABILITIES	
Government securities	$200	$100	Reserves	Reserves	$100	$500	Deposits
		$100	Currency	Loans	$400		

Note: Money supply (M1) = Currency + Deposits = $600.

PANEL 2: REQUIRED RESERVE RATIO = 12.5%

FEDERAL RESERVE				COMMERCIAL BANKS			
ASSETS		LIABILITIES		ASSETS		LIABILITIES	
Government securities	$200	$100	Reserves	Reserves	$100	$800	Deposits (+$300)
		$100	Currency	Loans (+$300)	$700		

Note: Money supply (M1) = Currency + Deposits = $900.

port $800 billion in deposits. The total money supply would then be $800 billion in deposits plus the $100 billion in currency, for a total of $900 billion.[7]

Put another way, with the new lower reserve ratio, banks have excess reserves of $37.5 billion. At a required reserve ratio of 20%, they needed $100 billion in reserves to back their $500 billion in deposits. At the lower required service ration of 12.5%, they now need only $62.5 billion of reserves to back their $500 billion of deposits, so the remaining $37.5 billion of the existing $100 billion in reserves are "extra." With that $37.5 billion of excess reserves, banks can lend out more money. If we assume that the system loans money and creates deposits to the *maximum* extent possible, the $37.5 billion of reserves will support an additional $300 billion of deposits ($37.5 billion × the money multiplier of 8 = $300 billion). The change in the required reserve ratio has thus injected an additional $300 billion into the banking system, at which point the banks will be fully loaned up and unable to increase their deposits further.

In sum:

> Decreases in the required reserve ratio allow banks to have more deposits with the existing volume of reserves. As banks create more deposits by making loans, the supply of money (currency + deposits) increases. The reverse is also true: If the Fed wants to restrict the supply of money, it can raise the required reserve ratio, in which case banks will find that they have insufficient reserves and must therefore reduce their deposits by "calling in" some of their loans.[8] The result is a decrease in the money supply.

---

[7]*To find the maximum volume of deposits (D) that can be supported by an amount of reserves (R), simply divide R by the required reserve ratio. If the required reserve ratio is g, since R = gD, then D = R/g.*
[8]*In fact, banks never really have to "call in" loans before they are due in order to reduce the money supply. First, the Fed is almost always expanding the money supply slowly because the real economy grows steadily and, as we shall see, growth brings with it the need for more circulating money. So when we speak of "contractionary monetary policy," we mean that the Fed is slowing down the rate of money growth, not reducing the money supply. Second, even if the Fed were actually to cut reserves (rather than merely curb their expansion), banks would no doubt be able to comply by reducing the volume of new loans that they make while old ones are coming due.*

For a variety of reasons, the Fed has tended not to use changes in the reserve requirement as a means of controlling the money supply. In part, this reluctance stems from the era when only some banks were members of the Federal Reserve System and thus subject to reserve requirements. The Fed reasoned that if it raised the reserve requirement in order to contract the money supply, banks might choose to stop being members. (Since reserves pay no interest, the higher the reserve requirement, the more the penalty imposed on those banks holding reserves.) This argument, however, no longer applies. Since the passage of the Depository Institutions Deregulation and Monetary Control Act in 1980, all depository institutions are subject to Federal Reserve requirements.

It is also true that changing the reserve requirement ratio is a fairly crude tool. Because of lags in banks' reporting to the Fed on their reserve and deposit positions, a change in the requirement today does not affect banks for about two weeks. (However, the fact that changing the reserve requirement expands or reduces credit in every bank in the country makes it a very powerful tool when the Fed does use it.) A much better tool for controlling week-to-week changes in the money supply, as we shall see shortly, is open market operations.

THE DISCOUNT RATE

Banks are allowed to borrow from the Fed. The interest rate that they pay the Fed for this privilege is called the **discount rate.** When banks increase their borrowing, the money supply increases.

discount rate *Interest rate that banks pay to the Fed to borrow from it.*

To simplify our analysis, let us assume that there is only one bank in the country and that the required reserve ratio is 20%. The initial position of the bank and the Fed appear in Panel 1 of Table 11.3 on the next page, where the money supply (currency + deposits) is $480. In Panel 2, the bank has borrowed $20 from the Fed. By using this $20 as a reserve, the bank can increase its loans by $100, from $320 to $420. (Remember that a required reserve ratio of 20% gives a money multiplier of 5. Thus, excess reserves of $20 allows the bank to create an additional $20 × 5, or $100, in deposits.) Thus,

> Bank borrowing from the Fed leads to an increase in the money supply.

Of course, banks that borrow from the Fed must eventually repay their borrowings. When they do, the money supply goes back down by exactly the amount by which it initially increased.

The Fed can exercise some influence over bank borrowing through the discount rate:

> The higher the discount rate, the higher the cost of borrowing, and the less borrowing banks will want to do.

If the Fed wants to curtail the growth of the money supply, for example, it raises the discount rate, discourages banks from borrowing from it, and thus restricts the growth of reserves (and ultimately deposits).

In practice, the Fed does not use the discount rate very often to control the money supply. It does change the discount rate from time to time to keep it in line with other interest rates, but most often the discount rate follows the other rates rather than leads them.

Changing the discount rate in order to control the supply of money has several problems associated with it. First, although raising the discount rate does dis-

TABLE 11.3 — THE EFFECT ON THE MONEY SUPPLY OF COMMERCIAL BANK BORROWING FROM THE FED
(ALL FIGURES IN BILLIONS OF DOLLARS)

PANEL 1: NO COMMERCIAL BANK BORROWING FROM THE FED

FEDERAL RESERVE				COMMERCIAL BANKS			
ASSETS		LIABILITIES		ASSETS		LIABILITIES	
Securities	$160	$80	Reserves	Reserves	$80	$400	Deposits
		$80	Currency	Loans	$320		

Note: Money supply (*M1*) = Currency + Deposits = $480.

PANEL 2: COMMERCIAL BANK BORROWING $20 FROM THE FED

FEDERAL RESERVE				COMMERCIAL BANKS			
ASSETS		LIABILITIES		ASSETS		LIABILITIES	
Securities	$160	$100	Reserves (+$20)	Reserves (+$20)	$100	$500	Deposits (+$100)
Loans	$20	$80	Currency	Loans (+$100)	$420	$20	Amount owed to Fed (+$20)

Note: Money supply (*M1*) = Currency + Deposits = $580.

courage borrowing by banks (and therefore reduces their ability to expand the money supply), it is never clear in advance exactly how much of an effect any given change in the discount rate will have. If banks are very short of reserves, they may decide to borrow from the Fed even though the discount rate is quite high. In short:

> The discount rate cannot be used to control the money supply with great precision, because its effects on banks' demand for reserves are uncertain.

Second, changes in the discount rate can be largely offset by movements in other interest rates. For example, if the discount rate is set at 10% and the rate paid by Treasury bills is 9%, banks will obviously not find it profitable to borrow from the Fed to purchase Treasury bills. Since they would be paying more in borrowing costs than they would be making in interest revenue, they would lose by borrowing from the Fed. If the Treasury bill rate were to rise to 11%, however, then banks could profitably borrow from the Fed to purchase Treasury bills. Thus, a discount rate that is high enough to discourage borrowing in some circumstances may not be high enough in others.

You may be wondering whether the discount rate can ever be below the rate banks charge their customers for loans or below the rate offered on Treasury bills. If this were the case, wouldn't banks borrow enormous quantities from the Fed at the lower rate and lend at the higher rate? In practice, the discount rate is at times lower than the rate that banks charge for their loans, and yet this kind of behavior is not common. This is because the Fed places other constraints on the borrowing behavior of banks. The Fed practices what is sometimes called **moral suasion** to discourage heavy borrowing. Because member banks know that the Fed would look askance at heavy borrowing, they do not borrow heavily, and the amount that they do borrow responds only slightly to changes in the discount rate.

moral suasion *The pressure exerted by the Fed on member banks to discourage them from borrowing heavily from the Fed.*

OPEN MARKET OPERATIONS

By far the most significant of the Fed's tools for controlling the supply of money is **open market operations.** Congress has authorized the Federal Reserve to buy and sell U.S. government securities in the open market. When the Fed purchases a security, it pays for it by writing a check which, when cleared, *expands* the quantity of reserves in the system and thus the money supply. When the Fed sells a bond, private citizens or institutions pay for it with a check which, when cleared, *reduces* the quantity of reserves in the system.

Before we look at how open market transactions and reserve controls work, however, we need to review several key ideas.

■ **Two Branches of Government Deal in Government Securities** The fact that the Fed is able to buy and sell government securities—bills and bonds—is a source of much confusion to students. In fact, *two* branches of government deal in financial markets for very different reasons, and it is critical that you keep the two separate in your mind.

First, keep in mind that the Treasury Department is responsible for collecting taxes and paying the federal government's bills. Salary checks paid to government workers, payments to General Dynamics for a new Navy ship, social security checks to retirees, and so forth are all written on accounts maintained by the Treasury. Tax receipts collected by the Internal Revenue Service, a Treasury branch, are deposited to these accounts.

If total government spending exceeds tax receipts, the law requires the Treasury to borrow the difference. Recall that the government deficit is $(G - T)$, or government purchases minus net taxes. $(G - T)$ is the amount the Treasury must borrow each year to finance the deficit. This means that:

> The Treasury *cannot* print money to finance the deficit.

The Treasury borrows by issuing bills, bonds, and notes that pay interest. These government securities, or IOUs, are sold to individuals and institutions. Often foreign countries, as well as U.S. citizens, buy them. The total amount of outstanding government securities is the **federal debt.** At the end of 1994, the federal debt stood at about $3.4 trillion.

The Fed is not the Treasury. Rather, it is a quasi-independent agency authorized by Congress to buy and sell *outstanding* (that is, preexisting) U.S. government securities on the open market. The bonds and bills initially sold by the Treasury to finance the deficit are continuously resold and traded among ordinary citizens, firms, banks, pension funds, and so forth. The Fed's participation in that trading affects the quantity of reserves in the system, as we will see below.

Because the Fed owns some government securities, some of what the government owes, it owes to itself. Recall that the Federal Reserve System's largest single asset is government securities. These securities are nothing more than bills and bonds initially issued by the Treasury to finance the deficit. They were acquired by the Fed over time through direct open market purchases that the Fed made in order to expand the money supply as the economy expanded.

■ **The Mechanics of Open Market Operations** How do open market operations affect the money supply? Look again at Table 11.1. As you can see, most of the Fed's assets consist of the government securities we have just been talking about.

open market operations *The purchase and sale by the Fed of government securities in the open market; a tool used to expand or contract the amount of reserves in the system and thus the money supply.*

federal debt *The total amount owed by the federal government.*

Suppose, now, that the Fed wants to decrease the supply of money. If it can reduce the volume of bank reserves on the liabilities side of its balance sheet, it will force banks in turn to reduce their own deposits (in order to meet the required reserve ratio). Since these deposits are part of the supply of money, the supply of money will contract.

We must now ask ourselves what will happen if the Fed sells some of its holdings of government securities to the general public. Clearly, the Fed's holdings of government securities must decrease, since some of the securities it used to own will now be owned by someone else. How do the purchasers of securities pay for what they have bought? Quite simply, by writing checks that are drawn on their banks and payable to the Fed.

Let's look a bit more carefully at how this process works, with the help of Table 11.4. In Panel 1, the Fed initially has $100 billion of government securities. Its liabilities consist of $20 billion of deposits (which, you recall, are the reserves of commercial banks) and $80 billion of currency. With the required reserve ratio at 20%, the $20 billion of reserves can support $100 billion of deposits in the commercial banks. The commercial banking system is thus fully loaned up. Panel 1 also shows the financial position of a private citizen, Jane Q. Public. Jane has assets of $5 billion (a rather large checking account deposit in the bank) and no debts, so her net worth is $5 billion.

Now imagine that the Fed sells $5 billion in government securities to Jane. Jane pays for the securities by writing a check to the Fed, drawn on her bank. The Fed then reduces the reserve account of her bank by $5 billion. The balance sheets of all the participants after this transaction are shown in Panel 2. Note that the supply of money (currency plus deposits) has fallen from $180 billion to $175 billion.

This is not the end of the story, however. As a result of the Fed's sale of securities, the amount of reserves has fallen from $20 billion to $15 billion, while deposits have fallen from $100 billion to $95 billion. With a required reserve ratio of 20%, banks must have .20 × $95 billion, or $19 billion in reserves. Banks are thus under their required reserve ratio by $4 billion ($19 billion [the amount they should have] minus $15 billion [the amount they do have]). In order to comply with the federal regulations, therefore, banks must decrease their loans and their deposits.[9]

The final equilibrium position is shown in Panel 3, where commercial banks have reduced their loans by $20 billion. Notice that the change in deposits from Panel 1 to Panel 3 is $25 billion, which is five times the size of the change in reserves that the Fed brought about through its $5 billion open market sale of securities. This corresponds exactly to our earlier analysis of the money multiplier. The change in money (−$25 billion) is equal to the money multiplier (five) times the change in reserves (−$5 billion).

Now consider what happens when the Fed *purchases* a government security. Suppose that I hold $100 in Treasury bills, which the Fed buys from me. The Fed writes me a check for $100, and I turn in my Treasury bills. I then take the $100 check and deposit it in my local bank. This increases the reserves of my bank by $100 and begins a new episode in the money expansion story. With a reserve requirement of 20%, my bank can now lend out $80. If that $80 is spent and ends up back in a bank, that bank can lend $64, and so forth. (Review Figure 26.3.) The Fed can thus expand the money supply by buying government securities from people who own them, just the way it reduces the money supply by selling these securities.

Each business day, the Open Market Desk in the New York Federal Reserve Bank buys or sells millions of dollars' worth of securities, usually to large security

---

[9]*Once again, banks never really have to call in loans. Loans and deposits would probably be reduced by slowing the rate of new lending as old loans come due and are paid off.*

TABLE 11.4 — OPEN MARKET OPERATIONS
THE NUMBERS IN PARENTHESES IN PANELS 2 AND 3 SHOW THE DIFFERENCES BETWEEN THOSE PANELS AND PANEL 1. ALL FIGURES IN BILLIONS OF DOLLARS

PANEL 1

FEDERAL RESERVE				COMMERCIAL BANKS				JANE Q. PUBLIC			
ASSETS		LIABILITIES		ASSETS		LIABILITIES		ASSETS		LIABILITIES	
Securities	$100	$20	Reserves	Reserves	$20	$100	Deposits	Deposits	$5	$0	Debts
		$80	Currency	Loans	$80					$5	Net Worth

Note: Money supply (M1) = Currency + Deposits = $180.

PANEL 2

FEDERAL RESERVE				COMMERCIAL BANKS				JANE Q. PUBLIC			
ASSETS		LIABILITIES		ASSETS		LIABILITIES		ASSETS		LIABILITIES	
Securities (−$5)	$95	$15 (−$5)	Reserves	Reserves (−$5)	$15	$95 (−$5)	Deposits	Deposits (−$5)	$0	$0	Debts
		$80	Currency	Loans	$80			Securities (+$5)	$5	$5	Net Worth

Note: Money supply (M1) = Currency + Deposits = $175.

PANEL 3

FEDERAL RESERVE				COMMERCIAL BANKS				JANE Q. PUBLIC			
ASSETS		LIABILITIES		ASSETS		LIABILITIES		ASSETS		LIABILITIES	
Securities (−$5)	$95	$15 (−$5)	Reserves	Reserves (−$5)	$15	$75 (−$25)	Deposits	Deposits (−$5)	$0	$0	Debts
		$80	Currency	Loans (−$20)	$60			Securities (+$5)	$5	$5	Net Worth

Note: Money supply (M1) = Currency + Deposits = $155.

dealers who act as intermediaries between the Fed and the private markets. We can sum up the effect of these open market operations this way:

- An open market *purchase* of securities by the Fed results in an increase in reserves and an *increase* in the supply of money by an amount equal to the money multiplier times the change in reserves.

- An open market *sale* of securities by the Fed results in a *decrease* in reserves and a *decrease* in the supply of money by an amount equal to the money multiplier times the change in reserves.

Open market operations are the Fed's preferred means of controlling the money supply for several reasons. First, open market operations can be used with some precision. If the Fed needs to change the money supply by just a small amount, it can buy or sell a small volume of government securities. If it wants a larger change in the money supply, it can simply buy or sell a larger amount. Second, open market operations are extremely flexible. If the Fed decides to reverse course, it can easily switch from buying securities to selling them. Finally, open market operations have a fairly predictable effect on the supply of money. Since banks are obliged to meet their reserve requirements, an open market sale of $100 in government securities will reduce reserves by $100, which will reduce the supply of money by $100 times the money multiplier.

But where does the Fed get the money to buy government securities when it wants to expand the money supply? The Fed simply creates it. In effect, it tells the bank from which it has bought a $100 security that its reserve account (deposit) at the Fed now contains $100 more than it did previously. This is where the power of the Fed, or any central bank, lies. The Fed has the ability to create money at will. In the United States, the Fed exercises this power when it creates money to buy government securities.

THE SUPPLY CURVE FOR MONEY

The main point of our discussion thus far is that the Fed can control the money supply by controlling the amount of reserves in the economy. If the Fed wants the quantity of money to be $900 billion on a given date, it can aim for this target by changing the discount rate, by changing the required reserve ratio, or by engaging in open market operations. In this sense, the supply of money is completely determined by the Fed, and we can draw the money supply curve in Figure 11.5 as a vertical line.

A vertical money supply curve says that the Fed sets the money supply independent of the interest rate. In other words, a vertical money supply curve means that the interest rate does not affect the Fed's decision on how much money to supply. We will see in Chapter 16 that the Fed's money supply behavior is in fact influenced by the state of the economy, and perhaps by the interest rate. In practice, then, the money supply curve is not likely to be vertical. It would, however, complicate matters too much at this stage of our analysis to consider Fed behavior in more detail, so we will assume for now that the money supply curve is vertical. This assumption is relaxed in Chapter 16.[10]

FIGURE 11.5

The Supply of Money

If the Fed's money supply behavior is not influenced by the interest rate, the money supply curve is a vertical line.

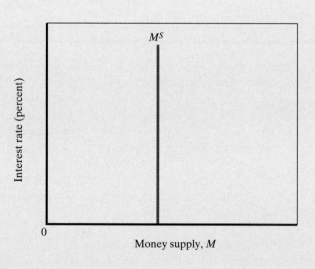

[10]*There is another reason that the money supply curve may not be vertical. If bank borrowing from the Fed responds positively to the difference between the market interest rate and the discount rate, then as the market interest rate rises (with the discount rate fixed), banks will borrow more. We have seen that an increase in bank borrowing leads to an increase in the money supply. Therefore, the supply of money responds positively to the market interest rate, so the money supply schedule should have a positive slope. In practice this effect is fairly small, and for the sake of simplicity we will ignore it. The Fed could, of course, offset this effect completely if it raised the discount rate in line with the market interest rate.*

LOOKING AHEAD

This chapter has discussed only the supply side of the money market. We have seen what money is, how banks create money by making loans, and how the Fed controls the money supply. In the next chapter we turn to the demand side of the money market. There we examine the demand for money and how the supply of and demand for money determine the equilibrium interest rate.

SUMMARY

AN OVERVIEW OF MONEY

1. Money has three distinguishing characteristics. It is (1) a means of payment, or medium of exchange, (2) a store of value, and (3) a unit of account. The alternative to using money is a *barter* system, in which goods are exchanged directly for other goods. Barter is costly and inefficient in an economy with many different kinds of goods.

2. *Commodity monies* are those items used as money that also have an intrinsic value in some other use (for example, gold and cigarettes). *Fiat monies* are intrinsically worthless apart from their use as money. In order to ensure the acceptance of fiat monies, governments use their power to declare money *legal tender* and promise the public that they will not debase the currency by expanding its supply rapidly.

3. There are various definitions of money. Currency plus demand deposits plus travelers checks plus other checkable deposits comprise M1, or *transactions money*—money that can be used directly to buy things. The addition of savings accounts and money market accounts (*near monies*) to M1 gives M2, or *broad money*.

HOW BANKS CREATE MONEY

4. The *required reserve ratio* is the percentage of a bank's deposits that must be kept as reserves at the nation's central bank, the Federal Reserve.

5. Banks create money by making loans. When a bank makes a loan to a customer, it simply creates a deposit in that customer's account. This deposit becomes part of the money supply. Banks can create money only when they have *excess reserves*—that is, reserves in excess of the amount set by the required reserve ratio.

6. The *money multiplier* is the multiple by which the total supply of money can increase for every dollar increase in reserves. The money multiplier is equal to 1/Required reserve ratio.

THE FEDERAL RESERVE SYSTEM

7. The Fed's most important function is controlling the nation's money supply. However, the Fed also performs several other important functions: It clears interbank payments, is responsible for many of the regulations governing banking practices and standards, and acts as a *lender of last resort* for troubled banks that cannot find any other sources of funds. The Fed also acts as the bank for the U.S. government.

HOW THE FED CONTROLS THE MONEY SUPPLY

8. The key to understanding how the Fed controls the money supply is an appreciation of the role of reserves. If the Fed wants to increase the supply of money, it creates more reserves, thereby freeing banks to create additional deposits. If it wants to decrease the money supply, it reduces reserves.

9. The Fed has three tools at its disposal to control the money supply. It can (1) change the required reserve ratio, (2) change the *discount rate* (the interest rate that member banks pay when they borrow from the Fed), or (3) engage in *open market operations* (that is, the buying and selling of already-existing government securities). To increase the money supply, the Fed can create additional reserves by lowering the discount rate or by buying government securities. Alternatively, the Fed can increase the number of deposits that can be created from a given quantity of reserves by lowering the required reserve ratio. To decrease the money supply, the Fed can reduce reserves by raising the discount rate or by selling government securities. Alternatively, it can raise the required reserve ratio.

10. If the Fed's money supply behavior is not influenced by the interest rate, the supply curve for money is a vertical line.

barter 242

commodity monies 243

currency debasement 244

discount rate 261

excess reserves 251

federal debt 263

Federal Open Market Committee (FOMC) 254

Federal Reserve System (the Fed) 250

fiat, or token, money 244

financial intermediaries 247

legal tender 244

lender of last resort 257

liquidity property of money 243

M1, or transactions money 245

M2, or broad money 245

medium of exchange, or means of payment 242

money multiplier 253

moral suasion 262

near monies 245

Open Market Desk 254

open market operations 263

required reserve ratio 250

reserves 250

run on a bank 249

store of value 243

unit of account 243

Equations:

1. $M1 \equiv$ Currency held outside banks + Demand deposits + Travelers checks + Other checkable deposits

2. $M2 \equiv M1 +$ Savings accounts + Money market accounts + Other near monies

3. Assets $\equiv$ Liabilities + Capital (or Net Worth)

4. Excess reserves $\equiv$ Actual reserves $-$ Required reserves

5. Money multiplier $\equiv \dfrac{1}{\text{Required reserve ratio}}$

PROBLEM SET

1. In November 1994, the Federal Reserve moved decisively to slow the rate of U.S. money growth by changing the discount rate and engaging in open market operations. Describe how the Fed could use these tools to slow money growth or to reduce the money supply.

2. In 1993, the U.S. money supply (M1) was $1,128 billion, broken down as follows: $321 billion in currency, $8 billion in travelers checks, and $799 billion in checking deposits. Suppose that the Fed has decided to reduce the money supply by increasing the reserve requirement from 10% to 11 percent. Assuming all banks were initially loaned up (had no excess reserves) and that currency held outside of banks did not change, how large a change in the money supply would have resulted from the change in the reserve requirement?

3. As King of Medivalia, you are constantly strapped for funds to pay your army. Your chief economic wizard suggests the following plan: "When you collect your tax payments from your subjects, insist on being paid in gold coins. Take these gold coins, melt them down, and then remint them with an extra 10% of brass thrown in. You will then have 10% more money than you started with." What do you think of the plan? Will it work?

4. Why is M2 sometimes a more stable measure of money than M1? Explain in your own words, using the definitions of M1 and M2.

5. Do you agree or disagree with each of the following statements? Explain your answers.
   a. "When the Treasury of the United States issues bonds and sells them to the public to finance the deficit, the money supply remains unchanged because every dollar of money taken in by the Treasury goes right back into circulation through government spending. This is not true when the Federal Reserve System sells bonds to the public."
   b. "The money multiplier depends on the marginal propensity to save."
   c. "In 1994 the Federal Reserve moved to raise the discount rate. This move was designed to expand the supply of money in circulation."

*6. When the Fed adds new reserves to the system, some of these new reserves find their way out of the country into foreign banks or foreign investment funds. In addition, some portion of new reserves ends up in people's pockets and mattresses rather than in bank vaults. These "leakages" reduce the money multiplier and sometimes make it very difficult for the Fed to control the money supply precisely.

a. Explain why this is true.

b. Suppose that the reserve requirement is 12%, but that 25% of *M1* is held as currency. If the Fed buys $1000 worth of securities on the open market, how much will the money supply expand? What is the impact of a 25% leakage on the size of the money multiplier?

7. You are given the following simplified T account for a bank:

ASSETS		LIABILITIES	
Reserves	$500	$3500	Deposits
Loans	3000		

The required reserve ratio is 10 percent.

a. How much is the bank required to hold as reserves, given its deposits of $3500?

b. How much are its excess reserves?

c. By how much can the bank increase its loans?

d. Suppose a depositor comes to the bank and withdraws $200 in cash. Show the bank's new balance sheet, assuming that the bank obtains the cash by drawing down its reserves. Does the bank now hold excess reserves? Is it meeting the required reserve ratio? If not, what can it do?

8. What are the major functions of the Federal Reserve? Do you think any of these functions could be performed by private banks, or is the central bank the only agent capable of filling these roles? Explain.

12

monetary policy *The behavior
of the Federal Reserve regarding
the money supply.*

interest *The fee that a borrower
pays to a lender for the use of
his or her funds.*

interest rate *The annual interest
payment on a loan expressed as
a percentage of the loan. Equal
to the amount of interest
received per year divided by the
amount of the loan.*

MONEY DEMAND, THE EQUILIBRIUM INTEREST RATE, AND MONETARY POLICY

HAVING DISCUSSED THE *SUPPLY* OF MONEY IN THE LAST CHAPTER, WE now turn to a discussion of the *demand* for money. One of the main goals of this chapter and the previous chapter is to provide a theory of how the interest rate is determined in the macroeconomy. Once we have seen how the interest rate is determined, we can turn to the question of how the Fed affects the interest rate through **monetary policy.**

Because the interest rate plays such an important role in the economy, it is important that you understand exactly what it is. **Interest** is the fee that a borrower pays to a lender for the use of his or her funds. Firms and the government borrow funds by issuing bonds, and they pay interest to the firms and households (the lenders) that purchase those bonds. Households and firms that have borrowed from a bank must pay interest on those loans to the bank.

The **interest rate** is the annual interest payment on a loan expressed as a percentage of the loan. For example, a $1000 bond (representing a $1000 loan from a household to a firm) that pays $100 in interest per year has an interest rate of 10 percent. Note that the interest rate is expressed as an *annual* rate. It is the amount of interest received *per year* divided by the amount of the loan.

While there are many different interest rates, for the purposes of our analysis we will assume that there is only one interest rate in the economy. This simplifies our analysis but still provides us with a valuable tool for understanding how the various parts of the macroeconomy relate to one another. Appendix A to this chapter provides a more detailed discussion of the various types of interest rates.

THE DEMAND FOR MONEY

The question of what factors and forces determine the demand for money is one of the central issues in macroeconomics. As we shall see, the interest rate and the level of national income (Y) are important in determining how much money households and firms wish to hold.

Before we proceed, however, we must stress one point that students often find troublesome. When we speak of the demand for money, we are not asking "How much cash do you wish you could have?" or "How much income would you like to earn?" or "How much wealth would you like?" (The answer to these questions is presumably "as much as possible.") Rather, we are concerned with the question of how much of your financial assets you want to hold *in the form of money,* which does not earn interest, versus how much you want to hold in interest-bearing securities, such as bonds. We take as given the *total* amount of financial assets; our concern here is with how these assets are divided between money and interest-bearing securities.

THE TRANSACTION MOTIVE

The choice of how much money to hold involves a trade-off between the liquidity of money and the interest income offered by other kinds of assets. The main reason for holding money instead of interest-bearing assets is that money is useful for buying things. Economists call this rather obvious motive the **transaction motive.** This rationale for holding money is at the heart of the discussion that follows.[1]

■ **Assumptions**   To keep our analysis of the demand for money clear, we need to make a few simplifying assumptions. First, we assume that there are only two kinds of assets available to households: bonds and money. By "bonds" we mean interest-bearing securities of all kinds. By "money" we mean currency in circulation and deposits, neither of which is assumed to pay interest.[2]

Second, we assume that income for the typical household is "bunched up." It arrives once a month, at the beginning of the month. Spending, by contrast, is spread out over time; we assume that spending occurs at a completely uniform rate throughout the month—that is, that the same amount is spent each day (see Figure 12.1, page 272). The mismatch between the timing of money inflow and the timing of money outflow is sometimes called the **nonsynchronization of income and spending.**

Finally, we assume that spending for the month is exactly equal to income. Because we are focusing on the transactions demand for money and not on its use as a store of value, this assumption is perfectly reasonable.

transaction motive *The main reason that people hold money—to buy things.*

nonsynchronization of income and spending *The mismatch between the timing of money inflow to the household and the timing of money outflow for household expenses.*

---

[1]*The model that we discuss here is known in the economics profession as the Baumol/Tobin model, after the two economists who independently derived it, William Baumol of Princeton University and James Tobin of Yale University.*

[2]*Remember that the category "deposits" includes checking accounts. Many checking accounts do pay interest. This turns out not to matter for the purposes of our discussion, however. Suppose that bonds pay 10% interest and checking accounts pay 5 percent. (Checking accounts must pay less than bonds. Otherwise, everyone would hold all their wealth in checking accounts and none in bonds, because checking accounts are more convenient.) When it comes to choosing whether to hold bonds or money, it is the difference in the interest rates on the two that matters. People are concerned about how much extra interest they will get from holding bonds rather than money. Therefore, in the example above, we could just as well say that bonds pay 5% and money pays 0%, which makes our discussion simpler.*

FIGURE 12.1

The Nonsynchronization of
Income and Spending
Income arrives only once a
month, but spending takes
place continuously.

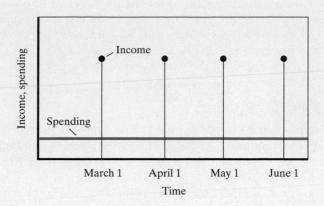

MONEY MANAGEMENT AND THE OPTIMAL BALANCE

Given the assumptions above, how would a rational person (household) go about deciding how much of his or her monthly income to hold as money and how much to hold as interest-bearing bonds? Suppose our hypothetical person, Jim, decides to deposit his entire paycheck in his checking account. Let us say that Jim earns $1200 per month. The pattern of Jim's bank account balance is illustrated in Figure 12.2. At the beginning of the month, Jim's balance is $1200. As the month rolls by, Jim draws down his balance, writing checks or withdrawing cash to pay for the things he buys. At the end of the month, Jim's bank account balance is down to zero. Just in time, he receives his next month's paycheck, deposits it, and the process begins all over again.

One useful statistic that we will need to calculate is the *average balance* in Jim's account. Jim spends his money at a constant $40 per day ($40 per day times 30 days per month = $1200). His average balance is just his starting balance ($1200) plus his ending balance (0) divided by 2, or ($1200 + 0)/2 = $600. For the first half of the month Jim has more than his average of $600 on deposit, and for the second half of the month he has less than his average.

Is there anything wrong with Jim's strategy? The answer is clearly yes. If he follows the plan described above, Jim is giving up interest on his funds, interest that he could be earning if he held some of his funds in interest-bearing bonds instead of in his checking account. How could he manage his funds to give himself more interest?

FIGURE 12.2

Jim's Monthly Checking
Account Balances: Strategy 1
Jim could decide to deposit
his entire paycheck ($1200)
into his checking account at
the start of the month and
run his balance down to zero
by the end of the month. In
this case, his average balance
would be $600.

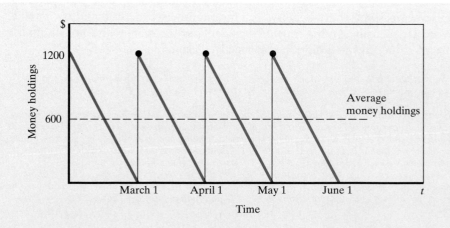

Instead of depositing his entire paycheck in his checking account at the beginning of the month, Jim could put half his paycheck into his checking account and buy a bond with the other half. If he followed this strategy, though, he would run out of money in his checking account halfway through the month. At a spending rate of $40 per day, his initial deposit of $600 would last him only 15 days. Obviously, then, Jim would have to sell his bond halfway through the month and deposit the $600 from the sale of the bond in his checking account in order to pay his bills during the second half of the month.

Jim's money holdings (checking account balances) if he follows this strategy are shown in Figure 12.3. When he follows the buy-a-$600-bond strategy, Jim reduces the average amount of money in his checking account. In fact, comparing the dashed green lines (old strategy) with the solid green lines (new strategy), his average bank balance is exactly half of what it was with the first strategy.[3]

The buy-a-$600-bond strategy seems sensible. After all, the whole object of this strategy was to keep some of his funds in bonds, where they could earn interest, instead of as "idle" money. But why stop there? Another possibility would be for Jim to put only $400 into his checking account on the first of the month and buy two $400 bonds with the rest. The $400 in his account will last him only 10 days if he spends $40 per day, so after 10 days he must sell one of the bonds and deposit the $400 from the sale of the bond in his checking account. This will last him through the 20th of the month, at which point he must sell the second bond and deposit the other $400. This strategy lowers Jim's average money holding (checking account balance) even further, reducing his money holdings to an average of only $200 per month, with correspondingly higher average holdings of interest-earning bonds.

You can imagine Jim going even further. Why not hold all wealth in the form of bonds (where it earns interest) and make transfers from bonds to money every time a purchase has to be made? If selling bonds, transferring funds to checking accounts, and making trips to the bank were without cost, Jim would never hold money for more than an instant. Each time he needed to pay cash for something or write a check, he would go to the bank or call the bank, transfer the exact amount of the transac-

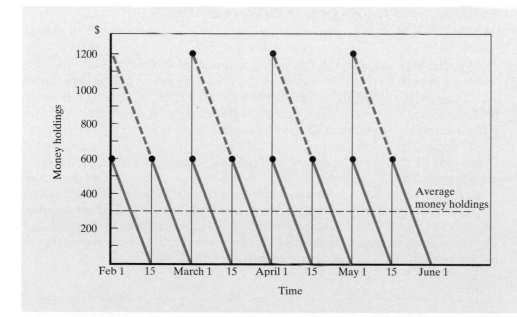

FIGURE 12.3
Jim's Monthly Checking Account Balances: Strategy 2
Jim could also choose to put one half of his paycheck into his checking account and buy a bond with the other half of his income. At mid-month, Jim would sell the bond and deposit the $600 into his checking account to pay the second half of the month's bills. Following this strategy, Jim's average money holdings would be $300.

---

[3]Jim's average balance for the first half of the month is (starting balance + ending balance)/2, or ($600 + 0)/2 = $300. His average for the second half of the month is also $300. His average for the month as a whole is thus $300.

tion to his checking account, and either withdraw the cash or write the check to complete the transaction. If he did this constantly, he would squeeze the most interest possible out of his funds because he would never hold assets that did not earn interest.

In practice, however, money management of this kind is costly. There are brokerage fees and other costs when one buys or sells bonds, and time must be spent waiting in line at the bank. At the same time, though, it is also costly to hold assets in non-interest-bearing form, because they lose potential interest revenue.

We thus have a standard trade-off problem of the type that is so pervasive in economics. Switching more often from bonds to money raises the interest revenue Jim earns (since the more times he switches, the less, on average, he has to hold in his checking account and the more he can keep in bonds), but doing this increases his money management costs. Less switching means more interest revenue lost (because average money holdings are higher) but lower money management costs (fewer purchases and sales of bonds, less time spent waiting in bank lines, fewer trips to the bank, and so on).

■ **The Optimal Balance**   It is not hard to demonstrate that there is some level of average money balances that earns Jim the most profit, taking into account both the interest earned on bonds and the costs paid for switching from bonds to money. This level is his *optimal balance*.

The really important question we wish to answer is: How does the interest rate affect the number of switches that Jim makes and thus the average money balance he chooses to hold? It is easy to see why an increase in the interest rate lowers the optimal money balance. If the interest rate were only 2%, it would not be worthwhile to give up much liquidity by holding bonds instead of cash or checking balances. But if the interest rate were 30%, the opportunity cost of holding money instead of bonds would be quite high, and we would expect people to keep most of their funds in bonds and thus to spend considerable time in managing their money balances. This leads us to conclude the following:

> When interest rates are high, people want to take advantage of the high return on bonds, so they choose to hold very little money.

Appendix B to this chapter provides an extended numerical example of this important principle.

Another way of looking at this situation is to note that the interest rate represents the opportunity cost of holding money (and therefore not holding bonds, which pay interest). The higher the interest rate, the higher the opportunity cost of holding money, and the less money people will want to hold. In other words, when interest rates rise, the amount of money people wish to hold goes down.

A demand curve for money, with the interest rate representing its "price," would look like the curve labeled M^d in Figure 12.4. At higher interest rates, bonds are more attractive than money, so people hold less money because they must make a larger sacrifice in interest for each dollar of money they hold. At lower interest rates, the interest earned on bonds is lower, so people choose to hold more money. The curve in Figure 12.4 thus slopes downward, just like an ordinary demand curve for, say, oranges or shoes. In other words, there is an inverse relationship between the interest rate and the quantity of money demanded.[4]

---

[4]*The theory of money demand presented here assumes that a person knows the exact timing of her or his income path and spending path. In practice, both paths have some uncertainty attached to them. For example, some income payments may be unexpectedly delayed a few days or weeks, and some expenditures may arise unexpectedly (such as an unexpected plumbing problem). Because people know that this uncertainty exists, they may choose to hold more money than the strict transactions motive would suggest they would hold, as a precaution against unanticipated delays in income receipts or unanticipated expenses. This reason for holding money is sometimes called the* precautionary motive.

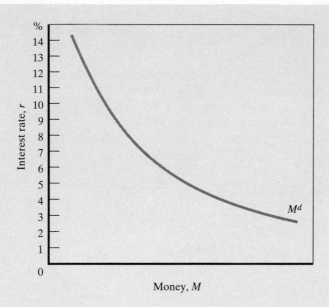

FIGURE 12.4
The Demand Curve for Money Balances

The quantity of money demanded (the amount of money households and firms wish to hold) is a function of the interest rate. Because the interest rate is the opportunity cost of holding money balances, increases in the interest rate will reduce the quantity of money that firms and households want to hold, and decreases in the interest rate will increase the quantity of money that firms and households want to hold.

THE SPECULATION MOTIVE

A number of alternative theories have been offered to explain why the quantity of money that households desire to hold may rise when interest rates fall, and fall when interest rates rise. One of these theories involves household expectations and the relationship of interest rates to bond values.

To understand this theory, it is important to understand that the market value of most interest-bearing bonds is inversely related to the interest rate. Suppose, for example, that I bought an 8% bond a year ago for $1000. Now suppose that the interest rate rises to 10 percent. If I offered to sell my bond for $1000, no one would buy it because anyone can buy a new bond and earn 10% rather than 8 percent. But at some lower price, my bond becomes attractive to buyers. This is true because a lower price increases the actual yield to the buyer of my bond. Suppose I were to sell you my bond for $500. Since the bond is paying 8% annually on the original $1000 (that is, $80 per year), it is actually paying you an annual amount that comes to 16% of your investment in the bond ($500 × .16 = $80). If you bought that same bond from me for about $800, it would effectively pay you 10% interest ($800 × .10 = $80).

The key point here is simple:

> When interest rates fall, bond values rise; when interest rates rise, bond values fall.

Now consider my desire to hold money balances rather than bonds. If interest rates are higher than normal, I may expect them to come down in the future. If and when interest rates fall, the bonds that I bought when interest rates were high will increase in value. Thus, when interest rates are high, the opportunity cost of holding cash balances is high and there is a **speculation motive** for holding bonds in lieu of cash. I am "speculating" that interest rates will fall in the future.

Similarly, when interest rates are lower than normal, I may expect them to rise in the future. Rising interest rates will bring about a decline in the value of bonds.

speculation motive *One reason for holding bonds instead of money: Because the market value of interest-bearing bonds is inversely related to the interest rate, investors may wish to hold bonds when interest rates are high with the hope of selling them when interest rates fall.*

THE PRIMARY MOTIVE FOR HOLDING CASH IS TO ENGAGE IN TRANSACTIONS. MOST PEOPLE WALK AROUND WITH SOME MONEY IN THEIR POCKETS AND KEEP SOME MONEY IN THEIR CHECKING ACCOUNTS, BUT USUALLY NOT THOUSANDS OF DOLLARS. THE COST OF HOLDING MONEY IS FORGONE INTEREST.

Thus, when interest rates are low, it is a good time to be holding money and not bonds. When interest rates are low, not only is the opportunity cost of holding cash balances low, but there is also a speculative motive for holding a larger amount of money. Why should I put money into bonds now when I expect interest rates to rise in the future? (For more details on the interaction between the bond market and the money market, see the Application Box titled "The Bond Market, the Money Market, and the Speculation Motive.")

THE TOTAL DEMAND FOR MONEY

So far we have talked only about household demand for checking account balances. But the total quantity of money demanded in the economy is the sum of the demand for checking account balances *and cash* by both households *and firms*.

The trade-off for firms is the same as it was for Jim. Like households, firms must manage their money. They have payrolls to meet and purchases to make; they receive cash and checks from sales; and many firms that deal with the public must make change—they need cash in the cash register. Thus, just like Jim, firms need money to engage in ordinary transactions.

But firms as well as households can hold their assets in interest-earning form. As was true for Jim, holding cash and maintaining checking account balances has an opportunity cost for firms. Firms manage their assets just as households do, keeping some in cash, some in their checking accounts, and some in bonds. A higher interest rate raises the opportunity cost of money for firms as well as for households and thus reduces the demand for money. A lower interest rate reduces the opportunity cost of holding money and increases the demand for it.

The same trade-off holds for cash. We all walk around with some money in our pockets, but not thousands of dollars, for routine transactions. We carry, on average, about what we think we will need. Why not more? Because there are costs—risks of being robbed and forgone interest.

People are often confused when business-page headlines read "Bonds Fall, Pushing up Interest Rates" or "Bonds Rise, Driving Yields Down." Nonetheless, it is true that the current market price or value of all fixed-rate bonds, whether U.S. Treasury Bonds or German corporate bonds, fall in value when interest rates rise, and rise in value when interest rates fall.

To see why this is so, consider Heidi, a German house painter who bought for $1000 a 10-year German government bond with a fixed rate of 10 percent. By buying that bond, Heidi has agreed to accept a return on her money of 10% for ten years. This translates in simple terms into a check for $100 every year with a promise that her $1000 will be returned at the end of 10 years.

While the German government has no obligation to pay the $1000 back before the bond matures in ten years, Heidi may need the money before ten years is up. To get her money back earlier, she can call a broker and sell the bond. In fact, there is a huge market for existing bonds, and existing bond prices are posted in the newspapers everyday. To sell the bond, the broker has to find a buyer, and the amount that a buyer would be willing to pay depends on the current rate of interest.

An example will help here. Suppose Heidi wants to sell her bond two years after she purchased it. The bond still has eight years left to maturity. Assume further that for some reason the Bundesbank (the German central bank) has pushed rates for eight-year bonds to 12 percent. If someone paid $1000 for Heidi's bond today, they would be getting only $100 (10%) interest per year. The same person could be getting interest of $120 per year, or 12% by buying a newly issued $1000 bond. The result is that Heidi's broker will not be able to sell her bond for $1000. Instead, Heidi will have to take a loss because her bond's value has fallen.

Do bond values really fall in the real world? Absolutely. When the Federal Reserve raised U.S. interest rates in 1994, the value of outstanding bonds traded in the market fell by nearly $1.7 trillion! Similarly, during Mexico's peso crises in 1995, Mexican interest rates shot up sharply, and Mexican government bonds lost a lot of their value. (U.S. holders of Mexican securities got hit even harder because the value of the peso fell too—but that's a story to be covered later in the chapter on open-market macroeconomics.)

Another way to see the same connection between the bond market and the money market is to think of a case in which the demand for bonds increases. Suppose that because of excess demand for bonds in Germany, the value of Heidi's bond goes up to $1100. Someone who is willing to pay $1100 for Heidi's bond *must reveal that he is willing to accept an annual yield of less than 10 percent*. After all, $100 is only 9.1% of $1100. In addition, the buyer who pays $1100 will get back only $1000 when the bond matures. Thus it is clear that higher bond prices mean that the interest rate that bond buyers are willing to accept is lower than before! Clearly if buyers are willing to accept 9% on old bonds, they will accept 9% on new bonds.

The bottom line is that bond prices and interest rates are simply two sides of the same coin. A "rally" in the bond market means that bond prices have gone up and that interest rates, or bond "yields," have gone down. Similarly, when the bond market "drops," interest rates, or yields, have gone up.

These effects have important implications for money demand. Assume that households choose only between holding their assets as money (which does not earn interest) or as bonds (which do earn interest). If households and firms believe that interest rates are historically high and that they are likely to fall, it is a *good* time to hold bonds. Why? Because a drop in rates means that bond values will rise, in a sense earning bondholders a bonus. Thus, when interest rates are high and expected to fall, demand for bonds is likely to be high and money demand is likely to be low. Similarly, if people see interest rates as being low and expect them to rise, it is *not* a good time to be holding bonds. Why? Because if interest rates rise, bond holders suffer losses. Thus, when interest rates are low, money demand is likely to be high and the demand for bonds is likely to be low. Thus, we have another reason for the negative relationship between interest rates and money demand. As we mentioned in the text, this is the *speculation motive* for holding money.

In sum:

> At any given moment, there is a demand for money—for cash and checking account balances. Although households and firms need to hold balances for everyday transactions, their demand has a limit. For both households and firms, the quantity of money demanded at any moment depends on the opportunity cost of holding money, a cost determined by the interest rate.

TRANSACTIONS VOLUME AND THE PRICE LEVEL

The money demand curve in Figure 12.4 is drawn as a function of the interest rate. There are other factors besides the interest rate, however, that influence total desired money holdings. One of the most important of these is the dollar value of transactions made during a given period of time.

Suppose that Jim's income were to double. Instead of making $1200 in purchases each month, he now makes $2400 in purchases. Clearly, he needs to hold more money. Why? The answer is simple: If you want to buy more things, you need more money to buy things with.

What is true for Jim in this case is true for the economy as a whole. The total demand for money in the economy depends on the total dollar volume of transactions made. The total dollar volume of transactions in the economy, in turn, depends on two things: the total *number* of transactions and the average transaction *amount*. While there are no data on the actual number of transactions in the economy, a reasonable indicator is likely to be aggregate output (income) (Y). A rise in aggregate output—real GDP—means that there is more economic activity. Firms are producing and selling more output, more people are on payrolls, and household incomes are higher. In short, there are more transactions, and firms and households together will hold more money when they are engaging in more transactions. Thus, an increase in aggregate output (income) will increase the demand for money.

Figure 12.5 shows a shift of the money demand curve resulting from an increase in Y:

> For a given interest rate, a higher level of output means an increase in the *number* of transactions and thus more demand for money. The money demand curve shifts to the right when Y rises. Similarly, a decrease in Y means a decrease in the number of transactions and a lower demand for money. The money demand curve shifts to the left when Y falls.

The amount of money needed by firms and households to facilitate their day-to-day transactions also depends on the average *dollar amount* of each transaction. In turn, the average amount of each transaction depends on prices, or rather, on the *price level*. If all prices, including the price of labor (the wage rate) were to double, firms and households would need more money balances to carry out their day-to-day transactions—each transaction would require twice as much money. If the price of your lunch increases from $3.50 to $7.00, you will no doubt begin carrying more cash. If your end-of-the-month bills are twice as high as they used to be, you will keep more money in your checking account. Thus:

> Increases in the price level shift the money demand curve to the right, and decreases in the price level shift the money demand curve to the left. Even though the number of transactions may not have changed, the quantity of money needed to engage in them has.

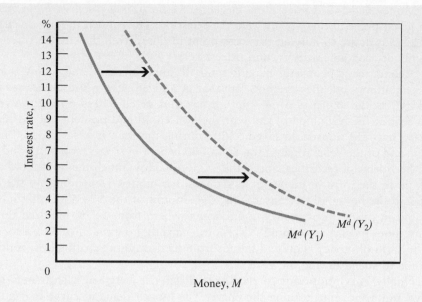

An increase in Y means that there is more economic activity. Firms are producing and selling more, and households are earning more income and buying more. There are thus more transactions, for which money is needed. As a result, both firms and households are likely to increase their holdings of money balances at a given interest rate.

THE DETERMINANTS OF MONEY DEMAND (REVIEW)

Figure 12.6 summarizes everything we have said about the demand for money. First, because the interest rate (r) is the opportunity cost of holding money balances for both firms and households, increases in the interest rate are likely to decrease the quantity of money demanded. Similarly, decreases in the interest rate will increase the quantity of money demanded. Thus, the quantity of money demanded is a negative function of the interest rate.

The demand for money also depends on the dollar volume of transactions in a given period. The dollar volume of transactions depends on both aggregate output (income), Y, and the price level, P. The relationship of money demand to Y and the relationship of money demand to P are both positive. Increases in Y or in P will shift the money demand curve to the right, and decreases in Y or P will shift the money demand curve to the left.

■ **Some Common Pitfalls** Before we go on, we need to note several pitfalls that people often encounter in thinking about money demand. First, when we spoke in earlier chapters about the demand for goods and services, we were speaking of demand as a *flow variable*. A flow variable, you will recall, is measured over a period of time. For example, if you say that your demand for coffee is three cups, you need to specify whether you are talking about three cups per hour, three cups per day, three cups per week, and so forth. In macroeconomics, consumption and saving are flow variables. We consume and save continuously, but we express consumption and saving in time-period terms, such as $600 *per month*.

1. The interest rate: r (negative effect)
2. The dollar volume of transactions (positive effect)
   a. Aggregate output (income): Y (positive effect)
   b. The price level: P (positive effect)

FIGURE 12.6

Determinants of Money Demand

Money demand is *not* a flow measure. Rather it is a *stock variable,* measured at a given point in time. It answers the question: How much money do firms and households desire to hold at a specific point in time, given the current interest rate, volume of economic activity, and price level?

Second, many people mistakenly think of money demand and saving as roughly the same thing, but they are not. Say that in a given year a household has income of $50,000 and expenses of $47,000. It has thus saved $3000 during the year. Say also that at the beginning of the year the household had no debt and $100,000 in assets. Since the household saved $3000 during the year, it has $103,000 in assets at the end of the year. Some of the $103,000 is held in stocks, some in bonds, some in other forms of securities, and some in money. How much the household chooses to hold in the form of money is its demand for money. Depending on the interest rate and the household's transactions, the amount of the $103,000 that it chooses to hold in the form of money could be anywhere from a few hundred dollars to many thousands. A household's decision regarding how much of its assets to hold in the form of money is quite different from its decision regarding how much of its income to spend during the year.

Finally, it is important to recall the difference between a shift in a demand curve and a movement along the curve. The money demand curve in Figure 12.4 shows optimal money balances as a function of the interest rate *ceteris paribus,* all else equal. Changes in the interest rate cause movements *along* the curve—*changes in the quantity of money demanded.* Changes in real GDP (Y) or in the price level (P) cause shifts of the curve as shown in Figure 12.5—*changes in demand.*

THE EQUILIBRIUM INTEREST RATE

We are now in a position to consider one of the key questions in macroeconomics: How is the interest rate determined in the economy?

Financial markets (what we are calling the money market) work very well in the United States. Almost all financial markets clear—that is, almost all reach an equilibrium where quantity demanded equals quantity supplied. In the money market,

> The point at which the quantity of money demanded equals the quantity of money supplied determines the equilibrium interest rate in the economy.

As simple as this sounds, the point requires some elaboration.

SUPPLY AND DEMAND IN THE MONEY MARKET

We saw in the previous chapter that the Fed controls the money supply through its manipulation of the amount of reserves in the economy. Because we are assuming that the Fed's money supply behavior does not depend on the interest rate, the money supply curve is simply a vertical line. (Review Figure 11.5.) In other words, we are assuming that the Fed uses its three tools (the required reserve ratio, the discount rate, and open market operations) to achieve its fixed target for the money supply.

Figure 12.7 superimposes the vertical money supply curve on the downward-sloping money demand curve. Only at interest rate r^* is the quantity of money in circulation (the money supply) equal to the quantity of money demanded. To understand why r^* is an equilibrium, we need to ask what adjustments would take place if the interest rate were not r^*.

To understand the adjustment mechanism, we need to keep in mind that borrowing and lending is a continuous process. The Treasury sells U.S. government

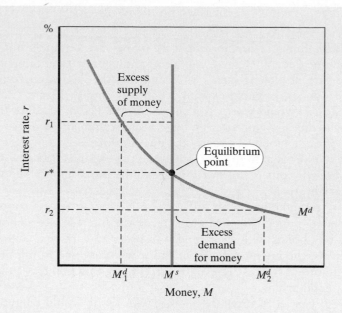

FIGURE 12.7
Adjustments in the Money Market

Equilibrium exists in the money market when the supply of money is equal to the demand for money: $M^d = M^s$. At r_1, the quantity of money supplied exceeds the quantity of money demanded, and the interest rate will fall. At r_2, the quantity demanded exceeds the quantity supplied, and the interest rate will rise. Only at r^* is equilibrium achieved.

securities (bonds) more or less continuously to finance the deficit. When it does so, it is borrowing, and it must pay interest to attract bond buyers. Buyers of government bonds are, in essence, lending money to the government, just as buyers of corporate bonds are lending money to corporations that wish to finance investment projects.

Consider first r_1 in Figure 12.7. At r_1, the quantity of money demanded is M_1^d, and the quantity of money supplied exceeds the quantity of money demanded. This means that there is more money in circulation than households and firms want to hold. At r_1, then, firms and households will attempt to reduce their money holdings by buying bonds. When there is money in circulation looking for a way to earn interest—that is, when demand for bonds is high—those looking to borrow money by selling bonds will find that they can do so at a lower interest rate. Thus:

> If the interest rate is initially high enough to create an excess supply of money, the interest rate will immediately fall, thus discouraging people from moving out of money and into bonds.

Now consider r_2. At interest rate r_2, the quantity of money demanded (M_2^d) exceeds the supply of money currently in circulation. In such a circumstance, households and firms do not have enough money on hand to facilitate ordinary transactions. As a result, they will try to adjust their holdings by shifting assets out of bonds and into their checking accounts. At the same time, the continuous flow of new bonds being issued must also be absorbed. The Treasury and corporations can sell bonds in an environment where people are adjusting their asset holdings to shift *out* of bonds only by offering a higher interest rate to the people who buy them. Thus:

> If the interest rate is initially low enough to create an excess demand for money, the interest rate will immediately rise, thus discouraging people from moving out of bonds and into money.

THE FED: CHANGING THE MONEY SUPPLY TO AFFECT THE INTEREST RATE

With an understanding of equilibrium in the money market under our belts, we can now see how the Federal Reserve can affect the interest rate. Suppose, for example, that the current interest rate is 14% and that the Fed wants to reduce the interest rate. To do so, it would expand the money supply. Figure 12.8 shows how such an expansion would work. To expand M^s, the Fed can reduce the reserve requirement, cut the discount rate, or buy U.S. government securities on the open market. All of these practices expand the quantity of reserves in the system. Banks can thus make more loans, and the money supply expands. (Review Chapter 11 if you are unsure why this is so.) In Figure 12.8, the initial money supply curve, M_0^s, shifts to the right, to M_1^s.

At the initial interest rate of 14%, there is now an excess supply of money. This immediately puts downward pressure on the interest rate as households and firms try to buy bonds with their money in order to earn that high interest rate. As this happens, the interest rate falls, and it will continue to fall until it reaches the new equilibrium interest rate of 7 percent. At this point, $M_1^s = M^d$, and the market is in equilibrium.

If the Fed wanted to drive the interest rate *up,* it would contract the money supply. It could do so by increasing the reserve requirement, by raising the discount rate, or by selling U.S. government securities in the open market. Whichever tool the Fed chooses, the result would be lower reserves and a lower supply of money. M_0^s in Figure 12.8 would shift to the left, and the equilibrium interest rate would rise. (As an exercise, draw a graph of this situation.)

INCREASES IN Y AND SHIFTS IN THE MONEY DEMAND CURVE

Changes in the supply of money are not the only factors that influence the equilibrium interest rate. Shifts in money demand can do the same thing.

Recall that the demand for money depends on both the interest rate and the volume of transactions. As a rough measure of the volume of transactions, we use Y, the level of aggregate output (income). Remember that the relationship between money demand and Y is positive. That is, increases in Y mean a higher level of real

FIGURE 12.8

The Effect of an Increase in the Supply of Money on the Interest Rate

An increase in the supply of money from M_0^s to M_1^s lowers the rate of interest from 14% to 7 percent.

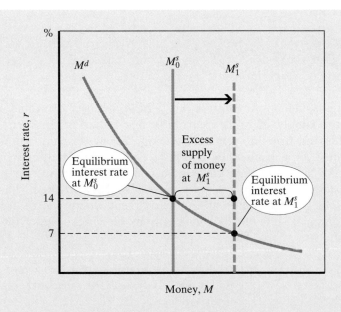

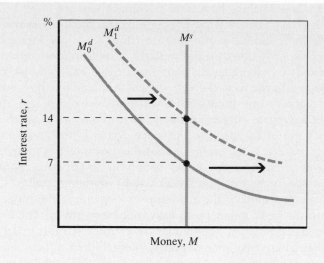

FIGURE 12.9

The Effect of an Increase in Income on the Interest Rate

An increase in aggregate output (income) shifts the money demand curve from M_0^d to M_1^d, which raises the equilibrium interest rate from 7% to 14 percent.

economic activity. More is being produced, income is higher, and there are more transactions in the economy. Consequently, the demand for money on the part of firms and households in aggregate is higher. Thus,

An increase in Y shifts the money demand curve to the right.

Figure 12.9 illustrates such a shift. Y increases, causing money demand to shift from M_0^d to M_1^d. The result is an increase in the equilibrium level of the interest rate from 7% to 14 percent. Similarly, a decrease in Y would shift M^d to the left, and the equilibrium interest rate would fall.

We saw earlier that the money demand curve also shifts when the price level changes. If the price level rises, the money demand curve shifts to the right, because people need more money to engage in their day-to-day transactions. With the quantity of money supplied unchanged, however, the interest rate must rise in order to reduce the quantity of money demanded to the unchanged quantity of money supplied. (This is a movement *along* the money demand curve.) Thus, it follows that:

An increase in the price level is like an increase in Y in that both events increase the demand for money. The result is an increase in the equilibrium interest rate.

If the price level *falls,* the money demand curve shifts to the left, because people need less money for their transactions. But with the quantity of money supplied unchanged, the interest rate must fall in order to increase the quantity of money demanded to the unchanged quantity of money supplied. Therefore,

A decrease in the price level leads to a decrease in the equilibrium interest rate.

We explore this relationship in more detail in Chapter 14.

LOOKING AHEAD: FED BEHAVIOR AND MONETARY POLICY

We now know that the Fed can change the interest rate by changing the quantity of money supplied. If the Fed increases the quantity of money, the interest rate falls; if it decreases the quantity of money, the interest rate rises.

Thus far, however, we have said nothing about *why* the Fed might want to change the interest rate or what happens to the economy when the interest rate changes. We have hinted at the reason, though. A low interest rate stimulates spending, particularly investment. Similarly, a high interest rate reduces spending. This means that by changing the interest rate the Fed can also change aggregate output (income). In the next chapter, we will combine our discussions of the goods and money markets and discuss the ways that the interest rate affects the equilibrium level of aggregate output (income) (Y) in the goods market.

The Fed's use of its power to influence events in the goods market, as well as in the money market, is the centerpiece of the government's monetary policy. When the Fed moves to contract the money supply in an effort to restrain the economy, economists refer to the Fed's policy as a **tight monetary policy.** Conversely, when the Fed moves to stimulate the economy by expanding the money supply, economists refer to the Fed's policy as an **easy monetary policy.** The Fed moved aggressively to expand the money supply and lower interest rates in 1975, in 1982, and early in 1991. These easy money policies contributed to economic recovery from the recessions of those years. On the other side, tight money policies caused aggregate spending to decline in 1974 and 1981, thereby contributing to the recessions of those years. During the summer of 1981, tight money helped to push some key interest rates above 20 percent!

We will discuss the way in which the economy affects the Fed's behavior in Chapter 16. In that chapter, we'll also discuss some of the Fed's recent policies in more detail and examine the effects of these policies on the economy.

tight monetary policy *Fed policies that contract the money supply in an effort to restrain the economy.*

easy monetary policy *Fed policies that expand the money supply in an effort to stimulate the economy.*

SUMMARY

1. *Interest* is the fee that a borrower pays to a lender for the use of his or her funds. The *interest rate* is the annual interest payment on a loan expressed as a percentage of the loan; it is equal to the amount of interest received per year divided by the amount of the loan. Although there are many different interest rates in the United States, we assume that there is only one interest rate in the economy. This simplifies our analysis but still provides us with a valuable tool for understanding how the various parts of the macroeconomy relate to each other.

THE DEMAND FOR MONEY

2. The demand for money depends negatively on the interest rate. The higher the interest rate, the higher the opportunity cost (more interest forgone) from holding money, and the less money people will want to hold. Thus, an increase in the interest rate reduces the demand for money, and the money demand curve slopes downward.

3. Increases in the volume of transactions in the economy increase money demand. The total dollar volume of transactions depends on both the total number of transactions and the average transaction amount.

4. A reasonable measure of the number of transactions in the economy is aggregate output (income) (Y). When Y rises, there is more economic activity, more is being produced and sold, and more people are on payrolls—in short, there are more transactions in the economy. Thus, an increase in Y causes the money demand curve to shift to the right. This follows because households and firms need more money when they are engaging in more transactions. A decrease in Y causes the money demand curve to shift left.

5. Changes in the price level affect the average dollar amount of each transaction. *Increases* in the price level will increase the demand for money (shift the money demand curve to the right) because

households and firms will need more money for their expenditures. *Decreases* in the price level will decrease the demand for money (shift the money demand curve to the left).

THE EQUILIBRIUM INTEREST RATE

6. The point at which the quantity of money supplied equals the quantity of money demanded determines the equilibrium interest rate in the economy. An excess supply of money will cause households and firms to attempt to buy more bonds and will drive the interest rate down. An excess demand for money will cause households and firms to attempt to move out of bonds and will drive the interest rate up.

7. The Fed can affect the equilibrium interest rate by changing the supply of money using one of its three tools—the required reserve ratio, the discount rate, or open market operations.

8. An increase in the price level is like an increase in *Y* in that both events cause an increase in money demand. The result is an increase in the equilibrium interest rate. A decrease in the price level leads to reduced money demand and a decrease in the equilibrium interest rate.

9. *Tight monetary policy* refers to Fed policies that contract the money supply in an effort to restrain the economy. *Easy monetary policy* refers to Fed policies that expand the money supply in an effort to stimulate the economy. The Fed chooses between these two types of policies for different reasons at different times.

REVIEW TERMS AND CONCEPTS

easy monetary policy 284
interest 270
interest rate 270

monetary policy 270
nonsynchronization of income and spending 271

speculation motive 275
tight monetary policy 284
transaction motive 271

PROBLEM SET

1. During the fourth quarter of 1993, real GDP in the United States grew at an annual rate of over 7 percent. During 1994, the economy continued to expand with modest inflation (*Y* rose at a rate of 4% and *P* increased about 3 percent). At the beginning of 1994, the prime interest rate (the interest rate that banks offer their best, least risky customers) stood at 6%, where it remained for over a year. By the beginning of 1995, the prime rate had increased to over 8.5 percent.
   a. Using money supply and money demand curves, show the effects of the increase in *Y* and *P* on interest rates assuming *no change* in the money supply.
   b. On a separate graph, show that the interest rate can rise even if the Federal Reserve expands the money supply as long as it does so more slowly than money demand is increasing.

2. At the beginning of 1995, interest rates in Japan were very low. However, households believed that interest rates were likely to rise eventually. This implies that the quantity of money demanded in Japan at the beginning of 1995 was quite high. Using the concepts of speculative motive and transaction motive for money, explain why.

3. Illustrate the following situations using supply and demand curves for money:
   a. The Fed buys bonds in the open market during a recession.
   b. During a period of rapid inflation, the Federal Reserve increases the reserve requirement.
   c. The Fed acts to hold interest rates constant during a period of high inflation.
   d. During a period of no growth in GDP and zero inflation, the Federal Reserve lowers the discount rate.
   e. During a period of rapid real growth of GDP, the Fed acts to increase the reserve requirement.

4. During a recession, interest rates may fall even if the Federal Reserve takes no action to expand the money supply. Why is this true? Use a graph to explain your answer.

5. The demand for money in a country is given by the equation

$$M^d = 10,000 - 10,000r + Y,$$

where M^d is money demand in dollars, r is the interest rate (a 10% interest rate means $r = 0.1$), and Y is national income. Assume that Y is initially equal to 5000.

  a. Graph the amount of money demanded (on the horizontal axis) against the interest rate (on the vertical axis).

  b. Suppose the money supply (M^s) is set by the Central Bank at $10,000. On the same graph you drew for part a, add the money supply curve. What is the equilibrium rate of interest? Explain how you arrived at your answer.

  c. Suppose that income rises from $Y = 5000$ to $Y = 7500$. What happens to the money demand curve you drew in part a? Draw the new curve, if there is one. What happens to the equilibrium interest rate if the Central Bank doesn't change the supply of money?

  d. If the Central Bank wants to keep the equilibrium interest rate at the same value as it was in part b, by how much should it increase or decrease the supply of money given the new level of national income?

  e. Suppose that the shift in part b has occurred, and the money supply remains at $10,000, but there is no observed change in the interest rate. What might have happened that could explain this?

6. In February of 1993, Alan Greenspan, Chair of the Federal Reserve Board of Governors, was very supportive of President Clinton's proposed deficit reduction plan. The Clinton plan, as presented to the Congress in March, called for substantial cuts in government purchases (G) and increases in taxes (T). Greenspan declared himself ready to act to keep this contractionary fiscal policy from dragging the economy back into recession. What specific steps might he have chosen to take? What would you expect to see happening to interest rates assuming that Congress had passed the Clinton plan?

APPENDIX A TO CHAPTER 12 THE VARIOUS INTEREST RATES IN THE U.S. ECONOMY

At the beginning of this chapter, we noted that there are many different interest rates in the economy. Although these different interest rates tend to move up or down with one another, it is useful to have some knowledge of their differences. In this Appendix, we will first discuss the relationship between interest rates on securities with different *maturities,* or terms. We then discuss briefly some of the main interest rates in the U.S. economy.

THE TERM STRUCTURE OF INTEREST RATES

The *term structure of interest rates* is the relationship between the interest rates offered on securities of different maturities. The key question here is: How are these different rates related? Does a two-year security (that is, an IOU that promises to repay principal, plus interest, after two years) pay a lower annual rate than a one-year security (an IOU to be repaid, with interest, after one year)? What happens to the rate of interest offered on one-year securities if the rate of interest on two-year securities increases?

For the sake of example, assume that you want to invest some money for two years and that at the end of the two years you want it back. Assume also that you

want to buy government securities. For the purposes of this analysis, we will restrict your choices to two: (1) You can buy a two-year security today and simply hold on to it for two years, at which time you cash it in (we will assume that the interest rate on the two-year security is 9% per year), or (2) you can buy a one-year security today. At the end of one year, you must cash this security in; you can then buy another one-year security. At the end of the second year, you will cash in the second security. We will assume that the interest rate on the first one-year security is 8 percent.

Which of these choices would you prefer? Currently, you don't have enough data to answer this question. To consider choice 2 sensibly, you need to know the interest rate on the one-year security that you intend to buy in the second year. This rate, however, will not be known until the second year. All you know now is the rate on the two-year security and the rate on the current one-year security. To decide what to do, you must form an *expectation* of the rate on the one-year security a year from now. If you expect the one-year rate (8%) to remain the same in the second year, you should obviously buy the two-year security. You would earn 9% per year on the two-year security but only 8% per year on the two one-year securities. If, on the other hand, you expect the one-year rate to rise to 12% a year from now, you should make the second choice. You would earn 8% in the first year, and you expect to earn 12% in the second year. The expected rate of return over the two years is thus about 10%, which is better than the 9% you can get on the two-year security. If you expected the one-year rate a year from now to be 10%, it would not matter very much which of the two choices you made. The rate of return over the two-year period would be roughly 9% for both choices.

We must now alter the focus of our discussion to get to the topic we are really interested in—how the two-year rate is determined. Let us assume that the one-year rate has been set by the Fed and that it is 8 percent. Let us also assume that people expect the one-year rate a year from now to be 10 percent. What, then, is the two-year rate? According to a theory called the *expectations theory of the term structure of interest rates,* the two-year rate is equal to the average of the current one-year rate and the one-year rate expected a year from now. In this example, the two-year rate would be 9% (the average of 8% and 10 percent).

If the two-year rate were lower than the average of the two one-year rates, people would not be indifferent as to which security they held. They would want to hold only the short-term, one-year securities. Thus, in order to find a buyer for a two-year security, the seller would be forced to increase the interest rate it offers on the two-year security until it is equal to the average of the current one-year rate and the expected one-year rate for next year. The interest rate on the two-year security will continue to rise until people are once again indifferent between one two-year security and two one-year securities.[1]

Let us now return to Fed behavior. We know that the Fed can affect the short-term interest rate by changing the money supply. But does it also affect long-term interest rates? The answer is "somewhat." Since the two-year rate is an average of the current one-year rate and the expected one-year rate a year from now, the Fed influences the two-year rate to the extent that it influences the current one-year rate. The same holds for three-year rates and beyond. In other words, the current short-term rate is a means by which the Fed can influence longer-term rates.

In addition, Fed behavior may directly affect people's expectations of the future short-term rates, which will then affect long-term rates. If the chair of the Federal Reserve testifies before Congress that he or she is thinking about raising short-term interest rates, people's ex-

pectations of higher future short-term interest rates are likely to increase. These expectations will then be reflected in current long-term interest rates.

TYPES OF INTEREST RATES

The following are some of the most widely followed interest rates in the United States.

■ **Three-month Treasury Bill Rate** Government securities that mature in less than a year are called *Treasury bills,* or sometimes *T bills.* The interest rate on three-month Treasury bills is probably the most widely followed short-term interest rate.

■ **Government Bond Rate** Government securities with terms of one year or more are called *government bonds.* There are 1-year bonds, 2-year bonds, and so on up to 30-year bonds. Bonds of different terms have different interest rates. The relationship among the interest rates on the various maturities is the term structure of interest rates that we discussed in the first part of this Appendix.

■ **Federal Funds Rate** Banks borrow not only from the Fed but also from each other. If one bank has excess reserves, it can lend some of those reserves to other banks through the federal funds market. The interest rate in this market is called the *federal funds rate*—the rate banks are charged to borrow reserves from other banks.

The federal funds market is really a desk in New York City. From all over the country, banks with excess reserves to lend and banks in need of reserves call the desk and negotiate a rate of interest. Account balances with the Fed are changed for the period of the loan without any physical movement of money.

This borrowing and lending, which takes place near the close of each working day, is generally for one day ("overnight"), so the federal funds rate is a one-day rate. It is the rate that the Fed controls most closely through its open market operations.

■ **Commercial Paper Rate** Firms have several alternatives for raising funds. They can sell stocks, issue bonds, or borrow from a bank. Large firms can also borrow directly from the public by issuing "commercial paper," which are essentially short-term corporate IOUs that offer a designated rate of interest. The interest rate offered on commercial paper depends on the financial condition of the firm and the maturity date of the IOU.

■ **Prime Rate** Banks charge different interest rates to different customers. You would expect to pay a higher

---

[1]For longer terms, additional future rates must be averaged in. For a three-year security, for example, the expected one-year rate a year from now and the expected one-year rate two years from now are added to the current one-year rate and averaged.

interest rate for a car loan than General Motors would pay for a $1 million loan to finance investment. Also, you would pay more interest for an unsecured loan, a "personal" loan, than for one that was secured by some asset, such as a house or car, to be used as collateral.

The *prime rate* is a benchmark that banks often use in quoting interest rates to their customers. A very low-risk corporation might be able to borrow at (or even below) the prime rate. A less well-known firm might be quoted a rate of "prime plus three fourths," which means that if the prime rate is say, 10%, the firm would have to pay interest of 10.75 percent. Since the prime rate depends on the cost of funds to the bank, it moves up and down with changes in the economy.

■ **AAA Corporate Bond Rate** Corporations finance much of their investment by selling bonds to the public. Corporate bonds are classified by various bond dealers according to their degree of risk. Bonds issued by General Motors are in less risk of default than bonds issued by a new, risky biotech research firm. Bonds differ from commercial paper in one important way: Bonds have a longer maturity.

Bonds are graded in much the same way students are. The highest grade is AAA, the next highest AA, and so on. The interest rate on bonds rated AAA is the *triple A corporate bond rate,* the rate that the least risky firms pay on the bonds that they issue.

PROBLEM SET

1. The following table gives three key U.S. interest rates in 1980 and again in April 1993:

	1980	1993
Three-month U.S. government bills	11.39%	2.92%
Long-term U.S. government bonds	10.81%	6.85%
Prime rate	15.26%	6.00%

Can you give an explanation for the extreme differences that you see? Specifically, comment on the following: (1) the fact that rates in 1980 were much higher than they were in 1993, and (2) the long-term rate was higher than the short-term rate in 1993 but below it in 1980.

APPENDIX B TO CHAPTER 12   THE DEMAND FOR MONEY: A NUMERICAL EXAMPLE

This Appendix presents a numerical example showing how optimal money management behavior can be derived.

We have seen that the interest rate represents the opportunity cost of holding funds in non-interest-bearing checking accounts (as opposed to bonds, which yield interest). We have also seen that there are costs involved in switching from bonds to money. Given these costs, our objective is to determine the optimum amount of money for an individual to hold. The optimal average level of money holdings is the amount that maximizes the profits from money management. Interest is earned on average bond holdings, but the cost per switch multiplied by the number of switches must be subtracted from interest revenue to obtain the net profit from money management.

Suppose the interest rate is .05 (5%), it costs $2 each time a bond is sold,[1] and the proceeds from the sale are deposited in one's checking account. Suppose also that the individual's income is $1200 and that this income is spent evenly throughout the period. This situation is depicted in the top half of Table 12A.1. The optimum value for average money holdings is the value that achieves the largest possible profit in column 6 of the table. When the interest rate is 5%, the optimum average money holdings are $150 (which means the individual makes three switches from bonds to money).

In the bottom half of Table 12A.1, the same calculations are performed for an interest rate of 3% rather than 5 percent. In this case, the optimum average money holding is $200 (which means the person/household makes two switches from bonds to money rather than three). The lower interest rate has thus led to an increase in the optimum average money holdings. Under the assumption that people behave optimally, the demand for money is thus a negative function of the interest rate: The lower the rate, the more money on average is held, and the higher the rate, the less money on average is held.

---

[1]*In this example we will assume that the $2 cost does not apply to the original purchase of bonds.*

TABLE 12A.1 OPTIMUM MONEY HOLDINGS

1 NUMBER OF SWITCHES[1]	2 AVERAGE MONEY HOLDINGS[2]	3 AVERAGE BOND HOLDINGS[3]	4 INTEREST EARNED[4]	5 COST OF SWITCHING[5]	6 NET PROFIT[6]
Assumptions: Interest rate $r = 0.05$. Cost of switching from bonds into money equals $2 per transaction.					
		$r = 5$ percent			
0	$600.00	$ 0.00	$ 0.00	$ 0.00	$0.00
1	300.00	300.00	15.00	2.00	13.00
2	200.00	400.00	20.00	4.00	16.00
3	150.00*	450.00	22.50	6.00	16.50
4	120.00	480.00	24.00	8.00	16.00
Assumptions: Interest rate $r = 0.03$. Cost of switching from bonds into money equals $2 per transaction.					
		$r = 3$ percent			
0	$600.00	$ 0.00	$ 0.00	$0.00	$0.00
1	300.00	300.00	9.00	2.00	7.00
2	200.00*	400.00	12.00	4.00	8.00
3	150.00	450.00	13.50	6.00	7.50
4	120.00	480.00	14.40	8.00	6.40

*Optimum money holdings. [1]That is, the number of times you sell a bond. [2]Calculated as 600/(col. 1 + 1). [3]Calculated as 600 − col. 2. [4]Calculated as $r \times$ col. 3, where r is the interest rate. [5]Calculated as $t \times$ col. 1, where t is the cost per switch ($2). [6]Calculated as col. 4 − col. 5.

PROBLEM SET

1. Sherman Peabody earns a monthly salary of $1500, which he receives at the beginning of each month. He spends the entire amount each month, at the rate of $50 per day. (Assume that there are 30 days in a month.) The interest rate paid on bonds is 10% per month. It costs $4 every time Peabody sells a bond.
   a. Describe briefly how Mr. Peabody should go about deciding how much money to hold.
   b. Calculate Peabody's optimal money holdings. (*Hint:* It may help to formulate a table such as the one in this Appendix. You can round to the nearest $.50, and you need to consider only average money holdings of more than $100.)
   c. Suppose the interest rate rises to 15 percent. Find Peabody's optimal money holdings at this new interest rate. What would happen if the interest rate increases to 20 percent?
   d. Graph your answers to b. and c. with the interest rate on the vertical axis and the amount of money demanded on the horizontal axis. Explain why your graph slopes downward.

CLIPPED COINS, COUNTERFEITING, AND CURRENCY DEBASEMENT

Throughout history we find people who take it upon themselves to print their own money. Typically, we find them on the wrong side of the law. Governments, however, have the privilege of issuing a nation's money and can print more when they need it. Printing money to finance the state's spending needs, however, usually compromises money's integrity as a standard of value and leads to inflation.

From medieval to early modern times, silver was the monetary standard. Money's unit-of-account function was quoted in terms of metal weights—for example, the British "pound" of silver. Such metal-based commodity monies contained metal approximately equal in value to the coin's face value. The earliest form of currency debasement took place when governments began issuing new coins of reduced weight and purity, thus lowering the coin's intrinsic value far below face value. Debased coin often had a different "ring" than full-bodied coin, not unlike the hollow sound of U.S. copper-filled quarters that now replace their silver ancestors. It is said that Charles II of England debased the currency to the embarrassing extent that rubbing one's nose on the coin would turn it red as a result of the coin's excessive copper content. Debasement reduced minting costs and thus helped governments finance their wars while avoiding the levy of unpopular direct taxes.

The Swedish government's ownership of one of the largest copper mines in Europe led it in 1625 to adopt a copper standard instead of silver. State ownership of the money facilitated government finances. Worth only 100th the value of silver, however, copper proved to be unsatisfactory for coinage because of its great weight: While difficult to steal, it made transactions cumbersome. Ten dollars' worth of silver in copper coins weighed nearly 50 pounds, not a terribly convenient means of exchange. The Swedish Riksbank, the first central bank in the world, was also the first to substitute bank notes for coin (in 1668) because of the inconveniences of copper.

In sixteenth-century England, the public played its part in the debasement of the nation's money by "clipping" and counterfeiting coins. Not until 1663 were English coins marked or milled along the edges to discourage the clipping or shaving of metal off coins. (Offenders melted down the shavings for bullion.) In 1695 the national monetary crisis prompted John Locke to write, "Clipping . . . has contributed more to sink us than all the forces of our enemies could do." By that time the clippers had reduced the coinage by one third its weight. The threat to the monetary system was so great that the crime was made punishable by death. So important was it to the state that the coinage not be clipped or counterfeited that Locke saw to it that Sir Isaac Newton was appointed Warden and Master of the Mint. Beyond assuring the currency's weight and purity, it is said that Newton spent 50 days a year prosecuting clippers and counterfeiters on the state's behalf.

The move to fiat money, where paper is substituted for metal, generates large savings in resources that would otherwise be expended for mining and smelting metal. Since producing the paper is virtually costless, the temptation to overissue bank notes is strong, and the result is likely to be inflation. During the Napoleonic Wars the British government borrowed heavily, issuing Bank of England notes to cover its debts. The Bank prohibited the redemption of paper notes for gold. As inflation developed, forgers and counterfeiters began "copying" the Bank of England's seemingly profitable scheme of fiat money issue. By 1821 the quantity of forged notes presented to the Bank reached nearly 31,000. Records show that Bank directors took up more time with problems of forgery than the key issues of monetary policy. Government response was severe—nearly 400 men and women hanged from the gallows between 1797 and 1815 for passing forged notes!

Efforts to eradicate forgery resulted in a Bank contest for the "men of science and eminent artists" to design a note that could not be imitated. George Cruikshank's "Bank Note—not to be imitated" was the most controversial submission. Designed in protest to reflect public indignation at the Bank of England hangings, Cruikshank's note (see photo on page 291) de-

DESIGNED TO PROTEST THE NUMBER OF FORGERY-RELATED HANGINGS IN NINETEENTH-CENTURY ENGLAND, GEORGE CRUIKSHANK'S BANK NOTE DEPICTED ELEVEN CORPSES SUSPENDED FROM A SCAFFOLD. THE NOTE WAS SIGNED BY "JACK KETCH," THE HANGMAN PERSONIFIED.

picted eleven corpses suspended from a scaffold and was signed by the hangman, "Jack Ketch." Public outcry did put an end to the hangings, though the problem of counterfeiting remains to this day.

A 1992 Federal Bureau of Investigation (FBI) study estimated the cost of forgery to U.S. financial institutions to be around $4.2 billion. In Moscow, over one fifth of an enormous circulation of U.S. dollar bills is said to be fake. This longstanding problem has prompted the Federal Reserve to study proposals to "make selected design changes to improve the resistance of currency to counterfeiting" in the new world of color copy machines and scanners. As in previous centuries, deals have been struck with convicted counterfeiters to turn their creativity to designing forgery-resistant money. By 2000, all denominations will be redesigned bearing a portrait-shaped watermark and small iridescent disks that cannot be reproduced. In Australia, the central bank has already introduced plastic money, incorporating complex optical tricks that cannot be photocopied. Singapore and Kuwait have asked the Australians to produce some plastic

bills to replace their high-denomination notes.

And how will governments protect the emerging forms of digital cash that can be loaded onto hard drives or wallet cards to be used as freely and anonymously as cash? With the projected explosion of Internet commerce, the demand for secure and private digital money will grow. As was the case with Newton in the seventeenth century, eminent scientists will be recruited to design and protect the currency. It is likely that the marriage of cryptology and quantum physics can produce "money" that is physically impossible to counterfeit. Indeed, the modern counterfeiter will have to be a truly extraordinary high-tech hacker.

Questions for Analytical Thinking

1. Who are the winners and losers when a currency is debased? When analyzing debasement, does it make any difference whether the currency consists of commodity money or fiat money?

2. Why did it make sense for the Swedish government to adopt a

copper standard in 1625? Why did copper fail in its role as a medium of exchange?

3. Suppose you redeem all your U.S. paper money in pennies. Does this mean the United States is on a copper standard?

4. Why have counterfeiters and clippers been so severely punished? What are the economic impacts of counterfeit note circulation?

Sources: Murray Teigh Bloom, *Money of Their Own: The Great Counterfeiters* (New York, Scribner's, 1957); Murray Teigh Bloom, *The Brotherhood of Money: The Secret World of Bank Note Printers* (Port Clinton, Ohio: BNR Press, 1983); Louis Dembitz Brandeis, *Other People's Money, and How the Bankers Use It* (New York: Stokes, 1914); Constantine George Caffentzis, *Clipped Coins, Abused Words, and Civil Government: John Locke's Philosophy of Money* (Brooklyn, NY: Autonomedia, 1989); *Coin World*, "British Illustrator Parodies Hangings," August 13, 1986; Frank Whitson Fetter, *Development of British Monetary Orthodoxy, 1797–1875* (Cambridge, MA: Harvard University Press, 1965); Charles P. Kindleberger, *A Financial History of Western Europe* (London: George Allen & Unwin, 1985); Peter Linebaugh, *The London Hanged: Crime and Civil Society in the Eighteenth Century* (Cambridge and New York: Cambridge University Press, 1992); A.D. MacKenzie, *The Bank of England Note: A History of Its Printing* (Cambridge and New York: Cambridge University Press, 1953).

goods market *The market in which goods and services are exchanged and in which the equilibrium level of aggregate output is determined.*

money market *The market in which financial instruments are exchanged and in which the equilibrium level of the interest rate is determined.*

Money, the Interest Rate, and National Income: Analysis and Policy

I N Chapters 9 and 10, we discussed the market for goods and services—the **goods market**—without ever mentioning money, the money market, or the interest rate. We described in some detail how the equilibrium level of aggregate output (income) (Y) is determined in the goods market. At given levels of planned investment spending (I), government spending (G), and net taxes (T), we were able to determine the equilibrium level of output in the economy.

In Chapters 11 and 12, we discussed the financial market, or **money market,** with only passing references to the goods market. In those chapters, we explained how the equilibrium level of the interest rate is determined in the money market.

The goods market and the money market do not operate independently, however. Events in the money market have important effects on the goods market, and events in the goods market have important effects on the money market. Only by analyzing the two markets together can we determine the values of aggregate output (income) (Y) and the interest rate (r) that are consistent with the existence of equilibrium in *both* markets.

Looking at both markets simultaneously also reveals how fiscal policy affects the money market and how monetary policy affects the goods market. This is our task in this chapter. By establishing how the two markets affect each other, we will be able to show how open market purchases of government securities (which expand the money supply) affect the equilibrium level of national output and income. Similarly, we will be able to show how fiscal policy measures (such as tax cuts) affect interest rates and investment spending.

The Links Between the Goods Market and the Money Market

There are two key *links*, or connections, between the goods market and the money market.

■ **Link 1: Income and the Demand for Money** The first link between the goods market and the money market exists because the demand for money depends on income. As aggregate output (income) (Y) increases, the number of transactions requiring the use of money increases. (This point should be fresh in your mind from the previous chapter.) Thus, an increase in output, with the interest rate held constant, leads to an increase in money demand. This leads us to conclude that:

> Income, which is determined in the goods market, has an important influence on the demand for money in the money market.

■ **Link 2: Planned Investment Spending and the Interest Rate** The second link between the goods market and the money market exists because planned investment spending (I) depends on the interest rate (r). In Chapters 9 and 10 we assumed that planned investment spending is fixed at a certain level, but we did so only to simplify our initial discussion. In practice, investment is not fixed. Rather, it depends on a number of key economic variables. One of these variables is the interest rate. The higher the interest rate, the lower the level of planned investment spending. Therefore,

> The interest rate, which is determined in the money market, has important effects on planned investment in the goods market.

We examine these links in more detail in the sections that follow.

INVESTMENT, THE INTEREST RATE, AND THE GOODS MARKET

It should come as no surprise to you that the relationship between the level of planned investment and the interest rate is a negative one. Stated simply,

> When the interest rate falls, planned investment rises.
> When the interest rate rises, planned investment falls.

It is easy to see why this is so. Recall that *investment* refers to the purchase of new capital—new machines and plants. Firms undertake investment projects because they expect those projects to yield profits in the future. Thus, whether a firm decides to invest in a project depends upon whether the expected profits from the project justify its costs. One of the important costs of an investment project is the interest cost.

Consider, for example, a firm that is opening a new plant, or the investment required to open a new ice-cream store. When a manufacturing firm builds a new plant, the contractor must be paid at the time the plant is built. When an entrepreneur decides to open a new ice-cream parlor, she needs freezers, tables, chairs, light fixtures, and signs. These too must be paid for when they are installed.

The money needed to carry out such projects is generally borrowed and paid back over an extended period of time. Thus, the real cost of an investment project

HIGHER INTEREST RATES BEGIN TO HIT INVESTMENT: MORTGAGES AND HOUSING IN 1994

One component of planned investment spending that is quite sensitive to interest rate changes is investment in housing. Home purchases are generally financed with a mortgage. A mortgage is a long-term loan. Higher mortgage rates increase the cost of buying and owning a home. Between January and December of 1994, the interest rate on 30-year fixed-rate mortgages jumped from 6.75% to 9.25%, largely as the result of an expanding economy (which was shifting the money demand curve to the right) and an increasingly resistant Fed holding the line on money supply growth.

Consider the effect of such an interest rate hike on the cost of buying and owning a home. A potential buyer considering a $100,000 home requiring a 20% down payment faced a monthly payment of $519 at the 6.75% rate in January. By December, the same potential buyer faced a monthly payment of $658 at a rate of 9.25 percent. (These numbers assume a 30-year fixed-rate mortgage.) The hike in rates has the same impact as a 25% increase in the price of the house. It is not surprising that by the summer of 1994, higher rates were beginning to have an effect on the housing market.

The following excerpt from *Business Week* tells the story:

Home sales were stunningly weak in June. Demand for existing homes fell 3.6%, to an annual rate of 3.96 million, while sales of new single-family homes plunged 14.1% in the month, to a two-year low of just 591,000. All regions shared in the decline in new-home sales.

As a result, just like retailers and wholesalers, homebuilders ended last quarter carrying more inventory than they probably wanted. The supply of unsold homes jumped to 6.1 months from 4.7 months in May.

Demand is caving in to higher interest rates. Mortgage applications to buy a home popped up in the week ended July 22, but for the first four weeks of the month, the pace of applications was way below the average of June, which was down from May.

Source: James C. Cooper and Kathleen Madigan, "This Expansion has Slowed to a Summer Stroll," *Business Week,* August 15, 1994, p. 24.

WHEN INTEREST RATES GO UP, IT BECOMES HARDER TO PURCHASE A HOME. AS A RESULT, MORE HOMES REMAIN ON THE MARKET LONGER THAN THEY WOULD IF INTEREST RATES WERE LOWER.

To summarize the effects of an expansionary fiscal policy, we can write:

Effects of an Expansionary Fiscal Policy:	$G \uparrow \rightarrow Y \uparrow \rightarrow M^d \uparrow \rightarrow r \uparrow \rightarrow I \downarrow$
	Y increases less than if r did not increase.

Exactly the same reasoning holds for changes in net taxes. The ultimate effect of a tax cut on the equilibrium level of output depends on how the money market reacts. The expansion of Y that a tax cut brings about will lead to an increase in the interest rate and thus a decrease in planned investment spending. The ultimate increase in Y will therefore be less than it would be if the interest rate did not rise.

■ **Expansionary Monetary Policy: An Increase in the Money Supply**   Now let us consider what will happen when the Fed decides to increase the supply of money through open market operations. At first, open market operations inject new reserves into the system and expand the quantity of money supplied (that is, the money supply curve shifts to the right). Because the quantity of money supplied is now greater than the amount households want to hold, the equilibrium rate of interest falls. Planned investment spending (which is a component of planned aggregate expenditure) increases when the interest rate falls.

Increased planned investment spending means that planned aggregate expenditure is now greater than aggregate output. Firms experience unplanned decreases in inventories, and they raise output (Y). An increase in the money supply thus decreases the interest rate and increases Y. However, the higher level of Y increases the demand for money (that is, the demand for money curve shifts to the right), and this keeps the interest rate from falling as far as it otherwise would.

If you review the sequence of events that follows the monetary expansion, you can see a number of links between the injection of reserves by the Fed into the economy and the increase in output. First, the increase in the quantity of money supplied pushes down the interest rate. Second, the lower interest rate causes planned investment spending to rise. Third, the increased planned investment spending means higher planned aggregate expenditure, which means increased output as firms react to unplanned decreases in inventories. Fourth, the increase in output (income) leads to an increase in the demand for money (the demand for money curve shifts to the right), which means that the interest rate decreases less than it would have if the demand for money had not increased. These connections can be summarized as:

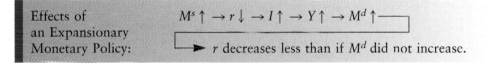

Effects of an Expansionary Monetary Policy:	$M^s \uparrow \rightarrow r \downarrow \rightarrow I \uparrow \rightarrow Y \uparrow \rightarrow M^d \uparrow$ ─────┐
	└──► r decreases less than if M^d did not increase.

The power of monetary policy to affect the goods market depends on how much of a reaction occurs at each link in this chain. Perhaps the most critical link is the link between r and I. Monetary policy can be effective *only* if I reacts to changes in r. If firms sharply increase the number of investment projects undertaken when the interest rate falls, expansionary monetary policy works well at stimulating the economy. If, however, firms are reluctant to invest even at a low interest rate, expansionary monetary policy will have limited success. In other words, the effectiveness of monetary policy depends on the shape of the investment function. If it is nearly vertical, indicating very little responsiveness of investment to the interest rate, the middle link in this chain is weak, rendering monetary policy ineffective.

■ **Expansionary Policy in Action: The Recessions of 1974–1975, 1980–1982, and 1990–1991**   The United States has experienced three recessions since 1970. In two of these recessions, 1974–1975 and 1980–1982, the government engaged in tax cuts that had the effect of stimulating consumer spending (C). Because C is a component of planned aggregate expenditure, these tax cuts had the effect of increasing aggregate output (income) (Y).

Consider the recession of 1974–1975. The Tax Reduction Act of 1975 resulted in a 1974 tax rebate of $8 billion that was paid to consumers in the second quarter of 1975. This rebate and other tax reductions led to increased consumer spending, which contributed to the economic recovery that began soon after the new tax laws went into effect.

But what about the crowding-out effect? Did the 1975 expansionary fiscal policy drive up interest rates and crowd out private spending? The answer in this case is no. At the same time that Congress was cutting taxes to stimulate spending, the Fed was trying to stimulate the economy by expanding the money supply. Thus, even though the increased output during the expansion caused the *demand* for money to rise, the Fed was simultaneously expanding the *supply* of money, and interest rates did not change very much. This situation is illustrated in Figure 13.6.

A similar sequence of events took place during the recession of 1980–1982. On the recommendation of President Reagan, Congress passed a huge tax cut during the summer of 1981. Like the 1975 tax cut, the 1981 tax cut led to an increase in consumer spending, which helped lift the economy out of the recession.

Recovery from the 1980–1982 recession was also helped along by the Fed, which began to increase the supply of money sharply in the spring of 1982. So, even though output and income were expanding by late 1982, thereby increasing the demand for money, interest rates actually *declined* because the supply of money was expanding at the same time. There was thus no crowding-out effect.

The recession of 1990–1991 began soon after Iraq's invasion of Kuwait in the late summer of 1990. The recession was short-lived and fairly shallow compared with the two previous recessions. Real GDP actually began to rise in the second quarter of 1991. But this recover was to become known as the "jobless recovery." Because productivity increased and large firms continued to trim payrolls even as output was expanding, the unemployment rate stayed high right into the presidential election of 1992.

President Bush had debated calling for a tax cut to stimulate the economy, but concern with the already large government deficit and pressure from the Fed

FIGURE 13.6

Fed Accommodation of an Expansionary Fiscal Policy

An expansionary fiscal policy, like the 1975 tax cut, will increase aggregate output (income) and shift the money demand curve to the right, from M_0^d to M_1^d. If the money supply were unchanged, the interest rate would rise from r_0 to r_1 and planned investment would be negatively affected. But if the Fed were to "accommodate" the fiscal expansion by increasing the money supply from M_0^s to M_1^s, the interest rate would not rise.

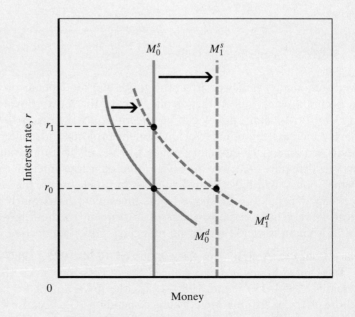

convinced him to wait. However, the Fed did push interest rates lower in an effort to get the economy moving. Even so, little response was evident by election time.

President Clinton called for some modest fiscal stimulus when he took office, but the Congress balked. Then, in the summer of 1993, Congress passed the Clinton deficit reduction package, which *increased* taxes and *reduced* government spending. In the meantime, monetary policy continued to be expansionary. Eventually, interest rates hit 30-year lows! For much of 1993, the three-month T-bill rate was under 3% for the first time since 1962, and the 30-year bond rate fell below 6% for the first time since the government began selling 30-year-bonds.

In late 1994, the slow-growth recovery ended and a real expansion began. To the extent that policy was responsible for the expansion, it was monetary (rather than fiscal) policy that finally got things moving.

CONTRACTIONARY POLICY EFFECTS

Any government policy that is aimed at reducing aggregate output (income) (Y) is said to be *contractionary*. Where expansionary policy is used to boost the economy, contractionary policy is used to slow the economy.

Considering that one of the four major economic goals is economic growth (see Chapter 1), why would the government adopt policies designed to reduce aggregate spending? As we will see in more detail in the next two chapters, one of the ways to fight inflation is to reduce aggregate spending. Thus, when the inflation rate is high, the government may feel compelled to use its powers to contract the economy. Before we discuss the contractionary policies that the government has undertaken in recent years, however, we need to discuss how contractionary fiscal and monetary policy work.

■ **Contractionary Fiscal Policy: A Decrease in Government Spending (G) or an Increase in Net Taxes (T)**   A **contractionary fiscal policy** is a decrease in government spending (G) or an increase in net taxes (T) aimed at decreasing aggregate output (income) (Y). The effects of this policy are the opposite of the effects of an expansionary fiscal policy.

A decrease in government purchases or an increase in net taxes leads to a decrease in aggregate output (income) (Y), a decrease in the demand for money (M^d), and a decrease in the interest rate (r). The decrease in Y that accompanies a contractionary fiscal policy is less than it would be if we did not take the money market into account because the decrease in r also causes planned investment (I) to *increase*. This increase in I offsets some of the decrease in planned aggregate expenditure brought about by the decrease in G. (Of course, this also means that the multiplier effect is smaller than it would be if we did not take the money market into account.) The effects of a decrease in G, or an increase in T, can be summarized as follows:

Effects of a Contractionary Fiscal Policy:	$G \downarrow$ or $T \uparrow \rightarrow Y \downarrow \rightarrow M^d \downarrow \rightarrow r \downarrow \rightarrow I \uparrow$
	Y decreases less than if r did not decrease.

■ **Contractionary Monetary Policy: A Decrease in the Money Supply**   A **contractionary monetary policy** is a decrease in the money supply aimed at decreasing aggregate output (income) (Y). As you recall, the level of planned investment spending is a negative function of the interest rate: The higher the interest rate, the less

contractionary fiscal policy *A decrease in government spending or an increase in net taxes aimed at decreasing aggregate output (income) (Y).*

contractionary monetary policy *A decrease in the money supply aimed at decreasing aggregate output (income) (Y).*

planned investment there will be. The less planned investment there is, the lower planned aggregate expenditure will be, and the lower the equilibrium level of output (income) (Y) will be. The lower equilibrium income results in a decrease in the demand for money, which means that the increase in the interest rate will be less than it would be if we did not take the goods market into account. The effects of a decrease in the money supply can be summarized as:

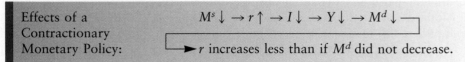

Effects of a Contractionary Monetary Policy:

$$M^s \downarrow \rightarrow r \uparrow \rightarrow I \downarrow \rightarrow Y \downarrow \rightarrow M^d \downarrow$$
r increases less than if M^d did not decrease.

■ **Contractionary Policy in Action: 1973–1974, 1979–1980, and 1994** The Fed has pursued strong contractionary policies twice in the last two decades: first in 1973–1974 and again in 1979–1980. In both cases, the tight monetary policies led to very high interest rates. In 1974, short-term rates exceeded 12%, and in 1981, some short-term rates exceeded 20 percent! These high interest rates had a negative effect on planned aggregate expenditure and contributed to the recessions that followed. The Fed's purpose in following a tight monetary policy was to slow the inflation rate. (We will see in the next chapter why a contractionary policy may bring the inflation rate down.)

In 1994, worries about inflation surfaced again as the economy began to push toward full employment. Once again, the Fed began to pull on the reins. In February, it announced the first of several increases in the discount rate and the target federal funds rate. By the end of the year, the prime rate had jumped from 6% to 8.5 percent.

THE MACROECONOMIC POLICY MIX

Thus far, we've been treating fiscal and monetary policy separately. However, it should be clear that fiscal and monetary policy can be used simultaneously. For example, both government purchases (G) and the money supply (M^s) can be increased at the same time. We have seen that an increase in G by itself raises both Y and r, while an increase in M^s by itself raises Y but lowers r. Therefore, if the government wanted to increase Y without changing r, it could do so by increasing both G and M^s by the appropriate amounts.

policy mix *The combination of monetary and fiscal policies in use at a given time.*

The term **policy mix** refers to the combination of monetary and fiscal policies in use at a given time. A policy mix that consists of a decrease in government spending and an increase in the money supply would favor investment spending over government spending. This is because both the increased money supply and the fall in government purchases would cause the interest rate to fall, which would lead to an increase in planned investment. The opposite is true for a mix that consists of an expansionary fiscal policy and a contractionary monetary policy. This mix favors government spending over investment spending. Such a policy will have the effect of increasing government spending and reducing the money supply. Tight money and expanded government spending would drive the interest rate up and planned investment down.

There is no hard-and-fast rule about what constitutes the "best" policy mix or the "best" composition of output. On this, as on many other issues, economists (and others) disagree. In part, one's preference for a certain composition of output—say, one weighted heavily toward private spending with relatively little government spending—depends on how one stands on such issues as the proper role of government in the economy.

Figure 13.7 summarizes the effects of various combinations of policies on several important macroeconomic variables. If you can explain the reasoning underlying each of the effects shown in the figure, you can be satisfied that you have a good understanding of the links between the goods market and the money market.

OTHER DETERMINANTS OF PLANNED INVESTMENT

We have assumed in this chapter that planned investment depends only on the interest rate. In reality, however, planned investment depends on other factors as well. We will discuss these factors in more detail in Chapter 17, but provide a brief description of them here.

■ **Expectations and Animal Spirits**   Firms' expectations about their future sales play an important role in their investment decisions. When a firm invests, it adds to its capital stock, and capital is used in the production process. If a firm expects that its sales will increase in the future, it may begin to build up its capital stock (that is, to invest) now so that it will be able to produce more in the future to meet the increased level of sales. The optimism or pessimism of entrepreneurs about the future course of the economy can thus have an important effect on current planned investment. Keynes used the phrase *animal spirits* to describe the feelings of entrepreneurs, and he argued that these feelings affect investment decisions.

■ **Capital Utilization Rates**   The degree of utilization of a firm's capital stock is also likely to affect planned investment. If the demand for a firm's output has been decreasing and the firm has been lowering output in response to this decline, the firm may have a low rate of capital utilization. It can be costly to get rid of capital quickly once it is in place, and firms sometimes respond to a fall in output by keeping the capital in place but utilizing it less (for example, by running machines fewer hours per day or at slower speeds). For obvious reasons, firms tend to invest less in new capital when their capital utilization rates are low than when they are high.

■ **Relative Labor and Capital Costs**   The cost of capital (of which the interest rate is the main component) *relative* to the cost of labor can affect planned investment. If labor is expensive relative to capital (high wage rates), firms tend to substitute away from labor toward capital. They aim to hold more capital relative to labor when wage rates are high than when they are low.

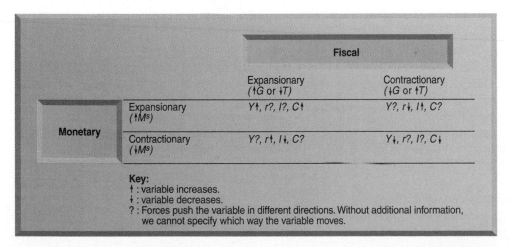

FIGURE 13.7
The Effects of the Macroeconomic Policy Mix

To summarize:

The Determinants of Planned Investment:	■ The interest rate ■ Expectations of future sales ■ Capital utilization rates ■ Relative capital and labor costs

LOOKING AHEAD: THE PRICE LEVEL

Our discussion of aggregate output (income) and the interest rate in the goods market and the money market is now complete. By now you should have a good understanding of how the two markets work together. Thus far, however, we have not yet discussed the price level in any detail.

One cannot begin to understand the economic events of the last two decades without an understanding of the aggregate price level. The two periods of rapid increases in the price level, 1974–1975 and 1979–1981, had dramatic effects on the economy. What causes the price level to change? Are there policies that might prevent large changes in the price level or stop them once they have started? Before we can answer such questions, we must understand the factors that affect the overall price level. This is the task of the next chapter. Up to this point we have taken the price level as fixed, and it is now time to relax this assumption.

SUMMARY

1. The *goods market* and the *money market* do not operate independently. Events in the money market have important effects on the goods market, and events in the goods market have important effects on the money market.

THE LINKS BETWEEN THE GOODS MARKET AND THE MONEY MARKET

2. There are two important links between the goods market and the money market. First, the level of real output (income) (Y), which is determined in the goods market, determines the volume of transactions each period and thus affects the demand for money in the money market. Second, the interest rate (r), which is determined in the money market, affects the level of planned investment spending in the goods market.

3. There is a negative relationship between planned investment and the interest rate because the interest rate determines the cost of investment projects.

When the interest rate rises, planned investment will decrease; when the interest rate falls, planned investment will increase.

4. For every value of the interest rate, there is a different level of planned investment spending and a different equilibrium level of output. The final level of equilibrium output depends on what the interest rate turns out to be, which depends on events in the money market.

5. For a given quantity of money supplied the interest rate depends on the demand for money. Money demand depends on the level of output (income). With a given money supply, then, increases and decreases in Y will affect money demand, which will affect the equilibrium interest rate.

COMBINING THE GOODS MARKET AND THE MONEY MARKET

6. An *expansionary fiscal policy* is an increase in government spending (G) or a reduction in net taxes

(T) aimed at increasing aggregate output (income) (Y). An expansionary fiscal policy based on increases in government spending tends to lead to a *crowding-out effect*: Because increased government expenditures mean more transactions in the economy and thus an increased demand for money, the interest rate will rise. The decrease in planned investment spending that accompanies the higher interest rate will then partially offset (crowd out) the increase in aggregate expenditures brought about by the increase in G.

7. The size of the crowding-out effect, and thus the size of the government-spending multiplier, depends on two things: the assumption that the Fed does not change the quantity of money supplied and the *sensitivity* or *insensitivity of planned investment* to changes in the interest rate.

8. An *expansionary monetary policy* is an increase in the money supply aimed at increasing aggregate output (income) (Y). An increase in the money supply leads to a lower interest rate, increased planned investment, increased planned aggregate expenditure, and ultimately a higher equilibrium level of aggregate output (income) (Y). Expansionary policies have been used to lift the economy out of recessions.

9. A *contractionary fiscal policy* is a decrease in government spending or an increase in net taxes aimed at decreasing aggregate output (income) (Y). A decrease in government spending or an increase in net taxes leads to a decrease in aggregate output (income) (Y), a decrease in the demand for money, and a decrease in the interest rate. However, the decrease in Y is somewhat offset by the additional planned investment that is undertaken as a result of the lower interest rate.

10. A *contractionary monetary policy* is a decrease in the money supply aimed at decreasing aggregate output (income) (Y). The higher interest rate brought about by the reduced money supply causes a decrease in planned investment spending and a lower level of equilibrium output. However, the lower equilibrium level of output brings about a decrease in the demand for money, which means that the increase in the interest rate will be less than it would be if we did not take the goods market into account. Contractionary policies have been used to fight inflation.

11. The *policy mix* is the combination of monetary and fiscal policies in use at a given time. There is no hard-and-fast rule about what constitutes the best policy mix or the best composition of output. In part, one's preference for a certain composition of output depends on one's stance regarding such issues as the proper role of government in the economy.

OTHER DETERMINANTS OF PLANNED INVESTMENT

12. In addition to the interest rate, the level of planned investment in the economy also depends on expectations and animal spirits, capital utilization rates, and relative capital and labor costs.

REVIEW TERMS AND CONCEPTS

contractionary fiscal policy 303
contractionary monetary policy 303
crowding-out effect 298
expansionary fiscal policy 298

expansionary monetary policy 298
goods market 292
interest sensitivity or **insensitivity of planned investment** 299

money market 292
policy mix 304

PROBLEM SET

1. Some economists argue that the "animal spirits" of investors are so important in determining the level of investment in the economy that interest rates don't matter at all. Suppose that this were true—that investment in no way depends on interest rates.

   a. How would the first figure in this chapter be different?
   b. What would happen to the level of planned aggregate expenditures if the interest rate were to change?

c. What would be different about the relative effectiveness of monetary and fiscal policy?

2. For each of the following, tell a story and predict the effects on the equilibrium levels of aggregate output (Y) and the interest rate (r):

a. The Republicans, who gained control of Congress in the elections of 1994, pass a major tax reduction bill and a bill to reduce government spending. The President vetoes the spending cuts, and the Federal Reserve maintains a slow-growth policy (essentially holding M^s constant).

b. In 1993, the Congress and the President raised taxes. At the same time, the Federal Reserve was pursuing an expansionary monetary policy.

c. In 1990, the Perisan Gulf War led to a sharp drop in consumer confidence and a drop in consumption. Assume that the Fed holds the money supply constant.

d. The Federal Reserve attempts to increase the money supply to stimulate the economy, but plants are operating at 65% of their capacities and businesses are very pessimistic about the future.

3. Occasionally, the Federal Reserve Open Market Committee sets a policy designed to "track" the interest rate. This means that the OMC is pursuing policies designed to keep the interest rate constant. If, in fact, the Fed were acting to counter any increases or decreases in the interest rate to keep it constant, what specific actions would you expect to see the Fed take if the following were to occur? (In answering, indicate the effects of each set of events on Y, C, S, I, M^s, M^d, and r.)

a. There is an unexpected increase in investor confidence, leading to a sharp increase in orders for new plant and equipment.

b. A major New York bank fails, causing a number of neurotic people (not trusting even the FDIC)

to withdraw a substantial amount of cash from other banks and put it in their cookie jars.

4. Paranoia, the largest country in Central Antarctica, receives word of an imminent penguin attack. The news causes expectations about the future to be shaken. As a consequence, there is a sharp decline in investment spending plans.

a. Explain in detail the effects of such an event on the economy of Paranoia, assuming no response on the part of the Central Bank or the Treasury (M^s, T, and G all remain constant). Be sure to discuss the adjustments in the goods market and the money market.

b. To counter the fall in investment, the king of Paranoia calls for a proposal to increase government spending. To finance the program, the Chancellor of the Exchequer has proposed three alternative options:

(1) Finance the expenditures with an equal increase in taxes.

(2) Keep tax revenues constant and borrow the money from the public by issuing new government bonds.

(3) Keep taxes constant and finance the expenditures by printing new money.

Consider the three financing options and rank them from most expansionary to least expansionary. Explain your ranking.

5. Why might investment not respond positively to low interest rates during a recession? Why might investment not respond negatively to high interest rates during a boom?

6. In the early 1980s, the Federal Reserve was tightening the money supply in order to fight inflation at the same time that President Reagan was increasing defense spending and reducing taxes. What would you expect the effects of this policy mix to be?

APPENDIX TO CHAPTER 13   **THE *IS-LM* DIAGRAM**

There is a useful way of depicting graphically the determination of aggregate output (income) and the interest rate in the goods and money markets. Two curves are involved in this diagram, the *IS* curve and the *LM* curve. In this appendix, we will derive these two curves and use them to see how changes in government purchases (G) and the money supply (M^s) affect the equilibrium values of aggregate output (income) and the interest rate. The effects we describe here are the same as the effects we described in the main text; the only difference

is that here we illustrate the effects graphically rather than verbally.

THE *IS* CURVE

We know that in the goods market, there is an equilibrium level of aggregate output (income) (Y) for each value of the interest rate (r). For a given value of r, we can determine the equilibrium value of Y. We also know from Figure 13.5 that the equilibrium value of Y falls when r rises and rises when r falls. There is thus a *negative* relationship between the equilibrium value of Y and r. The reason for this negative relationship is the negative relationship between planned investment and the interest rate. When the interest rate rises, planned investment (I) falls, and this decrease in I leads to a decrease in the equilibrium value of Y. The negative relationship between the equilibrium value of Y and r is shown in Figure 13A.1. This curve is called the **IS curve**.[1] Each point on the IS curve represents the equilibrium point in the goods market for the given interest rate.

We also know from our earlier analysis of the goods market that when government purchases (G) increase with a constant interest rate, the equilibrium value of Y increases. This means that the IS curve shifts to the right when G increases. With the same value of r and a higher value of G, the equilibrium value of Y is larger. Conversely, when G decreases, the IS curve shifts to the left.

THE *LM* CURVE

In the money market, as we know, there is an equilibrium value of the interest rate (r) for every value of aggregate output (income) (Y). The equilibrium value of r is determined at the point at which the quantity of money demanded equals the quantity of money supplied. For a given value of Y, then, we can determine the equilibrium value of r in the money market. We also know from Figure 13.4 that the equilibrium value of r rises when Y rises and falls when Y falls. There is thus a *positive* relationship between the equilibrium value of r and Y. The reason for this positive relationship is the positive relationship between the demand for money and Y. When Y increases, the demand for money increases because more money is demanded for the increased volume of transactions in the economy. An increase in the demand for money, in turn, increases the equilibrium value of r. There is thus a positive relationship between the equilibrium value of r and Y.

The positive relationship between the equilibrium value of r and Y is shown in Figure 13A.2. This curve is called the **LM curve**.[2] Each point on the LM curve represents equilibrium in the money market for the given value of aggregate output (income).

We also know from our analysis of the money market that when the money supply (M^s) increases with a constant level of Y, the equilibrium value of r decreases. As Figure 13A.2 shows, this means that the LM curve shifts to the right when M^s increases. With the same value of Y and a higher value of M^s, the equilibrium

---

FIGURE 13A.1 **THE IS CURVE**

Each point on the IS curve corresponds to the equilibrium point in the goods market for the given interest rate. When government spending (G) increases, the IS curve shifts to the right, from IS_0 to IS_1.

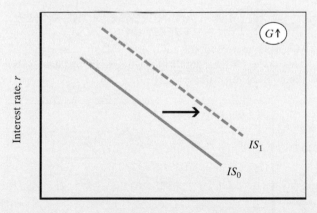

FIGURE 13A.2 **THE LM CURVE**

Each point on the LM curve corresponds to the equilibrium point in the money market for the given value of aggregate output (income). When the money supply (M^s) increases, the LM curve shifts to the right, from LM_0 to LM_1.

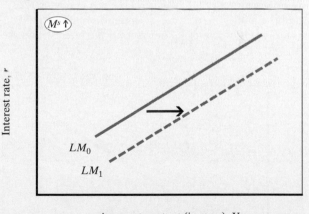

---

[1] *The letter* I *stands for investment, and the letter* S *stands for saving.* IS *refers to the fact that in equilibrium in the goods market, planned investment equals saving.*
[2] *The letter* L *stands for liquidity, a characteristic of money, and the letter* M *stands for money.*

value of r is lower. Conversely, when M^s decreases, the *LM* curve shifts to the left.

THE *IS-LM* DIAGRAM

Figure 13A.3 shows the *IS* and *LM* curves together on one graph. The point at which the two curves intersect is the point at which equilibrium exists in *both* the goods market and the money market. There is equilibrium in the goods market because the point is on the *IS* curve, and there is equilibrium in the money market because the point is on the *LM* curve.

We now have only two tasks left. The first is to see how the equilibrium values of Y and r are affected by changes in G—that is, by fiscal policy. This is easy to do. We have just seen that an increase in G shifts the *IS* curve to the right. Thus, an increase in G leads to higher equilibrium values of Y and r. This situation is illustrated in Figure 13A.4. Conversely, a decrease in G leads to lower equilibrium values of Y and r because the lower level of G causes the *IS* curve to shift to the left. (The effects are similar for changes in net taxes, T.)

Our second task is to see how the equilibrium values of Y and r are affected by changes in M^s—that is, by monetary policy. This is also easy to do. We have just seen that an increase in M^s shifts the *LM* curve to the right. Thus, an increase in M^s leads to a higher equilibrium value of Y and a lower equilibrium value of r.

FIGURE 13A.3 THE *IS-LM* DIAGRAM

The point at which the *IS* and *LM* curves intersect corresponds to the point at which both the goods market and the money market are in equilibrium. The equilibrium values of aggregate output and the interest rate are Y_0 and r_0.

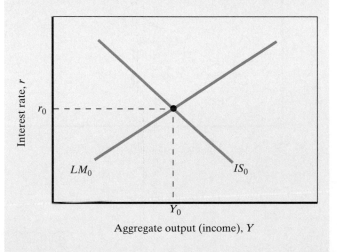

FIGURE 13A.4 AN INCREASE IN GOVERNMENT PURCHASES (G)

When G increases, the *IS* curve shifts to the right. This increases the equilibrium value of both Y and r.

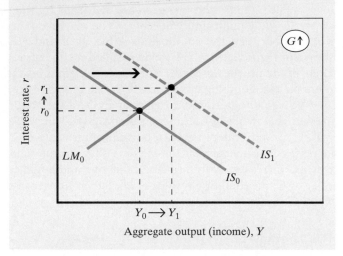

This is illustrated in Figure 13A.5. Conversely, a decrease in M^s leads to a lower equilibrium value of Y and a higher equilibrium value of r because a decreased money supply causes the *LM* curve to shift to the left.

The *IS-LM* diagram is a useful way of seeing the effects of changes in monetary and fiscal policies on equilibrium aggregate output (income) and the interest rate through shifts in the two curves. You should always keep in mind, however, the economic theory that lies *behind* the two curves. Do not just memorize what curve

FIGURE 13A.5 AN INCREASE IN THE MONEY SUPPLY (M^S)

When M^s increases, the *LM* curve shifts to the right. This increases the equilibrium value of Y and decreases the equilibrium value of r.

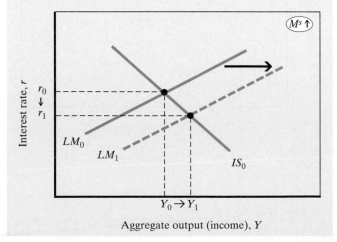

shifts when, but always be able to go back and explain *why* the curves shift as they do. This means always going back to the behavior of households and firms in the goods and money markets.

On a final note, it is easy to use the *IS-LM* diagram to see how there can be a monetary and fiscal policy mix that leads to, say, an increase in aggregate output (income) but no increase in the interest rate. If both *G* and *M^s* increase, both curves shift to the right, and the shifts can be controlled in such a way as to bring about no change in the equilibrium value of the interest rate.

SUMMARY

1. An *IS curve* illustrates the negative relationship between the equilibrium value of aggregate output (income) (*Y*) and the interest rate in the goods market. An *LM curve* illustrates the positive relationship between the equilibrium value of the interest rate and aggregate output (income) (*Y*) in the money market. The point at which the *IS* and *LM* curves intersect is the point at which equilibrium exists in both the goods market and the money market.

REVIEW TERMS AND CONCEPTS

IS curve A curve illustrating the negative relationship between the equilibrium value of aggregate output (income) (*Y*) and the interest rate in the goods market.   308

LM curve A curve illustrating the positive relationship between the equilibrium value of the interest rate and aggregate output (income) (*Y*) in the money market.   309

PROBLEM SET

1. Illustrate each of the following situations with *IS/LM* curves:
   a. An increase in *G* with the money supply held constant by the Fed.
   b. An increase in *G* with Fed accommodation designed to hold interest rates constant.
   c. The president cuts *G* and increases *T* while the chair of the Fed expands *M^s*.
   d. The president increases *G* and holds *T* constant while the chair of the Fed holds *M^s* constant during a period of inflation.

Thus, the *AD* curve in Figure 14.2 embodies everything we have learned about the goods market and the money market up to now.

To reiterate:

> The *AD* curve is *not* the sum of all the market demand curves in the economy. It is *not* a market demand curve.

OTHER REASONS FOR A DOWNWARD-SLOPING AGGREGATE DEMAND CURVE

In addition to the effects of money supply and money demand on the interest rate, two other factors lie behind the downward slope of the *AD* curve. These are the consumption link and the real wealth effect.

■ **The Consumption Link** We noted in Chapter 9 (and will discuss in detail in Chapter 17) that, in reality, both consumption (C) and planned investment (I) depend on the interest rate. Other things being equal, consumption expenditures tend to rise when the interest rate falls and to fall when the interest rate rises—just as planned investment does. This tendency is another link between the goods market and the money market. If something happens to change the interest rate in the money market, both consumption and planned investment are affected in the goods market.

The *consumption* link provides another reason for the *AD* curve's downward slope. An increase in the price level increases the demand for money, which leads to an increase in the interest rate, which leads to a decrease in consumption (as well as planned investment), which leads to a decrease in aggregate output (income). The initial decrease in consumption (brought about by the increase in the interest rate) contributes to the overall decrease in output. Thus:

> Planned investment does not bear all the burden of providing the link from a higher interest rate to a lower level of aggregate output. Decreased consumption brought about by a higher interest rate also contributes to this effect.

■ **The Real Wealth Effect** We also noted in Chapter 9 (and will discuss in detail in Chapter 17) that consumption depends on wealth. Other things being equal, the more wealth households have, the more they consume. Wealth includes holdings of money, shares of stock, bonds, and housing, among other things. If household wealth decreases, the result will be less consumption both now and in the future.

The price level has an effect on some kinds of wealth. Suppose, for example, that you are holding $1000 in a checking account or in a money market fund and that the price level rises by 10 percent. Your holding is now worth 10% less because the prices of the goods that you could buy with your $1000 have all increased by 10 percent. In other words, the purchasing power (or "real value") of your holding has decreased by 10 percent.

An increase in the price level may also lower the real value of stocks and housing, although whether it does so depends on what happens to stock prices and housing prices when the overall price level rises. If stock prices and housing prices rise by the same percentage as the overall price level, the real value of stocks and housing will remain unchanged. The main point here, however, is that:

> An increase in the price level lowers the real value of *some* types of wealth.

The fact that the price level lowers the real value of wealth provides another reason for the downward slope of the *AD* curve. An increase in the price level lowers the real value of wealth. This, in turn, leads to a decrease in consumption, which leads to a decrease in aggregate output (income). There is thus a negative relationship between the price level and output through this **real wealth effect** or **real balance effect**.

real wealth, or **real balance, effect** *The change in consumption brought about by a change in real wealth that results from a change in the price level.*

AGGREGATE EXPENDITURE AND AGGREGATE DEMAND

Throughout our discussion of macroeconomics so far, we have referred to the total planned spending by households (C), firms (I), and the government (G) as planned aggregate expenditure. At equilibrium, planned aggregate expenditure ($AE \equiv C + I + G$) and aggregate output (Y) are equal:[1]

$$\text{Equilibrium condition: } C + I + G = Y$$

How does planned aggregate expenditure relate to aggregate demand?

> At every point along the aggregate demand curve, the aggregate quantity demanded is exactly equal to planned aggregate expenditure, $C + I + G$.

You can see this in Figures 14.1 and 14.2. When the price level rises, it is planned aggregate expenditure that decreases, thus moving us down the aggregate demand curve.

But the aggregate demand curve represents more than just planned aggregate expenditure. Each point on the *AD* curve represents the *particular* level of planned aggregate expenditure that is consistent with equilibrium in the goods market and money market. Notice that the variable on the horizontal axis of the aggregate demand curve in Figure 14.2 is Y. At every point along the *AD* curve, $Y = C + I + G$.

SHIFTS OF THE AGGREGATE DEMAND CURVE

The aggregate demand curve in Figure 14.2 is based on the assumption that the government policy variables G, T, and M^s are fixed. If any of these variables change, the aggregate demand curve will shift.

Consider, for example, an increase in the quantity of money supplied. If the quantity of money is expanded at any given price level, the interest rate will fall, causing planned investment spending (and thus planned aggregate expenditure) to rise. The result is an increase in output at the given price level. Thus, as Figure 14.3 on page 318 shows:

> An increase in the quantity of money supplied at a given price level shifts the aggregate demand curve to the right.

An increase in government purchases or a decrease in net taxes also increases aggregate output (income) at each possible price level, even though some of the increase will be crowded out if the money supply is held constant. (If you are unsure of what the crowding-out effect is, review the last chapter.) An increase in government purchases directly increases planned aggregate expenditure, which leads to an increase in output. A decrease in net taxes results in a rise in consumption, which increases planned aggregate expenditure, which also leads to an increase in output. Thus, as Figure 14.4 on the next page shows:

> An increase in government purchases or a decrease in net taxes shifts the aggregate demand curve to the right.

---

[1]*If we include the rest of the world, the equilibrium condition is* $C + I + G + (EX - IM) = Y$.

FIGURE 14.3

The Effect of an Increase in Money Supply on the *AD* Curve

An increase in the money supply (M^s) causes the aggregate demand curve to shift to the right, from AD_0 to AD_1. This shift occurs because the increase in M^s lowers the interest rate, which increases planned investment (and thus planned aggregate expenditure). The final result is an increase in output at each possible price level.

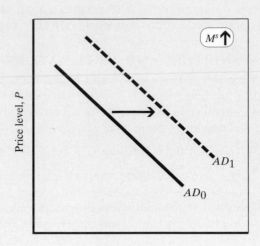

The same kind of reasoning applies to decreases in the quantity of money supplied, decreases in government purchases, and increases in net taxes. All of these shift the aggregate demand curve to the left.

Figure 14.5 summarizes the ways in which the aggregate demand curve shifts in response to changes in M^s, G, and T. A good way to test your understanding of the *AD* curve is to go through the figure piece by piece and explain each of its components.

FIGURE 14.4

The Effect of an Increase in Government Purchases or a Decrease in Net Taxes on the *AD* Curve

An increase in government purchases (G) or a decrease in net taxes (T) causes the aggregate demand curve to shift to the right, from AD_0 to AD_1. The increase in G increases planned aggregate expenditure, which leads to an increase in output at each possible price level. A decrease in T causes consumption to rise. The higher consumption then increases planned aggregate expenditure, which leads to an increase in output at each possible price level.

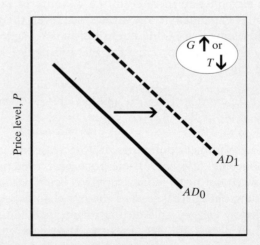

FIGURE 14.5
Shifts in the Aggregate
Demand Curve: A Summary

Expansionary monetary policy
$M^s \uparrow \rightarrow AD$ curve shifts to the right.

Contractionary monetary policy
$M^s \downarrow \rightarrow AD$ curve shifts to the left.

Expansionary fiscal policy
$G \uparrow \rightarrow AD$ curve shifts to the right.
$T \downarrow \rightarrow AD$ curve shifts to the right.

Contractionary fiscal policy
$G \downarrow \rightarrow AD$ curve shifts to the left.
$T \uparrow \rightarrow AD$ curve shifts to the left.

THE AGGREGATE SUPPLY CURVE

Aggregate supply is the total supply of goods and services in an economy. While there is little disagreement among economists about the logic behind the aggregate demand curve, there is a great deal of disagreement about the logic behind the aggregate supply curve. There is also disagreement about its shape.

aggregate supply *The total supply of all goods and services in an economy.*

THE AGGREGATE SUPPLY CURVE: A WARNING

The **aggregate supply (AS) curve** shows the relationship between the aggregate quantity of output supplied by all the firms in an economy and the overall price level. To understand the aggregate supply curve, we need to understand something about the behavior of the individual firms that make up the economy.

aggregate supply (AS) curve *A graph that shows the relationship between the aggregate quantity of output supplied by all firms in an economy and the overall price level.*

It may seem logical to think that we can derive the aggregate supply curve by simply adding together the supply curves of all the individual firms in the economy. However, the logic behind the relationship between the overall price level in the economy and the level of aggregate output (income)—that is, the *AS* curve—is very different from the logic behind an individual firm's supply curve. The aggregate supply curve is *not* a market supply curve, and it is *not* the simple sum of all the individual supply curves in the economy. (Recall that a similar warning holds for the aggregate demand curve.)

To understand why this is so, recall the logic behind a simple supply curve, which we first introduced in Chapter 4. A supply curve shows the quantity of output that an individual firm would supply at each possible price *ceteris paribus,* or all else equal. When we draw a firm's supply curve, we assume that input prices, including wage rates, are constant. Thus, an individual firm's supply curve shows what would happen to the firm's output if the price of its output changes with *no* corresponding increase in costs. Such an assumption for an individual firm is reasonable because an individual firm is small relative to the economy as a whole. (It is unlikely that one firm raising the price of its output will lead to significant increases in input prices in the economy.) If the price of a profit-maximizing firm's output rises with *no* increase in the costs of any inputs, the firm is likely to increase output.

But what would happen if there were an increase in the overall price level? It is unrealistic to believe that costs are constant for individual firms if the overall price level is increasing, for two reasons. First, the outputs of some firms are the inputs of other firms. Therefore, if output prices rise, there will be an increase in at least some input prices. Second, it is unrealistic to assume that wage rates (an important input cost) do not rise at all when the overall price level rises. Because all input prices (including wage rates) are not constant as the overall price level changes, individual firms' supply curves *shift* as the overall price level changes, so we cannot sum them to get an aggregate supply curve.

Another reason that the aggregate supply curve cannot be the sum of the supply curves of all the individual firms in the economy is that many firms (some would argue most firms) do not simply respond to prices determined in the market. Rather, they actually *set prices*. Only in perfectly competitive markets do firms simply react to prices determined by market forces. Firms in other kinds of industries (imperfectly competitive industries, to be exact) make both output *and* price decisions based on their perceptions of demand and costs. Price-setting firms do not have individual supply curves because these firms are choosing both output and price at the same time. To derive an individual supply curve, we need to imagine calling out a price to a firm and having the firm tell us how much output it will supply at that price. We cannot do this if firms are also setting prices. Thus, if supply curves do not exist for imperfectly competitive firms, we certainly cannot add them together to get an aggregate supply curve!

What, then, can we say about the relationship between aggregate output and the overall price level? Because input prices change when the overall price level changes and because many firms in the economy set prices as well as output, it is clear that an "aggregate supply curve" in the traditional sense of the word *supply* does not exist. What does exist is what one might call a "price/output response" curve—that is, a curve that traces out the price decisions and output decisions of all the markets and firms in the economy under a given set of circumstances.

What might such a curve look like?

AGGREGATE SUPPLY IN THE SHORT RUN

Many would argue that the aggregate supply curve (or the "price/output response" curve) has a positive slope, at least in the short run. (We will discuss the short-run/long-run distinction in more detail later in this chapter.) In addition, many would argue that at very low levels of aggregate output (for example, when the economy is in a recession), the aggregate supply curve is fairly flat, and at high levels of output (for example, when the economy is experiencing a boom), it is vertical or nearly vertical. Such a curve is shown in Figure 14.6.

To understand the logic behind the shape of the *AS* curve in Figure 14.6, consider the output and price response of markets and firms to a steady increase in aggregate demand brought about by an increasingly expansionary fiscal or monetary policy. The reaction of firms to such an expansion is likely to depend on two important factors: (1) how close the economy is to capacity at the time of the expansion, and (2) how rapidly input prices (such as wage rates) respond to increases in the overall price level.

■ **Capacity Constraints** In microeconomics, the term "short run" is used to describe the period of time in which firms' decisions are constrained by some *fixed factor of production*. For example, a farmer is constrained in the short run by the number of acres of land on his or her farm—the amount of land owned is the fixed factor of production. Manufacturing firms' short-run production decisions are constrained by the size of their physical production facilities. In the longer run, individual firms can overcome these types of constraints by investing in greater capacity—for example, by purchasing more acreage or building a new factory.

The idea of a fixed capacity in the short run also plays a role in macroeconomics. Macroeconomists tend to focus on the question of whether or not *individual firms* are producing at or close to full capacity. A firm is producing at full capacity if it is fully utilizing the capital and labor that it has on hand. As we

FIGURE 14.6

The Short-Run Aggregate Supply Curve

In the short run, the aggregate supply curve (the price/output response curve) has a positive slope. At low levels of aggregate output, the curve is fairly flat. As the economy approaches capacity, the curve becomes nearly vertical. At capacity, the curve is vertical.

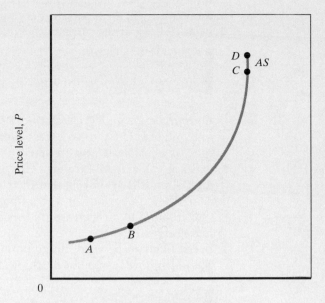

will discuss in detail in Chapter 17, firms may at times have *excess capital* and *excess labor* on hand—that is, capital and labor that are not needed to produce the current level of output. If, for example, there are costs of getting rid of capital once it is in place, a firm may choose to hold on to some of this capital, even if the economy is in a downturn and the firm has decreased its output. In this case, the firm will not be fully utilizing its capital stock. Firms may be especially likely to behave this way if they expect that the downturn will be short and that they will need the capital in the future to produce a higher level of output. Firms may have similar reasons for holding excess labor. It may be costly, both in worker morale and administrative costs, to lay off a large number of workers.

The Federal Reserve reports on the nation's "capacity utilization rate" monthly. In December of 1990, for example, during the recession of 1990–1991, the capacity utilization rate for manufacturing firms was 79.3 percent. This suggests that about 20% of the nation's factory capacity was idle. During the recessions of 1974–1975 and 1980–1982, capacity utilization fell below 75 percent. At the beginning of 1995, with real output growing at a healthy pace, U.S. capacity utilization stood at 85% for the first time since 1979.

Macroeconomists also focus on the question of whether or not the *economy as a whole* is operating at full capacity.

WHEN FIRMS ARE HOLDING EXCESS LABOR, THE ECONOMY MAY BE OPERATING BELOW CAPACITY. FIRMS WITH EXCESS LABOR CERTAINLY WILL NOT HIRE MORE LABOR IMMEDIATELY WHEN AN ECONOMIC DOWNTURN ENDS.

If there is cyclical unemployment (that is, unemployment above the frictional and structural amounts), the economy is not fully utilizing its labor force. There are people who want to work at the current wage rates who cannot find jobs. Therefore,

> Even if firms are not holding excess labor and capital, the economy may be operating below its capacity if there is cyclical unemployment.

Output Levels and Price/Output Responses At low levels of output in the economy, there is likely to be excess capacity both in individual firms and in the economy as a whole. Firms are likely to be producing at levels of output below their existing capacity constraints. That is, they are likely to be holding excess capital and labor. It is also likely that there will be cyclical unemployment in the economy as a whole in periods of low output. When this is the case, it is likely that firms will respond to an increase in demand by increasing output much more than they increase prices. Firms are below capacity, so the extra cost of producing more output is likely to be small. In addition, firms can get more labor (from the ranks of the unemployed) without much, if any, increase in wage rates. Thus,

> An increase in aggregate demand when the economy is operating at low levels of output is likely to result in an increase in output with little or no increase in the overall price level. That is, the aggregate supply (price/output response) curve is likely to be fairly flat at low levels of aggregate output.

Refer again to Figure 14.6. Aggregate output is considerably higher at point *B* than at point *A*, but the price level at point *B* is only slightly higher than it is at point *A*.

If aggregate output continues to expand, however, things will change. As firms and the economy as a whole begin to move closer and closer to capacity, firms' response to an increase in demand is likely to change from one of primarily increasing output to one of primarily increasing prices. Why? As firms continue to increase their output, they will begin to bump into their short-run capacity constraints. In addition, unemployment will be falling as firms hire more workers to produce the increased output, so the economy as a whole will be approaching its capacity. As aggregate output rises, the prices of labor and capital (that is, input costs) will begin to rise more rapidly, thus leading firms to increase their output prices.

At some level of output, it is virtually impossible for firms to expand any further. At this level, all sectors are fully utilizing their existing factories and equipment. Plants are running double shifts, and many workers are on overtime. In addition, there is little or no cyclical unemployment in the economy. At this point, firms will respond to any further increases in demand only by raising prices. In other words:

> When the economy is producing at its maximum level of output—that is, at capacity—the aggregate supply curve becomes vertical.

Look again at Figure 14.6. Between points *C* and *D*, the *AS* curve is vertical. Moving from point *C* to point *D* results in no increase in aggregate output but a large increase in the price level.

■ **The Response of Input Prices to Changes in the Overall Price Level** Whether or not the economy is producing a level of output close to capacity, there must be some time lag between changes in input prices and changes in output prices for the aggregate supply (price/output response) curve to slope upward. If input prices changed at exactly the same rate as output prices, the *AS* curve would be vertical.

It is easy to see why this is so. It is generally assumed that firms make decisions with the objective of maximizing profits. If all output and input prices increase 10%, no firm would find it advantageous to change its level of output. Why? Because the output level that maximized profits before the 10% increase will be the same as the level that maximizes profits after the 10% increase.[2] Thus, if input prices adjusted immediately to output prices, the aggregate supply (price/output response) curve would be vertical.

Wage rates may increase at exactly the same rate as the overall price level if the price-level increase is *fully anticipated*. For example, if inflation were expected to be 5% this year, this expected increase might be built into wage and salary contracts. Most employees, however, do not receive automatic pay raises as the overall price level increases, and sometimes increases in the price level are unanticipated. In fact, input prices—particularly wage rates—tend to lag behind increases in output prices for a variety of reasons. (We discuss these in the next chapter.) At least in the short run, wage rates tend to be slow to adjust to overall macroeconomic changes. It is precisely this point that has led to an important distinction between the *AS* curve in the long run and the *AS* curve in the short run.[3] We will return to this distinction shortly, but for now we will assume that the *AS* curve is shaped like the one in Figure 14.6.

SHIFTS OF THE SHORT-RUN AGGREGATE SUPPLY CURVE

Just as the aggregate demand curve can shift, so too can the aggregate supply (price/output response) curve. Recall the individual firm behavior that we have just considered in describing the shape of the short-run *AS* curve. Firms with the power to set prices choose the price/output combinations that maximize their profits. Firms in perfectly competitive industries choose the quantities of output to supply at given price levels. The *AS* curve traces out these price/output responses to economic conditions.

Anything that affects these individual firm decisions can shift the *AS* curve. Some of these factors include cost shocks, economic growth, stagnation, public policy, and natural disasters.

■ **Cost Shocks** Firms' decisions are heavily influenced by costs. Some costs change at the same time that the overall price level changes, some costs lag behind changes in the price level, and some may not change at all. Changes in costs that occur at the same time that the price level changes are built into the shape of the short-run *AS* curve. For example, when the price level rises, wage rates might rise by half as much in the short run. (This could happen if half of all wage contracts in the economy had cost-of-living increase clauses and half did not.) The shape of the short-run *AS* curve would reflect this response.

---

[2]*All prices going up by the same percentage is analogous to changing the monetary unit of account from, say, green dollars to red dollars, where 1.1 red dollars equals one green dollar. A change in the monetary unit of account has no effect on the firms' profit-maximizing decisions. If the nominal value of all output and input prices increases by 10%, then nothing real happens. When all nominal values go up by 10%, firms' decisions regarding real output will not change.*

[3]*Some textbooks derive the short-run aggregate supply curve by assuming that all input prices are fixed. "Fixed input prices" means that input prices do not change as the overall price level changes. This assumption is obviously not realistic because the outputs of some firms (such as intermediate goods and capital goods) are the inputs of other firms. It is also unrealistic to assume that wage rates do not respond at all to changes in the overall price level. It is more realistic to assume that wage rates do not fully respond in the short run than it is to assume no response at all.*

But sometimes cost changes occur that are *not* the result of changes in the overall price level. Perhaps the best recent example is the cost of energy. During the fall of 1990, world crude oil prices doubled from about $20 to $40 a barrel. Once it became clear that the Persian Gulf War would not lead to the destruction of the Saudi Arabian oil fields, the price of crude oil on world markets fell back to below $20 per barrel. In contrast, in 1973–1974 and again in 1979, the price of oil increased substantially and remained at a higher level. Oil is an important input in many firms and industries, and when the price of firms' inputs rises, firms respond by raising prices and lowering output. At the aggregate level, this means that an increase in the price of oil (or a similar cost increase) *shifts* the AS curve to the left, as shown in Figure 14.7a. A leftward shift of the AS curve means a higher price level for a given level of output. Conversely, a decrease in costs shifts the AS curve to the right, as shown in Figure 14.7b. A rightward shift of the AS curve means a lower price level for a given level of output. Shifts in the AS curve brought about by a change in costs are referred to as **cost shocks** or **supply shocks**.

cost shock, or **supply shock** *A change in costs that shifts the aggregate supply* (AS) *curve.*

■ **Economic Growth**   Economic growth shifts the AS curve to the right. Recall that the vertical part of the short-run AS curve represents the economy's maximum (capacity) output. This maximum output is determined by the economy's existing resources and the current state of technology. If the supply of labor increases or the stock of capital grows, the AS curve will shift to the right. The

FIGURE 14.7
Shifts of the Aggregate Supply Curve

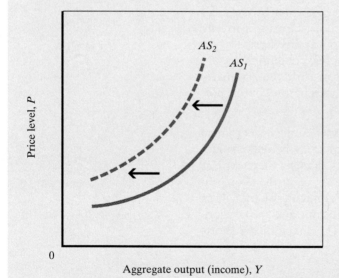

a. A decrease in aggregate supply

A leftward shift of the AS curve from AS_1 to AS_2 could be caused by an increase in costs (for example, an increase in wage rates or energy prices), natural disasters, economic stagnation, and the like.

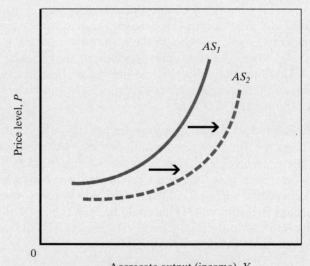

b. An increase in aggregate supply

A rightward shift of the AS curve from AS_1 to AS_2 could be caused by a decrease in costs, economic growth, public policy that stimulates supply, and the like.

labor force grows naturally with the population, but it can also increase for other reasons. Since the 1960s, for example, the percentage of women in the labor force has grown sharply. This increase in the supply of women workers has shifted the *AS* curve to the right.

Immigration can also shift the *AS* curve. During the 1970s, Germany, faced with a serious labor shortage, opened its borders to large numbers of "guest workers," largely from Turkey. The United States has recently experienced significant immigration, legal and illegal, from Mexico, other Central and South American countries, and Asia. Increases in the stock of capital over time and technological advances can also shift the *AS* curve to the right. We will discuss economic growth in more detail in Chapter 20.

■ **Stagnation and Lack of Investment** The opposite of economic growth is stagnation and decline. Over time, capital deteriorates and eventually wears out completely if it is not properly maintained. If an economy fails to invest in both public capital (sometimes called *infrastructure*) and private capital (plant and equipment) at a sufficient rate, the stock of capital will decline. If the stock of capital declines, the *AS* curve will shift to the left.

■ **Public Policy** Public policy can also be used to shift the *AS* curve. In the 1980s, for example, the Reagan administration put into effect a form of public policy based on supply-side economics. The idea behind these supply-side policies was to deregulate the economy and reduce taxes to increase the incentives to work, engage in entrepreneurial activity, and invest. The main purpose of these policies was to shift the *AS* curve to the right. (We discuss supply-side economics in Chapter 19.)

■ **Weather, Wars, and Natural Disasters** Changes in weather can also shift the *AS* curve. A severe drought, for example, will reduce the supply of agricultural goods, while the perfect mix of sun and rain will produce a bountiful harvest. If an economy is damaged by war or natural disaster, the *AS* curve will shift to the left. Whenever part of the resource base of an economy is reduced or destroyed, the *AS* curve shifts to the left.

Figure 14.8 summarizes some of the factors that might cause the *AS* curve to shift.

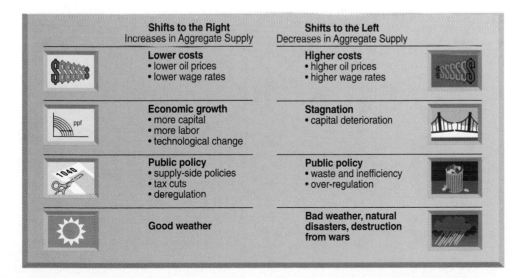

Shifts to the Right Increases in Aggregate Supply	Shifts to the Left Decreases in Aggregate Supply
Lower costs • lower oil prices • lower wage rates	**Higher costs** • higher oil prices • higher wage rates
Economic growth • more capital • more labor • technological change	**Stagnation** • capital deterioration
Public policy • supply-side policies • tax cuts • deregulation	**Public policy** • waste and inefficiency • over-regulation
Good weather	**Bad weather, natural disasters, destruction from wars**

FIGURE 14.8

Factors That Shift the Aggregate Supply Curve

THE EQUILIBRIUM PRICE LEVEL

equilibrium price level *The point at which the aggregate demand and aggregate supply curves intersect.*

The **equilibrium price level** in the economy occurs at the point at which the *AD* curve and the *AS* curve intersect. This equilibrium is shown in Figure 14.9, where the equilibrium price level is P_0 and the equilibrium level of aggregate output (income) is Y_0.

Although Figure 14.9 looks simple, it is a powerful device for analyzing a number of important macroeconomic questions. Consider first what is true at the intersection of the *AS* and *AD* curves. Each point on the *AD* curve corresponds to equilibrium in both the goods market and the money market. Each point on the *AS* curve represents the price/output responses of all the firms in the economy. Thus, we can conclude that:

> The point at which the *AS* and *AD* curves intersect corresponds to equilibrium in the goods and money markets and to a set of price/output decisions on the part of all the firms in the economy.

We will use this *AS/AD* framework to analyze the effects of monetary and fiscal policy on the economy and to analyze the various causes of inflation. Before turning to these topics, however, we need to return to the *AS* curve and discuss its shape in the long run.

THE LONG-RUN AGGREGATE SUPPLY CURVE

As we noted earlier, for the *AS* curve not to be vertical, some costs must lag behind increases in the overall price level. If all prices (that is, both input and output prices) change at the same rate, the level of aggregate output does not change. We have assumed that in the short run at least some cost changes lag behind price level changes. But what happens in the long run?

Many economists believe that costs lag behind price-level changes in the short run but ultimately move with the overall price level. For example, wage rates tend to move very closely with the price level *over time*. If the price level increases at a steady rate, inflation may come to be fully anticipated and built into most labor contracts.

FIGURE 14.9

The Equilibrium Price Level

At each point along the *AD* curve, both the money market and the goods market are in equilibrium. Each point on the *AS* curve represents the price/output decisions of all the firms in the economy. P_0 and Y_0 correspond to equilibrium in the goods market and the money market and to a set of price/output decisions on the part of all the firms in the economy.

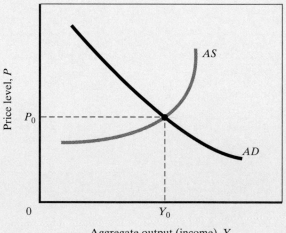

If costs and the price level move in tandem in the long run, the AS curve is vertical. To see why this is so, look carefully at Figure 14.10. Initially, the economy is in equilibrium at a price level of P_0 and aggregate output of Y_0 (the point at which AD_0 and AS_0 intersect). Now imagine a shift of the AD curve from AD_0 to AD_1. In response to this shift, both the price level and aggregate output rise in the short run, to P_1 and Y_1 respectively. But recall that the movement along the upward-sloping AS curve as Y increases from Y_0 to Y_1 assumes that some costs lag behind the increase in the overall price level.

Now suppose that costs fully adjust to prices in the long run. For example, suppose that labor unions renegotiate wage contracts to catch up with the increase in prices. These kinds of cost increases, which come in later periods, cause the AS curve to shift to the left, from AS_0 to AS_1. If, in the final analysis, costs and prices have risen by exactly the same percentage, aggregate output will be back at Y_0 (the point at which AD_1 and AS_1 intersect). Thus,

> If wage rates and other costs fully adjust to changes in prices in the long run, then the long-run AS curve is vertical.

POTENTIAL GDP

Recall that even the short-run AS curve becomes vertical at some particular level of output. The vertical portion of the short-run AS curve exists because there are physical limits to the amount that an economy can produce in any given time period. At the physical limit, all plants are operating around the clock, many workers are on overtime, and there is no cyclical unemployment.

Note that the vertical portions of the short-run AS curves in Figure 14.10 are to the right of Y_0. If the vertical portions of the short-run AS curves represent "capacity," then what is the nature of Y_0, the level of output corresponding to the long-run AS curve?

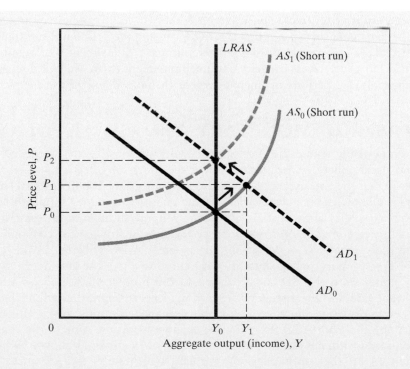

FIGURE 14.10

The Long-Run Aggregate Supply Curve

When the AD curve shifts from AD_0 to AD_1, the equilibrium price level initially rises from P_0 to P_1 and output rises from Y_0 to Y_1. Costs respond in the longer run, shifting the AS curve from AS_0 to AS_1. If costs ultimately increase by the same percentage as the price level, the quantity supplied will end up back at Y_0. Y_0 is sometimes called "potential GDP."

Y_0 represents the level of aggregate output that can be *sustained* in the long run without inflation. It is sometimes called **potential output** or **potential GDP.** Output can be pushed above Y_0 under a variety of circumstances, but when it is, there is upward pressure on costs. As the economy approaches short-run capacity, wage rates tend to rise as firms try to attract more people into the labor force and to induce more workers to work overtime. Rising costs shift the short-run *AS* curve to the left (in Figure 14.10, from AS_0 to AS_1) and drive output back to Y_0. The Application box titled "Was the United States at Potential GDP in 1994–1995?" discusses the Fed's recent attempts to prevent the U.S. economy from exceeding potential GDP.

The underlying idea here is simple. It is possible to try to squeeze too much from an existing resource base. Labor can be overemployed. In recent years, some states experienced unemployment rates below 3 percent. When the unemployment rate is this low, there is an upward pressure on wages that ultimately constrains growth.

■ **Short-Run Equilibrium below Potential GDP**   Thus far we have argued that if the short-run aggregate supply and aggregate demand curves intersect to the right of Y_0 in Figure 14.10, wages and other input prices will rise, causing the short-run *AS* curve to shift left and pushing GDP back down to Y_0. Although different economists have different opinions on how to determine whether an economy is operating at or above potential GDP, there is general agreement that there is a maximum level of output (below the vertical portion of the short-run aggregate supply curve) that can be sustained without inflation.

But what about short-run equilibria that ocur to the *left* of Y_0? If the short-run aggregate supply and aggregate demand curves intersect at a level of output below potential GDP, what will happen? Here again economists disagree. Those who believe that the aggregate supply curve is vertical in the long run believe that when short-run equilibria exist below Y_0, GDP will tend to rise—just as GDP tends to fall when short-run equilibrium exists above Y_0. The argument is that when the economy is operating below full employment with excess capacity and high unemployment, input prices (including wages) are likely to *fall*. A decline in input prices shifts the aggregate supply curve to the *right,* causing the price level to fall and the level of real GDP to rise back to Y_0. This automatic adjustment works only if input prices fall when excess capacity and unemployment exist. We will discuss wage adjustment during periods of unemployment in more detail in the next chapter.

AD, AS, AND MONETARY AND FISCAL POLICY

We are now ready to use the *AS/AD* framework to consider the effects of monetary and fiscal policy. We will first consider the short-run effects.

Recall that the two fiscal policy variables are government purchases (G) and net taxes (T). The monetary policy variable is the quantity of money supplied (M^s). An *expansionary* policy aims at stimulating the economy through an increase in G or M^s or a decrease in T. A *contractionary* policy aims at slowing the economy down through a decrease in G or M^s or an increase in T. We saw earlier in this chapter that an expansionary policy shifts the *AD* curve to the right and that a contractionary policy shifts the *AD* curve to the left. But how do these policies affect the equilibrium values of the price level (P) and the level of aggregate output (income)?

When considering the effects of a policy change, we must be careful to note where along the (short-run) *AS* curve the economy is at the time of the change. If the economy is initially on the flat portion of the *AS* curve, as shown by point A in Figure 14.11, then an expansionary policy, which shifts the *AD* curve to the right, results in a small price increase relative to the output increase: The increase in equilibrium Y (from Y_0 to Y_1) is much greater than the increase in equilibrium

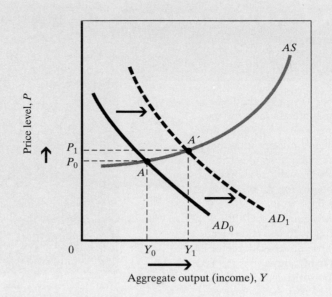

FIGURE 14.11

A Shift of the Aggregate Demand Curve When the Economy Is on the Nearly Flat Part of the AS Curve

Aggregate demand can shift to the right for a number of reasons, including an increase in the money supply, a tax cut, or an increase in government spending. If the shift occurs when the economy is on the nearly flat portion of the AS curve, the result will be an increase in output with little increase in the price level.

P (from P_0 to P_1). This is the case in which an expansionary policy works well. There is an increase in output with little increase in the price level.

However, if the economy is initially on the steep portion of the AS curve, as shown by point B in Figure 14.12, then an expansionary policy results in a small increase in equilibrium output (from Y_0 to Y_1) and a large increase in the equilibrium price level (from P_0 to P_1). In this case, an expansionary policy does not work well. It results in a much higher price level with little increase in output. The multiplier is therefore close to zero: Output is initially close to capacity, and attempts to increase it further lead mostly to a higher price level.

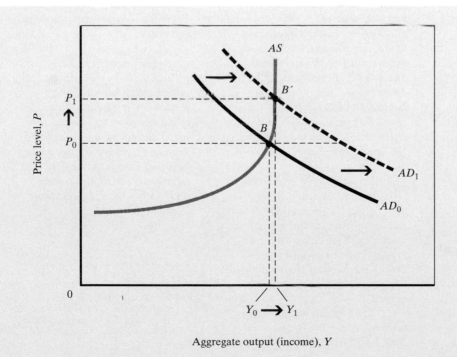

FIGURE 14.12

A Shift of the Aggregate Demand Curve When the Economy Is Operating at or Near Maximum Capacity

If a shift of aggregate demand occurs while the economy is operating near full capacity, the result will be an increase in the price level with little increase in output.

APPLICATION

WAS THE UNITED STATES AT POTENTIAL GDP IN 1994–1995?

On November 16, 1994, the Federal Reserve raised interest rates for the sixth time that year. Its goal: to slow the economy and prevent inflation. Open market operations to restrain money supply growth caused the short-term borrowing rate to jump from 3% at the beginning of 1994 to 5.5% by the beginning of 1995.

Interestingly, these actions were taken with little direct evidence of inflation, and many argue that the Fed was being too cautious. In response, the Fed argued that the country was beginning to creep above potential GDP. As evidence it cited historical levels of capacity utilization and unemployment immediately prior to past periods of inflation. Here are some excerpts from the debate as reported in *The New York Times:*

ALAN GREENSPAN, CHAIRMAN OF THE FEDERAL RESERVE, STRIKES A PENSIVE POSE. MANY BELIEVE THE CHAIR OF THE FED IS THE SECOND MOST POWERFUL PERSON IN THE UNITED STATES.

WASHINGTON, Nov. 15—Determined to prevent strong economic growth from feeding inflation, the Federal Reserve raised short-term interest rates today by the largest amount since 1981 and left open the possibility of further increases. Banks followed by raising the rates they charge for loans.

. . .

The decision by the Federal Reserve came five hours after it reported that American factories operated at 84.9 percent of capacity in October, the highest level in nearly 15 years. When factories work at top speed, production bottlenecks often occur and can lead to inflation as companies bid up the prices of scarce materials and skilled workers.

"These measures were taken against the background of evidence of persistent strength in economic activity

and high and rising levels of resource utilization," the Federal Reserve said in a statement.

The Federal Reserve's decision to increase interest rates by the largest amount in years intensified a debate that focuses not so much on the amount of the rise but whether the Federal Reserve should have acted at all.

On one side are those who applauded the Federal Reserve's action, most of them on Wall Street. They are challenged by an unlikely coalition of manufacturers and labor leaders who charged that yesterday's increase would slow the economy too much, cutting back sales and eliminating jobs.

. . .

[For] Jerry Jasinowski, president of the National Association of Manufacturers, yesterday's Fed move may prove to be the straw that breaks the back of the economy. And unnecessarily so, he argued.

"The Fed is fundamentally misreading the American economy," Mr. Jasinowski said.

"They ought to get out from behind their desks and see what is really happening in plants and on factory floors across the country."

. . .

"There is no evidence of capacity pressures," said Mr. Jasinowski of the manufacturers association. "The Federal Reserve's measurements are too restrictive."

. . .

Alan Greenspan, the Federal Reserve's chairman, has said that the central bank should err, if at all, on the side of raising rates too much. It is easier to reverse an unexpected drop in economic output by lowering interest rates than it is to stop an inflationary spiral with higher rates, he testified last summer.

Sources: Keith Bradsher, "Federal Reserve Increases Interest Rates by 3/4 Point," *The New York Times,* November 16, 1994, p. A1; Louis Uchitelle, "A Debate Arises on the Need to Take Any Action on Rates," *The New York Times,* November 16, 1994, p. A1.

Figures 14.11 and 14.12 show clearly that it is important to know where the economy is *before* a policy change is put into effect. The economy is producing on the nearly flat part of the *AS* curve if most firms are producing well below capacity. When this is the case, firms will respond to an increase in demand by increasing output much more than they increase prices. The opposite is true if the economy is producing on the steep part of the *AS* curve. In this case, firms are close to capacity, and they will respond to an increase in demand by increasing prices much more than they increase output.

To see what happens when the economy is on the steep part of the *AS* curve, consider the effects of an increase in *G* with no change in the money supply. Why, since *G* is increased, will there be virtually no increase in *Y*? In other words, why will the expansionary fiscal policy fail to stimulate the economy? To answer this question, we need to go back to the analysis we did in Chapter 13 and consider what is behind the *AD* curve.

The first thing that happens when *G* increases is an unanticipated decline in firms' inventories. However, because firms are very close to capacity output when the economy is on the steep part of the *AS* curve, they cannot increase their output very much. The result, as Figure 14.12 shows, is a substantial increase in the price level. The increase in the price level increases the demand for money, which (with a fixed money supply) leads to an increase in the interest rate and thus a decrease in planned investment. *There is nearly complete crowding out of investment.* If firms are producing at capacity, prices and interest rates will continue to rise until the increase in *G* is completely matched by a decrease in planned investment and there is complete crowding out.

LONG-RUN AGGREGATE SUPPLY AND POLICY EFFECTS

We have so far been considering monetary and fiscal policy effects in the short run. Regarding the long run, it is important to note that:

> If the *AS* curve is vertical in the long run, neither monetary policy nor fiscal policy has any effect on aggregate output in the long run.

Look back at Figure 14.10. Monetary and fiscal policy shift the *AD* curve. If the long-run *AS* curve is vertical, output always comes back to Y_0. In this case, policy affects *only* the price level in the long run, and the multiplier effect of a change in government spending on aggregate output in the long run is zero. Under the same circumstances, the tax multiplier is also zero.

The conclusion that policy has no effect on aggregate output in the long run is perhaps startling. Do most economists agree that the aggregate supply curve is vertical in the long run?

Most economists do agree that input prices tend to lag behind output prices in the short run, thus giving the *AS* curve some positive slope. Most also agree that the *AS* curve is likely to be steeper in the long run. The pressing question is: How long is the long run? The longer the lag time, the greater the potential impact of monetary and fiscal policy on aggregate output. If the long run is only three to six months, policy has little chance to affect output, but if the long run is three or four years, policy can have significant effects. It should not be surprising that a good deal of research in macroeconomics focuses on the length of time lags between input and output prices. In a sense, the length of the long run is one of the most important open questions in macroeconomics.

Another source of disagreement centers on whether equilibria below potential GDP, Y_0 in Figure 14.10, are self-correcting. Recall that those who believe in a vertical long-run *AS* curve believe that slack in the economy will put downward pressure on input prices (including wages), causing the short-run *AS* curve to shift to the right and pushing GDP back toward Y_0. However, some argue that wages and other input prices do *not* fall during slack periods and that the economy can get "stuck" at an equilibrium below potential GDP. In this case, monetary and fiscal policy would be necessary to restore full employment. We will return to this debate in the next chapter.

The "new classical" economics, which we discuss at length in Chapter 19, assumes that prices and wages are fully flexible and adjust very quickly to changing conditions. New classical economists believe, for example, that wage rate changes do not lag behind price changes. The new classical view is thus consistent with the existence of a vertical AS curve, even in the short run. At the other end of the spectrum is what is sometimes called the simple "Keynesian" view of aggregate supply. Those who hold this view believe that there is a kink in the AS curve at capacity output, as we discuss in the Issues and Controversies box titled "The Simple 'Keynesian' Aggregate Supply Curve."

CAUSES OF INFLATION

We now turn to the question of inflation and use the AS/AD framework to consider the various causes of inflation.

inflation *An increase in the overall price level.*

sustained inflation *Occurs when the overall price level continues to rise over some fairly long period of time.*

■ **Inflation Versus Sustained Inflation: A Reminder**   Before we discuss the specific causes of inflation, it is important to recall the distinction we made in Chapter 8. **Inflation,** as you know, is an increase in the overall price level. Thus, anything that shifts the AD curve to the right or the AS curve to the left causes inflation. But it is often useful to distinguish between a *one-time increase* in the price level (that is, a one-time inflation) and an inflation that is sustained. A **sustained inflation** occurs when the overall price level continues to rise over some fairly long period of time. When we speak of an inflation rate of 7%, for example, we generally mean that the price level has been rising at a rate of 7% per year over a number of years.

It is generally accepted that there are many possible causes of a one-time increase in the price level. (We discuss the main causes below.) But for the price level to continue to increase period after period, most economists believe that it must be "accommodated" by an expanded money supply. This leads to the assertion that a sustained inflation, whatever the initial cause of the increase in the price level, is essentially a monetary phenomenon.

DEMAND-PULL INFLATION

demand-pull inflation *Inflation that is initiated by an increase in aggregate demand.*

Inflation that is initiated by an increase in aggregate demand is called **demand-pull inflation.** You can see how demand-pull inflation works by looking back at Figures 14.11 and 14.12. In both figures, the inflation begins with a shift of the aggregate demand schedule from AD_0 to AD_1, which causes the price level to increase from P_0 to P_1. (Output also increases, from Y_0 to Y_1.) If the economy is operating on the steep portion of the AS curve at the time of the increase in aggregate demand, as it is in Figure 14.12, most of the effect will be an increase in the price level rather than an increase in output. If the economy is operating on the flat portion of the AS curve, as it is in Figure 14.11, most of the effect will be an increase in output rather than an increase in the price level.

Remember that in the long run the initial increase in the price level will cause the AS curve to shift to the left as input prices (costs) respond to the increase in output prices. If the long-run AS curve is vertical, as depicted in Figure 14.10, the increase in costs will shift the short-run AS curve (AS_0) to the left to AS_1, pushing the price level even higher, to P_2. Thus, if the long-run AS curve is vertical, a shift in aggregate demand from AD_0 to AD_1 will result, in the long run, in *no* increase in output and a price-level increase from P_0 to P_2.

As noted in the text, there is a great deal of disagreement regarding the shape of the *AS* curve. One view of the aggregate supply curve, often called the simple "Keynesian" view, holds that at any given moment, the economy has a clearly defined capacity, or maximum, output. This maximum output, denoted by the term Y_F is defined by the existing labor force, the current capital stock, and the existing state of technology. If planned aggregate expenditure increases when the economy is producing *below* this maximum capacity, this view holds, inventories will be lower than planned and firms will increase output, but the price level will not change. Firms are operating with underutilized plants (excess capacity) and there is unemployment. Thus, expansion does not exert any upward pressure on prices. However, if planned aggregate expenditure increases when the economy is producing near or at its maximum (Y_F), inventories will be lower than planned, but firms cannot increase their output. The result will be an increase in the price level, or inflation.

This view is illustrated in Figure 1. In the top half of the diagram, aggregate output (income) (Y) and planned aggregate expenditure ($C + I + G \equiv AE$) are initially in equilibrium at AE_1, Y_1, and price level P_1. Now suppose that a tax cut or an increase in government spending increases planned aggregate expenditure. If such an increase shifts the *AE* curve from AE_1 to AE_2 and the corresponding aggregate demand curve from AD_1 to AD_2, the equilibrium level of output will rise from Y_1 to Y_F. (Remember that an expansionary policy shifts the *AD* curve to the right.) Since we were initially producing be-

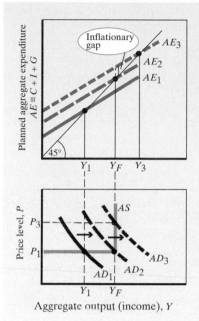

low capacity output (Y_1 is lower than Y_F), the price level will be unaffected, remaining at P_1.

But now consider what would happen if *AE* were to increase even further. For example, suppose that planned aggregate expenditure were to shift from AE_2 to AE_3, with a corresponding shift of AD_2 to AD_3. If the economy were producing below capacity output, the equilibrium level of output would rise to Y_3. But the output of the economy cannot exceed the maximum output of Y_F. Thus, as inventories fall below what was planned, firms encounter a fully employed labor market and fully utilized plants. Therefore, they cannot increase their output. The result is that the aggregate supply curve becomes vertical at Y_F, and the price level is driven up to P_3.

FIGURE 1

With planned aggregate expenditure of AE_1 and aggregate demand of AD_1, equilibrium output is Y_1. A shift of planned aggregate expenditure to AE_2, corresponding to a shift of the *AD* curve to AD_2, causes output to rise but the price level to remain at P_1. If planned aggregate expenditure and aggregate demand exceed YF, however, there is an inflationary gap and the price level rises to P_3.

The difference between planned aggregate expenditure and aggregate output at full capacity is sometimes referred to as an **inflationary gap.** You can see the inflationary gap in the top half of Figure 1. At Y_F (capacity output), planned aggregate expenditure (shown by AE_3) is greater than Y_F. Thus, the price level rises to P_3 until the aggregate quantity supplied and the aggregate quantity demanded are equal.

Despite the fact that the kinked aggregate supply curve provides some insights, most economists find it unrealistic. It does not seem likely that the whole economy suddenly runs into a capacity "wall" at a specific level of output. As output expands, some firms and industries will hit capacity before others.

COST-PUSH, OR SUPPLY-SIDE, INFLATION

cost-push, or **supply-side, inflation** *Inflation caused by an increase in costs.*

Inflation can also be caused by an increase in costs. Such inflation is referred to as **cost-push,** or **supply-side, inflation.** As we noted above, several times in the last two decades oil prices on world markets increased sharply. Because oil is used in virtually every line of business, costs increased.

An increase in costs (a cost shock) shifts the AS curve to the left, as Figure 14.13 shows. If we assume that the government does not react to this shift in AS by changing fiscal or monetary policy, the AD curve will not shift. The supply shift will cause the equilibrium price level to rise (from P_0 to P_1) and the level of aggregate output to decline (from Y_0 to Y_1). Recall from Chapter 6 that **stagflation** occurs when output is falling at the same time that prices are rising—in other words, when the economy is experiencing both a contraction and inflation simultaneously. Figure 14.13 thus shows that one possible cause of stagflation is an increase in costs.

stagflation *Occurs when output is falling at the same time that prices are rising.*

To return to monetary and fiscal policy for a moment, note from Figure 14.13 that the government could counteract the increase in costs (the cost shock) by engaging in an expansionary policy (an increase in G or M^s or a decrease in T). This would shift the AD curve to the right, and the new AD curve would intersect the new AS curve at a higher level of output. The problem with this policy, however, is that the intersection of the new AS and AD curves would take place at a price even higher than P_1 in Figure 14.13.

In sum:

> Cost shocks are bad news for policy makers. The only way they can counter the output loss brought about by a cost shock is by having the price level increase even more than it would without the policy action.

This situation is illustrated in Figure 14.14.

FIGURE 14.13

Cost-Push, or Supply-Side, Inflation

An increase in costs shifts the AS curve to the left. Assuming the government does not react to this shift the AD curve does not shift, the price level rises and output falls.

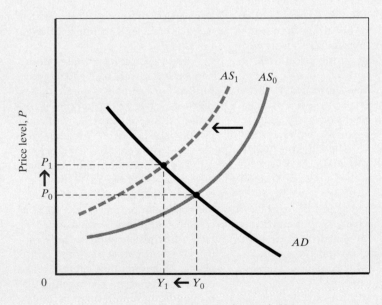

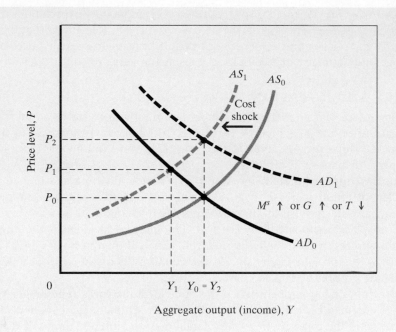

FIGURE 14.14

Cost Shocks Are Bad News for Policy Makers

A cost shock with no change in monetary or fiscal policy would shift the aggregate supply curve from AS_0 to AS_1, lower output from Y_0 to Y_1, and raise the price level from P_0 to P_1. Monetary or fiscal policy could be changed enough to have the AD curve shift from AD_0 to AD_1. This would prevent output from falling, but it would raise the price level further, to P_2.

EXPECTATIONS AND INFLATION

When firms are making their price/output decisions, their *expectations* of future prices may affect their current decisions. If a firm expects that its competitors will raise their prices, it may raise its own price in anticipation of this.

Take, for example, a firm that manufactures toasters. The toaster maker must decide what price to charge retail stores for its toaster. If it overestimates price and charges much more than other toaster manufacturers are charging, it will lose many customers. Conversely, if it underestimates price and charges much less than other toaster makers are charging, it will gain customers but at a considerable loss in revenue per sale. The firm's *optimum price*—that is, the price that maximizes the firm's profits—is presumably not too far from the average of its competitors' prices. If it does not know its competitors' projected prices before it sets its own price, as is often the case, it must base its price on what it expects its competitors' prices to be.

Suppose that inflation has been running at a rate of about 10% per year. Our firm probably expects that its competitors will raise their prices about 10% this year, so it is likely to raise the price of its own toaster by about 10 percent. This is how expectations can get "built into the system." If every firm expects every other firm to raise prices by 10%, every firm will raise prices by about 10 percent. Thus, every firm ends up with the price increase it expected.

The story is the same for the pricing of an economics textbook. Every publisher finds the optimal price for its textbook close to the price that other publishers are charging for their economics textbooks. A publisher thus bases its price on what its competitors are doing now and what it expects them to do in the future. At the same time, the publisher's competitors base *their* prices on what their rivals are doing now and what they expect them to do in the future.

The fact that expectations can affect the price level is vexing. Expectations can lead to an inertia that makes it difficult to stop an inflationary spiral. If prices have been rising, and if people's expectations are *adaptive*—that is, if they form their expectations on the basis of past pricing behavior—then firms may continue raising prices even if demand is slowing or contracting.

In terms of the *AS/AD* diagram, an increase in inflationary expectations that causes firms to increase their prices shifts the *AS* curve to the left. Remember that the *AS* curve represents the price/output responses of firms. If firms increase their prices because of a change in inflationary expectations, the result is a leftward shift of the *AS* curve.

MONEY AND INFLATION

It is easy to see that an increase in the money supply can lead to an increase in the aggregate price level. As Figures 14.11 and 14.12 show, an increase in the money supply (M^s) shifts the *AD* curve to the right and results in a higher price level. This is simply a demand-pull inflation.

But the supply of money may also play a role in creating a sustained inflation. Consider an initial increase in government spending (G) with the money supply (M^s) unchanged. Because the money supply is unchanged, this is an increase in G that is not "accommodated" by the Fed. The increase in G shifts the *AD* curve to the right and results in a higher price level. This is shown in Figure 14.15 as a shift from AD_0 to AD_1. (In Figure 14.15, the economy is assumed to be operating on the vertical portion of the *AS* curve.)

Remember what happens when the price level increases. The higher price level causes the demand for money to increase. With an unchanged money supply and an increase in the quantity of money demanded, the interest rate will rise, and the result will be a decrease in planned investment (I) spending. The new equilibrium corresponds to higher G, lower I, a higher interest rate, and a higher price level.

Now let's take our example one step further. Suppose that the Fed is sympathetic to the expansionary fiscal policy (the increase in G we just discussed) and decides to expand the supply of money to keep the interest rate constant. Thus, as the higher price level pushes up the demand for money, the Fed expands the supply of money with the goal of keeping the interest rate unchanged and thus eliminating the crowding-out effect of a higher interest rate.

FIGURE 14.15

Sustained Inflation from an Initial Increase in G and Fed Accommodation

An increase in G with the money supply constant shifts the *AD* curve from AD_0 to AD_1. Although not shown in the figure, this leads to an increase in the interest rate and crowding out of planned investment. If the Fed tries to keep the interest rate unchanged by increasing the money supply, the *AD* curve will shift farther and farther to the right. The result is a sustained inflation, perhaps a hyperinflation.

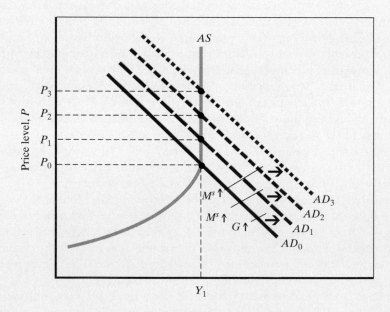

When the supply of money is expanded, the AD curve shifts to the right again, from AD_1 to AD_2. This shift of the AD curve, brought about by the increased money supply, pushes prices up even further. Higher prices in turn increase the demand for money further, which requires a further increase in the money supply, and so on.

What would happen if the Fed tried to keep the interest rate constant when the economy is operating on the steep part of the AS curve? The situation could lead to a **hyperinflation,** a period of very rapid increases in the price level. If no more output can be coaxed out of the economy and if planned investment is not allowed to fall (because the interest rate is kept unchanged), then it is not possible to increase G. As the Fed keeps pumping more and more money into the economy to keep the interest rate unchanged, the price level will keep rising.

hyperinflation *A period of very rapid increases in the price level.*

SUSTAINED INFLATION AS A PURELY MONETARY PHENOMENON

As we mentioned earlier, virtually all economists agree that an increase in the price level can be caused by anything that causes the AD curve to shift to the right or the AS curve to shift to the left. These include expansionary fiscal policy actions, monetary expansion, cost shocks, changes in expectations, and so forth. It is also generally agreed, however, that for a *sustained* inflation to occur, the Federal Reserve must accommodate it. In this sense, a sustained inflation can be thought of as a purely monetary phenomenon.

This argument, first put forth by monetarists (see Chapter 19), has gained wide acceptance. It is easy to show, as we just did, how expanding the money supply can continuously shift the AD curve. However, it is not as easy to come up with other reasons for continued shifts of the AD curve if the money supply is constant. One possibility is for the government to increase spending continuously without increasing taxes. But this process cannot continue forever. To finance spending without taxes, the government must borrow. Without any expansion of the money supply, the interest rate will rise dramatically, making the cost of borrowing very high. But more importantly, the public must be willing to buy the government bonds that are being issued to finance the spending increases. At some point, the public may be unwilling to buy any more bonds even though the interest rate is very high.[4] At this point, the government is no longer able to increase non-tax-financed spending without the Fed's cooperation. If this is true, then a sustained inflation cannot exist without the Fed's cooperation.

In recent years, the governments of several struggling eastern European and Latin American nations have expanded their money supplies significantly. The result has been very high inflation in those countries. For more details, see the Global Perspective box titled "Inflation and Monetary Growth in Eastern Europe and Latin America."

LOOKING AHEAD

Let us review where we have been and where we are going. In Chapters 9 and 10, we discussed the concept of an equilibrium level of aggregate output and income, the idea of the multiplier, and the basics of fiscal policy. Our discussion in those two chapters centered on the workings of the goods market alone.

In Chapters 11 and 12, we analyzed the money market by discussing the supply of money, the demand for money, the equilibrium interest rate, and the basics of monetary policy. Chapter 13 brought our analysis of the goods market together with our analysis of the money market.

---

[4]*This means that the public's demand for money no longer depends on the interest rate. Even though the interest rate is very high, the public cannot be induced to have its real money balances fall any further. In other words, there is a limit regarding how much the public can be induced to have its real money balances fall.*

In this chapter, we used everything learned up to this point to discuss the aggregate supply and aggregate demand curves, first mentioned in Chapter 6. Using aggregate supply and aggregate demand curves, we can determine the equilibrium price level in the economy and understand some of the causes of inflation.

There is still one piece missing to our story, however. We have said little about employment, unemployment, and the functioning of the labor market in the macroeconomy. The next chapter will link everything we have done so far to this third major market arena—the labor market—and to the problem of unemployment.

GLOBAL PERSPECTIVE

INFLATION AND MONETARY GROWTH IN EASTERN EUROPE AND LATIN AMERICA

AD and *AS* analysis shows clearly that a sustained high level of inflation is not possible without expansion of the money supply. When the price level rises, the demand for money schedule shifts to the right. If the money supply is held constant, the interest rate will rise. The rise in the interest rate decreases planned aggregate expenditure, which leads to a reduction in real output (*Y*). The only way to prevent the rise in the interest rate (and thus the decrease in real output) is to expand the money supply. However, if the economy is at potential output and if the money supply is expanded as the price level rises to accommodate the increased money demand, the price level will simply continue to rise.

In fragile growing economies, an expanding money supply is often the result of political pressures. Governments have bills to pay and commitments to meet, and they find it difficult to raise the money needed to balance the budget from taxes.

They end up running deficits and financing the shortfall with central bank purchases of bonds, which expands the money supply.

The following two excerpts from the *Economist* indicate that during the fall of 1994, this was exactly what was happening in Poland and Venezuela.

Despite progress, the Polish economy is only precariously stable and its transformation is incomplete. Inflation is still too high. The goal for this year is to get annual price increases below 24%, which is bad enough. But in June annualised inflation was over 30% and few believe it will come down much in the next few months. This is much higher than targeted and much higher than in Western Europe.[1]

* * *

Venezuela looks increasingly like Latin America's odd man out. In a report on September 16th the UN's Economic Commission for Latin America and the Caribbean said the region's economic growth this year would average 3%, inflation (excluding stratospheric Brazil) had fallen from 49% in 1991 to about 16% this year, and large inward capital flows were continuing.

By contrast, Venezuela's banking crisis . . . caused (many Venezuelans would say forced) the government to inject money—in the event $7 billion, about 91/2% of GDP—into a system that was about to collapse. These measures have led to inflation, now estimated at 65% for this year.[2]

Sources: [1]"Poland: Not There Yet," *The Economist*, September 3, 1994, p. 52.
[2]"Venezuela, Crisis Manager," *The Economist*, September 17, 1994, p. 42.

THE AGGREGATE DEMAND CURVE

1. Money demand is a function of three variables: (1) the interest rate (r); (2) the level of real income (Y); and (3) the price level (P). Money demand will increase if the real level of output (income) increases, the price level increases, or the interest rate declines.

2. At a higher price level, households and firms need to hold larger money balances than they did before. If the money supply remains the same, this increased demand for money will cause the interest rate to increase and planned investment spending to fall. As a result, planned aggregate expenditure will be lower, inventories will be greater than planned, firms will cut back on output, and Y will fall. Thus, an increase in the price level causes the level of aggregate output (income) to fall. Conversely, a decrease in the price level causes the level of aggregate output (income) to rise.

3. *Aggregate demand* is the total demand for goods and services in the economy. The *aggregate demand (AD) curve* illustrates the negative relationship between aggregate output (income) and the price level. Each point on the *AD* curve is a point at which both the goods market and the money market are in equilibrium. The *AD* curve is *not* the sum of all the market demand curves in the economy.

4. At every point along the aggregate demand curve, the aggregate quantity demanded in the economy is exactly equal to planned aggregate expenditure.

5. An increase in the quantity of money supplied, an increase in government purchases, or a decrease in net taxes at a given price level shifts the aggregate demand curve to the right. A decrease in the quantity of money supplied, a decrease in government purchases, or an increase in net taxes shifts the aggregate demand curve to the left.

THE AGGREGATE SUPPLY CURVE

6. *Aggregate supply* is the total supply of goods and services in an economy. The *aggregate supply (AS) curve* shows the relationship between the aggregate quantity of output supplied by all the firms in an economy and the overall price level. The *AS* curve is *not* a market supply curve, and it is *not* the simple sum of all the individual supply curves in the economy. For this reason, it is helpful to think of the *AS* curve as a "price/output response" curve—that is, a curve that traces out the price decisions and output decisions of all the markets and firms in the economy under a given set of circumstances.

7. The shape of the short-run *AS* curve is a source of much controversy in macroeconomics. Many economists believe that at very low levels of aggregate output the *AS* curve is fairly flat, and at high levels of aggregate output the *AS* curve is vertical or nearly vertical. Thus, the *AS* curve slopes upward and becomes vertical when the economy reaches its capacity, or maximum, output.

8. Anything that affects individual firms' decisions can shift the *AS* curve. Some of these factors include cost shocks, economic growth, stagnation, public policy, and natural disasters.

THE EQUILIBRIUM PRICE LEVEL

9. The *equilibrium price level* in the economy occurs at the point at which the *AS* and *AD* curves intersect. The intersection of the *AS* and *AD* curves corresponds to equilibrium in the goods and money markets *and* to a set of price/output decisions on the part of all the firms in the economy.

THE LONG-RUN AGGREGATE SUPPLY CURVE

10. For the *AS* curve to slope upward, some input prices must lag behind increases in the overall price level. If wage rates and other costs fully adjust to changes in prices in the long run, then the long-run *AS* curve is vertical.

11. The level of aggregate output that can be sustained in the long run without inflation is called *potential output* or *potential GDP*.

AD, AS, AND MONETARY AND FISCAL POLICY

12. If the economy is initially producing on the flat portion of the *AS* curve, an expansionary policy—which shifts the *AD* curve to the right—will result in a small increase in the equilibrium price level relative to the increase in equilibrium output. If the economy is initially producing on the steep portion of the *AS* curve, an expansionary policy results in a small increase in equilibrium output and a large increase in the equilibrium price level.

13. If the *AS* curve is vertical in the long run, neither

monetary nor fiscal policy has any effect on aggregate output in the long run. For this reason, the exact length of the long run is one of the most pressing questions in macroeconomics.

CAUSES OF INFLATION

14. *Inflation* is an increase in the overall price level. A *sustained inflation* occurs when the overall price level continues to rise over some fairly long period of time. Most economists believe that sustained inflations can occur only if the Fed continuously increases the money supply.

15. *Demand-pull inflation* is inflation initiated by an increase in aggregate demand. *Cost-push, or supply-side, inflation* is inflation initiated by an increase in costs. An increase in costs may also lead to *stagflation*—the situation in which the economy is experiencing both a contraction and inflation simultaneously.

16. Inflation can become "built into the system" as a result of expectations. If prices have been rising and people form their expectations on the basis of past pricing behavior, firms may continue raising prices even if demand is slowing or contracting.

17. When the price level increases, so too does the demand for money. If the economy is operating on the steep part of the *AS* curve and the Fed tries to keep the interest rate constant by increasing the supply of money, the result could be a hyperinflation—a period of very rapid increases in the price level.

REVIEW TERMS AND CONCEPTS

aggregate demand 313
aggregate demand (AD) curve 314
aggregate supply 319
aggregate supply (AS) curve 319
cost-push, or supply-side, inflation 334

cost shock, or supply shock 324
demand-pull inflation 332
equilibrium price level 326
hyperinflation 337
inflation 332
inflationary gap 333

potential output, or potential GDP 328
real wealth, or real balance, effect 317
stagflation 334
sustained inflation 332

PROBLEM SET

1. "The aggregate demand curve slopes downward, because when the price level is lower, people can afford to buy more, and aggregate demand rises. When prices rise, people can afford to buy less, and aggregate demand falls." Is this a good explanation of the shape of the *AD* curve? Why or why not?

2. Using aggregate supply and demand curves to illustrate your points, discuss the impacts of the following events on the price level and on equilibrium GDP (*Y*) in the *short run*:
   a. A tax cut holding government purchases constant with the economy operating at near full capacity.
   b. An increase in the money supply during a period of high unemployment and excess industrial capacity.
   c. An increase in the price of oil caused by a war in the Middle East, assuming that the Fed attempts to keep interest rates constant by accommodating inflation.
   d. The Clinton plan from early 1993: an increase in

taxes and a cut in government spending, supported by a cooperative Fed acting to keep output from falling.

3. During 1995, a debate raged over whether the United States was at or above potential GDP (see Application box in this chapter). At the same time that the Fed was raising interest rates to prevent inflation, Republicans who took control of Congress vowed to fight President Clinton over fiscal policy. Illustrate the following scenarios with aggregate supply and aggregate demand curves. What would happen to *Y, P,* and *r* in each case?
   a. The Fed is wrong. The United States was not above potential GDP and a needless recession is caused.
   b. The Fed is right; the economy was above potential GDP. The Fed succeeds in slowing the economy down just enough to hold GDP at its potential.
   c. The Congress passes a major tax cut without a

corresponding cut in spending at the same time that the Fed increases its resolve to prevent inflation.

4. Using aggregate supply and aggregate demand curves to illustrate, describe the effects of the following events on the price level and on equilibrium GDP in the *long run* assuming that input prices fully adjust to output prices after some lag:
   a. An increase in the money supply above potential GDP.
   b. A decrease in government spending and in the money supply with GDP above potential GDP.
   c. Starting with the economy at potential GDP, a war in the Middle East pushes up energy prices temporarily. The Fed expands the money supply to accommodate the inflation.

5. Two separate capacity constraints are discussed in this chapter: (1) the actual physical capacity of existing plants and equipment, shown as the vertical portion of the short-run *AS* curve, and (2) potential GDP, leading to a vertical *LRAS* curve. Explain the difference between the two. Which is greater, full-capacity GDP or potential GDP? Why?

6. In country A, all wage contracts are indexed to inflation. That is, each month wages are adjusted to reflect increases in the cost of living as reflected in changes in the price level. In country B, there are no cost-of-living adjustments to wages, but the work force is completely unionized. Unions negotiate three-year contracts. In which country is an expansionary monetary policy likely to have a larger effect on aggregate output? Explain your answer using aggregate supply and aggregate demand curves.

7. In an effort to fight inflation in 1974 and 1975, the U.S. government acted with contractionary monetary policy. Using aggregate supply and aggregate demand curves, illustrate the effects that the government expected this policy to have on aggregate output and on the price level.

The contractionary monetary policy had the effect of reducing aggregate output; the United States experienced a recession in 1975. But although output was reduced, prices continued to increase throughout the recession. Give two alternative explanations for why prices might continue to rise even though output is falling.

15

unemployment rate *The ratio of the number of people unemployed to the total number of people in the labor force.*

The Labor Market, Unemployment, and Inflation

In Chapter 6, we stressed that there are three broadly defined markets in which households, firms, the government, and the rest of the world interact: (1) the *goods market,* which we discussed in Chapters 9 and 10, (2) the *money market,* which we discussed in Chapters 11 and 12, and (3) the *labor market.* In Chapter 8 we described some of the features of the U.S. labor market and explained how the unemployment rate is measured. Then, in Chapter 14, we considered the labor market briefly in our discussion of the aggregate supply curve. Because labor is an input, the workings of the labor market affect the shape of the *AS* curve. If wages and other input costs lag behind price increases, the *AS* curve will be upward-sloping; if wages and other input costs are completely flexible and rise every time prices rise by the same percentage, the *AS* curve will be vertical.

In this chapter we take a closer look at the labor market's role in the macroeconomy. First, we consider the classical view, which holds that wages always adjust to clear the labor market. We then consider why the labor market may not always clear and why unemployment may sometimes exist. Finally, we discuss the relationship between inflation and unemployment.

■ **The Labor Market: Basic Concepts** Before beginning, it is useful to review briefly what the unemployment rate measures. Recall that the **unemployment rate** is the number of people unemployed as a percentage of the labor force. To be unemployed, a person must be out of a job and actively

342

looking for work. When a person stops looking for work, he or she is considered *out of the labor force* and is no longer counted as unemployed.

It is important to remember that even if the economy is running at or near full capacity, the unemployment rate will never be zero. The economy is dynamic. Students graduate from schools and training programs; some businesses make profits and grow, while others suffer losses and go out of business; people move in and out of the labor force and change careers. It takes time for people to find the right job and for employers to match the right worker with the jobs they have to fill. This **frictional** and **structural unemployment** is inevitable and in many ways desirable. (Review Chapter 8 if these terms are hazy to you.)

In this chapter, we are concerned with **cyclical unemployment,** the increase in unemployment that occurs during recessions and depressions. When the economy contracts, the number of people unemployed and the unemployment rate rise. The United States has experienced several periods of high unemployment. During the Great Depression, the unemployment rate remained over 17% for nearly a decade. In December of 1982, more than 12 million people were unemployed, putting the unemployment rate at 10.8 percent.

In one sense, the reason that employment falls when the economy experiences a downturn is obvious. When firms cut back on production, they need fewer workers, so people get laid off. Thus,

> Employment tends to fall when aggregate output falls and rise when aggregate output rises.

But a decline in the demand for labor does not necessarily mean that unemployment will rise. If markets work as we described in Chapters 4 and 5, a decline in the demand for labor will initially create an excess supply of labor. As a result, the wage rate will fall until the quantity of labor supplied again equals the quantity of labor demanded, thus restoring equilibrium in the labor market. At the new lower wage rate, everyone who wants a job will have one.

If the quantity of labor demanded and the quantity of labor supplied are brought into equilibrium by rising and falling wage rates, there should be no persistent unemployment above the frictional and structural amount. Indeed, this was the view held by the classical economists who preceded Keynes, and it is still the view of a number of economists today.

THE CLASSICAL VIEW OF THE LABOR MARKET

The classical view of the labor market is illustrated in Figure 15.1 on page 344. Classical economists assumed that the wage rate adjusts to equate the quantity of labor demanded with the quantity of labor supplied, thereby implying that unemployment does not exist. To see how this adjustment takes place, assume that there is a decrease in the demand for labor that shifts the demand curve in Figure 15.1 from D_0 to D_1. This decreased demand will cause the wage rate to fall from W_0 to W and the amount of labor demanded to fall from L_0 to L. The decrease in the quantity of labor supplied is a movement along the labor supply curve.

Each point on the **labor supply curve** in Figure 15.1 represents the amount of labor that households want to supply at the particular wage rate. Each household's decision regarding how much labor to supply is part of the overall consumer choice problem of a household. Each household member looks at the market wage rate,

frictional unemployment *The portion of unemployment that is due to the normal working of the labor market; used to denote short-run job/skill matching problems.*

structural unemployment *The portion of unemployment that is due to changes in the structure of the economy that result in a significant loss of jobs in certain industries.*

cyclical unemployment *The increase in unemployment that occurs during recessions and depressions.*

labor supply curve *A graph that illustrates the amount of labor that households want to supply at the particular wage rate.*

If our carpenter decides to continue looking for a job paying more than $20,000 per year, he will be considered unemployed because he is actively looking for work. This does not necessarily mean, however, that the labor market is not working properly. The carpenter has *chosen* not to work for a wage of $20,000 per year, but if his value to any firm outside the construction industry is no more than $20,000 per year, we would not expect him to find a job paying more than $20,000. The unemployment rate as measured by the government is thus not necessarily an accurate indicator of whether the labor market is working properly.

If the degree to which industries are changing in the economy fluctuates over time, there will be more people like our carpenter at some times than at others. This will cause the measured unemployment rate to fluctuate. Thus, some economists argue, the measured unemployment rate may sometimes *seem* high even though the labor market is working well. The quantity of labor supplied at the current wage is equal to the quantity demanded at the current wage. The fact that there are people willing to work at a wage higher than the current wage does not mean that the labor market is not working. Whenever there is an upward-sloping supply curve in a market (as is usually the case in the labor market), the quantity supplied at a price higher than the equilibrium price is always greater than the quantity supplied at the equilibrium price.

Economists who view unemployment in this way do not see it as a major problem. Yet the images of the bread lines in the 1930s are still with us, and many find it difficult to believe that everything was optimal when over 12 million people were looking for work at the end of 1982. Not surprisingly, there are other views of unemployment, and to these we now turn.

SOME CLASSICAL ECONOMISTS BELIEVE THAT UNEMPLOYMENT IS NOT A MAJOR PROBLEM. YET THE IMAGES OF THE BREADLINES OF THE 1930s ARE STILL WITH US, AND MORE THAN 12 MILLION PEOPLE WERE LOOKING FOR WORK DURING THE RECESSION OF 1982.

EXPLAINING THE EXISTENCE OF UNEMPLOYMENT

If unemployment is a major macroeconomic problem—and many economists believe that it is—then it is worthwhile to explore some of the reasons that have been suggested for its existence. Among these are sticky wages, efficiency wage theory, imperfect information, and minimum wage laws.

STICKY WAGES

One explanation for unemployment (above and beyond normal frictional and structural unemployment) is that wages are **"sticky"** on the downward side. That is, the equilibrium wage gets stuck at a particular level and does not fall when the demand for labor falls. This situation is illustrated in Figure 15.2, where the equilibrium wage gets stuck at W_0 (the original wage) and does not fall to W^* when demand decreases from D_0 to D_1. The result is unemployment of the amount $L_0 - L_1$, where L_0 is the quantity of labor that households want to supply at wage rate W_0 and L_1 is the amount of labor that firms want to hire at wage rate W_0. $L_0 - L_1$ is thus the number of workers who would like to work at wage rate W_0 but cannot find jobs.

Unfortunately, the sticky wage explanation of unemployment begs the question. We need to know *why* wages are sticky, if they are, and why wages do not fall to clear the labor market during periods of high unemployment. Many answers to this question have been proposed, but as yet no one answer has been agreed upon. This is one of the reasons that macroeconomics has been in a state of flux for so long. The existence of unemployment continues to be a puzzle. Although we will discuss the major theories that have been proposed to explain why wages may not clear the labor market, we can offer no conclusions. The question is still very much open.

■ **Social, or Implicit, Contracts** One explanation for downwardly sticky wages is that firms enter into **social,** or **implicit, contracts** with workers not to cut wages.

sticky wages *The downward rigidity of wages as an explanation for the existence of unemployment.*

social, or implicit, contracts *Unspoken agreements between workers and firms that firms will not cut wages.*

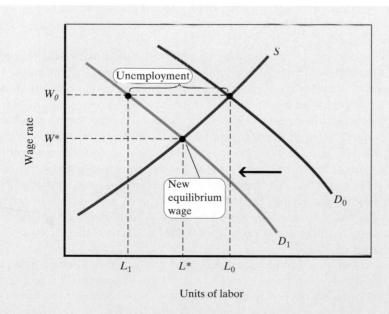

FIGURE 15.2

Sticky Wages

If wages "stick" at W_0 rather than fall to the new equilibrium wage of W^* following a shift of demand from D_0 to D_1, the result will be unemployment equal to $L_0 - L_1$.

It seems that extreme events—a deep recession, deregulation, or threat of bankruptcy—are necessary for firms to cut wages. Wage cuts did occur during the Great Depression, in the airline industry following deregulation of the industry in the 1980s, and recently when some U.S. manufacturing firms found themselves in danger of bankruptcy from stiff foreign competition. These are exceptions to the general rule, however. For reasons that may be more sociological than economic, cutting wages seems close to being a taboo.

A related argument, the **relative-wage explanation of unemployment,** holds that workers are concerned about their wages *relative* to the wages of other workers in other firms and industries and may be unwilling to accept wage cuts unless they know that other workers are receiving similar cuts. Because it is difficult to reassure any one group of workers that all other workers are in the same situation, workers may resist any cut in their wages. There may thus be an implicit understanding between firms and workers that firms will not do anything that would make their workers worse off relative to workers in other firms.

■ Explicit Contracts

Many workers—in particular, unionized workers—sign one- to three-year employment contracts with firms. These contracts stipulate the workers' wages for each year of the contract. Wages set in this way do not fluctuate with economic conditions, either upward or downward. Thus, if the economy slows down and firms demand fewer workers, the wage will not fall. Rather, some workers will be laid off.

Although the existence of **explicit contracts** can explain why some wages are sticky, a deeper question must also be considered. Workers and firms surely know at the time a contract is signed that unforeseen events may cause the wages set by the contract to be too high or too low. Why, then, do firms and workers bind themselves in this way? One explanation is that negotiating wages is a costly process. Negotiations between unions and firms can take a considerable amount of time—time that could be spent producing output—and it would be very costly to negotiate wages weekly or monthly. Contracts are a way of bearing these costs at no more than one-, two-, or three-year intervals. There is thus a trade-off between the costs of locking workers and firms into contracts for long periods of time and the costs of wage negotiations. The length of contracts that minimizes negotiation costs seems to be (from what we observe in practice) between one and three years.

Nonetheless, even if it is optimal to negotiate only once a year or every other year, contracts could be written to take unforeseen events into account. Consider what happens when wages are fixed for the next two years by an employment contract and there is an unanticipated contraction in the economy during that period. The contraction causes a decrease in demand for the firm's product, which leads to a decrease in the firm's demand for labor. If wages were allowed to adjust to clear the labor market, wages would fall and equilibrium would be restored. If wages cannot fall because they are set in advance by a contract, some workers will be laid off. But that contract could have been written to allow wages to fall during a contraction, thus allowing layoffs to be avoided. In other words, workers and firms could have agreed to a fixed *employment* level rather than a fixed *wage* level in their contract. This would guarantee the level of jobs rather than the level of wages.

Contracts that guarantee jobs rather than wages are exceedingly rare, however. Why? One theory postulates that there are two basic types of workers: senior workers and junior workers. *Senior workers* are those workers who have been with a firm for a long time and have seniority. *Junior workers* are relatively new workers. When layoffs take place, it is usually the junior workers who are laid off. If

relative-wage explanation of unemployment *An explanation for sticky wages (and therefore unemployment): If workers are concerned about their wages relative to other workers in other firms and industries, they may be unwilling to accept a wage cut unless they know that all other workers are receiving similar cuts.*

explicit contracts *Employment contracts that stipulate workers' wages, usually for a period of one to three years.*

senior workers have most of the power in the union (or other bargaining unit), they may be quite content to write a contract that calls for layoffs rather than wage cuts during hard times. Clearly, if you do not need to worry about being laid off, it is better to have wages stay where they are than to have them fall.

Another theory about why workers sign contracts that in effect call for layoffs instead of wage cuts during hard times centers on the *monitoring of information*. Suppose, for example, that there is a shift of demand away from a firm's product because of a decrease in aggregate expenditure. If the firm could reduce wages immediately, it might be able to lower the price of its product and restore some or all of the lost demand. If the strategy worked, no layoffs would be necessary. But this plan requires wage concessions from workers. To accept pay cuts, workers must believe that the firm will really cut prices, and they may not believe this. Monitoring prices is often difficult because many firms produce different versions of the same product and sometimes different products. Workers may simply not agree to an arrangement in which their wages are cut (which they can definitely see) and in which prices may or may not be cut.

In the case of layoffs, the information available to workers is much clearer. It is obvious to workers when output is cut, and most workers understand that layoffs are necessary when output falls. At any rate, in practice it certainly seems that workers more readily accept layoffs than wage cuts.

It should be mentioned that some contracts adjust for unforeseen events by **cost-of-living adjustments (COLAs)** written into the contract. COLAs tie wages to changes in the cost of living: The greater the rate of inflation, the more wages are raised. COLAs thus protect workers from unexpected inflation. Not all contracts contain COLAs, however. Many contracts provide workers with little or no protection from unanticipated inflation, and many COLAs end up adjusting wages by a smaller percentage than the percentage increase in prices.

cost-of-living adjustments (COLAs) *Contract provisions that tie wages to changes in the cost of living. The greater the inflation rate, the more wages are raised.*

EFFICIENCY WAGE THEORY

Another explanation for unemployment centers on the **efficiency wage theory**, which holds that the productivity of workers increases with the wage rate. If this is indeed true, firms may have an incentive to pay wages *above* the wage at which the quantity of labor supplied is equal to the quantity of labor demanded.

An individual firm has an incentive to hire workers as long as the value of what they produce is equal to or greater than the wage rate. With no efficiency effects, the market illustrated in Figure 15.1 would produce an equilibrium wage of W^*. But suppose that the firm could increase the productivity of all its workers by raising the wage rate above W^*. The firm's demand for labor would be no lower, but the higher wage rate would cause the quantity of labor supplied to increase. The quantity of labor supplied would thus exceed the quantity of labor demanded at the new higher wage—the *efficiency wage*—and the result is unemployment.

A number of empirical studies of labor markets have identified several potential benefits that firms receive from paying workers more than the market-clearing wage. Among them are lower turnover, improved morale, and reduced "shirking" of work.[1] But even though the efficiency wage theory predicts the existence of some unemployment, it is unlikely that the behavior it is describing accounts for much of the observed large cyclical fluctuations in unemployment over time.

efficiency wage theory *An explanation for unemployment that holds that the productivity of workers increases with the wage rate. If this is so, firms may have an incentive to pay wages above the market-clearing rate.*

---

[1] *For a good summary, see George Akerlof and Janet Yellen,* Efficiency Wage Models of the Labor Market *(Cambridge: Cambridge University Press, 1986).*

IMPERFECT INFORMATION

Thus far we have been assuming that firms know exactly what wage rates they need to set to clear the labor market. They may not choose to set their wages at this level, but at least they know what the market-clearing wage is. In practice, however, firms may not have enough information at their disposal to know what the market-clearing wage is. In this case, firms are said to have *imperfect information*. If firms have imperfect or incomplete information, they may simply set wages wrong—wages that do not clear the labor market.

If a firm sets its wages too high, more workers will want to work for that firm than the firm wants to employ, and some potential workers will be turned away. The result is, of course, unemployment. One objection to this explanation is that it explains the existence of unemployment only in the very short run. As soon as a firm sees that it has made a mistake, why wouldn't it immediately correct its mistake and adjust its wage to the correct, market-clearing level? In other words, why would unemployment *persist?*

If the economy were simple, it should take no more than a few months for firms to correct their mistakes. But in fact the economy is very complex. Although firms may be aware of their past mistakes and may try to correct them, new events are happening all the time. Because constant change—including a constantly changing equilibrium wage level—is characteristic of the economy, firms may find it hard to adjust wages to the market-clearing level. The labor market is not like the stock market or the market for wheat, where prices are determined in organized exchanges every day. Rather, thousands of firms are setting wages and millions of workers are responding to these wages. It may take considerable time for the market-clearing wages to be determined after they have been disturbed from an equilibrium position.

MINIMUM WAGE LAWS

minimum wage laws *Laws that set a floor for wage rates—that is, a minimum hourly rate for any kind of labor.*

The existence of **minimum wage laws** explains at least a small fraction of unemployment. These laws set a floor for wage rates—that is, a minimum hourly rate for any kind of labor. In 1995, the federal minimum wage was $4.25 per hour. If the market-clearing wage for some groups of workers is below this amount, this group will be unemployed. Refer again to Figure 15.2. If the minimum wage is W_0 and the market-clearing wage is W^*, then the number of unemployed will be $L_0 - L_1$.

Teenagers, who have relatively little job experience, are most likely to be hurt by minimum wage laws. If some teenagers can produce only $4.00 worth of output per hour, no firm would be willing to hire them at a wage of $4.25. To do so would be to incur a loss of $0.25 per hour. In an unregulated market, these teenagers would be able to find work at the market-clearing wage of $4.00 per hour. If the minimum wage laws prevent the wage from falling below $4.25, however, these workers will not be able to find jobs, and they will be unemployed.

In response to this argument against the minimum wage, Congress established a subminimum wage for teenagers. The subminimum wage was set at 85% of the minimum wage and is payable to teenagers in entry-level training programs for up to six months. As of April 1, 1991, the subminimum wage was $3.61 per hour.

Minimum wage laws setting rates of $4.25 and $3.61 per hour are clearly not important to steelworkers earning $17.00 per hour or for doctors, lawyers, and most economists. It is possible, however, that the existence of minimum wage laws (even with the subminimum wage provision in place) is one of the factors contributing to high unemployment rates among teenagers.

AN OPEN QUESTION

As we've seen, there are many explanations for why the labor market may not clear. The theories we have just set forth are not necessarily mutually exclusive, and there may be elements of truth in all of them. The aggregate labor market is very complicated, and there are no simple answers to the question of unemployment. In fact, much current work in macroeconomics is concerned directly or indirectly with this question, and it is an exciting area of study. Which argument or arguments will win out in the end is an open question.

THE RELATIONSHIP BETWEEN THE UNEMPLOYMENT RATE AND INFLATION

As you know, two of the most important variables in macroeconomics are the unemployment rate and the inflation rate. The relationship between these two variables is thus of considerable interest, and it has been the subject of much debate. We now have enough knowledge of the macroeconomy to explore this relationship.

We must begin by considering the relationship between aggregate output (income) (Y) and the unemployment rate (U). An increase in Y means that firms are producing more output. In order to produce more output, more labor is needed in the production process. Therefore, an increase in Y leads to an increase in employment. An increase in employment means more people working (fewer people unemployed) and thus a lower unemployment rate. An increase in Y thus corresponds to a *decrease* in U. Thus U and Y are *negatively* related:[2]

> When Y rises, the unemployment rate falls, and when Y falls, the unemployment rate rises.

Next consider an upward-sloping aggregate supply (AS) curve, as shown in Figure 15.3. This curve represents the relationship between Y and the overall price

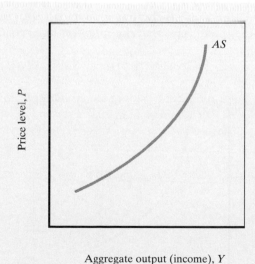

Aggregate output (income), Y

FIGURE 15.3

The Aggregate Supply Curve
The AS curve shows a positive relationship between the price level (P) and aggregate output (income) (Y).

---

[2] *We will see in Chapter 18 that this relationship is not a simple one, but all we need to know for now is that the two variables are negatively related.*

level (P). The relationship is a positive one: When Y increases, P increases, and when Y decreases, P decreases.

As you will recall from the last chapter, the shape of the AS curve is determined by the behavior of firms and how they react to an increase in demand. If aggregate demand shifts to the right and the economy is operating on the nearly flat part of the AS curve—far from capacity—output will increase but the price level will not change much. However, if the economy is operating on the steep part of the AS curve—close to capacity—an increase in demand will drive up the price level, but output will be constrained by capacity and will not increase much.

Now think carefully about what will happen following an event that leads to an increase in aggregate demand. First, firms experience an unanticipated decline in inventories. They respond by increasing output (Y) and hiring workers. Thus, the unemployment rate falls. If the economy is not close to capacity, there will be little increase in the price level. But if aggregate demand continues to grow, the ability of the economy to increase output will eventually reach its limit. As aggregate demand shifts further and further to the right along the AS curve, the price level increases more and more, and output begins to reach its limit. At the point at which the AS curve becomes vertical, output cannot rise any further. If output cannot grow, the unemployment rate cannot be pushed any lower. Thus, we can see that:

> There is a negative relationship between the unemployment rate and the price level. As the unemployment rate declines in response to the economy moving closer and closer to capacity output, the overall price level rises more and more, as shown in Figure 15.4.

The curve depicted in Figure 15.4 has *not* been a major focus of attention in macroeconomics. Rather, the curve that has been extensively studied is shown in Figure 15.5, which plots the inflation rate on the vertical axis and the unemployment rate on the horizontal axis. The **inflation rate** is the percentage change in the price level, not the price level itself.

The implications of Figures 15.4 and 15.5 are different. Figure 15.4 says that the *price level* remains the same if the unemployment rate remains unchanged. Figure 15.5, on the other hand, says that the *inflation rate* remains the same if the

inflation rate *The percentage change in the price level.*

FIGURE 15.4

The Relationship between the Price Level and the Unemployment Rate

There is a negative relationship between the price level (P) and the unemployment rate (U). As the unemployment rate declines in response to the economy's moving closer and closer to capacity output, the price level rises more and more.

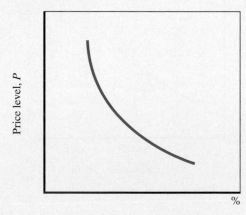

Price level, P

Unemployment rate, U

%

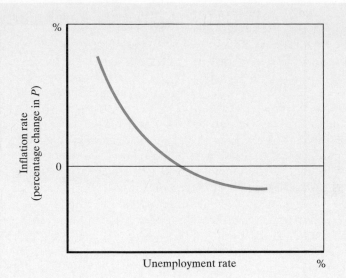

unemployment rate remains unchanged. The curve in Figure 15.5 is called the **Phillips Curve,** after A. W. Phillips, who first examined it using data for the United Kingdom. In simplest terms, the Phillips Curve is a graph showing the relationship between the inflation rate and the unemployment rate.

The rest of this chapter focuses on the Phillips Curve depicted in Figure 15.5 because it is the macroeconomic relationship that has been studied the most. You should keep in mind, however, that it is not easy to go from the *AS* curve to the Phillips Curve. We have moved from graphs in which the price level is on the vertical axis (Figures 15.3 and 15.4) to a graph in which the *percentage change* in the price level is on the vertical axis (Figure 15.5). Put another way, the theory behind the Phillips Curve is somewhat different from the theory behind the *AS* curve. Fortunately, however, most of the insights gained from the *AS/AD* analysis regarding the behavior of the price level also apply to the behavior of the inflation rate.

Phillips Curve *A graph showing the relationship between the inflation rate and the unemployment rate.*

THE PHILLIPS CURVE: A HISTORICAL PERSPECTIVE

In the 1950s and 1960s, there was a remarkably smooth relationship between the unemployment rate and the rate of inflation, as Figure 15.6 shows for the 1960s. As you can see, the data points fit fairly closely around a downward-sloping curve; in general, the higher the unemployment rate, the lower the rate of inflation. The Phillips Curve in Figure 15.6 thus shows a trade-off between inflation and unemployment. To lower the inflation rate, we must accept a higher unemployment rate, and to lower the unemployment rate, we must accept a higher rate of inflation.

Textbooks written in the 1960s and early 1970s relied on the Phillips Curve as the main explanation of inflation. Things seemed fairly simple—inflation appeared to respond in a fairly predictable way to changes in the unemployment rate. For this reason, policy discussions in the 1960s revolved around the Phillips Curve. The role of the policy maker, it was thought, was to choose a point on the curve. Conservatives usually argued for choosing a point with a low rate of inflation and were willing to accept a higher unemployment rate in exchange for this. Liberals usually argued for accepting more inflation to keep unemployment at a low level.

FIGURE 15.6

Unemployment and Inflation, 1960–1969

(Source: *Economic Report of the President*, 1995.)

During the 1960s there seemed to be an obvious trade-off between inflation and unemployment. Policy debates during the period revolved around this apparent trade-off.

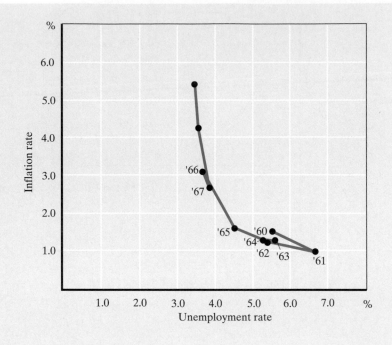

Life did not turn out to be quite so simple, however. The Phillips Curve broke down in the 1970s and 1980s. This is easily seen in Figure 15.7, which graphs the unemployment rate and inflation rate for the period from 1970 to 1994. The points in Figure 15.7 show no particular relationship between inflation and unemployment.

FIGURE 15.7

Unemployment and Inflation, 1970–1994

(Source: *Economic Report of the President*, 1995.)

During the 1970s and 1980s, it became clear that the relationship between unemployment and inflation was anything but simple.

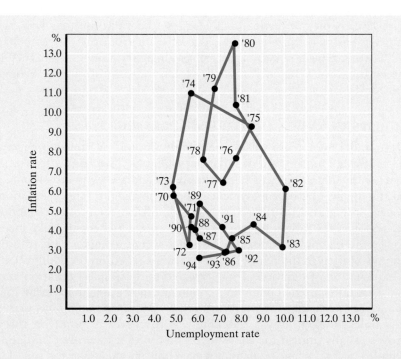

AS/AD ANALYSIS AND THE PHILLIPS CURVE

How can we explain the stability of the Phillips Curve in the 1950s and 1960s and the lack of stability after that? To answer this question, we need to turn back to AS/AD analysis.

If the AD curve shifts from year to year but the AS curve does not, the values of P and Y each year will lie along the AS curve (Figure 15.8a). The plot of the relationship between P and Y will thus be upward-sloping. Correspondingly, the plot of the relationship between the unemployment rate (which decreases with increased output) and the rate of inflation will be a curve that slopes downward. In other words, we would expect to see a negative relationship between the unemployment rate and the inflation rate.

But the relationship between the unemployment rate and the inflation rate will look different if the AS curve shifts from year to year but the AD curve does not. A leftward shift of the AS curve will cause an *increase* in the price level (P) and a *decrease* in aggregate output (Y) (Figure 15.8b). Thus, when the AS curve shifts to the left, the economy experiences both inflation *and* an increase in the unemployment rate (because decreased output means increased unemployment). In other words, if the AS curve is shifting from year to year, we would expect to see a positive relationship between the unemployment rate and the inflation rate.

If both the AS and the AD curves are shifting simultaneously, however, there is no systematic relationship between P and Y (Figure 15.8c) and thus no systematic relationship between the unemployment rate and the inflation rate.

■ **The Role of Import Prices**   One of the main factors that causes the AS curve to shift is the price of imports. (Remember that the AS curve shifts when input prices

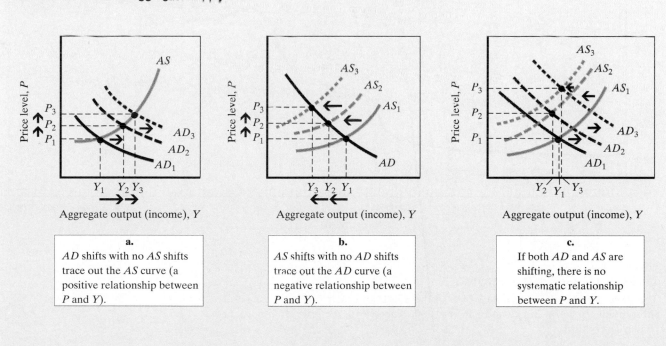

FIGURE 15.8

Changes in the Price Level and Aggregate Output Depend on Both Shifts in Aggregate Demand and Shifts in Aggregate Supply

a.
AD shifts with no AS shifts trace out the AS curve (a positive relationship between P and Y).

b.
AS shifts with no AD shifts trace out the AD curve (a negative relationship between P and Y).

c.
If both AD and AS are shifting, there is no systematic relationship between P and Y.

change, and input prices are affected by the price of imports, particularly the price of imported oil.) The price of imports is plotted in Figure 15.9 for the 1960 I–1994 IV period. As you can see, the price of imports changed very little between 1960 and 1970. There were thus no large shifts in the *AS* curve in the 1960s due to changes in the price of imports. There were also no other large changes in input prices in the 1960s, so overall the *AS* curve shifted very little during the decade. The main variation in the 1960s was in aggregate demand, so the shifting *AD* curve traced out points along the *AS* curve.

Figure 15.9 also shows that the price of imports increased dramatically in the 1970s. This led to large shifts in the *AS* curve during the decade. But the *AD* curve was also shifting throughout the 1970s. With both curves shifting, the data points for *P* and *Y* were scattered all over the graph, and the observed relationship between *P* and *Y* was not at all systematic.

This story about import prices and the *AS* and *AD* curves in the 1960s and 1970s carries over to the Phillips Curve. The Phillips Curve was stable in the 1960s because the primary source of variation in the economy was demand, not costs. In the 1970s (and the 1980s), however, both demand *and* costs were varying, so no obvious relationship between the unemployment rate and the inflation rate was apparent.

To some extent, what is remarkable about the Phillips Curve is not that it was not smooth after the 1960s but that it ever was smooth.

EXPECTATIONS AND THE PHILLIPS CURVE

Another reason that the Phillips Curve is not stable concerns expectations. We saw in the last chapter that if a firm expects other firms to raise their prices, the firm

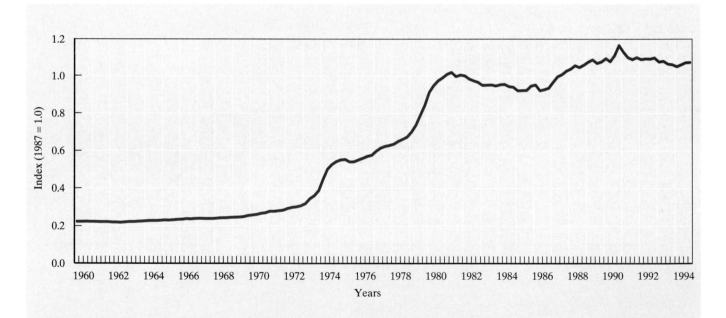

FIGURE 15.9

The Price of Imports, 1960 I–1994 IV

The price of imports changed very little in the 1960s and early 1970s. It increased substantially in 1974 and again in 1979–1980. Since 1981, the price of imports has changed very little.

may raise the price of its own product. If all firms are behaving in this way, then prices will rise because they are expected to rise. In this sense, expectations are self-fulfilling. Similarly, if inflation is expected to be high in the future, negotiated wages are likely to be higher than if inflation is expected to be low. Wage inflation is thus affected by expectations of future price inflation. Because wages are input costs, prices rise as firms respond to the higher wage costs. Thus, price expectations that affect wage contracts eventually affect prices themselves.

If the rate of inflation depends on expectations, then the Phillips Curve will shift as expectations change. For example, if inflationary expectations increase, the result will be an increase in the rate of inflation even though the unemployment rate may not have changed. In this case, the Phillips Curve will shift to the right. Conversely, if inflationary expectations decrease, the Phillips curve will shift to the left—there will be less inflation at any given level of the unemployment rate.

It so happened that inflationary expectations were quite stable in the 1950s and 1960s. The inflation rate was moderate during most of this period, and people expected it to remain moderate. With inflationary expectations not changing very much, there were no major shifts of the Phillips Curve, which helps explain its stability during the period.

Near the end of the 1960s, however, inflationary expectations began to increase, primarily in response to the actual increase in inflation that was occurring because of the tight economy caused by the Vietnam War. Inflationary expectations increased even further in the 1970s as a result of large oil price increases. These changing expectations led to shifts of the Phillips Curve, which is another reason the curve was not stable during the 1970s.

IS THERE A TRADE-OFF BETWEEN INFLATION AND UNEMPLOYMENT?

Does the fact that the Phillips Curve broke down during the 1970s and 1980s mean that there is no trade-off between inflation and unemployment? Not at all. It simply means that other things affect inflation aside from unemployment. Just as the relationship between price and quantity demanded along a standard demand curve shifts when income or other factors change, so too does the relationship between unemployment and inflation change when other factors change.

In 1975, for example, inflation and unemployment were both high. As we explained earlier, this stagflation was caused partly by an increase in oil costs that shifted the aggregate supply curve to the left and partly by expectations of continued inflation that kept prices rising despite high levels of unemployment. In response to this situation, the Fed pursued a contractionary monetary policy, which shifted the *AD* curve to the left and led to even higher unemployment. This resulted in a lower inflation rate. By 1977, the rate of inflation had dropped from over 11% to about 6 percent. In sum:

> There *is* a trade-off between inflation and unemployment, but other factors besides unemployment affect inflation. Policy involves much more than simply choosing a point along a nice, smooth curve.

Back in Chapter 8, we mentioned that recessions may be the price that the economy pays to eliminate inflation. We can now understand this statement better. When unemployment rises, *other things being equal,* inflation falls. We explore the trade-off between inflation and unemployment in other nations—and caution against generalizing too much—in the Global Perspective box titled "Inflation and Unemployment around the World, 1990–1992."

GLOBAL PERSPECTIVE

INFLATION AND UNEMPLOYMENT AROUND THE WORLD, 1990–1992

Table 1 presents unemployment and inflation figures for a number of industrial economies. The countries are ranked by unemployment rate in 1990 from highest to lowest.

These numbers make it clear that economic generalizations across countries can be hazardous. This is true for two reasons. First, the economic events experienced by one country in a given time period may be very different than the economic events experienced by another country during the same period. (For example, one country may encounter a supply shock that shifts its aggregate supply curve at the same time that another is experiencing demand-pull inflation.) Second, the trade-off between inflation and unemployment, to the extent that one exists, is determined by the institutions within the country. For example, Japan had a tradition of "lifetime" employment for male workers in the country's largest industries. Although 1992 and 1993 saw the rules beginning to change, Japanese firms are still more reluctant than their U.S. counterparts to lay off workers during economic hard times. This means that Japanese workers do much less "job searching" and that Japan probably has a lower natural rate of unemployment than the United States. The opposite is true in the Netherlands, which has a very liberal unemployment insurance program that pays virtually 100% of lost wages to the unemployed for an extended period of time. Such a system is likely to lead to a higher natural rate because it makes the cost of being unemployed quite low.

However, a number of clear patterns do emerge from the numbers. Seven of the ten countries in the group experienced an increase in unemployment between 1990 and 1992. Those same seven countries experienced a simultaneous decline in inflation. Only Germany and the

UNEMPLOYMENT HAS EMERGED AS A SERIOUS PROBLEM IN EUROPE IN THE 1990s. HERE, LONDONERS CALL ATTENTION TO THE FACT THAT THE NUMBER OF ENGLISH UNEMPLOYED ROSE TO MORE THAN 3 MILLION IN 1993.

Netherlands saw unemployment decline, and both experienced an increase in inflation. Japan had no change in the unemployment rate. Thus, all nine countries seemed to exhibit a trade-off between inflation and unemployment.

The similarity of patterns across the seven countries experiencing higher unemployment and lower inflation demonstrates that linkages across economies do exist. All countries experienced falling commodity prices (including oil) on world markets during 1991 and 1992. In addition, countries are linked through imports and exports and through capital flows. For example, one of the reasons that the U.S. economy did not grow more quickly following the 1990–1991 recession was that its major trading partners (Europe and Japan) were experiencing recessions of their own and were buying less from the United States.

TABLE 1	UNEMPLOYMENT AND INFLATION RATES IN SELECTED COUNTRIES, 1990–1992			
	UNEMPLOYMENT RATE		**INFLATION RATE**	
	1990	1992	1990	1992
Canada	8.1	11.3 ↑	5.0	2.0 ↓
Australia	6.9	10.8 ↑	7.0	1.0 ↓
France	9.2	10.1 ↑	3.1	2.3 ↓
United Kingdom	6.8	9.6 ↑	6.4	4.3 ↓
Italy	11.4	11.6 ↑	7.6	4.5 ↓
United States	5.5	6.8 ↑	5.0	3.0 ↓
Netherlands	8.0	6.6 ↓	3.0	4.0 ↑
Sweden	1.5	4.7 ↑	11.0	2.0 ↓
Germany	6.2	5.8 ↓	3.1	4.4 ↑
Japan	2.2	2.2 -	2.2	1.6 ↓

Sources: OECD, IMF, and *Statistical Abstract of the United States*, 1994, Tables 1379, 1381.

THE LONG-RUN *AS* CURVE, POTENTIAL GDP, AND THE NATURAL RATE OF UNEMPLOYMENT

Recall from the previous chapter that many economists believe that the *AS* curve is vertical in the long run. In the short run, we know that some input prices (which are costs to firms) lag behind increases in the overall price level. If the price level rises without a full adjustment of costs, firms' profits will be higher and output will increase. In the long run, however, input prices may catch up to output price increases. If input prices rise in subsequent periods, thus driving up costs, the short-run aggregate supply curve will shift to the left, and aggregate output will fall.

This situation is illustrated in Figure 15.10. Assume that the initial equilibrium is at the intersection of AD_0 and the long-run aggregate supply curve. Now consider a shift of the aggregate demand curve from AD_0 to AD_1. If input prices lag behind changes in the overall price level, aggregate output will rise from Y_0 to Y_1. (This is a movement along the short-run *AS* curve AS_0.) But in the longer run, input prices

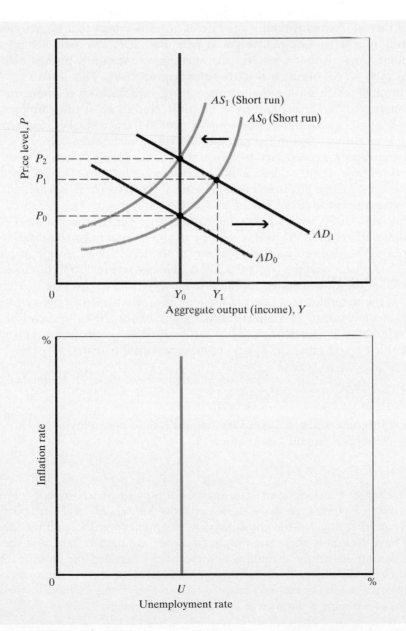

FIGURE 15.10

The Long-Run Phillips Curve: The Natural Rate of Unemployment

If the *AS* curve is vertical in the long run, so is the Phillips Curve. In the long run, the Phillips Curve corresponds to the natural rate of unemployment—that is, the unemployment rate that is consistent with the notion of a fixed long-run output at potential GDP.

may catch up. For example, next year's labor contracts may make up for the fact that wage increases did not keep up with the cost of living this year. If input prices catch up in the longer run, the AS curve will shift from AS_0 to AS_1 and drive aggregate output back to Y_0. If input prices ultimately rise by exactly the same percentage as output prices, firms will produce the same level of output as they did before the increase in aggregate demand.

In the last chapter, we said that Y_0 is sometimes called *potential GDP*. Aggregate output can be pushed above Y_0 in the short run. When aggregate output exceeds Y_0, however, there is upward pressure on input prices and costs. The unemployment rate is already quite low, firms are beginning to encounter the limits of their plant capacities, and so forth. At levels of aggregate output above Y_0, costs will rise, the AS curve will shift to the left, and the price level will rise. Thus potential GDP is the level of aggregate output that can be sustained in the long run without inflation.

This story is directly related to the Phillips Curve. Those who believe that the AS curve is vertical in the long run at potential GDP also believe that the Phillips Curve is vertical in the long run at some natural rate of unemployment. The **natural rate of unemployment** is the rate of unemployment that is consistent with the notion of a fixed long-run output at potential GDP. The logic behind the vertical Phillips Curve is that whenever the unemployment rate is pushed below the natural rate, wages begin to rise, thus pushing up costs. This leads to a *lower* level of output, which pushes the unemployment rate back up to the natural rate. At the natural rate, the economy can be considered to be at full employment.

Why is the natural rate of unemployment (if it exists) higher than zero? We have said several times that in the normal functioning of a healthy economy, some firms are contracting while others are expanding. Some people switch jobs; others graduate from high school or college and begin looking for jobs. This means that even in good times, there are people out looking for work. These normal frictional and structural unemployment rates make up the natural rate. The measured unemployment rate can be pushed below the natural rate, but only in the short run and not without inflation. Many believe that the natural rate of unemployment in the United States is 6%, give or take a few tenths of a percentage point. As the Application box titled "Approaching the Natural Rate of Unemployment: 1995" discusses, many believe that the United States appeared to be very close to this rate in 1994.

If the natural rate is fixed in the long run, what role can policy play in reducing unemployment? If some event like a cost shock drives the level of unemployment above the natural rate, policy can be used to accelerate its return to the sustainable natural rate. The key point here, however, is that:

> There is a limit to how low the unemployment rate can be pushed without setting off a round of inflation.

We will return to the notion of the natural rate of unemployment when we discuss new classical economics in Chapter 19.

LOOKING AHEAD

This chapter concludes our basic analysis of how the macroeconomy works. In the last seven chapters, we have examined how households and firms behave in the three market arenas—the goods market, the money market, and the labor market. We have seen how aggregate output (income), the interest rate, and the price level are determined in the economy, and we have examined the relationship between two of the most important macroeconomic variables, the inflation rate and the unemployment rate. In the next chapter, we use everything we have learned up to this point to examine a number of important policy issues.

natural rate of unemployment
A concept consistent with the notion of a fixed long-run output at potential GDP. Generally considered the sum of the frictional and structural unemployment rates.

APPROACHING THE NATURAL RATE OF UNEMPLOYMENT: 1994

In December 1994, the U.S. Labor Department announced that the unemployment rate had dropped to 5.6% in November from 5.8% the month before. During the month, the labor force expanded by 100,000 while the number of employed rose by 372,000. The number of unemployed fell by 272,000 to a level of 7.3 million. Only two years earlier, the unemployment rate had been 7.6% with nearly 10 million unemployed.

Even though more than 7 million workers were still looking for a job, the Federal Reserve Board worried that the United States was actually *below* the natural rate of unemployment and that inflation would soon follow. *The New York Times* reported the following rationale for the Fed's interest rate hikes in November 1994:

The most compelling cause for concern, many analysts believe, is that the economy is operating at full employment or maybe even past that point. Full employment does not mean everybody who wants a job necessarily finds one in a reasonable period of time. It simply means a rate below which inflationary pressures start to build.

That threshold, experience and studies suggest, may be about 6 percent, give or take a few tenths. Not only is unemployment now 5.8 percent, but growth is also sufficiently rapid to drive it down further.

"We're just a little bit on the other side of safety," [one analyst] said. "If you believe that full employment is 6 percent, and you understand the

economy is growing 3.5 to 4 percent, then you can understand the Fed's action. They've got to slow the economy down to 2.5 percent growth or below."[1]

In addition, there were already signs that the falling unemployment rate was having an effect on wages:

Americans' average weekly paychecks jumped 1.5 percent in October. The increase was the largest since a 2.3 percent gain in February 1982, the Labor Department said. In September, earnings showed a rise of seven-tenths of a percent.[2]

Sources: [1]Sylvia Nasar, "Thinking as the Fed Thinks," *The New York Times*, November 17, 1994, p. D1., [2]"Consumer Price Index Barely Rose Last Month," *The New York Times*, November 17, 1994, p. D6.

SUMMARY

1. Because the economy is dynamic, *frictional* and *structural unemployment* are inevitable and in some ways desirable. Nonetheless, there are times of *cyclical unemployment* that concern macroeconomic policy makers.

2. In general, employment tends to fall when aggregate output falls and rise when aggregate output rises.

THE CLASSICAL VIEW OF THE LABOR MARKET

3. Classical economists believe that the interaction of supply and demand in the labor market brings about equilibrium and that unemployment (beyond the frictional and structural amounts) does not exist.

4. The classical view of the labor market is consistent with the theory of a vertical aggregate supply curve.

EXPLAINING THE EXISTENCE OF UNEMPLOYMENT

5. Some economists argue that the unemployment rate is not an accurate indicator of whether the labor market is working properly. Unemployed people who are considered part of the labor force may be offered jobs but may be unwilling to take those jobs at the offered salaries. Thus, some of the unemployed may have chosen not to work, but this does not mean that the labor market has malfunctioned.

6. Those who do not subscribe to the classical view of the labor market have suggested several reasons why unemployment exists. Downwardly *sticky wages* may be brought about by *implicit* or *explicit contracts* not to cut wages. If the equilibrium wage rate falls but wages are prevented from falling also, the result will be unemployment.

7. *Efficiency wage theory* holds that the productivity of workers increases with the wage rate. If this is true, firms may have an incentive to pay wages above the wage at which the quantity of labor supplied is equal to the quantity of labor demanded. At all wages above the equilibrium, there will be an excess supply of labor and therefore unemployment.

8. If firms are operating with incomplete or imperfect information, they may not know what the market-clearing wage is. As a result, they may set their wages incorrectly and bring about unemployment. Because the economy is so complex, it may take considerable time for firms to correct these mistakes.

9. *Minimum wage laws,* which set a floor for wage rates, are one of the factors contributing to unemployment among teenagers. If the market-clearing wage for some groups of workers is below the minimum wage, some members of this group will be unemployed.

THE RELATIONSHIP BETWEEN THE UNEMPLOYMENT RATE AND INFLATION

10. There is a negative relationship between the unemployment rate (U) and aggregate output (income) (Y): When Y rises, U falls. When Y falls, U rises.

11. The relationship between the unemployment rate and the price level is negative: As the unemploy-ment rate declines and the economy moves closer to capacity, the price level rises more and more.

12. The *Phillips Curve* is a graph illustrating the relationship between the *inflation rate* and the *unemployment rate*. During the 1950s and 1960s, this relationship was fairly stable, and there seemed to be a predictable trade-off between inflation and unemployment. As a result of import price increases (which led to shifts in aggregate supply) and shifts in aggregate demand brought about partially by inflationary expectations, however, the relationship between the inflation rate and the unemployment rate since 1970 has been erratic. There *is* a trade-off between inflation and unemployment, but other things besides unemployment affect inflation.

13. Those who believe that the *AS* curve is vertical in the long run also believe that the Phillips Curve is vertical in the long run at the *natural rate of unemployment*. The natural rate is generally taken to be the sum of the frictional and structural rates. If the Phillips Curve is vertical in the long run, then there is a limit to how low government policy can push the unemployment rate without setting off inflation.

REVIEW TERMS AND CONCEPTS

PROBLEM SET

1. Obtain monthly data on the unemployment rate and the inflation rate for the last two years. (These data can be found in a recent issue of the *Survey of Current Business* or in the *Monthly Labor Review* or *Employment and Earnings,* all published by the government and available in many college libraries.)
   a. What trends do you observe? Can you explain what you see using aggregate supply and aggregate demand curves?
   b. Plot the 24 monthly rates on a graph with the unemployment rate measured on the X axis and the inflation rate on the Y axis. Is there evidence of a trade-off between these two variables? Can you offer an explanation?

2. Japan has traditionally had a substantially lower unemployment rate than the United States, at least since the 1960s. Japanese workers rarely move from one city to another and rarely switch employers, staying with one firm for their entire career. How, if at all, do these factors help to explain the difference in unemployment rates between the two countries?

3. In 1996, the country of Ruba was suffering a period of high unemployment. The newly elected President Clang appointed as his chief economist Laurel Tiedye. Ms. Tiedye and her staff estimated the following supply and demand curves for labor from data obtained from the secretary of labor, Robert Small:

$$Q_D = 100 - 5W$$

$$Q_S = 10W - 20,$$

where Q is the quantity of labor supplied/demanded in millions of workers and W is the wage rate in slugs, the currency of Ruba.
   a. Currently, the law in Ruba states that no worker shall be paid less than nine slugs per hour. Estimate the quantity of labor supplied, the number of unemployed, and the unemployment rate in Ruba.
   b. President Clang, over the objection of Secretary Small, has recommended to the Congress that the law be changed to allow the wage rate to be determined in the market. If such a law were passed, and the market adjusted quickly, what would happen to total employment, the size of the labor force, and the unemployment rate? Show the results graphically.
   c. Do you think that the Rubanese labor market would adjust quickly to such a change in the law? Why or why not?

4. The following policies have at times been advocated for coping with the problem of unemployment. Briefly explain how each policy might work, and explain which type or types of unemployment (frictional, structural, or cyclical) the policy is designed to alter.
   a. Developing a computer list of job openings and a service that matches employees with job vacancies (sometimes called an "economic dating service").
   b. Lowering the minimum wage for teenagers.
   c. Retraining programs for workers who need to learn new skills in order to find employment.

   d. Public employment for people without jobs.
   e. Improving information about available jobs and current wage rates.
   f. The President goes on nationwide TV and attempts to convince firms and workers that the inflation rate next year will be low.

5. Your boss offers you a wage increase of 10 percent. Is it possible that you are worse off, even with the wage increase, than you were before?

6. How will the following affect labor-force participation rates? Labor supply? Unemployment?
   a. Because the retired elderly are comprising a larger and larger fraction of the U.S. population, Congress and the President decide to raise the social security tax on individuals in order to continue paying benefits to the elderly.
   b. A national child care program is enacted, requiring employers to provide free child care services.
   c. The U.S. government reduces restrictions on immigration into the United States.
   d. The welfare system is eliminated.
   e. The government subsidizes the purchase of new capital by firms (an investment tax credit).

7. Draw a graph to illustrate the following:
   a. A Phillips Curve based on the assumption of a vertical long-run aggregate supply curve.
   b. The effect of accelerating inflationary expectations on a recently stable Phillips Curve.
   c. Unemployment caused by a recently enacted minimum wage law.

8. Suppose economists have predicted an upcoming recession. Also suppose that, as a result, firms plan to reduce workers' wages, but also expect the price level to fall (thus keeping the real wage constant). Would you expect to observe an increase in unemployment? Why or why not?

9. Obtain data on "average hourly earnings of production workers" and the unemployment rate for your state or area over a recent two-year period. Has unemployment increased or decreased? What has happened to wages? Does the pattern of unemployment help explain the movement of wages? Can you offer an explanation?

10. Suppose that the inflation-unemployment relationship depicted by the Phillips Curve was, in fact, stable. Do you think that the U.S. trade-off and the Japanese trade-off would be identical? If not, what kinds of factors might make the trade-offs dissimilar?

16

The Federal Deficit and the Federal Debt
The Size of the Federal Debt
The Burden of the Debt

Deficit Reduction and Macropolicy
The Effects of Government Spending Cuts on the Deficit
Economic Stability and Deficit Reduction

The Fed's Response to the State of the Economy

Lags in the Economy's Response to Monetary and Fiscal Policy
Recognition Lags
Implementation Lags
Response Lags

Business Cycles in Other Countries

federal deficit *The difference between what the federal government spends and what it collects in taxes in a given period $(G - T)$.*

federal debt *The total of all accumulated federal deficits minus surpluses over time, or the total amount owed by the federal government.*

DEFICIT REDUCTION, STABILIZATION POLICY, AND MACRO ISSUES ABROAD

A S WE'VE NOTED THROUGHOUT THIS BOOK, MACROECONOMICS IS filled with important policy questions. Newspapers carry articles dealing with macroeconomic problems daily, and macroeconomic issues play an important role in many political campaigns. Using what we've learned about how the macroeconomy works, we can now examine some current issues and problems in greater depth.

In this chapter, we take up four issues: (1) the federal deficit, the federal debt, and legislation that is concerned with setting targets for the deficit; (2) the way the Fed reacts to the state of the economy; (3) the lags that exist in the economy's response to monetary and fiscal policy changes; and (4) the cyclical behavior since 1980 of the economies of Japan and five European countries.

THE FEDERAL DEFICIT AND THE FEDERAL DEBT

We noted in Chapter 10 that the size of the federal deficit since the early 1980s has been a subject of great concern. Recall that the **federal deficit** is the difference between what the federal government spends and what it collects in tax in a given period: $(G - T)$. In 1994, the federal deficit was $159.1 billion. Recall also that the **federal debt** is the total of all accumulated federal deficits minus surpluses over time. It is the total amount owed by the federal government. Because the U.S. Treasury must borrow by issuing securities when the government spends more than it collects in taxes, the federal debt is also the total amount of U.S. government obligations (bills, notes, and bonds) outstanding.

Some of the securities that the government issues end up being held by the federal government itself at the Federal Reserve or in trust funds. The term **federal debt held by the public** refers only to the *privately held* debt of the U.S. government. At the end of 1994, total outstanding U.S. government obligations amounted to $4,643.7 billion, of which $3,432.2 billion was privately held.

federal debt held by the public *The privately held (non-government-owned) debt of the U.S. government.*

THE SIZE OF THE FEDERAL DEBT

One way to measure the size of the federal debt is to compare it to the size of national output (income) (Y). Figure 16.1 shows the total privately held debt as a percentage of GDP between the years 1940 and 1994. (A similar figure is found in Chapter 10, Figure 10.5, where the percentage is shown for each quarter between 1970 I and 1994 IV.) A large debt was incurred to fight World War II, pushing the debt-to-GDP ratio from 44.8% in 1940 to 113.8% in 1946. After 1946, the ratio dropped each year for nearly 30 years to a low of 24.5% in 1974. Between 1974 and 1981, there was little change. But between 1981 and 1994, the debt increased dramatically. The large deficits of the 1980s began with the significant tax cuts and military spending increases in the early years of the Reagan administration. As Congress and the President fought over the budget throughout the 1980s, the debt grew to over $2 trillion by the end of the 1980s. As just noted, by the end of 1994, the debt was $3,432.2 billion, or 51.7% of GDP.

Table 16.1 on page 366 shows the federal deficit in billions of dollars and as a percentage of GDP for 1970 to 1994. The sharp increases after 1980 are obvious. The deficit hit 4.7% of GDP in 1986. After 1986 the deficit as a percentage of GDP fell to 2.3% in 1992, rose to 4.7% in 1992, and then fell to 2.4% in 1994.

THE BURDEN OF THE DEBT

It is easy to determine where the burden of a household's debt falls. When a family borrows to buy a house or a car or to finance college for one or more of its members, it takes out loans that must be paid off over time. Interest must be paid on these loans. The more a household must spend on principal and interest payments, the less it has to spend elsewhere.

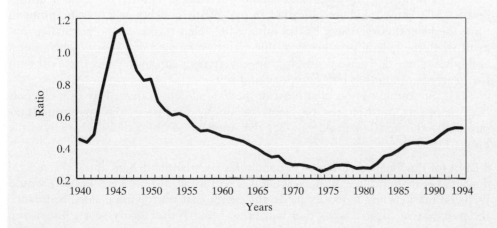

FIGURE 16.1

Ratio of Privately Held U.S. Government Debt to GDP, 1940–1994

(Source: *Economic Report of the President, 1995,* Table B-78.)

The large deficits of the 1980s began with the tax cuts and military spending increases in the early years of the Reagan administration. By the end of 1994, the debt stood at 51.7% of U.S. GDP.

TABLE 16.1			DEFICIT AND INTEREST PAYMENTS, 1970–1994		
(1) YEAR	(2) FEDERAL DEFICIT (BILLIONS OF $)	(3) DEFICIT AS A % OF GDP	(4) NET INTEREST PAYMENTS (BILLIONS OF $)	(5) INTEREST AS A % OF GDP	(6) INTEREST AS A % OF FEDERAL EXPENDITURES
1970	13.3	1.3	14.1	1.4	6.9
1972	17.3	1.4	14.4	1.2	5.8
1974	11.5	0.8	20.7	1.4	6.8
1976	52.8	3.0	26.8	1.5	6.8
1978	28.1	1.3	34.6	1.6	7.4
1980	60.0	2.2	52.7	1.9	8.6
1982	135.6	4.3	84.4	2.7	11.0
1984	166.8	4.4	113.1	3.0	12.7
1986	201.1	4.7	131.0	3.1	12.7
1987	151.8	3.3	136.5	3.0	12.8
1988	136.6	2.8	146.0	3.0	13.2
1989	122.3	2.3	164.7	3.1	13.9
1990	163.5	2.9	176.5	3.2	13.8
1991	202.9	3.5	187.8	3.3	14.1
1992	282.7	4.7	186.8	3.1	12.8
1993	241.4	3.8	183.6	2.9	12.2
1994	159.1	2.4	191.5	2.8	12.5

Source: U.S. Department of Commerce, Bureau of Economic Analysis.

In some respects, the federal government is like a household. In order to borrow, it must pay interest. The more debt it incurs, the higher its interest payments will be. Columns 5 and 6 of Table 16.1 show the annual interest cost of financing the federal debt as a percentage of GDP and as a percentage of total federal expenditures. Interest payments represented less than 10% of total federal expenditures and less than 2% of GDP until 1982. By 1991, the figures had jumped to 14.1% of total federal expenditures and 3.3% of GDP, and they have fallen only slightly since then. Interest payments now rank third behind national defense and social security payments as a percentage of the total federal budget, and they far exceed total federal expenditures on education, employment training, social services, and housing assistance.

In another sense, however, the federal government is different from a household. While households are obligated to pay off their debts at a specific point in time, the federal government has an infinite life. That is, there is no particular moment when the federal debt becomes due and must be paid off. Specific bills, notes, and bonds come due periodically, but the government can simply pay these off with the proceeds of another bill, note, or bond sale.

It is interesting to note that most of the federal debt is owned by U.S. citizens. Because of this, most interest payments are simply a transfer from one group (taxpayers) to another (bondholders). (See the Application box titled "Who Owns the Public Debt?")

■ **Debt for the Finance of Capital Expenditures** Often the debate about the federal debt makes it sound like all borrowing is a bad thing. If that were so, why would financial markets and banks exist? To the extent that borrowing is done to finance the purchase of capital assets that will bring benefits over many years, borrowing money and issuing debt are perfectly logical and appropriate ways to finance acquisitions by households, firms, and governments. It makes sense to borrow if the return on the investment exceeds the borrowing rate.

At the end of 1994, the total U.S. government debt was $4,643.7 billion, of which $3,432.2 billion was privately held. The difference between the total debt and the privately held debt—$1,211.5 billion—is the amount of the debt held by the government itself. Of the government-held debt, the Federal Reserve System held $355.2 billion and various government trust funds (such as the trust funds administered by the Social Security Administration) held the rest. Other federal trust funds that own U.S. Treasury obligations include federal employees' retirement funds, highway trust funds, the military retirement fund, and the airport and airway trust fund.

Why does the Federal Reserve hold so much of the debt? The Fed is responsible for controlling the U.S. money supply. As the economy grows, the money supply must be expanded to accommodate that growth. In December 1985, the money supply (M1) was $619.9 billion; by December 1994 it had grown to $1,147.8 billion.

The Fed expands the money supply primarily through open market operations—that is, by buying U.S. government securities in the open market. The Fed pays for these securities by writing a check or by expanding a bank's reserve account at the Fed. In either case, reserves are injected into the system. These additional reserves allow banks to lend more money, which ultimately expands the money supply. In essence, the Fed is creating money when it buys securities.

As a result, the Fed has come to own more than $355 billion worth of

TABLE 1	ESTIMATED PRIVATE OWNERSHIP OF PUBLIC DEBT SECURITIES, SEPTEMBER 1994	
	BILLIONS OF $	% OF TOTAL
Commercial banks	325.0	10.4
Individuals	327.2	10.5
Insurance companies	250.0	8.0
Money market funds	59.9	1.9
Corporations	229.3	7.3
State and local governments	521.0	16.7
Foreigners	653.8	20.9
Other*	761.6	24.3
Total	3127.8	100.0

*Note: Includes savings and loans, credit unions, mutual savings banks, and pension funds.

Source: *Economic Report of the President, 1995*, Table B-89.

Treasury securities. The Fed uses the interest it receives on these obligations to finance its operations. It turns the excess interest back to the Treasury each year.

What happens to the funds held by the various government trust funds? They are used to buy Treasury securities! This makes deficit accounting a very tricky business. Table 16.1 shows that the federal government deficit as reported in the National Income and Product Accounts was $159.1 billion in 1994. However, the social security system ran a surplus of $53.1 billion that year. If we remove this surplus from the official numbers, the 1994 deficit was $212.2 billion.

Most privately held government debt is held in "public debt securities." Table 1 presents the breakdown of the private ownership of these securities in September 1994. "Private ownership" includes state and local governments. Most of the $521.0 billion owned by states and localities is

held in pension funds administered by those governments for their employees. For example, many states have a teachers' retirement fund, and many of the dollars in those funds are invested in Treasury securities. These funds are not really owned by the government because each dollar in them represents an obligation of the state or local government to a retiree.

You can see from Table 1 that the private ownership of Treasury obligations is widespread. Individuals directly own $327.2 billion, or 10.5% of the total. Commercial banks account for 10.4%, insurance companies for 8.0%, and money market funds for 1.9 percent.

In recent years there has been some concern that the United States is relying too much on foreign countries (particularly Japan) to finance its deficits. The table shows that foreigners accounted for 20.9% of the total private ownership of public debt securities.

Consider a household that borrows $100,000 to finance a home purchase. Because the house will bring benefits over many years, it is appropriate to pay for it out of future years' incomes by borrowing (signing a mortgage) and agreeing to pay back the loan over many years. When a large German corporation decides to build a new production facility, it will more than likely borrow the money by issuing corporate bonds. Those bonds and the interest on them will be paid out of the company's future earnings. Students borrow to pay for education on the grounds that the future return on the acquired human capital will be sufficient to cover the interest expense.

The same logic can be applied to capital acquisitions made by the government. When the state of Maine builds a bridge, the benefits will be enjoyed by both future generations and people in the present. Most states finance such projects—as well as other capital projects like school buildings, highways, and hospitals—by borrowing and issuing debt. Even states whose constitutions mandate a balanced budget allow for the issue of debt to cover capital expenditures.[1]

Unfortunately, the federal government does not distinguish between capital expenditures and current spending in the budget process. Thus there is no way to know how much government borrowing can be justified as capital purchases that will bring benefits in the future. Some have called for the establishment of a federal capital budget, although it is highly unlikely that "capital acquisition" would justify the amount of borrowing being done by the federal government today. Critics of the idea argue that it would just provide an excuse for the government to borrow even more.

■ **The Deficit and the Future Standard of Living**   It is sometimes argued that one of the burdens of large government deficits (which lead to a large government debt) is the crowding out of investment. Recall from Chapter 13 that when government spending (G) increases or the level of net taxes (T) decreases (both of which increase the deficit, $G - T$) with the money supply unchanged, the interest rate rises and crowds out (decreases) planned investment spending. The cost of decreased investment spending is then a smaller capital stock.

As you know, one of the key decisions all economies make is how much to consume today and how much to consume in the future. Put another way, resources must be allocated between consumption goods and capital goods. Capital goods (investment in plant and equipment) increase future productivity and lead to economic growth. Our friends Bill and Colleen faced this decision on their desert island. They had to decide how to allocate their time between building a boat (capital investment) and gathering food (consumption). If the government through its tax and expenditure policies is crowding out investment (by spending more than it receives in tax revenues), future economic growth is being hurt. This is why many argue that the real burden of the government deficits will fall on U.S. children, whose standards of living will be lower in the future than they would have been if the government had not spent so much relative to its income in the past.

■ **What Does the Deficit Measure?**   Much of the concern over the federal debt centers around the fact that it represents a claim on the government in the future. Recent economic analysis of the federal budget suggests that the annual budget deficit may be a misleading indicator of the impact of the overall government budget, however. This may be true because the borrowing undertaken in a given year is only one aspect of the total "obligations" that the government incurs in that year.

---

[1]*Sometimes, noncapital expenditures also benefit future generations. The United States borrowed more than 120% of its GDP to fight World War II to save future generations from Nazi tyranny.*

As an extreme example, suppose that the government decides to reduce the level of social security benefits for retirees starting in 1999. Such a policy would have no impact on the actual budgets between now and 1999, but the government's total obligations are now lower. Similarly, changes in loan guarantee programs (such as government guarantees of the mortgages of some veterans) or in deposit insurance laws can have significant impacts on the future obligations of the federal government. Expanding loan guarantees may cost us nothing today but lead to large expenses in the future. If the government were a corporation, accountants would insist that all future obligations be recognized on the books, just as if a bond had been issued.

DEFICIT REDUCTION AND MACROPOLICY

The size of the federal government's deficit has been a concern to policy makers for many years. The deficit problem began in the early 1980s, when huge increases in the deficit occurred, and has continued unabated since that time. When the deficit reached 4.7% of GDP in 1986, the U.S. Congress passed and President Reagan signed a bill known popularly as the **Gramm-Rudman-Hollings Bill,** after its three congressional sponsors. Hereafter, we will refer to this bill as the GRH legislation, or just GRH.

In essence, GRH set a target for reducing the federal deficit by a set amount each year. As Figure 16.2 shows, the deficit was to decline by $36 billion per year between 1987 and 1991, with a deficit of zero slated for fiscal year 1991. What was particularly interesting about the GRH legislation was that the targets were not merely guidelines. If Congress, through its decisions about taxes and spending programs, produced a budget with a deficit larger than the targeted amount, GRH called for automatic spending cuts. The cuts were divided proportionately among most federal spending programs, so that a program that comprised 5% of total spending was to endure a cut equal to 5% of the total spending cut.[2]

In 1986, the U.S. Supreme Court declared part of the GRH bill unconstitutional. In effect, the court said that the Congress would have to approve the "automatic" spending cuts before they could take place. The law was changed in 1986 to meet the Supreme Court ruling and again in 1987, when new targets were established. The new targets had the deficit reaching zero in 1993 rather than 1991. The targets were changed again in 1991, when the year to achieve a zero deficit was changed from 1993 to 1996.

You can see from the actual deficit values in Table 16.1 that these targets never came close to being achieved. As time wore on even the revised targets became completely unrealistic, and by the end of the 1980s the GRH legislation was not taken seriously.

But the deficit problem continued in the 1990s, and one of President Clinton's goals when he took office in January of 1992 was to reduce the deficit. The first step in this direction was the Omnibus Budget Reconciliation Act of 1993. The act, which barely made it through Congress, was projected to reduce the deficit in the five fiscal years 1994–1998 by a total of $504.8 billion. About half of this amount ($254.7 billion) would come from cuts in federal spending, and about half ($250.1 billion) would come from tax increases. Most of the tax increases were to be levied on high-income taxpayers.

Once the act passed, the Clinton administration began focusing on health-care reform, and much of the political discussion in 1994 centered on this issue.

Gramm-Rudman-Hollings Bill
Passed by the U.S. Congress and signed by President Reagan in 1986, this law set out to reduce the federal deficit by $36 billion per year, with a deficit of zero slated for 1991.

FIGURE 16.2
Deficit Reduction Targets under Gramm-Rudman-Hollings
The GRH legislation, passed in 1986, set out to lower the federal deficit by $36 billion per year. If the plan had worked, a zero deficit would have been achieved by 1991.

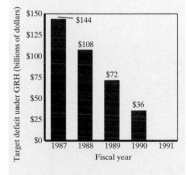

---

[2]*Certain programs, notably Social Security, were exempt from cuts or were treated somewhat differently. Interest payments on the federal debt were also immune from cuts.*

THE U.S. DEFICIT BEGAN TO INCREASE DRAMATICALLY IN THE EARLY 1980s, AND IT REMAINS AN IMPORTANT ISSUE TODAY.

Discussions got very heated. Many people feared that large tax increases would be needed to fund the reforms, and others worried that the reforms would lead to even more government bureaucracy. No health-care legislation was passed in 1994, and in November of that year the Republicans were voted into the majority in both houses of Congress. Many political commentators believe that the Republican victory was the result of a widespread concern that the Democrats wanted more government programs (especially in the health-care area) and more taxes to fund the programs. The Republicans' "Contract with America" called for less government and lower taxes.

Two of the Republicans' main goals in 1995 were (1) a cut in taxes and government spending and (2) a decrease in the federal government deficit. Clearly, to achieve the second goal, government spending has to be cut more than taxes, and this is where things get difficult. Almost everyone likes tax cuts, but spending cuts hurt at least some groups of people. How can one ensure that the late 1990s will not be a replay of the early 1980s, where taxes were cut much more than spending and huge deficits resulted? The Contract with America called for a "balanced-budget amendment," which it was hoped would prevent Congress from doing what it did in the 1980s. The balanced-budget amendment passed the House in early 1995, but it failed by one vote in the Senate. It is unlikely, however, that we have heard the last of this amendment.

Many economists who favor deficit reduction were opposed to the GRH legislation and are opposed to the balanced-budget amendment. As we will now see, some of the macroeconomic consequences of the GRH legislation and the balanced-budget amendment are undesirable, and many feel that they are a high price to pay for deficit reduction. Whatever one's view about deficit targeting proposals like the GRH legislation and the balanced-budget amendment, the proposals provide an excellent framework for analyzing macroeconomic effects.

THE EFFECTS OF GOVERNMENT SPENDING CUTS ON THE DEFICIT

Suppose that the terms of the balanced-budget amendment or some other deficit-reduction measure dictate that the deficit must be cut by $20 billion. By how much must government spending be cut to achieve this goal? You might be tempted to think that the spending cuts should simply add up to the amount by which the deficit is to be cut—in this case, $20 billion. (This is in fact what GRH dictated: If the deficit needed to be cut by a certain amount, automatic spending cuts were to be equal to this amount.) This course of action seems reasonable from an individual household's point of view. If you decrease your personal spending by $100 over the course of a year, your personal deficit will fall by the full $100 of your spending cut.

But the government is not an individual household. A cut in government spending shifts the *AD* curve to the left and results in a decrease in aggregate output (income) (*Y*) and thus a contraction in the economy. When the economy contracts, both the taxable income of households and the profits of firms fall. This means that revenue from the personal income tax and the corporate profits tax will fall.

How do these events affect the size of the deficit? To estimate the response of the deficit to changes in government spending, we need to go through two steps. First, we must decide how much a $1 change in government spending will change GDP. In other words, we need to know the size of the government spending multiplier. (Recall that the government spending multiplier measures the increase [or decrease] in GDP [*Y*] brought about by a $1 increase [or decrease] in government spending.) Based on empirical evidence, a reasonable value for the government spending multiplier seems to be around 1.4 after one year, and this is the value that we will use here. This means that a $1 billion decrease in government spending lowers GDP by about $1.4 billion after one year.

Next, we must see what happens to the deficit when GDP changes. We have just noted that when GDP falls (that is, when the economy contracts), taxable income and corporate profits fall and thus tax revenues fall. In addition, some categories of government expenditures tend to rise when the economy contracts. For example, unemployment insurance benefits (a transfer payment) rise as the economy contracts because more people become unemployed and thus eligible for unemployment benefits. Both the decrease in tax revenues and the rise in government expenditures cause the deficit to increase. Thus,

> The deficit tends to rise when GDP falls. Conversely, the deficit tends to fall when GDP rises.

For the sake of illustration, let us assume that the **deficit response index (DRI)** is −.22. That is, for every $1 billion decrease in GDP, the deficit rises by $0.22 billion. This number seems close to what is true in practice.

We can now use the multiplier and the DRI to answer the question that began this section. Suppose that government spending is reduced by $20 billion, the exact amount of the necessary deficit reduction. This will lower GDP by 1.4 × $20 billion, or $28 billion, if the value of the multiplier is 1.4. A $28 billion fall in GDP will increase the deficit by .22 × $28 billion, or $6.2 billion, if the value of the DRI is −.22. Because we initially cut government spending (and therefore lowered the deficit from this source) by $20 billion, the net effect of the spending cut is to lower the deficit by $20 billion − $6.2 billion = $13.8 billion.

A $20 billion government spending cut thus does not lower the deficit by the required $20 billion. To lower the deficit by the full $20 billion, we need to cut government spending by about $30 billion. Using 1.4 as the value of the government

deficit response index (DRI) *The amount by which the deficit changes with a one dollar change in GDP.*

spending multiplier and $-.22$ as the value of the DRI, we see that a spending cut of $30 billion lowers GDP by $1.4 \times \$30$ billion, or $42 billion. This raises the deficit by $.22 \times \$42$ billion, or $9.2 billion. The net effect on the deficit is thus $-\$30$ billion (from the government spending cut) + $9.2 billion, which is $-\$20.8$ billion (an amount slightly larger than the necessary $20 billion reduction). This means that the spending cut must be nearly 50% larger than the deficit reduction we wish to achieve! Clearly, then, Congress would have had trouble achieving the deficit targets under the GRH legislation even if it had allowed GRH's automatic spending cuts to take place.

■ **Monetary Policy to the Rescue?** Is Congress really so poorly informed about macroeconomics that it would pass legislation that could not possibly work? In other words, are there any conditions under which it would be reasonable to assume that a spending cut needs to be only as large as the desired reduction in the deficit? If the government spending multiplier is zero, government spending cuts will not contract the economy and there will be no effect from this source on the deficit. In this case, the only effect on the deficit will be the initial cut in government spending.

But are there times when it is reasonable to assume that the government spending multiplier is zero? Before the GRH bill was passed, some argued that there were. The argument went as follows: If households and firms are worried about the large government deficits and hold back on consumption and investment because of these worries, the passage of GRH might make them more optimistic and induce them to consume and invest more. This increased consumption and investment, the argument continued, would offset the effects of the decreased government spending, and the net result would be a multiplier effect of zero.

Another argument in favor of the GRH bill centered on the Fed and monetary policy. We know from Chapter 14 that an increase in the money supply shifts the AD curve to the right. Because a cut in government spending shifts the AD curve to the left, the Fed could respond to the spending cut by increasing the money supply enough to shift the AD curve back (to the right) to its original position, thus preventing any change in aggregate output (income). Some argued that the Fed would be likely to behave in this way after the passage of the GRH bill because it would see that Congress finally "got its house in order."

We know from Chapter 13 that an increase in the money supply leads to a decrease in the equilibrium interest rate. Therefore, if the Fed were to offset the effects of a decrease in government spending by increasing the money supply, the interest rate would fall, thus stimulating planned investment and offsetting the effects of the decrease in G. Again, this would be a multiplier of zero. However, studies done at the time of the original GRH bill showed that the decrease in the interest rate that would be necessary to have the multiplier be zero (that is, for a government spending cut to have no effect on aggregate output [income]) is quite large. The Fed would have had to engage in extreme behavior with respect to interest rate changes for the multiplier to be zero.

To summarize:

A zero multiplier can come about through renewed optimism on the part of households and firms or through very aggressive behavior on the part of the Fed. But because neither of these situations is very plausible, the multiplier is likely to be greater than zero. Thus, it is likely that in order to lower the deficit by a certain amount, the cut in government spending must be larger than that amount.

ECONOMIC STABILITY AND DEFICIT REDUCTION

We have seen that lowering the deficit by a given amount is likely to require a government spending decrease larger than this amount. However, this is not the only important point to take away from our analysis of deficit targeting. We will now see how deficit targeting can adversely affect the way the economy responds to a variety of stimuli.

In a world with no GRH, balanced-budget amendment, or similar deficit targeting measure, the Congress and the President make decisions each year about how much to spend and how much to tax. The federal government deficit is a result of these decisions and the state of the economy. With GRH or the balanced budget amendment, in contrast, the size of the deficit is set in advance. Taxes and government spending must be adjusted to produce the required deficit. In this situation, the deficit is no longer a consequence of the tax and spending decisions. Rather, taxes and spending become a consequence of the deficit decision.

What difference does it make whether Congress chooses a target deficit and adjusts government spending and taxes to achieve this target or decides how much to spend and tax and lets the deficit adjust itself? The difference may be substantial. Consider a leftward shift of the *AD* curve caused by some negative demand shock. A **negative demand shock** is something that causes a negative shift in consumption or investment schedules or that leads to a decrease in U.S. exports.

We know that a leftward shift of the *AD* curve lowers aggregate output (income), which causes the government deficit to increase. In a world without deficit targeting, the increase in the deficit during contractions provides an **automatic stabilizer** for the economy. (Review Chapter 10 if this term is hazy to you.) The contraction-induced decrease in tax revenues and increase in transfer payments tends to boost consumer incomes and stimulate consumer spending at a time when spending would otherwise be weak. Thus, the decrease in aggregate output (income) caused by the negative demand shock is lessened somewhat by the growth of the deficit (Figure 16.3a).

negative demand shock
Something that causes a negative shift in consumption or investment schedules or that leads to a decrease in U.S. exports.

automatic stabilizers *Revenue and expenditure items in the federal budget that automatically change with the economy in such a way as to stabilize GDP.*

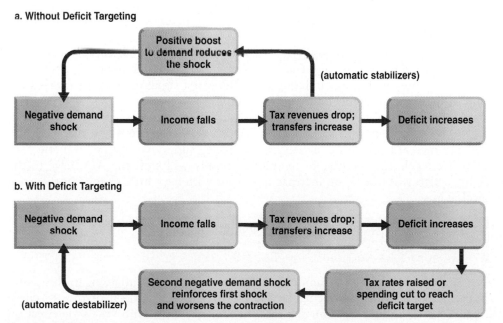

a. Without Deficit Targeting

b. With Deficit Targeting

FIGURE 16.3

Deficit Targeting as an Automatic Destabilizer

Deficit targeting changes the way the economy responds to negative demand shocks because it does not allow the deficit to increase. The result is a smaller deficit, but a larger decline in income than would have otherwise occurred.

In a world with deficit targeting, the deficit is not allowed to rise. Some combination of tax increases and government spending cuts would be needed to offset what would have otherwise been an increase in the deficit. We know that increases in taxes or cuts in spending are contractionary in themselves. The contraction in the economy will therefore be larger than it would have been without deficit targeting, because the initial effect of the negative demand shock is worsened by the rise in taxes or the cut in government spending required to keep the deficit from rising. As Figure 16.3b shows, deficit targeting acts as an **automatic destabilizer.** It requires taxes to be raised and government spending to be cut during a contraction. This reinforces, rather than counteracts, the shock that started the contraction.

■ **Summary**   The preceding discussion should make it clear that the GRH legislation, the balanced-budget amendment, and similar deficit targeting measures have some undesirable macroeconomic consequences. Deficit targeting requires cuts in spending or increases in taxes at times when the economy is already experiencing problems. This is not to say that Congress should ignore the deficit. Rather, it means that locking the economy into spending cuts during periods of negative demand shocks, as deficit targeting measures do, is not a good way to manage the economy.

Nonetheless, some people believe that a balanced-budget amendment is the only way to induce Congress to keep the deficit low. If it is true that a balanced-budget amendment is the only way to discipline Congress, then there is clearly a trade-off. One can have the discipline and bear the macroeconomic costs or not have the discipline and not bear the costs. This trade-off is an important part of the debate regarding the balanced-budget amendment.

THE FED'S RESPONSE TO THE STATE OF THE ECONOMY

We know from Chapter 11 that the Fed can control the money supply through open market operations, and we know from Chapters 13 and 14 that changes in the money supply can affect aggregate output (income) (Y), the interest rate, and the price level. The Fed thus has the power to affect the economy through open market operations. But what factors affect its decisions? Why does the Fed sometimes choose to increase the money supply and sometimes choose to decrease the money supply?

Two of the Fed's main goals are high levels of output and employment and a low rate of inflation. From the Fed's point of view, the best situation is a fully employed economy with a low inflation rate. The worst situation is *stagflation*—a period of high unemployment and high inflation.

If the economy is in a low output/low inflation situation, it will be producing on the relatively flat portion of the *AS* curve (Figure 16.4). In this case, the Fed can increase output by increasing the money supply with very little effect on the price level. The increase in the money supply will shift the *AD* curve to the right, which will lead to an increase in output with very little change in the price level. Thus:

> The Fed is likely to increase the money supply during times of low output and low inflation.

The opposite is true in times of high output and high inflation. In this situation, the economy is producing on the relatively steep portion of the *AS* curve (Figure 16.5), and the Fed can decrease the money supply with very little effect on

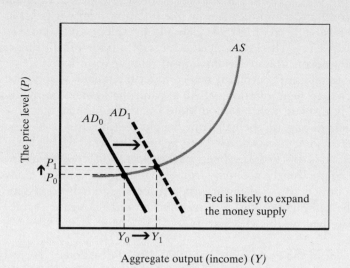

FIGURE 16.4

The Fed's Response to Low Output/Low Inflation

During periods of low output/low inflation, the economy is on the relatively flat portion of the AS curve. In this case, the Fed is likely to expand the money supply. This will shift the AD curve to the right, from AD_0 to AD_1, and lead to an increase in output with very little increase in the price level.

output. The decrease in the money supply will shift the AD curve to the left, which will lead to a fall in the price level and little effect on output.[3] Thus:

The Fed is likely to decrease the money supply during times of high output and high inflation.

FIGURE 16.5

The Fed's Response to High Output/High Inflation

During periods of high output/high inflation, the economy is on the relatively steep portion of the AS curve. In this case, the Fed is likely to contract the money supply. This will shift the AD curve to the left, from AD_0 to AD_1, and lead to a decrease in the price level with very little decrease in output.

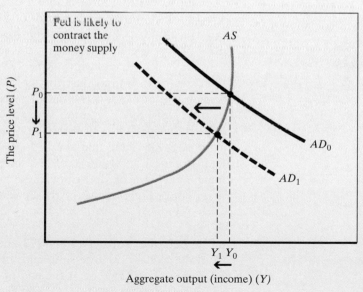

[3]*In practice, the price level rarely falls. What the Fed actually achieves in this case is a decrease in the rate of inflation (that is, in the percentage change in the price level), not a decrease in the price level itself. The discussion here is sliding over the distinction between the price level and the rate of inflation. Recall our discussion of this distinction in Chapter 15.*

Stagflation is a more difficult problem to solve. If the Fed expands the money supply, output will rise, but so will the inflation rate (which is already too high). If the Fed contracts the money supply, the inflation rate will fall, but so will output (which is already too low). (You should be able to draw *AS/AD* diagrams to see why this is true.) The Fed is thus faced with a trade-off. In this case, the Fed's decisions depend on how it weighs output relative to inflation. If it dislikes high inflation more than low output, it will contract the money supply; if it dislikes low output more than high inflation, it will expand the money supply. In practice, the Fed probably dislikes high inflation more than low output, but how the Fed behaves depends in part on the beliefs of the chair of the Fed.

The Fed is sometimes said to "lean against the wind." This means that as the economy expands, the Fed uses open market operations to raise interest rates gradually to try to prevent the economy from expanding too quickly. Conversely, as the economy contracts, the Fed lowers interest rates gradually to lessen (and eventually stop) the contraction. This type of stabilization is not easily achieved, however, as we will see later in this chapter.

■ **The Behavior of the Fed During the 1990–1991 Recessions**   Table 16.2 presents data on selected variables for the 1989 I–1994 IV period. We can use this table to see how the Fed behaved both before and after the 1990–1991 recession. In the first quarter of 1990 the growth rate was 3.3%, the unemployment rate 5.3%, the inflation rate 5.1%, and the three-month Treasury bill rate 7.8 percent. You can see that the Fed kept the bill rate fairly high in 1989. The economy was at or close to full employment, and the Fed wanted to keep the inflation rate in check.

In the second half of 1990, the economy went into a recession. Since inflation seemed to be under control at this time, experts expected that the Fed would begin following an expansionary monetary policy to lessen the contraction of the economy. At the end of 1990, the Fed began to follow exactly this policy. Table 16.2 shows that the three-month T-bill rate fell from 7.0% in the fourth quarter of 1990 to 6.1% in the first quarter of 1991. By the fourth quarter of 1991, the bill rate was down to 4.6 percent. This lowering of interest rates was designed to stimulate private spending and bring the economy out of the recession.

The Fed's behavior during the 1990–1991 recession is thus a clear example of its tendency to lean against the wind. After the Fed became convinced that a recession was at hand, it responded by engaging in open market operations to lower interest rates. Since inflation was not a problem, the Fed could expand the economy in this way without worrying much about the inflationary consequences of its actions. Some argue that the Fed should have acted sooner, but with the Persian Gulf situation uncertain until February 1991, the Fed did not want to expand too much in the face of a possibly lengthy war that could have led to inflationary pressures. Once the outcome of the Persian Gulf War was known, the Fed responded fairly rapidly.

■ **The Behavior of the Fed in 1993 and 1994**   The economy was slow to recover from the 1990–1991 recession, and the growth rate did not pick up much until the beginning of 1992. Even at the end of 1992, the unemployment rate was still high at 7.3% (see again Table 16.2). The Fed kept the bill rate relatively low in 1992 and 1993 in an attempt to stimulate the economy. This was simply an extension of its expansionary policy in 1991. Again, inflation was not a problem in 1992 and 1993, so the Fed had room to stimulate. By the fourth quarter of 1993 the unemployment rate had fallen to 6.5% and the growth rate was 5.1 percent.

TABLE 16.2

QUARTER	REAL GDP GROWTH RATE (%)	UNEMPLOYMENT RATE (%)	INFLATION RATE (%)	THREE-MONTH T-BILL RATE	AAA BOND RATE	FEDERAL GOVERNMENT DEFICIT	DEFICIT/GDP
1989 I	3.6	5.2	4.8	8.5	9.7	110.1	0.021
II	1.7	5.2	4.6	8.4	9.5	109.6	0.021
III	0.2	5.3	3.6	7.8	9.0	128.1	0.024
IV	1.5	5.4	3.5	7.6	8.9	141.4	0.026
1990 I	3.3	5.3	5.1	7.8	9.2	166.5	0.031
II	1.4	5.3	4.8	7.8	9.4	152.0	0.027
III	−1.2	5.6	4.6	7.5	9.4	144.7	0.026
IV	−2.5	6.0	3.4	7.0	9.3	191.0	0.035
1991 I	−2.3	6.5	5.2	6.1	8.9	144.5	0.026
II	1.7	6.7	3.2	5.6	8.9	207.6	0.036
III	0.8	6.7	3.1	5.4	8.8	213.6	0.037
IV	0.1	7.0	2.4	4.6	8.4	245.9	0.042
1992 I	3.1	7.3	3.8	3.9	8.3	279.8	0.047
II	2.0	7.5	3.1	3.7	8.3	284.6	0.048
III	2.6	7.5	2.3	3.1	8.0	293.9	0.049
IV	5.9	7.3	2.4	3.1	8.0	272.2	0.044
1993 I	0.4	7.0	4.0	3.0	7.7	283.3	0.045
II	1.8	7.0	2.3	3.0	7.4	237.1	0.038
III	1.9	6.7	1.9	3.0	6.9	224.9	0.035
IV	5.1	6.5	2.5	3.1	6.8	220.1	0.034
1994 I	2.8	6.6	3.2	3.3	7.2	176.2	0.027
II	4.3	6.2	2.7	4.0	7.9	145.1	0.022
III	3.4	6.0	2.8	4.5	8.2	154.0	0.023
IV	3.7	5.6	2.5	5.3	8.6	161.1	0.023

Note: The inflation rate is the percentage change in the GDP price index.

At the end of 1993 the Fed decided to begin contracting the economy. The T-bill rate rose from 3.1% in the fourth quarter of 1993 to 5.3% in the fourth quarter of 1994. Although not shown in the table, the T-bill rate at the beginning of February 1995 was 5.8 percent. Why was the Fed pursuing a contractionary policy? You can see from the table that the inflation rate in 1993 and 1994 was quite low, and there were no signs even at the end of 1994 of any inflationary pressures building in the economy. But the Fed was worried about inflation picking up in the future. The growth rate in 1994 was relatively high (about 3.5%) and the unemployment rate was down to 5.6% by the fourth quarter, and the Fed felt that these trends might spell inflation problems in the future. The survey used to construct the unemployment rate was changed slightly at the end of 1993, and some felt that the measured unemployment rates in 1994 would have been even smaller had the old process still been in effect. This caused further concerns that the unemployment rate was getting too low and that inflationary pressures would follow.

The Fed's behavior in 1994 is thus an example of leaning against the wind quite far in advance, long before any observed sign of increasing inflation. Indeed, some people felt that the Fed was acting too hastily and that it should have waited for direct signs of inflationary pressures before tightening.

LAGS IN THE ECONOMY'S RESPONSE TO MONETARY AND FISCAL POLICY

One of the main objectives of monetary and fiscal policy is stabilization of the economy. Consider the two possible time paths for aggregate output (income) (Y) shown in Figure 16.6 on the next page. In path B (the dashed line), the fluctuations in GDP are smaller than those in path A (the solid line). One aim of

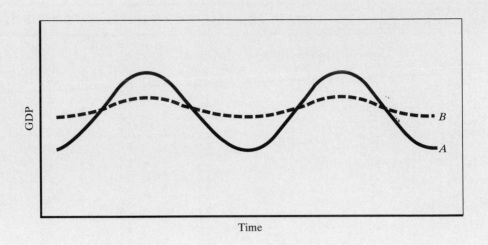

FIGURE 16.6

Two Time Paths for GDP

Path *A* is less stable—that is, it shows more variation over time—than path *B*. Other things being equal, society prefers path *B* to path *A*.

stabilization policy *A term used to describe both monetary and fiscal policy, the goals of which are to smooth out fluctuations in output and employment and to keep prices as stable as possible.*

time lags *Delays in the economy's response to stabilization policies.*

stabilization policy is to smooth out fluctuations in output, to try to move the economy along a path like B instead of A. Stabilization policy is also concerned with the stability of prices. Here the goal is not to prevent the overall price level from rising at all but rather to achieve an inflation rate that is as low as possible given the government's other goals of high and stable levels of output and employment.

Stabilization goals are not easy to achieve. The existence of various kinds of **time lags,** or delays in the response of the economy to stabilization policies, can make the economy difficult to control. Economists generally recognize three kinds of time lags: recognition lags, implementation lags, and response lags. We will consider each of these in turn, but it is useful to begin with an analogy.

■ **"The Fool in the Shower"**   Milton Friedman, a leading critic of stabilization policy, once likened the government's attempts to stabilize the economy to a "fool in the shower." The shower starts out too cold, because the pipes have not yet warmed up. So the fool turns up the hot water. Nothing happens right away, so he turns up the hot water a bit further. The hot water then comes on and scalds him. He immediately turns up the cold water. Again, nothing happens right away, so he turns up the cold still further. When the cold water finally starts to come up, he has succeeded in making the shower too cold. And so it goes.

In Friedman's view, the government is constantly behaving like the fool in the shower, stimulating or contracting the economy at the wrong time. An example of how this might happen is shown in Figure 16.7. Suppose the economy reaches a peak and begins to slide into recession at point A (at time t_0). Policy makers do not observe the decline in GDP until it has sunk to point B (at time t_1). By the time they have begun to stimulate the economy (point C, time t_2), the recession is well advanced and the economy has almost bottomed out. When the policies finally begin to take effect (point D, time t_3), the economy is already on its road to recovery. The policies thus push the economy to point F'—a much greater fluctuation than point F, which is where the economy would have been without the stabilization policy. Sometime after point D, policy makers may begin to realize that the economy is expanding too quickly. But by the time they have implemented contractionary policies and the policies have made their effects felt, the economy is starting to weaken. The contractionary policies therefore end up pushing GDP to point G' instead of point G.

In short: Because of the various time lags, the expansionary policies that should have been instituted at time t_0 do not begin to have an effect until time t_3, when

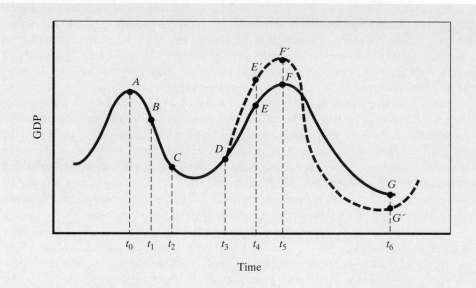

FIGURE 16.7

"The Fool in the Shower"—How Government Policy Can Make Matters Worse

Attempts to stabilize the economy can prove destabilizing because of time lags. An expansionary policy that should have begun to take effect at point *A* does not actually begin to have an impact until point *D*, when the economy is already on an upswing. Hence the policy pushes the economy to points *F'* and *G'* (rather than points *F* and *G*). Income varies more widely than it would have if no policy had been implemented.

they are no longer needed. The dashed lines in Figure 16.7 show how the economy behaves as a result of the "stabilization" policies; the solid lines show the time path of GDP if the economy had been allowed to run its course and no stabilization policies had been attempted. In this case, stabilization policy clearly succeeds in making income more erratic rather than less erratic—the policy results in a peak income of *F'* as opposed to *F* and a trough income of *G'* instead of *G*.

Critics of stabilization policy argue that the situation described in Figure 16.7 is typical of the interaction between the government and the rest of the economy. This is not necessarily true, however. We need to know more about the exact nature of the various kinds of lags before deciding whether stabilization policy is good or bad. We will now consider these lags.

RECOGNITION LAGS

It takes time for policy makers to recognize the existence of a boom or a slump. For one thing, many important data—those from the national income and product accounts, for example—are available only quarterly. It usually takes several weeks to compile and prepare even the preliminary estimates for these figures. Thus, if the economy goes into a slump on January 1, the recession may not show up until the data for the first quarter are available at the end of April.

Moreover, the early national income and product accounts data are only preliminary, based on an incomplete compilation of the various data sources. These estimates can, and often do, change as better data become available. This makes the interpretation of the initial estimates difficult, and **recognition lags** are the result.

recognition lag *The time it takes for policy makers to recognize the existence of a boom or a slump.*

IMPLEMENTATION LAGS

The problems that lags pose for stabilization policy do not end once economists and policy makers recognize that the economy is in a slump or a boom. Even if everyone knows that the economy needs to be stimulated or reined in, it takes time to put the desired policy into effect, especially for actions that involve fiscal policy. **Implementation lags** are the result.

implementation lag *The time that it takes to put the desired policy into effect once economists and policy makers recognize that the economy is in a boom or a slump.*

Each year Congress decides on the federal government's budget for the coming year. The tax laws and spending programs embodied in this budget are not subject to change once they are in place. If it becomes clear that the economy is entering a recession and is in need of a fiscal stimulus during the middle of the year, there is relatively little that can be done. Until Congress authorizes more spending or a cut in taxes, changes in fiscal policy are not possible.[4]

Implementation lags vary in length. In May of 1975, for example, it was clear that the U.S. economy was in the midst of a deep recession and needed immediate stimulation. Although many economists had called for government action earlier, general agreement that action was necessary did not come about until late spring. Once the consensus emerged, President Ford asked Congress for an immediate tax cut retroactive to 1974. (See the Application box on this topic in Chapter 10.) Congress responded, and rebate checks were mailed to millions of people within weeks. As those dollars were spent, the economy began to recover.

Monetary policy is less subject to the kinds of restrictions that slow down changes in fiscal policy. As we saw in Chapter 11, the Fed's chief tool to control the supply of money or the interest rate is open market operations—the buying and selling of government securities. Transactions in these securities take place in a highly developed market, and if the Fed wishes, it can buy or sell a large volume of securities in a very short period of time. Therefore:

> The implementation lag for monetary policy is generally much shorter than it is for fiscal policy.

Whenever the Fed wishes to increase the supply of money, it simply goes into the open market and purchases government securities. This instantly increases the stock of money (that is, bank reserves held at the Fed), and an expansion of the money supply begins.

RESPONSE LAGS

response lag *The time that it takes for the economy to adjust to the new conditions after a new policy is implemented; the lag that occurs because of the operation of the economy itself.*

Even after a macroeconomic problem has been recognized and the appropriate policies to correct it have been implemented, another set of lags remains. These are **response lags**—the lags that occur because of the operation of the economy itself. Even after the government has formulated a policy and put it into place, the economy takes time to adjust to the new conditions.

Although monetary policy can be adjusted and implemented more quickly than fiscal policy, it may actually take longer to make its effect felt on the economy. What is most important is the total lag between the time a problem first occurs and the time the corrective policies are felt. Even if monetary policy has a smaller implementation lag than does fiscal policy, it may nevertheless have a longer lag in total, once response lags are also considered.

■ **Response Lags for Fiscal Policy** One way to think about the response lag in fiscal policy is through the concept of the government spending multiplier. Remember that this multiplier measures the change in GDP caused by a given change in government spending or net taxes. It takes time for the multiplier to reach its full value. There is thus a lag between the time a fiscal policy action is first initiated and the time when the full change in GDP is realized.

---

[4]*Don't forget, however, about the existence of automatic stabilizers. Many programs contain built-in countercyclical features that expand spending or cut tax collections automatically (without the need for congressional or executive action) during a recession.*

The reason for the response lag in fiscal policy—the delay in the multiplier process—is quite simple. During the first few months after an increase in government spending or a tax cut, there simply is not enough time for the firms or individuals who benefit directly from the extra government spending or the tax cut to increase their own spending. A simple example will help to make this clear.

Suppose that you are the owner of Transylvania Trucking, a small fleet of trucks. The government decides to increase its spending, and one of the things it spends more on is trucking services, including some extra purchases from your company. In the first months after you receive this extra business from the government, however, you are unlikely to increase your own purchases. Most of the things you buy—trucks, office furniture, stationery—are already contained in your inventories. It will generally take you some time before your own purchases are increased to reflect the extra income that you have received, and the multiplier effect of government spending will not be felt until this occurs. In short:

> Neither individuals nor firms revise their spending plans instantaneously. Until they can make those revisions, extra government spending does not stimulate extra private spending.

Changes in government purchases have the virtue of being a component of aggregate expenditure. When G rises, aggregate expenditure increases directly; when G falls, aggregate expenditure decreases directly. When personal taxes are changed, however, an additional step intervenes, and this gives rise to another lag. Suppose that a tax cut has lowered personal income taxes across the board. Each household must now decide what portion of its tax cut to spend and what portion to save. This decision is the extra step. Before the tax cut gets translated into extra spending, households must take the step of increasing their spending, and it usually takes some time for this to be done.

With a business tax cut, there is a further complication. Firms must decide what to do with their added after-tax profits. If they pay out their added profits to households as dividends, the result is the same as that of a personal tax cut. Households must decide whether to spend or to save the extra funds. Firms may also retain their added profits and use them for investment, but investment is a component of aggregate expenditure that requires planning and time.

In practice, it takes about a year for a change in taxes or in government spending to have its full effect on the economy. This means that if we increase spending to counteract a recession today, the full effects will not be felt for 12 months. By that time, the state of the economy might be very different from what it is now.

■ **Response Lags for Monetary Policy** As you know, monetary policy works by changing interest rates, which then change planned investment. Interest rates can also affect consumption spending, as we discuss in more detail in the next chapter. For now, though, it is enough to know that lower interest rates usually stimulate consumption spending and higher interest rates decrease consumption spending.

The response of consumption and investment to interest rate changes takes time. Even if interest rates were to drop by five percentage points overnight, firms would not immediately increase their investment purchases. Firms generally make their investment plans several years in advance. For example, if General Motors wants to respond to a decrease in interest rates by investing more, it will take some time—perhaps up to a year—for the firm to come up with plans for a new factory or assembly line. While such plans are being drawn up, GM may spend very little on new investments. Thus, the effect of the decrease in interest rates may not make itself felt for quite some time.

It is likely that the response lags for monetary policy will be even longer than those for fiscal policy. When government spending changes, there is a direct change in the sales of firms, which sell more as a result of the increased government purchases. When interest rates change, however, the sales of firms do not change until households change their consumption spending and/or firms change their investment spending. As we have just said, it takes time for households and firms to respond to interest rate changes. In this sense, interest rate changes are like tax-rate changes. The resulting change in firm sales must wait for households and firms to change their purchases of goods.

■ **Summary**   From this analysis it should be clear that stabilization is not easily achieved. It takes time for policy makers to recognize the existence of a problem, more time for them to implement a solution, and yet more time for firms and households to respond to the stabilization policies taken. Monetary policy can be adjusted more quickly and easily than taxes or government spending, and this makes it a useful instrument in stabilizing the economy. But because the economy's response to monetary changes is probably slower than its response to changes in fiscal policy, tax and spending changes can also play a useful role in macroeconomic management.

BUSINESS CYCLES IN OTHER COUNTRIES

We have examined the ups and downs of the U.S. economy in considerable detail in this text. But the United States is not the only developed nation to have business cycles. We now turn to a discussion of inflation and unemployment in six other developed economies: Japan, the United Kingdom, (West) Germany, France, Italy, and Spain. Figure 16.8 gives data for the 1980–1993 period for each country's growth rate, (2) inflation rate, (3) unemployment rate, and (4) short-term interest rate.

Consider Japan first. The overall performance of the Japanese economy in the 1980–1993 period was quite good. The unemployment rate never rose above 2.9%, and inflation was above 3% only in 1980 and 1981. The only real weakness occurred in 1992 and 1993, where the growth rates were only 1.1% and 0.1%, respectively. The unemployment rate rose from 2.1% in 1991 to 2.5% in 1993. The Bank of Japan eased monetary policy during this period in an attempt to stimulate the economy, and as a result the short-term interest rate fell substantially from 1991 to 1993. The Bank of Japan's "leaning against the wind" behavior is similar to the behavior of the Fed we discussed earlier in this chapter. Clearly, the Japanese economy does have some ups and downs, but overall its cyclical fluctuations have been fairly mild by U.S. standards.

(In 1995, the Bank of Japan faced a dilemma after an earthquake hit the city of Kobe. For more details, see the Global Perspective box on page 384 titled "The Bank of Japan and the Kobe Earthquake.")

The Japanese fluctuations are also mild by European standards, as the rest of the figure shows. Consider the United Kingdom's economy, which shows distinct cycles. The U.K. growth rate was negative in 1980–1981 and then again in 1991–1992, while the growth rate in the mid-1980s was strong. Note that inflation was very high in 1980 and 1981 even though growth was negative, a clear period of stagflation. By 1990 the unemployment rate had fallen to 6.8%, but it then began rising again as the growth rate turned negative. The interest rate dropped substantially during the 1991–1993 period, which reflects the Bank of England's easing of monetary policy to try to stimulate the economy.

The general U.K. pattern of low or negative growth in the early 1980s and then again in the early 1990s also holds for the other four European countries in the figure. In addition, the inflation rate has been generally falling over time in the European countries, except for Germany, where it as always been fairly low. Another general pattern is the fairly high level of unemployment across all the European countries for most of the 1980–1993 period, with Spain experiencing the worst problems in this area.

FIGURE 16.8

Data for Selected Variables for Selected Nations, 1980–1993

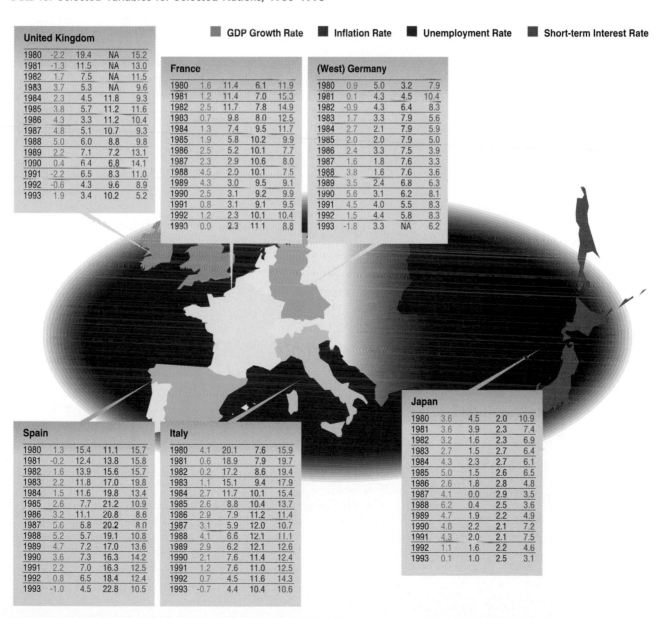

■ GDP Growth Rate   ■ Inflation Rate   ■ Unemployment Rate   ■ Short-term Interest Rate

United Kingdom

Year	GDP	Infl	Unemp	Int
1980	-2.2	19.4	NA	15.2
1981	-1.3	11.5	NA	13.0
1982	1.7	7.5	NA	11.5
1983	3.7	5.3	NA	9.6
1984	2.3	4.5	11.8	9.3
1985	3.8	5.7	11.2	11.6
1986	4.3	3.3	11.2	10.4
1987	4.8	5.1	10.7	9.3
1988	5.0	6.0	8.8	9.8
1989	2.2	7.1	7.2	13.1
1990	0.4	6.4	6.8	14.1
1991	-2.2	6.5	8.3	11.0
1992	-0.6	4.3	9.6	8.9
1993	1.9	3.4	10.2	5.2

France

Year	GDP	Infl	Unemp	Int
1980	1.6	11.4	6.1	11.9
1981	1.2	11.4	7.0	15.3
1982	2.5	11.7	7.8	14.9
1983	0.7	9.8	8.0	12.5
1984	1.3	7.4	9.5	11.7
1985	1.9	5.8	10.2	9.9
1986	2.5	5.2	10.1	7.7
1987	2.3	2.9	10.6	8.0
1988	4.5	2.9	10.1	7.5
1989	4.3	3.0	9.5	9.1
1990	2.5	3.1	9.2	9.9
1991	0.8	3.1	9.1	9.5
1992	1.2	2.3	10.1	10.4
1993	0.0	2.3	11.1	8.8

(West) Germany

Year	GDP	Infl	Unemp	Int
1980	0.9	5.0	3.2	7.9
1981	0.1	4.3	4.5	10.4
1982	-0.9	4.3	6.4	8.3
1983	1.7	3.3	7.9	5.6
1984	2.7	2.1	7.9	5.9
1985	2.0	2.0	7.9	5.0
1986	2.4	3.3	7.5	3.9
1987	1.6	1.8	7.6	3.3
1988	3.8	1.6	7.6	3.6
1989	3.5	2.4	6.8	6.3
1990	5.6	3.1	6.2	8.1
1991	4.5	4.0	5.5	8.3
1992	1.5	4.4	5.8	8.3
1993	-1.8	3.3	NA	6.2

Spain

Year	GDP	Infl	Unemp	Int
1980	1.3	15.4	11.1	15.7
1981	-0.2	12.4	13.8	15.8
1982	1.6	13.9	15.6	15.7
1983	2.2	11.8	17.0	19.8
1984	1.5	11.6	19.8	13.4
1985	2.6	7.7	21.2	10.9
1986	3.2	11.1	20.8	8.6
1987	5.6	6.8	20.2	8.0
1988	5.2	5.7	19.1	10.8
1989	4.7	7.2	17.0	13.6
1990	3.6	7.3	16.3	14.2
1991	2.2	7.0	16.3	12.5
1992	0.8	6.5	18.4	12.4
1993	-1.0	4.5	22.8	10.5

Italy

Year	GDP	Infl	Unemp	Int
1980	4.1	20.1	7.6	15.9
1981	0.6	18.9	7.9	19.7
1982	0.2	17.2	8.6	19.4
1983	1.1	15.1	9.4	17.9
1984	2.7	11.7	10.1	15.4
1985	2.6	8.8	10.4	13.7
1986	2.9	7.9	11.2	11.4
1987	3.1	5.9	12.0	10.7
1988	4.1	6.6	12.1	11.1
1989	2.9	6.2	12.1	12.6
1990	2.1	7.6	11.4	12.4
1991	1.2	7.6	11.0	12.5
1992	0.7	4.5	11.6	14.3
1993	-0.7	4.4	10.4	10.6

Japan

Year	GDP	Infl	Unemp	Int
1980	3.6	4.5	2.0	10.9
1981	3.6	3.9	2.3	7.4
1982	3.2	1.6	2.3	6.9
1983	2.7	1.5	2.7	6.4
1984	4.3	2.3	2.7	6.1
1985	5.0	1.5	2.6	6.5
1986	2.6	1.8	2.8	4.8
1987	4.1	0.0	2.9	3.5
1988	6.2	0.4	2.5	3.6
1989	4.7	1.9	2.2	4.9
1990	4.8	2.2	2.1	7.2
1991	4.3	2.0	2.1	7.5
1992	1.1	1.6	2.2	4.6
1993	0.1	1.0	2.5	3.1

THE BANK OF JAPAN AND THE KOBE EARTHQUAKE

In January 1995, the city of Kobe, Japan, was hit by a massive earthquake. Thousands died in what was Japan's worst natural disaster of the century. In the aftermath of the quake, the city of Kobe and the surrounding area had to be rebuilt largely with government money. The tremendous expenditure required to rebuild represented a shift of the aggregate demand curve to the right, which put upward pressure on prices.

This situation left the Bank of Japan (the Japanese central bank) with a difficult choice: Should it risk inflation by accommodating the expanded demand for money by increasing the money supply, or should it hold the money supply in check, thus allowing interest rates to rise

and slowing the economy precisely when a recovery from recession was beginning? The following excerpt from *The New York Times* lays out the dilemma:

> Perhaps the greatest challenge to be faced by the Japanese authorities will be for the central bank, which must decide whether it wants to tighten monetary policy—and thus help to offset the inflationary aspects of government spending—or keep it relatively loose for fear of damaging a banking system that has not fully recovered from bad loans made in earlier years.
>
> "Japan is the only country in the world with substantial

savings," said William Sterling, an international economist at Merrill Lynch. "Now it has a very pressing need.". . .

> There are those who doubt the thesis that interest rates will be pushed up[.] Certainly, rates generally have not risen since the quake, and there is not a fixed supply of capital in the world. Banks can create credit, and may do so in this case.
>
> But the demand for money still seems likely to have at least some effect, simply because the quake's damage was so large.

Source: Floyd Norris, "From Japan's Quake, Fear of Higher Interest Rates," *The New York Times,* January 19, 1995, p. D1.

There has been much discussion in Europe as to why the unemployment rates have remained so high for so long. Some argue that the problem is caused by the generous social welfare benefits in Europe—especially unemployment benefits—which may lead the unemployed not to search very hard for a job. Others argue that the problem has mushroomed as people who are laid off lose more work skills the longer they remain unemployed and thus face over time a lower likelihood of being hired again. Others argue that because of union power the real wage rate has been kept higher than it should be to achieve full employment. Finally, some argue that monetary and fiscal policies, especially monetary policies, have not been expansionary enough. They argue, for example, that more expansionary monetary policies could have led to lower unemployment rates without much of an increase in inflation. (Note that short-term interest rates were fairly high in Europe throughout the period, even after the inflation rates fell substantially.)

It is hard to resolve these debates, and it could be that each explanation has some validity. What they do show is that macro problems are not unique to the United States. Although customs and institutions differ across countries, the basic tools of macroeconomics can be applied to many countries.

THE FEDERAL DEFICIT AND THE FEDERAL DEBT

1. The *federal deficit* is the difference between what the federal government spends and what it collects in taxes $(G - T)$. In 1994, the federal deficit was $159.1 billion. To finance the deficit, the U.S. Treasury issues government securities (bills, notes, and bonds).

2. The *federal debt* is the total of all accumulated federal deficits minus surpluses over time. The current federal debt is over $4 trillion. The term *federal debt held by the public* refers to the privately held (non-government-held) debt of the U.S. government. Because most of the federal debt is owned by U.S. citizens, most interest payments on the federal debt are simply a transfer from one group (taxpayers) to another (bondholders).

3. Debt is not necessarily a bad thing. To the extent that borrowing is done to finance the purchase of capital assets that will bring benefits over many years, borrowing money and issuing debt are logical ways to finance acquisitions, whether by households, firms, or governments. Unfortunately, the federal government does not distinguish between capital expenditures and current spending. There is thus no way to know how much government borrowing can be justified as capital purchases that will bring benefits in the future.

4. When government spending increases or the level of net taxes decreases (both of which increase the deficit, $G - T$) with the money supply unchanged, the interest rate rises and crowds out planned investment spending. Less investment means less capital stock, which means decreased future productivity and lower economic growth. Thus large deficits may cause future standards of living to be lower than they would have been if the government had not incurred such large deficits.

5. Recent economic analysis of the federal budget suggests that the annual budget deficit may be a misleading indicator of the impact of the overall government budget. This may be true because the borrowing undertaken in a given year is only one aspect of the total obligations that the government incurs in that year.

DEFICIT REDUCTION AND MACROPOLICY: GRAMM-RUDMAN-HOLLINGS

6. In fiscal year 1986, Congress passed and President Reagan signed the *Gramm-Rudman-Hollings Bill*, which set out to reduce the federal deficit by $36 billion per year, with a zero deficit slated for fiscal year 1991. If Congress passed a budget with a deficit larger than the targeted amount, the law called for automatic spending cuts. A Supreme Court ruling later overturned this provision, and the actual figures for each year never came close to the targets. Recent attempts to get the deficit under control include the Omnibus Budget Reconciliation Act and the proposed balanced-budget amendment.

7. The deficit tends to rise when GDP falls, and to fall when GDP rises. The *deficit response index (DRI)* is the amount by which the deficit changes with a one dollar change in GDP.

8. For spending cuts of a certain amount to reduce the deficit by the same amount, the government spending multiplier must be zero. Before GRH was passed, some argued that a government spending multiplier of zero can be achieved through renewed optimism on the part of households or through very aggressive behavior by the Fed to decrease the interest rate. Empirical evidence has shown that neither of these situations is very plausible. Therefore, in order to lower the deficit by a certain amount, government spending cuts must be larger than that amount.

9. Deficit targeting measures that call for automatic spending cuts to eliminate or reduce the deficit may have the effect of destabilizing the economy because they prevent automatic stabilizers from working. Nonetheless, some argue that a balanced-budget amendment is the only way to control Congress' spending activities and that there is a trade-off between fiscal discipline and economic stability.

THE FED'S RESPONSE TO THE STATE OF THE ECONOMY

10. Because the Fed can control the money supply through open market operations, it has the ability to affect aggregate output (income) (Y), the interest rate, and the price level. The Fed is likely to increase the money supply during times of low output and low inflation, and to decrease the money supply during periods of high output and high inflation. The Fed's behavior during stagflation (periods of high unemployment and high inflation) depends on how the Fed weighs output relative to inflation.

11. As the economy expands, the Fed tends to use open market operations to raise interest rates gradually to try to prevent the economy from expanding too quickly. Conversely, the Fed lowers interest rates gradually to lessen (and eventually stop) a contraction. This tendency is called "leaning against the wind."

LAGS IN THE ECONOMY'S RESPONSE TO MONETARY AND FISCAL POLICY

12. *Stabilization policy* is an inclusive term used to describe both fiscal and monetary policy, the goals of which are to smooth out fluctuations in output and employment and to keep prices as stable as possible. Stabilization goals are not necessarily easy to achieve because of the existence of certain *time lags,* or delays in the response of the economy to macropolicies.

13. A *recognition lag* is the time it takes for policy makers to recognize the existence of a boom or slump. An *implementation lag* is the time it takes to put the desired policy into effect once economists and policy makers recognize that the economy is in a boom or a slump. A *response lag* is the time that it takes for the economy to adjust to the new conditions after a new policy is implemented—in other words, a lag that occurs because of the operation of the economy itself. In general, monetary policy can be implemented more rapidly than fiscal policy, but fiscal policy generally has a shorter response lag than monetary policy.

BUSINESS CYCLES IN OTHER COUNTRIES

14. The United States is not the only developed country to experience business cycles. Since 1980, the nations of Europe have shown great fluctuation in growth rates, unemployment rates, and inflation rates. Japan's business cycles have been mild compared to those of the United States and Europe.

15. Several explanations have been offered for the persistence of high unemployment in Europe: (1) generous social welfare benefits, (2) structural unemployment as workers lose more skills the longer they are laid off, (3) union-imposed above-equilibrium wages, and (4) monetary and fiscal policies that have not been expansionary enough. Each explanation may have some validity.

REVIEW TERMS AND CONCEPTS

automatic destabilizer 374
automatic stabilizer 373
deficit response index (DRI) 371
federal debt 364
federal debt held by
  the public 365

federal deficit 364
Gramm-Rudman-Hollings Bill 369
implementation lag 379
negative demand shock 373
recognition lag 379

response lag 380
stabilization policy 378
time lag 378

PROBLEM SET

1. Some people argue that the U.S. debt is not a problem because the country "owes the debt to itself." Who actually owns the U.S. debt? Does this mean that the debt is not a problem?

2. You are given the following information about the economy in 1996 (all amounts are in billions of dollars):
   (1) Consumption function: $C = 100 + (0.8 \times Y_d)$
   (2) Taxes: $T = -150 + (0.25 \times Y)$
   (3) Investment function: $I = 60$
   (4) Disposable income: $Y_d = Y - T$
   (5) Government spending: $G = 80$
   (6) Equilibrium: $Y = C + I + G$

   Hint: Deficit is $D = G - T = G - [-150 + (0.25 \times Y)]$

   a. Find equilibrium income. Show that the government budget deficit (the difference between government spending and tax revenues) is $5 billion.
   b. Congress passes the Foghorn-Leghorn amendment, which requires that the deficit be zero this year. If the budget adopted by Congress has a deficit that

is larger than zero, the deficit target must be met by cutting spending. Suppose spending is cut by $5 billion (to $75 billion). What is the new value for equilibrium GDP? What is the new deficit? Explain carefully why the deficit is not zero.

c. What is the deficit response index and how is it defined? Explain why the DRI must equal 0.25 in this example. Using this information, by how much must we cut spending to achieve a deficit of zero?

d. Suppose that the Foghorn-Leghorn amendment was not in effect and that planned investment falls to $I = 55$. What is the new value of GDP? What is the new government budget deficit? What happens to GDP if the F-L amendment is in effect and spending is cut to reach the deficit target? (*Hint:* Spending must be cut by $21.666 billion to balance the budget.)

3. During the first six months of 1995, the U.S. economy appeared to slow significantly. Many people point to Federal Reserve decisions made during 1994. What specific actions did the Fed take that might have caused economic slowing during 1995? Why were such actions taken? In retrospect, was the Fed right or wrong in doing what it did? Was the Fed a "fool in the shower?"

4. Some states are required to balance their budgets. Is this measure stabilizing or destabilizing? Suppose all states were committed to a balanced-budget philosophy and the economy moved into a recession. What effects would this philosophy have on the size of the federal deficit?

5. Describe the Fed's tendency to "lean against the wind." Do the Fed's policies tend to stabilize or destabilize the economy?

6. Explain why stabilization policy may be difficult to carry out. How is it possible that stabilization policies can actually be destabilizing?

7. It takes about one year for the multiplier to reach its full value. How can you explain this phenomenon? Does this fact have any implications for fiscal policy?

8. The unemployment rate in Japan has been much lower than the unemployment rate in the United States, and the unemployment rate in the United States has been much lower than unemployment rates in European countries. Look up the most recent unemployment figures for Europe, Japan, and the United States. Does this pattern still hold? Why might unemployment rates be consistently lower in one country *vis-à-vis* another?

THE VENEZUELAN BANKING CRISIS: 1994–1995

Venezuela, a lush tropical country on the north coast of South America, holds some of the best and worst economic world records. From 1950 to 1980, it held the record for the world's lowest inflation rate. Over the 30-year period, average annual inflation was only 3.1%, while annual growth averaged a robust 6 percent. Rich in energy resources, the country's state-owned oil company, Petroleos de Venezuela (PDVSA), ranked as the world's third largest oil company and the second largest exporter of oil to the United States. Within Latin America, Venezuela's world-class economic performance generated the region's highest per capita living standards. In 1991, with GDP roaring along at 10% annual growth rates, the International Finance Corporation named Venezuela the world's number-one emerging capital market. Money fund managers throughout the world turned to Venezuela to invest in its rapidly appreciating equities markets.

Yet, in recent years Venezuela suffered a peculiar reversal of fortune that rapidly turned its opulence into impoverishment and economic distress. As one of the country's former finance ministers commented, it seemed the country was plagued with a reverse Midas touch—that oil richness produced poverty instead of gold. While blessed with one of the highest income levels in Latin America, the country is also cursed with one of the region's worst income distributions. Sixty percent of the population lives in relative poverty, earning less than 30% of

VENEZUELA IS A COUNTRY OF CONTRASTS: MOUNTAINS AND CITIES, JUNGLES AND URBAN AREAS, AND GREAT WEALTH AND POVERTY.

the average per capita income, while 30% are critically poor, lacking in basic daily nutritional requirements. In 1992, social unrest (which included two aborted coup attempts) brought the stock market crashing down as fast as it had rocketed up. In 1993, then-president Carlos Andres Perez was impeached for corruption involving the misuse of public funds. By 1994, the high-octane growth of 1991 had gone into reverse and real GDP growth registered negative 4 percent. The crunch hit hardest in the real estate and construction sectors, which depended heavily on large amounts of bank credit.

All of these factors conspired to put Venezuela in the record-breaking category of what economist Francisco Faraco called the "world's biggest financial crisis since the 1930s Great Depression." By January 1995, 16 of the country's 40 private banks had failed. The Venezuelan banking collapse was roughly 10 times as severe as the failure of the U.S. savings and loans institutions in the early 1990s. Direct losses absorbed by the deposit insurance system totaled more than U.S. $7 billion—the equivalent of more than 16% of Venezuela's GDP and 75% of the government's 1994 national budget. These losses were financed by new money creation.

Over and above these problems, the Venezuelan economy suffers from severe unpredictable booms and busts in economic activity driven by chronic swings in world oil prices. This is due, in part, to the country's excessive dependence on oil as the primary source of national income. When oil prices fell between 1981 and 1986, the country's export earnings decreased from U.S. $19.3 billion to U.S. $7.6 billion. This collapse produced a great deal of painful belt tightening for the general population and led to riots in 1989.

The early 1990s boom was fueled by a 30% increase in government spending in real terms over the two years 1990–1992. This strong demand stimulus could not be sustained, however, due to political instability and the costly breakdown of the banking system that unfolded. The banking crisis (which began in 1994) burst the "bubble growth" that occurred between 1990 and 1992.

The Banking Crisis: How It Happened

The enormous failure of Venezuela's small banking sector was rooted in the freeing of government-regulated interest rates in 1989. Until that time, the Central Bank fixed interest rates and real interest rates on deposits in the nation's currency, the bolivar, were often negative. As a result, people preferred to convert their money into dollars and take it out of the country for deposit into U.S. bank accounts. (This phenomenon is known as *capital flight*.)

Because few people wanted to hold bolivars, deposits in Venezuelan banks dropped to historic lows by 1989. Without deposits, banks cannot make loans, hurting profits. When the government finally set interest rates free, interest rates rose and bolivar deposits began piling up in Venezuelan banks. Rising interest rates also attracted large amounts of foreign capital. These large money flows helped bid up prices on Venezuela's stock exchange. But even while banks were intoxicated with deposits, the demand for loans did not increase greatly because most large investors could raise money more cheaply by drawing on their dollar holdings abroad. To make returns sufficient to cover the interest owed to depositors, banks increasingly chose more risky investments. With virtually no regulation to contend with in the new climate of deregulation, bankers took the depositors' funds to speculate in the stock market or buy junk bonds. Skyrocketing real estate prices made speculation in office and luxury housing construction another favorite pastime of bank portfolio managers. To keep the balance sheets looking healthy, the banks and their parent companies would often buy and sell the same office building back and forth to artificially push up its price. Banco Latino, the nation's second largest bank, built a real estate empire of 500 office buildings. It was the first to crash when the market fell.

Bank deregulation also took on new meaning as bankers used their institutions as personal *cajas chicas*, or petty-cash drawers. Government investigations revealed that hundreds of loans went to relatives and friends of bank managers and directors, as well as to real estate operators with important political connections. "Insider lending" was rampant, and no extravagance was spared. Only weeks before its collapse, Banco Latino chartered an Air France Concorde supersonic jetliner at a cost of $300,000 to transport friends of the bank to a party celebrating the opening of a Paris branch. Lavish high-rise headquarters were filled with expensive artwork. Members of the board of directors had private jets, which proved quite handy for fleeing the country when authorities closed the bank's doors in January 1994. Yet, even after the doors were closed, bank officers logged into the bank's computers from offshore refuges to electronically transfer remaining funds abroad and alter or destroy records.

As stock, bond, and real estate markets collapsed, artificially inflated bank assets collapsed as well, exposing the banks' negative net worth throughout the financial system. To cover their backs, banks attempted to forestall default by offering sky-high interest rates—up to 18 points above going rates—to attract new depositors. The scheme only served to run up bank losses and deepen the recession. By the time the government reintroduced bank supervision in 1994, the Venezuelan economy was in serious trouble.

Questions for Analytical Thinking

1. How does the Venezuelan banking crisis compare to the U.S. savings and loan crisis during the 1980s? What role does bank deregulation play in banking crises?

2. What other developing countries experience dramatic business fluctuations associated with changing market conditions for their major export product? How does an economy adjust to a major loss in revenues from an export product?

3. Why must banks do more than simply take in large volumes of deposits? Should U.S. commercial banks be allowed to invest in the stock market?

4. What do you expect will happen to prices in Venezuela as a result of the central bank's financed bailout?

Sources: James Brooke, "Failure of High-Flying Banks Shakes Venezuelan Economy," *The New York Times,* May 16, 1994, p.1; Francisco J. Faraco and Roman Suprani, *La Crisis Bancaria Venezolana* (Caracas, Venezuela: Editorial Panapro, 1995); Michael S. Serrill, "We're All Going to Pay: *The Toll in the Banking Scandal Reaches $7 Billion, Leaving Everyone Asking, 'Who Stole Venezuela?'"* *Time* (International), February 20, 1995, pp. 22–23.

17

PART FIVE

HOUSEHOLD AND FIRM BEHAVIOR IN THE MACROECONOMY: A CLOSER LOOK

HOUSEHOLD AND FIRM BEHAVIOR IN THE MACROECONOMY

IN CHAPTERS 9 THROUGH 15, WE CONSIDERED THE INTERACTIONS of households, firms, the government, and the rest of the world in the goods, money, and labor markets. The macroeconomy is complicated, and there is a lot to learn about these interactions. To keep our discussions as uncomplicated as possible, we have so far assumed fairly simple behavior on the part of households and firms—the two basic decision-making units in the economy. For example, we assumed that household consumption (C) depends only on income and that firms' planned investment (I) depends only on the interest rate. Furthermore, we did not consider the fact that households make consumption and labor supply decisions simultaneously and that firms make investment and employment decisions simultaneously.

Now that we have an understanding of the basic interactions in the economy, we are in a position to relax these restrictive assumptions. In the first part of this chapter, we present a more realistic picture of the influences on households' consumption and labor supply decisions. In the second part, we present a more detailed and realistic picture of the influences on firms' investment and employment decisions. In the next chapter, we use what we've learned in this chapter to analyze some more macroeconomic issues.

HOUSEHOLDS: CONSUMPTION AND LABOR SUPPLY DECISIONS

Before discussing the theories of household behavior in the macroeconomy, it is useful to review what we have learned up to this point.

THE KEYNESIAN THEORY OF CONSUMPTION: A REVIEW

The assumption that household consumption (C) depends on income, which we have used as the basis of our analysis so far, is one that Keynes stressed in his *General Theory of Employment, Interest, and Money*. While Keynes believed that many factors, including interest rates and wealth, are likely to influence the level of consumption spending, he focused on current income:

> The amount of aggregate consumption depends mainly on the amount of aggregate income. The fundamental psychological law, upon which we are entitled to depend with great confidence both . . . from our knowledge of human nature and from the detailed facts of experience, is that men [and women, too] are disposed, as a rule and on average, to increase their consumption as their incomes increase, but not by as much as the increase in their income.[1]

Keynes is making two points here. First, he suggests that consumption is a positive function of income. That is, the more income one has, the more consuming one is likely to do. Except for a few rich misers who save scraps of soap and bits of string despite million-dollar incomes, this proposition seems to make sense. Rich people typically consume more than poor people do.

Second, Keynes suggests, high-income households consume a smaller proportion of their income than low-income households. (If rich households consume relatively less of their incomes, then by definition they save a higher proportion of their incomes than poor households do.) The proportion of income that households spend on consumption is measured by the **average propensity to consume (APC)**.[2] The APC is defined as consumption divided by income:

$$APC \equiv \frac{C}{Y}$$

average propensity to consume (APC) *The proportion of income households spend on consumption. Determined by dividing consumption (C) by income (Y).*

If, for example, a household earns $30,000 per year and spends $25,000 (and thus saves the remaining $5000), it has an *APC* of $25,000/$30,000, or 0.833. Keynes argues that someone who earns, say, $30,000 is likely to spend a larger portion of his or her income than is someone who earns $100,000.

Although the idea that consumption depends on income is a useful starting point, it is far from a complete description of the consumption decision. We need to consider other theories of consumption.

THE LIFE-CYCLE THEORY OF CONSUMPTION

The **life-cycle theory of consumption** is an important extension of Keynes's theory. The fundamental idea of the life-cycle theory is that people make lifetime consumption plans. Realizing that they are likely to earn more in their prime working years than they earn earlier or later, they make consumption decisions based on their expectations

life-cycle theory of consumption *A theory of household consumption: Households make lifetime consumption decisions based on their expectations of lifetime income.*

---

[1] *John Maynard Keynes,* The General Theory of Employment, Interest, and Money (1936), *First Harbinger Ed. (New York: Harcourt Brace Jovanovich, 1964), p. 96.*
[2] *While the APC measures the proportion of total income households spend on consumption, the marginal propensity to consume (MPC), which we introduced in Chapter 9, measures the proportion of a change in income that households spend on consumption. One could interpret Keynes's theory as implying that the marginal propensity to consume falls as income rises. If the MPC falls as income rises, it follows that the average propensity to consume (APC) falls also.*

of lifetime income. People tend to consume less than they earn during their main working years—that is, they *save* during those years—and they tend to consume more than they earn during their early and later years—that is, they *dissave,* or use up savings, during those years. For example, students in medical school, generally have very low current incomes, but few live in the poverty that those incomes might predict. Instead, they borrow now and plan to pay back later when their incomes improve.

The lifetime income and consumption pattern of a representative individual is shown in Figure 17.1. As you can see, this person has a low income during the first part of her life, high income in the middle, and low income again in retirement. Her income in retirement is not zero because she has income from sources other than her own labor—social security payments, interest and dividends, and the like.

The consumption path as drawn in Figure 17.1 is constant over the person's life. This is an extreme assumption, but it illustrates an important point, namely that the path of consumption over a lifetime is likely to be much more stable than the path of income. We consume an amount greater than our incomes during our early working careers. We do this by borrowing against future income, by taking out a car loan, a mortgage to buy a house, or a loan to pay for college. This debt is repaid when our incomes have risen and we can afford to use some of our income to pay off past borrowing without substantially lowering our consumption. The reverse is true for our retirement years. Here, too, our incomes are low. But because we consume less than we earn during our prime working years, we can save up a "nest egg" that allows us to maintain an acceptable standard of living during retirement.

Fluctuations in wealth are also an important component of the life-cycle story. Many young households go into debt by borrowing in anticipation of higher income in the future. Some households actually have *negative wealth*—the value of their assets is less than the debts they owe. A household in its prime working years saves to pay off debts and to build up assets for its later years, when income typically goes down. Such households, whose assets are greater than the debts they owe, are said to have *positive wealth*. With its wage earners retired, a household consumes its accumulated wealth. Generally speaking, wealth starts out negative, turns positive, and then approaches zero near the end of life. Wealth, therefore, is intimately linked to the cumulative saving and dissaving behavior of households.

FIGURE 17.1

Life-Cycle Theory of Consumption

In their early working years, people consume more than they earn. This is also true in the retirement years. In between, people save (consume less than they earn) to pay off debts from borrowing and to accumulate savings for retirement.

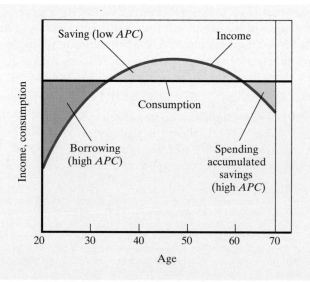

The key difference between the Keynesian theory of consumption and the life-cycle theory is that the life-cycle theory suggests that consumption and saving decisions are likely to be based not just on current income but on expectations of future income as well. The consumption behavior of households immediately following World War II clearly supports the life-cycle story. Just after the war ended, income fell as wage earners moved out of war-related work. However, consumption spending did not fall commensurately, as Keynesian theory would predict. People expected to find jobs in other sectors eventually, and they did not adjust their consumption spending to the temporarily lower incomes they were earning in the meantime.

The phrase **permanent income** is sometimes used to refer to the average level of one's expected future income stream. If you expect that your income will be high in the future (even though it may not be high now), your permanent income is said to be high. With this concept, we can sum up the life-cycle theory by saying that current consumption decisions are likely to be based on permanent income rather than on current income.[3]

permanent income *The average level of one's expected future income stream.*

But although this insight enriches our understanding of the consumption behavior of households, the analysis is still missing a number of important pieces. To complete the picture, we need to bring in the other main decision of households: the labor supply decision.

THE LABOR SUPPLY DECISION

Households decide not only how much to consume but also how much to work. These decisions are not made separately. Rather,

> Households make consumption and labor supply decisions simultaneously. Consumption cannot be considered separately from labor supply, because it is precisely by selling one's labor that one earns the income that makes consumption possible.

This may seem obvious to you, but it is an important point that is sometimes forgotten.

Clearly, then, it does not make sense to have one theory that explains consumption and another that explains labor supply. Consumption requires income (either current income or the promise of future income that can be borrowed against), and to earn income one must supply labor. Unless you are lucky enough to have a large inheritance or to win a lottery, you are going to have to work to buy the things you need and want. If you want more, you are going to have to work more.

The theories of consumption that we have discussed so far assume that consumption depends on current or permanent income. The view that consumption and labor supply are determined jointly complicates matters somewhat. If households make decisions about consumption and labor supply together, then it is not (strictly speaking) correct to say that income determines consumption. Rather, income is the byproduct of the labor supply/consumption decisions.

The theory of consumer choice in microeconomics treats consumption and labor supply decisions together. This is an important area where we can gain macroeconomic insights from microeconomic theory. The following is a brief discussion of what microeconomics tells us about the factors that affect consumption and labor supply decisions.

---

[3]*The pioneering work on this topic was done by Milton Friedman,* A Theory of the Consumption Function *(Princeton, N.J.: Princeton University Press, 1957). In the mid-1960s, Franco Modigliani did closely related work that included the formulation of the life-cycle theory.*

■ **Wages** The wage rate that a household is paid and the prices of the goods that it buys affect the household's consumption and labor supply decisions. If you work, you are paid a wage. Your wage income is the number of hours that you work times your hourly wage rate. Wage income enables you to buy market-produced goods and services. If you do not work, you may engage in leisure activities or you may work at tasks that do not pay a wage. People may choose not to do paid work for a variety of reasons—because they are bringing up children, keeping house, going to school, and so forth. Thus,

> There is a trade-off between the goods and services that wage income will buy and leisure or other nonmarket activities. The wage rate is the key variable that determines how a household responds to this trade-off.

Consider what would happen if the wage rate were to increase. First, an increase in the wage rate means that the opportunity cost of leisure (or of nonmarket production) is higher. The opportunity cost of leisure is the bundle of market-produced goods and services that you give up by not working—in other words, your wage rate. If the wage rate rises, the true price of each additional hour of leisure you consume is higher. That is, when the wage rate increases, you must sacrifice a larger bundle of market-produced goods and services for each hour of leisure you consume. Since leisure is now more costly, you are likely to engage in less of it, which means you will work more after the wage rate increase. This effect is called the **substitution effect of a wage rate increase,** and it should lead to an increase in the quantity of labor supplied and a decrease in leisure (or nonmarket production).

If the wage rate declines, the substitution effect takes the opposite turn. A lower wage rate means the opportunity cost of leisure (or of nonmarket production) is lower. In this case, a decision to spend more hours at home in the garden or with the kids means less of a sacrifice in terms of market-produced goods and services. Thus, the substitution effect suggests that a lower wage rate should lead to a decrease in the quantity of labor supplied.

But the substitution effect is only part of the story. A higher wage rate also means that a person can earn a higher amount of income for a given number of hours worked. This higher income may be spent on more goods, or it may be spent on leisure. If we assume that leisure is a *normal good* (that is, a good for which demand increases when income increases and for which demand decreases when income decreases), we would expect to see a higher wage rate lead to more leisure and thus less labor supplied. This effect is called the **income effect of a wage rate increase.** Conversely, the income effect of a wage rate decrease is less leisure and therefore more labor supplied.

When we combine the income and substitution effects, we are left with an ambiguous result. A higher wage rate means that the opportunity cost of not working is higher. This leads to more work—a larger quantity of labor supplied. But a higher wage rate also means that people can earn more wage income for a given number of hours worked, and they spend some of this added income on leisure. The evidence suggests that the substitution effect seems to dominate for most people, which means that the aggregate labor supply responds positively to an increase in the wage rate.[4]

Let us now return to the consumption of goods-and-services decision. If the wage rate rises, *both* the income and substitution effects work in the same direction to increase consumption. There is a positive income effect, which leads to more consumption, and there is a substitution effect away from leisure toward

---

[4]*Keep in mind, however, that this need not be the case. There may be times when the income effect dominates the substitution effect, in which case the aggregate labor supply falls when the wage rate rises.*

work (and therefore higher income and increased consumption of goods and services). Thus,

Consumption increases when the wage rate increases.

■ **Prices**   Prices also play a major role in the consumption/labor supply decision. As we have been discussing the possible effects of an increase in the wage rate, we have been implicitly assuming that the prices of goods and services do not rise at the same time. If the wage rate and all other prices rise simultaneously, the story is different. To keep the two cases clear, we need to distinguish between the nominal wage rate and the real wage rate.

The **nominal wage rate** is the wage rate in current dollars. When we adjust the nominal wage rate for changes in the price level, we obtain the **real wage rate**. The real wage rate measures the amount that wages can buy in terms of goods and services. Workers do not care about their nominal wage per se; they care about the purchasing power of this wage—that is, the real wage.

For example, suppose that skilled workers in Indianapolis were paid a wage rate of $15 per hour in 1995. Now suppose that their wage rate rose to $18 in 1996, a 20% increase. If the prices of goods and services were exactly the same in 1996 as they were in 1995, the real wage rate would have increased by 20 percent. That is, an hour of work in 1996 ($18) buys 20% more than an hour of work in 1995 ($15).

But what if the prices of all goods and services also increased by 20% between 1995 and 1996? In this case, the purchasing power of an hour's wages has not changed. That is, the real wage rate has not increased at all. Eighteen dollars in 1996 buys the same quantity of goods and services that $15 bought in 1995.

To measure the real wage rate, we simply adjust the nominal wage rate with a price index. As we saw in Chapter 8, there are several such indexes that we might use, including the consumer price index and the GDP price index.[5]

We can now apply what we have learned from the life-cycle theory to our wage/price story. Recall that life-cycle theory holds that people look ahead in making their decisions. Translated to real wage rates, this idea says that:

Households look at expected future real wage rates as well as the current real wage rate in making their current consumption and labor supply decisions.

Consider again the medical student who expects that his or her real wage rate will be higher in the future. This expectation obviously has an effect on current decisions about things like how much to buy and whether or not to take a part-time job.

■ **Wealth and Nonlabor Income**   Life-cycle theory holds that wealth fluctuates over the life cycle. Households accumulate wealth during their working years to pay off debts accumulated when they were young and to support themselves in retirement. This role of wealth is clear, but the existence of wealth also poses another question. Consider two households that are at the same stage in their life cycle and have pretty much the same expectations about future wage rates, prices, and so forth. They expect to live the same length of time, and both plan to leave the same amount to their children. They

nominal wage rate *The wage rate in current dollars.*

real wage rate *The amount that the nominal wage rate can buy in terms of goods and services.*

---

[5]*To calculate the real wage rate, we simply divide the nominal wage rate by the price index. For example, suppose that the wage rate rose from $5.00 per hour in 1984 to $9.00 per hour in 1994 and that the price level rose 50% during the same period. Using 1984 as the base year, the price index would be 1.00 in 1984 and 1.50 in 1994. The real wage rate is W/P, where W is the nominal wage rate and P is the price level. The real wage rate is thus $5.00 in 1984 ($5.00/$1.00) and $6.00 in 1994 ($9.00/$1.50), using 1984 as the base year.*

differ only in their wealth. Because of a past inheritance, Household 1 has more wealth than Household 2. Which household is likely to have a higher consumption path for the rest of its life? The answer should be obvious: Household 1 would, because it has more wealth to spread out over the rest of its life. In other words:

> Holding everything else constant (including the stage in the life cycle), the more wealth a household has, the more it will consume, both now and in the future.

Now consider a household that has a sudden unexpected increase in wealth, perhaps an inheritance from a distant relative. How will the household's consumption pattern be affected? It should be obvious that the household will increase its consumption, both now and in the future, as it spends the inheritance over the course of the rest of its life.

An increase in wealth can also be looked upon as an increase in nonlabor income. **Nonlabor, or nonwage, income** is income that is received from sources other than working—inheritances, interest, dividends, and transfer payments such as welfare payments and social security payments. As with wealth:

nonlabor, or nonwage, income
Any income that is received from sources other than working—inheritances, interest, dividends, transfer payments, and so on.

> An unexpected increase in nonlabor income will have a positive effect on a household's consumption.

But what about the effect of an increase in wealth or nonlabor income on labor supply? We already know that an increase in income results in an increase in the consumption of normal goods, including leisure (see page 394). Therefore, an unexpected increase in wealth or nonlabor income results in both an increase in consumption and an increase in leisure. With leisure increasing, labor supply must fall, so we see that:

> An unexpected increase in wealth or nonlabor income leads to a *decrease* in labor supply.

This point should be fairly obvious. If I suddenly win a million dollars in the state lottery, I will probably work less in the future than I otherwise would have.

One major source of fluctuations in the wealth of the household sector is the stock market. Stock prices change considerably over time. Many households hold much of their wealth in stocks, and as stock prices rise or fall, so does household wealth. This is one of the ways in which the stock market affects the economy. By increasing or decreasing household wealth, the stock market influences how much households decide to spend and how much they decide to work. (We shall have more to say about this point in the next chapter.)

MANY HOUSEHOLDS HOLD MUCH OF THEIR WEALTH IN STOCKS. WHEN THE STOCK MARKET TAKES A MAJOR TURN FOR THE WORSE, WEALTH DECLINES IN VALUE. WHEN THE STOCK MARKET PLUNGED IN OCTOBER 1987, MORE THAN HALF A TRILLION DOLLARS WAS LOST. A FEW DAYS AFTER THE CRASH, A NEW YORK CITY PERFORMANCE ARTIST PERFORMED A ONE-MAN SHOW IN FRONT OF THE NEW YORK STOCK EXCHANGE, SETTING FIRE TO SOME OVERSIZED $100 BILLS TO SYMBOLIZE ALL THE MONEY THAT WENT "UP IN SMOKE."

INTEREST RATE EFFECTS ON CONSUMPTION

We saw earlier that the interest rate affects planned investment (I). The interest rate can also affect consumption. In fact, a change in the interest rate has both income and substitution effects on consumption. Consider first the substitution effect. A change in the interest rate affects households' choices between present and future consumption. Every dollar I earn today can either be spent—that is, used for present consumption—or saved, allowing me to buy things in the future. Suppose I put a dollar of my income in the bank now at an interest rate of 5% per year. A year from now, my dollar will have earned $0.05 in interest, and I can then spend the $1.05 on whatever

I choose. If my bank offers a 10% rate instead of a 5% interest rate, my dollar will grow to $1.10 at the end of a year.

The rate of interest thus represents one type of opportunity cost. Each dollar I spend today means either $1.05 or $1.10 less of future consumption, depending on the interest rate. If the interest rate rises from 5% to 10%, the opportunity cost of present consumption rises. Instead of sacrificing $1.05 of future consumption each time I spend (fail to save) a dollar today, I must now sacrifice $1.10 worth of future consumption. Hence, an increase in the interest rate should encourage me to spend less (save more) than before. Put another way, when the interest rate rises, households substitute away from current consumption toward future consumption due to the increase in the relative price of current consumption. Through this *substitution effect,* an increase in the interest rate has a negative effect on current consumption.

Now consider the *income effect,* which works in the opposite direction from the substitution effect for households that have positive wealth. Consider a household that has positive wealth and is earning interest on that wealth. When the interest rate rises, the household earns more in interest income than it did before. This is an increase in its nonlabor income. As we saw above, a rise in nonlabor income has a positive effect on consumption. This is the income effect at work. The interest rate rises, interest (nonlabor) income rises, and consumption increases due to the increase in nonlabor income. Thus:

> An increase in the interest rate thus has a negative effect on consumption through the substitution effect and a positive effect on consumption through the income effect.

Which effect dominates for a given household varies from situation to situation. The only time the total effect is unambiguous is when a household is a debtor, in which case an increase in the interest rate leads to a corresponding increase in the interest payments that the household must make. This situation is similar to a decrease in nonlabor income, which has a negative effect on consumption. In this case, the income effect is in the same direction as the substitution effect.

The income and substitution effects are not just theoretical niceties that have nothing important to say about the real world. In fact, they may help to explain why monetary policy was less effective in stimulating the U.S. economy after the 1990–1991 recession than it was after previous recessions.

Why is this so? Households as a group have positive wealth, and they own a considerable fraction of the federal debt. Although some of the increase in the government debt has been financed by foreigners, most of this increase has been financed by domestic households. Because the government debt is so much larger now than it was ten years ago, the effect of a change in the interest rate on government interest payments is also much larger now than it used to be.

All this means that the larger a decrease in government interest payments today (as a result of a given decrease in the interest rate), the larger the decrease in households' interest income. This in turn means that the income effect on households is larger now than it used to be. In fact, some experiments have suggested that the income effect is now almost as large as the substitution effect. A given change in interest rates may thus have less effect on consumption today than in the past, which would help to explain why the easing of monetary policy in 1991 and 1992 was not very effective in stimulating the economy.

Interestingly, the news media have been busy reporting the income effect at work. As interest rates fell in 1991 and 1992, there were numerous newspaper articles and television programs interviewing retirees who were hurt by the decrease in their interest income. Interest income for many retirees is a fairly large fraction of their total income. These individuals undoubtedly consume less when their interest income falls, which at least partly offsets the stimulative effect that the Fed tries to achieve when it lowers the interest rate.

GOVERNMENT EFFECTS ON CONSUMPTION AND LABOR SUPPLY: TAXES AND TRANSFERS

The government influences household behavior mainly through tax rates and transfer payments.

When the government raises tax rates, after-tax real wages decrease. This, in turn, lowers consumption. Conversely, when the government lowers tax rates, after-tax real wages increase. The result is an increase in consumption.

A change in tax rates also affects labor supply. If the substitution effect dominates, as we are generally assuming, then an increase in tax rates, which lowers after-tax wages, will lower labor supply (see p. 394). Conversely, a decrease in tax rates will increase labor supply.

Recall that *transfer payments* are payments such as social security benefits, veterans benefits, and welfare benefits. An increase in transfer payments is an increase in nonlabor income, and we have seen that nonlabor income has a positive effect on consumption and a negative effect on labor supply. Increases in transfer payments thus increase consumption and decrease labor supply, while decreases in transfer payments decrease consumption and increase labor supply. Figure 17.2 summarizes these results.

Precisely how labor supply responds to transfer payments is a question that greatly concerns government policy makers, whose objective is a welfare system that helps people truly in need while maintaining an incentive to work for those who are able to do so. Because welfare payments are a form of nonlabor income, we expect some accompanying decrease in work, but the key question for government policy is how large this effect is. A number of income maintenance experiments have attempted to estimate the size of this response. In general, the response seems fairly small.

Using this information, we can again come back to the life-cycle theory and the idea that people look ahead to make lifetime consumption decisions:

> If people look ahead, then changes in tax rates that are expected to be permanent have a greater effect on current consumption than those that are expected to be temporary. If tax rates are lowered this year, but people expect them to go back up next year, the effect of the tax cut on current consumption is likely to be small.

FIGURE 17.2

The Effects of Government on Household Consumption and Labor Supply

	Tax rates		Transfer payments	
	Increase	**Decrease**	**Increase**	**Decrease**
Effect on consumption	Negative	Positive	Positive	Negative
Effect on labor supply	Negative*	Positive*	Negative	Positive

*If the substitution effect dominates.

A POSSIBLE EMPLOYMENT CONSTRAINT ON HOUSEHOLDS

Our discussion of the labor supply decision has so far proceeded as if households were free to choose how much to work each period. For example, if a member of a household decides to work five additional hours a week at the current wage rate, we have implicitly assumed that the person *can* work five hours more—that work is available. If someone who has not been working decides to work at the current wage rate, we have assumed that the person *can find a job.*

As we've said all along, however, there are times when these assumptions do not hold. Indeed, it was the Great Depression, when unemployment rates reached 25% of the labor force, that led to the birth of macroeconomics in the 1930s. Since the mid-1970s, the United States has experienced three recessions, with millions of unemployed workers unable to find work.

All households face a budget constraint, regardless of the state of the economy. This budget constraint, which separates those bundles of goods that are available to a household from those that are not, is determined by income, wealth, and prices. When there is unemployment, some households feel an additional constraint on their behavior. Some people may want to work 40 hours per week at the current wage rates but can find only part-time work. Others may not find any work at all.

How does a household respond when it is constrained from working as much as it would like? Most importantly, it consumes less than it otherwise would. This should be fairly obvious. If your current wage rate is $10 per hour and you normally work 40 hours a week, your normal income from wages is $400 per week. If your average tax rate is 20%, your after-tax wage income is $320 per week. You are likely to spend much of this income during the week. If you are prevented from working, this income will not be available to you, and you will have less to spend.

You will spend something, of course. You may receive some form of nonlabor income, and you may have assets, such as savings deposits or stocks and bonds, that can be withdrawn or sold. You may also be able to borrow during your period of unemployment. But even though you will spend something during the week, it is almost certain that you will spend less than you would have if you had your usual income of $320 in after-tax wages. Thus,

> Households consume less if they are constrained from working.

A household constrained from working as much as it would like to at the current wage rate faces a different decision from the one facing a household that can work as much as it wants to. The work decision of the former household is, in effect, forced on it. The household works as much as it can—a certain number of hours per week or perhaps none at all—but this amount is less than the household would choose to work at the current wage rate if it could find more work. The amount that a household would like to work at the current wage rate if it could find the work is called its **unconstrained supply of labor.** The amount that the household actually works in a given period at current wage rates is called its **constrained supply of labor.**

A household's constrained supply of labor is not a variable over which it has any control. The amount of labor the household supplies is imposed on it from the outside by the workings of the economy. However, the household's consumption *is* under its control. We have just seen that the less a household works—that is, the smaller the household's constrained supply of labor–the lower its consumption is.

unconstrained supply of labor
The amount a household would like to work within a given period at the current wage rate if it could find the work.

constrained supply of labor
The amount a household actually works in a given period at the current wage rate.

Constraints on the supply of labor are thus an important determinant of consumption when there is unemployment.

■ **Keynesian Theory Revisited**   Recall the simple Keynesian theory that current income determines current consumption. We now know that the consumption decision is made jointly with the labor supply decision and that the two depend on the real wage rate. Thus, it is incorrect to argue that consumption depends only on income, at least when there is full employment. But if there is unemployment, Keynes's simple story is closer to being correct because income is not determined by households. When there is unemployment, the level of income (at least workers' income) depends exclusively on the employment decisions made by firms. There are unemployed workers who are willing to work at the current wage rate, and their income is in effect determined by firms' hiring decisions. This income in turn affects current consumption, which is consistent with Keynes's theory. This is one of the reasons that Keynesian theory is generally considered to pertain to periods of unemployment. It was, of course, precisely during such a period that the theory was developed.

A SUMMARY OF HOUSEHOLD BEHAVIOR

This completes our discussion of household behavior in the macroeconomy. Clearly, household consumption depends on more than current income. Households determine consumption and labor supply simultaneously, and they look ahead in making their decisions. To summarize:

> The following factors affect household consumption and labor supply decisions:
> ■ current and expected future real wage rates
> ■ the initial value of wealth
> ■ current and expected future nonlabor income
> ■ interest rates
> ■ current and expected future tax rates and transfer payments

If households are constrained in their labor supply decisions, income is directly determined by firms' hiring decisions. In this case, we can say (in the traditional, Keynesian way) that "income" affects consumption.

THE HOUSEHOLD SECTOR SINCE 1970

To gain a better understanding of household behavior, it is useful to examine how some of the aggregate household variables have changed over time. We will confine our discussion here to the period 1970 I–1994 IV. (Remember that the Roman numerals refer to quarters. 1970 I means the first quarter of 1970.) Within this time span, there have been three recessionary periods, 1974 I–1975 IV, 1980 II–1983 I, and 1990 III–1991 I. How did the household variables behave during each of these three periods?

■ **Consumption**   Data on the total consumption of the household sector are available from the national income accounts. As we saw in Table 7.2, personal consumption expenditures accounted for about 68.7% of GDP in 1994. The three basic categories of consumption expenditures are services, nondurable goods, and durable goods.

Figure 17.3 presents the data for consumption of services and nondurable goods combined and for durable goods. The variables are in real terms. You can see from the figure that expenditures on services and nondurable goods are "smoother" over time than expenditures on durable goods. For example, the decrease in expenditures on services and nondurable goods was much smaller during the three recessionary periods than the decrease in expenditures on durable goods.

Why do expenditures on durables fluctuate more than expenditures on services and nondurables? The reason is simple. When times are bad, people can postpone the purchase of durable goods, and they do. It follows, then, that expenditures on these goods change the most. When times are tough, you do not *have* to have a new car or a new washer-dryer; you can make do with your old Chevy or Maytag until things get better. But when your income falls, it is less easy to postpone the service costs of day care or health care. Nondurables fall into an intermediate category, with some items (new clothes, for example) easier to postpone than others (food, for example).

■ **Housing Investment** Another important expenditure of the household sector is housing investment (purchases of new housing), plotted in Figure 17.4. This

FIGURE 17.3

Consumption Expenditures, 1970 I–1994 IV

Over time, expenditures for services and nondurable goods are "smoother" than expenditures for durable goods.

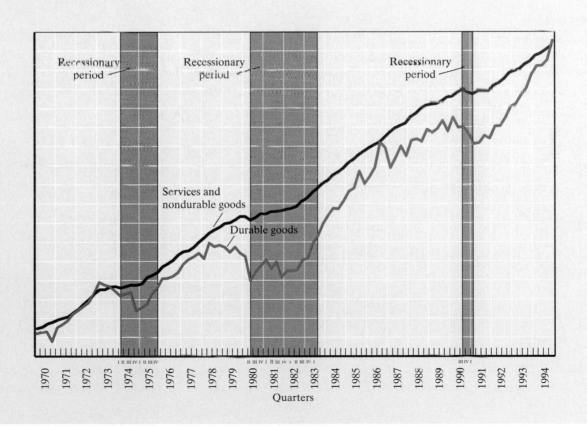

variable fluctuates greatly, for at least two reasons. First, housing investment is the most easily postponable of all household expenditures. Second, housing investment is sensitive to the general level of interest rates, and interest rates fluctuate considerably over time. When interest rates are low, housing investment is generally high, and vice versa.

■ **Labor Supply**   As we noted in Chapters 8 and 15, a person is considered a part of the labor force when he or she either is working or has been actively looking for work in the past few weeks. The ratio of the labor force to the total working-age population—those 16 and over—is the *labor-force participation rate.*

It is informative to divide the labor force into three categories: males 25–54, females 25–54, and all others 16 and over. Ages 25–54 are sometimes called "prime" ages, presumably on the assumption that one is in the prime of one's working life during these ages. The participation rates for these three groups are plotted in Figure 17.5.

As the figure shows, most men of prime age work, although the participation rate has fallen slightly since 1970—from .961 in 1970 I to .920 in 1994 IV. (A rate of .920 means that 92.0% of prime-age men were in the labor force.) The participation rate for prime-age women, on the other hand, has risen dramatically since 1970—from .501 in 1970 I to .756 in 1994 IV. Although economic factors account for some of this increase, a change in social attitudes and preferences probably explains most of the increase. Although the participation rate of prime-age women is still below the rate for prime-age men, this difference will narrow even further in the future if the rate for men keeps falling and the rate for women keeps rising.

FIGURE 17.4

Housing Investment of the Household Sector, 1970 I–1994 IV

Housing investment fell sharply during the three recessionary periods since 1970. Like expenditures for durable goods, expenditures for housing investment are postponable.

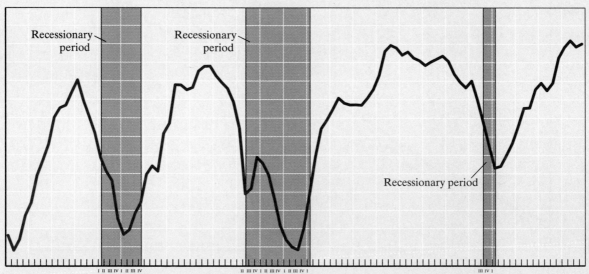

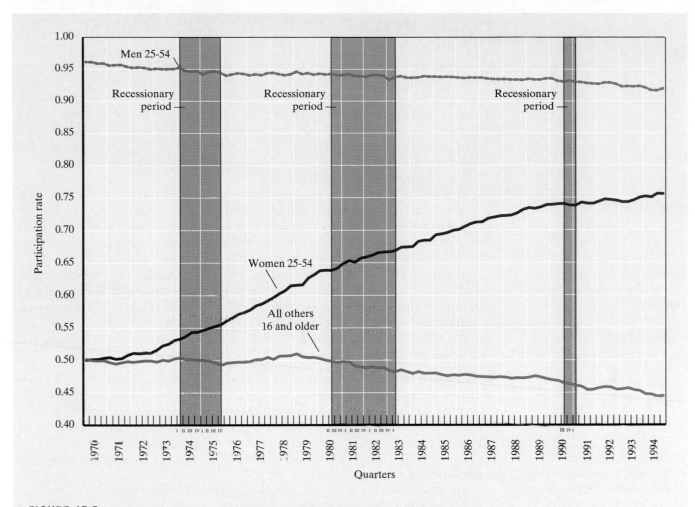

FIGURE 17.5

Labor-Force Participation Rates for Men 25–54, Women 25–54, and All Others 16 and Over, 1970 I–1994 IV

Since 1970, the labor-force participation rate for prime-age men has been decreasing slightly. The rate for prime-age women has been increasing dramatically. The rate for all others 16 and over has been declining since 1979 and shows a tendency to fall during recessions (the discouraged-worker effect).

Figure 17.5 also shows the participation rate for all individuals 16 and over except prime-age men and women. This rate has some cyclical features—it tends to fall in recessions and to rise or fall less during expansions. These features reveal the operation of the *discouraged-worker effect,* which we discussed in Chapter 8. During recessions, some people get discouraged about ever finding a job. As a result, they stop looking and are then not considered a part of the labor force. During expansions, people become encouraged again. Once they begin looking for jobs, they are again considered a part of the labor force. Because prime-age women and men are likely to be fairly attached to the labor force, the discouraged-worker effect for them is quite small.

The participation rate for non-prime-age men and women has fallen since 1970. Part of this decrease reflects an increase in early retirement. When someone retires, he or she is no longer considered a part of the labor force.

FIRMS: INVESTMENT AND EMPLOYMENT DECISIONS

Having taken a closer look at the behavior of households in the macroeconomy, we now turn to a closer look at the behavior of firms—the second major decision-making unit in the economy. In discussing firm behavior earlier, we simply assumed that planned investment depends only on the interest rate. However, there are several other determinants of planned investment. We now turn to a discussion of these factors. We will also discuss the factors that affect firms' employment decisions. Once again, microeconomic theory can help us gain some insights into the working of the macroeconomy.

In a market economy, firms determine which goods and services are available to consumers today and which will be available in the future, how many workers are needed for what kinds of jobs, and how much investment will be undertaken. Stated in macroeconomic terms, the decisions of firms, taken together, determine output, labor demand, and investment.

inputs *The goods and services that firms purchase and turn into output.*

In this section, we concentrate on the input choices made by firms. By **inputs,** we mean the goods and services that firms purchase and turn into output. Two important inputs that firms use are capital and labor. (Other inputs are energy, raw materials, and semifinished goods.) Each period, firms must decide how much capital and labor they wish to use in producing output. Let us first look at the decision about how much capital to use.

plant-and-equipment investment *Purchases by firms of additional machines, factories, or buildings within a given period.*

■ **Investment Decisions** At any point in time a firm has a certain stock of capital on hand. By *stock of capital* we mean the factories and buildings (sometimes called "plant") that firms own, the equipment they need to do business, and their inventories of partly or wholly finished goods. There are two basic ways that a firm can add to its capital stock. One way is to buy more machinery or build new factories or buildings. This kind of addition to the capital stock is called **plant-and-equipment investment.**

inventory investment *Occurs when a firm produces more output than it sells within a given period.*

The other way for a firm to add to its capital stock is to increase its inventories. When a firm produces more than it sells in a given period, the firm's stock of inventories increases.[6] This type of addition to the capital stock is called **inventory investment.** Recall from Chapter 9 that unplanned inventory investment is quite different from planned inventory investment. When a firm sells less than it expected to, it experiences an unplanned increase in its inventories and is thus forced to invest more than it planned to. Unplanned increases in inventories result from factors beyond the firm's control. (We take up inventory investment in more detail later in this chapter.)

■ **Employment Decisions** In addition to investment decisions, firms also make *employment* decisions. At the beginning of each period, a firm has a certain number of workers on its payroll. On the basis of its current situation and its upcoming plans, the firm must decide whether it wants to hire additional workers, keep the same number of workers, or reduce its work force by laying off some employees.

Until this point, our description of firm behavior has been quite simple. In Chapter 9 we argued that firms increase production when they experience unplanned decreases in inventory and reduce production when they experience

---

[6]*The change in inventories is exactly equal to the difference between production and sales. If a firm sells 20 units more than it produces in the course of a month, its inventories fall by 20 units; if it produces 20 units more than it sells, its inventories rise by 20 units.*

unplanned increases in inventory. We have also alluded to the fact that the demand for labor increases when output grows. In reality, however, the set of decisions facing firms is much more complex. A decision to produce additional output is likely to involve additional demand for both labor *and* capital.

The demand for labor is of obvious importance in macroeconomics. If the demand for labor increases at a time of less-than-full employment, the unemployment rate will fall. If the demand for labor increases when there is full employment, wage rates will rise. The demand for capital (which, as you know, is partly determined by the interest rate) is important as well. Recall that planned investment spending is a component of planned aggregate expenditure. When planned investment spending (*I*, the demand for new capital) increases, the result is additional output (income). We discussed the investment multiplier effect in Chapter 9. Another important aspect of capital is that it increases labor's productivity and leads to growth.

■ **Decision Making and Profit Maximization**   To understand the complex behavior of firms in input markets, it is important to assume that firms make decisions to maximize their profits. One of the most important profit-maximizing decisions that a firm must make is how to produce its output. In most cases, a firm must choose among alternative methods of production, or *technologies*. Different technologies generally require different combinations of capital and labor.

Take, for example, a factory that manufactures shirts. Shirts can be made entirely by hand, with workers cutting the pieces of fabric and sewing them together. But those same shirts can also be made on huge complex machines that cut and sew and produce shirts with very little human supervision. Between these two extremes are dozens of alternative technologies. For example, shirts can be partly hand sewn, with the stitching done on electric sewing machines.

All of this is to say that firms' decisions regarding the amount of capital and labor that they will use in production are closely related. If firms maximize profits, they will choose the technology that minimizes the cost of production. That is, it is logical to assume that firms will choose the technology that is most efficient.

Clearly, the most efficient technology depends on the relative prices of capital and labor. A shirt factory in the Philippines that decides to increase its production faces a large supply of relatively inexpensive labor. Wage rates in the Philippines are quite low. Capital equipment, in contrast, must be imported and is very expensive. A shirt factory in the Philippines is thus likely to choose a **labor-intensive technology**—that is, one that uses a large amount of labor relative to capital. When labor-intensive technologies are used, expansion is likely to increase the demand for labor substantially while increasing the demand for capital only modestly.

Conversely, a shirt factory in Germany that decides to expand production is likely to buy a large amount of capital equipment and to hire relatively few new workers. In other words, it will probably choose a **capital-intensive technology**—that is, a technique that uses a large amount of capital relative to labor. German wage rates are quite high, higher in many occupations than in the United States. Capital, however, is in plentiful supply.

In sum:

labor-intensive technology *A production technique that uses a large amount of labor relative to capital.*

capital-intensive technology *A production technique that uses a large amount of capital relative to labor.*

> Firms' decisions about labor demand and investment are likely to depend on the relative costs of labor and capital. The relative impact of an expansion of output on employment and on investment demand depends on the wage rate and the cost of capital.

EXPECTATIONS AND ANIMAL SPIRITS

In addition to the cost of capital and the cost of labor, firms' expectations about the future play an important role in investment and employment decisions. This should not come as a surprise to you, given the importance we have attached to expectations in this book.

Time is a key factor in investment decisions. Capital has a life that typically extends over many years. A developer who decides to build an office tower is making an investment that will be around (barring earthquakes, floods, or tornadoes) for several decades. In deciding where to build a plant, a manufacturing firm is committing a large amount of resources to purchase capital that will presumably yield services over a long period of time. Furthermore, the decision to build a building or to purchase a piece of large equipment must often be made years before the actual project is completed. While the acquisition of a small business computer may take only a few days, the planning process for downtown developments in large U.S. cities has been known to take decades.

For these reasons, investment decisions necessarily involve looking into the future and forming expectations about it. In forming their expectations, firms consider numerous factors. At a minimum, they usually gather information about the demand for their specific line of products, about what their competitors are planning to do, and about the macroeconomy's overall health. A firm is not likely to increase its production capacity if it does not expect to sell more of its product in the future. Hilton will not put up a new hotel if it does not expect to fill the rooms at a profitable rate. Ford will not build a new plant if it expects the economy to enter a prolonged recession.

Of course, forecasting the future is fraught with dangers. Many important events simply cannot be foreseen. Investments are therefore always made with imperfect knowledge. Keynes pointed this out in 1936:

> The outstanding fact is the extreme precariousness of the basis of knowledge on which our estimates of prospective yield have to be made. Our knowledge of the factors which will govern the yield of an investment some years hence is usually very slight and often negligible. If we speak frankly, we have to admit that our basis of knowledge for estimating the yield ten years hence of a railway, a copper mine, a textile factory, the goodwill of a patent medicine, an Atlantic liner, a building in the City of London amounts to little and sometimes nothing.

animal spirits of entrepreneurs
A phrase coined by Keynes to describe investors' feelings.

Keynes concludes from this that much investment activity depends on psychology and on what he calls the **animal spirits of entrepreneurs:**

> Our decisions . . . can only be taken as a result of animal spirits. In estimating the prospects of investment, we must have regard, therefore, to nerves and hysteria and even the digestions and reactions to the weather of those upon whose spontaneous activity it largely depends.[7]

Because expectations about the future are, as Keynes points out, subject to great uncertainty, they may change quite often. Thus animal spirits help to make investment a volatile component of GDP.

■ **The Accelerator Effect** It is clear that expectations at least in part determine the level of planned investment spending. At any given interest rate, the level of investment is likely to be higher if businesses are optimistic and confident. If businesses are pessimistic and gloomy, the level of planned investment will be lower. But what determines expectations?

---

[7]John Maynard Keynes, The General Theory of Employment, Interest, and Money (1936), *First Harbinger Ed. (New York: Harcourt Brace Jovanovich, 1964), pp. 149, 152.*

One possibility that seems to be borne out empirically is that expectations are optimistic when aggregate output (Y) is rising and pessimistic when aggregate output is falling. In other words:

> At any given level of the interest rate, expectations are likely to be more optimistic and planned investment is likely to be higher when output is growing rapidly than when it is growing slowly or falling.

It is not difficult to see why this is so. If firms expect future output to grow, they must plan now to add productive capacity. One indicator of future prospects is the current growth rate.

If this is indeed the case in reality, and the evidence indicates that it is, the ultimate result will be an **accelerator effect**. If aggregate output (income) (Y) is rising, investment will increase even though the level of Y may be low. Higher investment spending leads to an added increase in output, further "accelerating" the growth of aggregate output. Conversely, if Y is falling, expectations are dampened, and investment spending will be cut even though the level of Y may be high, thus accelerating the decline.

accelerator effect *The tendency for investment to increase when aggregate output increases and decrease when aggregate output decreases, thus accelerating the growth or decline of output.*

EXCESS LABOR AND EXCESS CAPITAL EFFECTS

We need to make one further point about firms' investment and employment decisions: Firms may sometimes choose to hold **excess labor** and/or **excess capital**. A firm holds excess labor (or capital) if it could reduce the amount of labor it employs (or capital it holds) and still produce the same amount of output.

excess labor, excess capital *Labor and capital that are not needed to produce the firm's current level of output.*

Why would a firm ever want to employ more workers or have more capital on hand than it needs? After all, both labor and capital are costly—a firm has to pay wages to its workers, and it forgoes interest on its funds if they are tied up in machinery or buildings. Why would a firm want to incur costs that do not yield it anything in the way of revenue?

A simple example may help to shed some light on this question. Suppose that a firm suffers a sudden and fairly large decrease in sales, but that it expects the lower sales level to last only a few months, after which it believes that sales will pick up again. In this case, the firm is likely to lower production in response to the sales change in order to avoid too large an increase in its stock of inventories. This decrease in production means that the firm could get rid of some workers and some machines, because it now needs less labor and less capital to produce the now-lower level of output.

But things are not this simple. Decreasing its work force and capital stock quickly can be quite costly for a firm. Abrupt cuts in the work force hurt worker morale and may increase personnel administration costs, and abrupt reductions in capital stock may be disadvantageous because of the difficulty of selling used machines. These types of costs are sometimes called **adjustment costs** because they are the costs of adjusting to the new level of output. There are also adjustment costs to increasing output. For example, it is usually costly to recruit and train new workers.

adjustment costs *The costs that a firm incurs when it changes its production level—for example, the administration costs of laying off employees or the training costs of hiring new workers.*

Adjustment costs may be large enough that a firm chooses not to decrease its work force and capital stock when production falls. In other words, the firm may at times choose to have more labor and capital on hand than it needs to produce its current amount of output, simply because it would be more costly to get rid of them than to keep them. In practice, excess labor takes the form of workers not working at their normal level of activity (more coffee breaks and more idle time, for instance). Some of this excess labor may receive new training so that productivity will be higher when production picks up again. This is exactly what happened to the staff at the Honda plant in Marysville, Ohio in 1993. (See the Global Perspective box titled "Honda Puts Labor into the Classroom" for more details.) Excess capital takes the form of fully or partially idle machines.

The existence of excess labor and capital at any given moment is likely to affect future employment and investment decisions. Suppose that a firm already has excess labor and capital due to a fall in its sales and production. When production picks up again, the firm will not need to hire as many new workers or acquire as much new capital as it otherwise would have. In general:

> The more excess capital a firm already has, the less likely it is to invest in new capital in the future. The more excess labor it has, the less likely it is to hire new workers in the future. In fact, if the firm finds itself holding excess capital, it may try to decrease its capital stock in the future, even if demand is actually increasing. The same is true for excess labor.

INVENTORY INVESTMENT

We now turn to a brief discussion of the inventory-investment decision. This decision is quite different from the plant-and-equipment investment decision.

■ **The Role of Inventories** Recall that there is an important distinction between a firm's sales and its output. If a firm can hold goods in inventory, which is usually the case unless the good is perishable or unless the firm produces services, then within a given period it can sell a quantity of goods that differs from the quantity of goods it produces during that period. When a firm sells more than it produces, its stock of inventories decreases; when it sells less than it produces, its stock of inventories increases. The following relationship thus holds:

> Stock of inventories (end of period) = Stock of inventories (beginning of period) + Production − Sales

For example, if a firm starts a period with 100 umbrellas in inventory, produces 15 umbrellas during the period, and sells 10 umbrellas in this same interval of time, it will have 105 umbrellas (100 + 15 − 10) left in inventory at the end of the period. A change in the stock of inventories is actually investment because inventories are counted as part of a firm's capital stock. In our example, inventory investment during the period is a positive number, five umbrellas (105 − 100). When the number of goods produced is less than the number of goods sold, inventory investment is negative.

■ **The Optimal Inventory Policy** We can now consider firms' inventory decisions. Firms are, of course, concerned with what they are going to sell and produce in the future, as well as what they are selling and producing currently. At each point in time, a firm has some idea of how much it is going to sell in the current period and in future periods. Given these expectations and its knowledge of how much of its good it already has in stock, a firm must decide how much to produce in the current period.

Inventories are costly to a firm because they take up space and they tie up funds that could otherwise be earning interest. However, if a firm's stock of inventories gets too low, the firm may have difficulty meeting the demand for its product, especially if demand increases unexpectedly. The firm may lose sales as a result. The point between too low a stock of inventory and too high a stock of inventory is called the **desired, or optimal, level of inventories.** This is the level at which the

desired, or optimal, level of inventories *The level of inventory at which the extra cost (in lost sales) from lowering inventories by a small amount is just equal to the extra gain (in interest revenue and decreased storage costs).*

HONDA PUTS EXCESS LABOR INTO THE CLASSROOM

Not all firms announce layoffs when demand for their products decreases. The following excerpt from *The New York Times* is a perfect example of a firm willing to hold "excess labor" during a period of slack demand:

MARYSVILLE, Ohio–For the 5,400 workers who assemble the popular Honda Accord at a factory here, the unthinkable finally happened. Tougher competition from the Big Three and tepid demand for cars has forced the Honda Motor Company to trim production significantly for the first time in the plant's 10-year history. . . .

But instead of laying off hundreds of workers until business improves, or spreading the pain by imposing a holiday on everyone, as American car makers often do in similar situations, Honda is using the extra time to intensify training.

"We've never guaranteed there won't be layoffs," Roger Lambert, a Honda spokesman, said. Nevertheless, "when we decided we would have to reduce output, we didn't see this as a way to cut 200 workers, we saw it as 5 percent more time for training."

In Big Three plants, workers who are laid off receive what amounts to a paid vacation under their union contracts. Honda decided to use

RATHER THAN LAY OFF WORKERS WHEN THE DEMAND FOR ITS CARS DECREASED, MANAGERS OF THE HONDA PLANT IN MARYSVILLE, OHIO SENT ASSEMBLY-LINE WORKERS BACK TO THE CLASSROOM FOR ADDITIONAL TRAINING.

this time to teach its workers new skills, reasoning that it would be an investment in future productivity.

Honda says its commitment to training is a strategy for enlarging the capability of its work force so that its rebound will be magnified when tough times improve. For Honda and other Japanese auto makers operating factories in the United States, constant training has been a key tactic in their battle against American auto makers. . . .

Last fall, Honda announced it would build 110,000 Accords in the first quarter of 1993, down almost 11 percent from the 123,483 built in the first quarter last year. The rate translates to about 200 fewer cars a day. Rather than stopping production, Honda slowed assembly slightly–which allowed it to move people from the assembly line to the classroom.

Source: Doron P. Levin, "Back to School for Honda Workers," *The New York Times,* March, 1993.

extra cost (in lost sales) from decreasing inventories by a small amount is just equal to the extra gain (in interest revenue and decreased storage costs).

A firm that had no costs other than inventory costs would always aim to produce in a period exactly the volume of goods necessary to make its stock of inventories at the end of the period equal to the desired stock. If the stock of inventory fell lower than desired, the firm would produce more than it expected to sell to bring the stock up. If the stock of inventory grew above the desired level, the firm would produce less than it expected to sell in order to reduce the stock.

There are other costs to running a firm besides inventory costs, however. In particular, large and abrupt changes in production can be extremely costly because it is often disruptive to change a production process geared to a certain rate of output. If production is to be increased, there may be adjustment costs involved in hiring more labor and in increasing the capital stock. If production is to be decreased, there may be adjustment costs in laying off workers and decreasing the capital stock.

Because holding inventories and changing production levels are both costly, firms face a trade-off between these two courses of action. Because of adjustment costs, a firm is likely to smooth its production path relative to its sales path. This means that a firm is likely to have its production fluctuate less than its sales, with changes in inventories being used to absorb the difference each period. However, because there are incentives not to stray too far from the optimal level of inventories, fluctuations in production are not eliminated completely. Production is still likely to fluctuate somewhat, just not as much as sales fluctuate.

Two other points need to be made here. First, if a firm's stock of inventories is unusually or unexpectedly high, the firm is likely to produce less in the future than it otherwise would have, in order to decrease its high stock of inventories. In other words, although the stock of inventories fluctuates over time because production is smoothed relative to sales, at any point in time inventories may be unexpectedly high or low because sales have been unexpectedly low or high. An unexpectedly high stock will have a negative effect on production in the future, and an unexpectedly low stock will have a positive effect on production in the future.

> An unexpected increase in inventories has a negative effect on future production, and an unexpected decrease in inventories has a positive effect on future production.

Second, firms do not know their future sales exactly. In practice, firms have only expectations of future sales, and these expectations may not turn out to be exactly right.

This fact has important consequences. If sales turn out to be less than expected, inventories will be higher than expected, and there will be less production in the future. Furthermore, *future* sales expectations are likely to have an important effect on *current* production. If a firm expects its sales to be high in the future, it will adjust its planned production path accordingly. Even though a firm smoothes production relative to sales, over a long period of time it must produce as much as it sells. If it did not, it would have an indefinitely falling stock of inventories.

> The level of a firm's planned production path depends on the level of its expected future sales path. If a firm's expectations of the level of its future sales path decrease, the firm is likely to decrease the level of its planned production path, including its actual production in the current period. Thus, current production depends on expected future sales.

Because production is likely to depend on expectations of the future, animal spirits may once again play an important role. If firms become more optimistic about the future, they are likely to produce more now. Thus, Keynes's view that animal spirits affect investment is also likely to pertain to output.

A SUMMARY OF FIRM BEHAVIOR

To summarize our discussion of firm behavior:

The following factors affect firms' investment and employment decisions:

- the wage rate and the cost of capital. (An important component of the cost of capital is the interest rate.)
- firms' expectations of future output.
- the amount of excess labor and excess capital on hand.

The most important points to remember about the relationship between production, sales, and inventory investment are:

- inventory investment (that is, the change in the stock of inventories) equals production minus sales.
- an unexpected increase in the stock of inventories has a negative effect on future production.
- current production depends on expected future sales.

THE FIRM SECTOR SINCE 1970

To close our discussion of firm behavior in the macroeconomy, we now turn to an examination of some aggregate investment and employment variables for the period 1970 I–1994 IV.

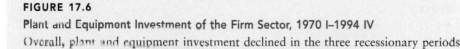

■ **Plant and Equipment Investment** Plant and equipment investment by the firm sector is plotted in Figure 17.6. As you can see, investment fared poorly in the three

FIGURE 17.6

Plant and Equipment Investment of the Firm Sector, 1970 I–1994 IV

Overall, plant and equipment investment declined in the three recessionary periods since 1970.

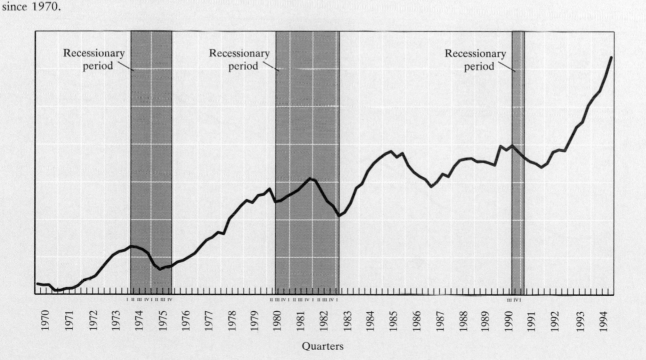

recessionary periods after 1970. This observation is consistent with the observation that investment depends in part on output. An examination of the plot of real GDP in Figure 6.6 and the plot of investment in Figure 17.6 shows clearly that investment generally does poorly when GDP does poorly and that investment generally does well when GDP does well.

Figure 17.6 also shows that investment fluctuates greatly. This is not surprising. The animal spirits of entrepreneurs are likely to be volatile, and if animal spirits affect investment, it follows that investment too will be volatile.

Despite the volatility of plant and equipment investment, however, it is still true that housing investment fluctuates more than plant and equipment investment (as you can see by comparing Figures 17.4 and 17.6). Plant and equipment investment is not the most volatile component of GDP.

■ **Employment** Employment in the firm sector is plotted in Figure 17.7, which shows that employment fell in all three recessionary periods. This is consistent with the theory that employment depends in part on output. Otherwise, employment has grown over time in response to the growing economy. Employment in the firm sector rose from 71.8 million in 1970 I to 111.1 million in 1994 IV.

■ **Inventory Investment** Recall that *inventory investment* is the difference between the level of output and the level of sales. Recall also that some inventory investment is usually unplanned. This occurs when the actual level of sales is different from the expected level of sales.

Inventory investment of the firm sector is plotted in Figure 17.8. Also plotted

FIGURE 17.7

Employment in the Firm Sector, 1970 I–1994 IV

Growth in employment was generally negative in the three recessions the U.S. economy has experienced since 1970.

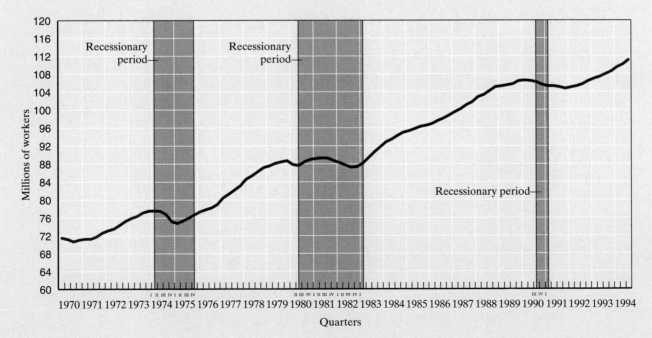

in this figure is the ratio of the stock of inventories to the level of sales—the *inventory/sales ratio*. The figure shows that inventory investment is very volatile—more volatile, in fact, than housing investment and plant and equipment investment. Some of this volatility is undoubtedly due to the unplanned component of inventory investment, which is likely to fluctuate greatly from one period to the next.

When the inventory/sales ratio is high, the actual stock of inventories is likely to be larger than the desired stock. In such a case, firms have overestimated demand and produced too much relative to sales, and they are likely to want to produce less in the future in order to draw down their stock. You can find several examples of this phenomenon in Figure 17.8, the clearest of which occurred during the 1974–1975 period. At the end of 1974, the stock of inventories was very high relative to sales, which means that firms probably had undesired inventories at the end of 1974. In 1975, firms worked off these undesired inventories by producing less than they sold. Thus inventory investment was very low in 1975. The year 1975 is clearly a year in which output would have been higher had the stock of inventories at the beginning of the year not been so high.

On average the inventory/sales ratio has been declining over time, which suggests that firms are becoming more efficient in their management of inventory stocks. They are becoming more efficient in the sense of being able (other things equal) to hold smaller and smaller stocks of inventories relative to sales.

FIGURE 17.8

Inventory Investment of the Firm Sector and the Inventory/Sales Ratio, 1970 I–1994 IV

The inventory/sales ratio is the ratio of the firm sector's stock of inventories to the level of sales. Inventory investment is very volatile.

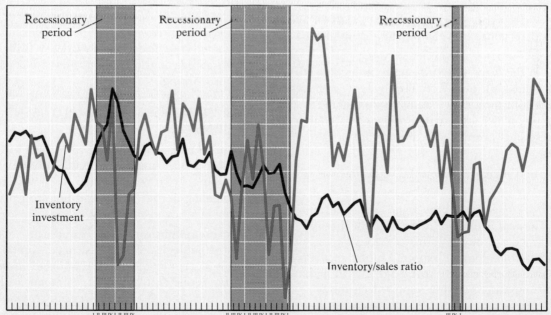

HOUSEHOLDS: CONSUMPTION AND LABOR SUPPLY DECISIONS

1. The Keynesian theory of consumption holds that household consumption (C) is positively related to income: The more income one has, the more consumption one is likely to do. Keynes also believed that high-income households consume a smaller proportion of their income than do low-income households. The proportion of income that households spend on consumption is measured by the *average propensity to consume (APC),* which is equal to consumption divided by income (C/Y).

2. The *life-cycle theory of consumption* holds that households make lifetime consumption decisions based on their expectations of lifetime income. Generally, households consume an amount less than their incomes during their prime working years and an amount greater than their incomes during their early working years and after they have retired.

3. Households make consumption and labor supply decisions simultaneously. Consumption cannot be considered separately from labor supply, because it is precisely by selling one's labor that one earns the income that makes consumption possible.

4. There is a trade-off between the goods and services that wage income will buy and leisure or other nonmarket activities. The wage rate is the key variable that determines how a household responds to this trade-off.

5. Changes in the wage rate have both an income effect and a substitution effect. The evidence suggests that the substitution effect seems to dominate for most people, which means that the aggregate labor supply responds positively to an increase in the wage rate.

6. Consumption increases when the wage rate increases.

7. The *nominal wage rate* is the wage rate in current dollars. The *real wage rate* is the amount that the nominal wage can buy in terms of goods and services. Households look at expected future real wage rates as well as the current real wage rate in making their consumption and labor supply decisions.

8. Holding all else constant (including the stage in the life cycle), the more wealth a household has, the more it will consume, both now and in the future.

9. An unexpected increase in *nonlabor income* (that is, any income that is received from sources other than working, such as inheritances, interest, and dividends) will have a positive effect on a household's consumption and will lead to a decrease in labor supply.

10. The interest rate also affects consumption, although the direction of the total effect depends on the relative sizes of the income and substitution effects. There is some evidence that the income effect is larger now than it used to be, thus making monetary policy less effective than it used to be.

11. The government influences household behavior mainly through tax rates and transfer payments. If the substitution effect dominates, an increase in tax rates lowers after-tax income, decreases consumption, and decreases the labor supply; a decrease in tax rates raises after-tax income, increases consumption, and increases labor supply. Increases in transfer payments increase consumption and decrease labor supply, while decreases in transfer payments decrease consumption and increase labor supply.

12. During times of unemployment, households' labor supply may be constrained. That is, households may wish to work a certain number of hours at current wage rates but may not be allowed to do so by firms. In this situation, the level of income (at least workers' income) depends exclusively on the employment decisions made by firms. Households consume less if they are constrained from working.

FIRMS: INVESTMENT AND EMPLOYMENT DECISIONS

13. Firms purchase *inputs* and turn them into outputs. Each period, firms must decide how much capital and labor (two major inputs) they wish to use in producing output. Firms can invest in plants and equipment or in inventory.

14. Because output can be produced using many different technologies, firms must make capital and labor decisions simultaneously. A *labor-intensive technique* is one that uses a large amount of labor relative to capital. A *capital-intensive technique* is one that uses a large amount of capital relative to labor. The ultimate decision of which technology to use depends on the wage rate and the cost of capital.

15. Expectations play an important role in investment and employment decisions. Keynes used the term *animal spirits of entrepreneurs* to refer to investors' feelings.

16. At any given level of the interest rate, expectations are likely to be more optimistic and planned investment is likely to be higher when output is growing rapidly than when it is growing slowly or falling. The ultimate result is an *accelerator effect* that can cause the economy to expand more rapidly during an expansion and contract more quickly during a recession.

17. *Excess labor and capital* are labor and capital that are not needed to produce a firm's current level of output. Holding excess labor and capital may be more efficient than laying off workers or selling used equipment. The more excess capital a firm already has, the less likely it is to invest in new capital in the future. The more excess labor it has, the less likely it is to hire new workers in the future.

18. Holding inventories is costly to a firm because they take up space and because they tie up funds that could otherwise be earning interest. However, not holding inventories can cause a firm to lose sales if demand increases. The *desired*, or *optimal*, *level of inventories* is the level at which the extra cost (in lost sales) from lowering inventories by a small amount is just equal to the extra gain (in interest revenue and decreased storage costs).

19. An unexpected increase in inventories has a negative effect on future production, and an unexpected decrease in inventories has a positive effect on future production.

20. The level of a firm's planned production path depends on the level of its expected future sales path. If a firm's expectations of its future sales path decrease, the firm is likely to decrease the level of its planned production path, including its actual production in the current period.

REVIEW TERMS AND CONCEPTS

accelerator effect 407

adjustment costs 407

animal spirits of entrepreneurs 406

average propensity to consume (APC) 391

capital-intensive technology 405

constrained supply of labor 399

desired, or **optimal, level of inventories** 408

excess capital 407

excess labor 407

income effect of a wage rate increase 394

inputs 404

inventory investment 404

labor-intensive technology 405

life-cycle theory of consumption 391

nominal wage rate 395

nonlabor, or **nonwage, income** 396

permanent income 393

plant-and-equipment investment 404

real wage rate 395

substitution effect of a wage rate increase 394

unconstrained supply of labor 399

Equation:

$$APC \equiv \frac{C}{Y}$$

PROBLEM SET

1. During 1994 and 1995, the Federal Reserve Bank raised interest rates steadily in an effort to slow the U.S. economy's rate of growth. Its goal: to prevent inflation.
   a. What direct effects do higher interest rates have on household and firm behavior?
   b. One of the consequences of higher interest rates was that the value of existing bonds (both corporate bonds and government bonds) fell by more than $1.7 trillion. Briefly explain why higher interest rates would reduce the value of existing fixed rate bonds held by the public.
   c. Some economists argue that the wealth effect of higher interest rates on consumption is as important as the direct effect of higher interest rates on consumption. Explain what economists mean by

"wealth effects on consumption" and illustrate with *AS/AD* curves.

2. In 1993, President Clinton proposed and Congress enacted an increase in taxes. One of the increases was in the income tax rate for higher-income wage earners. Republicans claimed that reducing the rewards for working (the net after-tax wage rate), would lead to less work effort and a lower labor supply. Supporters of the tax increase replied that this criticism was baseless because it "ignored the income effect of the tax increase (net wage reduction)." Explain what these supporters meant.

3. Graph the following two consumption functions:
   (1) $C = 300 + 0.5 Y$
   (2) $C = 0.5 Y$.
   a. For each function, calculate and graph the average propensity to consume (*APC*) when income is $100, $400, and $800.
   b. In both examples, what happens to the *APC* as income rises?
   c. In both examples, what is the relationship between the *APC* and the marginal propensity to consume?
   d. Under consumption function (1), a family with an income of $50,000 consumes a smaller proportion of its income than a family with an income of $20,000; yet if we take a dollar of income away from the rich family and give it to the poor family, total consumption by the two families does not change. Explain how this could be so.

4. During the late 1980s the price of houses increased dramatically in both the Northeast and California. During the early 1990s home prices dropped sharply in both of these regions. During the late 1980s the economies of both the Northeast and California boomed, and during the 1990s both went into deep recessions.

   What impact would you expect increases and decreases in home value to have on the consumption behavior of home owners? Explain. In what ways might events in the housing market have influenced the rest of the economy through their effects on consumption spending? Be specific.

5. Adam Smith is 45 years old. He has assets (wealth) of $20,000 and has no debts or liabilities. He knows he will work for 20 more years and that he will live five years after that, and during those five years he will earn nothing. His salary each year for the rest of his working career is $14,000. (There are no taxes.) He wants to distribute his consumption over the rest of his life in such a way that he consumes the same amount each year. Of course, he cannot consume in total more than his current wealth plus the sum of his income for the next 20 years. Assume that the rate of interest is zero and that Smith decides not to leave any inheritance to his children.
   a. How much will Adam consume this year? Next year? How did you arrive at your answer?
   b. Plot on a graph Adam's income, consumption, and wealth from the time he is 45 until the time he is 70 years old. What is the relationship between the annual increase in Adam's wealth and his annual saving (income minus consumption)? In what year does Adam's wealth start to decline? Why? How much wealth does he have when he dies?
   c. Suppose that Adam receives a tax rebate of $100 per year, so that his income is $14,100 per year for the rest of his working career. By how much does his consumption increase this year? Next year?
   d. Now suppose that Adam receives a one-year-only tax refund of $100. That is, his income this year is $14,100, but in all succeeding years his income is back to $14,000. What happens to his consumption this year? In succeeding years?

6. Explain why a household's consumption and labor supply decisions are interdependent. What impact does this interdependence have on the way in which consumption and income are related?

7. Compile a list of factors that are important in determining how much labor you will supply during the summer. How might your list differ from that of a 40-year-old breadwinner?

8. Why do expectations play such an important role in investment demand? How, if at all, does this explain why investment is so volatile?

9. Explain why the size of its existing stock of inventories is negatively related to the amount of output a firm wishes to produce in a period.

10. How can a firm maintain a smooth production schedule even when sales are fluctuating? What are the benefits of a smooth production schedule? What are the costs?

FURTHER TOPICS IN MACROECONOMIC ANALYSIS

THE LAST CHAPTER PRESENTED A MORE COMPLETE AND REALISTIC picture of the behavior of households and firms in the macroeconomy. Using what we learned there, we can now analyze the effects of fiscal and monetary policy on the macroeconomy in more detail. We can also consider some interesting new topics, including the impact of the stock market on the economy and the relationship between aggregate output and the unemployment rate. We begin our discussion with a brief review of basic monetary and fiscal policy.

MONETARY AND FISCAL POLICY REVISITED

A major focus of our discussion of macroeconomics has been on the role of government. As you know, the federal government can influence the behavior of the economy through **fiscal policy**—that is, through its taxing and spending decisions. About 20% of U.S. GDP goes to the federal government in the form of taxes. In recent years, the government has been spending a good deal more than it has been collecting in taxes. The result has been high annual budget deficits and a large national debt.

The government can also influence the economy by using **monetary policy** to change the interest rate. In the United States, the Federal Reserve controls the money supply. By expanding and contracting the quantity of money in circulation, the Fed indirectly controls the interest rate and thus influences the behavior of households and firms.

Let us now consider monetary and fiscal policy in more detail.

fiscal policy *The spending and taxing policies used by the government to influence the economy.*

monetary policy *The behavior of the Federal Reserve regarding the money supply.*

TEMPORARY VERSUS PERMANENT CHANGES IN TAXES AND SPENDING

Thus far, our analysis of fiscal policy has been quite simple. If the government cuts taxes, we said, households consume more. The cut in taxes shifts the aggregate expenditure (*AE*) curve up and the aggregate demand (*AD*) curve to the right. The result is a higher level of equilibrium national output, at least in the short run, and a higher price level.

With the expanded discussion of household and firm behavior in the previous chapter, we are in a position to understand better the full impacts of fiscal policy. Consider, for example, the effect of a tax cut on household behavior. We now know that household consumption and saving behavior is influenced not by current income alone, but also by households' expectations about future income. Thus,

> If a tax cut is expected to be temporary rather than permanent, it will have less of an effect on household behavior because it will have less of an impact on households' permanent income.

ALTHOUGH THE U.S. SOCIAL SECURITY SYSTEM IS EXPECTED TO HAVE MORE THAN $2 TRILLION IN RESERVES BY THE YEAR 2020, MANY ARE CONCERNED THAT THE SYSTEM WILL GO BANKRUPT WHEN THE BABY BOOM GENERATION BEGINS TO RETIRE. IF PEOPLE IN THEIR 30S AND 40S EXPECT THE SYSTEM TO BE BANKRUPT WITHIN 30 YEARS, THEY MIGHT ALTER THEIR CONSUMPTION AND SAVING BEHAVIOR.

Examples of temporary tax changes include the lump-sum tax rebate on 1974 income granted by the Ford administration in 1975 and the temporary income tax "surcharge" enacted in the late 1960s by the Nixon administration to help pay for the Vietnam War. In contrast, the tax cuts in 1981 and 1986 (which we have discussed several times in this book) were intended by Congress to be permanent. (With hindsight, of course, many of these tax cuts were not permanent. As discussed in Chapter 16, tax rates were raised in 1993.)

The fact that household decisions depend on expectations also means that changes in government policies that have little or no impact on this year's budget, but that do have impacts in the future, can affect behavior. Perhaps the most important example of this is social security policy. As we discussed briefly in Chapter 3, virtually everyone employed in the United States belongs to the social security system. Employers and employees are required to pay a fairly stiff social security tax out of each week's pay. When a worker retires, he or she receives a check from the Social Security Administration every month for as long as he or she lives.

Some economists believe that the saving rate in the United States is low partly because of the social security system. If workers expect to receive social security benefits, they may decrease their personal saving for retirement and consume more today. In this sense, the social security system may act as a substitute for private saving.

The effects of tax changes on firm behavior also depend on whether these changes are perceived to be permanent or temporary. Even more than consumption decisions, investment decisions are based on expectations of the future. Clearly, the future returns on an investment project depend, at least in part, on the tax laws that will be in effect in the future. Nothing is more frustrating to private business than a government that is constantly changing the rules. In 1986, Roger Smith, then chairman of the board of General Motors, decided to speak out in favor of the Tax Reform Act of 1986 despite the fact that the act increased corporation income taxes by about $120 billion and despite opposition from many other chief executive officers. He did so because members of Congress promised that if the act were passed, they would strongly resist changing the tax laws again for a long time.

POLICIES THAT AFFECT REAL WAGES VERSUS POLICIES THAT AFFECT NONLABOR INCOME

The analysis we did in the last chapter makes it clear that policies that affect real after-tax wages are likely to have a different effect on labor supply *and* consumption than policies that affect income alone. Remember that households make both labor supply decisions and consumption decisions simultaneously.

In 1991, in testing the waters for a possible run for the presidency in 1992, Senator John D. Rockefeller suggested a $1000 "refundable income tax credit." Through this credit, everyone's taxes would be cut by $1000, regardless of their income. If a taxpayer paid less than $1000 in taxes, he or she would receive a check for the difference.

Now imagine the effect of a tax cut of the same magnitude enacted in the form of reduced tax *rates* rather than as a lump-sum credit. When tax rates are cut, the after-tax wage rate rises (because workers take home a bigger part of each hour's wages). Thus, the rewards of an added hour of work are higher when tax rates are cut. The rewards of an added hour of work do *not* change if the tax cut is simply $1000, regardless of how much one works.

Assuming that both the $1000 across-the-board tax cut and the rate reduction increase disposable income by the same amount initially, one might think that both would have the same impact on consumption spending and ultimately on output. But this is not the case. Why? Because the two proposals can have very different effects on the labor supply. Both proposals make households better off, and this *income effect* leads workers to consume more leisure (that is, to work less). But the reduced tax rate also produces a *substitution effect* away from leisure, while the lump-sum reduction does not. The lower tax rate means that the opportunity cost (or the "price") of leisure is higher, which may cause people to work more. The lump-sum tax reduction, however, does *not* affect the trade-off between work and leisure. (Review the last chapter if you are unsure of how the income and substitution effects work.)

This is precisely the point made by policy makers during the Reagan administration. Between 1981 (when President Reagan first took office) and 1986, Congress sharply reduced personal income tax rates twice. In 1981, the highest income tax rate was reduced from 70% to 50 percent. Then, in 1986, it was reduced from 50% to 33 percent. The expressed purpose of these cuts was to "increase the incentive to work." This was part of the logic of what came to be called *supply-side economics*. (We touched briefly on supply-side economics earlier and will return to the topic in the next chapter.)

TRANSFER PAYMENTS AND OTHER NONLABOR INCOME

The refundable credit we discussed above is a **transfer payment.** Other transfer payments include social security payments, welfare benefits, and unemployment compensation. (Review Chapter 3 if necessary.) Transfer payments, in turn, are part of a larger category of income called **nonlabor income**—income received from non-wage-earning activities. Interest income received by households is one type of nonlabor income.

The effect of a change in nonlabor income on households is a pure income effect. There is no substitution effect because a change in nonlabor income does not change the trade-off between work and leisure. (In other words, a change in nonlabor income does not affect the wage rate.) Therefore:

> Any increase in nonlabor income unambiguously leads to an increase in consumption and a decrease in labor supply. Conversely, any decrease in nonlabor income unambiguously leads to a decrease in consumption and an increase in labor supply.

transfer payments *Cash payments made by the government directly to households.*

nonlabor income *Any income that is received from sources other than working.*

dividends *The portion of a corporation's profits the firm pays out each period to shareholders.*

Dividend payments by firms to households are part of nonlabor income. When the economy expands, firms' profits increase, and some of these profits go to households in the form of **dividends.** This increase in nonlabor income then leads households to consume more and work less. Firm profits are thus another channel through which policy changes can affect the economy. Any policy change that initially stimulates the economy and increases firms' profits will lead to an increase in the nonlabor income of households, which will further affect the economy through the (increased) consumption and (decreased) labor supply responses of households.

THE IMPORTANCE OF INTEREST RATES

We know that monetary policy works primarily through changes in the interest rate. Until the last chapter, we focused on the effects of changes in the interest rate on firms' planned investment spending (I) by firms. We assumed that lower interest rates stimulate I and that higher interest rates reduce I. In the last chapter, however, we saw that consumption (C) is also likely to depend on the interest rate. If the substitution effect is greater than the income effect, then a decrease in the interest rate has a positive effect on consumption. If the income effect is greater than the substitution effect, a decrease in interest rates has a negative effect on consumption. Because the interest rate affects both investment and consumption, there are two channels through which monetary policy can influence behavior in the goods market.

In the last chapter, we also discussed the fact that the income effect of a change in the interest rate on consumption may be larger today than it was in the past. For this reason monetary policy may now be less effective than before. The income effect may be larger today due to the recent huge increase in the government debt, much of which is owned by households. A decrease in the interest rate leads to a large decrease in the interest income of households; this has a negative effect on consumption. Current evidence suggests that this effect offsets much of the positive substitution effect on consumption and the positive effect on investment from a decrease in the interest rate.

POLICY EFFECTS IN HIGH-OUTPUT VERSUS LOW-OUTPUT PERIODS

When we discussed the short-run aggregate supply curve in Chapter 14, we argued that the *AS* curve is likely to be fairly flat at low levels of output and fairly steep at high levels of output. This means that policies designed to stimulate or contract the economy are likely to have a larger impact on output when output is low rather than high.

We are now in a position to understand exactly why this is so. At low levels of output, firms may be holding excess capital and excess labor. That is, firms may have idle plant capacity and workers who are not working at their potential even though they are on the payroll. If firms believe that a downturn in sales and output is temporary and that increased output will be needed in the future, they may choose to close a plant temporarily or to reassign workers rather than to sell off the plant and fire the workers. If firms behave this way, then an expansionary policy can lead to more output without the need for more workers or more plant capacity. Existing plants and current workers can simply be put back to work.

Recall that when output is low, there is likely to be unemployment. During periods of unemployment, households are constrained from working as much as they would like to at current wage rates. Thus, when firms expand during such periods, labor is available from the ranks of the unemployed, and higher wages are not needed to attract them. For this reason, output can be expanded with little or no increase in wage rates, input costs, or the overall price level.

At high levels of output, however, firms are holding very little excess capital and labor, and the unemployment rate is low. In this case, an expansionary policy can work only if the labor supply expands. The policy will create an excess demand for labor, which will push up wages (labor/input costs). Higher wages are required to induce the needed number of workers away from leisure and into the work force. This means upward pressure on wages and on the aggregate price level.

The size of the multiplier depends on whether excess labor and capital exist and whether workers are willing to take jobs at the current wage rate. If output can expand with little or no increase in costs, the multiplier is likely to be large. However if added output leads to higher wages and other costs, firms are not likely to expand output as much. Thus:

> During periods of high output and low unemployment, the multiplier is likely to be smaller.

THE ROLE OF INVENTORIES

Finally, the effectiveness of monetary and fiscal policy also depends on the size of inventory stocks. During periods of low output, inventory stocks are likely to be high (because sales have presumably been weak), so part of any increase in sales brought about by an expansionary policy can come out of inventories. In periods of high output inventory stocks are likely to be low, so sales increases are likely to be matched fairly closely by output increases. Thus:

> Output is likely to respond more to sales increases in high-output periods than in low-output periods, provided that firms have enough capital and labor to support the output increase.

If firms do not have sufficient capital and labor to support an output increase, their inventory stocks will fall further as sales increase, even though they would like to build their stocks back up. In this case, the economy is in effect on the steep part of the *AS* curve, and there is likely to be a large price response to any increase in aggregate demand.

THE EFFECTS OF THE STOCK MARKET ON THE ECONOMY

In the last chapter, we pointed out that one of the factors that affects consumption is wealth. If a household has a sudden increase in wealth, its current and future consumption levels will increase. One of the main components of household wealth is the value of stocks held by households. When stock prices rise, household wealth increases, and when stock prices fall, household wealth decreases. Stock prices thus affect the economy by affecting household wealth, which affects household consumption. (This chapter's Application boxes explain in detail how to follow both the bond market and the stock market by reading the financial pages of the daily newspaper.)

WHAT IS A BOND?

When a business wishes to make a large purchase—to build a new factory, for example, or to buy an expensive piece of machinery—it often finds that it cannot pay for the purchase all at once, entirely out of its normal revenues. The obvious solution is to borrow the money, make the purchase, and then repay the lender of the funds over a longer period of time. This process is called "financing" an investment, and the "pieces of paper" that are involved in these transactions are called **financial instruments.** *Bonds* are one type of financial instrument that firms issue in exchange for cash. If you buy a bond, you are making a loan to the firm that sold it to you.

Bonds have several important properties. First, they are issued with a *face value,* typically in denominations of $1000, that represent the amount you (the buyer) agree to lend the bond issuer. They also come with a *maturity date* on which the firm promises to pay back the funds you lent it. (However, you can sell the bond to someone else before the maturity date if you want.) Finally, there is a fixed payment of a specified amount (usually made annually), paid by the bond issuer to the bondholder. This payment, known as the *coupon,*

is calculated using the prevailing interest rate at the time the bond is issued. Even if interest rates change over the life of the bond, which they almost always do, the amount you receive as interest on your bond remains fixed. (This is why bonds are sometimes referred to as fixed-income securities. The bondholder receives a set amount, known in advance, no matter what happens to interest rates, stock prices, and so on.)

For example, if you bought a $10,000, 10%, 15-year bond from Company XYZ on January 1, 1995, this is what would happen. You would give XYZ, or perhaps your broker, a check for $10,000. Every January for the next 14 years, XYZ would send you a check for $1000 (10% of the $10,000 face value). On January 1, 2010, XYZ would send you a check for the face value of the bond—$10,000—plus the interest for that year—$1000—and that would square all accounts.

Does the fact that the annual interest payment (coupon) on a bond does not change with fluctuations in the interest rate mean that bonds are completely insulated from interest rate movements? Absolutely not! Instead of the coupon responding to a change in the interest rate, it is the *price of the bond* that changes. To see why this is so, suppose you had a choice

of putting $10,000 into the bond described above or into a bank account that pays 10% per year interest. In either case, you would earn $1000 per year in interest payments, so you should be indifferent between the two choices.

But now suppose that the interest rate on the bank account goes up to 20% instead of 10 percent. The bond still promises to pay $1000 per year. If you want to earn $1000 in interest, you need to put only $5000 into the bank account (since .20 × $5000 = $1000). You would obviously prefer to put $5000 into the bank rather than tie up $10,000 in the bond. The only way anyone would willingly buy the bond is if it cost no more than other investments that yield the same stream of income in the future. The bond would thus be worth much less than $10,000 if the interest rate were 20 percent. It follows, then, that when interest rates rise, bond prices fall, and bondholders suffer a *capital loss*—that is, a reduction in the value of the securities they own.

HOW TO READ A BOND TABLE

Figure 1 shows a small section of *The New York Times's* corporate bond price quotations for February 2, 1995. What do all these signs and symbols mean?

As you should recall from Chapter 3, one of the key aspects of the modern corporation is its limited liability feature. Stockholders are entitled to a share of the firm's profits, but if the firm incurs losses, stockholders' liability is limited to the amount of their initial contribution. This is not true with partnerships or proprietorships.

To see how events in the stock market affect the economy, it is informative to consider a particular episode in the history of the stock market, namely the stock market crash of October 1987. The value of stocks in the United States fell by

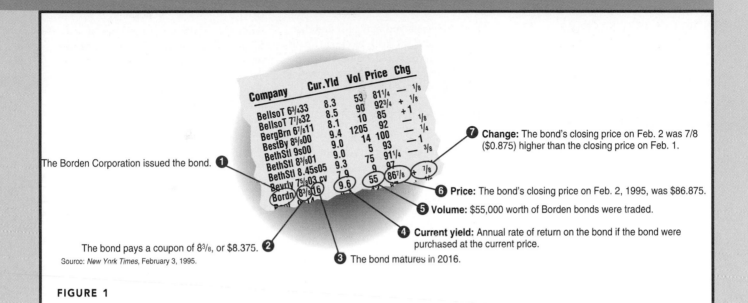

The Borden Corporation issued the bond. **1**

7 Change: The bond's closing price on Feb. 2 was 7/8 ($0.875) higher than the closing price on Feb. 1.

6 Price: The bond's closing price on Feb. 2, 1995, was $86.875.

5 Volume: $55,000 worth of Borden bonds were traded.

4 Current yield: Annual rate of return on the bond if the bond were purchased at the current price.

The bond pays a coupon of 8³/₈, or $8.375. **2**

Source: *New York Times*, February 3, 1995.

3 The bond matures in 2016.

FIGURE 1

New York Stock Exchange Bonds

The first column, under the heading "Company," gives the name of the corporation that issued the bond and certain information about the terms under which the bond was originally issued. Let's take the last bond listed in the figure as an example. This bond was issued by the Borden Corporation. The "8³/₈" means that the bond pays a coupon of 8³/₈, or $8.375, per $100 of face value of the bond. The "16" means that the bond matures in 2016. The column titled "Cur. Yld" shows the annual rate of return on the bond if the bond were purchased at the current price. If the current price were $100, then the annual rate of return would be 8.375 percent. Since the bond yields 9.6%, however, the current price of the bond must be lower than its face value of $100. (Remember that an increase in the interest rate lowers the value of a bond.) The third column, "Vol," tells how many thousands of dollars in bonds were traded during the day in question. Here we see that $55,000 (at face value) of the Borden bond was traded on February 2, 1995.

"Price" is the closing price of the bond. This is how much you would have to pay for the bond per $100 of face value. The Borden bond's closing price was 86⅞, which means that the bond was worth $86.875 at the end of the trading day. The last column, "Chg," tells us by how much the closing bond price differs from the closing price on the previous day. In this case, the price of the Borden bond rose by seven eighths of a point—that is, by $0.875.

about a trillion dollars between August 1987 and the end of October 1987. In one day—October 19, 1987—the value of stocks fell nearly $700 billion. This corresponded to a large drop in household wealth.

In practice, it seems to be the case that a $1.00 decrease in wealth leads roughly to a $0.05 decrease in consumption spending per year. In other words, consumption seems to be lower in each future year by about 5% of the decrease in wealth. Using this estimate, we can see that the $1 trillion decrease in wealth in 1987 implies a

WHAT IS A STOCK?

In addition to issuing bonds, firms can finance investments by borrowing money directly from a bank or other lending institution. A third alternative is for firms to issue additional shares of stock. When a corporation issues new shares of stock, it does not add to its debt. Instead, it brings in additional "owners" of the firm, owners who agree to supply it with funds. The contributions of such owners are treated differently from loans made by outsiders, which are considered liabilities.

What is a share of stock, exactly? If you buy one share of Company QRS, and the firm has 1 million total shares outstanding, you have purchased a one-millionth ownership of the firm. You have a right—along with the owners of the other 999,999 shares—to select the management of the firm and to share in its profits. (This is not true of bondholders and other creditors of the firm, who have no say in its management.) Unlike bonds or direct borrowing, however, your stock does not promise a fixed annual payment. Rather, the returns you receive on your investment depend on how well Company QRS performs. If its profits are high, the firm may elect to pay dividends to its shareholders, although it is not required to do so. If the firm does well, you may also find that the price of QRS stock has gone up, in which case you could realize a *capital gain* by selling your stock for more than you originally paid for it.

HOW TO READ THE STOCK PAGE

Once you buy a stock, you are free to sell it to someone else at any time. Developments in the stock market, where such transactions take place, are constantly followed in the news.

Figure 1 reproduces part of the stock quotations from *The New York Times* for February 2, 1995. Let us take the stock of American Health Properties and see what information the stock pages provide.

The first two columns, under the general heading "52-Week," give the stock's highest and lowest prices over the past year. The price of a share of American Health stock reached a high of 27 and a low of $18\frac{1}{2}$ during this period. (Stock prices are quoted in dollars per share, so "$18\frac{1}{2}$" means that the stock sold for $18.50 per share at its low point during the past 52 weeks.) The column labeled "Div" gives the dividend paid (in dollars) per share over the past year. If you had owned a share of American Health stock, you would have received a payment of $2.30 during the year. What sort of return is this? The next column, "Yld %" (yield percent), takes the dividend as a percentage of the day's closing price. (The day's closing price in this case is $21\frac{1}{2}$, which is given in the column titled "Last.") If you had purchased a share of stock for $21.50 and received a dividend of $2.30 for the year, your investment would be returning, or "yielding," 10.7% per year.

The column labeled "P/E" (price-earnings ratio) calculates the ratio of the price of a share of stock to the company's *total earnings per share* (which includes not only dividends paid to shareholders but also retained earnings). The PE ratio is a widely used measure of how highly a stock is valued. American Health's PE ratio is 48. The column labeled "Sales 100s" tells how many hundreds of shares changed hands during the day's trading. On February 2, 1995, 40,000 shares of American Health's stock were traded. The last four columns of the table give the stock's highest, lowest, and closing price during the day's trading, as well as the change in the closing price from the closing price of the previous day.

Source: *New York Times*, February 3, 1995.

FIGURE 1

New York Stock Exchange Issues

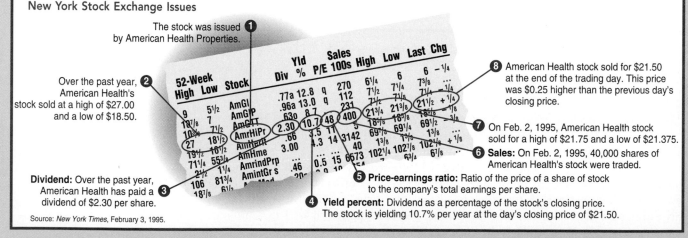

① The stock was issued by American Health Properties.

② Over the past year, American Health's stock sold at a high of $27.00 and a low of $18.50.

③ **Dividend:** Over the past year, American Health has paid a dividend of $2.30 per share.

④ **Yield percent:** Dividend as a percentage of the stock's closing price. The stock is yielding 10.7% per year at the day's closing price of $21.50.

⑤ **Price-earnings ratio:** Ratio of the price of a share of stock to the company's total earnings per share.

⑥ **Sales:** On Feb. 2, 1995, 40,000 shares of American Health's stock were traded.

⑦ On Feb. 2, 1995, American Health stock sold for a high of $21.75 and a low of $21.375.

⑧ American Health stock sold for $21.50 at the end of the trading day. This price was $0.25 higher than the previous day's closing price.

Source: *New York Times*, February 3, 1995.

IT'S EASY TO SEE WHY EMOTIONS RUN SO HIGH ON MOST STOCK AND MERCANTILE EXCHANGES. MILLIONS OF DOLLARS CAN LITERALLY BE MADE OR LOST IN THE BLINK OF AN EYE.

$50 billion lower level of consumption in 1988. The level of GDP was around $4 trillion in 1987, so a $50 billion decrease in consumption is around 1.25% of GDP. A multiplier effect would also be at work in this case. A decrease in consumption spending leads to a decrease in aggregate output (income), which leads to a further decrease in spending, and so on. The total decrease in GDP would thus be somewhat larger than the initial decrease in consumption of $50 billion. If the multiplier is 1.4, the total decrease in GDP would be about 1.4 × $50 billion = $70 billion, or about 1.75% of GDP.

While 1.75% of GDP is a large amount, it is not large enough to imply that a recession would necessarily result from the crash. The life-cycle theory we discussed in the previous chapter is useful for understanding why this is so. If households are making lifetime decisions and want to have as smooth a consumption path as possible over their lifetimes, they will respond to a decrease in wealth by cutting consumption a little each year. They certainly will *not* decrease their consumption in the current year by the full amount of the decrease in wealth. As we noted in the previous paragraph, it has been estimated that households adjust their consumption by about 5% of the decrease in wealth each year.

Why, then, were people predicting that the economy would go into a severe recession, if not a depression, after the crash? The reasons all pertain to expectations. If households and firms expected that the economy would contract sharply after the crash, they probably would have cut back on consumption and investment. (This would be Keynes's animal spirits at work.) These expectations would have become self-fulfilling in the sense that the economy would have gone into a recession because of the cuts in consumption and investment brought about by lowered expectations.

In fact, the economy did not go into a recession in 1988. It seems that expectations were not changed drastically following the crash. The Fed helped out by easing monetary policy right after the crash to counteract any large negative reaction. The three-month Treasury bill rate fell from 6.4% to 5.8% between October and November of 1987. In addition, the value of stocks gradually increased over time to their earlier levels. Because the initial decrease in wealth turned out to be temporary, the negative wealth effect was not nearly as large as it otherwise would have been. In the end, the crash affected consumption only slightly.

PRODUCTIVITY AND THE BUSINESS CYCLE

productivity, or **labor productivity** *Output per worker hour; the amount of output produced by an average worker in one hour.*

Productivity, sometimes called **labor productivity,** is defined as output per worker hour. If output is Y and the number of hours worked in the economy is H, then productivity is Y/H. Simply stated, productivity measures how much output an average worker produces in one hour.

Productivity fluctuates over the business cycle, tending to rise during expansions and fall during contractions. In the previous chapter, we discussed why firms may at times choose to hold excess labor. This facet of firm behavior explains why productivity fluctuates in the same direction that output does.

A simple example will help to explain how the existence of excess labor can explain cyclical movements in productivity. Consider what happens at The Feed Bag restaurant over the course of the business cycle. We will assume that The Feed Bag produces and sells only one item, hamburgers. This makes it easy to keep track of its total output—simply the number of hamburgers sold.

When times are good, The Feed Bag maintains a staff of 12 people and serves an average of 960 burgers each day. Labor productivity is therefore 10 burgers per person/hour (960 burgers/[12 people × 8 hours each]). If the economy goes into a slump, however, the demand for burgers tends to fall off. Instead of selling 960 burgers per day, the restaurant sells only 720—a drop in sales of 25 percent. But what happens to the work force at The Feed Bag when the slump hits?

If the restaurant is typical of most firms in the economy, it will lay off some workers or cut back on the length of the work shift. However, these cuts are almost always smaller than they need to be. In other words, if output falls by 25%, the number of work hours should also fall by 25% if the same level of productivity is to be maintained. However, the number of work hours will probably fall by less than this amount—say by only 12.5% (or by 12 hours, since .125 × 96 = 12).[1] The restaurant therefore uses only 84 hours of labor (instead of 96), perhaps by employing 10 workers for eight hours each and one additional worker for four hours, or 12 workers for seven hours each, or some other combination.

Why should The Feed Bag hold excess labor? As we discussed in the last chapter, it is costly to fire and hire workers. Furthermore, if a firm is unsure whether a decrease in sales is temporary or permanent, it may decide to keep "extra" workers on hand for the not-so-distant future when they will again be needed.

The implications of excess labor with regard to labor productivity should be clear. In good times, The Feed Bag used 96 hours of labor per day to produce 960 hamburgers, for a labor productivity ratio of 10 burgers per hour worked. In a slump, the restaurant sells only 720 burgers and uses 84 worker hours each day.

---

[1] *In terms of the notation we developed above, Y, (or output), falls by more than H, (or labor hours). It follows, then, that the ratio Y/H, or labor productivity, must fall when the numerator falls by more than the denominator.*

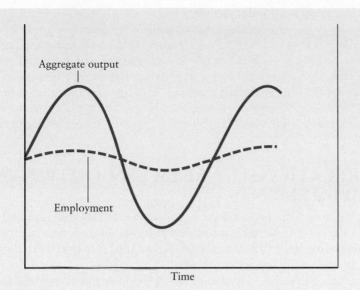

FIGURE 18.1

Employment and Output over the Business Cycle

In general, employment does not fluctuate as much as output over the business cycle. As a result, measured productivity (the output-to-labor ratio) tends to rise during expansionary periods and decline during contractionary periods.

Output per worker hour during the slump is therefore 720/84 = 8.57 burgers per worker hour—lower than the previous figure of 10 burgers per hour.

Figure 18.1 shows the pattern of employment and output for a hypothetical economy over time. The figure shows that employment does not fluctuate as much as output over the business cycle. It is precisely this pattern that leads to higher productivity during periods of high output and lower productivity during periods of low output. During expansions in the economy, output rises by a larger percentage than employment, and the ratio of output to workers rises. During downswings, output falls faster than employment and the ratio of output to workers falls.

The existence of excess labor when the economy is in a slump means that productivity as measured by the ratio Y/H tends to fall at such times. Does this mean that labor is in some sense "less productive" during recessions than it was previously? Not really: It means only that firms choose to employ more labor than they need. For this reason, some workers are in effect idle some of the time, even though they are considered employed. They are not less productive in the sense of having less potential to produce output; they are merely not working part of the time that they are *counted* as working.

■ **Productivity in the Long Run**   Theories of long-run economic behavior, which attempt to explain how and why economies grow over time, focus a great deal of attention on productivity. *Output per worker,* or its closely related measure, *GDP per capita,* is the key index of an economy's performance over the long run. For example, in comparing how the economies of the United States and Japan have performed over the past 90 years, we would probably begin by noting that while the United States had a substantially higher income per person in 1900, the two countries' incomes per person are now comparable. As we shall see in Chapter 20, the growth of output per worker depends on technological progress and on the growth of the capital stock, both of which have been more rapid in Japan than in the United States.

For now, the crucial point is this:

> Productivity figures can be misleading when used to diagnose the health of the economy over the short run, because business cycles can distort the meaning of productivity measurements. Output per worker falls in recessions simply because firms hold excess labor during slumps. Output per worker rises in expansions because firms put the excess labor back to work. Neither of these conditions has anything to do with the economy's long-run potential to produce output.

THE RELATIONSHIP BETWEEN OUTPUT AND UNEMPLOYMENT

Okun's Law *The theory, put forth by Arthur Okun, that the unemployment rate decreases about one percentage point for every 3% increase in real GDP. Later research and data have shown that the relationship between output and unemployment is not as stable as Okun's "law" predicts.*

When we discussed the connections between the *AS/AD* diagram and the Phillips Curve in Chapter 15, we mentioned that output (Y) and the unemployment rate (U) are inversely related. When output rises, the unemployment rate falls, and when output falls, the unemployment rate rises.

At one time, it was believed that the relationship between the two variables was fairly stable. **Okun's Law** (named after Arthur Okun, who first studied the relationship) stated that the unemployment rate decreased about one percentage point for every 3% increase in real GDP. As with the Phillips Curve, however, Okun's Law has not turned out to be a "law" at all. The economy is far too complex for there to be such a simple and stable relationship between two macroeconomic variables.

Although the relationship between output and the unemployment rate is not the simple relationship Okun believed it to be, it is true that a 1% increase in output tends to correspond to a less than 1% decrease in the unemployment rate. In other words, there are a number of "slippages" between changes in output and changes in the unemployment rate. It is useful to consider what these slippages are.

The first slippage is between the change in output and the change in the number of jobs in the economy. When output increases by 1%, the number of jobs does not tend to rise by 1% in the short run. There are two reasons why this is so. First, a firm is likely to meet some of the increase in output by increasing the number of hours worked per job. Instead of having the labor force work 40 hours per week, the firm may pay overtime and have the labor force work 42 hours per week. Second, if a firm is holding excess labor at the time of the output increase, at least part of the increase in output can come from putting the excess labor back to work. For both of these reasons, the number of jobs is likely to rise by a smaller percentage than the increase in output.

The second slippage is between the change in the number of *jobs* and the change in the *number of people employed*. If I have two jobs, I am counted twice in the job data but only once in the persons-employed data. Because some people have two jobs, there are more jobs in the economy than there are people employed. When the number of jobs increases, some of the new jobs are filled by people who already have one job (rather than by people who are unemployed). This means that the increase in the number of people employed is less than the increase in the number of jobs. This is a slippage between output and the unemployment rate because the unemployment rate is calculated from data on the number of people employed, not the number of jobs.

The third slippage concerns the response of the labor force to an increase in output. Let E denote the number of people employed, let L denote the number of people in the labor force, and let U denote the unemployment rate. In these terms, the unemployment rate is equal to

$$U = 1 - E/L.$$

In other words, the unemployment rate is one minus the employment rate, E/L.

When we discussed how the unemployment rate is measured in Chapter 8, we introduced the notion of the **discouraged-worker effect.** A discouraged worker is one who would like a job but who has stopped looking for one because the prospects seem so bleak. When output increases, job prospects begin to look better, and some people who had stopped looking for work begin looking again. When they do so, they are once again counted as part of the labor force. Thus, the labor force increases when output increases because discouraged workers are moving back into the labor force. This is another reason that the unemployment rate does not fall as much as one might expect when output increases: As the economy expands, more people enter the labor force, and this means that the measured unemployment rate does not fall as much as it would have if discouraged workers had not reentered the labor force.

These three slippages show that the link from changes in output to changes in the unemployment rate is fairly complicated. All three slippages combine to make the change in the unemployment rate less than the percentage change in output in the short run. They also show that the relationship between changes in output and changes in the unemployment rate is not likely to be stable. The size of the first slippage, for example, depends on how much excess labor is being held at the time of the output increase, and the size of the third slippage depends on what else is affecting the labor force (like changes in real wage rates) at the time of the output increase. In general:

> The relationship between output and unemployment depends on the state of the economy at the time of the output change

Table 18.1 shows the percentage change in aggregate output (real GDP) and the change in the unemployment rate for each year between 1975 and 1994. You can see that increases in the level of real output tend to be associated with decreases in the unemployment rate, and vice versa. But you can also see that the pattern is anything but uniform.

THE SIZE OF THE MULTIPLIER

We mentioned in Chapter 9 that much of the analysis we would do after deriving the simple multiplier would have the effect of decreasing the size of the multiplier. Now that we have a better understanding of how the macroeconomy works, we can review why the multiplier is smaller than the analysis in Chapter 9 might indicate.

- First, there are *automatic stabilizers.* We saw in the Appendix to Chapter 10 that if taxes are not a fixed amount but rather depend on income (which is surely the case in practice), the size of the multiplier is decreased. When the economy expands and income increases, the amount of taxes collected increases. This acts to offset some of the expansion (thus a smaller multiplier). Conversely, when the economy contracts and income decreases, the amount of taxes collected decreases. This helps to lessen the contraction. Some transfer payments also respond to the state of the

discouraged-worker effect *The decline in the measured unemployment rate that results when people who want to work but cannot find work grow discouraged and stop looking for jobs, thus dropping out of the ranks of the unemployed and the labor force.*

TABLE 18.1

THE RELATIONSHIP BETWEEN OUTPUT AND UNEMPLOYMENT

YEAR	% CHANGE IN REAL GDP	CHANGE IN UNEMPLOY-MENT RATE
1975	−0.7	+2.9
1976	5.4	−0.8
1977	4.9	−0.6
1978	5.2	−1.0
1979	2.8	−0.3
1980	−0.2	+1.2
1981	2.5	+0.5
1982	−2.3	+2.1
1983	3.8	−0.1
1984	7.1	−2.1
1985	3.2	−0.3
1986	2.9	−0.2
1987	3.1	−0.8
1988	3.9	−0.7
1989	2.7	−0.2
1990	1.2	+0.2
1991	−0.7	+1.2
1992	2.1	+0.7
1993	2.5	−0.6
1994	3.5	−0.7

Sources: *Economic Report of the President,* February 1995, and U.S. Department of Commerce, Bureau of Economic Analysis.

economy and act as automatic stabilizers, thus lowering the value of the multiplier. Unemployment benefits are the best example of transfer payments that increase during contractions and decrease during expansions.

- Second, there is the *interest rate.* We saw in Chapter 13 that if government spending increases and the money supply remains unchanged, the interest rate increases, which decreases planned investment and thus aggregate output (income). This *crowding out* of planned investment decreases the value of the multiplier. And, as we saw in Chapter 17, increases in the interest rate also have a negative effect on consumption. Consumption is thus also crowded out in the same way that planned investment is, and this lowers the value of the multiplier even further.

- Third, there is the response of the *price level.* We saw in Chapter 14 that some of the effect of an expansionary policy is to increase the price level. The multiplier is smaller than it otherwise would be because of this price response. The multiplier is particularly small when the economy is on the steep part of the *AS* curve, where most of the effect of an expansionary policy is to increase prices.

- Fourth, there is the existence of *excess capital* and *excess labor.* If firms are holding excess labor and capital, then part of any output increase can come from putting the excess labor and capital back to work rather than from increasing employment and investment. This lowers the value of the multiplier because (1) investment increases less than it would have if there were no excess capital, and (2) consumption increases less that it would have if employment (and thus household income) had increased more.

- Fifth, there is the existence of *inventories.* Part of any initial increase in sales can come from drawing down inventories rather than increasing output. To the extent that firms draw down their inventories in the short run, the value of the multiplier is lower because output does not respond as quickly to demand changes.

- Sixth, there is the *life-cycle story* and *expectations.* People look ahead, and they respond less to temporary changes than to permanent changes. The multiplier effects for policy changes that are perceived to be temporary are smaller than those for policy changes that are perceived to be permanent.

- Finally, the fact that the United States imports a good deal of what it consumes makes the multiplier smaller than it would be if the U.S. economy were closed. Consider the effects of an increase in government purchases. Initially, most government spending is spending on domestically produced goods and services. But the multiplier effect results from consumption spending by those who earn more income as a result of the additional government spending. Consumers in the United States buy automobiles from Germany and Japan, electronics from Korea, and textiles from the Philippines. When spending "leaks" into imports, the size of the multiplier is reduced. (We will discuss this topic fully in Chapter 22.)

■ **The Size of the Multiplier in Practice** In practice, the multiplier probably has a value of around 1.4. Its size also depends on how long ago the spending increase began. For example, in the first quarter of an increase in government spending, the multiplier is only about 1.1. If government spending rises by $1 billion, then GDP increases by only about $1.1 billion during the first quarter. In the second quarter, the multiplier rises to about 1.3. The multiplier then rises to its peak of about 1.4 in the third or fourth quarter.

One of the main points to remember here is that if the government is contemplating a monetary or fiscal policy change, the response of the economy to the change is not likely to be large and quick. It takes time for the full effects to be felt, and in the final analysis the effects are much smaller than the simple multiplier we discussed in Chapter 9 would lead one to believe.

A good way to review much of the material since Chapter 9 is to make sure that you clearly understand how the value of the multiplier is affected by each of the additions to the simple model in Chapter 9. We have come a long way since then, and this review may help you to put all the pieces together.

SUMMARY

MONETARY AND FISCAL POLICY REVISITED

1. The government influences the economy through *fiscal policy* (its taxing and spending behavior) and through *monetary policy* (the behavior of the Fed regarding the money supply).

2. Changes in taxes and spending that are expected to be permanent have a larger effect on household and firm behavior than changes that are expected to be temporary.

3. Policies that change tax rates have both an income *and* a substitution effect because they change the trade-off between work and leisure. Thus, reducing tax rates may lead to a *decrease* in the quantity of labor supplied through a dominant income effect or to an *increase* in the quantity of labor supplied through a dominant substitution effect.

4. Income received from non-wage-earning activities is called *nonlabor income.* The effect of a change in nonlabor income on households is a pure income effect. Any increase in nonlabor income therefore unambiguously leads to an increase in consumption and a decrease in labor supply. Conversely, any decrease in nonlabor income unambiguously leads to a decrease in consumption and an increase in labor supply.

5. The interest rate affects consumption as well as investment, and so there are two channels through which monetary policy can affect the economy.

6. Policies designed to stimulate or contract the economy are likely to have a larger impact when output is low rather than high. During periods of high output and low unemployment, the multiplier is likely to be smaller.

7. Output is likely to respond more to sales increases in high-output periods than in low-output periods, provided that firms have enough capital and labor to support the output increase. If firms do not have excess capacity to support an output increase, their inventory stocks will fall further as sales increase. In this case, the economy is on the steep part of the *AS* curve.

THE EFFECTS OF THE STOCK MARKET ON THE ECONOMY

8. When stock prices rise, household wealth increases. When stock prices fall, household wealth decreases. Stock prices thus affect the economy by affecting household wealth, which affects household consumption.

PRODUCTIVITY AND THE BUSINESS CYCLE

9. *Productivity,* or *labor productivity,* is defined as output per worker. It is the amount of output produced by an average worker in one hour. Productivity fluctuates over the business cycle, tending to rise during expansions and fall during contractions. The fact that workers are less productive during contractions does not mean that workers have less potential to produce output; it simply means that excess labor exists and that workers are not working at their capacity.

THE RELATIONSHIP BETWEEN OUTPUT AND UNEMPLOYMENT

10. There is a negative relationship between output and unemployment: When output (Y) rises, the unemployment rate (U) falls, and when output falls, the unemployment rate rises. *Okun's Law* stated that the unemployment rate decreases about one percentage point for every 3% increase in GDP. However, Okun's Law is not a "law" at all—the

economy is far too complex for there to be such a stable relationship between two macroeconomic variables. In general, the relationship between output and unemployment depends on the state of the economy at the time of the output change.

THE SIZE OF THE MULTIPLIER

11. There are several reasons why the actual value of the multiplier is smaller than the size that would be predicted by a simple model of a closed economy: (1) Automatic stabilizers help to offset contractions or limit expansions. (2) When government spending increases, the increased interest rate crowds out planned investment and consumption spending. (3) Expansionary policies increase the price level. (4) Firms sometimes hold excess capital and excess labor. (5) Firms may meet increased demand by drawing down inventories rather than increasing output. (6) Households and firms change their behavior less when they expect changes to be temporary rather than permanent. (7) A significant portion of spending is spent on foreign-produced goods.

12. In practice, the size of the multiplier at its peak is about 1.4.

REVIEW TERMS AND CONCEPTS

dividends 420

discouraged-worker effect 429

financial instruments 422

fiscal policy 417

monetary policy 417

nonlabor income 419

Okun's Law 428

productivity, or **labor productivity** 426

transfer payments 419

PROBLEM SET

1. Real GDP began to rise during the second quarter of 1991 and rose fairly steadily through the first part of 1995. Employment grew erratically during the same period. Get a copy of the latest issue of the *Economic Report of the President*. Most libraries have it.
   a. Record the percentage change in real GDP for each quarter between the second quarter of 1991 and the present.
   b. Calculate the percentage change in employment by quarter for the same time period. To do this you will have to look at changes June–September, September–December, December–March, and March–June.
   c. Calculate the ratio of the percentage change in GDP to the percentage change in employment.
   d. What can you conclude about the relationship between output growth and employment growth over the period? What do your answers say about Okun's Law?

2. The chair of the Council of Economic Advisors has recommended several options for dealing with a recession that currently exists in the economy. The President has asked you, as a member of the domestic policy staff, to evaluate the options. For each of the following options, describe the likely effects on consumer spending, labor supply, planned aggregate investment, the overall price level, aggregate output, and the unemployment rate.
   a. A temporary tax cut of 10% in place for two years or until the recession ends, with a continued tight monetary policy
   b. A permanent tax cut of 5% with a continued tight monetary policy
   c. An expansionary monetary policy with no change in fiscal policy
   d. An increase in transfer payments (unemployment benefits) with no tax cut and a continued tight monetary policy

3. Between January and July of 1993, the Dow Jones Industrial Average rose by 300 points, from 2700 to 3000. Assume that the household sector held $2 trillion worth of stocks in January of 1993 and that these stocks increased in value at about the same rate as the Dow increased. How much of an effect would you expect such an increase to have on annual consumer spending? How would such an increase affect the supply of labor? The unemployment rate?

4. Okun's Law suggests that a fairly simple negative relationship exists between the rate of unemployment and the level of aggregate output—that an increase

in aggregate output should lead to a decrease in the unemployment rate. Between 1980 and 1981, aggregate output in the United States rose by 1.9%, but the unemployment rate *increased* from 7% to 7.5 percent. Give several possible explanations for this phenomenon.

5. Do you agree or disagree with the following statements? Explain your answers.

   a. The primary reason that productivity tends to increase during periods of increased output is that higher wages attract better workers into the labor force.

   b. The fact that the United States exports nearly a tenth of its total output and imports a good deal of what it consumes implies that the multiplier is significantly larger than what it otherwise would be.

   c. If an economy is operating at a level of output along its short-run *AS* curve above the level of potential GDP, the multiplier is likely to be large and output is likely to increase.

THE UNDERGROUND ECONOMY AND THE TAX GAP

Underground economic activity has existed for as long as taxes have existed—which is to say, all of recorded history. In ancient Greece 2500 years ago, Plato wrote, "When taxes fall due, it is the just who will pay more than the unjust." The Ducal Palace in Renaissance Venice had a hole through which informers could anonymously snitch on tax deadbeats. In modern times, the underground economy is often associated with hard crime and drug rings, yet to become a member you need only to participate in any activity that generates income that goes unreported to either the Internal Revenue Service (IRS) or the Labor Department. The unreported income from summer odd jobs, paying the plumber, or housekeeper with checks made out to "cash"—all constitute part of the underground economy.

Recent attention on the underground economy in the United States derives from efforts to reduce the nation's enormous fiscal deficits. Part of the focus has been on reducing the "tax gap"—unrealized tax revenues from underreporting income or overstating deductions—as an alternative to raising taxes or cutting spending. The IRS estimates that the tax gap ran as high as $127 billion in 1992, fully one third of the $300 billion budget deficit for that year.

To measure the amount of lost revenue to the Treasury's coffers one must estimate the size of the underground economy. These estimates are tricky business and results vary widely, from 5% to 28% of GDP. One conservative estimate concludes that the total value of U.S. underground activity was $337 billion in 1990, 6.2% of GDP. Of this, $268 billion is estimated to be unreported income from legal activities, with the remainder derived from illegal activity. A recent Labor Department study using IRS data puts the annual income from underground activity at more than $500 billion, or roughly 10% of GDP. These figures, which do not include $200 billion worth of additional criminal activity, suggest that a "tax-free" covert economic sector the size of Canada exists within the overall U.S. economy.

The underground economy is not static. Rather, it expands and contracts as individuals weigh the expected costs and benefits of evading taxes and circumventing government regulations. The gain is the expected value of the taxes not paid or the extra income earned. The cost is determined by both the size of the penalty and the probability of being caught. The government might try to drive more people "above ground" by raising the fines for underground activity, but this plan can backfire if the likelihood of being caught is low. Indeed, one IRS study revealed that people who know someone who is being audited are more likely to cheat, figuring the odds are now in their favor. Similarly, governments that raise taxes may find that revenues increase less than proportionately as more people jump into the underground economy to escape the new taxes. Opportunities for tax evasion vary by sector—underground activity typically concentrates itself in the service sector, where income is easier to hide. Self-employed professionals and establishments like the neighborhood grocery store account for over $205 billion in unreported income every year.

An important telltale sign of the underground economy's size can be gleaned from monetary data. Because U.S. law allows government prosecutors access to bank records in criminal investigations, underground activity is rarely conducted with checks, which are traceable. The preferred means of payment for underground transactions seems to be cash, which leaves no audit trail. If we examine the ratio of currency to deposits (C/D, Figure 1) we have an index of the public's demand for currency, which is positively related to the volume of underground activity. Historically, we find two major increases in the C/D ratio associated with the two world wars. In 1917 the United States raised taxes to finance its entry into World War I. It did the same for World War II during the 1940s. The evidence suggests the public dramatically increased cash payments for goods and services to avoid the burden of the war taxes. Curiously, the Vietnam war of the late 1960s did not produce a sharp rise in underground transactions. This is due, in part, to the fact that the war was financed by deficit spending instead of the imposition of stringent new taxes.

The explosion in underground activity since the 1960s is reflected in the steady climb in currency demand up until the early 1980s. Part of this increased demand can be explained by the increased taxes the public paid due to inflation, a phenomenon known as *bracket creep*. In a progressive tax system, such as

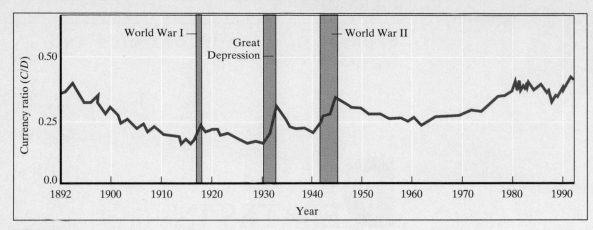

FIGURE 1
Currency Ratio, 1892–1993

Source: Federal Reserve *Bulletin; Banking and Monetary Statistics.*

that of the Untied States, tax rates rise as income rises. Inflation pushes nominal incomes into higher tax brackets, so the public is taxed harder even though there is no change in the tax schedule. As a result, people may turn to currency as a way of evading taxes by not declaring income.

More troublesome, however, is the growth in illegal drug trade. The Drug Enforcement Agency (DEA) estimates the retail value of illegal drug trade in the United States at over $100 billion. A closer look at the demand for currency reflects this as well. A 1981 study showed that the Florida Federal Reserve's Miami and Jacksonville branch offices both exhibited unusual currency flows: Both offices consistently received more currency than they paid out, a trait observed in only seven of the Fed's 37 branches. These Florida branches also received a much higher proportion of large denomination ($100) bills than the other branches, even after correcting for the effects of tourism.

While underground activity in the United States is pervasive, it ranks low compared to most industrialized countries. According to *Business*

Week (February 15, 1993), high tax rates in the Netherlands have created a huge "off-the-books" economy, and 40% of taxpayers in Italy evade taxes regularly. In many developing countries, not paying taxes is common. It is also true, however, that many developing nations experience difficulty in creating formal sector employment, leaving 25 to 40% of the labor force to fend for themselves in the underground economy.

Questions for Analytical Thinking

1. Do any signs of the underground economy exist in your area? Is there an underground economy on campus? If so, what impacts does it have on the local economy?

2. Given the cost-benefit logic of those who participate in the underground economy, what legal changes would you recommend to your Congressperson to reduce the tax gap from the underground economy? How might tax simplification reduce the size of the underground economy and the government budget deficit?

3. Why might the sharp growth in the demand for currency during the Great Depression of the 1930s reflect something other than an increase in the underground economy?

4. If a country's underground economy is large, how might its official GDP and employment statistics be distorted? What impact can these activities have on policy making? Should illegal activity be included in GDP?

Sources: Edgar L. Feige, "Defining and Estimating the Underground and Informal Economies: The New Institutional Economic Approach," *World Development* 19, No. 7, 1990; Harry Greenfield, *Invisible, Outlawed and Untaxed: America's Underground Economy* (Greenwich, CT: Praeger, 1993); Peter M. Gutman, "Statistical Illusions, Mistaken Policies," *Challenge* 22, November–December 1979; Ralph C. Kimbal, "Trends in the Use of Currency," *New England Economic Review,* September–October 1981; Karen Pennar and Christopher Farrel, "Notes from the Underground Economy," *Business Week,* February 15, 1993; Vito Tanzi and Parthasasrathi Shome, "A Primer on Tax Evasion," *IMF Staff Papers,* Vol. 40, No. 4, December 1993; U.S. Department of Labor, "The Underground Economy in the United States," Occasional Paper No. 2, September 1992.

19

PART SIX

DEBATES IN MACROECONOMICS AND ECONOMIC GROWTH

DEBATES IN MACROECONOMICS: MONETARISM, NEW CLASSICAL THEORY, AND SUPPLY-SIDE ECONOMICS

T HROUGHOUT THIS BOOK, WE HAVE NOTED THAT THERE ARE MANY disagreements and open questions in macroeconomics. For example, economists disagree on whether the aggregate supply curve is vertical, either in the short run or the long run. (Some even doubt that the aggregate supply curve is a useful macroeconomic concept!) There are also different views on whether cyclical employment exists and, if it does, what causes it. Economists disagree as well about whether monetary and fiscal policies are effective at stabilizing the economy, and they espouse different views on the primary determinants of consumption and investment spending.

We discussed some of these disagreements in previous chapters, but only briefly. In this chapter, we discuss in more detail a number of alternative views of how the macroeconomy works.

KEYNESIAN ECONOMICS

John Maynard Keynes's *General Theory of Employment, Interest and Money,* first published in 1936, remains one of the most important works in the history of economics. While a great deal of the material in the previous ten chapters is drawn from modern research that postdates Keynes, much of it is built around a framework first constructed by Keynes.

But what exactly is *Keynesian economics?* In one sense, Keynesian economics is the foundation of all of macroeconomics. Keynes was the first to stress aggregate demand and the links between the money market and the goods market. In addition, it was Keynes who stressed the possible problem of sticky wages. In fact, virtually all the debates that we discuss in this chapter can be understood in terms of the aggregate output/aggregate expenditure framework suggested by Keynes.

In recent years, the term "Keynesian" has been used more narrowly. Keynes believed in an activist federal government. That is, he believed that the government had an important role to play in fighting inflation and unemployment, and he argued that monetary and fiscal policy should be used to manage the macroeconomy. Thus, the term "Keynesian" is sometimes used to refer to economists who advocate active government intervention in the macroeconomy.

During the 1970s and 1980s, it became clear that managing the macroeconomy was much more easily accomplished on paper than in practice. The inflation problems of the 1970s and early 1980s and the seriousness of the recessions of 1974–1975 and 1980–1982 led many economists to challenge the idea of active government intervention in the economy. Some of these challenges were simple attacks on the bureaucracy's ability to act in a timely manner. Others were theoretical assaults that claimed to show that monetary and fiscal policy could have *no effect whatsoever* on the economy, even if it were efficiently managed.

In particular, in recent years two major schools of thought that are decidedly *against* government intervention have developed: monetarism and new classical economics. It is to these schools of thought that we now turn.

MONETARISM

Much has been written about the debate between "monetarist" and "Keynesian" economics. This debate is complicated by the fact that these terms mean different things to different people. If one takes the main monetarist message to be that "money matters," then almost all economists would agree. In the *AS/AD* story, for example, an increase in the money supply shifts the *AD* curve to the right, which leads to an increase in both aggregate output (Y) and the price level (P). Monetary policy thus has an effect on output and the price level. **Monetarism,** however, is usually considered to go beyond the notion that money matters.

THE VELOCITY OF MONEY

To understand monetarist reasoning, you must understand a new term, the **velocity of money.** You can think of velocity as the number of times a dollar bill changes hands, on average, during the course of a year.

For example, suppose that on January 1 you buy a new ballpoint pen with a $5 bill. The owner of the stationery store does not spend your $5 right away. She may hold on to it until, say, May 1, at which point she uses it to buy a dozen doughnuts. The doughnut store owner, in turn, does not spend the $5 he receives until July 1, when he uses it (along with other cash) to buy 100 gallons of oil. The oil distributor uses the bill to buy an engagement ring for his fiancée on September

velocity of money *The number of times a dollar bill changes hands, on average, during the course of a year; the ratio of nominal GDP to the stock of money.*

1, but the $5 bill is not used again in the remaining three months of the year. Because this $5 bill has changed hands four times during the year, its velocity of circulation is four. Stated another way, a velocity of four means that the $5 bill stays with each owner for an average of three months, or one quarter of a year.

In practice, we usually use GDP, rather than the total value of all transactions in the economy, to measure velocity,[1] simply because GDP data are more readily available. The income velocity of money (V) is the ratio of nominal GDP to the stock of money (M):

$$V \equiv \frac{GDP}{M}$$

If $6 trillion worth of final goods and services are produced in a year and if the money stock is $1 trillion, then the velocity of money is $6 trillion ÷ $1 trillion, or 6.0.

We can expand this definition slightly by noting that nominal income (GDP) is equal to real output (income) (Y) times the overall price level (P):

$$GDP \equiv P \cdot Y$$

Through simple substitution, we can write

$$V \equiv \frac{P \cdot Y}{M}$$

or

$$M \cdot V \equiv P \cdot Y$$

At this point, it is worth pausing to ask if our definition has provided us with any insights into the workings of the economy. The answer is no. Because we defined V as the ratio of GDP to the money supply, the statement $M \cdot V \equiv P \cdot Y$ is an identity—that is, it is true by definition. It contains no more useful information than the statement "a bachelor is an unmarried man." The definition does not, for example, say anything about what will happen to $P \cdot Y$ when M changes. The final value of $P \cdot Y$ depends on what happens to V. If V falls when M increases, the product $M \cdot V$ could stay the same, in which case the change in M would have had no effect on nominal income. To give monetarism some economic content, we turn to a simple version of monetarism known as the **quantity theory of money.**

quantity theory of money *The theory based on the identity* $M \cdot V \equiv P \cdot Y$ *and the assumption that the velocity of money (V) is constant (or virtually constant).*

THE QUANTITY THEORY OF MONEY

The key assumption of the quantity theory of money is that the velocity of money is constant (or virtually constant) over time, an assumption that has a long history in economics. If we let $\overline{V}$ denote the constant value of V, the equation for the quantity theory can be written:

$$M \cdot \overline{V} = P \cdot Y$$

Note that the double equal sign has replaced the triple equal sign because the equation is no longer an identity. The equation is true if velocity is constant (and equal

---

[1]*Recall that GDP does not include transactions in intermediate goods (such as the flour sold to a baker to be made into bread) or in existing assets (such as the sale of a used car). If these transactions are made using money, however, they do influence the number of times money changes hands during the course of a year. GDP is thus an imperfect measure of transactions to use in calculating the velocity of money.*

to $\bar{V}$), but not otherwise. If the equation is true, it provides an easy and accurate way to explain nominal GDP. Given M, which can be considered a policy variable set by the Federal Reserve, nominal GDP is just $M \cdot \bar{V}$. In this case, the effects of monetary policy are very clear. Changes in M cause equal percentage changes in nominal GDP. For example, if the money supply doubles, nominal GDP also doubles. If the money supply remains unchanged, nominal GDP remains unchanged.

Of course, the key question is whether the velocity of money is really constant. Early economists believed that the velocity of money was determined largely by institutional considerations, such as how often people are paid and how the banking system clears transactions between banks. Because these factors change gradually, early economists believed that velocity was essentially constant.

If there is equilibrium in the money market, then the quantity of money supplied is equal to the quantity of money demanded. One can thus think about M in the quantity-theory equation as equaling both the quantity of money supplied and the quantity of money demanded. If the quantity-theory equation is looked upon as a demand-for-money equation, it says that the demand for money depends on nominal income (GDP, or $P \cdot Y$), but *not* on the interest rate.[2] If the interest rate changes and nominal income does not, the equation says that the quantity of money demanded will not change. This is contrary to the theory of the demand for money we presented in Chapter 12, which had the demand for money depending on both income and the interest rate.

■ **Testing the Quantity Theory of Money** One way to test the validity of the quantity theory of money is to look at the demand for money using recent data on the U.S. economy. The key question is: Does money demand depend on the interest rate? Most empirical work finds that the answer is yes. When demand-for-money equations are estimated (or "fit to the data"), the interest rate usually turns out to be an important explanatory variable. The demand for money does not appear to depend only on nominal income.

Another way of testing the quantity theory is simply to plot velocity over time and see how it behaves. Figure 19.1 on page 440 plots the velocity of money for the 1960 I–1994 IV period. The data in the figure clearly show that velocity is far from constant. There is a long-term trend—on average, velocity has been rising during these years—but fluctuations around this trend have also occurred, and some of them have been quite large. Velocity rose from 6.8 in 1980 III to 7.2 in 1981 III; fell to 6.7 in 1983 I; rose to 7.0 in 1984 III; and fell to 6.1 in 1986 IV. Changes of a few tenths of a point may seem small, but they are actually quite large. For example, the money supply in 1986 IV was \$709 billion. If velocity changes by 0.3 with a money supply of this amount, and if the money supply is unchanged, we have a change in nominal GDP ($P \cdot Y$) of \$213 billion ($0.3 \times \$709$ billion), which is about 5% of GDP.

The debate over monetarist theories is more subtle than our discussion so far indicates, however. First, there are many definitions of the money supply. $M1$ is the money supply variable used for the graph in Figure 19.1, but there may be some other measure of the money supply that would lead to a smoother plot. For example, many people shifted their funds from checking account deposits to money market accounts when the latter became available in the late 1970s. Because GDP did not change as a result of this shift while $M1$ decreased, velocity—the ratio of GDP to $M1$—must have gone up. But suppose instead that we measured the supply of money by $M2$ (which includes both checking accounts and money market accounts). In this case, the decrease in checking deposits would be exactly offset by the rise in money market account deposits, and $M2$ would remain unchanged. With

---

[2]*In terms of the Appendix to Chapter 13, this means that the* LM *curve is vertical.*

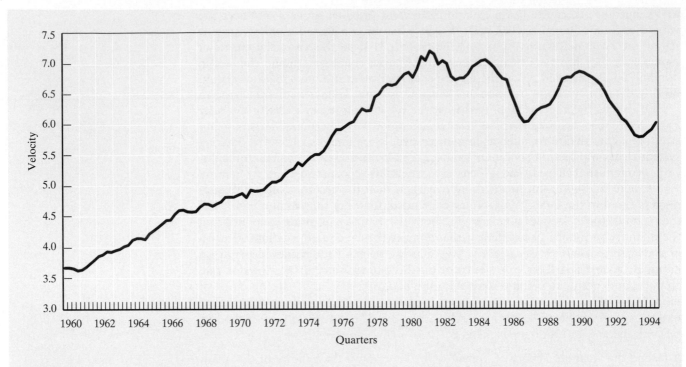

FIGURE 19.1

The Velocity of Money, 1960 I–1994 IV

Velocity has not been constant over the period from 1960 to 1994. There is a long-term trend—velocity has been rising. There are also fluctuations, some of them quite large.

no change in GDP and no change in *M2*, the velocity of money would not change either. Thus, whether velocity is constant or not may depend partly on how we choose to measure the money supply.

Second, there may be a time lag between a change in the money supply and its effects on nominal GDP. Suppose that we experience a 10% increase in the money supply today, but that it takes one year for nominal GDP to increase by 10 percent. If we measured the ratio of today's money supply to today's GDP, it would seem that velocity had fallen by 10 percent. But if we measured today's money supply against GDP one year from now, when the increase in the supply of money had its full effect on income, then velocity would prove to have been constant after all.

The debate over the usefulness of monetarist theory is thus primarily an empirical one. That is, it is a debate that can be resolved by looking at facts about the real world and seeing whether they are in accord with the predictions of theory. Is there a measure of the money supply and a choice of the time lag between a change in the money supply and its effects on nominal GDP such that *V* is in effect constant? If so, then the monetarist theory is a useful approach to understanding how the macroeconomy works. If not, then some other theory is likely to be more appropriate. (We discuss the testing of alternative theories at the end of this chapter.)

INFLATION AS A PURELY MONETARY PHENOMENON

So far we have talked only about nominal output (*P·Y*). We have said nothing about how a monetarist would break down a change in nominal output (due to a money-supply change) into a change in *P* and a change in *Y*. Here again it is not possible to make a general statement about what all monetarists believe. Some may believe that all of the change occurs in P, and others may believe that at least sometimes some of the change occurs in Y. If all of the change occurs in P, then there is a proportional relationship between changes in the money supply and changes in the price level. For example, a 10% change in M will lead to a 10% change in P if Y remains unchanged. In this case, inflation (an increase in P) is always a purely monetary phenomenon. The price level will not change if the money supply does not change. We will call this view, that changes in M affect only P and not Y, the "strict monetarist" view.

There is considerable disagreement in the profession as to whether the strict monetarist view is a good approximation of reality. For example, the strict view is not compatible with a non-vertical AS curve in the AS/AD model in Chapter 14. In the case of a non-vertical AS curve, an increase in M, which shifts the AD curve to the right, increases both P and Y. (You may want to review why this is so.)

Almost all economists would agree, however, that *sustained* inflation, which is inflation that continues over many periods, is a purely monetary phenomenon. We pointed out in Chapter 14 in the context of the AS/AD framework that inflation cannot continue indefinitely unless the Fed "accommodates" it by increasing the money supply. It is useful to review this argument here.

Consider the case of a continuously increasing level of government spending (G) without any corresponding increase in taxes. The increases in G keep shifting the AD curve to the right, which leads to an increasing price level (P). (You may find it useful to draw a graph here.) With a fixed money supply, the increases in P lead to a higher and higher interest rate, but there is a limit to how far this process can go. Because taxes are unchanged, the government must finance the increases in G by issuing bonds, and there is a limit to how many bonds the public is willing to hold regardless of how high the interest rate goes. At the point at which the public cannot be induced to hold any more bonds, the government will be unable to borrow any more to finance its expenditures. Only if the Fed is willing to increase the money supply (that is, buy some of the government bonds) can the government spending (with its inflationary consequences) continue. In sum:

> Inflation cannot continue indefinitely without increases in the money supply.

THE KEYNESIAN/MONETARIST DEBATE

The leading spokesman for monetarism over the last few decades has been Professor Milton Friedman, formerly of the University of Chicago and currently at the Hoover Institute in California. Most monetarists, including Friedman, blame most of the instability in the economy on the federal government, arguing that the inflation that the United States encountered over the years could have been avoided if only the Fed had not expanded the money supply so rapidly.

Interestingly, most monetarists do not advocate an activist monetary stabilization policy. That is, they do not advocate expanding the money supply during bad times and slowing the growth of the money supply during good times. By and large, monetarists tend to be very skeptical of the government's ability to "manage" the macroeconomy. The argument against such management that is most often voiced is the one expressed in Chapter 16: That time lags make it likely that conscious attempts to stimulate and contract the economy make the economy more, not less, unstable.

Friedman has for many years advocated a policy of steady and slow money growth. Specifically, he argues that the money supply should grow at a rate equal to the average growth of real output (income) (Y). That is, the Fed should pursue a constant policy that accommodates real growth but not inflation.

It is clear, then, that Keynesianism and monetarism are at odds with each other. As we said earlier, many Keynesians advocate the application of coordinated monetary and fiscal policy tools to reduce instability in the economy—that is, to fight inflation and unemployment. It is important to point out, though, that not all Keynesians advocate an activist federal government. Some Keynesian economists reject the strict monetarist position that only money matters in favor of the view that both monetary and fiscal policies make a difference and *at the same time* believe that the best possible policy for government to pursue is basically noninterventionist.

Most Keynesians do agree after the experience of the 1970s that monetary and fiscal tools are not finely calibrated. The notion that monetary and fiscal expansions and contractions can "fine-tune" the economy is gone forever. Still, many feel that the experiences of the 1970s also show that stabilization policies can help prevent even bigger economic disasters. Had the government not cut taxes and expanded the money supply in 1975 and in 1982, they argue, the recessions of those years might have been significantly worse. The same people would argue that had the government not resisted the inflations of 1974–1975 and 1979–1981 with tight monetary policies, they would probably have become much worse.

In 1994 and early 1995, the Fed raised the discount rate eight times and began tightening the rate of money growth because it was worried about inflation as the economy continued to expand near capacity. If the Fed

MANY KEYNESIANS BELIEVE THAT MONETARY AND FISCAL POLICY TOOLS ARE NOT FINELY CALIBRATED, BUT THAT STABILIZATION POLICIES CAN HELP PREVENT EVEN WIDER SWINGS IN THE BUSINESS CYCLE. IN ADDITION, MANY DEFEND GOVERNMENT INVOLVEMENT ON EQUITY GROUNDS: IN A SOCIETY AS RICH AS THE UNITED STATES, THEY ARGUE, THE GOVERNMENT HAS THE RESPONSIBILITY TO PROVIDE ALL PEOPLE WITH BASIC NECESSITIES OF LIFE—FOOD, CLOTHING, AND SHELTER.

had not taken these actions, the argument goes, inflation would have been the result. Despite the continuing debate, monetary policy is pursued in much the same way that it has been pursued for decades.

Thirty years ago, the debate between Keynesians and monetarists was the central controversy in macroeconomics. That controversy, while still alive today, is no longer at the forefront. For the past two decades, the focus of current thinking in macroeconomics has been on the new classical macroeconomics.

NEW CLASSICAL MACROECONOMICS

The key challenge to Keynesian and related theories has come from a school that is sometimes referred to as the **new classical macroeconomics**.[3] Like the terms "monetarism" and "Keynesianism," this term is somewhat vague. No two new classical macroeconomists think exactly alike, and no single model completely represents this school. The following discussion, however, conveys the general flavor of the new classical views.

THE DEVELOPMENT OF NEW CLASSICAL MACROECONOMICS

New classical macroeconomics has developed from two different, though related, sources. These sources are the theoretical and the empirical critiques of existing, or traditional, macroeconomics.

---

[3]The term "new classical" is used because many of the assumptions and conclusions of this group of economists resemble those of the classical economists—that is, those who wrote before Keynes.

On the theoretical level, there has been growing dissatisfaction with the way traditional models treat expectations. Keynes himself recognized that expectations (in the form of "animal spirits") play an important role in economic behavior. The problem is that traditional models have generally assumed that expectations are formed in rather naive ways. A common assumption, for example, is that people form their expectations of future inflation by assuming a continuation of present inflation. If they turn out to be wrong, they adjust their expectations by some fraction of the difference between their original forecast and the actual inflation rate. Suppose that I expect 10% inflation next year. When next year rolls around, the inflation rate turns out to be only 5%, so I have made an error of five percentage points. I might then predict an inflation rate for the following year of 7.5%, halfway between my earlier expectation (10%) and actual inflation last year (5%).

The problem with this traditional treatment of expectation formation is that it is not consistent with the assumptions of microeconomics. Specifically, it implies that people systematically overlook information that would allow them to make better forecasts, even though there are costs to being wrong. If, as microeconomic theory assumes, people are out to maximize their satisfaction and firms are out to maximize their profits, they should form their expectations in a smarter way. Instead of just blindly or naively assuming that the future will be like the past, they should actively seek to forecast the future. Any other behavior is not in keeping with the microeconomic view of the forward-looking, rational people who compose households and firms.

On the empirical level, there was the existence of stagflation in the U.S. economy during the 1970s. Remember that stagflation is the simultaneous existence of high unemployment and rising prices. The Phillips Curve theory of the 1960s predicted that demand pressure pushes up prices, so that when demand is weak—in times of high unemployment, for example—prices should be stable (or perhaps even falling). The new classical theories were an attempt to explain the apparent breakdown in the 1970s of the simple inflation-unemployment trade-off predicted by the Phillips Curve. Just as the Great Depression of the 1930s motivated the development of Keynesian economics, so the stagflation of the 1970s helped motivate the formulation of new classical economics.

RATIONAL EXPECTATIONS

In previous chapters, we stressed the importance of households' and firms' expectations about the future. A firm's decision to build a new plant depends on its expectations of future sales. The amount of saving a household chooses to undertake today depends on its expectations about future interest rates, wages, and prices. The list of situations in which expectations come into play could be greatly expanded.

How are expectations formed? Do people simply assume that things will continue as they are at present? (This would be equivalent to predicting rain tomorrow because it is raining today.) What information do people use to make their guesses about the future? Questions like these have become central to current macroeconomic thinking and research. One theory, the **rational-expectations hypothesis,** offers a powerful way of thinking about expectations.

Suppose we want to forecast inflation. What does it mean to say that my expectations of inflation are "rational"? The rational-expectations hypothesis assumes that people know the "true model" that generates inflation—that is, they know how inflation is determined in the economy—and that they use this model to forecast future inflation rates. If there were no random, unpredictable events in

rational-expectations hypothesis *The hypothesis that people know the "true model" of the economy and that they use this model to form their expectations of the future.*

EVEN THOUGH UNCERTAINTY EXISTS, IF YOU KNOW THE "MODEL" GENERATING THE UNCERTAINTY, IT IS POSSIBLE TO HAVE EXPECTATIONS ABOUT THE FUTURE THAT ARE "ON AVERAGE" CORRECT. YOU DON'T KNOW WHETHER A RANDOM COIN TOSS WILL COME UP HEADS OR TAILS. BUT YOU DO KNOW THAT IF YOU TOSS A FAIR COIN A THOUSAND TIMES, IT WILL COME UP HEADS ABOUT 500 TIMES.

the economy, and if people knew the true model generating inflation, then their forecasts of future inflation rates would be perfect. Because it is true, the model would not permit mistakes, and thus the people using it would not make mistakes either.

In practice, however, many events that affect the inflation rate are not predictable—they are, in fact, random. By "true" model, then, we mean a model that is *on average* correct in forecasting inflation. Sometimes the random events have a positive effect on inflation, which means that the model underestimates the inflation rate, and sometimes they have a negative effect, which means that the model overestimates the inflation rate. On average, however, the model is correct. Therefore, rational expectations are correct on average, even though their predictions are not exactly right all the time.

A noneconomic example may help at this point. Suppose that you have to make a forecast about how many times a fair coin will come up heads out of 100 tosses. The true model in this case is that the coin has a 50–50 chance of coming up heads on any one toss. Because the outcome of the 100 tosses is random, you cannot be sure of guessing correctly. If you know the true model, namely that the coin is fair, your rational expectation of the outcome of 100 tosses is 50 heads. You are not likely to be exactly right—the actual number of heads is likely to be slightly higher or slightly lower than 50—but *on average* you will be correct.

Sometimes people are said to have rational expectations if they use "all available information" in forming their expectations. This definition is somewhat vague, because it is not always clear what the phrase "all available information" means. The definition is precise, however, if by "all available information" we mean that people know and use the true model. One cannot have more or better information than the true model.

If information can be obtained at no cost, then someone is not behaving rationally if he or she fails to use all available information. Because there are almost always costs to making a wrong forecast, it is not rational to overlook information that could help improve the accuracy of one's estimate as long as the costs of acquiring that information do not outweigh the benefits of improving the accuracy of one's forecasts.

■ **Rational Expectations and Market Clearing** If firms have rational expectations and if they set prices and wages on this basis, then, on average, prices and wages will be set at levels that ensure equilibrium in the goods and labor markets. When a firm has rational expectations, it knows the demand curve for its output and the supply curve of labor that it faces, except when random shocks disrupt those curves. Therefore, on average the firm will set the market-clearing prices and wages. The firm knows the true model, and it will not set wages different from those it expects will attract the number of workers it wants. If all firms behave this way, then wages will be set in such a way that the total amount of labor supplied will, on average, be equal to the total amount of labor that firms demand. In other words, on average there will be no unemployment.

In Chapter 15, we argued that there might be disequilibrium in the labor market (either in the form of unemployment or in excess demand for workers) because firms may make mistakes in their wage-setting behavior because of expectation errors. If, on average, firms do not make errors, then, on average, there is equilibrium. In other words, when expectations are rational, disequilibrium exists only temporarily as a result of random, unpredictable shocks. This is obviously an important conclusion. If true, it means that disequilibrium in any market is only a temporary phenomenon, because firms, on average, set market-clearing wages and prices.

The assumption that expectations are rational radically changes the way one views the economy. We go from a world in which unemployment can exist for substantial periods of time and the multiplier can operate to a world in which (on average) all markets clear and there is full employment. In this new world there is no need for government stabilization policies. Unemployment is not a problem that governments need to worry about; if it exists at all, it is simply because of unpredictable shocks which, on average, amount to zero. There is no more reason for the government to try to change the outcome in the labor market than there is for it to change the outcome in the banana market. On average, prices and wages are being set at market-clearing levels.

THE LUCAS SUPPLY FUNCTION

The **Lucas supply function,** named after Robert E. Lucas of the University of Chicago, is an important part of a number of new classical macroeconomic theories. It yields, as we shall see, a surprising policy conclusion. The function is deceptively simple. It says that real output (Y) depends on (is a function of) the difference between the actual price level (P) and the expected price level (P^e):

$$Y = f(P - P^e)$$

The actual price level minus the expected price level ($P - P^e$) is the **price surprise.** Before considering the policy implications of this function, we should look at the theory behind it.

Lucas begins by assuming that people and firms are specialists in production but generalists in consumption. Take, for example, someone you know. If she is a manual laborer, the chances are she sells only one thing—labor. If she is a lawyer, she sells only legal services. And so on. In contrast, people buy a large bundle of goods—ranging from gasoline to ice cream and pretzels—on a regular basis. The same is true for firms. Most companies tend to concentrate on producing a relatively small range of products, but they typically buy a much larger range of inputs—raw materials, labor, energy, capital. According to Lucas, this divergence between people's buying and selling experience creates an asymmetry. People know much more about the prices of the things they sell than they do about the prices of the things they buy.[4]

At the beginning of each period, a firm has some expectation of the average price level for that period. If the actual price level turns out to be different from what the firm expected, there is a price surprise. Say that the average price level is higher than expected. Because the firm learns about the actual price level slowly, some time goes by before it realizes that all prices have gone up. The firm does learn rather quickly, however, that the price of its *output* has gone up. The firm thus perceives—incorrectly, as it turns out—that its price has risen relative to other prices, and this leads it to produce more output.

A similar argument holds for workers. When there is a positive price surprise, workers at first believe that their "price"—that is, their wage rate—has increased relative to other prices. In other words, workers believe that their real wage rate has risen. We know from theory that an increase in the real wage is likely to encourage workers to work more hours.[5] The real wage has not actually risen, but it takes workers a while to figure this out. In the meantime, they will supply more hours of work than they otherwise would have. This means

Lucas supply function *The supply function, named after Robert Lucas, that embodies the idea that output (Y) depends on the difference between the actual price level and the expected price level.*

price surprise *The actual price level minus the expected price level.*

---

[4]*It is not entirely obvious why this should be true, and, indeed, some critics of the new classical school have argued that this assumption is unrealistic. Some have also criticized the Lucas supply function as being too simple, arguing that other things besides price surprises affect aggregate output.*
[5]*This is true if we assume that the substitution effect dominates the income effect (see Chapter 17).*

that the economy will produce more output when prices are unexpectedly higher than when prices are at their expected level.

This, in essence, is the rationale for the Lucas supply function. Unexpected increases in the price level can fool workers and firms into thinking that relative prices have changed, however, and this causes them to alter the amount of labor or goods they choose to supply.

■ **Policy Implications of the Lucas Supply Function**   The Lucas supply function in combination with the assumption that expectations are rational implies that anticipated policy changes have no effect on real output. Consider, for example, a change in monetary policy. In general, such a change will have some effect on the average price level. If the policy change is announced to the public, then people know what the effect on the price level will be, because they have rational expectations (and thus know the way that changes in monetary policy affect the price level). This means that the change in monetary policy affects both the actual price level and the expected price level in the same way. The new price level minus the new expected price level is thus zero—there is no price surprise. In such a case, there will be no change in real output, because the Lucas supply function states that real output can change from its fixed level only if there is a price surprise.

The general conclusion is thus that *any* announced policy change—in fiscal policy or any other policy—has no effect on real output, because the policy change affects both actual and expected price levels in the same way. In other words, if people have rational expectations, known policy changes can produce no price surprises and thus no increases in real output. The only way that any change in government policy can affect real output is if it is kept in the dark so that it is not generally known. Government policy can affect real output only if it surprises people; otherwise, it cannot. Thus rational-expectations theory combined with the Lucas supply function proposes a very small role for government policy in the economy.

EVALUATING RATIONAL-EXPECTATIONS THEORY

What are we to make of all this? It should be clear by now that the key question regarding the new classical macroeconomics is how realistic the assumption of rational expectations is. If it does approximate the way that expectations are actually formed, then it calls into question any theory that relies at least in part on expectation errors for the existence of disequilibrium. The arguments in favor of the rational-expectations assumption sound persuasive from the perspective of microeconomic theory. If expectations are not rational, there are likely to be unexploited profit opportunities around, and most economists believe that such opportunities are rare and short-lived.

The argument *against* the rational-expectations assumption is that it requires households and firms to know too much. According to this argument, it is unrealistic to think that these basic decision-making units know as much as they need to know in order to form rational expectations. People must know the true model (or at least a good approximation of the true model) to form rational expectations, and this is a lot to expect. Even if firms and households are smart enough in principle to learn the true model, it may be costly to take the time and gather the relevant information to do so. The gain from learning the true model (or a good approximation of it) may not be worth the cost. In this sense, there may not be unexploited profit opportunities around. Gathering information and learning economic models may simply be too costly to bother with, given the expected gain from improving one's forecasts.

Although the assumption that expectations are rational seems consistent with the satisfaction-maximizing and profit-maximizing postulates of microeconomics, the rational-expectations assumption is more extreme and demanding because it requires more information on the part of households and firms. Consider a firm engaged in maximizing profits. In some way or other, it forms expectations of the relevant future variables, and given these expectations, it figures out the best thing to do from the point of view of maximizing profits. Given a set of expectations, the problem of maximizing profits may not be too hard. What may be hard, however, is forming accurate expectations in the first place. This requires firms to know much more about the overall economy than they are likely to, so the assumption that their expectations are rational is not necessarily realistic. Firms, like the rest of us—so the argument goes—grope around in a world that is difficult to understand, trying to do their best but not always understanding enough to avoid mistakes.

In the final analysis, the issue is an empirical one. Does the assumption of rational expectations stand up well against empirical tests? This is a difficult question to answer, and much work is currently proceeding along these lines. There are no conclusive results as yet, but it is one of the questions that makes macroeconomics an exciting area of research.

REAL BUSINESS CYCLE THEORY

Recent work in new classical macroeconomics has been concerned with whether the existence of business cycles can be explained under the assumptions of complete price and wage flexibility (market clearing) and rational expectations. This work has come to be called **real business cycle theory.** As we discussed in Chapter 14, if prices and wages are completely flexible, then the *AS* curve is vertical, even in the short run. If the *AS* curve is vertical, then events or phenomena that shift the *AD* curve (such as changes in the money supply, changes in government spending, and shocks to consumer and investor behavior) have no effect on real output. Since real output does fluctuate over time, the puzzle is how these fluctuations can be explained if they are not due to policy changes or other shocks that shift the *AD* curve. Solving this puzzle is one of the main missions of real business cycle theory.

real business cycle theory *An attempt to explain business-cycle fluctuations under the assumptions of complete price and wage flexibility and rational expectations. It emphasizes shocks to technology and other shocks.*

It is clear that if shifts of the *AD* curve cannot account for real output fluctuations (because the *AS* curve is vertical), then shifts of the *AS* curve must be responsible. However, the key task is to come up with convincing stories as to what causes these shifts and why they persist over a number of periods. The problem is particularly difficult when it comes to the labor market. If prices and wages are completely flexible, then there is never any unemployment aside from frictional unemployment. For example, since the measured U.S. unemployment rate was 9.7% in 1982 and 6.1% in 1994, the puzzle is to explain why so many more people choose not to work in 1982 than in 1994.

Early real business cycle theorists emphasized shocks to the production technology. Say there is a negative shock in a given year that causes the marginal product of labor to decline. This leads to a fall in the real wage, which leads to a decrease in labor supply. People have been led to work less because the negative technology shock has led to a lower return from working. The opposite happens when there is a positive shock: The marginal product of labor rises, the real wage rises, and people choose to work more. This early work was not as successful as some had hoped because it required what seemed to be unrealistically large shocks to explain the observed movements in labor supply over time.

Since this initial work, different types of shocks have been introduced, and work is actively continuing in this area. To date, fluctuations of some variables, but not all of them, have been explained fairly well. Some argue that this work is doomed to failure because it is based on the unrealistic assumption of complete price and wage flexibility, while others hold more hope. Real business cycle theory is clearly another example of the current state of flux in macroeconomics.

SUPPLY-SIDE ECONOMICS

If you think back to our discussion of equilibrium in the goods market, beginning with the simple multiplier in Chapter 9 and continuing through Chapter 14, you will recall that we have focused primarily on *demand*. Supply increases and decreases in response to changes in aggregate expenditure (which, as you recall, is closely linked to aggregate demand). Fiscal policy works by influencing aggregate expenditure through tax policy and government spending. Monetary policy works by influencing investment and consumption spending through increases and decreases in the interest rate. In essence, the theories we have been discussing are "demand oriented."

As we have said a number of times, the 1970s were difficult times for the U.S. economy. The United States found itself in 1974–1975 with stagflation—high unemployment and inflation. The late 1970s saw inflation return to the high levels of 1974–1975. It seemed as if policy makers were incapable of controlling the business cycle.

As a result of these seeming failures, orthodox economics came under fire. One assault was from a group of economists who expounded what came to be called **supply-side economics.** The essential argument of the supply-siders was quite simple. Basically, they said, all the attention to demand in orthodox macro theory distracted our attention from the real problem with the U.S. economy. The real problem, according to the supply-siders, was that high rates of taxation and heavy regulation had reduced the incentive to work, to save, and to invest. What was needed was not a demand stimulus but rather better incentives to stimulate *supply*.

If we cut taxes so that people take home more of their paychecks, the argument continued, they will work harder and save more. If businesses get to keep more of their profits and can get away from government regulations, they will invest more. This added labor supply and investment, or capital supply, will lead to an expansion of the supply of goods and services, which, in turn, will reduce inflation and unemployment at the same time. The ultimate solution to the economy's woes, the supply-siders concluded, was to be found on the *supply side* of the economy.

At their most extreme, supply-siders argued that the incentive effects of supply-side policies were likely to be so great that a major cut in tax rates would actually *increase* tax revenues. That is, even though tax *rates* would be lower, more people would be working and earning income and firms would earn more profits, so that the increases in the *tax bases* (profits, sales, and income) would outweigh the decreases in rates, resulting in increased government revenues.

■ **The Laffer Curve** Figure 19.2 presents one of the key diagrams of supply-side economics. The tax rate is measured on the vertical axis, and tax revenue is measured on the horizontal axis. The assumption behind this curve is that there is some tax rate beyond which the supply response is large enough to lead to a decrease in tax revenue for further increases in the tax rate. There is obviously some tax rate between zero and 100% at which tax revenue is at a maximum. At a tax rate of zero, work effort is high, but there is no tax revenue. At a tax rate of 100, the labor supply is presumably zero, since no one is allowed to keep any of his or her income. Somewhere in between zero and 100 is the maximum-revenue rate.

The major debate in the 1980s was whether tax rates in the United States put the country on the upper or lower part of the curve in Figure 19.2. The supply-side

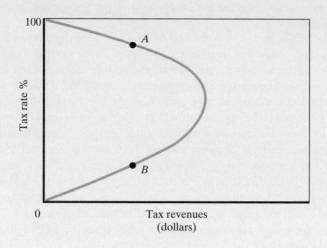

FIGURE 19.2

The Laffer Curve

The Laffer Curve shows that the amount of revenue that the government collects is a function of the tax rate. It also shows that when tax rates are very high, an increase in the tax rate could cause tax revenues to fall. Similarly, under the same circumstances, a cut in the tax rate could generate enough additional economic activity to cause revenues to rise.

school claimed that the United States was at a point like *A* and that taxes should be cut. Others argued that the United States was at a point like *B* and that tax cuts would lead to lower tax revenue.

The diagram in Figure 19.2 is called the **Laffer Curve,** after Arthur Laffer, who, legend has it, first drew it on the back of a napkin at a cocktail party. The Laffer Curve had some influence on the passage of the Economic Recovery Tax Act of 1981, the tax package put forward by the Reagan administration that brought with it substantial cuts in both personal and business taxes. The individual income tax was to be cut 25% over three years. Corporate taxes were cut sharply in a way designed to stimulate capital investment. The new law allowed firms to depreciate their capital at a very rapid rate for tax purposes, and the bigger deductions led to taxes that were significantly lower than before.

Laffer Curve *The graph, named after Arthur Laffer, with the tax rate measured on the vertical axis and tax revenue measured on the horizontal axis. The Laffer Curve shows that there is some tax rate beyond which the supply response is large enough to lead to a decrease in tax revenue for further increases in the tax rate.*

EVALUATING SUPPLY-SIDE ECONOMICS

Supply-side economics has been criticized on a number of counts. Critics point out that it is unlikely that a tax cut would increase the supply of labor substantially.

Supporters of supply-side economics claim that Reagan's tax policies were quite successful in stimulating the economy. They point to the fact that almost immediately after the tax cuts of 1981 were put into place, the economy expanded and the recession of 1980–1982 came to an end. In addition, inflation rates fell sharply from the high rates of 1980 and 1981. And, except for one year, federal receipts continued to rise throughout the 1980s despite the cut in tax rates.

Critics of supply-side policies do not dispute these facts but offer an alternative explanation of how the economy recovered. The Reagan tax cuts were enacted just as the U.S. economy was in the middle of its deepest recession since the Great Depression. The unemployment rate stood at 10.8% in the fourth quarter of 1982. It was the recession, critics argue, that was responsible for the reduction in inflation—not the supply-side policies. In addition, in theory, a tax cut could even lead to a *reduction* in labor supply. Recall our discussion of income and substitution effects in Chapter 4. While it is true that a higher after-tax wage rate provides a higher reward for each hour of work and thus more incentive to work, a tax cut also means that households receive a higher income for a given number of hours of work. Because they can earn the same amount of money working fewer hours, households might actually choose to work *less*. In other words, they might spend some of their added income on leisure. Research done during the 1980s suggests that tax cuts do seem to increase the supply of labor somewhat but that the increases are very modest.

But what about the recovery from the recession? Why did real output begin to grow rapidly in late 1982, precisely when the supply-side tax cuts were taking effect? Two reasons have been suggested. First, the supply-side tax cuts had large *demand*-side effects that stimulated the economy. Second, the Federal Reserve dramatically expanded the money supply and drove interest rates down at the same time that the tax cuts were being put into effect. The money supply expanded about 20% between 1981 and 1983, and interest rates dropped dramatically. In 1981, the average three-month U.S. Treasury bill paid 14% interest. In 1983, the figure had dropped to 8.6 percent.

Certainly, traditional theory suggests that a huge tax cut will lead to an increase in disposable income and, in turn, an increase in consumption spending (a component of aggregate expenditure). In addition, although an increase in planned investment (brought about by a lower interest rate) leads to added productive capacity and added supply in the long run, it also increases expenditures on capital goods (new plant and equipment investment) in the short run.

Whether the recovery from the 1981–1982 recession was the result of supply-side expansion or supply-side policies that had demand-side effects, one thing is clear: The extreme promises of the supply-siders did not materialize. President Reagan argued that because of the effect depicted in the Laffer Curve, the government could maintain expenditures (and even increase defense expenditures sharply), cut tax rates, *and* balance the budget. This was clearly not the case. Government revenues fell sharply from levels that would have been realized without the tax cuts. After 1982, the federal government ran huge deficits, with nearly $2 trillion added to the national debt between 1983 and 1992.

After dying down in the late 1980s and early 1990s, supply-side economics experienced a resurgence in 1995. For more details, see the Issues and Controversies box titled "The Supply-Side Debate: Then and Now."

TESTING ALTERNATIVE MACROECONOMIC MODELS

At this point, you may be wondering why there is so much disagreement in macroeconomics. Why cannot macroeconomists simply test their models against one another and see which one performs best?

One problem is that macroeconomic models differ in ways that are hard to standardize for. If, for example, one model takes the price level to be given, or not explained within the model, and another one does not, the model with the given price level may do better in, say, predicting output—not because it is a better model but simply because the errors in predicting prices have not been allowed to affect the predictions of output. The model that takes prices as given has a head start, so to speak.

Another problem arises in the testing of the rational-expectations assumption. Remember that if people have rational expectations, they are using the true model to form their expectations. Therefore, to test this assumption one needs the true model. One is never sure, of course, that whatever model is taken to be the true model is in fact the true one. Any test of the rational-expectations hypothesis is therefore a *joint* test (1) that expectations are formed rationally, and (2) that the model that is being used is the true one. If the test rejects the hypothesis, it may be that the model is wrong rather than that expectations are not rational.

THE SUPPLY-SIDE DEBATE: THEN AND NOW

THEN

In 1979 the Consumer Price Index rose 11.3% and in 1980 it rose 13.5 percent. So, in 1980 the Fed began pursuing a policy of slowing the rate of money growth to fight inflation. As the Fed tightened, interest rates rose. In 1978 the 90-day T-Bill interest rate stood at 7.2 percent. It rose to an average level of 10.0% in 1979, to 11.5% in 1980, and to over 14% in 1981.

Ronald Reagan was elected in 1980 on an economic platform based on supply-side principles, and he promised to get the economy under control. Because Keynesian economics focuses on demand, Keynesian economists believe that the appropriate fiscal-policy response to inflation is to increase taxes and reduce government spending. The idea is to reduce aggregate expenditure and shift the aggregate demand curve to the left. But supply-siders believe that the policy prescription is exactly the opposite: *Cut* taxes and shift the aggregate supply curve to the right! The clearest statement of this logic is contained in the following excerpt from the *Joint Economic Report* of the 96th Congress:

> [The policy of the United States should be to increase] real economic growth through tax reductions designed, not to pump money into the economy, but to restructure the tax code to in-

crease the reward to additional saving, investment and employment. . . . The tax cuts to stimulate saving, investment, and competitiveness will put more goods on the shelves and lower prices, thus reinforcing anti-inflation monetary policy.[1]

NOW

In 1995, the Federal Reserve was once again raising interest rates to fight inflation. In January of that year, the Fed raised the discount rate for the eighth time as the economy approached what the Fed believed to be potential GDP (the maximum level of output that is consistent with stable prices).

Also in January 1995, the 104th Congress was sworn into office and immediately proposed a series of tax and expenditure reductions. Under the Congress' proposed budget rules, any tax reduction had to be accompanied by a dollar-for-dollar reduction in expenditures. Many members proposed that in accounting for the revenue losses from tax cuts, a system of "dynamic scoring" be implemented to anticipate the "supply-side responses" to the tax cuts. They argued, for example, that a tax cut that leads to increased work effort, more saving, or greater investment could actually increase tax revenues (see discussion of the Laffer Curve in the text) and that these effects should be taken into ac-

count in the budget rules.

The Clinton administration responded to these supply-side arguments in the *1995 Economic Report of the President*:

> . . . different assumptions about the sensitivity of labor-supply decisions to changes in income tax rates, and about the sensitivity of saving to changes in the after-tax rate of return, can lead to very different conclusions about the extent of revenue loss resulting from a reduction in the income tax rate or the capital gains tax rate. Unfortunately, existing empirical techniques make it impossible to determine which estimates are the best predictions of behavioral responses to tax-rate changes with the appropriate degree of precision necessary for reliable dynamic analysis. . . . It is not hard to imagine how dynamic scoring techniques could be used to justify generous tax cuts on the grounds that they would pay for themselves, when it is all too likely that they would cause a large increase in the deficit.[2]

So the debate continues.

Sources: 1. *The 1980 Joint Economic Report*, the 96th Congress, March 1980. 2. *The Economic Report of the President*, February 1995, p. 75.

Another problem that macroeconomists have is that the amount of data available is fairly small. Most empirical work uses data beginning in about 1950, which in 1996 was about 46 years' (184 quarters) worth of data. While this may seem like a lot of data, it is not. Macroeconomic data are fairly "smooth," which means that a typical variable does not vary all that much from quarter to quarter or year to year. For example, the number of business cycles within this 46-year period is quite small, about seven. Testing various macroeconomic hypotheses on the basis of seven business cycle observations is not easy, and any conclusions drawn from such an exercise must be interpreted with considerable caution.

To give an example of the problem of a small number of observations, consider trying to test the hypothesis that import prices affect domestic prices. Import prices changed very little in the 1950s and 1960s. Because of this, it would have been very difficult at the end of the 1960s to estimate the effect of import prices on domestic prices. The variation in import prices was simply not great enough to show any effects. One cannot demonstrate that changes in import prices explain changes in domestic prices if import prices do not change! The situation was quite different by the end of the 1970s, however, because by then import prices had varied considerably. By the end of the 1970s, there were fairly good estimates of the import price effect, but not before then. This kind of problem is encountered again and again in empirical macroeconomics. In many cases there are simply not enough observations for much to be said, and thus there is considerable room for disagreement.

We pointed out in Chapter 1 that it is difficult in economics to perform controlled experiments. Economists are for the most part at the mercy of the historical data. If we were able to perform experiments, we could probably learn more about the economy in a shorter period of time. Since this is not the case, we must wait. In time, the current range of disagreements in macroeconomics should be considerably narrowed.

SUMMARY

KEYNESIAN ECONOMICS

1. In a broad sense, Keynesian economics is the foundation of modern macroeconomics. In a narrower sense, the term *Keynesian* is used to refer to economists who advocate active government intervention in the economy.

MONETARISM

2. The monetarist analysis of the economy places a great deal of emphasis on the *velocity of money*, which is defined as the number of times a dollar bill changes hands, on average, during the course of a year. The velocity of money is the ratio of nominal GDP to the stock of money, or $V \equiv GDP/M \equiv P \cdot Y/M$. Alternately, $M \cdot V \equiv P \cdot Y$.

3. The *quantity theory of money* assumes that velocity is constant (or virtually constant). This implies that changes in the supply of money will lead to equal percentage changes in nominal GDP. The quantity theory of money equation is $M \cdot \overline{V} = P \cdot Y$. The equation says that the demand for money does not depend on the interest rate.

4. Most economists believe that sustained inflation is a purely monetary phenomenon. Inflation cannot continue indefinitely unless the Fed "accommodates" it by expanding the money supply.

5. Most monetarists blame most of the instability in the economy on the federal government and are skeptical of the government's ability to manage the macroeconomy. They argue that the money supply should grow at a rate equal to the average growth of real output (income) (Y). That is, the Fed should expand the money supply to accommodate real growth but not inflation.

NEW CLASSICAL MACROECONOMICS

6. The *new classical macroeconomics* has developed from two different but related sources: the theoretical and the empirical critiques of traditional macroeconomics. On the theoretical level, there has been growing dissatisfaction with the way traditional models treat expectations. On the empirical level, the stagflation in the U.S. economy during the 1970s caused many people to look for alternative theories to explain the breakdown of the Phillips Curve.

7. The *rational-expectations hypothesis* assumes that people know the "true model" that generates economic variables. For example, rational expectations

assumes that people know how inflation is determined in the economy and use this model to forecast future inflation rates.

8. The *Lucas supply function* assumes that real output (Y) depends on the actual price level minus the expected price level, or the *price surprise*. This function in combination with the assumption that expectations are rational implies that anticipated policy changes have no effect on real output.

9. *Real business cycle theory* is an attempt to explain business-cycle fluctuations under the assumptions of complete price and wage flexibility and rational expectations. It emphasizes shocks to technology and other shocks.

SUPPLY-SIDE ECONOMICS

10. *Supply-side economics* focuses on incentives to stimulate supply. Supply-side economists believe that if we lower taxes, workers will work harder and save more and firms will invest more and produce more. At their most extreme, supply-siders argue that in-

centive effects are likely to be so great that a major cut in taxes will actually increase tax revenues.

11. The *Laffer Curve* shows the relationship between tax rates and tax revenues collected. Supply-side economists use it to argue that it is possible to generate higher revenues by cutting tax rates, but evidence does not appear to support this proposition. The lower tax rates put into place by the Reagan administration decreased tax revenues significantly and contributed to the massive increase in the federal debt during the 1980s.

TESTING ALTERNATIVE MACROECONOMIC MODELS

12. Economists disagree about which macroeconomic model is best for several reasons: (1) macroeconomic models differ in ways that are hard to standardize for; (2) when testing the rational-expectations assumption, one is never sure that whatever model is taken to be the true model is in fact the true one; (3) the amount of data available is fairly small.

REVIEW TERMS AND CONCEPTS

Laffer Curve 449

Lucas supply function 445

monetarism 437

new classical macroeconomics 442

price surprise 445

quantity theory of money 438

rational-expectations hypothesis 443

real business cycle theory 447

supply-side economics 448

velocity of money (V) 437

Equations:

$$V \equiv \frac{GDP}{M}$$

$$M \cdot V \equiv P \cdot Y$$

$$M \cdot \overline{V} = P \cdot Y$$

PROBLEM SET

1. The three diagrams in Figure 1 on page 454 represent in a simplified way the predictions of the three theories presented in this chapter about the likely effects of a major tax cut.
   a. Match each of the following three theories with a graph: (1) Keynesian economics, (2) supply-side economics, (3) rational expectations/monetarism. Briefly explain the logic behind the three graphs.
   b. Which of the three theories do you find the most convincing? Explain your choice.

2. When Bill Clinton took office in January 1993, he faced two major economic problems: a large federal budget deficit and high unemployment resulting from a very slow recovery from the recession of 1990–1991. In his first State of the Union message,

the President called for spending cuts and substantial tax increases to reduce the deficit. Most of these proposed spending cuts were in the defense budget. The following day, Alan Greenspan, chair of the Federal Reserve Board of Governors, signaled his support for the President's plan. Many elements of the President's original plan were later incorporated into the deficit reduction bill passed in August 1993.
   a. Some said at the time that without the Fed's support, the Clinton plan would be a disaster. Explain this argument.
   b. Supply-side economists and monetarists were very worried about the plan and the support that it received from the Fed. Why were these

FIGURE 1

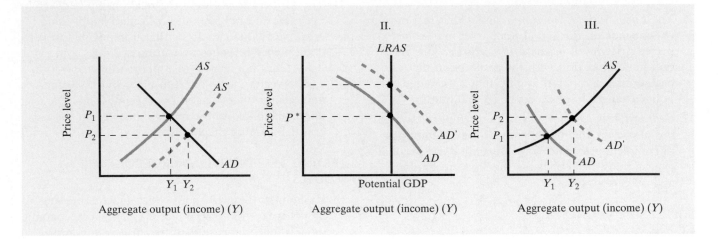

I. II. III.

two groups worried? What specific problems might a monetarist worry about? A supply-side economist?

c. Suppose that you were hired by the Federal Reserve Bank of St. Louis to report on the events of 1995 and 1996. What specific evidence would you look for to see if the Clinton plan was effective or whether the critics were right to be skeptical?

3. A cornerstone of new classical economics is the notion that expectations are "rational." What do you think will happen to the prices of single-family homes in your community over the next several years? On what do you base your expectations? Is your thinking consistent with the notion of rational expectations? Explain.

4. You are a monetarist, and you are given the following information. The money supply is $1000. The velocity of money is five. What is nominal income? What is real income? What happens to nominal income if the money supply is doubled? What happens to real income?

5. "In an economy with reasonably flexible prices and wages, full employment is almost always maintained." Explain why this statement is true.

6. During the 1980 presidential campaign, Ronald Reagan promised to cut taxes, increase expenditures on national defense, and balance the budget. During the New Hampshire primary of 1980, George Bush called this policy "voodoo economics." The two men were arguing about the relative merits of supply-side economics. Explain their disagreement.

*7. Assume that in a hypothetical economy there is a simple proportional tax on wages imposed at a rate t. Suppose further that there are plenty of jobs around so that if people enter the labor force they can find work. We define total government receipts from the tax as

$$T = t \cdot W \cdot L$$

where t = the tax rate, W = the gross wage rate, and L = the total supply of labor. The net wage rate is

$$W_n = (1 - t)W.$$

The elasticity of labor supply is defined as

$$\frac{\text{percentage change in } L}{\text{percentage change in } W_n} = \frac{\Delta L/L}{\Delta W_n/W_n}$$

Suppose that t were cut from .25 to .20. For such a cut to *increase* total government receipts from the tax, how elastic must the supply of labor be? (Assume a constant gross wage and full employment.) What does your answer imply about the supply-side assertion that a cut in taxes can increase tax revenues?

ECONOMIC GROWTH AND PRODUCTIVITY

A s YOU MAY RECALL FROM CHAPTER 1, **economic growth** OCCURS when an economy experiences an increase in total output. However, the increase in real output that began in the Western World with the Industrial Revolution and continues today has been so sustained and so rapid that economists have given the period a special name: **modern economic growth.** These three simple words describe the complex phenomenon that is the subject of this chapter.

Modern economic growth is the subject of much debate. It is through economic growth that living standards improve. But growth also brings change. New things are produced, while others become obsolete. Some believe that growth is the fundamental objective of a society, because it lifts people out of poverty and enhances the quality of their lives. Others argue that economic growth erodes traditional values and leads to exploitation, environmental destruction, and corruption.

The first part of this chapter describes the economic growth process in some detail and identifies some sources of economic growth. After a review of the U.S. economy's growth record since the nineteenth century, we turn to an examination of the role of public policy in the growth process. The chapter concludes with a review of the debate over the benefits and costs of growth.

THE GROWTH PROCESS: FROM AGRICULTURE TO INDUSTRY

The easiest way to understand the growth process and to identify its causes is to think about a simple economy. Recall from Chapter 2 our friends Colleen and Bill, who were washed up on a deserted island. At first they had only a few simple tools and whatever human capital they brought with them to the island. They gathered nuts and berries and built a small cabin. Their "GDP" consisted of basic food and shelter.

economic growth *An increase in the total output of an economy. Defined by some economists as an increase of real GDP per capita.*

modern economic growth *The period of rapid and sustained increase in real output per capita that began in the Western World with the Industrial Revolution.*

Over time, things improved. The first year, they cleared some land and began to cultivate a few vegetables that they found growing on the island. They made some tools and dug a small reservoir to store rainwater. As their agricultural efforts became more efficient, they shifted their resources (that is, their time) into building a larger, more comfortable home.

Colleen and Bill were accumulating capital in two forms. First, they built *physical capital,* material things used in the production of goods and services—a better house, tools, and a water system. Second, they acquired more *human capital*—knowledge, skills, and talents. Through trial and error, they learned about the island, its soil and its climate, what worked and what didn't. Both kinds of capital made them more efficient and increased their productivity. Because it took less time to produce the food that they needed to survive, they could devote more energy to producing other things or to leisure.

At any given time, Colleen and Bill faced limits on what they could produce. These limits were imposed by the existing state of their technical knowledge and the resources at their disposal. Over time, they expanded their possibilities, developed new technologies, accumulated capital, and made their labor more productive. In Chapter 2, you will recall, we defined a society's *production possibilities frontier (ppf),* which shows all possible combinations of output that can be produced given present technology and if all available resources are fully and efficiently employed. Economic growth expands those limits and shifts society's production possibilities frontier out to the right, as Figure 20.1 shows.

■ **From Agriculture to Industry: The Industrial Revolution** Before the Industrial Revolution in Great Britain, every society in the world was agrarian. Towns and cities existed here and there, but almost everyone lived in rural areas. People spent most of their time producing food and other basic subsistence goods. Then, beginning in England around 1750, technical change and capital accumulation increased

FIGURE 20.1

Economic Growth Shifts Society's Production Possibility Frontier Up and to the Right

The production possibility frontier shows all the combinations of output that can be produced if all of society's scarce resources are fully and efficiently employed. Economic growth expands society's production possibilities, shifting the ppf up and to the right.

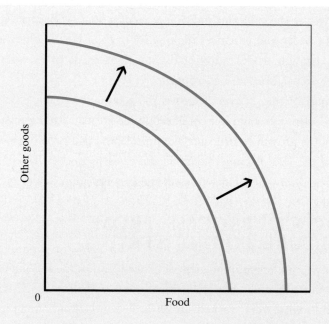

productivity dramatically in two very important industries: agriculture and textiles. New and more efficient methods of farming were developed. New inventions and new machinery in spinning, weaving, and steel production meant that more could be produced with fewer resources. Just as new technology, capital equipment, and the resulting higher productivity made it possible for Colleen and Bill to spend time working on other projects and new "products," the British turned from agricultural production to industrial production. In both cases, growth meant new products, more output, and wider choice.

There was one major difference, however. Colleen and Bill were fully in charge of their own lives. But peasants and workers in eighteenth-century England ended up with a very different set of choices. It was no longer possible to make a living as a peasant farmer. The cities offered the only real alternative, and a rural agrarian society was very quickly transformed into an urban industrial society.

■ **Growth in an Industrial Society**   The process of economic growth in an industrial society such as the United States is more complex but follows the same steps we have just described for growth in an agrarian society.

Consider the development of the electronic calculator. Prior to 1970, calculators that could add, subtract, multiply, and divide weighed fifty pounds, performed calculations very slowly, and were very expensive (a good calculator cost hundreds of dollars). Today, electronic calculators retail for as low as $3 or come free with a magazine subscription. Some are even small enough to fit into a wristwatch.

Everyone with a checkbook knows the value of owning a small calculator. The increase in the efficiency and speed with which calculators perform basic mathematical functions saves us all time and effort that can be spent doing other things. Tasks that once took days now take minutes, and one accountant today can do what it took 10 accountants to do 20 years ago.

Technological change, innovation, and capital production (calculators, computers, and software) have increased productivity. If a diner spends less on accounting, its sandwiches will cost less. Sandwich buyers thus may go to see another movie or have another soda. The entertainment and soft drink sectors expand, and so on. That is economic growth.

THE SOURCES OF ECONOMIC GROWTH

Economic growth occurs either when (1) society acquires more resources, or (2) society discovers ways of using available resources more efficiently. For economic growth to increase living standards, the rate of growth must exceed the rate of population increase. Thus, some economists define economic growth as *an increase in real GDP per capita.*

As we discuss the factors that contribute to economic growth, it will be helpful to think of an **aggregate production function.** An individual firm's production function is a mathematical representation of the relationship between the firm's inputs and its output. Output for an aggregate production function is national output, or gross domestic product. Stated simply, gross domestic product (output) (Y), depends upon the amount of labor (L) and the amount of capital (K) available in the economy (assuming that the amount of land is fixed).[1]

aggregate production function
The mathematical representation of the relationship between inputs and national output, or gross domestic product.

---

[1] *All the numbers in the tables to follow were derived from the simple production function:* $Y = 3 \cdot K^{1/3} L^{2/3}$.

If you think of GDP as a function of both labor and capital, you can see that:

> An increase in GDP can come about in three ways: (1) through an increase in the labor supplies, (2) through an increase in physical or human capital, or (3) through an increase in productivity (the amount of product produced by each unit of capital or labor).

AN INCREASE IN LABOR SUPPLY

It stands to reason that an increasing labor supply can generate more output. Consider, for example, what would happen if another person joined Colleen and Bill on the island. She would join in the work and produce, and so GDP would rise. Or suppose that a person who had not been a part of the labor force were to begin to work and use his time and energy to produce pottery. Real output would rise in this case also.

Whether output *per capita* rises when the labor supply increases is another matter. If the capital stock remains fixed while labor increases, it is likely that the new labor will be less productive than the old labor. This phenomenon is called *diminishing returns,* and it worried Thomas Malthus, David Ricardo, and other early economists.

Malthus and Ricardo, who lived in England during the nineteenth century, were concerned that the fixed supply of land would ultimately lead to diminishing returns. With land in strictly limited supply, the ppf could be pushed out only so far as population increased. To increase agricultural output, people would be forced to farm less productive land or to farm land more intensively. In either case, the returns to successive increases in population would diminish. Both Malthus and Ricardo predicted a gloomy future as population outstripped the land's capacity to produce. What both economists left out of their calculations, however, was technological change and capital accumulation. New and better farming techniques have raised agricultural productivity so dramatically that less than 3% of the U.S. population now provides enough food for the country's entire population.

Diminishing returns can also occur if a nation's capital stock grows more slowly than its work force. Capital enhances workers' productivity. A person with a shovel digs a bigger hole than a person without one, and a person with a steam shovel outdoes them both. If a society's stock of plant and equipment does not grow and the technology of production does not change, additional workers will not be as productive, because they do not have machines to work with.

Table 20.1 illustrates how growth in the labor force, without a corresponding increase in the capital stock or technological change, might lead to growth of output but declining productivity and a lower standard of living. As labor increases, output rises from 300 units in Period 1 to 320 in Period 2, to 339 in Period 3, and so forth, but **labor productivity** (output per worker hour) falls. Output per worker hour, Y/L, is a measure of labor's productivity.

labor productivity *Output per worker hour; the amount of output produced by an average worker in one hour.*

The fear that new workers entering the labor force will displace existing workers and generate unemployment has been with us for a long time. New workers can come from many places. They might be immigrants, young people looking for their first jobs, or older people entering the labor force for the first time. Between 1947 and 1994, the number of women in the labor force more than tripled, jumping from 17 million to 60 million. Table 20.2 shows that in the United States since World War II, the civilian noninstitutional population (that is, those not in jails or

TABLE 20.1	ECONOMIC GROWTH FROM AN INCREASE IN LABOR—MORE OUTPUT BUT DIMINISHING RETURNS AND LOWER LABOR PRODUCTIVITY			
PERIOD	QUANTITY OF LABOR L (HOURS)	QUANTITY OF CAPITAL K (UNITS)	TOTAL OUTPUT Y (UNITS)	MEASURED LABOR PRODUCTIVITY Y/L
1	100	100	300	3.0
2	110	100	320	2.9
3	120	100	339	2.8
4	130	100	357	2.7

mental institutions) over 16 years of age grew by 93.3%, while the labor force more than doubled. The U.S. economy, however, has shown a remarkable ability to expand right along with the labor force. The number of persons employed jumped by 66.1 million—116.0%—during the same period.

As long as the economy and the capital stock are expanding rapidly enough, new entrants into the labor force do not displace other workers.

INCREASES IN PHYSICAL CAPITAL

An increase in the stock of capital can also increase output, even if it is not accompanied by an increase in the labor force. Physical capital both enhances the productivity of labor and provides valuable services directly.

It is easy to see how capital provides services directly. Consider what happened on Bill and Colleen's island. In the first few years, they built a house, putting many hours of work into it that could have gone into producing other things for immediate consumption. With the house for shelter, Colleen and Bill live in relative comfort and can thus spend time on other things. In the same way, capital equipment produced in one year can add to the value of a product over

TABLE 20.2	EMPLOYMENT, LABOR FORCE, AND POPULATION GROWTH, 1947–1994			
	CIVILIAN NONINSTITUTIONAL POPULATION OVER 16 YEARS OLD (MILLIONS)	CIVILIAN LABOR FORCE NUMBER (MILLIONS)	PERCENTAGE OF POPULATION	EMPLOYMENT (MILLIONS)
1947	101.8	59.4	58.3	57.0
1960	117.3	69.6	59.3	65.8
1970	137.1	82.8	60.4	78.7
1980	167.7	106.9	63.7	99.3
1990	188.0	124.8	66.4	117.9
1994	196.8	131.1	66.6	123.1
Percentage change, 1947–1994	+93.3%	+120.7%		+116.0%
Annual Rate	+1.4%	+1.7%		+1.7%

Source: Department of Labor, Bureau of Labor Statistics, *Monthly Labor Review*, February 1995.

many years. For example, we still derive use and value from bridges and tunnels built decades ago.

It is also easy to see how capital used in production enhances the productivity of labor. Computers enable us to do almost instantly tasks that once were impossible or might have taken several years to complete. An airplane with a relatively small crew can transport hundreds of people thousands of miles in a few hours. A bridge over a river at a critical location may save thousands of labor hours that would be spent transporting materials and people the long way around. It is precisely this yield in the form of future valuable services that provides both private and public investors with the incentive to devote resources to capital production.

Table 20.3 shows how an increase in capital without a corresponding increase in labor might increase output. Several things about these numbers are notable. First, additional capital increases measured productivity; output per worker hour (Y/L) increases from 3.0 to 3.1, to 3.2, and finally to 3.3 as the quantity of capital (K) increases. Second, there are diminishing returns to capital. Increasing capital by 10 units first increases output by 10 units—from 300 in Period 1 to 310 in Period 2. But the second increase of 10 units yields only 9 units of output, and the third increase yields only eight.

Table 20.4 shows the value of nonresidential capital stocks in the United States since 1960. The increase in capital stock is the difference between gross investment and depreciation. (Remember that some capital becomes obsolete and some capital wears out every year.) Over the last 32 years, the capital stock has increased at a rate of 3.5% per year. The stock of equipment has increased faster than the stock of structures.

By comparing Tables 20.2 and 20.4, you can see that capital has been increasing faster than labor since 1960. In all economies experiencing modern economic growth, capital expands at a more rapid rate than labor. That is, the ratio of capital to labor (K/L) increases, and this too is a source of increasing productivity. Another important source of increased productivity is public capital, the subject of the Application box on page 462 titled "Infrastructure and Economic Growth."

INCREASES IN HUMAN CAPITAL

Investment in human capital is another important source of economic growth. People in good health are more productive than people in poor health; people with skills are more productive than people without them.

WORKERS REPAIR THE BROOKLYN BRIDGE, WHICH CONNECTS THE NEW YORK CITY BOROUGHS OF MANHATTAN AND BROOKLYN. MAINTENANCE AND DEVELOPMENT OF INFRASTRUCTURE PLAY AN IMPORTANT ROLE IN ECONOMIC GROWTH.

TABLE 20.3	ECONOMIC GROWTH FROM AN INCREASE IN CAPITAL—MORE OUTPUT, DIMINISHING RETURNS TO ADDED CAPITAL, HIGHER MEASURED LABOR PRODUCTIVITY			
PERIOD	QUANTITY OF LABOR L (HOURS)	QUANTITY OF CAPITAL K (UNITS)	TOTAL OUTPUT Y (UNITS)	MEASURED LABOR PRODUCTIVITY Y/L
1	100	100	300	3.0
2	100	110	310	3.1
3	100	120	319	3.2
4	100	130	327	3.3

TABLE 20.4	FIXED NONRESIDENTIAL BUSINESS CAPITAL STOCK, ALL INDUSTRIES, 1960–1992		
	NET STOCK	EQUIPMENT	STRUCTURES
1960	1637	656	982
1970	2544	1076	1473
1980	3677	1709	1968
1990	4773	2202	2571
1992	4871	2260	2611
Percentage change, 1960–1992	98%	245%	166%
Annual rate	3.5%	3.9%	3.1%

Source: *Survey of Current Business*, January 1992, Table 4, p. 137, and *Statistical Abstract of the United States, 1994*, Table 862.

Human capital can be produced in a number of ways. Individuals can invest in themselves by going to college or vocational training programs. Firms can invest in human capital through on-the-job training. The government invests in human capital with programs to improve health, to underwrite schooling, and to provide job training.

Table 20.5 shows that the level of educational attainment has risen significantly since 1940. The percentage of the population with at least a four-year college degree rose from under 5% in 1940 to 21.9% in 1993. In 1940 fewer than one person in four had completed a high school education; in 1993, more than eight in ten had.

INCREASES IN PRODUCTIVITY

Growth that cannot be explained by increases in the *quantity* of inputs can be explained only by an increase in the *productivity* of those inputs. In this case, each unit of input must be producing more output. The **productivity of an input** can be affected by several factors, including technological change, other advances in knowledge, and economies of scale.

productivity of an input *The amount of output produced per unit of an input.*

TABLE 20.5	YEARS OF SCHOOL COMPLETED BY PEOPLE OVER 25 YEARS OLD, 1940–1993		
	PERCENTAGE WITH LESS THAN FIVE YEARS OF SCHOOL	PERCENTAGE WITH FOUR YEARS OF HIGH SCHOOL OR MORE	PERCENTAGE WITH A BACHELOR'S DEGREE OR HIGHER
1940	13.7	24.5	4.6
1950	11.1	34.3	6.2
1960	8.3	41.1	7.7
1970	5.5	52.3	10.7
1980	3.6	66.5	16.2
1993	NA	80.2	21.9

Source: *Statistical Abstract of the United States, 1990*, Table 215; and *1992*, Table 219; and *1994*, Table 234. NA = not available.

A major source of economic growth is the accumulation of capital. When we think of capital's role in economic growth, we tend to focus on private capital—the plant, equipment, and inventory of business firms. But what about *public* capital?

Recall from our earlier discussions that *capital goods* are used to produce other goods and services over time. One form of capital is infrastructure. **Infrastructure,** also called **public capital,** refers to the roads, bridges, water treatment plants, fire stations, and so on that collectively contribute to the public good.

Infrastructure has the potential for increasing productivity and growth. Good highways and bridges reduce transportation costs and make it easier to transport goods. Readily available clean water improves health and is often essential for production.

Governments are usually responsible for putting public capital into place. Throughout the 1980s, however, there was strong pressure to reduce government spending and to increase growth in the private sector. One of the consequences of these pressures was a significant slowdown in public infrastructure investment. Some have pointed to this slowdown as a cause of the slower economic growth in the 1980s.

In June 1990, the Federal Reserve Bank of Boston held a conference on the topic of infrastructure and growth. Professor David Aschauer of Bates College opened the conference with the following challenge:

> As the decade of the 1990s begins, new challenges present themselves to the citizenry of the United States. Among the most important are concerns about the environment, economic productivity, and international competitiveness, and a re-arrangement of standing strategic military relationships. Our future quality of life, economic prosperity, and security depend crucially on how we choose to meet these new challenges.
>
> The apparent failure of the communist economic system and the associated relaxation of Cold War tensions offer the potential for a significant reallocation of the nation's resources from military to other uses. A crucial question then arises whether these resources should be channeled to the private sector, effecting overall government expenditure reduction, or kept within the public sector, thereby inducing an alteration in the composition of government spending.
>
> The first direction, expenditure reduction, certainly has merit to a broad class of individuals. Many would point to the fact that total federal government outlays, expressed relative to gross national product, rose from 14.8 percent in 1950 to 21.6 percent in 1980 and, in 1989, to 21.8 percent. Others would point to the persistence of federal budget deficits. To both groups, expenditure reduction would be of benefit to economic performance, either by reducing the overall scale of government activity in the economy or by allowing a reduction in interest rates and an expansion in domestic investment activity.
>
> But the second direction, expenditure reorientation, may also have merit. It could well be the case that quality of life and economic performance would be best served by retaining the resources within the public sector and expanding expenditure in certain critical areas. One candidate area is infrastructure, the public stock of social and economic overhead capital. Indeed, it has been claimed in the popular press that "it's hard to escape America's crumbling infrastructure" and that "even though the deterioration of U.S. highways, bridges, airports, harbors, sewage systems, and other building blocks of the economy has been exhaustively documented in recent years, there has been scant progress" in addressing the postulated need to renew the public capital stock (Industry Week, May 21, 1990).

Clearly, someone was listening. Prior to taking office, President Bill Clinton held an economic summit to discuss ideas for stimulating economic growth. A major focus of the discussion was infrastructure, and it led to Clinton's call for $16 billion in public works spending in his 1993 State of the Union address.

The president's proposal was defeated by Congress, which argued that the infrastructure's role in economic growth is not significant enough to justify spending such huge sums of money. The debate continues to rage. In his 1995 *Economic Report*, Clinton summarized this situation as follows: "Declining trends in public capital suggest that infrastructure investment has been a net drag on the growth of productivity since 1970, but there is no consensus as to the quantitative importance of this effect."

Source: "Is There a Shortfall in Public Capital Investment?" Proceedings of a Conference sponsored by the Federal Reserve Bank of Boston, Alicia Munnell, Editor, June 1990.

■ Technological Change The Industrial Revolution was in part sparked by important new technological developments. The development of new techniques of spinning and weaving—the invention of the "mule" and the "spinning jenny," for example—were critical. The high-tech boom that swept the United States in the early 1980s was driven by the rapid development and dissemination of semiconductor technology.

Technological change affects productivity in two stages. First, there is an advance in knowledge, or an **invention.** But knowledge by itself does nothing unless it is used. When new knowledge is used to produce a new product or to produce an existing product more efficiently, there is **innovation.**

invention *An advance in knowledge.*

innovation *The use of new knowledge to produce a new product or to produce an existing product more efficiently.*

Technological change cannot be measured directly. Some studies have presented data on "indicators" of the rate of technical change—the number of new patents, for example—but none are very satisfactory. Still, we know that technological changes that have improved productivity are all around us. Computer technology has revolutionized the office, hybrid seeds have dramatically increased the productivity of land, and more efficient and powerful aircraft have made air travel routine and relatively inexpensive.

■ Other Advances in Knowledge Over and above invention and innovation, advances in other kinds of knowledge can also improve productivity. One important category of knowledge is what we might call "managerial knowledge." For example, because of the very high cost of capital during the early 1980s, firms learned to manage their inventories much better. Many were able to keep production lines and distribution lines flowing with a much lower stock of inventories. Inventories are part of a firm's capital stock, and trimming them reduces costs and raises productivity. This is an example of a *capital-saving* innovation; many of the advances that we are used to thinking about, such as the introduction of robotics, are *labor-saving.*

In addition to managerial knowledge, improved personnel management techniques, accounting procedures, data management, and the like can also make production more efficient, reduce costs, and increase measured productivity.

■ Economies of Scale *External economies of scale* are cost savings that result from increases in the size of industries. The economies that accompany growth in size may arise from a variety of causes. For example, as firms in a growing industry build plants at new locations, they may have lower transport costs. There may also be some economies of scale associated with R&D (research and development) spending and job-training programs.

■ Other Influences on Productivity In addition to technological change, other advances in knowledge, and economies of scale, other forces may affect productivity. During the 1970s and 1980s, for example, the U.S. government required many firms to reduce the air and water pollution they were producing. These requirements diverted capital and labor from the production of measured output and thus *reduced* measured productivity. Similarly, in recent years requirements imposed by the Occupational Safety and Health Act (OSHA) have required firms to protect workers better from accidental injuries and potential health problems. These laws also divert resources from measured output.

It is important to understand that negative effects such as these are more a problem of *measurement* than of truly declining productivity. The EPA (Environmental Protection Agency) regulates air and water quality because clean air and water presumably have a value to society. Thus, the resources diverted to produce that value are not wasted. A perfect measure of output produced that is of value to society would include environmental quality and good health.

The list of factors that can affect productivity could go on and on. Weather can have an enormous impact on agricultural productivity. The early 1990s saw huge floods and massive crop losses in the Midwest. Floods in California in 1995 had similar effects.

Having presented the major factors that influence productivity, we now turn to the growth record for the United States and to an estimate of how these factors have combined to produce a record of steady growth that has lasted well over 100 years.

GROWTH AND PRODUCTIVITY IN THE U.S. ECONOMY

Modern economic growth in the United States began in the middle of the nineteenth century. After the Civil War, the railroads spread out across the country and the economy took off. Table 20.6 shows the rate of growth of real output in the United States since 1871.

The conventional wisdom is that over the long haul, real output in the United States has been growing at about 3.0% annually. Between 1871 and 1909, the growth rate was very healthy, ranging from 4.0% to 5.5% per year. Because of the dislocations of the Great Depression, growth was slower during the 1930s and 1940s, but the 1950s and 1960s saw renewed growth and vigor in the economy. Although the 1970s contained some good years and some bad, during the decade output rose by an average of 2.8% per year, a credible performance. Between 1980 and 1994, the rate of growth fell to 2.5%, a below-average performance.

Figure 20.2 shows growth rates of real GDP since 1961 for the United States and several other countries. Growth has been slowing everywhere. Virtually all the countries in the table experienced less growth during the 1970s than during the 1960s and continued to grow even more slowly during the 1980s. The early 1990s saw a recession sweep across the world; in 1991, GDP declined in many countries, including the United States. In most of the countries of the European Union, recession lasted through 1993, but by 1994 virtually all of the world's industrial countries were growing again. Not shown directly in the table is the collapse of the economies of the former Soviet Union, where GDP fell 40% between 1990 and 1994.

TABLE 20.6	GROWTH OF REAL GDP IN THE UNITED STATES, 1871–1994			
PERIOD	**AVERAGE GROWTH RATE PER YEAR**		**PERIOD**	**AVERAGE GROWTH RATE PER YEAR**
1871–1889	5.5		1960–1970	3.8
1889–1909	4.0		1970–1980	2.8
1909–1929	2.9		1980–1994	2.5
1929–1950	2.7		1950–1994	3.1
1950–1960	3.2			

Sources: *Historical Statistics of the United States: Colonial Times to 1970*, Tables F47-70, F98-124; U.S. Department of Commerce, Bureau of Economic Analysis.

FIGURE 20.2

Average Annual Growth Rates of Real GDP for Selected Countries, 1961–1994 (percentage)

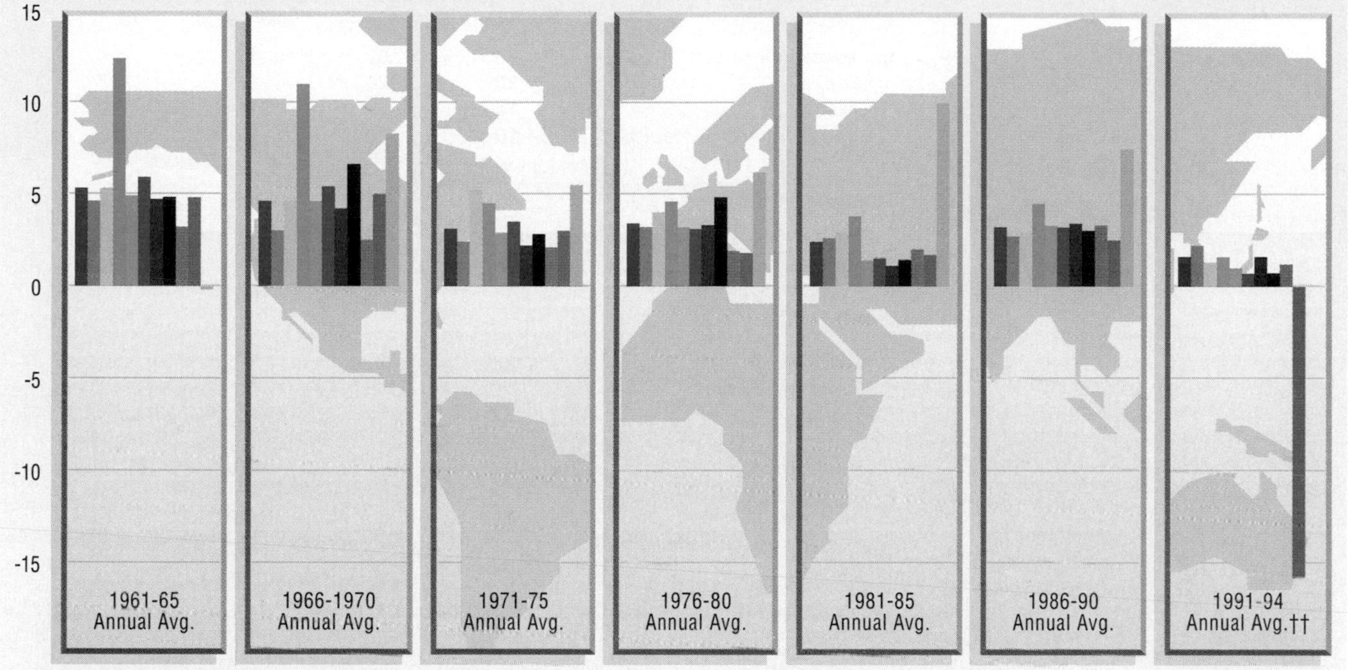

*OECD (Organization for Economic Cooperation and Development) includes Australia, Austria, Belgium, Canada, Denmark, Finland, France, Germany, Greece, Japan, Iceland, Ireland, Italy, Luxembourg, Netherlands, New Zealand, Norway, Portugal, Spain, Sweden, Switzerland, Turkey, United Kingdom, and the United States.
**Includes Austria, Belgium, Denmark, Finland, France, Germany, Greece, Ireland, Italy, Luxembourg, Netherlands, Portugal, Spain, Sweden, and the United Kingdom.
†Formerly West Germany   ††Data for Former USSR: 1992-1993 only   NA = not available

Source: *Economic Report of the President, 1991*, Table B-110, and *Economic Report of the President, 1995*, Table B-113

OECD countries*	European Union **	United Kingdom
United States	France	Former USSR††
Canada	Germany†	China
Japan	Italy	

SOURCES OF GROWTH IN THE U.S. ECONOMY SINCE 1929

For many years, Edward Denison of the Brookings Institution in Washington has been studying the growth process in the United States and sorting out the relative importance of the various causal factors. Table 20.7 on page 466 presents the results of his most recently published major work.

Denison estimates that about half of U.S. growth in output over the entire period from 1929 to 1982 has come from increases in factors of production and the other half from increases in productivity. Growth in the labor force accounted for about 20% of overall growth, while growth in capital stock (both human and physical) accounted for 33 percent. Of the capital stock growth figure, human capital (that is, education and training) accounted for 19% of the total, and physical capital accounted for 14 percent. Growth of knowledge was the single most important factor contributing to increases in the productivity of inputs.

The relative importance of these causes of growth varied considerably over the years. Between 1929 and 1948, for example, physical capital played a much smaller role than it did in other periods. But each of the separate periods included times that were atypical for one reason or another. The period between 1929 and

TABLE 20.7	**SOURCES OF GROWTH IN THE UNITED STATES, 1929–1982**			
	PERCENT OF GROWTH ATTRIBUTABLE TO EACH SOURCE			
	1929–1982	1929–1948	1948–1973	1973–1979
Increases in inputs	53	49	45	94
Labor	20	26	14	47
Capital	14	3	16	29
Education (human capital)	19	20	15	18
Increases in productivity	47	51	55	6
Advances in knowledge	31	30	39	8
Other factors*	16	21	16	−22
Total	100	100	100	100
Annual growth rate in real national income	2.8	2.4	3.6	2.6

*Note: Economies of scale, weather, pollution abatement, worker safety and health, crime, labor disputes, and so forth.

Source: Edward Denison, *Trends in American Economic Growth, 1929–1982* (Washington: Brookings Institution, 1985).

1948 included the dislocations and uncertainties of the Great Depression and World War II. From 1948 to 1973, the economy enjoyed a period of unusual stability and expansion.

THE PRODUCTIVITY "PROBLEM"

The years since 1973 have deserved much of the special attention they have received. During the early years of the Reagan administration, the "productivity problem" was much discussed. Some economics textbooks published in the early 1980s had entire chapters discussing the decline in productivity that seemed to be taking place during the late 1970s. In January of 1981, the Congressional Budget Office published a report entitled "The Productivity Problem: Alternatives for Action."

What exactly was this productivity problem? While the overall growth rate in the United States remained at 2.5% between 1973 and 1979—not far off the long-run average for the United States—the growth rate of *measured output per hour of labor* dropped precipitously in the same period. Figure 20.3 chronicles the decline from a labor-productivity growth rate of 3.5% in the 1960–1964 period to 1.0% for 1985–1989.

Many explanations were offered for the productivity decline of the late 1970s. Some economists pointed to the low rate of saving in the United States compared to other parts of the world. Others blamed increased environmental and government regulation of U.S. businesses. Still others argued that the country was not spending as much on research and development as it should have been. Finally, some suggested, high energy costs in the 1970s led to investment designed to save energy rather than to enhance productivity. (We discuss exactly how each of these factors influence growth later in this chapter.)

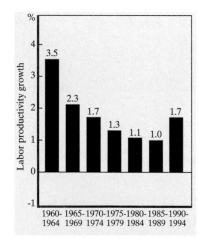

FIGURE 20.3

Labor Productivity Growth: Rate of Change of Real Output per Hour of Labor in the United States, 1960–1994

Source: *Economic Report of the President, 1995*, Table B-48

During the 1980s many of these factors seemed to turn around. Private investment in plant and equipment increased from long-run levels of under 8% of GDP to nearly 10% during the decade. Energy prices fell dramatically. There was some reduction in regulation under the Reagan administration. Research and development spending rose to its highest percentage of GDP since 1970. Despite these changes, though, measured growth in labor productivity grew at only a 1.0% rate during 1980–1989.

Between the recession of 1990–1991 and 1994, productivity rose at a rate of 1.7% per year. GDP grew for sixteen consecutive quarters beginning in the spring of 1991, but total employment hardly grew at all during the first two years. Many economists believe that U.S. firms became "lean and mean," keeping payrolls down and pushing productivity up, during this period

To conclude our discussion of productivity, it is important to point out that the productivity statistics we have been examining are hotly debated. For more details, see the Issues and Controversies Box on page 468 titled "Can We Really Measure Productivity Changes?".

ECONOMIC GROWTH AND PUBLIC POLICY

The decline in productivity that has caused so much concern has led to a protracted national discussion about the role of government in stimulating economic growth. This debate was spurred in part by increasing concern in the United States regarding Japanese competition. The enormous success of the Japanese in world markets and their extraordinary postwar annual rates of growth have led more and more people to look to the Far East for economic instruction.

Several strategies for increasing the rate of growth in the United States have been suggested, and some have even been enacted into law. These strategies include policies aimed toward improving the quality of education, increasing the saving rate, stimulating investment, increasing research and development, reducing regulation, and pursuing an industrial policy.

■ **Policies to Improve the Quality of Education** The Denison study, discussed earlier, shows that the contribution of education and training (human capital production) to growth in the United States has remained relatively constant at about 20% since 1929.

During the 1970s, public education came under siege. Teachers' salaries declined sharply in real terms, while property tax limitations and cuts in federal programs forced the curtailment of school budgets. In the last few years, battles have been waged in Congress over the amount of federal dollars set aside for scholarships and loans to college students. Whatever the policies of the moment, however, all federal, state, and local expenditures on education acknowledge the need to build the nation's stock of human capital.

■ **Policies to Increase the Saving Rate** The amount of capital accumulation in an economy is ultimately constrained by its rate of saving. The more saving in an economy, the more funds are available for investment. The national saving rate in Japan is twice as high as it is in the United States, and investment is a much higher fraction of GDP in Japan than it is in the United States. Many people have argued that the tax system and the social security system in the United States are biased against saving. Some public finance

NATIONAL POLICIES THAT MOTIVATE PEOPLE TO SAVE MORE CAN INCREASE ECONOMIC GROWTH. FOR MANY YEARS THE NATIONAL SAVING RATE IN JAPAN HAS BEEN TWICE AS HIGH AS THAT IN THE UNITED STATES. HIGHER SAVINGS MEANS MORE MONEY AVAILABLE FOR INVESTMENT IN PRODUCTIVITY-ENHANCING EQUIPMENT LIKE COMPUTERS AND OTHER TECHNOLOGY.

CAN WE REALLY MEASURE PRODUCTIVITY CHANGES?

When the government publishes numbers like those presented in Figure 20.3, most people take them as "true." Even though we don't really know much about how they are constructed, we assume that they are the best measurements we can get.

Yet such data are often the source of great controversy. In fact, some have argued that the mix of products produced in the United States and the increased pace of technological change in recent years have made it increasingly difficult to measure productivity changes accurately. The observed productivity decline in recent decades may thus simply be measurement error.

These arguments make a certain amount of sense at an intuitive level. Even in agriculture, where it is relatively easy to measure productivity growth, the possibility of mismeasurement exists. The output of a soybean farm can be measured in bushels, and labor, capital, and land inputs present no serious measurement problems. So, over time, as farming techniques improved and farmers acquired new and better machinery, output per acre and output per worker rose and have continued to rise. But today we have biotechnology. Genetic engineering now makes it possible to make soybeans higher in protein and more disease resistant. Clearly, technology has improved and "output" has increased, but these increases do not show up in the data because of our relatively crude measures of output.

A similar problem exists with computers. If you simply counted the number of personal computers produced and measured the cost of the inputs used in their production, you would no doubt see some productivity advances. But computers being produced for $1300 in 1995 contained processors capable of performing tasks literally thousands of times faster than computers produced a few years earlier. If we were to measure computer outputs not in terms of units produced but in terms of the actual "services" they provide to users, we would find massive productivity advances. Most new PCs now contain CD-ROM slots and can be easily connected to the new and growing "information superhighway," a source of cheap and plentiful information. In short, the problem is that many of the products that we now use are qualitatively different than the comparable products that we used only a few years ago, and the standard measures of productivity miss much of these quality changes.

The problems are even greater in the service sector, where output is extremely difficult to measure. It is easy to understand the problem if you think of what information technology has done for legal services. As recently as 10 years ago, a lawyer doing research to support a legal case might spend hundreds of hours looking through old cases and public documents. Today's lawyers can log on to a computer and in seconds do a key word search on a massive legal database. Such time- and labor-saving productivity advances are not counted in the official data.

One of the leading experts on technology and productivity estimates that we have reasonably good measures of output and productivity in only about 31% of the U.S. economy. Does this mean that productivity is not a problem? On this topic economists have agreed to disagree.*

---

*This argument was described most clearly by Professor Zvi Grilliches of Harvard in his Presidential Address to the American Economic Association in January of 1994. The full text, entitled "Productivity, R&D, and the Data Constraint," is published in the *American Economic Review,* March 1994. The counterargument is best advanced by Professor Dale Jorgenson in *Productivity* (Harvard University Press, 1995).

economists favor shifting to a system of consumption taxation rather than income taxation to reduce the tax burden on saving.

Others claim that the social security system, by providing guaranteed retirement incomes, reduces the incentive for people to save. Private pension plans make deposits to workers' accounts, the balances of which are invested in the stock market and bond market and are made available to firms for capital investment. Social security benefits, in contrast, are paid out of current tax receipts, and no such accumulations are available for investment. Thus, the argument goes, if social security substitutes for private saving, the national saving rate is reduced. Evidence on the extent to which taxes and social security reduce the saving rate has not been clear to date.

■ **Policies to Stimulate Investment** For the growth rate to increase, saving must be used to finance new investment. In an effort to revive a slowly growing economy in 1961, President Kennedy proposed and the Congress passed the *investment tax credit*. The ITC provided a tax reduction for firms that invest in new capital equipment. For most investments, the reduction took the form of a direct credit equal to 10% of the investment. Thus a firm investing in a new computer system costing $100,000 would have its tax liability reduced by $10,000. The investment tax credit was changed periodically over the years, and it was on the books until it was repealed in 1986. Many states have adopted investment tax credits against their state corporation taxes.

In 1982, the federal Economic Recovery Tax Act contained a number of provisions designed to encourage investment. Among them was the *Accelerated Cost Recovery System (ACRS),* which gave firms the opportunity to reduce their taxes by using artificially rapid rates of depreciation for purposes of calculating taxable profits. While these rules were complicated, their effect was similar to the effect of the investment tax credit. The government effectively reduced the cost of capital to firms that undertook investment in plant or equipment.

President Clinton proposed reinstating a modified version of the investment tax credit in 1994, but the measure was not passed by Congress.

■ **Policies to Increase Research and Development** As Table 20.7 shows, increases in knowledge accounted for 31% of total growth in the United States between 1929 and 1982. Although not shown in the table, during the years of high R&D expenditures, 1953 to 1973, the figure reached 40 percent. Research also shows that the rate of return on investment in R&D is quite high. Estimates place the rate of return at around 30 percent.[2]

It can be argued that new knowledge is like a public good. While the United States has a patent system to protect the gains of R&D for inventors and innovators, many of the benefits flow to imitators and others, including the public. This logic has been used to justify public subsidization of R&D spending.

■ **Reduced Regulations** One of the cornerstones of the Reagan and Bush administrations, and one of the items in the Republicans' "Contract with America" in 1995, was a commitment to reducing government regulation, which many believe stands in the way of U.S. industry.

Critics of these policies argue that many of the regulations on the books serve perfectly legitimate economic purposes. For example, environmental regulations, if properly administered, improve efficiency. Judicious use of antitrust laws can also improve the allocation of resources and stimulate investment and production.

Denison estimated that regulation of occupational health and safety, and of the environment, reduced the annual growth rate between 1973 and 1979 by 0.13 percentage points, from 2.74% to 2.61% per year. The question is: Has the value of the improved environment and increased safety been worth it?

■ **Industrial Policy** In the last few years, a number of economists have called for increased government involvement in the allocation of capital across manufactur-

---

[2]See M. Nadiri, "Contributions and Determinants of Research and Development Expenditures in the U.S. Manufacturing Industries," in Capital Efficiency and Growth, ed. George M. von Furstenberg, (Cambridge, Mass.: Ballinger Press, 1980).

industrial policy *Government involvement in the allocation of capital across manufacturing sectors.*

ing sectors, a practice known as **industrial policy.** Those who favor industrial policy argue that because governments of other countries are "targeting" industries for special subsidies and rapid investment, the United States should follow suit to avoid losing out in international competition. The Japanese Ministry of Trade and Industry, for example, picked the automobile industry very early on and decided to expand its role in world markets. The strategy succeeded very well—at the expense of the U.S. auto industry.

Critics of industrial policy argue that having the government involved in the allocation of capital would be disastrous. Investment always involves risk, they believe, and the best people to judge the extent and appropriateness of that risk are those making the investments and those actually involved in the industry.

GROWTH POLICY: A LONG-RUN PROPOSITION

When President Ford and Congress passed the dramatic tax cuts of 1975 in an effort to stimulate the economy and end the deep recession, the results were observable within a few months. Fiscal and monetary policies designed to counteract the cyclical up-and-down swings in the economy can produce measurable results in a short period of time.

However, the effects of policies designed to increase the rate of growth may not have observable effects for many years—they are by definition designed to mold the economy's long-run growth path. For example, a policy that succeeded in raising the rate of growth by one percentage point, say from 2.5% to 3.5%, would be viewed by all as a tremendous success. Yet it would be almost a decade before such a policy would raise GDP by 10 percent.

The fact that pro-growth policies can be costly in the short run and do not produce measurable results for a long time often pushes them far down on politicians' lists of priorities. Some economists who opposed the Tax Reform Act of 1986, argued that the elements of the tax code that had been favorable to capital investment and growth were cut for precisely these reasons. Defenders of the Tax Reform Act claim that it is indeed possible to oversubsidize investment and that the pre-1986 tax code had been doing just that.

But whether pro-growth policies work or not in the long run, are they worth pursuing? Not everyone agrees that the top priority in a developed economy should be continued growth. To close the chapter, we now turn to this debate.

THE PROS AND CONS OF GROWTH

As we said at the beginning of this chapter, there are those who believe that growth should be the primary objective of any society and those who believe that the costs of growth are too great. It is worth reviewing the arguments on both sides.

THE PRO-GROWTH ARGUMENT

Advocates of growth argue that growth *is* progress. Resources in a market economy are used to produce what people want; if you produce something that people do not want, you are out of business. Even in a centrally planned economy, resources are targeted to fulfill needs and wants. If a society is able to produce those things more efficiently and at less cost, how can that be bad?

By applying new technologies and better production methods, resources are freed to produce new and better products. Certainly, for Colleen and Bill accumulation of capital—a house, a water system, and so forth—and advancing knowledge were necessary to improve life on a formerly uninhabited island. In a modern industrial society as well, capital accumulation and new technology improve the quality of life.

One way to think about the benefits of growth is to compare two periods of time, say 1950 and 1995. In 1995, real GDP per capita was more than twice what it was in 1950. This means that incomes have grown twice as fast as prices so that we can buy that much more. (As we pursue this comparison, remember that no one is telling anyone what to buy, and most people can spend much more now than they could then.)

While it is true that the things available in both time periods are not exactly the same, growth has given us *more* choice, not less. Consider transportation. In the 1950s, the interstate highway system (social capital) had not been built. Driving from Chicago to New York took several days. We had automobiles, but the highway system did not compare to what we have today. And even more significant advances have been made in air travel. Flying between the two cities was possible, but more costly, less comfortable, and slower in 1950 than it is today. In the late 1990s, it is cheaper to get from New York to Chicago than it was in the 1950s, and it takes a fraction of the time.

Do these changes improve the quality of life? Yes, because they give us more freedom. We can travel more frequently. I can see my mother more often. I spend less time getting where I want to go so I can spend more time there. People are able to get to more places for less money.

What about consumer durables—dishwashers, microwave ovens, compact disc players, power lawn mowers, and so forth? Do they really enhance the quality of life? If they do not, why do we buy them? Few such things were around in the 1950s. In 1950, about 3% of all homes had dishwashers; today the figure is close to 50 percent. In 1950, less than 2% of all homes had air conditioners; today the figure is over 60 percent.

What makes a dishwasher worthwhile? It saves the most valuable commodity of all: *time.* Many consumer durables have no intrinsic value—that is, they don't provide satisfaction directly. They do free us from tasks and chores that are not fun, however—no one really likes to wash clothes or dishes. If a product allows us to perform these tasks more easily and quickly, it gives us more time for other things.

And think of the improvement in the *quality* of those things that do yield satisfaction directly. Record players in the 1950s reproduced sound very imperfectly; high fidelity was just being developed, and stereo was in the future. Today you can get a compact disc player for your car. Small "boxes" available at discount stores for under $30 reproduce sound far better than the best machines available in the early 1950s. And the range of tapes and compact discs available is extraordinary.

Growth also makes it possible to improve conditions for the less fortunate in society. The basic logic is simple: When there is more to go around, the sacrifice required to help the needy is smaller. With higher incomes, we can better afford the sacrifices needed to help the poor. Growth also produces jobs. When population growth is not accompanied by growth in output, unemployment and poverty increase.

It is easy for those in advanced societies to be complacent about growth, or even critical of it, but leaders of developing countries understand its benefits well. When 75% of a country's population is poor, redistributing existing incomes does not do much. The only hope for improvement in the long run is economic growth.

THE ANTI-GROWTH ARGUMENT

Those who argue against economic growth generally make four major points:

1. Any measure of output measures only the value of those things that are exchanged in the market. Many things that affect the quality of life are not traded in the market, and those things generally lose value when growth occurs.
2. For growth to occur, industry must cause consumers to develop new tastes and preferences. Therefore, we have no real need for many of the things we now consume. Wants are created, and consumers have become the servants, rather than the masters, of the economy.
3. The world has a finite quantity of resources, and rapid growth is consuming them at a rate that cannot continue. Because the available resources impose limits to growth, we should begin now to plan for the future, when growth will be impossible.
4. Growth requires that income be distributed unfairly.

Each of these points deserves some elaboration.

■ **Growth Has Negative Effects on the Quality of Life** Perhaps the most dramatic "unmeasurable" changes that affect the quality of life occur in the early stages of growth when societies become industrialized. It is true that more is produced: Agricultural productivity is higher, more manufactured goods are available, and so forth. But most people are crowded into cities, and their lives change drastically.

Before industrialization, most people in the Western World lived in small towns in the country. Most were poor, and they worked long hours to produce enough food to survive. After industrialization and urbanization in eighteenth-century England, men, women, and children worked long hours at routine jobs in hot, crowded factories. They were paid low wages and had very little control over their lives.

Even today, growth continues to change the quality of life in ways that are observable but that are not taken into account when we calculate growth rates. U.S. agriculture, for example, is becoming more and more productive every year. As productivity goes up, food prices drop, and fewer and fewer resources are needed in the agricultural sector. States such as those in New England that once had thriving farms have found their climates and soils simply not good enough to compete anymore. In 1959, 56,000 farms covered 9.3 million acres in the six New England states; in 1993, fewer than 30,000 farms covered fewer than five million acres. The agricultural sector had been cut in half.

During the early 1970s, small family farmers all over the United States found that making a living was becoming nearly impossible. The villain? Growth and progress. The cost? The decline of a lifestyle that many people want to maintain and that many others think of as an important part of America.

There are other consequences of growth that are not counted in the growth calculation. Perhaps the most significant is environmental damage. As the industrial engine is fed, waste is produced. Often both the feeding and the waste cause massive environmental damage. A dramatic example is the surface, or strip, mining of coal that has ravaged many parts of the United States. Another is the uncontrolled harvesting of U.S. forests. Modern growth requires paper and wood products, and large areas of timber in many states have been cleared and never replanted.

The disposal of industrial wastes has not begun to keep pace with industrial growth. It is now clear that growing and prosperous chemical companies have for decades been dumping hazardous, often carcinogenic, waste products into the nation's soil and water. It is costing billions to clean them up. Those costs were never taken into account when the market was allocating resources to the growing chemical industry.

Growth-related problems are by no means confined to the United States. Japan, for example, paid little attention to the environment during the early years of its rapid economic growth. Many of the results were disastrous. The best known of these results were the horrifying birth defects following the dumping of industrial mercury into the waters of Minamata Bay. In addition to birth defects, thousands of cases of "Minamata disease" in adults have been documented, and hundreds have died.

■ **Growth Encourages the Creation of Artificial Needs** The nature of preferences has been debated within the economics profession for many years. The orthodox view, which lies at the heart of modern welfare economics, is that preferences exist among consumers and that the economy's purpose is to serve those needs. According to the notion of **consumer sovereignty,** people are free to choose, and things that people do not want will not sell. Thus, the consumer rules.

The opposite view is that preferences are formed within the economic system. To continue growing, firms need a continuously expanding set of demands. To ensure that demand grows, firms create it by managing our minds and manipulating our behavior with elaborate advertising, fancy packaging, and other marketing techniques that persuade us to buy things for which we have no intrinsic need.

consumer sovereignty *The notion that people are free to choose, and that things that people do not want will not sell. Thus, "the customer rules."*

■ **Growth Means the Rapid Depletion of a Finite Quantity of Resources** In 1972, the Club of Rome, a group of "concerned citizens," contracted with a group at MIT to do a study entitled *The Limits to Growth.*[3] The book-length final report presented the results of computer simulations that assumed present growth rates of population, food, industrial output, and resource exhaustion. According to these data, sometime after the year 2000 the limits will be reached, and the entire world economy will come crashing down:

> Collapse occurs because of nonrenewable resource depletion. The industrial capital stock grows to a level that requires an enormous input of resources. In the very process of that growth, it depletes a large fraction of the resource reserves available. As resource prices rise and mines are depleted, more and more capital must be used for obtaining resources, leaving less to be invested for future growth. Finally, investment cannot keep up with depreciation and the industrial base collapses, taking with it the service and agricultural systems, which have become dependent on industrial inputs (such as fertilizers, pesticides, hospital laboratories, computers, and especially energy for mechanization. . . . Population finally decreases when the death rate is driven upward by the lack of food and health services.[4]

This argument is similar to one offered almost 200 years ago by Thomas Malthus, whom we mentioned earlier in this chapter.

In the early 1970s, many thought that the Club of Rome's predictions had come true. It seemed as if the world were starting to run up against the limits of world energy supplies; the prices of energy products shot up, and there were serious shortages. But dramatic changes have occurred in the years since. New reserves have been found, new sources of energy have been discovered and developed, and conservation measures have been tremendously successful (automobile gas mileage has been pushed up to levels that were inconceivable 15 years ago). Energy prices have fallen to levels that in real terms are about the same as they were before the oil price shocks of the 1970s.

---

[3]*Dennis L. Meadows, et al.,* The Limits to Growth *(Washington: Potomac Associates, 1972).*
[4]*Meadows,* Limits, *pp. 131–132.*

A variation of the depletion-of-resources argument stops short of predicting doomsday. It does point out, however, that unchecked growth in the developed world may have very undesirable distributional consequences. To fuel our growth, we are buying vast quantities of minerals and other resources from the developing countries, which have become dependent on the proceeds of those sales to buy food and other commodities on world markets. If this process continues, by the time these countries have grown to the point that they need mineral resources, their resources may be gone.

■ **Growth Requires an Unfair Income Distribution and Propagates It** One of the principal causes of growth is capital accumulation. Capital investment requires saving, and saving comes mostly from the rich. Certainly the rich save more than the poor, and in the developing countries most people are poor and need to use whatever income they have for survival.

Critics also claim that the real beneficiaries of growth are the rich. Choices open to the "haves" in society are greatly enhanced, but the choices open to the "have-nots" remain severely limited. If the benefits of growth trickle down to the poor, why are there more homeless today than there were 20 years ago?

■ **Summary: No Right Answer** We have presented the arguments for and against economic growth in overly simple and categorical terms. In reality, even those who take extreme positions in this debate acknowledge that there is no "right answer." To suggest that all economic growth is bad is wrong; to suggest that economic growth should run unchecked is equally wrong. The real question for society is: How can we derive the benefits of growth and at the same time minimize its undesirable consequences?

Society must make some hard choices, and there are many trade-offs. For example, we can grow faster if we pay less attention to environmental concerns. But how much environmental damage should we accept to get how much economic growth? Many argue that we can achieve an acceptable level of economic growth *and* protect the environment at the same time. There is also a trade-off between growth and the distribution of income. More financial inequality would probably lead to more saving and ultimately to more capital and faster growth. Using taxes and income transfers to redistribute some of the benefits of growth to the poor probably does slow the rate of growth. But it is not a question of all or nothing; society must decide how much inequality is desirable.

As long as these trade-offs exist, people will disagree. The debate in contemporary politics is largely about the costs and benefits of shifting more effort toward the goal of economic growth and away from environmental and social welfare goals.

SUMMARY

1. *Modern economic growth* is the period of rapid and sustained increase in real output per capita that began in the Western World with the Industrial Revolution.

THE GROWTH PROCESS: FROM AGRICULTURE TO INDUSTRY

2. All societies face limits imposed by the resources and technologies available to them. Economic growth expands these limits and shifts society's production possibilities frontier up and to the right.

THE SOURCES OF ECONOMIC GROWTH

3. If growth in output outpaces growth in population, and if the economic system is producing what people want, growth will increase the standard of living. Growth occurs either when (1) society acquires more resources, or (2) society discovers ways of using available resources more efficiently.

4. An *aggregate production function* embodies the relationship between inputs—the labor force and the stock of capital—and total national output.

5. A number of factors contribute to *economic growth*: (1) an increase in the labor supply; (2) an increase in physical capital—plant and equipment—and/or human capital—education, training, and health; (3) an increase in productivity brought about by technological change; other advances in knowledge (managerial skills and so forth); and/or economies of scale.

GROWTH AND PRODUCTIVITY IN THE U.S. ECONOMY

6. Modern economic growth in the United States dates to the middle of the nineteenth century. For the last 100 years, the nation's growth in real output has averaged about 3.0% per year. Between 1929 and 1982, about half of U.S. growth in output came from increases in factors of production and the other half from increases in productivity.

7. There has been much concern that the rate of growth in the United States is slowing. The growth rate of measured labor productivity decreased from 3.5% in the 1960–1964, period to 1.7% in the 1990–1994 period

ECONOMIC GROWTH AND PUBLIC POLICY

8. A number of public policies have been pursued with the aim of improving the growth of real output. These policies include efforts to improve the quality of education, to encourage saving, to stimulate investment, to increase research and development, and to reduce regulation. Some economists also argue for increased government involvement in the allocation of capital across manufacturing sectors, a practice known as *industrial policy*.

THE PROS AND CONS OF GROWTH

9. Advocates of growth argue that growth is progress. Growth gives us more freedom—that is, more choices. It saves time, improves the standard of living, and is the only way to improve conditions for the poor. Growth creates jobs and increases income simply because there is more to go around.

10. Those who argue against growth generally make four major points. First, many things that affect the quality of life are not traded in the market, and these things generally lose value when there is growth. Second, to have growth, industry must cause consumers to develop new tastes and preferences for many things that they have no real need for. Third, the world has a finite quantity of resources, and rapid growth is eating them up at a rate that cannot continue. Fourth, growth requires that income be distributed inequitably.

REVIEW TERMS AND CONCEPTS

aggregate production function 457

consumer sovereignty 473

economic growth 455

industrial policy 470

infrastructure, or **public capital** 462

innovation 463

invention 463

labor productivity 458

modern economic growth 455

productivity of an input 461

1. During 1994 and early 1995, real GDP in the United States was growing at a rate in excess of 3.5% per year. The Federal Reserve decided to raise interest rates in order to slow the growth rate to about 2.5% per year. If growth is a good thing for an economy, why would the Fed try to slow it down?

2. Tables 1, 2, and 3 present some data on three hypothetical economies. Complete the tables by figuring the measured productivity of labor and the rate of output growth. What do the data tell you about the causes of economic growth? (*Hint:* How fast are L and K growing?)

TABLE 1

PERIOD	L	K	Y	Y/L	GROWTH RATE OF OUTPUT
1	1052	3065	4506		
2	1105	3095	4674		
3	1160	3126	4842		
4	1218	3157	5019		

TABLE 2

PERIOD	L	K	Y	Y/L	GROWTH RATE OF OUTPUT
1	1052	3065	4506		
2	1062	3371	4683		
3	1073	3709	4866		
4	1084	4079	5055		

TABLE 3

PERIOD	L	K	Y	Y/L	GROWTH RATE OF OUTPUT
1	1052	3065	4506		
2	1062	3095	4731		
3	1073	3126	4967		
4	1084	3157	5216		

3. In earlier chapters, you learned that aggregate expenditure ($C + I + G$) must be equal to aggregate output for the economy to be in equilibrium. You also saw that when consumption spending rises, $C + I + G$ increases, inventories fall, and aggregate output rises. Thus, policies that simultaneously increase consumer spending and reduce saving would lead to a higher level of GDP. In this chapter, we have argued that a higher saving rate, even with lower consumption spending, is the key to long-run GDP growth. How can both of these arguments be correct?

4. Suppose that you have just been elected to Congress and that you find yourself on the Ways and Means Committee—the committee in the House that decides on tax matters. Suppose further that the committee is debating a bill that would make major changes in tax policy. First, the corporate tax would be lowered substantially in an effort to stimulate investment. The bill contains a 15% investment tax credit—firms would be able to reduce their taxes by 15% of the value of investment projects that they undertake. To keep revenues constant, the bill would impose a national sales tax that would raise the price of consumer goods and reduce consumption. What trade-offs do you see involved in this bill? What are the pros and cons? How would you vote?

5. If you wanted to measure productivity (output per worker) in the following sectors over time, how would you measure "output"? How easy is it to measure productivity in each of the sectors?
   a. Software
   b. Vegetable farming
   c. Education
   d. Airline transportation

6. Economists generally agree that high budget deficits today will reduce the growth rate of the economy in the future. Why is this the case? Do the reasons for the high budget deficit matter? In other words, does it matter whether the deficit is caused by lower taxes, increased defense spending, more job-training programs, and so on?

7. Why can growth lead to a more unequal distribution of income? Assuming this is true, how is it possible for the poor to benefit from economic growth?

INDUSTRIAL POLICY AND THE EAST ASIAN MIRACLE

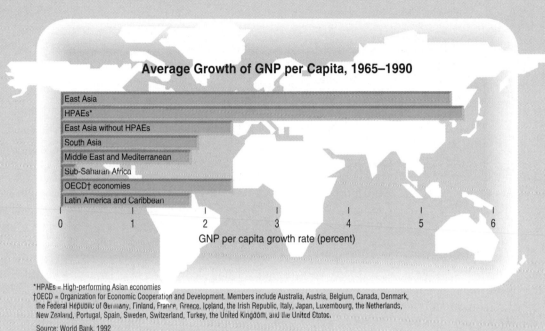

Average Growth of GNP per Capita, 1965–1990

East Asia
HPAEs*
East Asia without HPAEs
South Asia
Middle East and Mediterranean
Sub-Saharan Africa
OECD† economies
Latin America and Caribbean

0   1   2   3   4   5   6

GNP per capita growth rate (percent)

*HPAEs = High-performing Asian economies
†OECD = Organization for Economic Cooperation and Development. Members include Australia, Austria, Belgium, Canada, Denmark, the Federal Republic of Germany, Finland, France, Greece, Iceland, the Irish Republic, Italy, Japan, Luxembourg, the Netherlands, New Zealand, Portugal, Spain, Sweden, Switzerland, Turkey, the United Kingdom, and the United States.

Source: World Bank, 1992

FIGURE 1
Average Growth of GNP per Capita, 1965–1990

From 1965 to 1990 East Asia had a spectacular record of high and sustained economic growth (as measured by GDP per capita). For this reason references to the "Asian economic miracle" have become common. Over this period the 23 economies of East Asia grew faster than all other regions of the world (Figure 1). Most of this achievement is attributable to seemingly miraculous growth in just eight economies: Japan; the "Four Tigers"—Hong Kong, Singapore, the Republic of Korea, and Taiwan; and the three newly industrializing economies of Southeast Asia—Indonesia, Malaysia, and Thailand. In 1960, Japan, the richest country in Asia and one

that had been modernizing for nearly a century, had a GDP per capita of $380, or one eighth that of the United States. South Korea's GDP per head in 1962 was $110, about the same as Sudan, and Taiwan's was $160. By the 1990s Japan had become one of the world's richest countries, the Four Tigers had become a part of the developed world (Figure 2), and the newly industrialized economies are heading in the same direction.

No other group of developing countries has performed as well in sustaining rapid growth, reducing poverty, or raising standards of living. Nonetheless, the immense success of these countries has inspired a heated

debate on whether the East Asian success story can be imitated by other countries. Specifically, the debate has centered around whether East Asia's success can be attributed to a laissez-faire approach to economic policy making or to exceptionally clever industrial policy. To different degrees every nation pursues policies that significantly affect both the economy's aggregate productive capacity and its particular industrial structure. As we saw in the previous chapter, these policies are collectively known as *industrial policy*.

To shed light on the role of public policy in explaining economic growth in East Asia, the World Bank (an international agency that lends

	Life expectancy	GDP per capita	Exports (billions)	Imports (billions)	Foreign aid dispensed (millions)*
Hong Kong	80.0	$22,900	$135.2	$138.7	NA
Singapore	75.8	18,800	74.0	85.2	$12.4
South Korea	70.3	10,100	82.2	83.8	176.0
Taiwan	75.0	10,600	84.7	77.1	61.0

*For year ended March 31, 1994. NA = not available. Source: OECD, *CIA Handbook of International Economic Statistics*

FIGURE 2
Economic Performance of the Four Tigers, 1994

money to individual countries for projects that promote economic development) recently conducted a research project called *The East Asian Miracle*. The World Bank concludes that East Asia got the basics right. Macroeconomic performance was unusually stable, providing the necessary framework for private investment. The level of saving increased as a result of policies that enhanced the banking system's integrity while providing for the inclusion of the nontraditional savers. Universal provision of primary and secondary education generated immense increases in the quality of human capital. Price distortions were kept at a minimum, and all of the East Asian economies were open to foreign ideas and technology. In sum: East Asia's success can be explained by sound "market-friendly" policy making.

But the East Asian experience and the World Bank report do not make a clear case for a laissez-faire approach to economic policy making. Governments in most East Asian countries systematically intervened in the markets to foster development, and in some cases the development of specific industries. Policy interventions took many forms: targeting selected industries, offering these industries subsidized credit, keeping deposit rates low and maintaining ceilings on borrowing rates to increase profits and retained earnings, protecting domestic import substitutes, subsidizing declining industries, establishing and financially supporting government banks, making public investments in applied research, developing export marketing institutions, and sharing information widely between public and private sectors. All of this means that the East Asian success story is thus a result of governments using a combination of fundamental and selective interventions to (1) accumulate human and physical capital, (2) allocate this capital to high-yielding investments, and (3) promote productivity growth.

1. Accumulation of Human and Physical Capital. At the onset of its growth Asia began with an educational advantage over other developing countries and continued to maintain this advantage with explicit policies of investing in primary and secondary education. The limited public funding for postsecondary education was used primarily for science and technological education, while university education in the humanities and social sciences remained to a large extent in the hands of the private institutions. East Asian educational policies also contributed to a more equitable income distribution; by focusing on primary and secondary education they served a large segment of population that would have otherwise lacked access to education. An additional accomplishment of the East Asians was to provide the same educational opportunities to boys and girls. The difference in enrollments between boys and girls in primary and secondary education declined significantly and produced, among other benefits, lower fertility rates in these countries.

East Asia has also been spectacularly successful at accumulating capital. By the early 1990s the East Asian economies, excluding Japan, had increased their savings from 16% of GDP in the mid-1960s to more than 36% of GDP. Investment as a share of GDP also rose significantly over this period. The East Asian economies encouraged investment by several means. First, they provided good infrastructure to complement private investment. Second, they created an investment-friendly environment through a combination of tax policies and measures that kept relative prices of capital goods low; "strategic" companies were provided with subsidized loans and tax breaks. Third, private banks lent cheaply to officially favored firms. This practice was possible because of regulation, which kept interest rates below market-clearing levels (a practice known as *financial repression*).

2. Allocating Capital. High levels of physical and human capital do not guarantee high growth. Resources need to be channeled to highly productive investments. The East Asian economies used a combination of market mechanisms and selective interventions to guide the allocative decisions in both the labor and capital markets.

3. Promoting Productivity Growth. The East Asian economies promoted productivity growth by employing policies that increased the absorption of foreign technology, promoted selective industries, and encouraged rapid export growth

Effective policy making was aided by an effective bureaucracy. Governments in East Asia developed institutional mechanisms that enabled them to monitor the performance of policies and to establish clear performance criteria for the basis of selective interventions. Extensive coordination mechanisms between the private and public sector were created to help companies facing economic and political uncertainties. Japan and Korea set up deliberative councils and industrial associations to provide close coordination and consultation between the bureaucrats and businesses. This cooperation enabled the private sector to influence the design and the implementation of public policies relevant to their interests. Japan and Korea also helped individual firms in their investment decisions by supplying them with relevant market information about technological development, export prospects, and other market data. Last, but not least, policy making in East Asia was very pragmatic. When chosen public policies did not work, they were promptly reversed.

Questions for Analytical Thinking

1. What are the sources of East Asia's success?

2. What was the role of public policy in fostering East Asia's growth? Define the factors that promote growth. List some of the ways that the government influenced these factors in East Asia.

3. Can policies that were successful in East Asia be replicated by other economies? How would you design an industrial policy in order to minimize its inherent problems?

Sources: Alice Amsden, "Why Isn't the Whole World Experimenting with the East Asian Model to Develop?: Review of the East Asian Miracle," *World Development,* Vol. 22, No. 4, 1994, 627–633; "Asia's Four Tigers Spring into the First World," *The Wall Street Journal,* February 28, 1995; World Bank, *The East Asian Miracle: Economic Growth and Public Policy, Policy Research Report* (Washington D.C.: The World Bank, 1993); "Oriental Renaissance: A Survey of Japan," *The Economist,* July 9, 1994; John Page, "The East Asian Miracle: Building a Basis for Growth," *Finance and Development,* March 1994.

INTERNATIONAL ECONOMICS

PART SEVEN

THE GLOBAL ECONOMY

INTERNATIONAL TRADE, COMPARATIVE ADVANTAGE, AND PROTECTIONISM

O VER THE LAST 25 YEARS, INTERNATIONAL TRANSACTIONS HAVE become increasingly important to the U.S. economy. As recently as 1970, imports represented only about 7% of U.S. gross domestic product. The figure now stands at around 12 percent. In 1994, the United States imported $816.9 billion worth of goods and services. Chapter 3 presented an overview of the international sector in the United States.

The "internationalization" or "globalization" of the U.S. economy has occurred on all fronts—in the private and public sectors, in input and output markets, and in business firms and households. Once relatively uncommon, foreign products are now everywhere, from the utensils we eat with to the cars we drive. In 1970, for example, foreign-produced cars made up only a small percentage of all the cars in the United States. At that time, it was difficult to find mechanics who knew how to repair foreign cars, and replacement parts were hard to obtain. Today the roads are full of Toyotas and Nissans from Japan, Volvos from Sweden, and BMWs from Germany, and any service station that cannot repair foreign-produced automobiles probably won't get much business. Half of all the cars and 80% of all the consumer electronics (televisions, CD players, and so forth) that U.S. consumers buy are produced abroad.

At the same time, the United States exports billions of dollars worth of agricultural goods, aircraft, and industrial machinery. Financial capital flows smoothly and swiftly across international boundaries in search of high returns. In 1994, for example, German interest rates fell and U.S. interest rates rose. Almost immediately, billions of investor dollars shifted out of interest-bearing German securities and into U.S. securities.

The inextricable connection of the U.S. economy to the economies of the rest of the world has had a profound impact on the discipline of economics and is the basis of one of its most important insights:

> All economies, regardless of their size, depend to some extent on other economies and are affected by events outside their borders.

As a means of getting you more fully acquainted with the international economy, this chapter discusses the economics of international trade. First, we describe the recent tendency of the United States to import more than it exports. Next, we explore the basic logic of trade. Why should the United States or any other country engage in international trade? Finally, we address the controversial issue of protectionism. Should a country provide certain industries with protection in the form of import quotas, tariffs, or subsidies?

THE INTERNATIONAL ECONOMY: TRADE SURPLUSES AND DEFICITS

Until the 1970s, the United States generally exported more than it imported. When a country exports more than it imports, it runs a **trade surplus.** When a country imports more than it exports, it runs a **trade deficit.** Before 1975, the United States generally ran a trade surplus for goods and services as a whole, as well as for merchandise. Table 21.1 shows the U.S. balance of trade for merchandise and total goods and services for selected years since 1929.

In the mid-1970s, the United States began to import more merchandise than it exported. The merchandise deficit climbed steadily after 1975, reaching over $150 billion in 1987. It then fell until 1991, when it started to rise again. In 1994 it was $165.1 billion! The goods and services deficit shows a similar pattern, although not as extreme.

The large trade deficits that characterized the middle and late 1980s touched off serious political controversy that continues today. Foreign competition hit U.S. markets hard. Less expensive foreign goods—among them steel, textiles, and automobiles—began driving U.S. manufacturers out of business at an alarming rate, and thousands of jobs were lost in important industries. Cities such as Pittsburgh, Youngstown, and Detroit found themselves with major unemployment problems.

The natural reaction, of course, was to call for protection of U.S. industries. That is, many people wanted the President and Congress to impose taxes and import restrictions that would make foreign goods less available and more expensive, a situation that in turn would protect U.S. jobs. As you might guess, this argument was not new to the 1980s. For hundreds of years, industries have petitioned governments for protection, and societies have debated the pros and cons of free and open trade. For the last century and a half, the principal argument used against protection has been the theory of comparative advantage, which we first discussed in Chapter 2.

trade surplus *The situation when a country exports more than it imports.*

trade deficit *The situation when a country imports more than it exports.*

TABLE 21.1		
U.S. BALANCE OF TRADE (EXPORTS MINUS IMPORTS), 1929–1994 (BILLIONS OF DOLLARS)		
	MERCHANDISE	**GOODS AND SERVICES**
1929	+0.8	+0.3
1933	+0.2	+0.1
1945	+1.5	−0.8
1955	+2.6	+0.4
1960	+5.3	+2.5
1965	+5.6	+3.9
1970	+3.6	+1.2
1975	+10.6	+13.6
1976	−6.8	−2.2
1977	−28.9	−23.6
1978	−32.0	−26.2
1979	−28.6	−23.8
1980	−22.6	−14.7
1981	−28.4	−14.7
1982	−35.4	−20.6
1983	−65.2	−51.4
1984	−110.5	−102.7
1985	−120.9	−115.5
1986	−143.8	−132.5
1987	−157.1	−143.1
1988	−126.3	−108.0
1989	−113.5	−79.7
1990	−110.3	−71.4
1991	−74.3	−19.8
1992	−94.9	−30.3
1993	−131.1	−65.2
1994	−165.1	−98.2

Source: U.S. Department of Commerce, Bureau of Economic Analysis.

THE ECONOMIC BASIS FOR TRADE: COMPARATIVE ADVANTAGE

Perhaps the best-known debate on the issue of free trade took place in the British Parliament during the early years of the nineteenth century. At that time, the landed gentry—the landowners—controlled Parliament. For a number of years, imports and exports of grain had been subject to a set of tariffs, subsidies, and restrictions collectively called the **Corn Laws.** Designed to discourage imports of grain and encourage exports, the Corn Laws' purpose was to keep the price of food high. The landlords' incomes, of course, depended on the prices they got for what their land produced. The Corn Laws thus clearly worked to the advantage of those in power.

With the Industrial Revolution, a class of wealthy industrial capitalists began to emerge. The industrial sector had to pay workers at least enough to live on, and a living wage depended to a great extent on the price of food. Tariffs on grain imports and export subsidies that kept grain and food prices high increased the wages that capitalists had to pay, and these high wage payments cut into their profits. The political battle raged for years. But as time went by, the power of the landowners in the House of Lords was significantly reduced. When the conflict ended in 1848, the Corn Laws were repealed.

Participating in this battle on the side of repeal was David Ricardo, a businessman, economist, member of Parliament, and one of the fathers of modern economics. Ricardo's principal work, *Principles of Political Economy and Taxation,* was published in 1817, two years before he entered Parliament. Ricardo's **theory of comparative advantage,** which he used to argue against the Corn Laws, claimed that trade enables countries to specialize in producing the products that they produce best. According to the theory:

> Specialization and free trade will benefit all trading partners (real wages will rise), even those that may be absolutely less efficient producers.

This basic argument remains at the heart of free-trade debates even today. It was invoked numerous times by Presidents Reagan and Bush as they wrestled with Congress over various pieces of protectionist legislation.

■ **Specialization and Trade: The Two-Person Case**   Perhaps the easiest way to understand the theory of comparative advantage is to examine a simple two-person society. Recall Bill and Colleen, who were stranded on a deserted island in Chapter 2. Suppose that they have only two basic tasks to accomplish each week: gathering food to eat and cutting logs that will be used in constructing a house. If Colleen could cut more logs than Bill in a day and Bill could gather more berries and fruits, specialization would clearly benefit both of them.

But suppose that Bill is slow and somewhat clumsy and that Colleen is better at both cutting logs *and* gathering food. Ricardo's point is that it still pays for them to specialize. They can produce more in total by specializing than they can by sharing the work equally. (It may be helpful to review the discussion of comparative advantage in Chapter 2 before proceeding.)

ABSOLUTE ADVANTAGE VERSUS COMPARATIVE ADVANTAGE

A country is said to enjoy an **absolute advantage** over another country in the production of a product if it uses fewer resources to produce that product than the other country does. For example, suppose that country A and country B produce wheat, but that A's climate is more suited to wheat and its labor is more produc-

---

Corn Laws *The tariffs, subsidies, and restrictions enacted by the British Parliament in the early nineteenth century to discourage imports and encourage exports of grain.*

theory of comparative advantage *Ricardo's theory that specialization and free trade will benefit all trading partners (real wages will rise), even those that may be absolutely less efficient producers.*

absolute advantage *The advantage in the production of a product enjoyed by one country over another when it uses fewer resources to produce that product than the other country does.*

tive. Country A will therefore produce more wheat per acre than country B and use less labor in growing it and bringing it to market. Country A thus enjoys an absolute advantage over country B in the production of wheat.

A country enjoys a **comparative advantage** in the production of a good if that good can be produced at lower cost *in terms of other goods*. Suppose that countries C and D both produce wheat and corn and that C enjoys an absolute advantage in the production of both—that is, C's climate is better than D's, and fewer of C's resources are needed to produce a given quantity of both wheat and corn. Now C and D must each choose between planting land with either wheat or corn. To produce more wheat, either country must transfer land from corn production; to produce more corn, either country must transfer land from wheat production. Thus, the cost of wheat in each country can be measured in bushels of corn, and the cost of corn can be measured in bushels of wheat.

Suppose that in country C, a bushel of wheat has an opportunity cost of two bushels of corn. That is, to produce an additional bushel of wheat, C must give up two bushels of corn. At the same time, suppose that producing a bushel of wheat in country D requires the sacrifice of only one bushel of corn. Even though C has an *absolute* advantage in the production of both products, D enjoys a *comparative* advantage in the production of wheat because the *opportunity cost* of producing wheat is lower in D. Under these circumstances, Ricardo claims, D can benefit from trade if it specializes in the production of wheat.

■ **Gains from Mutual Absolute Advantage** To illustrate Ricardo's logic in more detail, let's start with a very simple case. Suppose that Australia and New Zealand each have a fixed amount of land and do not trade with the rest of the world. Suppose further that there are only two goods—wheat, used to produce bread, and cotton, used to produce clothing. This kind of two-country/two-good world does not exist, of course, but its operations can be generalized to many countries and many goods.

Before we proceed, we have to make some assumptions about the preferences of the people living in New Zealand and those living in Australia. If the citizens of both countries go around naked, there is no need to produce cotton at all; all the land can be used to produce wheat. For the sake of simplicity, however, let us assume that people in both countries have similar preferences with respect to food and clothing: The populations of both countries use both cotton and wheat. We will also assume that preferences for food and clothing are such that both countries consume equal amounts of wheat and cotton.

Finally, we shall assume that each country has only 100 acres of land for planting and that land yields are those given in Table 21.2. Notice that New Zealand can produce three times the wheat that Australia can on one acre of land, and that Australia can produce three times the cotton that New Zealand can in the same space. New Zealand thus has an absolute advantage in the production of wheat, and Australia has an absolute advantage in the production of cotton. In cases like this, we say that the two countries have *mutual absolute advantage*.

comparative advantage *The advantage in the production of a product enjoyed by one country over another when that product can be produced at lower cost in terms of other goods than it could be in the other country.*

TABLE 21.2	YIELD PER ACRE OF WHEAT AND COTTON	
	NEW ZEALAND	**AUSTRALIA**
Wheat	6 bushels	2 bushels
Cotton	2 bales	6 bales

TABLE 21.3	TOTAL PRODUCTION OF WHEAT AND COTTON ASSUMING NO TRADE, MUTUAL ABSOLUTE ADVANTAGE, AND 100 AVAILABLE ACRES	
	NEW ZEALAND	**AUSTRALIA**
Wheat	25 acres × 6 bushels/acre 150 bushels	75 acres × 2 bushels/acre 150 bushels
Cotton	75 acres × 2 bales/acre 150 bales	25 acres × 6 bales/acre 150 bales

If there is no trade and each country divides its land to obtain equal units of cotton and wheat production, each country produces 150 bushels of wheat and 150 bales of cotton. New Zealand puts 75 acres into cotton but only 25 acres into wheat, while Australia does the reverse. (See Table 21.3.)

We can organize the same information in a somewhat different way if we construct separate production possibilities frontiers for each country. In Figure 21.1, which presents the positions of the two countries before trade, each country is constrained by its own resources and productivity. If Australia put all its land into cotton, it would produce 600 bales of cotton (100 acres × 6 bales/acre) and no wheat; if it put all its land into wheat, it would produce 200 bushels of wheat (100 acres × 2 bu/acre) and no cotton. The opposite is true for New Zealand. As you recall from Chapter 2, a country's production possibilities frontier represents all combinations of goods that can be produced, given the coun-

FIGURE 21.1

Production Possibility Frontiers for Australia and New Zealand before Trade
Without trade, countries are constrained by their own resources and productivity.

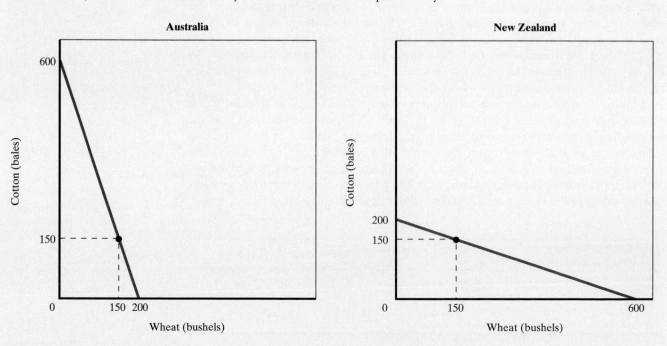

TABLE 21.4

PRODUCTION AND CONSUMPTION OF WHEAT AND COTTON AFTER SPECIALIZATION

	PRODUCTION			CONSUMPTION	
	New Zealand	Australia		New Zealand	Australia
Wheat	100 acres × 6 bu/acre 600 bushels	0 acres 0	Wheat	300 bushels	300 bushels
Cotton	0 acres 0	100 acres × 6 bales/acre 600 bales	Cotton	300 bales	300 bales

try's resources and state of technology. Each country must pick a point along its own production possibilities curve.

Because both countries have an absolute advantage in the production of one product, it is reasonable to expect that specialization and trade will benefit both countries. Clearly, Australia should produce cotton and New Zealand should produce wheat. Transferring all land to wheat production in New Zealand yields a total of 600 bushels; transferring all land to cotton production in Australia yields 600 bales. An agreement to trade 300 bushels of wheat for 300 bales of cotton would double both wheat and cotton consumption in both countries. (Remember, before trade both countries produced 150 bushels of wheat and 150 bales of cotton. After trade, each country will have 300 bushels of wheat and 300 bales of cotton to consume. Final production and trade figures are given in Table 21.4 and Figure 21.2.)

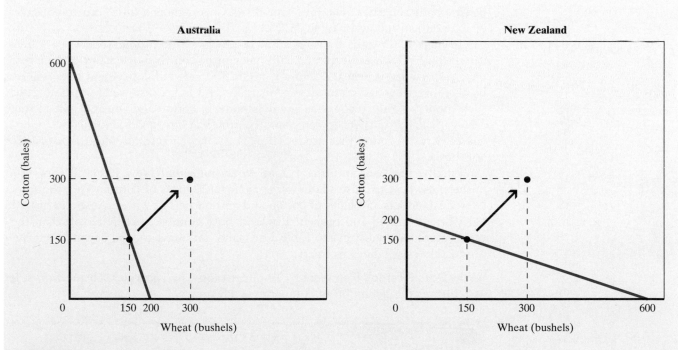

FIGURE 21.2

Expanded Possibilities after Trade

Trade enables both countries to move out beyond their own resource constraints— beyond their individual production possibility frontiers.

Thus,

> Trade enables both countries to move out beyond their previous resource and productivity constraints.

The advantages of specialization and trade seem obvious when one country is technologically superior at producing one product and another country is technologically superior at producing another product. Now, however, let us turn to the case in which one country has an absolute advantage in the production of *both* goods.

■ **Gains from Comparative Advantage**　Table 21.5 contains different land yield figures for New Zealand and Australia. In this new case, New Zealand has a considerable absolute advantage in the production of both cotton and wheat, with one acre of land yielding six times as much wheat and twice as much cotton as one acre in Australia. Ricardo would argue that *specialization and trade are still mutually beneficial.*

Assume again that preferences for food and clothing imply consumption of equal units of cotton and wheat in both countries. With no trade, New Zealand would divide its 100 available acres evenly, or 50/50, between the two crops. The result would be 300 bales of cotton and 300 bushels of wheat. Australia would divide its land 75/25. Table 21.6 shows that final production in Australia would be 75 bales of cotton and 75 bushels of wheat. (Remember, we are assuming that in each country, people consume equal amounts of cotton and wheat.) Once again, before any trade takes place each country is constrained by its own domestic production possibilities curve.

Now imagine that we are at a meeting of trade representatives of both countries. As a special adviser, David Ricardo is asked to demonstrate that trade can benefit both countries. The professor divides his demonstration into three stages, which you can follow in Table 21.7.

In stage 1, Australia transfers all its land into cotton production. When it does, it will have no wheat at all and 300 bales of cotton. New Zealand cannot completely specialize in wheat because it needs 300 bales of cotton and thus will not be able to get enough cotton from Australia. This is because we are assuming that each country wants to consume equal amounts of cotton and wheat. Thus, in stage 2 New Zealand transfers 25 acres out of cotton and into wheat. Now New Zealand has 25 acres in cotton that produce 150 bales and 75 acres in wheat that produce 450 bushels.

Finally, the two countries trade. We assume that New Zealand ships 100 bushels of wheat to Australia in exchange for 200 bales of cotton. After the trade, New Zealand has 350 bales of cotton and 350 bushels of wheat; Australia has 100 bales of cotton and 100 bushels of wheat. Both countries are better off than they were before the trade (review Table 21.6), and both have moved beyond their own production possibilities frontiers.

■ **Why Does Ricardo's Plan Work?**　To understand why Ricardo's scheme works, let us return to the definition of comparative advantage.

TABLE 21.5	YIELD PER ACRE OF WHEAT AND COTTON	
	NEW ZEALAND	AUSTRALIA
Wheat	6 bushels	1 bushel
Cotton	6 bales	3 bales

TABLE 21.6 **TOTAL PRODUCTION OF WHEAT AND COTTON ASSUMING NO TRADE AND 100 AVAILABLE ACRES**

	NEW ZEALAND	AUSTRALIA
Wheat	50 acres × 6 bushels/acre 300 bushels	75 acres × 1 bushels/acre 75 bushels
Cotton	50 acres × 6 bales/acre 300 bales	25 acres × 3 bales/acre 75 bales

The real cost of producing cotton is the wheat that must be sacrificed to produce it. *When we think of cost this way, it is less costly to produce cotton in Australia than to produce it in New Zealand, even though an acre of land produces more cotton in New Zealand.* Consider the "cost" of three bales of cotton in the two countries. In terms of opportunity cost, three bales of cotton in New Zealand cost three bushels of wheat; in Australia, however, three bales of cotton cost only one bushel of wheat. Because three bales are produced by one acre of Australian land, to get three bales an Australian must transfer one acre of land from wheat to cotton production. And because an acre of land produces a bushel of wheat, losing one acre to cotton implies the loss of one bushel of wheat. Thus, *Australia has a comparative advantage in cotton production* because its opportunity cost, in terms of wheat, is lower than New Zealand's. This situation is illustrated in Figure 21.3 on page 488.

Conversely, New Zealand has a comparative advantage in wheat production. A unit of wheat in New Zealand costs one unit of cotton; a unit of wheat in Australia costs three units of cotton.

> When countries specialize in producing those goods in which they have a comparative advantage, they maximize their combined output and allocate their resources more efficiently.

TABLE 21.7 **REALIZING A GAIN FROM TRADE WHEN ONE COUNTRY HAS A DOUBLE ABSOLUTE ADVANTAGE**

	STAGE 1			STAGE 2	
	New Zealand	Australia		New Zealand	Australia
Wheat	50 acres × 6 bushels/acre 300 bushels	0 acres 0	Wheat	75 acres × 6 bushels/acre 450 bushels	0 acres 0
Cotton	50 acres × 6 bales/acre 300 bales	100 acres × 3 bales/acre 300 bales	Cotton	25 acres × 6 bales/acre 150 bales	100 acres × 3 bales/acre 300 bales

	STAGE 3	
	New Zealand	Australia
Wheat	100 bushels (trade) ——→ 350 bushels 100 bushels (after trade)	
Cotton	200 bales (trade) ←—— 350 bales 100 bales (after trade)	

FIGURE 21.3

Comparative Advantage Means Lower Opportunity Cost

The real cost of cotton is the wheat that must be sacrificed to obtain it. The cost of three bales of cotton in New Zealand is three bushels of wheat (one-half acre of land must be transferred from wheat to cotton—refer to Table 21.5). But the cost of three bales of cotton in Australia is only one bushel of wheat (one acre of land must be transferred). Thus, Australia has a comparative advantage over New Zealand in the production of cotton, and New Zealand has a comparative advantage over Australia in wheat production.

Opportunity "cost" of wheat

	Bales of cotton given up		Bushels of wheat gained
New Zealand	1	→	1
Australia	3	→	1

New Zealand has a comparative advantage in wheat production

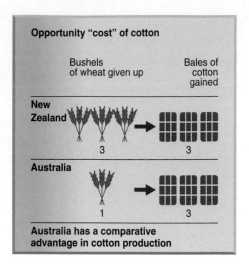

Opportunity "cost" of cotton

	Bushels of wheat given up		Bales of cotton gained
New Zealand	3	→	3
Australia	1	→	3

Australia has a comparative advantage in cotton production

TERMS OF TRADE

Ricardo might suggest a number of options open to the trading partners. The one we just examined benefited both partners; in percentage terms, Australia made out slightly better. Other deals might have been more advantageous to New Zealand.

terms of trade *The ratio at which a country can trade domestic products for imported products.*

The ratio at which a country can trade domestic products for imported products is called the **terms of trade.** The terms of the trade determine how the gains from trade are distributed among the trading partners. In the case we just considered, the agreed-upon terms of trade were one bushel of wheat for two bales of cotton. Such terms of trade benefit New Zealand, which can now get two bales of cotton for each bushel of wheat. If it were to transfer its own land from wheat to cotton, it would get only one. The same terms of trade benefit Australia, which can now get one bushel of wheat for two bales of cotton. A direct transfer of its own land would force it to give up three bales of cotton for one bushel of wheat.

If the terms of trade changed to three bales of cotton for every bushel of wheat, only New Zealand would benefit. In fact, at those terms of trade *all* the gains from trade would flow to New Zealand. Such terms do not benefit Australia at all because the opportunity cost of producing wheat domestically is *exactly the same* as the trade cost: One bushel of wheat costs three bales of cotton. If the terms of trade went the other way—one bale of cotton for each bushel of wheat—only Australia would benefit. New Zealand gains nothing, because it can already substitute cotton for wheat at that ratio. To get a bushel of wheat domestically, however, Australia must give up three bales of cotton, and one-for-one terms of trade would make wheat much less costly for Australia.

Clearly, both parties must have something to gain for trade to take place. In this case, you can see that both Australia and New Zealand will gain when the terms of trade are set between 1:1 and 3:1, cotton to wheat.

EXCHANGE RATES

The examples we have used thus far have shown that trade can result in gains to both parties. We have not yet discussed, however, how trade actually comes about.

> When trade is free (that is, unimpeded by government-instituted barriers), patterns of trade and trade flows result from the independent decisions of thousands of importers and exporters and millions of private households and firms.

Private households decide whether to buy Toyotas or Chevrolets, and private firms decide whether to buy machine tools made in the United States or machine tools made in Taiwan, raw steel produced in Germany or raw steel produced in Pittsburgh.

Before a citizen of one country can buy a product made in, or sold by, someone in another country, a currency swap must take place. Consider Shane, who buys a Volkswagen from a dealer in Boston. He pays in dollars, but the German workers who made the car receive their salaries in deutsche marks. Somewhere between the buyer of the car and the producer, a currency exchange must be made. The regional distributor probably takes payment in dollars and converts them into marks before remitting the proceeds back to Germany.

To buy a foreign-produced good, then, I in effect have to buy foreign currency. The price of Shane's Volkswagen in dollars depends on both the price of the car stated in deutsche marks and the price of deutsche marks. You probably know the ins and outs of currency exchange very well if you have ever traveled in another country. In March of 1995, a dollar exchanged for 4.9 French francs, making each franc worth $0.204. Now suppose that you are in France, and you see a nice bottle of Bordeaux wine for 120 francs. How can you figure out whether you want to buy it? You know what dollars will buy you in the United States, so you have to convert the price into dollars. Since each franc will cost you $0.204, 120 francs is worth $120 \times .204$, or $24.49.

The relative attractiveness of foreign goods to U.S. buyers, and of U.S. goods to foreign buyers, depends in part on **exchange rates,** the ratio at which two currencies are traded for each other. If the rate at which dollars could be converted into francs suddenly jumped to 10 francs for every dollar, that same bottle of wine would cost only $12.

Thus, to understand the patterns of trade that result from the actions of hundreds of thousands of independent buyers and sellers—households and firms—we must know something about the factors that determine exchange rates. Exchange rate determination is very complicated. Here, however, we can demonstrate two things:

exchange rate The ratio at which two currencies are traded for each other. The price of one currency in terms of another.

> First, for any pair of countries, there is a range of exchange rates that can lead automatically to both countries realizing the gains from specialization and comparative advantage. Second, within that range, the exchange rate will determine which country gains the most from trade. In short, exchange rates determine the terms of trade.

■ **Trade and Exchange Rates in a Two-Country/Two-Good World** Consider first a simple two-country/two-good model. Suppose that both the United States and Germany produce only two goods—raw timber and rolled steel. Table 21.8 gives the current prices of both goods as domestic buyers see them. In Germany timber is priced at three deutsche marks (DM) per foot, and steel is priced at four DM per meter. In the United States, timber costs $1 per foot and steel costs $2 per meter.

Now suppose that U.S. and German buyers have the option of buying at home or importing to meet their needs. The options they ultimately choose will depend

TABLE 21.8

DOMESTIC PRICES OF TIMBER (PER FOOT) AND ROLLED STEEL (PER METER) IN THE UNITED STATES AND GERMANY

	UNITED STATES	GERMANY
Timber	$1	3 DM
Rolled steel	$2	4 DM

on the exchange rate. For the time being, we will ignore transportation costs between countries and assume that German and U.S. products are of equal quality.

Let us start with the assumption that the exchange rate is $1 = 1 DM. From the standpoint of U.S. buyers, neither German steel nor German timber is competitive at this exchange rate. A dollar buys a foot of timber in the United States, but if converted into a mark, it will buy only one third of a foot. The price of German timber to an American is $3 because it will take $3 to buy the necessary three DM. Similarly, $2 buys a meter of rolled steel in the United States, but the same $2 buys only half a meter of German steel. The price of German steel to an American is $4, twice the price of domestically produced steel.

At this exchange rate, however, Germans find that U.S.-produced steel and timber are both less expensive than steel and timber produced in Germany. Timber at home costs three DM, but three DM buys $3, which buys three times as much timber in the United States. Similarly, steel costs four DM at home, but four DM buys $4, which buys twice as much U.S.-made steel. Thus, at an exchange rate of $1 = 1 DM, Germany will import steel and timber and the United States will import nothing.

But now suppose that the exchange rate is 1 DM = $0.25. We could thus say that the "price" of a DM is $0.25. This means that a dollar buys four DM. At this exchange rate, the Germans buy timber and steel at home and the Americans import both goods. At this exchange rate, Americans must pay a dollar for a foot of U.S. timber, but the same amount of timber can be had in Germany for the equivalent of $0.75. (Since one DM costs $0.25, three DM can be purchased for $0.75.) Similarly, steel that costs $2 per meter in the United States costs an American half as much in Germany, because $2 buys eight DM, which buys two meters of German steel. At the same time, Germans are not interested in importing, because both goods are cheaper when purchased from a German producer. In this case, the United States imports both goods and Germany imports nothing.

So far, we can see that at exchange rates of $1 = 1 DM and $1 = 4 DM we get trade flowing in only one direction. Let us now try an exchange rate of $1 = 2 DM, or 1 DM = $0.50. First, notice that Germans will buy timber in the United States. German timber costs three DM per foot, but three DM buys $1.50, which is enough to buy one and one half feet of U.S. timber. Buyers in the United States will find German timber too expensive, but Germany will import timber from the United States. At this same exchange rate, however, both German and U.S. buyers will be indifferent between German and U.S. steel. To U.S. buyers, domestically produced steel costs $2. Since $2 buys four DM, a meter of imported German steel also costs $2. German buyers also find that steel costs four DM, whether domestically produced or imported. Thus, there is likely to be no trade in steel.

But what happens if the exchange rate rises so that $1 buys 2.1 DM instead of just two? While U.S. timber is still cheaper to both Germans and Americans, German steel begins to look good to U.S. buyers. Steel produced in the United States costs $2 per meter, but $2 buys 4.2 DM, which buys more than a meter of steel in Germany. Thus, when the exchange rate rises above $1 = 2 DM, trade begins to flow in both directions: Germany will import timber and the United States will import steel.

If you examine Table 21.9 carefully, you will see that in fact trade flows in both directions as long as the exchange rate settles between $1 = 2 DM and $1 = 3 DM. Stated the other way around, trade will flow in both directions if the price of a DM is between $0.33 and $0.50.

■ **Exchange Rates and Comparative Advantage** Let us continue our example. If the foreign exchange market drives the exchange rate to anywhere between two and three DM per dollar, the countries will automatically adjust and comparative advantage will be realized. At these exchange rates, U.S. buyers begin buying all their

TABLE 21.9   TRADE FLOWS DETERMINED BY EXCHANGE RATES

EXCHANGE RATE	PRICE OF DM	RESULT
$1 = 1 DM	$ 1.00	Germany imports timber and steel.
$1 = 2 DM	$.50	Germany imports timber.
$1 = 2.1 DM	$.48	Germany imports timber; United States imports steel.
$1 = 2.9 DM	$.34	Germany imports timber; United States imports steel.
$1 = 3 DM	$.33	United States imports steel.
$1 = 4 DM	$.25	United States imports timber and steel.

steel in Germany. The U.S. steel industry finds itself in trouble. Plants close, and U.S. workers begin to lobby for tariff protection against German steel. At the same time, the U.S. timber industry does well, fueled by strong export demand from Germany. Thus, the timber-producing sector expands. Resources, including capital and labor, are attracted into timber production.

The opposite occurs in Germany. The German timber industry suffers losses as export demand dries up and Germans turn to cheaper U.S. imports. In Germany, lumber companies turn to the government and ask for protection from cheap U.S. timber. But steel producers in Germany are happy. Not only are they supplying 100% of the domestically demanded steel, but they are selling to U.S. buyers as well. Thus, the steel industry expands, and the timber industry contracts. Resources, including labor, flow into steel.

With this expansion-and-contraction scenario in mind, let us look again at our original definition of comparative advantage. If we assume that prices reflect resource use and that resources can be transferred from sector to sector, we can calculate the opportunity cost of steel/timber in both countries. In the United States, the production of a meter of rolled steel consumes twice the resources that the production of a foot of timber consumes. Assuming that resources can be transferred, the opportunity cost of a meter of steel is two feet of timber. (Refer again to Table 21.8.) In Germany, however, a meter of steel uses resources costing four DM, while a unit of timber costs three DM. Thus, to produce a meter of steel means the sacrifice of only four thirds, or one and one third, feet of timber. Because the opportunity cost of a meter of steel (in terms of timber) is lower in Germany, we say that Germany has a comparative advantage in steel production.

Conversely, consider the opportunity cost of timber in the two countries. Increasing timber production in the United States requires the sacrifice of half a meter of steel for every foot of timber—producing a meter of steel uses $2 worth of resources, while producing a foot of timber requires only $1 worth of resources. But each foot of timber production in Germany requires the sacrifice of three fourths of a meter of steel. Because the opportunity cost of timber is lower in the United States, the United States has a comparative advantage in the production of timber.

In short:

If exchange rates end up in the right ranges, the free market will drive each country to shift resources into those sectors in which it enjoys a comparative advantage. Only those products in which a country has a comparative advantage will be competitive in world markets.

THE SOURCES OF COMPARATIVE ADVANTAGE

You have now seen that specialization and trade can benefit all trading partners, even those that may be inefficient producers in an absolute sense. If markets are competitive, and if foreign exchange markets are linked to goods-and-services exchange, countries will specialize in producing those products in which they have a comparative advantage.

So far, however, we have said nothing about the sources of comparative advantage. What determines whether a country has a comparative advantage in heavy manufacturing or in agriculture? What explains the actual trade flows observed around the world? Various theories and empirical work on international trade have provided a number of partial answers to these questions. Most economists look to **factor endowments**—that is, to the quantity and quality of labor, land, and natural resources—as the principal sources of comparative advantage. Factor endowments seem to explain a significant portion of actual world trade patterns.

factor endowments *The quantity and quality of labor, land, and natural resources of a country.*

THE HECKSCHER-OHLIN THEOREM

Eli Heckscher and Bertil Ohlin, two Swedish economists who wrote in the first half of this century, expanded and elaborated on Ricardo's theory of comparative advantage. The **Heckscher-Ohlin theorem** ties the theory of comparative advantage to factor endowments. It assumes that products can be produced using differing proportions of inputs and that inputs are mobile between sectors in each economy, but that factors are not mobile *between* economies. According to the Heckscher-Ohlin theorem:

Heckscher-Ohlin theorem *A theory that explains the existence of a country's comparative advantage by its factor endowments: A country has a comparative advantage in the production of a product if that country is relatively well endowed with inputs used intensively in the production of that product.*

> A country has a comparative advantage in the production of a product if that country is relatively well endowed with inputs used intensively in the production of that product.

This idea is quite simple. A country with a lot of good fertile land is likely to have a comparative advantage in agriculture. A country with a large amount of accumulated capital is likely to have a comparative advantage in heavy manufacturing. A country with a lot of human capital is likely to have a comparative advantage in highly technical goods.

After an extensive study, Edward Leamer of UCLA has concluded that a relatively short list of factors accounts for a surprisingly large portion of world trade patterns. Natural resources, knowledge capital, physical capital, land, and skilled and unskilled labor, Leamer believes, explain "a large amount of the variability of net exports across countries."[1]

OTHER EXPLANATIONS FOR OBSERVED TRADE FLOWS

Comparative advantage is not the only reason that countries trade, of course. It does not explain why many countries both import and export the same kinds of goods. The United States, for example, both exports and imports automobiles.

Another explanation for international trade is that just as industries within a country differentiate their products to capture a domestic market, so too do they differentiate their products to please the wide variety of tastes that exists worldwide. The Japanese automobile industry, for example, began producing small, fuel-efficient cars long before U.S. automobile makers did. In doing so, they developed

---

[1]*Edward E. Leamer*, Sources of International Comparative Advantage: Theory and Evidence *(Cambridge, Mass: MIT Press, 1984), p. 187.*

expertise in creating products that attracted a devoted following and that elicited considerable brand loyalty. BMWs, made only in Germany, and Volvos, made only in Sweden, also have their champions in many countries. Just as product differentiation is a natural response to diverse preferences within an economy, it is also a natural response to diverse preferences across economies.

This idea is not inconsistent with the theory of comparative advantage. If the Japanese have developed skills and knowledge that gave them an edge in the production of fuel-efficient cars, that knowledge can be thought of as a very specific kind of capital not currently available to other producers. The Volvo company invested in a form of intangible capital that we call *goodwill*. That goodwill, which may come from establishing a reputation for safety and quality over the years, is one source of the comparative advantage that keeps Volvos selling on the international market. Some economists distinguish between gains from *acquired comparative advantages* and those acquired from *natural comparative advantages*.

Another explanation for international trade holds that some economies of scale may be available when producing for a world market that would not be available when producing only for a more limited domestic market. But because the evidence suggests that economies of scale are exhausted at relatively small size in most industries, it seems unlikely that they constitute a valid explanation of world trade patterns.

TRADE BARRIERS: TARIFFS, EXPORT SUBSIDIES, AND QUOTAS

Trade barriers—also called *obstacles to trade*—take many forms, the three most common of which are tariffs, export subsidies, and quotas. All of these are forms of **protection** through which some sector of the economy is shielded from foreign competition.

A **tariff** is a tax on imports. The average tariff on imports into the United States is now about 5%, although certain protected items have much higher tariffs. For example, the tariff rate on concentrated orange juice is a flat $0.35 per gallon. On rubber footwear, the tariff ranges from 20% to 48%, and on canned tuna it is 35 percent.

Export subsidies—government payments made to domestic firms to encourage exports—can also act as a barrier to trade. One of the provisions of the Corn Laws that stimulated Ricardo's musings in the nineteenth century was an export subsidy that was automatically paid to farmers by the British government when the price of grain fell below a specified level. The subsidy served to keep domestic prices high, but it flooded the world market with cheap subsidized grain. Foreign farmers who were not subsidized were driven out of the international marketplace by the artificially low prices.

Farm subsidies remain very much a part of the international trade landscape today. Many countries, especially those in Europe, continue to appease their farmers by heavily subsidizing exports of agricultural products. In fact, the political power of the farm lobby in many countries has had an important effect on recent international trade negotiations aimed at reducing trade barriers.

Closely related to subsidies is the practice of **dumping**. Dumping takes place when a firm or an industry sells products on the world market at prices *below* the cost of production. The charge has been levied against several specific Japanese industries, including automobiles, consumer electronics, and silicon computer chips.

Generally, a company dumps when it wants to dominate a world market. After the lower prices of the dumped goods have succeeded in driving out all the competition, the dumping company can exploit its position by raising the price of its

protection *The practice of shielding a sector of the economy from foreign competition.*

tariff *A tax on imports.*

export subsidies *Government payments made to domestic firms to encourage exports.*

dumping *Takes place when a firm or industry sells products on the world market at prices below the cost of production.*

product. Such practices, if committed by a U.S. firm in an attempt to monopolize a domestic market, are in violation of the Sherman Antitrust Act of 1890, which prohibits predatory pricing.

The current U.S. tariff laws contain several provisions aimed at counteracting the effects of dumping. The 1974 Trade Act contains a clause that qualifies an industry for protection if it has been "injured" by foreign competition. Building on that legislation, more recent trade bills, including the Comprehensive Trade Act of 1988, contain clauses that permit the President to impose trade sanctions when investigations reveal dumping by foreign companies or countries.

quota *A limit on the quantity of imports.*

A **quota** is a limit on the quantity of imports. Quotas can be mandatory or voluntary, and they may be legislated or negotiated with foreign governments. The best-known voluntary quota, or "voluntary restraint," was negotiated with the Japanese government in 1981. Japan agreed to reduce the number of automobiles it exported to the United States by 7.7%, from the 1980 level of 1.82 million units to 1.68 million units. In 1985, when President Reagan decided not to ask Japan to continue its restraints, auto imports jumped to 2.3 million units, nearly 20% of the U.S. market. Quotas currently apply to products as diverse as mushrooms, heavy motorcycles, and color television sets.

■ **U.S. Trade Policies and GATT** The United States has traditionally been a high-tariff nation, with average tariffs of over 50% for much of its history. The highest tariffs were in effect during the Great Depression following enactment of the **Smoot-Hawley tariff,** which pushed the average tariff rate to 60% in 1930. The Smoot-Hawley tariff set off an international trade war when the United States' trading partners retaliated with tariffs of their own. Many economists point to the decline in trade that followed as one of the causes of the worldwide depression of the 1930s.[2]

Smoot-Hawley tariff *The U.S. tariff law of the 1930s, which set the highest tariffs in U.S. history (60 percent). It set off an international trade war and caused the decline in trade that is often considered a cause of the worldwide depression of the 1930s.*

General Agreement on Tariffs and Trade (GATT) *An international agreement signed by the United States and 22 other countries in 1947 to promote the liberalization of foreign trade.*

In 1947 the United States, along with 22 other nations, agreed to reduce barriers to trade. It also established an organization to promote liberalization of foreign trade. This **General Agreement on Tariffs and Trade (GATT),** first considered an interim arrangement, continues in effect today and has been quite effective. The most recent round of world trade talks sponsored by the GATT, the "Uruguay Round," began in Uruguay in 1986. It was initialed by 116 countries on December 15, 1993, and was formally approved by the U.S. Congress after much debate just after the election in 1994. The "Final Act" of the Uruguay Round of negotiations is the most comprehensive and complex multilateral trade agreement in history. For more information, see the Global Perspective box titled "A New World Trade Agreement: GATT and the Final Act."

Every president who has held office since the first round of the General Agreement was signed has argued for free-trade policies, yet each one used his powers to protect one sector or another. Eisenhower and Kennedy restricted Japanese exports of textiles; Johnson restricted meat imports; Nixon restrained imports of steel and tightened restrictions on textiles; Carter protected steel, textiles, and footwear; Reagan restricted imports of sugar and automobiles. Both Bush and Clinton imposed new tariffs as well.

Despite these cases, however, the general movement in the United States has been away from tariffs and quotas and toward freer trade. The Reciprocal Trade Agreements Act of 1934 authorized the President to negotiate trade agreements on behalf of the United States. As part of trade negotiations, the President can confer

---

[2]*See especially Charles Kindleberger,* The World in Depression 1929–1939 *(London: Allen Lane, 1973).*

Launched in Punta del Este, Uruguay, in 1986, the Uruguay Round of multinational trade negotiations was concluded in Geneva on December 15, 1993, when 116 nations initialed what was called the "Final Act." In December 1994, a lame-duck U.S. Congress acted to approve the agreement for the United States.

The Final Act is a document of over 26,000 pages. It is the most comprehensive and complex trade agreement in history, and proponents argue that its implementation will increase the volume of world merchandise trade by 9 to 24% over what it would have been without the agreement.*

What are the provisions of the Final Act? First and foremost, it reduces tariffs and protection for agricultural products. Throughout history, agricultural goods have been the target of high import duties, large domestic subsidies, and outright trade restrictions. In many cases this was due to the farmers' political power. Talk of reducing subsidies going to agriculture in France led, on several occasions in the last decade, to highway blockades and violent demonstrations by French farmers. The agreement calls for an end to many agricultural subsidies, an end to nontariff barriers, such as quantitative restrictions and bans, and an average tariff reduction of 37% on agricultural imports. In general, developed countries have agreed to reduce tariffs on 64% of their imports by about 40%, from an average rate of 6.3% to 3.8 percent. The percentage of industrial imports allowed to enter the developed countries with no duties at all will increase from 20% to 44 percent. The developing countries have agreed to lower tariffs on about 33% of their imports.

Second, the Uruguay round is the first multilateral negotiation to reach

GATT, WHILE POPULAR WITH MANY ECONOMISTS, HAS MET WITH STRONG RESISTANCE IN MANY SECTORS. HERE, FRENCH FARMERS PROTEST FRANCE'S PARTICIPATION IN THE AGREEMENT, WHICH THEY BELIEVE WILL LEAD TO THE "DEATH OF AGRICULTURE."

a comprehensive agreement on international trade in services. It outlaws restrictions on the import of services such as banking, legal services, insurance, accounting, and computer consulting.

Third, the Final Act makes provisions for the protection of intellectual property. While existing patent and copyright laws usually protect artists, designers, computer software producers, authors, and the like from "theft" within their own countries, foreign pirating is commonplace. That is, while it is usually illegal to reproduce and sell pirated CDs, videotapes, books, and computer software packages produced within a country, there were no internationally applicable rules about

pirating across borders before the new agreement was signed. The new trade agreement requires all signatory countries to apply copyright and patent laws equally to foreign owners of intellectual property.

In addition, the Final Act established a Dispute Settlement Body designed to ensure compliance and to resolve conflicts between member countries. Some members of the U.S. Congress argued (in vain) that by signing the treaty the United States would be giving up its sovereignty to an international body.

*Source: See Norman S. Fieleke, "The Uruguay Round of Trade Negotiations: An Overview,: New England Economic Review, May–June 1995.

most-favored-nation status on individual trading partners. Exports from countries with most-favored-nation status are taxed at the lowest negotiated tariff rates. In addition, in recent years several successful rounds of tariff-reduction negotiations have reduced trade barriers to their lowest levels ever.

economic integration *Occurs when two or more nations join to form a free-trade zone.*

European Union (EU) *The European trading bloc composed of Austria, Belgium, Denmark, Finland, France, Germany, Greece, Ireland, Italy, Luxembourg, the Netherlands, Portugal, Spain, Sweden, and the United Kingdom.*

U.S.-Canadian Free-Trade Agreement *An agreement in which the United States and Canada agreed to eliminate all barriers to trade between the two countries by 1998.*

North American Free-Trade Agreement (NAFTA) *An agreement signed by the United States, Mexico, and Canada in which the three countries agreed to establish all of North America as a free-trade zone.*

■ **Economic Integration** **Economic integration** occurs when two or more nations join to form a free-trade zone. In 1991, the European Community (EC, or the Common Market) began the process of forming the largest free-trade zone in the world. The economic integration process began in December of that year, when the 12 original members (the United Kingdom, Belgium, France, Germany, Italy, the Netherlands, Luxembourg, Denmark, Greece, Ireland, Spain, and Portugal) signed the Maastricht Treaty. The treaty called for the end of border controls, a common currency, an end to all tariffs, and the coordination of monetary and even political affairs. In 1995, Austria, Finland, and Sweden became members of this **European Union (EU),** as the EC is now called, bringing the number of member countries to 15.

On January 1, 1993, all tariffs and trade barriers were dropped among the member countries. Border checkpoints were closed in early 1995. Citizens can now travel among member countries without passports. The most difficult step will be the adoption of a common currency. The goal is to have it in place by 1999, but most think it will take longer. Many economists believe that the advantages of free trade within the bloc, a reunited Germany, and the ability to work well as a bloc will make the EU the most powerful player in the international marketplace in the coming decades.

The United States is not a part of the EU. However, in 1988 the United States (under President Reagan) and Canada (under Prime Minister Mulroney) signed the **U.S.-Canadian Free-Trade Agreement**, which will remove all barriers to trade, including tariffs and quotas, between the two countries by 1998.

In addition, during the last days of the Bush administration, the United States, Mexico, and Canada signed the **North American Free-Trade Agreement (NAFTA)**, in which the three countries agreed to establish all of North America as a free-trade zone. The North American free-trade area will include 360 million people and a total output of over $7 trillion—a larger output than that of the European Union. The agreement will eliminate all tariffs over a 10- to 15-year period and remove restrictions on most investments.

During the presidential campaign of 1992, NAFTA was a hot topic of debate. Both Bill Clinton and George Bush supported the agreement; Ross Perot opposed it. Not surprisingly, industrial labor unions that might be affected by increased imports from Mexico (like those in the automobile industry) opposed the agreement, while industries whose exports to Mexico might increase as a result of the agreement (for example, the machine tool industry) supported it. Another concern raised by many was that Mexican companies were not subject to the same environmental regulations as U.S. firms and that U.S. firms might move to Mexico for this reason.

NAFTA was ratified by the U.S. Congress in late 1993 and went into effect on the first day of 1994. The U.S. Department of Commerce has estimated that as a result of NAFTA trade between the United States and Mexico increased by nearly $16 billion in 1994. In addition, exports from the United States to Mexico outpaced imports from Mexico during 1994. In 1995, however, the agreement fell under the shadow of a dramatic collapse of the value of the peso. U.S. exports to Mexico dropped sharply, and the United States shifted from a trade surplus to a large trade deficit with Mexico.

FREE TRADE OR PROTECTION?

As we pointed out earlier in this chapter, one of the great economic debates of all time revolves around the free-trade-versus-protection controversy. The arguments in favor of each are summarized briefly in the following discussion.

THE CASE FOR FREE TRADE

In one sense, the theory of comparative advantage *is* the case for free trade. Trade has potential benefits for all nations. A good is not imported unless its net price to buyers is below that of the domestically produced alternative. When the Germans in our earlier example found U.S. timber less expensive than their own, they bought it, yet they continued to pay the same price for homemade steel. Americans bought less-expensive German steel, but they continued to buy domestic timber at the same lower price. Under these conditions, *both Americans and Germans ended up paying less and consuming more.*

At the same time, resources (including labor) move out of steel production and into timber production in the United States. In Germany, resources (including labor) move out of timber production and into steel production. Thus, the resources in both countries are more efficiently used. Tariffs, export subsidies, and quotas, which interfere with the free movement of goods and services around the world, reduce or eliminate the gains of comparative advantage.

We can use supply and demand curves to illustrate this point. Suppose that Figure 21.4a on page 498 shows domestic supply and demand for textiles. In the absence of trade, the market clears at price of $4.20. At equilibrium, 450 million yards of textiles are produced and consumed.

Assume now that textiles are available at a world price of $2. This is the price in dollars that Americans must pay for textiles from foreign sources. If we assume that an unlimited amount of textiles is available at $2 and that there is no difference in quality between domestic and foreign textiles, no domestic producer will be able to charge more than $2. In the absence of trade barriers, the world price sets the price in the United States. As the price in the United States falls from $4.20 to $2.00, the quantity demanded by consumers increases from 450 million yards to 700 million yards, but the quantity supplied by domestic producers drops from 450 million yards to 200 million yards. The difference, 500 million yards, is the quantity of textiles imported.

The argument for free trade holds that each country should specialize in producing the goods and services in which it enjoys a comparative advantage. Clearly, if foreign producers can produce textiles at a much lower price than domestic producers, they have a comparative advantage. As the world price of textiles falls to $2, domestic (U.S.) supply drops and resources are transferred to other sectors. These other sectors, which may be export industries or domestic industries, are not shown in Figure 21.4a. It is clear, however, that the allocation of resources is more efficient at a price of $2. Why should the United States use domestic resources to produce what foreign producers can produce at a lower cost? U.S. resources should move into the production of the things it produces best.

Now consider what happens to the domestic price of textiles when a trade barrier is imposed. Figure 21.4b shows the effect of a set tariff of $1 per yard imposed on imported textiles. The tariff raises the domestic price of textiles to $2 + $1 = $3. The result is that some of the gains from trade are lost. First, consumers are forced to pay a higher price for the same good; the quantity of textiles demanded

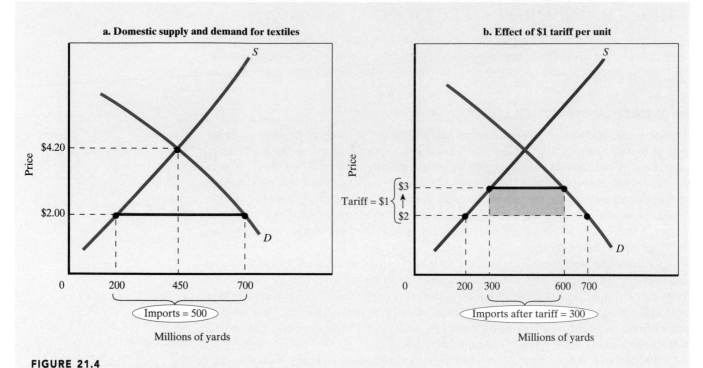

a. Domestic supply and demand for textiles

b. Effect of $1 tariff per unit

FIGURE 21.4

The Gains from Trade and Losses from the Imposition of a Tariff

A tariff of $1 increases the market price facing consumers from $2 per yard to $3 per yard. The government collects revenues equal to the gray shaded area. The loss of efficiency has two components. First, consumers must pay a higher price for goods that could be produced at lower cost. Second, marginal producers are drawn into textiles and away from other goods, resulting in inefficient domestic production.

drops from 700 million yards under free trade to 600 million yards because some consumers simply are not willing to pay the higher price.

At the same time, the higher price of textiles draws some marginal domestic producers who could not make a profit at $2 into textile production. (Remember, domestic producers do not pay a tariff.) As the price rises to $3, the quantity supplied by producers rises from 200 million yards to 300 million yards. The overall result is a decrease in imports from 500 million yards to 300 million yards.

Finally, the imposition of the tariff means that the government collects revenue equal to the shaded gray area in Figure 21.4b. This shaded area is simply equal to the tariff rate per unit, ($1), times the number of units that are imported after the tariff is in place (300 million yards). Thus, receipts from the tariff are $300 billion.

What is the final result of the tariff? The answer should be clear. Domestic producers that were receiving revenues of only $2 per unit before the tariff was imposed now receive a higher price and earn higher profits. But these higher profits are achieved at a loss of efficiency. All of this leads us to conclude that:

> Trade barriers prevent a nation from reaping the benefits of specialization, push it to adopt relatively inefficient production techniques, and force consumers to pay higher prices for protected products than they would otherwise pay.

THE CASE FOR PROTECTION

Arguments can also be made in favor of tariffs and quotas, of course. Over the course of U.S. history, these arguments have been made so many times by so many industries before so many congressional committees that it almost seems as if all pleas for protection share the same themes. The most frequently heard of these pleas are described below.

■ **Protection Saves Jobs** The main argument for protection is that foreign competition costs Americans their jobs. When Americans buy Toyotas, U.S. cars go unsold. This leads to layoffs in the domestic auto industry. When Americans buy Japanese or German steel, steelworkers in Pittsburgh lose their jobs. When Americans buy shoes or textiles from Korea or Taiwan, the millworkers in Maine and Massachusetts, as well as in South Carolina and Georgia, lose their jobs.

It is true that when we buy goods from foreign producers, domestic producers do suffer. But there is no reason to believe that the workers laid off in the contracting sectors will not be ultimately reemployed in other expanding sectors. Foreign competition in textiles, for example, has clearly meant the loss of U.S. jobs in that industry. Many thousands of textile workers in New England lost their jobs as the textile mills there closed down over the last 35 years. But with the tremendous expansion of high-tech industries, the unemployment rate in Massachusetts fell to one of the lowest in the country in the mid-1980s, and New Hampshire, Vermont, and Maine also boomed. By the 1990s, New England had suffered another severe downturn, due partly to the fact that high-technology hardware manufacturing had moved abroad. But in 1994 it became clear that small- to medium-sized companies in such newly developing areas as biotechnology and software were beginning to pick up steam just as hardware manufacturing had done a decade earlier.

The adjustment process is far from costless, however. The knowledge that some other industry, perhaps in some other part of the country, may be expanding is of little comfort to the person whose skills become obsolete or whose pension benefits are lost when his or her company abruptly closes a plant or goes bankrupt. The social and personal problems brought about by industry-specific unemployment, obsolete skills, and bankruptcy as a result of foreign competition are significant.

These problems can be addressed in two ways. We can ban imports and give up the gains from free trade, acknowledging that we are willing to pay premium prices to save domestic jobs in industries that can produce more efficiently abroad. Or we can aid the victims of free trade in a constructive way, helping to retrain them for jobs with a future. In some instances, programs to relocate people in expanding regions may be in order. Some programs deal directly with the transition without forgoing the gains from trade.

■ **Some Countries Engage in Unfair Trade Practices** Attempts by U.S. firms to monopolize an industry are illegal under the Sherman and Clayton acts. If a strong company decides to drive the competition out of the market by setting prices below cost, it would be aggressively prosecuted by the Antitrust Division of the Justice Department. But, the argument goes, if we won't allow a U.S. firm to engage in predatory pricing or monopolize an industry or market, can we stand by and let a German firm or a Japanese firm do so in the name of free trade? This is a legitimate argument and one that has gained significant favor in recent years. How should we respond when a large international company or a country behaves strategically against a domestic firm or industry? Free trade

PROTECTED BY THE GOVERNMENT, JAPAN'S POLITICALLY POWERFUL FARMERS TIE UP VERY VALUABLE LAND LIKE THESE FARMS. EFFICIENCY REQUIRES THAT LAND SHOULD BE ALLOCATED TO ITS MOST VALUABLE USE.

infant industry *A young industry which may need temporary protection from competition from the established industries of other countries in order to develop an acquired comparative advantage.*

may be the best solution when everybody plays by the rules, but sometimes we have to fight back.

■ **Cheap Foreign Labor Makes Competition Unfair**   Let us say that a particular country gained its "comparative advantage" in textiles by paying its workers low wages. How can U.S. automobile companies compete with companies that pay wages that are less than a quarter of what U.S. companies pay?

First, we need to remember that wages in a competitive economy reflect productivity. Workers in the United States earn higher wages because they are more productive. The United States has more capital per worker, and its workers are better trained. Second, trade flows not according to *absolute* advantage but according to *comparative* advantage: All countries benefit, even if one country is more efficient at producing everything.

■ **Protection Safeguards National Security**   Beyond simply saving jobs, certain sectors of the economy may appeal for protection for other reasons. The steel industry has argued for years with some success that it is vital to national defense. In the event of a war, the United States would not want to depend on foreign countries for products as vital as steel. Even if we acknowledge another country's comparative advantage, we may want to protect our own resources.

No industry has ever asked for protection without invoking the national defense argument. The testimony on behalf of the scissors and shears industry argued that "in the event of a national emergency and imports cutoff, the United States would be without a source of scissors and shears, basic tools for many industries and trades essential to our national defense." The question, then, lies not in the merit of the argument but in just how seriously it can be taken if *every* industry uses it.

■ **Protection Discourages Dependency**   Closely related to the national defense argument is the claim that countries, particularly small or developing countries, may come to rely too heavily on one or more trading partners for many items. If Lilliput comes to rely on a major power for food or energy or some important raw material in which the large nation has a comparative advantage, it may be difficult for the smaller nation to remain politically neutral. Some critics of free trade argue that the superpowers have consciously engaged in trade with smaller countries to create these kinds of dependencies.

Therefore, the argument goes, small independent countries should consciously avoid trading relationships that might lead to political dependence. This may involve developing domestic industries in areas where a country has a comparative disadvantage. To do so would mean protecting that industry from international competition.

■ **Protection Safeguards Infant Industries**   Young industries in a given country may have a difficult time competing with established industries in other countries. And in a dynamic world, a protected **infant industry** might mature into a strong one worldwide because of an acquired, but real, comparative advantage. If such an industry is undercut and driven out of world markets at the beginning of its life, that comparative advantage might never develop.

Yet efforts to protect infant industries can backfire. In July 1991, the U.S. government imposed a 62.67% tariff on imports of active-matrix liquid crystal display screens (also referred to as "flat-panel displays" and primarily used for laptop computers) from Japan. The Commerce Department and the International Trade Commission agreed that Japanese producers were selling their screens in the U.S. market at a price below cost and that this "dumping" threatened the survival of domestic laptop screen producers. The tariff was meant to protect the infant U.S. industry until it could compete head-on with the Japanese.

Unfortunately for U.S. producers of laptop computers and for consumers who purchase them, the tariff had an unintended (though predictable) effect on the industry. Because U.S. laptop screens were generally recognized to be of lower quality than their Japanese counterparts, imposition of the tariff left U.S. computer manufacturers with three options: (1) They could use the screens available from U.S. producers and watch sales of their final product decline in the face of *higher quality* competition from abroad; (2) they could pay the tariff for the higher quality screens and watch sales of their final product decline in the face of *lower priced* competition from abroad; or (3) they could do what was the most profitable for them to do—move their production facilities abroad in order to avoid the tariff completely. This is exactly what both Apple and IBM announced that they would do. In the end, not only were the laptop industry and its consumers hurt by the imposition of the tariff (due to higher costs of production and to higher laptop computer prices), but the U.S. screen industry was hurt as well (due to its loss of buyers for its product) by a policy specifically designed to help it.

■ **Protection Provides Protection During Temporary Currency Overvaluations** In 1983 and 1984, many people argued that the dollar was artificially strong—that is, that it bought more yen, DM, and francs than it should have. An overvalued dollar makes U.S. goods look undesirable to foreigners, who have to pay more to get dollars, and makes foreign goods look cheap to Americans.

When such a situation arises, whether artificially or normally but *temporarily*, protection might be required to help certain industries make it through the tough times. It is extremely difficult, however, to decide just what the "proper" exchange rate should be.

AN ECONOMIC CONSENSUS

You now know something about how international trade fits into the structure of the economy.

Critical to our study of international economics is the important debate between free-traders and protectionists. On one side is the theory of comparative advantage, formalized by David Ricardo in the early part of the nineteenth century. According to this view, all countries benefit from specialization and trade. The gains from trade are real, and they can be large; free international trade raises real incomes and improves the standard of living.

On the other side of the debate are the protectionists, who point to the loss of jobs and argue for the protection of workers from foreign competition. But although foreign competition can cause job loss in specific sectors, it is unlikely to cause net job loss in an economy, and workers will over time be absorbed into expanding sectors.

Foreign trade and full employment can be pursued simultaneously. Although economists disagree about many things, the vast majority of them favor free trade.

SUMMARY

1. All economies, regardless of their size, depend to some extent on other economies and are affected by events outside their borders.

THE INTERNATIONAL ECONOMY: TRADE SURPLUSES AND DEFICITS

2. Until the 1970s, the United States generally exported more than it imported—in other words, it ran a *trade surplus*. In the mid-1970s, the United States began to import more merchandise than it exported—a *trade deficit*.

THE ECONOMIC BASIS FOR TRADE: COMPARATIVE ADVANTAGE

3. The *theory of comparative advantage,* dating to the writings of David Ricardo in the nineteenth century, holds that specialization and free trade will benefit all trading partners, even those that may be absolutely less efficient producers.

4. A country enjoys an *absolute advantage* over another country in the production of a product if it uses fewer resources to produce that product than the other country does. A country has a *comparative advantage* in the production of a product if that product can be produced at a lower cost in terms of other goods.

5. Trade enables countries to move out beyond their previous resource and productivity constraints. When countries specialize in producing those goods in which they have a comparative advantage, they maximize their combined output and allocate their resources more efficiently.

6. When trade is free, patterns of trade and trade flows result from the independent decisions of thousands of importers and exporters and millions of private households and firms.

7. The relative attractiveness of foreign goods to U.S. buyers and of U.S. goods to foreign buyers depends in part on *exchange rates,* the ratios at which two currencies are traded for each other.

8. For any pair of countries, there is a range of exchange rates that will lead automatically to both countries realizing the gains from specialization and comparative advantage. Within that range, the exchange rate will determine which country gains the most from trade. This leads us to conclude that exchange rates determine the terms of trade.

9. If exchange rates end up in the right range (that is, in a range that facilitates the flow of goods between nations), the free market will drive each country to shift resources into those sectors in which it enjoys a comparative advantage. Only those products in which a country has a comparative advantage will be competitive in world markets.

THE SOURCES OF COMPARATIVE ADVANTAGE

10. The *Heckscher-Ohlin theorem* looks to relative *factor endowments* to explain comparative advantage and trade flows. According to the theorem, a country has a comparative advantage in the production of a product if that country is relatively well endowed with the inputs that are used intensively in the production of that product.

11. A relatively short list of inputs—natural resources, knowledge capital, physical capital, land, and skilled and unskilled labor—explains a surprisingly large portion of world trade patterns. But the simple version of the theory of comparative advantage cannot explain why many countries import and export the same goods.

12. Some theories argue that comparative advantage can be acquired. Just as industries within a country differentiate their products to capture a domestic market, so too do they differentiate their products to please the wide variety of tastes that exists worldwide. This theory is not inconsistent with the theory of comparative advantage.

TRADE BARRIERS: TARIFFS, EXPORT SUBSIDIES, AND QUOTAS

13. Trade barriers take many forms, the three most common of which are *tariffs, export subsidies,* and *quotas.* All of these are forms of *protection* through which some sector of the economy is shielded from foreign competition.

14. Although the United States has historically been a high-tariff nation, the general movement is now away from tariffs and quotas. *The General Agreement on Tariffs and Trade (GATT),* signed by the United States and 22 other countries in 1947, continues in effect today; its purpose is to reduce barriers to world trade and keep them down. Also important are the *U.S.-Canadian Free Trade Agreement,* signed in 1988, and the *North*

American Free-Trade Agreement, signed by the United States, Mexico, and Canada in the last days of the Bush administration, taking effect in 1994.

15. The *European Union (EU)* is a free-trade bloc composed of 15 nations: Austria, Belgium, Denmark, Finland, France, Germany, Greece, Ireland, Italy, Luxembourg, the Netherlands, Portugal, Spain, Sweden, and the United Kingdom. Many economists believe that the advantages of free trade within the bloc, a reunited Germany, and the ability to work well as a bloc will make the EU the most powerful player in the international marketplace in the coming decades.

FREE TRADE OR PROTECTION?

16. In one sense, the theory of comparative advantage is the case for free trade. Trade barriers prevent a nation from reaping the benefits of specialization, push it to adopt relatively inefficient production techniques, and force consumers to pay higher prices for protected products than they would otherwise pay.

17. The case for protection rests on a number of propositions, one of which is that foreign competition results in a loss of domestic jobs. But there is no reason to believe that the workers laid off in the contracting sectors will not be ultimately reemployed in other expanding sectors. This adjustment process is far from costless, however.

18. Other arguments for protection hold that cheap foreign labor makes competition unfair; that some countries engage in unfair trade practices; that it protects the national security and discourages dependency; and that it protects *infant industries.* Despite these arguments, however, most economists favor free trade.

REVIEW TERMS AND CONCEPTS

absolute advantage 482

comparative advantage 483

Corn Laws 482

dumping 493

economic integration 496

European Union (EU) 496

exchange rate 489

export subsidies 493

factor endowments 492

General Agreement on Tariffs and Trade (GATT) 494

Heckscher-Ohlin theorem 492

infant industry 500

North American Free-Trade Agreement 496

protection 493

quota 494

Smoot-Hawley tariff 494

tariff 493

terms of trade 488

theory of comparative advantage 482

trade deficit 481

trade surplus 481

U.S.-Canadian Free-Trade Agreement 496

PROBLEM SET

1. The United States imported $27.9 billion worth of "food feeds and beverages" in 1993 and exported $40.7 billion worth.
   a. Name some of the imported items that you are aware of in this category. Also name some of the exported items.
   b. The United States is said to have a comparative advantage in the production of agricultural goods. How would you go about testing this proposition? What data would you need?
   c. Are the numbers above consistent with the theory of comparative advantage? Suppose you had a more detailed breakdown of which items the United States imports and which it exports. What would you look for?

   d. What other theories of international trade might explain why the same goods are imported and exported?

2. The following table gives 1990 figures for yield per acre in Illinois and Kansas:

	WHEAT	SOYBEANS
Illinois	48	39
Kansas	40	24

Source: U.S. Dept. of Agriculture, *Crop Production,* 1992.

   a. If we assume that farmers in Illinois and Kansas use the same amount of labor, capital, and fertilizer, which state has an absolute advantage in wheat production? Soybean production?

b. If we transfer land out of wheat into soybeans, how many bushels of wheat do we give up in Illinois per additional bushel of soybeans produced? In Kansas?

c. Which state has a comparative advantage in wheat production? In soybean production?

The following table gives the distribution of land planted for each state in millions of acres in 1990:

	TOTAL ACRES UNDER TILL	WHEAT	SOYBEANS
Illinois	22.9	1.9 (8.3%)	9.1 (39.7%)
Kansas	20.7	11.8 (57.0%)	1.9 (9.2%)

Are these data consistent with your answer to part c? Explain.

3. The U.S. Congress ratified the North American Free-Trade Agreement (NAFTA) in September of 1993 by a very slim vote. The Agreement took effect on January 1, 1994. The same Congress ratified the Final Act of the Uruguay Round of the General Agreement on Tariffs and Trade (GATT) in December of 1994, and that Agreement took effect on January 1, 1995. Both were ratified over very strong political opposition from lobby groups. Using newspaper articles and periodicals at the time, write a short report about the opposition to each of these agreements. Who opposed them? Can you offer an explanation for their opposition? What logic did the Congress rely on to vote in favor?

4. You can think of the United States as a set of 50 separate economies with no trade barriers. In such an open environment, each state specializes in the products that it produces best.

a. What product or products does your state specialize in?

b. Can you identify the source of the comparative advantage that lies behind the production of one or more of these products (a natural resource, plentiful cheap labor, a skilled labor force, etc.)?

c. Do you think that the theory of comparative advantage and the Heckscher-Ohlin theorem help to explain why your state specializes in the way that it does?

5. Export subsidies have been proposed to prop up food prices and help struggling family farmers. Would you favor such subsidies?

6. Germany and France produce white and red wines. Current domestic prices for each are given in the following table:

	GERMANY	FRANCE
White wine	5 DM	10 francs
Red wine	10 DM	15 francs

Suppose that the exchange rate is 1 deutsche mark = 1 franc.

a. If the price ratios within each country reflect resource use, which country has a comparative advantage in the production of red wine? White wine?

b. Assume that there are no other trading partners and that the only motive for holding foreign currency is to buy foreign goods. Will the current exchange rate lead to trade flows in both directions between the two countries?

c. What adjustments might you expect in the exchange rate? Be specific.

d. What would you predict about trade flows between Germany and France in the long run?

7. The European Union (EU) is scheduled to remove all trade barriers within its member countries in the next 10 years. Its goal is to become one "common market" with one uniform currency. Explain the likely benefits and costs to the EU's member countries. Should the United States be concerned about the new common market? Why or why not?

OPEN-ECONOMY MACROECONOMICS: THE BALANCE OF PAYMENTS AND EXCHANGE RATES

WHEN WE BEGAN OUR DISCUSSION OF MACROECONOMICS, WE POINTED out that the economies of the world have become increasingly interdependent over the last two decades. No economy operates in a vacuum, and economic events in one country can have repercussions on the economies of other countries.

International trade is a major part of today's world economy. U.S. imports now account for over 12% of U.S. GDP, and billions of dollars flow through the international capital market each day. In the last chapter we explored the main reasons for the existence of international exchange. Countries trade with each other to obtain goods and services they cannot produce themselves or because other nations can produce goods and services at a lower cost than they can. You can see the various connections between the domestic economy and the rest of the world in Figure 6.2. Foreign countries supply goods and services, labor, and capital to the United States, and the United States supplies goods and services, labor, and capital to the rest of the world.

From a macroeconomic point of view, the main difference between an international transaction and a domestic transaction concerns currency exchange:

> When people in different countries buy from and sell to each other, an exchange of currencies must also take place.

French wine exporters, for example, cannot spend U.S. dollars in France—they need French francs. Nor can a U.S. wheat exporter use French francs to buy a tractor from a U.S. company or to pay the rent on her warehouse. Somehow, international exchange must be managed in a way that allows each partner in the transaction to wind up with his or her own currency.

exchange rate *The price of one country's currency in terms of another country's currency; the ratio at which two currencies are traded for each other.*

As you know from the previous chapter, the direction of trade between two countries depends on **exchange rates**—the price of one country's currency in terms of the other country's currency. If the German deutsche mark were very expensive, for example (thus making the dollar cheap), both Germans and Americans would buy from U.S. producers. If the deutsche mark were very cheap (thus making the U.S. dollar expensive), both Germans and Americans would buy from German producers. Within a certain range of exchange rates, trade flows in both directions, each country specializes in producing the goods in which it enjoys a comparative advantage, and trade is mutually beneficial.

Because exchange rates play such a major role in determining the flow of international trade, the way they are determined is very important. Since the turn of the century, the world monetary system has been changed on several occasions by international agreements and events. In the early part of the century, nearly all currencies were backed by gold. Their values were fixed in terms of a specific number of ounces of gold, which in turn determined their values in international trading (i.e., exchange rates).

In 1944, with the international monetary system in chaos as the end of World War II drew near, a large group of experts unofficially representing 44 countries met in Bretton Woods, New Hampshire, and drew up a number of agreements. One of these agreements established a system of essentially fixed exchange rates under which each country agreed to intervene in the foreign exchange market when necessary to maintain the agreed-upon value of its currency.

In 1971, most countries, including the United States, gave up trying to fix exchange rates formally and began allowing them to be determined essentially by supply and demand. For example, without government intervention in the marketplace, the price of British pounds in dollars is determined by the interaction of those who want to exchange dollars for pounds (those who "demand" pounds) and those who want to exchange pounds for dollars (those who "supply" pounds). If the quantity of pounds demanded exceeds the quantity of pounds supplied, the price of pounds will rise, just as the price of peanuts or paper clips would rise under similar circumstances. A more detailed discussion of the various monetary systems that have been in place since 1900 is found in the appendix to this chapter.

In this chapter, we explore what has come to be called "open-economy macroeconomics" in more detail. First, we discuss the *balance of payments*—that is, the record of a nation's transactions with the rest of the world. We then go on to consider how the analysis we presented in Chapters 9 through 18 changes when we allow for the international exchange of goods, services, and capital.

THE BALANCE OF PAYMENTS

We sometimes find it convenient to lump all foreign currencies—Swiss francs, Japanese yen, Brazilian cruzeiros, and so forth—together under the heading "foreign exchange." Specifically, **foreign exchange** is simply all currencies other than the domestic currency of a given country (in the case of the United States, the U.S. dollar). The United States' demand for foreign exchange arises because its citizens want to buy things whose prices are quoted in other currencies, such as Australian jewelry, vacations in France, and bonds or stocks issued by Sony Corporation of Japan. Whenever U.S. citizens make these purchases, Australians, French, and Japanese gain U.S. dollars, which, from their point of view, are foreign exchange.

But where does the *supply* of foreign exchange come from? The answer is simple: The United States (actually, U.S. citizens or firms) earns foreign exchange whenever it sells products, services, or assets to another country. Just as France earns foreign exchange when U.S. tourists go to visit the Eiffel Tower, the United States earns foreign exchange (in this case, French francs) when French tourists come to the United States to visit the Statue of Liberty. Similarly, Saudi Arabian purchases of stock in General Motors or Colombian purchases of real estate in Miami increase the U.S. supply of foreign exchange.

The record of a country's transactions in goods, services, and assets with the rest of the world is known as its **balance of payments.** The balance of payments is also the record of a country's sources (supply) and uses (demand) of foreign exchange.

Balance-of-payments accounting is quite straightforward if you remember the following simple rule:[1]

> Any transaction that brings in foreign exchange for a country is a credit (positive) item in that country's balance of payments; any transaction that causes a country to lose foreign exchange is a debit (negative) item.

Also keep in mind that the balance of payments is a record of all the ways a country earns foreign exchange and all the uses to which that foreign exchange is put.[2]

THE CURRENT ACCOUNT

The balance of payments is typically divided up into two major accounts, the *current account* and the *capital account,* and a number of subaccounts. These are shown in Table 22.1 on page 508, which provides data on the U.S. balance of payments for 1994. The balance of payments is subdivided in this manner because different kinds of transactions have different motivations, or causes, and imply different things for the functioning of the U.S. economy.

Consider first the current account. The first item in this account is U.S. trade in merchandise. This category includes exports of computer chips, potato chips, and Sting records and imports of Scotch whiskey, Japanese calculators, and Mexican oil. U.S. merchandise exports *earn* foreign exchange for the United States and are thus a credit (+) item on the balance of payments. U.S. merchandise imports *use up* foreign exchange (it must surrender some of its holdings of foreign currencies to purchase foreign-produced goods and services) and are thus debit (–) items. The difference between a country's merchandise exports and its merchandise imports is its

foreign exchange *All currencies other than the domestic currency of a given country.*

balance of payments *The record of a country's transactions in goods, services, and assets with the rest of the world; also the record of a country's sources (supply) and uses (demand) of foreign exchange.*

---

[1]*Bear in mind the distinction between the balance of payments and a balance sheet. A balance sheet for a firm or a country measures that entity's stock of assets and liabilities at a moment in time. The* balance of payments, *by contrast, measures* flows, *usually over a period of a month, a quarter, or a year. Despite its name, the balance of payments is* not *a balance sheet.*
[2]*As we shall see later, one of these uses is to add to existing stocks of foreign exchange. Thus, total uses of foreign exchange completely account for every unit of foreign exchange that is earned.*

TABLE 22.1	UNITED STATES BALANCE OF PAYMENTS, 1994

ALL TRANSACTIONS THAT BRING FOREIGN EXCHANGE INTO THE UNITED STATES ARE CREDITED (+) TO THE BALANCE OF PAYMENTS; ALL TRANSACTIONS THAT CAUSE THE UNITED STATES TO LOSE FOREIGN EXCHANGE ARE DEBITED (−) TO THE BALANCE OF PAYMENTS.

CURRENT ACCOUNT	
Merchandise exports	502.7
Merchandise imports	⁻669.1
(1) Balance of trade	⁻166.4
Exports of services	195.3
Imports of services	⁻135.3
(2) Net export of services	60.0
Income received on investments	134.9
Income payments on investments	⁻150.1
(3) Net investment income	⁻15.2
(4) Net transfer payments and other	⁻34.1
(5) Balance on current account (1 + 2 + 3 + 4)	⁻155.7
CAPITAL ACCOUNT	
(6) Change in private U.S. assets abroad (increase is −)	⁻130.8
(7) Change in foreign private assets in the United States	275.7
(8) Change in U.S. government assets abroad (increase is −)	5.1
(9) Change in foreign government assets in the United States	38.9
(10) Balance on capital account (6 + 7 + 8 + 9)	188.9
(11) Statistical discrepancy	⁻33.2
(12) Balance of Payments (5 + 10 + 11)	0

Source: U.S. Department of Commerce, *Survey of Current Business,* March 1995.

balance of trade *A country's merchandise exports minus its merchandise imports. Also called the* merchandise trade balance.

merchandise trade balance, more commonly called the **balance of trade.** If exports of goods are less than imports, as was the case in 1994 in the United States, the balance of trade is negative.

The second item in the current account concerns services. Like most other countries, the United States buys services from and sells services to other countries. For example, a U.S. firm shipping wheat to England might purchase insurance from a British insurance company. A Dutch flower grower may fly her flowers to the United States aboard an American airliner. In the first case, the United States is importing services and therefore using up foreign exchange; in the second, it is selling services to foreigners and earning foreign exchange. In 1994, the United States exported $60.0 billion more in services than it imported. If exports of goods and services are less than imports of goods and services, a country is said to run a **trade deficit.**

trade deficit *Occurs when a country's exports of goods and services are less than its imports of goods and services in a given period.*

The third item in the current account concerns *investment income*. U.S. citizens hold foreign assets (stocks, bonds, and real assets like buildings and factories). Dividends, interest, rent, and profits paid to U.S. asset holders are a source of foreign exchange. Conversely, when foreigners earn dividends, interest, and profits on assets held in the United States, foreign exchange is used up. In 1994, investment income paid to foreigners exceeded investment income received by the United States by $15.2 billion.

The fourth item in Table 22.1 is *net transfer payments and other*. Transfer payments from the United States to foreigners are another use of foreign exchange. Some of these transfer payments are from private U.S. citizens and some are from the U.S. government. You may send a gift to your aunt in Spain or the government may send a social security check to a retiree living in Italy. Conversely, some foreigners make transfer payments to the United States. "Net" refers to the difference between payments from the United States to foreigners and payments from foreigners to the United States. If we add the balance of trade, net export of services, net investment income, and net transfer payments and other,[3] we get the **balance on current account.**

The balance on current account is important because it shows how much a nation has spent on foreign goods, services, and transfers relative to how much it has earned from other countries. When the balance is negative, which it was for the United States in 1994, a nation has spent more on foreign products (plus investment income and transfers paid) than it has earned through the sales of its goods and services to the rest of the world (plus investment income and transfers received). If a nation has spent more on foreign goods and services than it has earned, its net asset position vis-à-vis the rest of the world must decrease. By "net" we mean a nation's assets abroad minus its liabilities to the rest of the world. A country's liabilities to the rest of the world are assets of foreigners. (A Japanese-owned building in Manhattan, for example, is a foreign liability of the United States and an asset of Japan.) A nation settles its accounts with the rest of the world through its capital account.

THE CAPITAL ACCOUNT

The second major account in a nation's balance of payments, the capital account, records the nation's capital inflows and outflows.

Governments and citizens around the world exchange physical assets (such as office buildings) and paper assets (such as stocks and bonds) across international boundaries. When a U.S. citizen buys a Canadian bond or a U.S. firm purchases an office tower in France, for example, foreign exchange is used up. Domestic banks also make loans to foreign countries. For instance, several New York banks made huge loans to developing countries during the 1970s. When a U.S. bank makes a loan to the Mexican National Oil Company or to a steel company in Korea, the bank receives an IOU in exchange. Thus a loan made to Mexico (or any other country) is a *use* of foreign exchange also. If U.S. citizens and banks increase their holdings of private assets abroad, the figure recorded in the capital account is negative (a debit). In 1994, U.S. citizens increased their private holdings abroad by $130.8 billion. (See item 6 in Table 22.1.)

Foreign purchases of domestic assets earn foreign exchange for a country. When a Japanese company bought Rockefeller Center in New York in 1990, for example, the transaction earned foreign exchange for the United States. Thus, when foreign citizens increase their holdings of private assets, the transactions are recorded in the capital account as positive figures (credits). As item 7 in Table 22.1 shows, foreign private investment in the United States increased by $275.7 billion in 1994.

Finally, governments hold foreign assets as well. Specifically, central banks, like the Federal Reserve in the United States and the Bundesbank in Germany, keep assets on hand that can be used to settle international obligations. An increase in the U.S. Federal Reserve Bank's holdings of German marks is considered an increase in U.S. government assets abroad (item 8 in Table 22.1). In 1994, the U.S. government

balance on current account
The balance of trade plus net exports of services, plus net investment income, plus the category "net transfer payments and other."

---

[3]*"Other" includes interest paid by the U.S. government to foreigners. Contrary to the treatment of private interest payments, government interest payments are not counted as imports of services. (This treatment is similar to that for government interest payments to domestic citizens, as discussed in Chapter 7.) These payments are a use of funds, however, so they must be included in computing the balance on current account.*

reduced its holdings of foreign assets by $5.1 billion, and foreign governments increased their holdings of U.S. assets by $38.9 billion. The sum of items 6 through 9 in Table 22.1 is the **balance on capital account.**

balance on capital account *In the United States, the sum of the following (measured in a given period): the change in private U.S. assets abroad, the change in foreign private assets in the United States, the change in U.S. government assets abroad, and the change in foreign government assets in the United States.*

THE STATISTICAL DISCREPANCY

Every use of foreign exchange must have a source. That is, every bit of foreign exchange that a country uses to buy foreign goods, services, or assets must come from somewhere. Thus,

> The overall sum of all the entries in the balance of payments must be zero.

This implies that if the current account is in *deficit,* there must be a *surplus* in the capital account. Similarly, if the current account is in surplus, the capital account must be in deficit.

To be more specific: Ignoring investment income and transfers, a country runs a current account deficit if it imports more than it exports. Where does the foreign exchange come from to pay for these imports? It must come from the sale of assets (or borrowing). When a country sells more of its assets than it buys abroad, it runs a capital account surplus. In essence, such a country is borrowing foreign exchange from abroad.

As you can see from Table 22.1, the $155.7 billion current account deficit in 1994 was offset by a surplus on the capital account of $188.9 billion. The difference between the balance on current account and the balance on capital account is listed as a *statistical discrepancy.* In 1994 it was −$33.2 billion. The statistical discrepancy is an error of measurement. If there were no errors in compiling the data, the statistical discrepancy would be zero.

THE UNITED STATES AS A DEBTOR NATION

When a Japanese bank buys a Treasury note, the note is an asset to the Japanese bank but a liability (debt) to the U.S. government. When a U.S. bank makes a loan to Poland, the loan is an asset to the bank but a liability to Poland, which is in debt to the U.S. bank. Thus:

> When foreign assets in the United States increase, the United States is increasing its debt to the rest of the world. Conversely, when the United States acquires assets abroad, it is in essence loaning money, and foreign debts to the United States increase.

Until the mid-1970s, the United States had invested heavily in foreign countries. U.S. multinational companies bought foreign firms and plants, and U.S. banks loaned money to foreign companies and governments. All the while, U.S. exports were competing well in world markets. The United States ran balance-of-trade surpluses year after year. In essence, the United States bought foreign assets and foreigners bought U.S. goods and services. A current account surplus balanced a capital account deficit, and the United States was a net creditor nation.

This situation turned around completely during the 1980s when the United States started importing much more than it was exporting. At the same time, the United States began borrowing from abroad. That is, foreigners began buying up U.S. assets. Funds from Japan, the Netherlands, England, and Hong Kong began to flood into U.S. asset markets. Foreign investors bought buildings, houses,

Treasury bills, stock, and bonds. As a result, the United States ran current account deficits and capital account surpluses in the second half of the 1980s and into the 1990s.

The consequence is that the United States is currently the largest debtor nation in the world. Foreign private citizens owned about $3.2 trillion worth of U.S. assets by the end of 1993, while private U.S. holdings of foreign assets totaled about $2.6 trillion that year.

EQUILIBRIUM OUTPUT (INCOME) IN AN OPEN ECONOMY

Everything that we have said so far has been descriptive. It is now time to turn to analysis. Just how are all these trade and capital flows determined, and what impacts do they have on the economies of the countries involved? To simplify our discussion in this part of the chapter, we will assume that exchange rates are fixed. We will relax this assumption a little later.

THE INTERNATIONAL SECTOR AND PLANNED AGGREGATE EXPENDITURE

Our earlier descriptions of the multiplier took into account the consumption behavior of households (C), the planned investment behavior of firms (I), and the spending of the government (G). We defined the sum of these three components as planned aggregate expenditure (AE):

$$AE \equiv C + I + G$$

Equilibrium is achieved when planned aggregate expenditure is equal to the total amount of product available to be purchased—that is, to aggregate output (income) (Y):

$$Y = C + I + G$$

To analyze the international sector, we must include the goods and services a country exports to the rest of the world, as well as those that it imports from abroad. If we call our exports of goods and services EX, it should be clear that EX is properly considered to be a component of total output and income. A U.S. razor blade that is sold to a buyer in Mexico is as much a part of U.S. production as a similar blade that is sold in Pittsburgh. Exports simply represent demand for domestic products not by domestic households and firms and the government but by the rest of the world.

But what about imports? Remember that imports are *not a part of domestic output (Y)*. The reason is quite simple. By definition, imports are not produced by the country that is importing them. Remember also that when we look at households' total consumption spending, firms' total investment spending, and total government spending, imports are included. Therefore, to calculate domestic output correctly, we must subtract the parts of consumption, investment, and government spending that constitute imports. Hence the definition of planned aggregate expenditure becomes:

Planned aggregate expenditure in an open economy:

$$AE \equiv C + I + G + EX - IM$$

net exports of goods and services (EX − IM) *The difference between a country's total exports and total imports.*

Note that if we look at the last two terms ($EX − IM$) together, we have the country's **net exports of goods and services.**

■ **Determining Import and Export Levels** We must now ask: What determines the level of exports and imports in a country? For present purposes, we will simply assume that imports are a function of income (Y). The rationale is simple: When U.S. income is higher, U.S. citizens buy more of everything, including U.S. cars and peanut butter, Japanese TV sets, and Korean steel and videocassette recorders. Thus, when income rises, imports tend to go up. Algebraically, we can write

$$IM = mY$$

where Y is income and m is some positive number.[4] Recall from Chapter 9 that the marginal propensity to consume (MPC) measures the change in consumption that results from a $1 change in income. Similarly, the **marginal propensity to import,** which we will abbreviate as MPM or m, is the change in imports caused by a $1 change in income. If $m = 0.2$, or 20%, and income is $1000, then imports, IM, are equal to $0.2 \times \$1000 = \$200$. If income rises by $100 to $1100, then the change in imports will be equal to $m \times$ (the change in income) $= 0.2 \times \$100 = \$20$.

marginal propensity to import (MPM) *The change in imports caused by a $1 change in income.*

Regarding exports, first note that one country's exports are other countries' imports. If a country's income (Y) affects its imports, as we have assumed, then the amount of goods and services that other countries import from the United States (U.S. exports) depends on the incomes of those countries. If foreign incomes go up, other countries' imports (and thus U.S. exports) should increase. For our purposes here, we will assume that exports (EX) are given. For now, we are simply assuming that U.S. exports are not affected, even indirectly, by the state of the U.S. economy. (We relax this assumption later in the chapter.)

■ **Solving for Equilibrium** With all this in mind, we can now solve for equilibrium income. This procedure is illustrated in Figure 22.1. Starting from the blue line (the consumption function) in Figure 22.1a, we gradually build up the components of planned aggregate expenditure. Assuming for simplicity's sake that planned investment, government purchases, and exports are all constant and do not depend on income, we move easily from the blue line to the brown line by simply adding the fixed amounts of I, G, and EX to consumption at every level of income. In this example, we take $I + G + EX$ to equal 80.

$C + I + G + EX$, however, includes spending on imports, which are not part of domestic production. To correct this problem, we must subtract the amount that is imported at each level of income. In Figure 22.1b, we assume that $m = .25$. That is, 25% of total income is spent on goods and services produced in foreign countries. Imports are a constant fraction of total income, and therefore at higher levels of income a larger amount is spent on foreign goods and services. For example, at $Y = 200$, $IM = .25Y$, or 50. Similarly, at $Y = 400$, $IM = .25Y$, or 100.

Remember that the AE function in Figure 22.1 must be planned aggregate expenditure on *domestically* produced goods and services. As income rises, some of the additional income is saved and the rest is spent. But not all of that added spending is on domestically produced goods and services. In fact, as income rises, some is saved and some is spent on imports. The brown dashed line in Figure 22.1b shows imports subtracted out of the AE function.

---

[4]*We usually assume that $0 < m < 1.0$. Otherwise, a $1 increase in income generates an increase in imports of more than $1, which does not make sense.*

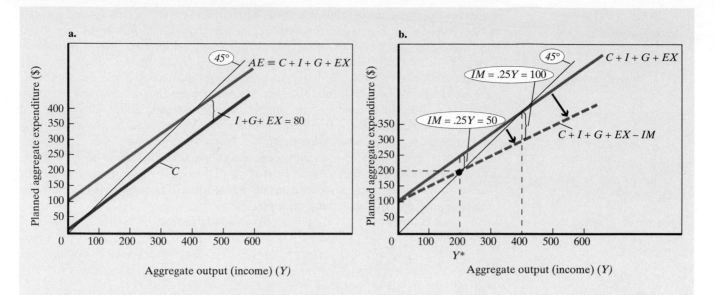

FIGURE 22.1

Determining Equilibrium Output in an Open Economy

In panel a, planned investment spending (*I*), government spending (*G*), and total exports (*EX*) are added to consumption (*C*) to arrive at planned aggregate expenditure. But *C* + *I* + *G* + *EX* includes spending on imports because imports are part of planned aggregate expenditure. In panel b, the amount that is imported at every level of income is subtracted from planned aggregate expenditure. Equilibrium output occurs at $Y^* = 200$, the point at which planned domestic aggregate expenditure crosses the 45° line.

As before, equilibrium is reached when planned aggregate expenditure on domestic output is equal to aggregate domestic output (income). This is true at only one level of aggregate output, $Y^* = 200$, in Figure 22.1b. If *Y* were below Y^*, planned expenditure would exceed output, inventories would be lower than planned, and output would rise. At levels above Y^*, output would exceed planned expenditure, inventories would be larger than planned, and output would fall.

■ **The Open-Economy Multiplier** All of this has implications for the size of the multiplier. Recall the multiplier story, which we first introduced in Chapter 9, and consider a sustained rise in government purchases (*G*). Initially, the increase in *G* will cause planned aggregate expenditure to be greater than aggregate output. Domestic firms will find their inventories to be lower than planned and thus will increase their output. But added output means more income. More workers are hired and profits are higher. Some of the added income is saved, and some is spent. The added consumption spending leads to a second round of inventories being lower than planned and raising output. Thus, equilibrium output rises by a multiple of the initial increase in government purchases. This is the multiplier.

In Chapters 9 and 10, we showed that the simple multiplier is equal to $1/(1 - MPC)$, or (1/*MPS*). That is, a sustained increase in government purchases equal to ΔG will lead to an increase in aggregate output (income) of $\Delta G[1/(1 - MPC)]$. For example, if the *MPC* were .75 and government purchases rose by $10 billion, equilibrium income would rise by 4 × $10 billion, or $40 billion. The multiplier is $[1/(1 - .75)] = [1/.25] = 4.0$.

In an open economy, however, some of the increase in income brought about by the increase in G is spent on imports rather than on domestically produced goods and services. The part of income that is spent on imports does not increase domestic income (Y) because imports are produced by foreigners. Thus, to compute the multiplier we need to know how much of the increased income is used to increase domestic consumption. (We are assuming here that all imports are consumption goods. In practice, some imports are investment goods and some are goods purchased by the government.) In other words, we need to know the marginal propensity to consume *domestic* goods. Domestic consumption is $C - IM$. So the marginal propensity to consume domestic goods is the marginal propensity to consume all goods (the MPC) minus the marginal propensity to import (the MPM). The marginal propensity to consume domestic goods is thus ($MPC - MPM$). Consequently, the open-economy multiplier is:

$$\text{Open-economy multiplier} \ = \ \frac{1}{1 - (MPC - MPM)}$$

If the MPC is .75 and the MPM is .25, then the multiplier is 1/.5, or 2.0. Note that this multiplier is smaller than the multiplier in which imports are not taken into account, which is 1/.25, or 4.0.

The major message of the open-economy multiplier model can be put quite succinctly:

The effect of a sustained increase in government spending (or investment) on income—that is, the multiplier—is smaller in an open economy than in a closed economy. The reason is simply that when government spending (or investment) increases and income and consumption rise, some of the extra consumption spending that results is on foreign products and not on domestically produced goods and services.

THE DETERMINANTS OF IMPORTS AND EXPORTS

When U.S. citizens buy U.S. cars, they generate income for the U.S. firm that sold the cars and thus increase U.S. output. When U.S. citizens buy Japanese cars, however, they generate income for a Japanese firm and have no effect on U.S. output.

But buying a Japanese car does provide a stimulus for the Japanese economy. This, in turn, leads to an increase in Japanese income and therefore to an increase in Japanese spending on imports, which include exports from the United States. In this section, we discuss the determinants of imports and exports.

■ **The Determinants of Imports**   For the sake of simplicity, we have thus far assumed that the amount of spending on imports depends only on income. In reality, however, the amount of spending on imports depends on factors other than income. In fact, the same factors that affect households' consumption behavior and firms' investment behavior are likely to affect the demand for imports because some imported goods are consumption goods and some are investment goods.

Anything that increases consumption spending is likely to increase the demand for imports. We saw in Chapters 9 and 17 that such factors as the after-tax real wage, after-tax nonlabor income, and interest rates affect consumption spending. These factors thus affect spending on imports also. For example, higher interest rates should discourage consumption of both domestically produced goods and foreign-produced goods.

There is one additional consideration in determining spending on imports: the *relative prices* of domestically produced and foreign-produced goods. If the prices of foreign goods are low relative to the prices of domestic goods, people will consume more foreign goods relative to domestic goods. Thus, when Japanese cars are cheap relative to U.S. cars, consumption of Japanese cars should be high. When U.S. cars are relatively inexpensive compared with Japanese cars, consumption of Japanese cars should be lower.

■ **The Determinants of Exports** Now let us relax our assumption that exports are fixed. The demand for U.S. exports by other countries is identical to their demand for imports from the United States. Germany imports goods, some of which are U.S. produced. So do France, Spain, and so on. Total expenditure on imports in Germany is a function of the factors we have just discussed, except that the variables are German variables rather than U.S. variables. This is true for all other countries as well. The demand for U.S. exports thus depends on economic activity in the rest of the world—rest-of-the-world real wages, wealth, nonlabor income, interest rates, and so on—as well as on the prices of U.S. goods relative to the price of rest-of-the-world goods.

If economic activity abroad is high and foreign GDPs are booming, U.S. exports tend to increase. U.S. exports also tend to increase when U.S. prices are low relative to those in the rest of the world.

■ **The Trade Feedback Effect** We can now combine what we know about the demand for imports and the demand for exports to discuss the **trade feedback effect.** Suppose that the United States finds its exports increasing, perhaps because the British suddenly decide they prefer U.S. hot dogs to British sausages. If U.S. exports to England rise by $100 million, will net U.S. exports (exports minus imports) increase by $100 million as well?

The answer is no. When U.S. exports increase, U.S. income rises, just as it would if consumption, investment, or government purchases were higher. This increase in U.S. income in turn increases U.S. demand for imports, so that some of the "extra" $100 million in export revenues goes to pay for additional purchases from abroad. For example, assume that a $1.00 increase in exports increases GDP by $1.40, and a $1.00 increase in income raises import spending by $0.15. In such a case, a $100 million increase in exports will raise imports by $21 million (or $100 million $\times$ 1.4 $\times$ .15). On balance, then, the $100 million in extra export revenues increases U.S. net exports by only $79 million, because $21 million of the $100 million is taken up by additional spending on imports.

But, there is still more to the story. Because U.S. imports are somebody else's exports, the extra import demand from the United States raises the exports of the rest of the world. When other countries' exports to the United States go up, their output and incomes also rise, which in turn leads to an increase in the demand for imports from the rest of the world. Some of the extra imports demanded by the rest of the world come from the United States, so U.S. exports increase. The increase in U.S. exports stimulates U.S. economic activity even more, which leads to a further increase in the U.S. demand for imports, and so on. To summarize:

> An increase in U.S. economic activity leads to a worldwide increase in economic activity, which then "feeds back" to the United States. An increase in U.S. imports increases other countries' exports, which stimulates those countries' economies and increases their imports, which increases U.S. exports, which stimulates the U.S. economy and increases its imports, and so on. This is the trade feedback effect.

trade feedback effect *The tendency for an increase in the economic activity of one country to lead to a worldwide increase in economic activity.*

■ **Import and Export Prices** We have talked about the price of imports, but we have not yet discussed the factors that influence import prices. The consideration of import prices is complicated by the fact that more than one currency is involved. When we talk about "the price of imports," do we mean the price in dollars, in francs, or in yen? And because the exports of one country are the imports of another, the same question holds for the price of exports. When France exports wine to the United States, for example, French wine growers are interested in the price of wine in terms of francs, because francs are what they use for transactions in France. U.S. consumers are interested in the price of wine in terms of dollars, because dollars are what they use for transactions in the United States. The link between the two prices is the dollar/franc exchange rate.

Suppose France is experiencing an inflation and the price of wine in French francs rises from 20 francs per bottle to 30 francs per bottle. France's export price for wine (in terms of francs) will in general go up by the same amount.[5] If the dollar/franc exchange rate remains unchanged at, say, $0.20 per franc, then France's export price for wine in terms of dollars will also rise, from $4 per bottle to $6 per bottle. Because France's exports to the United States are by definition U.S. imports from France, an increase in the dollar prices of French exports to the United States means an increase in the prices of U.S. imports from France. Therefore, when France's export prices rise with no change in the dollar/franc exchange rate, U.S. import prices rise. This holds for any country that trades with France. The point is clear:

> Export prices of other countries affect U.S. import prices.

A country's export prices tend to move fairly closely with the general price level in that country. If France is experiencing a general increase in prices, it is quite likely that this change will be reflected in price increases of all domestically produced goods, both exportable and nonexportable. Therefore,

> The general rate of inflation abroad is likely to affect U.S. import prices. If the inflation rate abroad is high, U.S. import prices are likely to rise.

■ **The Price Feedback Effect** We have just seen that when a country experiences an increase in domestic prices, the prices of its exports will increase. But it is also true that when the prices of a country's *imports* increase, the prices of domestic goods may increase in response. There are at least two mechanisms by which this can occur.

First, an increase in the prices of imported inputs will shift a country's aggregate supply curve to the left. In Chapter 14 we discussed the macroeconomy's response to a cost shock. Recall that a leftward shift in the aggregate supply curve due to a cost increase causes aggregate output to fall and prices to rise (stagflation).

Second, if import prices rise relative to domestic prices, households will tend to substitute domestically produced goods and services for imports. This is equivalent to a rightward shift of the aggregate demand curve. If the domestic economy is operating on the upward-sloping part of the aggregate supply curve, the overall domestic price level will rise in response to an increase in aggregate demand. Perfectly competitive firms will see market-determined prices rise, and imperfectly competitive firms will experience an increase in the demand for their

---

[5]*France's wine exporters could raise the export price but keep it less than the domestic price (to try to stay competitive with the rest of the world), but we ignore this possibility here.*

products. Studies have shown, for example, that the price of automobiles produced in the United States moves very closely with the price of cars imported from Japan and Europe.

But this is not the end of the story. Suppose that a particular country—say, Germany—experiences an increase in its domestic price level. This will increase the price of its exports to France (and to all other countries as well). In turn, the increase in the price of French imports from Germany will lead to an increase in domestic prices in France if the French economy is operating on the steep part of the *AS* curve. But France also exports to Germany. Thus, the increase in French prices causes an increase in the price of French exports to Germany, making the inflation in Germany even worse.

This process is called the **price feedback effect.** The price feedback effect shows that inflation is "exportable." An increase in the price level in one country can drive up prices in other countries; this, in turn, increases the price level in the first country. Through export and import prices, a domestic price increase can "feed back" on itself.

THE OPEN ECONOMY WITH FLEXIBLE EXCHANGE RATES

To a large extent, the fixed exchange rates set by the Bretton Woods agreements served as the centerpiece of international monetary arrangements until 1971. Then, in 1971 the United States and most other countries decided to abandon the fixed exchange rate system in favor of **floating, or market-determined, exchange rates.** While governments still intervene periodically to ensure that exchange rate movements are "orderly," exchange rates today are largely determined by the unregulated forces of supply and demand.

Understanding how an economy interacts with the rest of the world when exchange rates are not fixed is not as simple as it is when we assume fixed exchange rates. Exchange rates determine the price of imported goods relative to domestic goods and can have significant effects on the level of imports and exports. For example, consider a 20% drop in the value of the dollar against the deutsche mark. This means that dollars buy fewer marks and that marks buy more dollars. Both Germans, who now get more dollars for marks, and U.S. citizens, who get fewer marks for dollars, find that U.S. goods and services are more attractive. Thus, exchange rate movements can and do have important impacts on imports, exports, and the movement of capital between countries.

THE MARKET FOR FOREIGN EXCHANGE

What determines exchange rates under a floating rate system? To explore this issue, we will assume for now that there are just two countries, the United States and Great Britain. It is easier to understand a world with only two countries, and most of the points we will make can be generalized to a world with many trading partners.

■ **The Supply of and Demand for Pounds** Governments, private citizens, banks, and corporations exchange pounds for dollars and dollars for pounds every day. In our two-country case, those who *demand* pounds are holders of dollars seeking to exchange them for pounds. Those who *supply* pounds are holders of pounds seeking to exchange them for dollars. It is important not to confuse the supply of dollars (or pounds) on the foreign exchange market with the U.S. (or British) money supply. The latter is the sum of all the money currently in circulation. The supply of dollars on the foreign exchange market is the number of

price feedback effect *The process by which a domestic price increase in one country can "feed back" on itself through export and import prices. An increase in the price level in one country can drive up prices in other countries. This in turn increases the price level in the first country.*

floating, or **market-determined, exchange rates** *Exchange rates that are determined by the unregulated forces of supply and demand.*

dollars that holders seek to exchange for pounds in a given time period. The demand for, and supply of, dollars on foreign exchange markets determines *exchange* rates; the demand for money balances and the total domestic money supply determine the *interest* rate.

The most common reason for exchanging dollars for pounds is to buy something produced in Great Britain. U.S. importers who purchase Jaguar automobiles or Scotch whiskey must pay with pounds. U.S. citizens traveling in Great Britain who want to ride the train, stay in a hotel, or eat at a restaurant must acquire pounds for dollars to do so. If a U.S. corporation builds a plant in Great Britain, it must pay for that plant in pounds.

At the same time, some people may want to buy British stocks or bonds. Implicitly, when a U.S. citizen buys a bond issued by the British government or by a British corporation, he or she is making a loan, but the transaction requires a currency exchange. The British bond seller must ultimately be paid in pounds.

On the supply side of the market, the situation is reversed. Here we find people—usually British citizens—holding pounds with which they want to buy dollars. Again, the most common reason is to buy things produced in the United States. If a British importer decides to import golf carts made in Georgia, the producer must be paid in dollars. Similarly, British tourists visiting New York may ride in cabs, eat in restaurants, and tour Ellis Island. Doing these things requires dollars. When a British firm builds an office complex in Los Angeles, it must pay the contractor in dollars.

In addition to buyers and sellers who exchange money to engage in transactions, some people and institutions hold currency balances for speculative reasons. If I think that the U.S. dollar is going to decline in value relative to the pound, I may want to hold some of my wealth in the form of pounds. Table 22.2 summarizes some of the major categories of private foreign exchange demanders and suppliers in the two-country case of the United States and Great Britain.

EXCHANGE RATES ARE POSTED DAILY AT BANKS AND OTHER FINANCIAL INSTITUTIONS. THEY ARE ALSO AVAILABLE IN NEWSPAPERS, FROM ELECTRONIC INFORMATION SERVICES, AND ON THE INTERNET.

Figure 22.2 shows the demand curve for pounds in the foreign exchange market. When the price of pounds (the exchange rate) is lower, it takes fewer dollars to buy British goods and services, to build a plant in Liverpool, to travel to London, and so forth. Lower net prices (in dollars) should increase the demand for British-made products and encourage investment and travel in Great Britain. If prices (in pounds) in Britain do not change, an increase in the quantity of British goods and services demanded by foreigners will increase the quantity of pounds demanded. Thus, the demand-for-pounds curve in the foreign exchange market has a negative slope.

Figure 22.3 on page 520 shows a supply curve for pounds in the foreign exchange market. At a higher exchange rate, each pound buys more dollars, in which case the price of U.S.-produced goods and services is lower to the British. The British are thus more apt to buy U.S.-made goods when the price of pounds is high (the value of the dollar is low). An increase in British demand for U.S. goods and services is likely to increase the quantity of pounds supplied. Thus, the

TABLE 22.2	SOME PRIVATE BUYERS AND SELLERS IN INTERNATIONAL EXCHANGE MARKETS: UNITED STATES AND GREAT BRITAIN

THE DEMAND FOR POUNDS (SUPPLY OF DOLLARS)

1. Firms, households, or governments that import British goods into the United States or wish to buy British made goods and services
2. U.S. citizens traveling in Great Britain
3. Holders of dollars who want to buy British stocks, bonds, or other financial instruments
4. U.S. companies that want to invest in Great Britain
5. Speculators who anticipate a decline in the value of the dollar relative to the pound

THE SUPPLY OF POUNDS (DEMAND FOR DOLLARS)

1. Firms, households, or governments that import U.S. goods into Great Britain or wish to buy U.S.-made goods and sources
2. British citizens traveling in the United States
3. Holders of pounds who want to buy stocks, bonds, or other financial instruments in the United States
4. British companies that want to invest in the United States
5. Speculators who anticipate a rise in the value of the dollar relative to the pound

curve representing the supply of pounds in the foreign exchange market has a positive slope.

■ **The Equilibrium Exchange Rate** When exchange rates are allowed to float, they are determined the same way that other prices are determined:

The equilibrium exchange rate occurs at the point at which the quantity demanded of a foreign currency equals the quantity of that currency supplied.

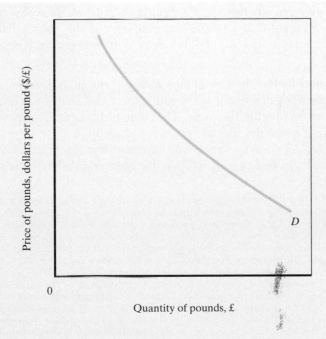

FIGURE 22.2

The Demand for Pounds in the Foreign Exchange Market

When the price of pounds falls, British-made goods and services appear less expensive to U.S. buyers. If British prices are constant, U.S. buyers will buy more British goods and services, and the quantity of pounds demanded will rise.

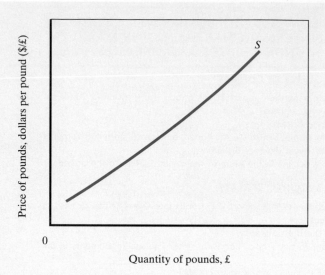

FIGURE 22.3

The Supply of Pounds in the Foreign Exchange Market

When the price of pounds rises, the British can obtain more dollars for each pound. This means that U.S.-made goods and services appear less expensive to British buyers. Thus, the quantity of pounds supplied is likely to rise with the exchange rate.

appreciation of a currency *The rise in value of one currency relative to another.*

depreciation of a currency *The fall in value of one currency relative to another.*

This is illustrated in Figure 22.4. An excess demand for pounds (quantity demanded in excess of quantity supplied) will cause the price of pounds to rise—that is, the pound will **appreciate** with respect to the dollar. An excess supply of pounds will cause the price of pounds to fall—that is, the pound will **depreciate** with respect to the dollar.[6]

The Mexican peso underwent a major depreciation in 1995. For more details on the factors that led to the crisis, see the Global Perspective box on page 522 titled "The Collapse of the Peso."

FACTORS THAT AFFECT EXCHANGE RATES

We now have enough information to discuss the factors likely to influence exchange rates. Anything that changes the behavior of the people listed in Table 22.2 can cause demand and supply curves to shift and the exchange rate to adjust accordingly.

■ **Purchasing Power Parity: The Law of One Price**   If the costs of transporting goods between two countries are small, we would expect the price of the same good in both countries to be roughly the same. The price of basketballs should be roughly the same in Canada and the United States, for example.

It is not hard to see why this is so. Suppose that the price of basketballs is cheaper in Canada. In this case, it will pay for someone to buy balls in Canada at

---

[6]*While Figure 22.3 shows the supply-of-pounds curve in the foreign exchange market with a positive slope, under certain circumstances the curve may bend back. Suppose, for example, that the price of a pound rises from $1.50 to $2.00. Consider a British importer who buys 10 Chevrolets each month at $15,000 each, including transportation costs. When a pound exchanges for $1.50, he will supply 100,000 pounds per month to the foreign exchange market—100,000 pounds brings $150,000, enough to buy 10 cars. Now suppose that the cheaper dollar causes him to buy 12 cars. Twelve cars will cost a total of $180,000, but at $2.00 = 1 pound, he will spend only 90,000 pounds per month. Thus, the supply of pounds on the market actually falls when the price of pounds rises. The reason for this seeming paradox is simple. The number of pounds a British importer needs to buy U.S. goods depends on both the quantity of goods he buys and the price of those goods in pounds. If demand for imports is inelastic so that the percentage decrease in price resulting from the depreciated currency is greater than the percentage increase in the quantity of imports demanded, importers will spend fewer pounds and the quantity of pounds supplied in the foreign exchange market will fall. The supply of pounds will slope upward as long as the demand for U.S. imports is elastic.*

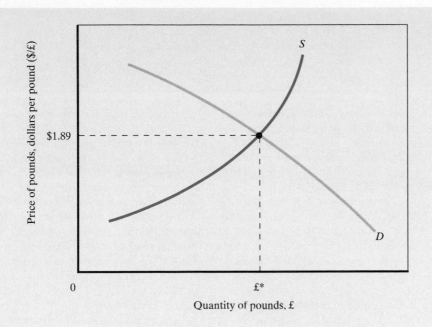

FIGURE 22.4
The Equilibrium Exchange Rate
When exchange rates are allowed to float, they are determined by the forces of supply
and demand. An excess de-
mand for pounds will cause
the pound to appreciate
against the dollar. An excess
supply of pounds will lead to
a depreciating pound.

a low price and sell them in the United States at a higher price. This decreases the supply and pushes up the price in Canada and increases the supply and pushes down the price in the United States. This process should continue as long as the price differential, and therefore the profit opportunity, persists. For a good with trivial transportation costs, therefore, we would expect this **law of one price** to hold. The price of a good should be the same regardless of where we buy it.

If the law of one price held for all goods, and if each country consumed the same market basket of goods, the exchange rate between the two currencies would be determined simply by the relative price levels in the two countries. If the price of a basketball were $10 in the United States and $12 in Canada, then the U.S.-Canada exchange rate would have to be $1 U.S. per $1.20 Canadian. If the rate were instead one-to-one, it would pay people to buy the balls in the United States and sell them in Canada. This would increase the demand for U.S. dollars in Canada, thereby driving up their price in terms of Canadian dollars to one U.S. dollar per 1.2 Canadian dollars, at which point no one could make a profit shipping basketballs across international lines, and the process would cease.[7]

The theory that exchange rates are set so that the price of similar goods in different countries is the same is known as the **purchasing-power-parity theory.** According to this theory, if it takes five times as many French francs to buy a pound of salt in France as it takes U. S. dollars to buy a pound of salt in the United States, then the equilibrium exchange rate should be five francs per dollar.

In practice, transportation costs for many goods are quite large, and the law of one price does not hold for these goods. (Haircuts are often cited as a good example. The transportation costs for a U.S. resident to get a French haircut are indeed large unless that person is an airline pilot.) Also, many products that are

law of one price *If the costs of transportation are small, the price of the same good in different countries should be roughly the same.*

purchasing-power-parity theory *A theory of international exchange that holds that exchange rates are set so that the price of similar goods in different countries is the same.*

---

[7]*Of course, if the rate were $1 U.S. to $2 Canadian, then it would pay people to buy basketballs in Canada (at $12 Canadian, or $6 U.S.) and sell them in the United States. This would weaken demand for the U.S. dollar, and its price would fall from $2 Canadian until it reached $1.20 Canadian.*

During the early months of 1995, newspapers were filled with stories of dramatic swings in foreign exchange markets. A large fall of the Mexican peso's value against the U.S. dollar made world currency traders and international investors particularly nervous.

On December 20, 1994, the value of the peso fell from $.29 to $.25. By March of 1995, the peso was down to a shocking $.135. A hotel room that cost a U.S. tourist $50 a night in December 1994 (172 pesos) cost a mere $23 a night in March.

What was behind the peso's large depreciation? The key to answering this question is an understanding of the forces that drive the supply of and demand for foreign currencies in foreign exchange markets.

The root of the peso's dramatic fall lies in the optimism about the Mexican economy that accompanied the signing of the North American Free-Trade Agreement (NAFTA), which went into effect in January of 1994 (see Chapter 21). The passage of NAFTA and the apparent strength of the Mexican economy sent a flood of investment into Mexico, mostly by U.S. investors and firms.

Always looking for international diversification, U.S. mutual funds snapped up Mexican stocks. Low U.S. interest rates and relatively high Mexican rates led many Americans to purchase Mexican bonds. U.S. companies moved aggressively into the Mexican market. Wal-Mart opened 22 Sam's Club discount stores and 11 su-

percenters, and General Motors built more than 40 parts-making plants at a cost in excess of $25 billion. All of this activity created a tremendous demand for pesos and drove their value up during 1993 and early 1994.

The expensive peso meant a cheap dollar. Mexico was hungry for U.S. products, including consumer goods like cars and investment goods like machine tools. (Ford alone exported 25,000 cars to Mexico, up from zero in 1992.) Mexico began running a large merchandise deficit and a large capital account surplus. That is, U.S. citizens and firms bought pesos (with dollars) to purchase stocks and bonds and other investments in Mexico, while Mexican citizens and firms sold pesos (for dollars) to buy goods produced in the United States. Thus most of the new jobs created as the result of expanded Mexican trade immediately following implementation of the NAFTA were created in the United States.

The bloom came off the Mexican rose in 1994 as the Mexican government faced a violent uprising by Chiapas Indians and the assassination of a presidential candidate. Fearing the worst, investors slowed their purchases of Mexican securities. At the same time, interest rates in the United States rose sharply, attracting many investors back to the United States.

As the depreciation problem became evident, the Mexican government decided to support the peso by using its foreign exchange reserves to buy pesos in hope that investors

would come back if the value of the peso held. But in December 1994, Mexico ran out of reserves and was forced to let the peso's value float. As the peso's value fell, those who had invested in Mexican securities lost money and made a dash for the door. As they sold securities, the stock market fell, further discouraging those holding peso-denominated assets, and the decline became a rout. Nobody wanted to hold anything denominated in pesos.

In January 1995, the Mexican government was forced to pay very high interest rates to raise the money needed to honor its obligations to bondholders whose bonds were coming due. To restore confidence in Mexican bonds and to stabilize the currency markets, the United States and the International Monetary Fund (see the appendix to this chapter) agreed to guarantee payment of Mexican government obligations up to $40 billion.

By March, markets had stabilized, and the Mexican government had not defaulted, but the peso remained at about $.14. Ultimately, with such a cheap peso, Americans will begin buying more Mexican goods and the currency markets are likely to stabilize. Much uncertainty remains, however, and the markets remained unstable in mid-1995.

Sources: *The Economic Report of the President,* February 1995; Anthony DePalma, "With Peso Freed, Mexican Currency Drops 20% More," *The New York Times,* December 23, 1994, p. A1.

potential substitutes for each other are not precisely identical. For instance, a Rolls Royce and a Mercedes Benz are both cars, but there is no reason to expect the exchange rate between the British pound and the deutsche mark to be set so

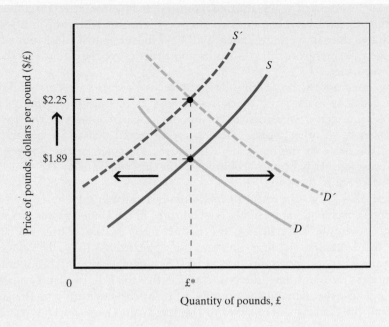

FIGURE 22.5

Exchange Rates Respond to Changes in Relative Prices

This figure shows the effects of an increase in the U.S. price level relative to the price level in Great Britain. The higher price level in the United States makes imports relatively less expensive. Thus, U.S. citizens are likely to increase their spending on imports from Britain, shifting the demand for pounds to the right, from *D* to *D'*. At the same time, the British see U.S. goods getting more expensive and reduce their demand for exports from the United States. Thus, the supply of pounds shifts to the left, from *S* to *S'*. The result is an increase in the price of pounds. The pound appreciates and the dollar is worth less.

that the prices of the two are equalized. In addition, countries consume different market baskets of goods, so we would not expect the aggregate price levels to follow the law of one price.

Nevertheless,

A high rate of inflation in one country relative to another puts pressure on the exchange rate between the two countries, and there is a general tendency for the currencies of relative high-inflation countries to depreciate.

Figure 22.5 shows the adjustments that are likely to take place following an increase in the U.S. price level relative to the price level in Great Britain. This change in relative prices will affect citizens of both countries. Higher prices in the United States make imports relatively less expensive. Thus, U.S. citizens are likely to increase their spending on imports from Britain, shifting the demand for pounds to the right, from *D* to *D'*. At the same time, the British see U.S. goods getting more expensive and reduce their demand for exports from the United States. Consequently, the supply of pounds shifts to the left, from *S* to *S'*. The result is an increase in the price of pounds. Before the change in relative prices, one pound sold for $1.89; after the change, one pound costs $2.25. The pound appreciates and the dollar is worth less.

■ **Relative Interest Rates** Another important factor that influences a country's exchange rate is the level of its interest rate relative to other countries' interest rates. If the interest rate is 7% in the United States and 9% in Germany, people with money to lend have an obvious incentive to buy German securities rather than U.S. securities. Although it is sometimes difficult for individuals in one country to buy securities in another country, it is quite easy for international banks and investment companies to do so. If the interest rate is lower in the United States than in Germany, there will be a movement of funds out of U.S. securities into German securities as banks and firms move their funds to the higher-yielding securities.

How does a U.S. bank buy German securities? It takes its dollars, buys German deutsche marks, and then uses the marks to buy the German securities. The bank's purchase of marks drives up the price of marks in the foreign exchange market. In other words, there is an increased demand for marks, which increases the price of the mark (and decreases the price of the dollar). Thus, a high interest rate in Germany relative to the interest rate in the United States tends to depreciate the dollar.

Figure 22.6 shows the effect of rising interest rates in the United States on the pound-dollar exchange rate. Higher interest rates in the United States attract British investors. To buy U.S. securities, the British need dollars. Thus, the supply of pounds (the demand for dollars) shifts to the right, from S to S'. The same relative interest rates affect the portfolio choices of U.S. banks, firms, and households. With higher interest rates at home, there is less incentive for U.S. residents to buy British securities. Thus, the demand for pounds drops at the same time as the supply increases and the demand curve shifts to the left, from D to D'. The net result is a depreciating pound and an appreciating dollar. The price of pounds falls from $1.89 to $1.25.

During the early 1980s, the Federal Reserve pursued a tight money policy to fight the inflation that began in the late 1970s. At the same time, Congress and the President were pursuing a loose fiscal policy. The result was very high interest rates, particularly in 1981. These high interest rates attracted a great deal of foreign

FIGURE 22.6

Exchange Rates Respond to Changes in Relative Interest Rates

If U.S. interest rates rise relative to British interest rates, British citizens holding pounds may be attracted into the U.S. securities market. To buy bonds in the United States, British buyers must exchange pounds for dollars. Thus, the supply of pounds shifts to the right, from S to S'. But U.S. citizens are less likely to be interested in British securities, because interest rates are higher at home. Thus, the demand for pounds shifts to the left, from D to D'. The result is a depreciated pound and a stronger dollar.

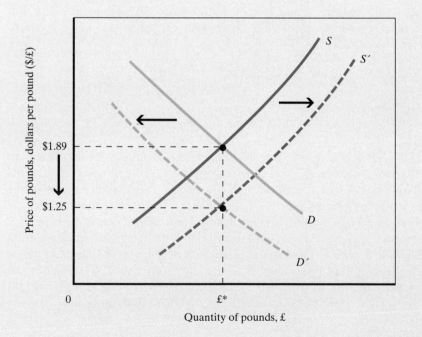

capital, particularly from Japan. The Japanese have had a very high saving rate for many years, and interest rates in Japan were very low at the time. To buy U.S. stocks and bonds, the Japanese had to buy dollars. This situation drove up both the demand for dollars and the value of the dollar sharply. In the early 1990s, this situation reversed itself, as the value of the dollar dropped sharply against the Japanese yen. For the complete story, see the Global Perspective box on page 526 titled "The Kobe Earthquake, the Dollar and the Yen."

THE EFFECTS OF EXCHANGE RATES ON THE ECONOMY

We are now ready to discuss some of the implications of floating exchange rates. Recall that when exchange rates are fixed, households spend some of their incomes on imports and the multiplier is smaller than it would otherwise be. Imports are a "leakage" from the circular flow, very much like taxes and saving are. Exports, in contrast, are like investment and government purchases; they represent spending on U.S.-produced goods and services ("injections" into the circular flow) and can stimulate output.

The world is far more complicated when exchange rates are allowed to float. First, the level of imports and exports depends on exchange rates as well as on income and other factors. Thus, when events cause exchange rates to adjust, the levels of imports and exports will change. Changes in exports and imports can in turn affect the level of real GDP and the price level. To complicate matters further, exchange rates themselves also adjust to changes in the economy. For example, suppose the government decides to stimulate the economy with an expansionary monetary policy. This will affect interest rates, which may in turn affect exchange rates.

■ **Exchange Rate Effects on Imports, Exports, and Real GDP**   As we already know, when a country's currency depreciates (falls in value), its import prices rise and its export prices (in foreign currencies) fall. When the U.S. dollar is cheap, U.S. products are more competitive with products produced in the rest of the world, and foreign-made goods look expensive to U.S. citizens.

A depreciation of a country's currency, then, can serve as a stimulus to the economy. Suppose, for example, that the U.S. dollar falls in value, as it did sharply between 1985 and 1988. If foreign buyers increase their spending on U.S. goods, and domestic buyers substitute U.S.-made goods for imports, aggregate expenditure on domestic output will rise, inventories will fall, and real GDP (Y) will increase. Thus,

A depreciation of a country's currency is likely to increase its GDP.[8]

■ **Exchange Rates and the Balance of Trade: The J Curve**   Because a depreciating currency tends to increase exports and decrease imports, you might think that it will also reduce a country's trade deficit. In fact, the effect of a depreciation on the balance of trade is ambiguous.

Many economists believe that when a currency starts to depreciate, the balance of trade is likely to worsen for the first few quarters (perhaps three to six). After that time, the balance of trade may improve. This effect is graphed in Figure 22.7.

---

[8]*For this reason, some counties are tempted at times to intervene in foreign exchange markets, depreciate their currencies, and thus stimulate their economies. If all countries attempted to lower the value of their currencies simultaneously, there will be no gain in income for any of them. Although the exchange rate system at the time was different, such a situation actually occurred during the early years of the Great Depression. So-called Beggar-thy-neighbor policies of competitive devaluations were practiced by many countries in a desperate attempt to maintain export sales and employment.*

One of the most important economic events of the last few years was the sharp drop in the value of the dollar against the Japanese yen (¥) beginning in late 1992. On March 12, 1995, the exchange rate closed on international markets at 89.05 yen—an all-time low. A year earlier, the dollar had been worth 111 yen; 10 years earlier, it had been worth 238 yen.

Why has the yen appreciated so sharply? Most economists point to changes in capital flows between the countries. Recall that the supply of yen (demand for dollars) and the demand for yen (supply of dollars) on foreign exchange markets is driven by both the demand for foreign-produced goods and the demand for stocks, bonds, and other investment opportunities. During the early 1980s the combination of a high saving rate and low interest rates in Japan and high interest rates in the United States produced a great demand for dollars that drove the dollar to more than 250 yen. This high exchange rate made Japanese goods seem inexpensive to Americans and made U.S. goods appear expensive to the Japanese. The result was a high trade deficit with Japan balanced by a large capital account surplus.

By 1993, however, interest rates in the United States were about the same as interest rates in Japan, whose economy was in recession and whose stock market had dropped dramatically. Having lost money and income at home, Japanese citizens were selling off some of their assets in the United States and sending a smaller portion of their net saving to the United States. Thus, the demand for dollars for capital-account transactions declined sharply, and so did the value of the dollar.

In 1995, a severe earthquake in the city of Kobe made matters worse. Huge claims against Japanese insurance companies had to be paid.

The earthquake that rocked Kobe, Japan in 1995 added to the yen's appreciation. To rebuild at home, the Japanese needed to sell foreign assets and convert them back into yen. The result was an increase in the demand for and price of yen, and a corresponding decrease in the demand for and price of the dollar.

Many of those insurance companies had bought investments in the United States, and some of those investments had to be sold to pay claims. Selling U.S. assets and bringing the money home means selling dollars and demanding yen.

Despite the dramatic fall of the dollar (increase in the price of the yen), U.S. citizens continue to buy more Japanese goods and services than the Japanese buy of U.S. goods and services. If the capital flows between the two countries do not even out over time, the trade flows must do so; otherwise, the dollar will continue to fall, making Japanese goods more and more expensive.

The curve in this figure resembles the letter J, and the movement in the balance of trade that it describes is sometimes called the **J-curve effect.** The main point of the J shape is that the balance of trade gets worse before it gets better following a currency depreciation.

How does the J curve come about? Recall that the balance of trade is equal to export revenue minus import costs, including exports and imports of services:

Balance of trade = Dollar price of exports × Quantity of Exports
− Dollar price of imports × Quantity of Imports.

A currency depreciation affects at least three of the items on the right-hand side of this equation. First, the quantity of exports increases and the quantity of imports decreases, both of which have a *positive* effect on the balance of trade (lowering the trade deficit or raising the trade surplus). Second, the dollar price of exports is not likely to change very much, at least not initially. The dollar price of exports changes when the U.S. price level changes, but the initial effect of a depreciation on the domestic price level is not likely to be large. Third, the dollar price of imports increases. Imports into the United States are more expensive, because one dollar buys fewer French francs and German deutsche marks than before. Thus, an increase in the dollar price of imports has a *negative* effect on the balance of trade.

An example may help to clarify this last point. The dollar price of a Japanese car that costs 2,000,000 yen rises from $10,000 to $15,000 when the exchange rate moves from 200 yen per dollar to 133 yen per dollar. Thus, after the currency depreciation, the United States ends up spending more (in dollars) for the Japanese car than it did before. Of course, the United States will end up buying fewer Japanese cars than it did before. But does the number of cars drop enough so that the quantity effect is bigger than the price effect, or vice versa? In other words, does the value of imports increase or decrease?

J-curve effect *Following a currency depreciation, a country's balance of trade may get worse before it gets better. The graph showing this effect is shaped like the letter J, hence the name "J-curve effect."*

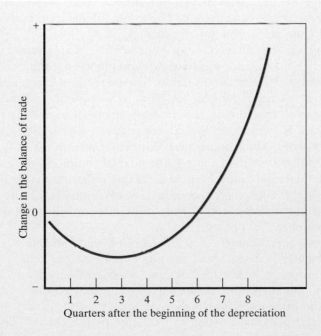

FIGURE 22.7

The Effect of a Depreciation on the Balance of Trade (the J Curve)

Initially, a depreciation of a country's currency may worsen its balance of trade. The negative effect on the price of imports may initially dominate the positive effects of an increase in exports and a decrease in imports.

Clearly, the net effect of a depreciation on the balance of trade could go either way. The depreciation stimulates exports and cuts back imports, but it also increases the dollar price of imports. It seems generally to be the case that the negative effect dominates initially. The impact of a depreciation on the price of imports is generally felt quickly, while it takes some time for export and import quantities to respond to price changes. In the short run, the value of imports increases more than the value of exports, so the balance of trade worsens. The initial effect is thus likely to be negative; but after exports and imports have had time to respond, the net effect turns positive. The more elastic the demand for exports and imports, the larger the eventual improvement in the balance of trade.

■ **Exchange Rates and Prices** The depreciation of a country's currency tends to increase its price level. There are two reasons for this. First, when a country's currency is less expensive, its products are more competitive on world markets, so exports rise. In addition, domestic buyers tend to substitute domestic products for the now-more-expensive imports. This means that planned aggregate expenditure on domestically produced goods and services rises, and the aggregate demand curve shifts to the right. The result is a higher price level, higher output, or both. (You may want to draw an *AS/AD* diagram to verify this.) If the economy is close to capacity, the result is likely to be higher prices. In 1994, exports took a big jump upward, and many people began to fear inflation, as the economy was operating near full employment.

Second, a depreciation makes imported inputs more expensive. If costs increase, the aggregate supply curve shifts to the left. If aggregate demand remains unchanged, the result is an increase in the price level.

■ **Monetary Policy with Flexible Exchange Rates** Let us now put everything we have learned in this chapter together and consider what happens when monetary policy is used first to stimulate the economy and then to contract the economy.

Suppose that the economy is below full employment and the Fed decides to expand the money supply. The volume of reserves in the system is expanded, perhaps through open-market purchases of U.S. government securities by the Fed. This results in a decrease in the interest rate. The lower interest rate stimulates planned investment spending and consumption spending.

This added spending causes inventories to be lower than planned and aggregate output (income) (Y) to rise. But there are two additional important effects. First, the lower interest rate has an impact in the foreign exchange market. A lower interest rate means a lower demand for U.S. securities by foreigners, and thus the demand for dollars drops off. In addition, U.S. investment managers will be more likely to buy foreign securities (which are now paying relatively higher interest rates), so the supply of dollars rises. These events push down the value of the dollar.

A cheaper dollar is a good thing if the goal of the monetary expansion is to stimulate the domestic economy, because a cheaper dollar means more U.S. exports and fewer imports. If consumers substitute U.S.-made goods for imports, both the added exports and the decrease in imports mean more spending on domestic products, so the multiplier actually increases.

Now suppose that inflation is a problem and that the Fed wants to slow it down with tight money. Here again, floating exchange rates help. Tight monetary policy works through a higher interest rate. A higher interest rate lowers investment and consumption spending, reducing aggregate expenditure, reducing output, and lowering the price level. The higher interest rate also attracts foreign buyers into U.S. financial markets, driving up the value of the dollar. This, in turn, increases the price of U.S. exports and reduces the price of imports. The reduction in the price of imports also helps fight the inflation.

■ Fiscal Policy with Flexible Exchange Rates The openness of the economy and flexible exchange rates do not always work to the advantage of policy makers. Consider, for example, a policy of cutting taxes to stimulate the economy. Suppose Congress enacts a major tax cut designed to raise output. Spending by households rises, but not all of this added spending is on domestic products. Some of this spending leaks out of the U.S. economy, and the multiplier is reduced.

As income rises, so too does the demand for money (M^d)—not the demand for dollars in the foreign exchange market, but the amount of money that people desire to hold for transactions. Unless the Fed is fully accommodating, the interest rate will rise. A higher interest rate tends to attract foreign demand for U.S. securities. This in turn tends to drive the price of the dollar up, which further blunts the effectiveness of the tax cut. If the value of the dollar rises, U.S. exports are less competitive in world markets, and the quantity of exports will decline. Similarly, a strong dollar makes imported goods look cheaper, and U.S. citizens spend more on foreign goods and less on U.S. goods. Again the multiplier is reduced.

All this leaves us with yet another caveat to add to the simple multiplier story of Chapters 9 and 10. Without a fully accommodating Fed, three factors work to reduce the multiplier: (1) A higher interest rate from the increase in money demand may crowd out private investment and consumption; (2) some of the increase in income from the expansion will be spent on imports; and (3) a higher interest rate may cause the dollar to appreciate, discouraging exports and further encouraging imports.

AN INTERDEPENDENT WORLD ECONOMY

The increasing interdependence of countries in the world economy has made the problems facing policy makers more difficult. We used to be able to think of the United States as a relatively self-sufficient region. Thirty years ago, economic events outside U.S. borders had relatively little effect on its economy. This is no longer true. If the events of the past three decades have taught us anything, it is that the United States is a part of a global economy and that the performance of the U.S. economy is heavily dependent on events outside its borders.

This chapter and the previous one have provided only the bare bones of open-market macroeconomics. If you continue your study of economics, as we hope you will, more will be added to the basic story we have presented.

The next two chapters keep us in the international arena. Chapter 23 deals with the problems of developing countries, and Chapter 24 explores special features of the economies of the former republics of the Soviet Union and some other nations.

SUMMARY

1. The main difference between an international transaction and a domestic transaction concerns currency exchange: When people in different countries buy from and sell to each other, an exchange of currencies must also take place.

2. The *exchange rate* is the price of one country's currency in terms of another country's currency.

THE BALANCE OF PAYMENTS

3. *Foreign exchange* is simply all currencies other than the domestic currency of a given country. The record of a nation's transactions in goods, services, and assets with the rest of the world is known as its *balance of payments*. The balance of payments is also the record of a country's sources (supply) and uses (demand) of foreign exchange.

EQUILIBRIUM OUTPUT (INCOME) IN AN OPEN ECONOMY

4. In an open economy, some income is spent on foreign-produced goods rather than domestically produced goods. Thus, to measure planned aggregate expenditure in an open economy, we must add total exports but subtract total imports: $AE \equiv C + I + G + EX - IM$. The open economy is in equilibrium when aggregate output (income) (Y) equals planned aggregate expenditure (AE).

5. In an open economy, the multiplier equals $1/1 - (MPC - MPM)$, where MPC is the marginal propensity to consume and MPM is the marginal propensity to import. The *marginal propensity to import* is the change in imports caused by a \$1 change in income.

6. In addition to income, other factors that affect the level of imports are the after-tax real wage rate, after-tax nonlabor income, interest rates, and the relative prices of domestically produced and foreign-produced goods. The demand for exports is determined by economic activity in the rest of the world and by relative prices.

7. An increase in U.S. economic activity leads to a worldwide increase in economic activity, which then "feeds back" to the United States. An increase in U.S. imports increases other countries' exports, which stimulates economies and increases their imports, which increases U.S. exports, which stimulates the U.S. economy and increases its imports, and so on. This is the *trade feedback effect*.

8. Export prices of other countries affect U.S. import prices. The general rate of inflation abroad is therefore likely to affect U.S. import prices. If the inflation rate abroad is high, U.S. import prices are likely to rise.

9. Because one country's exports are another country's imports, an increase in export prices in turn increases other countries' import prices. An increase in other countries' import prices in turn leads to an increase in their domestic prices and thus their export prices. In short, export prices affect import prices, and vice versa. This *price feedback effect* shows that inflation is "exportable"; an increase in the price level in one country can drive up prices in other countries, thus making inflation in the first country worse.

THE OPEN ECONOMY WITH FLEXIBLE EXCHANGE RATES

10. The equilibrium exchange rate occurs when the quantity demanded of a foreign currency in the foreign exchange market equals the quantity of that currency supplied in the foreign exchange market.

11. *Depreciation of a currency* occurs when a nation's currency falls in value relative to another country's currency. *Appreciation of a currency* occurs when a nation's currency rises in value relative to another country's currency.

12. According to the *law of one price,* if the costs of transportation are small, the price of the same good in different countries should be roughly the same. The theory that exchange rates are set so that the price of similar goods in different countries is the same is known as *purchasing-power-parity theory*. In practice, transportation costs are significant for many goods, and the law of one price does not hold for these goods.

13. A high rate of inflation in one country relative to another puts pressure on the exchange rate between the two countries. There is a general tendency for the currencies of relatively high-inflation countries to depreciate.

14. A depreciation of the dollar tends to increase U.S. GDP by making U.S. exports cheaper (and hence more competitive abroad) and by making U.S. imports more expensive (and thus encouraging consumers to switch to domestically produced goods and services).

15. The effect of a depreciation of a nation's currency on its balance of payments is unclear. In the short run, a currency depreciation may actually increase the balance-of-payments deficit, because it raises the price of imports. Although this price increase causes a decrease in the quantity of imports demanded, the impact of a depreciation on the price of imports is generally felt quickly, while it takes some time for export and import quantities to respond to price changes. The initial effect is thus likely to be negative; but after exports and imports have had time to respond, the net effect turns positive. The tendency for the balance-of-payments deficit to widen and then to decrease as the result of a currency depreciation is known as the *J-curve effect*.

16. The depreciation of a country's currency tends to raise its price level for two reasons. First, a currency depreciation increases planned aggregate expenditure, which shifts the aggregate demand curve to the right. If the economy is close to capacity, the result is likely to be higher prices. Second, a depreciation makes imported inputs more expensive. If costs increase, the aggregate supply curve shifts to

the left. If aggregate demand remains unchanged, the result is an increase in the price level.

17. When exchange rates are flexible, a U.S. expansionary monetary policy decreases the interest rate and stimulates planned investment and consumption spending. The lower interest rate leads to a lower demand for U.S. securities by foreigners, and a higher demand for foreign securities by U.S. in-

vestment-fund managers. As a result, the dollar depreciates. A U.S. contractionary monetary policy appreciates the dollar.

18. Flexible exchange rates do not always work to the advantage of policy makers. An expansionary fiscal policy can appreciate the dollar and work to reduce the multiplier.

REVIEW TERMS AND CONCEPTS

appreciation of a currency 520
balance of payments 507
balance of trade 508
balance on capital account 510
balance on current account 509
depreciation of a currency 520
exchange rate 506
floating, or **market-determined, exchange rates** 517

foreign exchange 507
J-curve effect 527
law of one price 521
marginal propensity to import (MPM) 512
net exports of goods and services (EX − IM) 512
price feedback effect 517
purchasing-power-parity theory 521

trade deficit 508
trade feedback effect 515

Equations:
Planned aggregate expenditure in an open economy:
$$AE \equiv C + I + G + EX - IM$$

Open-economy multiplier:
$$\frac{1}{1 - (MPC - MPM)}$$

PROBLEM SET

1. List the balance-of-payments account under which each of the following transactions would be classified and explain whether the item represents a credit or debit entry in the U.S. balance of payments.
   a. You go on vacation to Mexico and spend $300 there on a hotel room, food, transportation, and so forth.
   b. You bring back an Oriental carpet that you bought on a trip to the Middle East. The carpet is worth $10,000, but you do not declare it at customs, and no official record of the transaction exists.
   c. You buy a new Toyota (made in Japan) for $15,000.
   d. You send your cousin in Canada a birthday present worth $50.
   e. Volkswagen Inc. of Germany buys a factory in the United States for $100 million.
   f. Toyota of Japan buys 10% of all the shares in General Motors.
   g. You loan your uncle in Canada $5000.
   h. Your uncle pays you $500 in interest on the money you previously loaned him. He also repays $1000 of the principal.

2. Suppose that the following situation prevailed on the foreign exchange market in 1995 with floating exchange rates:

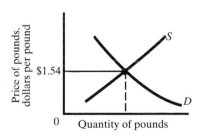

   a. Name three phenomena that might shift the demand curve to the right.
   b. Which, if any, of these three might cause a simultaneous shift of the supply curve to the left?
   c. What effects might the three phenomena have on the balance of payments if the exchange rate floats? On the balance of trade?

3. During 1981 and 1982, the President and the Congress were pursuing a very expansionary fiscal policy. In 1980 and 1981, the Federal Reserve was pursuing a very restrictive monetary policy in an attempt to rid the economy of inflation. Ultimately, the economy went into a deep recession, but before it did interest rates went to record levels with the prime rate topping out at over 21 percent.
   a. Explain how this policy mix led to very high interest rates.
   b. Show graphically the effect of the high interest rates on the foreign exchange market. What do you think would happen to the value of the dollar under these circumstances?
   c. What impact was such a series of events likely to have on the trade balance in countries like Japan? Explain your answer.

4. The exchange rate between the U.S. dollar and the Japanese yen is floating freely—neither government intervenes at all in the market for either currency. Suppose that because of a large trade deficit with Japan, the United States decides to impose quotas on certain Japanese products imported into the United States and, as a result, the value of these imports falls.
   a. The decrease in spending on Japanese products increases spending on U.S.-made goods. Why? What effect will this have on U.S. output and employment? On Japanese output and employment?
   b. What happens to U.S. imports from Japan when U.S. output (or income) rises? If the quotas initially reduce imports from Japan by $25 billion, why is the final reduction in imports likely to be less than $25 billion? Explain in terms of the trade feedback effect.
   c. Suppose that the quotas do succeed in reducing imports from Japan by $15 billion. What will happen to the demand for yen? Why?
   d. What will happen to the dollar-yen exchange rate, and why? (*Hint:* There is an excess supply of yen, or an excess demand for dollars.) What effects will the change in the value of each currency have on employment and output in the United States? What about the balance of payments? (You can ignore complications such as the J curve.)
   e. Considering the macroeconomic effects of a quota on Japanese imports, could a quota actually reduce employment and output in the United States, or have no effect at all? Explain.

5. What effect will each of the following events have on the balance of payments and the exchange rate if the exchange rate is fixed? If it is floating?
   a. The U.S. government cuts taxes, and income rises.
   b. The U.S. inflation rate increases, and prices in the United States rise faster than those in the countries with which the United States trades.
   c. The United States adopts an expansionary monetary policy. Interest rates fall (and are now lower than those in other countries), and income rises.
   d. Textile companies' "Buy American" campaign is successful, and U.S. consumers switch from purchasing imported products to those made in the United States.

*6. You are given the following model, which describes the economy of Hypothetica.

   (1) Consumption function: $C = 100 + .8Y_d$
   (2) Planned investment: $I = 38$
   (3) Government spending: $G = 75$
   (4) Exports: $EX = 25$
   (5) Imports: $IM = .05Y_d$
   (6) Disposable income: $Y_d \equiv Y - T$
   (7) Taxes: $T = 40$
   (8) Planned aggregate expenditure:
       $AE \equiv C + I + G + (EX - IM)$
   (9) Definition of equilibrium income: $Y = AE$.

   a. What is equilibrium income in Hypothetica? What is the government deficit? What is the current account balance?

b. If government spending is increased to $G = 80$, what happens to equilibrium income? Explain, using the government spending multiplier. What happens to imports?

Now suppose that the amount of imports is limited to $IM = 40$ by a quota on imports. If government spending is again increased from 75 to 80, what happens to equilibrium income?

Explain why the same increase in G has a bigger effect on income in the second case. What is it about the presence of imports that changes the value of the multiplier?

c. If exports are fixed at $EX = 25$, what must income be in order to ensure a current account balance of zero? (*Hint:* Imports depend on income, so what must income be for imports to be equal to exports?) By how much must we cut government spending to balance the current account? (*Hint:* Use your answer to the first part of this question to determine how much of a decrease in income is needed. Then use the multiplier to calculate the decrease in G needed to reduce income by that amount.)

7. The table below shows that over the course of a decade, the U.S. dollar has remained virtually constant against the British pound. In the same time period, the dollar fell dramatically against the yen; the price of yen rose 160% between 1983 and 1995. Explain why this might be so.

	MAY 1983	MARCH 1995
Pound sterling	$1.56	$1.58
Yen	.0042	.0111

Since the beginning of the twentieth century, the world has operated under a number of different monetary systems. This appendix provides a brief history of each and a description of how they worked.

THE GOLD STANDARD

The gold standard was the major system of exchange rate determination before 1914. All currencies were priced in terms of gold—that is, an ounce of gold was worth so much in each currency. When all currencies exchanged at fixed ratios to gold, exchange rates could be determined easily. For instance, one ounce of gold was worth $20 U.S.; that same ounce of gold exchanged for four British pounds. Since $20 and £4 were each worth one ounce of gold, the exchange rate between dollars and pounds was $20/£4, or $5 to £1.

For the gold standard to be effective, however, it had to be backed up by the country's willingness to buy and sell gold at the determined price. As long as countries maintain their currencies at a fixed value in terms of gold *and* as long as each is willing to buy and sell gold, exchange rates are fixed. If at the given exchange rate the number of U.S. citizens who want to buy things produced in Great Britain is equal to the number of British citizens who want to buy things produced in the United States, the currencies of the two countries will simply be exchanged. But what if U.S. citizens suddenly decide they want to drink imported Scotch instead of domestic bourbon? If the British do not in turn have an increased desire for U.S. goods, they would still accept U.S. dollars because they could be redeemed in gold. This gold could then be immediately turned into pounds.

As long as a country's overall balance of payments remained in balance, no gold would enter or leave the country, and the economy would be in equilibrium. If U.S. citizens bought more from the British than the British bought from the United States, however, the U.S. balance of payments would be in deficit, and the U.S. stock of gold would begin to fall. Conversely, Britain would start to accumulate gold because it would be exporting more than it spent on imports.

But under the gold standard, gold was an important determinant of the money supply.[1] An inflow of gold into a country caused that country's money supply to expand, and an outflow of gold caused that country's money supply to contract. If gold were flowing from the United States to Great Britain, the British money supply would expand and the U.S. money supply would contract.

Now recall from earlier chapters the impacts of a change in the money supply. An expanded money supply in Britain will lower British interest rates and stimulate aggregate demand. As a result, aggregate output (income) and the price level in Britain will increase. Higher British prices will discourage U.S. citizens from buying British goods. At the same time, British citizens will have more income and will face relatively lower import prices, causing them to import more from the States.

On the other side of the Atlantic, U.S. citizens will face a contracting domestic money supply. This will cause higher interest rates, declining aggregate demand, lower prices, and falling output (income). This, in turn, will lower demand in the United States for British goods. Thus, changes in relative prices and incomes that resulted from the inflow and outflow of gold would automatically bring trade back into balance.

PROBLEMS WITH THE GOLD STANDARD

Two major problems were associated with the gold standard. First, the gold standard implied that a country had little control over its money supply. The reason, as we have just seen, is that the money stock increased when the overall balance of payments was in surplus (gold inflow) and decreased when the overall balance was in deficit (gold outflow). A country that was experiencing a balance-of-payments deficit could correct the problem only by the painful process of allowing its money supply to contract. This brought on a slump in economic activity, a slump that would eventually restore balance-of-payments equilibrium, but only after reductions in income and employment. Countries could (and often did) act to protect their gold reserves, and this prevented the adjustment mechanism from correcting the deficit.

Making the money supply depend on the amount of gold available had another disadvantage as well. When major new gold fields were discovered (as in California in 1849 or South Africa in 1886), the world's supply of

---

[1] *In the days when currencies were tied to gold, changes in the amount of gold influenced the supply of money in two ways. A change in the quantity of gold coins in circulation had a direct effect on the supply of money; indirectly, gold served as a backing for paper currency. A decrease in the central bank's gold holdings meant a decline in the amount of paper money that could be supported.*

gold (and therefore of money) increased. The price level rose and income increased. When no new gold was discovered, the supply of money remained unchanged and prices and income tended to fall.

When President Reagan took office in 1981, he established a commission to consider returning the nation to the gold standard. The final commission report recommended against such a move. An important part of the reasoning behind this was that the gold standard puts enormous economic power in the hands of gold-producing nations.

FIXED EXCHANGE RATES AND THE BRETTON WOODS SYSTEM

As World War II drew to a close, a group of economists from the United States and Europe met to formulate a new set of rules for exchange rate determination that they hoped would avoid the difficulties of the gold standard. The rules they designed became known as the **Bretton Woods system,** after the town in New Hampshire where the delegates met. The Bretton Woods system was based on two (not necessarily compatible) premises. First, countries were to maintain fixed exchange rates with each other. Instead of pegging their currencies directly to gold, however, currencies were fixed in terms of the U.S. dollar, which was fixed in value at $35 per ounce of gold. The British pound, for instance, was fixed at roughly $2.40, which meant that an ounce of gold was worth approximately 14.6 pounds. As we shall see, the pure system of fixed exchange rates would work in a manner very similar to the pre-1914 gold standard.

The second aspect of the Bretton Woods system, however, added a new wrinkle to the operation of the international economy. Countries experiencing a "fundamental disequilibrium" in their balance of payments were allowed to change their exchange rates. (The term "fundamental disequilibrium" was necessarily vague, but it came to be interpreted as a large and persistent balance-of-payments deficit.) Thus, exchange rates were not really fixed under the Bretton Woods system; they were, as someone once remarked, only "fixed until further notice."

The point of allowing countries with serious balance-of-payments problems to alter the value of their currency was to avoid the harsh recessions that the operation of the gold standard would have produced under these circumstances. But the experience of the European economies in the years between World War I and World War II suggested that it might not be a good idea to give countries complete freedom to change their exchange rates whenever they wished.

During the Great Depression, many countries undertook so-called competitive devaluations to protect domestic output and employment. That is, countries would try to encourage exports—a source of output growth and employment—by attempting to set as low an exchange rate as possible, thereby making their exports competitive with foreign-produced goods. Unfortunately, such policies had a built-in flaw. A devaluation of the pound against the French franc may help encourage British exports to France, but if those additional British exports cut into French output and employment, France is likely to respond by devaluing the franc against the pound, which, of course, undoes the effects of the pound's initial devaluation.

To solve this problem of exchange rate rivalry, the Bretton Woods agreement created the International Monetary Fund (IMF). Its job was to assist countries experiencing temporary balance-of-payments problems.[2] It was also supposed to certify that a "fundamental disequilibrium" existed before a country was allowed to change its exchange rate. You can think of the IMF as an international economic traffic cop whose job is to ensure that all countries are playing the game according to the agreed-upon rules and to provide emergency assistance where needed.

"PURE" FIXED EXCHANGE RATES

Under a pure fixed exchange rate system, governments set a particular *fixed* rate at which their currencies will exchange for each other and then commit themselves to maintaining that rate. Thus, a true fixed exchange rate system is like the gold standard in that exchange rates are supposed to stay the same forever.[3] Because currencies are no longer backed by gold, however, they have no fixed, or standard, value relative to each other. There is therefore no automatic mechanism to keep exchange rates aligned with each other, as was the case with the gold standard.

[2]*The idea was that the IMF would make short-term loans to a country with a balance-of-payments deficit. The loans would enable the country to correct the balance-of-payments problem gradually, without bringing on a deep recession, running out of foreign exchange reserves, or devaluing the currency.*
[3]*Of course, "forever" is a very long time. Some countries in Central America have maintained fixed exchange rates with the U.S. dollar for almost 30 years, which is practically forever in the world of international finance.*

The result is that under a pure fixed exchange rate system, governments must at times intervene in the foreign exchange market to keep currencies aligned at their established values. Economists define government intervention in the foreign exchange market as the buying or selling of foreign exchange for the purpose of manipulating the exchange rate. What kind of intervention is likely to occur under a fixed exchange rate system, and how does it work?

We can see how intervention works by looking at Figure 22A.1. Initially, the market for Italian lira is in equilibrium. At the fixed exchange rate of $0.02 per lira, the supply of lira is exactly equal to the demand for lira. No government intervention is necessary to maintain the exchange rate at this level. Now suppose that Italian wines are found to be contaminated with antifreeze, and U.S. citizens decide to switch to California wines. This substitution away from the Italian product shifts the U.S. demand curve for lira to the left: The United States demands fewer lira at every exchange rate (cost of a lira) because it is purchasing less from Italy than it did before.

If the price of lira were set by a completely unfettered market, the shift in the demand curve would lead to a fall in the price of lira, just the way the price of wheat would fall if there was an excess supply of wheat. Remember, though, that the Italian and U.S. governments have committed themselves to maintaining the rate at $0.02 per lira. To do this, either the U.S. government or Italian government (or both) must buy up the excess supply of lira to keep the price of the lira from falling. In essence, the fixed exchange rate policy commits governments to making up any difference between the supply of a currency and the demand so as to keep the price of the currency (exchange rate) at the desired level. The government promises to act as the supplier (or demander) of last resort, who will ensure that the amount of foreign exchange demanded by the private sector will be equal to the supply at the fixed price.

PROBLEMS WITH THE BRETTON WOODS SYSTEM

As it developed after the end of World War II, the system of more-or-less fixed exchange rates had some important flaws that ultimately led to its abandonment in 1971.

First, there was a basic asymmetry built into the rules of international finance. Countries experiencing large and persistent balance-of-payments deficits—what the Bretton Woods agreements termed "fundamental disequilibria"—were obliged to devalue their currencies and/or take measures to cut their deficits by contracting their economies. Both of these alternatives were unpleasant, because devaluation meant rising prices and contraction meant rising unemployment. But a country with a balance-of-payments deficit had no choice. By definition, it was losing its stock of foreign currencies. When its stock of foreign currencies became exhausted, it had to change its exchange rate, because further intervention (selling off some of its foreign exchange reserves) became impossible.

Countries experiencing balance-of-payments surpluses were in a different position. By definition, they were gaining foreign exchange reserves. Although these countries were supposed to stimulate their economies and/or revalue their currencies to restore balance to their balance of payments, they were not obliged to do so. They could easily maintain their fixed exchange rate by buying up any excess supply of foreign exchange with their own currency, of which they had plentiful supply.

In practice, this meant that some countries—especially Germany and Japan—tended to run large and chronic balance-of-payments surpluses and were under no compulsion to take steps to correct the problem. The U.S. economy, stimulated by expenditures on the Vietnam War, experienced a large and prolonged balance-of-payments deficit (capital outflow) in the 1960s, which was the counterpart of these surpluses.

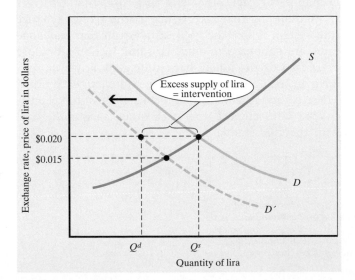

FIGURE 22A.1 **GOVERNMENT INTERVENTION IN THE FOREIGN EXCHANGE MARKET**

If the price of lira was set by a completely unfettered market, the price of a lira would be .020 when demand is D and .015 when demand is D'. If the government has committed itself to keeping the value of a lira at .020, it must buy up the excess supply of lira ($Q^s - Q^d$).

The United States was, however, in a unique position under the Bretton Woods system. The value of gold was fixed in terms of the U.S. dollar at $35 per ounce of gold. Other countries fixed their exchange rates in terms of U.S. dollars (and therefore only indirectly in terms of gold). This meant that the United States could never accomplish anything by devaluing its currency in terms of gold. If the dollar was devalued from $35 to $40 per ounce of gold, the yen, pegged at 200 yen per dollar, would move in parallel with the dollar (from 7000 yen per ounce of gold to 8000 yen per ounce), with the dollar-yen exchange rate unaffected. To correct its balance-of-payments deficits vis-á-vis Japan and Germany, then, it would be necessary for those two countries to adjust their currencies' exchange rates with the dollar. But these countries were reluctant to do so for a variety of reasons. As a result, the U.S. balance of payments was chronically in deficit throughout the late 1960s.

A second flaw in the Bretton Woods system was that it permitted devaluations only if a country had a "chronic" balance-of-payments deficit and was in danger of running out of foreign exchange reserves. This meant that devaluations could often be predicted quite far in advance, and they usually had to be rather large if they were to correct any serious balance-of-payments problem. The situation made it tempting for speculators to "attack" the currencies of countries with balance-of-payments deficits.

Problems like these eventually led the United States to abandon the Bretton Woods rules in 1971. Essentially, the U.S. government refused to continue pegging the value of the dollar in terms of gold. This meant that the prices of all currencies were free to find their own levels.

The alternative to fixed exchange rates is a system that allows exchange rates to move freely or flexibly in response to market forces. Two types of flexible exchange rate systems are usually distinguished. In a *freely floating system,* governments do not intervene at all in the foreign exchange market.[4] They do not buy or sell currencies with the aim of manipulating the rates. In a *managed floating system,* governments intervene if markets are becoming "disorderly"—that is, if they are fluctuating more than a government feels is desirable. Governments may also intervene if they think a currency is increasing or decreasing too much in value, even though the day-to-day fluctuations may be small.

Since the demise of the Bretton Woods system in 1971, the world's exchange rate system is probably best described as a managed floating one. One of the important features of this system has been times of large fluctuations in exchange rates. For example, the yen-dollar rate went from 347 in 1971 to 210 in 1978, to 125 in 1988, to 80 in 1995. These are very large changes, changes that have important effects on the international economy, some of which we have covered in this text.

SUMMARY

1. The gold standard was the major system of exchange rate determination before 1914. All currencies were priced in terms of gold. Difficulties with the gold standard led to the *Bretton Woods* agreement following World War II. Under this system, countries maintained fixed exchange rates with each other and fixed the value of their currencies in terms of the U.S. dollar. Countries experiencing a "fundamental disequilibrium" in their balance of payments were permitted to change their exchange rates.

2. The Bretton Woods system was abandoned in 1971. Since then, the world's exchange rate system has been one of managed floating rates. Under this system, governments intervene if foreign exchange markets are fluctuating more than the government thinks desirable.

REVIEW TERMS AND CONCEPTS

Bretton Woods The site in New Hampshire where a group of experts from 44 countries met in 1944 and agreed on an international monetary system of fixed exchange rates. 535

---

[4] *However, governments may from time to time buy or sell foreign exchange for their own needs (rather than to influence the exchange rate). For example, the U.S. government might need British pounds to buy land for a U.S. embassy building in London. For our purposes, we ignore this behavior since it is not "intervention" in the strict sense of the word.*

1. The currency of Atlantis is the wimp. In 1994, Atlantis developed a balance-of-payments deficit with the United States as a result of an unanticipated decrease in exports; U.S. citizens simply cut back on the purchase of Atlantean goods. Assume that Atlantis is operating under a system of fixed exchange rates.

   a. How does the drop in exports affect the market for wimps? Identify the deficit graphically.

   b. How must the government of Atlantis act (in the short run) to maintain the value of the wimp?

   c. If originally Atlantis was operating at full employment (potential GDP), what impact will these events have on its economy? Explain your answer.

   d. The chief economist of Atlantis suggests expansionary monetary policy to restore full employment; the secretary of commerce suggests a tax cut (expansionary fiscal policy). Given the fixed exchange rate system, describe the effects of these two policy options on Atlantis's balance of payments.

   e. How would your answers to a, b, and c change if the two countries operated under a floating rate system?

ECONOMIC GROWTH IN DEVELOPING NATIONS

OUR PRIMARY FOCUS IN THIS TEXT HAS BEEN ON ECONOMIC ISSUES facing the United States. Welfare and health-care reform, slow economic growth in recent years, antitrust action against Microsoft, and worries about the deficit are familiar to Americans. But the economics we have been studying also applies to other countries: Welfare reform is a big issue in the Netherlands, Japan is facing major fiscal deficits, and the German central bank has been wrestling with slow economic growth. We can analyze these and other issues in the Netherlands, Japan, and Germany with some confidence because these countries have so much in common with the United States. In spite of differences in languages and cultures, all these countries have modern industrialized economies that rely heavily on markets to allocate resources. But what about the economic problems facing Somalia or Haiti? Can we apply the same economic principles that we have been studying to these less-developed countries (sometimes called LDCs)?

The answer is yes. All economic analysis deals with the basic problem of making choices under conditions of scarcity, and the problem of satisfying their citizens' wants and needs is certainly as real for Somalia and Haiti as it is for the Netherlands, Germany, and Japan. The universality of scarcity is what makes economic analysis relevant to all nations, regardless of their level of material well-being or ruling political ideology.

The basic tools of supply and demand, theories about consumers and firms, and theories about the structure of markets all contribute to an understanding of the economic problems confronting the world's developing nations. However, these nations often face economic problems quite different from those faced by richer, more developed countries. In the developing nations, the economist may have to worry about chronic food shortages, explosive population growth, and hyperinflations that reach triple, and even quadruple, digits. The United States and other industrialized economies rarely encounter such difficulties.

The instruments of economic management also vary from nation to nation. The United States has well-developed financial market institutions and a strong central bank (the Federal Reserve) through which the government can control the macroeconomy to some extent. But even limited intervention is impossible in some of the developing countries. In the United States, tax laws can be changed to stimulate saving, to encourage particular kinds of investments, or to redistribute income. In most developing countries, there are neither meaningful personal income taxes nor effective tax policies.

But even though economic problems and the policy instruments available to tackle them vary across nations, economic thinking about these problems can be transferred quite easily from one setting to another. In this chapter we discuss several of the economic problems specific to developing nations in an attempt to capture some of the insights that economic analysis can offer.

LIFE IN THE DEVELOPING NATIONS: POPULATION AND POVERTY

By the year 2000, the population of the world will reach over 6.1 billion people. Most of the world's more than 200 nations belong to the developing world, in which about three fourths of the world's population lives.

In the early 1960s, the nations of the world could be assigned rather easily to categories: The *developed countries* included most of Europe, North America, Japan, Australia, and New Zealand; the *developing countries* included the rest of the world. The developing nations were often referred to as the "Third World" to distinguish them from the Western industrialized nations (the "First World") and the former Socialist bloc of Eastern European nations (the "Second World").

In the 1990s, however, the world does not divide into three neat parts as easily as it once did. Rapid economic progress has brought some developing nations closer to developed economies. Countries such as Argentina and Korea, while still considered to be "developing," are often referred to as middle-income, or newly industrialized, countries. Meanwhile, other countries, such as much of sub-Saharan Africa and some of South Asia, have stagnated and fallen so far behind the economic advances of the rest of the world that a new designation, the "Fourth World," has been coined to describe them. It is not clear yet where the republics of the former Soviet Union and other formerly Communist countries of Eastern Europe will end up. Production has fallen sharply in many of them. For example, between 1989 and 1992 industrial production fell 47.3% in Albania, 46% in Bulgaria, and 44% in the former East Germany. Between 1990 and 1994, real GDP in Russia fell nearly 50% and one estimate puts current per capita GDP in Russia at around $2500. Some of the new republics now have more in common with developing countries than with developed countries.

While the countries of the developing world exhibit considerable diversity, both in their standards of living and in their particular experiences of growth, marked differences continue to separate them from the developed nations. To begin with, the developed countries have a higher average level of material well-being. By material well-being, we mean the amounts of food, clothing, shelter, and other commodities consumed by the average person. Comparisons of gross national product (GNP) per capita—that is, of the value of goods and services produced per person in an economy—are often used as a crude index of the level of material well-being across nations. As you can see from Table 23.1, GNP per capita in the industrial market economies significantly exceeds that of both the low- and middle-income developing economies.

Other characteristics of economic development include improvements in basic health and education. The degree of political and economic freedom enjoyed by individual citizens might also be part of a comprehensive definition of what it means to be a developed nation. Some of these criteria are easier to quantify than others; Table 23.1 presents data for different types of economies according to some of the more easily measured indexes of development. As you can see, the industrial market economies enjoy higher standards of living according to whatever indicator of development is chosen.

Behind these statistics lies the reality of the very difficult life facing the people of the developing world. For most, meager incomes provide only the basic necessities of life. Most meals are the same, consisting of the region's food staple—typically rice, wheat, or corn. Shelter is primitive. Many people share a small room, usually with an earthen floor and no sanitary facilities. The great majority of the population lives in rural areas where agricultural work is hard and extremely time-consuming. Productivity (output produced per worker) is low because household plots are small and only the crudest of farm implements are available. Low productivity means that farm output per person is at levels barely sufficient to feed a farmer's own family, with nothing left over to sell to others. School-age children may receive some formal education, but illiteracy remains chronic for young and old alike. Infant mortality runs ten times higher than in the United States. Although

TABLE 23.1	INDICATORS OF ECONOMIC DEVELOPMENT				
COUNTRY GROUP	GNP PER CAPITA, 1992 (DOLLARS)	LIFE EXPECTANCY, 1992 (YEARS)	INFANT MORTALITY, 1992 (DEATHS BEFORE AGE ONE PER 1000 BIRTHS)	SECONDARY-SCHOOL ENROLLMENT, 1991 (NUMBER ENROLLED AS PERCENTAGE OF POPULATION AGED 12–17)	PERCENTAGE OF POPULATION IN URBAN AREAS, 1992
Low-income (e.g., China, Ethiopia, Haiti, India)	390	62	73	41	27
Lower middle-income (e.g., Guatemala, Poland, Philippines, Thailand)	1,732	67	45	53	53
Upper middle-income (e.g., Korea, Portugal, Venezuela, Mexico)	4,020	69	40	54	72
Industrial market economies (e.g., Japan, Germany, New Zealand, United States)	22,160	77	7	93	78

Note: GDP data not reported.

Source: World Bank, *World Development Report*, 1994. Note that all numbers refer to weighted averages for each country group, where the weights equal the populations of each nation in a specific country group.

parasitic infections are common and debilitating, there is only one physician per 5000 people. In addition, as the Global Perspective box on page 543 titled "The Challenges of Development in Sub-Saharan Africa" points out, many developing nations are engaged in civil and external warfare.

Life in the developing nations is a continual struggle against the circumstances of poverty, and prospects for dramatic improvements in living standards for most people are dim. However, as with all generalizations, there are important exceptions. Some nations are better off than others, and in any given nation an elite group always lives in considerable luxury. Just as in any advanced economy, income is distributed in a fashion that allows a small percentage of households to consume a disproportionately large share of national income. Income distribution in developing countries is often so skewed that the richest households surpass the living standards of many high-income families in the advanced economies. Table 23.2 presents some data on the distribution of income in some developing countries.

Clearly, poverty—not affluence—dominates the developing world. Recent studies suggest that 40% of the population of the developing nations have annual incomes insufficient to provide for adequate nutrition.

> While the developed nations account for only about one quarter of the world's population, they are estimated to consume three quarters of the world's output. This leaves the developing countries with about three fourths of the world's people, but only one fourth of the world's income. The simple result is that most of our planet's population is poor.

In the United States, the poorest one fifth (bottom 20%) of the families receives just over 4% of total income, while the richest one fifth receives about 45% of the income. But the inequality in the world distribution of income, is much greater. When we look at the population of the world, the poorest one fifth of the families earns about 0.5% of the total world income and the richest one fifth earn 79% of world income!

ECONOMIC DEVELOPMENT: SOURCES AND STRATEGIES

Economists have been trying to understand the process of economic growth and development since the days of Adam Smith and David Ricardo in the eighteenth and nineteenth centuries, but the study of development economics as it applies

TABLE 23.2	INCOME DISTRIBUTION IN SOME DEVELOPING COUNTRIES					
	UNITED STATES	**SRI LANKA**	**BOTSWANA**	**BRAZIL**	**PAKISTAN**	**INDONESIA**
Per Capita GNP 1992	$23,240	$540	$2790	$2770	$420	$670
Bottom 20%	4.4	2.9	3.6	2.1	8.4	8.7
Second 20%	10.5	13.1	6.9	4.9	12.9	12.1
Third 20%	16.5	16.9	11.4	8.9	16.9	15.9
Fourth 20%	24.0	21.7	19.2	16.8	22.2	21.1
Top 20%	44.6	39.3	58.9	67.5	39.7	42.3
Top 10%	29.2	25.2	42.9	51.3	25.2	27.9

Sources: World Bank, *World Development, 1994*, and *Statistical Abstract of the United States, 1994*, Table 716.

THE CHALLENGES OF DEVELOPMENT IN SUB-SAHARAN AFRICA

The following extract is taken from a speech given by Lawrence H. Summers, vice president and chief economist at the World Bank. Professor Summers was later appointed under secretary of the Treasury for international affairs by President Clinton.

Why in the face of so much development progress have 36 countries with a combined population of over half a billion people actually regressed? Any analysis of the right way forward for Nigeria and these other nations must start by answering this question. Broadly speaking, the 1991 World Development Report provides two explanations for development failure. First, national development failures are the fault of national policies—they cannot be blamed on a hostile international environment or on any kind of physical limits to growth. Second, national policies have failed when governments thwarted progress, supplanting markets rather than supporting them.

There is one simple but often neglected lesson that comes from any consideration of development failures. War stops development. Almost all of the 36 countries that have lost

CIVIL WARS IN THE AFRICAN NATION OF ANGOLA HAVE POSED MAJOR OBSTACLES TO ECONOMIC DEVELOPMENT. HOMES AND OTHER VALUABLE CAPITAL IN THAT COUNTRY ARE CONSTANTLY BEING DAMAGED OR DESTROYED BY WARTIME ACTIVITIES.

ground over the last 25 years have been involved in a substantial military conflict. Nowhere has war been more costly than in Africa, claiming 7 million victims directly in the last 30 years and millions more deaths indirectly by making the provision of food and basic social services difficult or impossible. The Middle East is often thought of as the world's tinderbox; yet relative to population, Africans have three times as high a war fatality rate. Today, after the Cold War, the threat of hot war in Africa persists: Sub-Saharan African governments spend four times as much on the military as on health and as much on the military as on education. It comes as no surprise that spending on both health and education far exceeds spending on the military in East Asia.

to the developing nations has a much shorter history. The geopolitical struggles that followed World War II brought increased attention to the developing nations and their economic problems. During this period, the central question of the new field of development economics was simply: Why are some nations poor and others rich? If economists could understand the barriers to economic growth that prevent nations from developing and the prerequisites that would help them to develop, then they could prescribe suitable strategies for achieving economic advancement.

THE SOURCES OF ECONOMIC DEVELOPMENT

While a general theory of economic development applicable to all nations has not emerged and probably never will, some basic factors that limit a poor nation's economic growth have been suggested. These include insufficient capital formation, a shortage of human resources and entrepreneurial ability, a lack of social overhead capital, and the constraints imposed by dependency on the already developed nations.

■ **Capital Formation**   One explanation for low levels of output in developing nations is the absence of sufficient quantities of necessary inputs. Developing nations have diverse resource endowments—Zaire, for instance, is abundant in natural resources, while Bangladesh is resource poor. Almost all developing nations have a scarcity of physical capital relative to other resources, especially labor. The small stock of physical capital (including factories, machinery, farm equipment, and other types of productive capital) constrains labor's productivity and holds back national output.

But citing capital shortages as the cause of low productivity does not really explain much. To get to the heart of the matter, we need to know why capital is in such short supply in developing countries. Many explanations have been offered. One, the **vicious-circle-of-poverty hypothesis,** suggests that a poor nation must consume most of its income just to maintain its already low standard of living. Just like a poor family, a poor nation finds that the opportunity cost of forgoing current consumption (that is, saving instead of consuming) is too high. Consuming most of national income implies limited saving, and this in turn implies low levels of investment. Without investment, the capital stock does not grow, income remains low, and the vicious circle is complete. Poverty becomes self-perpetuating.

The difficulty with the vicious-circle argument is that if it were true, no nation could ever develop. For example, Japanese GDP per capita at the turn of the century was well below that of many of today's developing nations. If the vicious-circle explanation were completely correct, Japan could never have grown into the industrial power it is today. The vicious-circle argument fails to recognize that every nation has some surplus above consumption needs that is available for investment. Often this surplus is most visible in the conspicuous-consumption habits of the nation's richest families. In short:

> Poverty alone cannot explain capital shortages, nor is poverty necessarily self-perpetuating.

In a developing economy, scarcity of capital may have more to do with a lack of incentives for citizens to save and invest productively than with any absolute scarcity of income available for capital accumulation. The inherent riskiness and uncertainty that surround a developing nation's economy and its political system tend to reduce incentives to invest in any activity, especially those that require long periods of time to yield a return. Many of the rich in developing countries take their savings and invest them in Europe or in the United States rather than risk holding them in what is often an unstable political climate. Savings transferred to the United States do not lead to physical capital growth in the developing countries. The term **capital flight** is often used to refer to the fact that both

vicious-circle-of-poverty hypothesis *Suggests that poverty is self-perpetuating because poor nations are unable to save and invest enough to accumulate the capital stock that would help them grow.*

capital flight *The tendency for both human capital and financial capital to leave developing countries in search of higher rates of return elsewhere.*

human capital and financial capital (domestic savings) often leave developing countries in search of higher rates of return elsewhere. In addition, a range of government policies in the developing nations—including price ceilings, import controls, and even outright appropriation of private property—tend to discourage investment activity.

Whatever the causes of capital shortages, it is clear that the absence of productive capital prevents income from rising in any economy. The availability of capital is a necessary, but not a *sufficient,* condition for economic growth. The Third World landscape is littered with idle factories and abandoned machinery. Clearly, other ingredients are required to achieve economic progress.

■ **Human Resources and Entrepreneurial Ability**   Capital is not the only factor of production required to produce output. Labor is an equally important input. But the quantity of available labor rarely constrains a developing economy. In most developing nations, rapid population growth for several decades has resulted in rapidly expanding labor supplies. The *quality* of available labor, however, may pose a serious constraint on the growth of income. Or, to put it another way, the shortage of *human capital*—the stock of knowledge and skill embodied in the work force—may act as a barrier to economic growth.

Human capital may be developed in a number of ways. Because malnutrition and the lack of basic health care can substantially reduce labor productivity, programs to improve nutrition and health represent one kind of human capital investment that can lead to increased productivity and higher incomes. The more familiar forms of human capital investment, including formal education and on-the-job training, may also play an important role. Basic literacy, as well as specialized training in farm management, for example, can yield high returns to both the individual worker and the economy. Education has grown to become the largest category of government expenditure in many developing nations, in part because of the belief that human resources are the ultimate determinant of economic advance.

Unfortunately, those lucky enough to get an education often leave developing countries because they can do better financially in the developed world. Just as financial capital seeks the highest and safest return, so does human capital. Thousands of students from developing countries, many of whom were supported by their governments, graduate every year from U.S. colleges and universities as engineers, doctors, scientists, economists, and the like. After graduation, these people face a difficult choice: to remain in the United States and earn a high salary or to return home and accept a job at a much lower salary. Many people choose to remain in the United States. This **brain drain** siphons off many of the most talented minds from developing countries.

Another frequently cited barrier to economic development is the apparent shortage of entrepreneurial activity in developing nations. Innovative entrepreneurs who are willing to take risks are an essential human resource in any economy. In a developing nation, new techniques of production rarely need to be invented, since they can usually be adapted from the technology already developed by the technologically advanced nations. But entrepreneurs who are willing and able to organize and carry out economic activity appear to be in short supply. Family and political ties often seem to be more important than ability when it comes to securing positions of authority. Whatever the explanation:

brain drain *The tendency for talented people from developing countries to become educated in a developed country and remain there after graduation.*

Development cannot proceed without human resources capable of initiating and managing economic activity.

■ **Social Overhead Capital** Anyone who has spent time in a developing nation knows how difficult it can be to send a letter, make a local phone call, or travel within the country itself. Add to this list of obstacles problems with water supplies, frequent electrical power outages—in the few areas where electricity is available at all—and often ineffective mosquito and pest control, and you soon realize how deficient even the simplest, most basic government-provided goods and services can be.

In any economy, Third World or otherwise, the government has considerable opportunity and responsibility for involvement where conditions encourage natural monopoly (as in the utilities industries) and where public goods (such as roads and pest control) must be provided. In a developing economy, the government must place particular emphasis on creating a basic infrastructure—roads, power generation, irrigation systems. There are often good reasons why such projects, referred to as **social overhead capital,** cannot successfully be undertaken by the private sector. First, many of these projects operate with economies of scale, which means that they can be efficient only if they are very large. In that case, they may be simply too large for any private company, or even a group of such companies, to carry out.

Second, many socially useful projects cannot be undertaken by the private sector because there is no way for private agents to capture enough of the returns to make such projects profitable. This so-called *free-rider problem* is common in the economics of the developed world. Consider as an example national defense. Since everyone in a country benefits from national defense, whether they have paid for it or not, anyone who attempted to go into the private business of providing national defense would quickly go broke. Why should I buy any national defense at all if your purchase of defense will also protect me? Why should you buy any if my purchase will also protect you?

> The governments of developing countries can do important and useful things to encourage development, but many of their efforts must be concentrated in areas that the private sector would never touch. If government action in these realms is not forthcoming, economic development may be curtailed by a lack of social overhead capital.

■ **Dependency Theories** In trying to understand why some nations are rich and others poor, some economists find the explanation within the developing nations themselves. In advanced industrial economies, these economists explain, the early merchant classes were responsible for breaking down traditional feudalism and replacing it with a market economy oriented toward growth and development. In many developing nations, however, the class that could foster capitalism has not followed the same path, perhaps out of fear of a socialist takeover. In the view of some analysts, potential capitalists have not transformed traditional societies but have instead acted to maintain the status quo and have thus retarded economic advancement.

Another position, **dependency theory,** holds that the poverty of the developing nations is due to the "dependence" of the developing world on nations that are already developed. (A *dependent country* is one whose economy is dependent on the development and expansion of another country's economy.) During the colonial period, European powers dominated much of the political and economic life of what is today the developing world. Colonial powers sometimes directly destroyed local industries, either by prohibiting certain economic activities or by flooding the colony's markets with manufactured goods from the parent country.

social overhead capital *Basic infrastructure projects such as roads, power generation, and irrigation systems.*

dependency theory *The theory that the poverty of the developing nations is due to the "dependence" of the developing world on nations that are already developed; it suggests that even after the end of colonialism, this dependence is maintained because developed countries are able to use their economic power to determine to their own advantage (and to the disadvantage of others) the relative prices and conditions under which the international exchange of goods takes place.*

Furthermore, by not developing basic physical infrastructure or local human capital and by draining mineral wealth from the colonies, colonialism created countries that had become helpless and economically dependent by the time they achieved political independence.

Some economists contend that economic dependency is maintained today, even though colonialism is long past, through the structure of international trade relations. Developed economies provide important markets for the exports of developing nations and often are their only sources of critical inputs. Industrialized economies also influence world interest rates, capital flows, and exchange rates. Through their economic power, it is argued, industrialized nations often determine to their own advantage (and the disadvantage of others) the relative prices and conditions under which the international exchange of goods takes place.

Dependency theorists argue that the unequal relationship between rich and poor nations in world markets works to the detriment of the developing world. This view has led many Third World leaders to call for a *new international economic order*. Such an arrangement would require agreements between developed and developing nations that would increase the gains that accrue to the developing world from international exchange. Plans for such a set of agreements have been widely discussed in the developing world. But because of divisions among the developing nations and a lack of cooperation from most developed countries there has been virtually no progress in reaching any sort of accord.

STRATEGIES FOR ECONOMIC DEVELOPMENT

Just as no single theory appears to explain lack of economic advancement, so too is it unlikely that one development strategy will succeed in all nations. In fact, many alternative development strategies have been proposed over the past 30 or 40 years. Although these strategies have been very different, they all share the recognition that a developing economy faces certain basic trade-offs. An insufficient amount of both human and physical resources dictates that choices must be made. Some of the basic trade-offs that underlie any development strategy include those between agriculture and industry, exports and import substitution, and central planning and free markets.

■ **Agriculture or Industry?** Most Third World countries began to gain political independence just after World War II. The tradition of promoting industrialization as the solution to the problems of the developing world dates from this time. The early five-year development plans of India called for promoting manufacturing; the current government in Ethiopia (an extremely poor country) has similar intentions.

Industry has several apparent attractions over agriculture. First, if it is true that capital shortages constrain economic growth, then the building of factories is an obvious step toward increasing a nation's stock of capital. Second, and perhaps most important, one of the primary characteristics of more developed economies is their structural transition away from agriculture and toward manufacturing and modern services. As Table 23.3 shows, agriculture's share in GDP declines substantially as per capita incomes increase. The share of services increases correspondingly, especially in the early phases of economic development.

Many economies have pursued industry at the expense of agriculture. In many countries, however, industrialization has been either unsuccessful or disappointing—that is, it has not brought the benefits that were expected. Experience suggests that simply trying to replicate the structure of developed economies does not in itself guarantee, or even promote, successful development.

TABLE 23.3		THE STRUCTURE OF PRODUCTION IN SELECTED DEVELOPED AND DEVELOPING ECONOMIES, 1992		
COUNTRY	PER CAPITA INCOME	PERCENTAGE OF GROSS DOMESTIC PRODUCT		
		AGRICULTURE	INDUSTRY	SERVICES
Uganda	$170	57	11	32
Bangladesh	$220	34	17	49
China	$470	27	34	38
Colombia	$1,330	16	35	49
Thailand	$1,840	12	39	49
Brazil	$2,770	11	37	52
Korea (Rep.)	$6,790	8	45	47
Germany	$23,030	2	39	60
Japan	$28,190	2	42	56

Source: World Bank, World Development Report, 1994, Tables 1 and 3.

Since the early 1970s, the agricultural sector has received considerably more attention. Agricultural strategies have had numerous benefits. Although some agricultural projects (such as the building of major dams and irrigation networks) are very capital intensive, many others (such as services to help teach better farming techniques and small-scale fertilizer programs) have low capital and import requirements. Programs like these can affect large numbers of households, and because their benefits are directed at rural areas, they are most likely to help a country's poorest families.

Experience over the last three decades suggests that some balance between these approaches leads to the best outcome—that is, it is important and effective to pay attention to both industry and agriculture. The Chinese have referred to this dual approach to development as "walking on two legs."

■ **Exports or Import Substitution?** As developing nations expand their industrial activities, they must decide what type of trade strategy to pursue. The choice usually boils down to one of two major alternatives: import substitution or export promotion.

import substitution *An industrial trade strategy that favors developing local industries that can manufacture goods to replace imports.*

Import substitution is an industrial trade strategy that favors developing local industries that can manufacture goods to replace imports. For example, if fertilizer is currently imported, import substitution calls for establishment of a domestic fertilizer industry to produce replacements for fertilizer imports. This strategy gained prominence throughout South America in the 1950s. At that time, most developing nations exported agricultural and mineral products, goods that faced uncertain and often unstable international markets. Furthermore, the *terms of trade* for these nations—the ratio of export to import prices—seemed to be on a long-run decline.[1] A decline in a country's terms of trade means that its imports of manufactured goods become relatively expensive in the domestic market, while its exports—mostly primary goods such as rubber and wheat and oil—become relatively inexpensive in the world market.

Under these conditions, the call for import-substitution policies was understandable. Special government actions, including tariff and quota protection and

[1]It now appears that the terms of trade for Third World countries as a group were not actually on a long-run decline. Of course, the prices of commodities have changed, with some doing very well and others doing quite poorly. During the 1950s, however, many policy makers believed that the purchasing power of developing-country exports was in a permanent slump.

subsidized imports of machinery, were set up to encourage new domestic industries. Multinational corporations were also invited into many countries to begin domestic operations.

Most economists believe that import-substitution strategies have failed almost everywhere they have been tried. With domestic industries sheltered from international competition by high tariffs (often as high as 200%), major economic inefficiencies were created. For example, Peru has a population of just over 22 million, only a tiny fraction of whom could ever afford to buy an automobile. Yet at one time the country had five or six different automobile manufacturers, each of which produced only a few thousand cars per year. Since there are substantial economies of scale in automobile production, the cost per car was much higher than it needed to be, and valuable resources that could have been devoted to another, much more productive, activity were squandered producing cars.

Furthermore, policies designed to promote import substitution often encouraged capital-intensive production methods, which limited the creation of jobs and hurt export activities. Obviously, a country like Peru could not export automobiles, since it could produce them only at a cost far greater than their price on the world market. Worse still, import-substitution policies encouraged the use of expensive domestic products, such as tractors and fertilizer, instead of lower-cost imports. These policies thus served to tax the very sectors that might have successfully competed in world markets. To the extent that the Peruvian sugar industry had to rely on domestically produced, high-cost fertilizer, for example, its ability to compete in international markets was reduced, because its production costs were artificially raised.

As an alternative to import substitution, some nations have pursued strategies of export promotion. **Export promotion** is simply the policy of encouraging exports. As an industrial market economy, Japan is a striking example to the developing world of the economic success that exports can provide. With an average annual per capita real GDP growth rate of roughly 6% per year since 1960, Japan's achievements are in part based on industrial production oriented toward foreign consumers.

export promotion *A trade policy designed to encourage exports.*

Several countries in the developing world have attempted to emulate Japan's success. Starting around 1970, Hong Kong, Singapore, Korea, and Taiwan (sometimes called the "four little dragons" between the two big dragons, China and Japan) all began to pursue export promotion of manufactured goods. Today their growth rates have surpassed even Japan's. Other nations, including Brazil, Colombia, and Turkey, have also had some success at pursuing a more outward-looking trade policy.

Government support of export promotion has often taken the form of maintaining an exchange rate that is favorable enough to permit exports to compete with products manufactured in developed economies. For example, many people believe that the Japanese kept the value of the yen artificially low during the 1970s. Because "cheap" yen means inexpensive Japanese goods in the United States, sales of Japanese goods (especially automobiles) increased dramatically. Governments also have provided subsidies to export industries.

Between 1992 and 1995, Japan slipped into recession and the yen became very expensive during 1994 and 1995. Overall, Japan's performance since 1990 has not been as strong as its pre-1990 performance. But its recent troubles do not diminish the incredible performance of the Japanese economic machine between 1960 and 1990.

■ **Central Planning or the Market?** As part of its strategy for achieving economic development, a nation must decide how its economy will be directed. Its basic choices lie between a market-oriented economic system and a centrally planned one.

In the 1950s and into the 1960s, development strategies that called for national planning commanded wide support. The rapid economic growth of the Soviet Union, a centrally planned economy, provided a historical example of the speed with which a less developed agrarian nation could be transformed into a modern industrial power. (The often appalling costs of this strategy—namely severe discipline, gross violation of human rights, and environmental damage—were less widely known.) In addition, the underdevelopment of many commodity and asset markets in the Third World led many experts to believe that market forces could not direct an economy reliably and that major government intervention was therefore necessary. Even the United States, with its commitment to free enterprise in the marketplace, supported early central planning efforts in many developing nations.

Today, planning takes many forms in the developing nations. In some settings, central planning has replaced market-based outcomes with direct, administratively determined controls over such economic variables as prices, output, and employment. In other situations, national planning amounts to little more than the formulation of general five- or ten-year goals that serve as rough blueprints for a nation's economic future.

The economic appeal of planning lies theoretically in its ability to channel savings into productive investment and to coordinate economic activities that private actors in the economy might not otherwise undertake. The reality of central planning, however, is that it is technically difficult, highly politicized, and a nightmare to administer. Given the scarcity of human resources and the unstable political environment in many developing nations, planning itself—let alone the execution of the plan—becomes a formidable task.

The failure of many central planning efforts has brought increasing calls for less government intervention and more market orientation in developing economies. The elimination of price controls, privatization of state-run enterprises, and reductions in import restraints are examples of market-oriented reforms that are frequently recommended by such international agencies as the **International Monetary Fund,** whose primary goals are to stabilize international exchange rates and to lend money to countries that have problems financing their international transactions, and the **World Bank,** which lends money to individual countries for projects that promote economic development.

Members' contributions to both organizations are determined by the size of their economies. Only 20% of the World Bank's funding comes from contributions; the other 80% comes from retained earnings and investments in capital markets. Throughout the developing world, a recognition of the value of market forces in determining the allocation of scarce resources appears to be increasing. Nonetheless, government still has a major role to play. In the decades ahead, the governments of developing nations will need to determine those situations where planning is superior to the market and those where the market is superior to planning.

GROWTH VERSUS DEVELOPMENT: THE POLICY CYCLE

Until now, we have used the words "growth" and "development" as if they meant essentially the same thing. But this may not always be the case. One can easily imagine instances in which a country has achieved higher levels of income (growth) with little or no benefit accruing to most of its citizens (development). Thus, one central question in evaluating alternative strategies for achieving economic development is whether economic growth necessarily brings about economic development.

International Monetary Fund
An international agency whose primary goals are to stabilize international exchange rates and to lend money to countries that have problems financing their international transactions.

World Bank *An international agency that lends money to individual countries for projects that promote economic development.*

In the past, most development strategies were aimed at increasing the growth rate of income per capita. Many still are, based on the theory that benefits of economic growth will "trickle down" to all members of society. If this theory is correct, then growth should promote development.

By the early 1970s, however, the relationship between growth and development was being questioned more and more. A major study by the World Bank in 1974 concluded that

> it is now clear that more than a decade of rapid growth in underdeveloped countries has been of little or no benefit to perhaps a third of their population. . . . Paradoxically, while growth policies have succeeded beyond the expectations of the first development decade, the very idea of aggregate growth as a social objective has increasingly been called into question.

The World Bank study indicated that increases in GDP per capita did not guarantee significant improvements in such development indicators as nutrition, health, and education. Although GDP per capita did indeed rise, its benefits trickled down to only a small minority of the population. This realization prompted a call for new development strategies that would directly address the problems of poverty. Such new strategies favored agriculture over industry, called for domestic redistribution of income and wealth (especially land), and encouraged programs to satisfy such basic needs as food and shelter.

In the late 1970s and early 1980s, the international macroeconomic crises of high oil prices, worldwide recession, and Third World debt forced attention away from programs designed to eliminate poverty directly.Then, during the 1980s and 1990s, the policy focus turned 180 degrees. The World Bank and the United States began demanding "structural adjustment" in the developing countries as a prerequisite for sending aid to them. **Structural adjustment** programs entail reducing the size of the public sector through privatization and/or expenditure reductions, substantially cutting budget deficits, reigning in inflation, and encouraging private saving and investment with tax reforms. These pro-market demands were an attempt to stimulate growth; distributional consequences took a back seat.

In recent years, foreign aid has become a source of some controversy. How much foreign aid does the United States provide, and who gets it? For the answers to these questions, see the Issues and Controversies box titled "Where Does U.S. Foreign Aid Go?".

structural adjustment *A series of programs in developing nations designed to (1) reduce the size of their public sectors through privatization and/or expenditure reductions, (2) decrease their budget deficits, (3) control inflation, and (4) encourage private saving and investment through tax reform.*

ISSUES IN ECONOMIC DEVELOPMENT

Every developing nation has a cultural, political, and economic history all its own and therefore confronts a unique set of problems. Still, it is possible to discuss common economic issues that each nation must face in its own particular way. These issues include rapid population growth, food shortages, agricultural output and pricing policies, and the Third World debt problem.

POPULATION GROWTH

The populations of the developing nations are estimated to be growing at a rate of about 1.7% per year. (Compare this with a population growth rate of only 0.5% per year in the industrial market economies.) If the Third World's population growth rate remains at 1.7%, it will take only 41 years for the population of the Third World to double from its 1990 level of 4.1 billion to over 8 billion by the year 2031. It will take the industrialized nations 139 years to double their populations. What is so immediately alarming about these numbers is that given the developing nations' current economic problems, it is hard

Many of the developed countries provide direct assistance in the form of grants and loans to developing nations. This aid is used to build infrastructure (roads, power plants, and so forth), drill wells, improve medical care facilities, teach everything from crop management to business development, help rural credit banks grow, and (when necessary) provide food and medical services directly to the people.

Many people think that foreign aid is a major part of U.S. government expenditures, and campaign rhetoric is often directed against it on the grounds that the United States should "help its own people first." In face, the total amount of direct development assistance in the *world* in 1991 was $56.7 billion, of which the United States contributed $11.3 billion. This figure amounted to only 8¢ out of every $10 of federal expenditures and only 2% of domestic transfer payments.

Table 1 presents some interesting statistics. In terms of official development aid per capita (that is, the amount of aid donated for each person in the donor country), the U.S. ranks 15th in the world. The Scandinavian countries spend the most on a per capita basis. The table also shows the top six countries that benefit from U.S. economic aid. Israel is the only country that receives more than $1 billion, and most countries receive only a small amount.

TABLE 1	FOREIGN AID, 1991

Official Development Assistance per capita, Selected Countries

COUNTRY	DOLLARS
Norway	$276
Sweden	245
Denmark	233
Finland	185
Netherlands	167
France	131
Canada	95
Japan	88
Germany	86
United States	45

Destination of Direct U.S. Economic Assistance, by Country

COUNTRY	MILLIONS OF DOLLARS
Israel	$1,850
Egypt	783
Philippines	328
Turkey	250
Nicaragua	215
El Salvador	180

Source: *Statistical Abstract of the United States, 1994*, Tables 1321, 1407, and 1408.

to imagine how they can possibly absorb so many more people in such a relatively short period.

Concern over world population growth is not new. The Reverend Thomas Malthus (who would one day become England's first professor of political economy) expressed his fears about the population increases he observed 200 years ago. Malthus believed that populations grow geometrically (that is, at a constant growth rate: thus the absolute size of the increase each year gets larger and larger), but that food supplies grow much more slowly because of the diminishing marginal productivity of land.[2] These two phenomena led Malthus to predict

---

[2]The law of diminishing marginal productivity says that with a fixed amount of some resource (land), additions of more and more of a variable resource (labor) will produce smaller and smaller gains in output.

the increasing impoverishment of the world's people unless population growth could be slowed.

Malthus's fears for Europe and America proved unfounded, because he neither anticipated the technological changes that revolutionized agricultural productivity nor the eventual decrease in population growth rates in Europe and North America. But Malthus's prediction may have been right, only premature. Do the circumstances in the developing world now fit his predictions? While some contemporary observers believe that the Malthusian view is correct and that the earth's population will eventually grow to a level that the world's resources will be unable to support, others argue that technological change and demographic transitions (to slower population growth rates) will permit further increases in global welfare.

■ **The Consequences of Rapid Population Growth**   Surprisingly, we know far less about the economic consequences of rapid population growth than you might expect. Conventional wisdom warns of dire economic consequences from the developing nations' "population explosion," but these predictions are difficult to substantiate with the available evidence. The rapid economic growth of the United States, for example, was accompanied by relatively rapid population growth by historical standards. Nor has any slowing of population growth been necessary for the economic progress achieved by many of the newly industrialized countries. Nonetheless, population expansion in many of today's poorest nations is of a magnitude unprecedented in world history, as Figure 23.1 clearly shows. From the year 1 A.D. until the mid-1600s, populations grew slowly, at rates of only about 0.04% per year. Since then, and especially since 1950, rates have skyrocketed. Today, populations are growing at rates of 1.5% to 4.0% per year throughout the developing world.

FIGURE 23.1

The Growth of World Population, Projected to 2020 A.D.

For thousands of years, population grew slowly. From 1 A.D. until the mid-1600s, population grew at about .04% per year. Since the Industrial Revolution, population growth has occurred at an unprecedented rate.

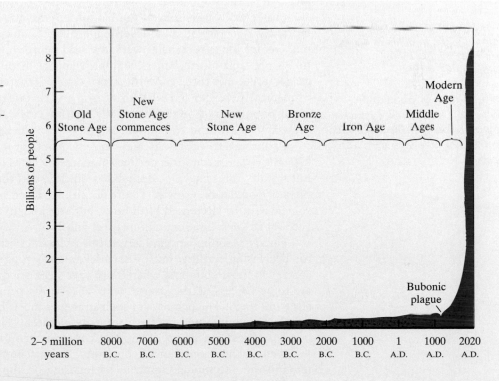

Because growth rates like these have never occurred before the twentieth century, no one knows what impact they will have on future economic development. But a basic economic concern is that such rapid population growth may limit investment and restrain increases in labor productivity and income. Rapid population growth changes the age composition of a population, generating many dependent children relative to the number of productive working adults. Such a situation may diminish saving rates, and hence investment, as the immediate consumption needs of the young take priority over saving for the future.

Even if low saving rates are not a necessary consequence of rapid population growth, as some authorities contend, other economic problems remain. The ability to improve human capital through a broad range of programs, from infant nutrition to formal secondary education, may be severely limited if the population explosion continues. Such programs are most often the responsibility of the state, and governments that are already weak cannot be expected to improve their services under the burden of population pressures that rapidly increase demands for all kinds of public goods and services.

For example, Mozambique's population growth rate—3.7%—is one of the highest in the world. It is likely that its 1994 population of over 28 million people will grow by about 3.6 million in the next five years and by 12 million in the next decade. This is a daunting prospect, and it is hard to imagine how in so little time Mozambique will be able to provide its population with the physical and human capital needed to maintain, let alone improve, already low standards of living.

■ Causes of Rapid Population Growth Population growth is determined by the relationship between births and deaths—that is, between **fertility rates** and **mortality rates.** The **natural rate of population increase** is defined as the difference between the birth rate and the death rate. If the birth rate is 4%, for example, and the death rate is 3%, the population is growing at a rate of 1% per year.

Historically, low rates of population growth were maintained because of high mortality rates despite high levels of fertility. That is, families had many children, but average life expectancies were low, and many children (and adults) died young. In Europe and North America, improvements in nutrition, in public health programs (especially those concerned with drinking water and sanitation services), and in medical practices have led to a drop in the mortality rate and hence to more rapid population growth. Eventually fertility rates also fell, returning population growth to a low and stable rate, as you can see in Figure 23.2a on page 555.

Public health programs and improved nutrition over the past 30 years have brought about precipitous declines in mortality rates in the developing nations also. But fertility rates have not declined as quickly, and the result has been high natural rates of population growth (Figure 23.2b). Reduced population growth depends to some extent on decreased birth rates, but attempts to lower fertility rates must take account of how different cultures feel and behave with regard to fertility.

Family planning and modern forms of birth control are important mechanisms for decreasing fertility, but by themselves such programs have had rather limited success in most countries where they have been tried. If family planning strategies are to be successful, they must make sense to the people who are supposed to benefit from them. The planners of such strategies must therefore understand why families in developing nations have so many children.

To a great extent, in developing countries people want large families because they believe they need them. Economists have attempted to understand fertility patterns in the developing countries by focusing on the determinants of the demand for children. In agrarian societies, children are important sources of farm labor, and

fertility rate *The birth rate. Equal to (the number of births per year divided by the population)* × *100.*

mortality rate *The death rate. Equal to (the number of deaths per year divided by the population)* × *100.*

natural rate of population increase *The difference between the birth rate and the death rate. It does not take migration into account.*

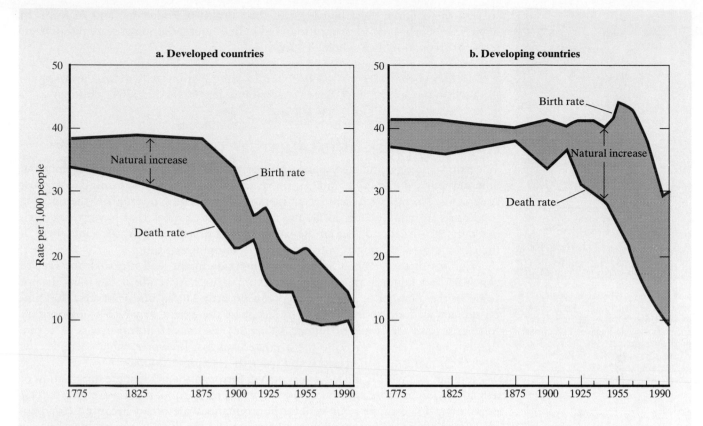

FIGURE 23.2

The Natural Rate of Population Increase, 1775–1990

they may thus make significant contributions to household income. In societies without public old-age support social security programs, children may also provide a vital source of income for parents who are too old to support themselves. With the high value of children enhanced by high rates of infant mortality, it is no wonder that families try to have many children to ensure that a sufficient number will survive into adulthood.

Cultural and religious values also affect the number of children families want to have, but the economic incentives to have large families are extremely powerful. Only when the relationship between the costs and benefits of having children changes will fertility rates decline. Expanding the opportunities for women in an economy increases the opportunity costs of child rearing (by giving women a more highly valued alternative to raising children) and often leads to lower birth rates. Government incentives for smaller families, such as subsidized education for families with fewer than three children, can have a similar effect. In general, rising incomes appear to decrease fertility rates, indicating that economic development itself reduces population growth rates.

Economic theories of population growth suggest that fertility decisions made by poor families should not be viewed as uninformed and uncontrolled. An individual family may find that having many children is a rational strategy for economic survival given the conditions in which it finds itself. This does not mean, however, that having many children is a net benefit to society as a whole. When a family decides to have a large number of children, it imposes costs on the rest of

SEVERAL AFRICAN NATIONS HAVE COME TO RELY ON FOREIGN SUPPORT TO PROVIDE FOOD FOR THEIR PEOPLE. HERE, MEMBERS OF THE FRENCH RED CROSS DISTRIBUTE GRAINS AND OTHER FOODSTUFFS TO THE PEOPLE OF RWANDA.

society; the children must be educated, their health provided for, and so forth. In other words, what makes sense for an individual household may create negative effects for the nation as a whole. Thus:

> Any nation that wants to slow its rate of population growth will probably find it necessary to have in place economic incentives for fewer children as well as family planning programs.

FOOD SHORTAGES: ACTS OF NATURE OR HUMAN MISTAKES?

Television footage and newspaper photos portraying victims of the famine in Somalia burned indelible images of starving people into the minds of most Americans. No other event in recent memory so forcefully dramatized the ongoing food crisis in many of the developing nations. The famines that have struck various parts of Africa and Asia in the past 15 years represent the most acute form of the chronic food shortage confronting the developing nations.

Pictures of the parched Somalian countryside might lead a casual observer to conclude that famines are ultimately acts of nature. After all, if the rains do not come or the locusts do, human beings can do little but sit and wait. But this simplistic view of food shortages fails to recognize the extent to which contemporary food crises are the result of human behavior. Even such natural events as severe flooding can often be traced to the overharvesting of firewood, which denudes the landscape, increases soil erosion, and exacerbates spring floods.

Human behavior is indeed a very strong factor in the inadequate distribution of available food to those who need it. India now grows enough grains to feed its vast population, for example, but malnutrition remains widespread because many people cannot afford to feed themselves. Other parts of the distribution problem involve failures to stockpile adequate food reserves in years of good harvests and transportation and communication barriers that prevent supplies from reaching those in need. World and domestic politics also heavily influence where, how, and whether food is available. During the Ethiopian famine in 1988, for example, the Ethiopian government blocked relief agencies from delivering food and medical supplies to the famine area because a civil war was being waged there. Similar events occurred when the United Nations attempted to aid Somalia in 1992. This led to U.S. military intervention in 1992 and 1993. War between the Hutu and the Tutsis in Rwanda in 1994 led to mass exodus into Zaire, loss of crops, and starvation.

While food shortages are recognized chronic problems, developing nations often pursue farm policies that actually discourage agricultural production. Agricultural production in sub-Saharan Africa today is lower than it was 20 years ago. Economists believe that misguided agricultural policies are responsible for much of this decline.

AGRICULTURAL OUTPUT AND PRICING POLICIES

Few governments in either industrialized or developing nations have permitted market forces alone to determine agricultural prices. In the United States and much of Europe, farm subsidies often encourage production that results in food surpluses rather than shortages. Some developing nations follow similar policies, maintaining high farm prices both to increase agricultural production and to maintain farm incomes. However, many developing nations follow a different route, offering farmers low prices for their output.

To appreciate the motives behind different pricing policies, you need to understand several things about the structure of agricultural markets in many developing nations. Often the government is the primary purchaser of both basic foodstuffs and export crops. Through **produce-marketing boards,** the governments of some developing countries buy farm output and sell it to urban residents at government-controlled prices. By setting the prices they pay to farmers at low levels, the government can afford to sell basic foodstuffs to urban consumers at low prices. Governments often find this an attractive course of action because the direct political influence of the relatively small urban population typically far outweighs the influence of the majority who live in the countryside. Because most city dwellers spend about half their incomes on food, low consumer prices bolster the real incomes of the urban residents and help keep them content. Urban food riots have been common in developing nations over the years, and whether a government is allowed to exist may hinge on its food-pricing strategy.

While we can easily appreciate the political motives behind food pricing, policies that set artificially low prices have significant pitfalls. Farmers react to these prices—often set so low that farmers cannot cover their production costs—by reducing the amount of output they produce. In the city, meanwhile, excess demand for food at the artificially low ceiling prices imposed by the government may promote the emergence of black markets.

Many developing economies that have followed low agricultural pricing policies have experienced exactly these results. Until recently, for example, Mexico kept corn prices low in order to hold down the price of tortillas, the staple in the diet of much of Mexico's urban population. As a result, corn production fell as farmers switched to crops whose prices the government did not control. Domestic corn shortages became widespread, and corn had to be imported to sustain urban demand.

■ Agricultural Output: The Supply Side

In 1995, a single U.S. farmer could provide enough food to feed 80 people. In most developing economies, a single farmer can provide barely enough food to feed his or her own family. While differences in agricultural pricing policies account for a part of this gap, other factors are also at work. Traditionally, low agricultural productivity in the developing world was blamed on the ignorance and laziness of peasant farmers. Today's more enlightened view traces the problem to a shortage of inputs, including land, fertilizer, irrigation, machinery, new seed varieties, and agricultural extension services (which provide credit and technical advice to farmers).

Modern agricultural science has created a so-called **Green Revolution** (not to be confused with the "environmental revolution") based on new, high-yield varieties of wheat, rice, and other crops. Using new, faster-growing varieties instead of the single-crop plants they have relied upon for centuries, some farmers can now grow three crops of rice a year. In Mexico, under ideal conditions, "miracle" wheat has produced 105 bushels of grain per acre, compared with traditional varieties that yield only 11.5 bushels per acre.

If the Green Revolution suggests that science can, in principle, solve world food shortages, the often disappointing history of developing countries' experiments with scientific agriculture offers a less optimistic outlook. Economic factors have greatly limited the adoption of Green Revolution techniques in developing countries. New seeds are expensive, and their cultivation requires the presence of many complementary inputs, including fertilizers and irrigation. With poorly developed rural credit markets, farmers often face interest rates so high that new technologies, regardless of their promise of higher crop yields, are out of reach or ultimately unprofitable. Although the reluctance of peasant farmers to adopt new agricultural techniques has often been blamed on superstition or lack of education, such deci-

produce-marketing boards *The channels through which the governments of some developing countries buy domestic farm output and then sell it to urban residents at government-controlled prices.*

Green Revolution *The agricultural breakthroughs of modern science, such as the development of new, high-yield crop varieties.*

The Green Revolution holds promise for developing nations looking to farm their land more productively. Here, Professor Wim VanCotthem of the University of Gand in Belgium demonstrates a new technique he devised to irrigate the arid zones of West Africa.

sions typically reflect a rational choice. Given the costs and benefits of new inputs and the inherent riskiness of any new method of cultivation, it is not surprising that it has been difficult to get farmers in the developing nations to accept the advances of the Green Revolution.

Peasant farmers in developing nations are also constrained by the amount of land they have to work. In some countries, high population density in the rural areas requires highly labor-intensive cultivation. In other countries, poor distribution of land decreases agricultural output. Throughout Latin America, for example, it is estimated that less than 2% of all landowners control almost 75% of the land under cultivation. Improved crop yields often follow land reforms that redistribute holdings, because owner households are often more productive than tenant farmers. Land reform has had positive effects on output in countries with economic systems as diverse as those of Korea and the People's Republic of China.

In sum:

> Although acts of nature will always threaten agricultural production, human actions, especially policies designed to support the agricultural sector, can have a major impact on reducing the food problems of the developing world.

THIRD WORLD DEBT

In the 1970s, development experts worried about many crises facing the developing world, but the debt crisis was not among them. Within a decade, this situation changed dramatically. The financial plight of nations such as Brazil, Mexico, and the Philippines has become front-page news. What alarmed those familiar with the debt situation was not only its potential impact on the developing nations, but a belief that it threatened the economic welfare of the developed nations as well.

Between 1970 and 1984, developing nations borrowed so much money from other nations that their combined debt increased by 1000%, to almost $700 billion. Three nations alone—Brazil, Mexico, and Venezuela—had outstanding loans to three major U.S. banks (Citibank, Chase-Manhattan, and Manufacturer's Hanover, now part of Chemical) that were more than double the net worth of those financial institutions. As recession took hold in the economically advanced countries during the early 1980s, growth in the exports of the debtor countries slowed, and many found they could no longer pay back the money they owed.

As the situation continued to deteriorate, many feared that debtor nations might simply repudiate their debts outright and default on their outstanding loans. When *default* (nonpayment) occurs with domestic loans, some collateral is usually available to cover all or part of the remaining debt. For loans to another country, however, such collateral is virtually impossible to secure. Given their extensive involvement with Third World borrowers, Western banks did not want to set in motion a pattern of international default. Nor did borrowers want to default. Leaders of the developing nations recognized that to default might result in the denial of access to developed-country banking facilities and to markets in the industrial countries. Such results would pose major obstacles to further development efforts.

Various countries rescheduled their debt as an interim solution. Under a **debt rescheduling** agreement, banks and borrowers negotiate a new schedule for the repayment of existing debt, often with some of the debt written off and with repayment periods extended. In return, borrowing countries are expected to sign an agreement with the International Monetary Fund to revamp their economic policies to provide incentives for higher export earnings and lower imports. This kind of agreement is often referred to as a **stabilization program,** and it usually requires painful austerity measures such as currency devaluations, a reduction in government expenditures, and an increase in tax revenues.

By the early 1990s, the debt crisis was not over but it had lessened somewhat, largely as a result of macroeconomic events that led to reduced interest rates. The international economy has revived somewhat, helping some nations to increase their export earnings. Other nations have benefited from new domestic policies. Still other countries, including Panama, and many African nations, however, continue to face debt burdens that are unmanageable in the short run. Table 23.4 presents figures for a selected group of countries in 1992.

The big news in recent years has been Mexico's monetary and debt situation. Mexico's total external debt in 1992, $113 billion, was second only to Brazil's. Following approval of the North American Free Trade Agreement (NAFTA), there was great optimism about Mexico, and massive amounts of capital flowed to Mexico to take advantage of the relatively high interest rates available on Mexican debt. As a result, Mexico's total external debt increased dramatically. Though the flow of capital pushed up the value of the peso during 1993 and early 1994, by mid-1994 investors had become nervous about the possibility of a decline in the peso's value and began to pull out of Mexico. The peso's value finally collapsed in early 1995, and the Mexican government's inability to get investors to buy Mexican bonds pushed it to the brink of defaulting on its obligations. A loan guarantee of $37 billion from the United States and the International Monetary Fund at least temporarily restored confidence and may have saved Mexico the embarrassment of a default in 1995.

One of the major economic lessons of the last ten years is that proper management of foreign capital in developing countries is essential. Much foreign borrowing

debt rescheduling *An agreement between banks and borrowers through which a new schedule of repayments of the debt is negotiated; often some of the debt is written off and the repayment period is extended.*

stabilization program *An agreement between a borrower country and the International Monetary Fund in which the country agrees to revamp its economic policies to provide incentives for higher export earnings and lower imports.*

TABLE 23.4	TOTAL (PUBLIC AND PRIVATE) EXTERNAL DEBT FOR SELECTED COUNTRIES, 1992 (BILLIONS OF DOLLARS)		
COUNTRY	**TOTAL EXTERNAL DEBT**	**TOTAL ARREARS**	**TOTAL DEBT AS A PERCENTAGE OF GDP**
Brazil	$121.1	$9.8	31.2
Russian Federation	78.7	7.7	NA
India	77.0	0	25.9
Argentina	67.6	14.7	30.3
Poland	48.5	6.1	55.2
Egypt	40.0	1.6	67.7
Thailand	39.4	0	35.2
Peru	20.3	6.7	92.7
Sudan	16.2	10.2	NA
Nicaragua	11.1	4.5	750.3

NA = Not available.

Source: World Bank, *World Development Report, 1994,* Tables 20, 23.

was wasted on projects that had little chance of generating the returns necessary to pay back their initial costs. In other cases, domestic policies that used debt as a substitute for adjusting to new economic circumstances proved to be harmful in the long run. And, overall, much of the optimism about the prospects of the developing economies was inappropriate. Whatever else we may have learned from these mistakes, the debt crisis underscored the growing interdependence of all economies—rich and poor, large and small.

SUMMARY

1. The economic problems facing the developing countries are often quite different from those confronting industrialized nations. The policy options available to governments may also differ. Nonetheless, the tools of economic analysis are as useful in understanding the economies of less developed countries as in understanding the U.S. economy.

LIFE IN THE DEVELOPING NATIONS: POPULATION AND POVERTY

2. The central reality of life in the developing countries is poverty. Although there is considerable diversity across the developing nations, most of the people in most developing countries are extremely poor by U.S. standards.

ECONOMIC DEVELOPMENT: SOURCES AND STRATEGIES

3. Almost all developing nations have a scarcity of physical capital relative to other resources, especially labor. The *vicious-circle-of-poverty hypothesis* argues that poor countries cannot escape from poverty because they cannot afford to postpone consumption (that is, to save) in order to make investments. In its crude form, the hypothesis is wrong inasmuch as some prosperous countries were at one time poorer than many developing countries are today. However, it is often difficult to mobilize savings efficiently in many developing nations.

4. Human capital—the stock of education and skills embodied in the work force—plays a vital role in economic development.

5. Developing countries are often burdened by inadequate *social overhead capital*, ranging from poor public health and sanitation facilities to inadequate roads, telephones, and court systems. Such social overhead capital is often expensive to provide, and many governments are simply not in a position to undertake many useful projects because they are too costly.

6. *Dependency theory* argues that the reason for the poverty of the developing nations is the relationship between the advanced industrial nations and the developing countries, a relationship designed by the former to work to their own advantage at the expense of the latter.

7. Because developed economies are characterized by a large share of output and employment in the industrial sector, many developing countries seem to believe that development and industrialization are synonymous. In many cases, developing countries have pursued industry at the expense of agriculture, with mixed results. Recent evidence suggests that some balance between industry and agriculture leads to the best outcome.

8. *Import substitution* policies, a trade strategy that favors developing local industries that can manufacture goods to replace imports, were once very common in the developing nations. In general, such policies have not succeeded as well as those promoting open, export-oriented economies.

9. The failure of many central planning efforts has brought increasing calls for less government intervention and more market orientation in developing economies.

ISSUES IN ECONOMIC DEVELOPMENT

10. Rapid population growth is characteristic of many developing countries. Large families can be economically rational for parents who need support in their old age, or because children offer an important source of labor. But the fact that parents find it in their interests to have large families does not mean that having many children is a net benefit to society as whole. Rapid population growth can put a strain on already overburdened public services, such as education and health.

11. Food shortages in developing countries are not simply the result of bad weather. Public policies

that depress the prices of agricultural goods, thereby lowering farmers' incentives to produce, are common throughout the developing nations, and human behavior is very much behind the inadequate distribution of available food to those who need it. While acts of nature will always threaten agricultural production, human actions, especially policies designed to support the agricultural sector, can have a major impact on reducing the food problems of the developing world.

12. Between 1970 and 1984 the debts of the developing countries grew tenfold. As recession took hold in the advanced countries during the early 1980s, growth in the exports of the debtor countries slowed, and many found they could no longer pay back money they owed. The prospect of loan defaults by Third World nations threatened the entire international financial system and transformed the debt crisis into a global problem. While Third World debt has not been in the press as much lately, the problem is still serious in many countries.

REVIEW TERMS AND CONCEPTS

brain drain 545
capital flight 544
debt rescheduling 559
dependency theory 546
export promotion 549
fertility rate 554
Green Revolution 557

import substitution 548
International Monetary Fund 550
mortality rate 554
natural rate of population increase 554
produce-marketing boards 557

social overhead capital 546
stabilization program 559
structural adjustment 551
vicious-circle-of-poverty hypothesis 544
World Bank 550

PROBLEM SET

1. Two developing countries that have been in the news lately are Argentina and Mexico. Both countries were experiencing excellent growth during the early 1990s but fell on hard times in 1995. Argentina's banking system nearly collapsed while a precipitous decline in the value of the Mexican peso was at the center of Mexico's difficulties. Choose either Mexico or Argentina, and using indexes to the popular press (like *The Wall Street Journal* or *The New York Times*) write a chronology of events starting in mid-1994. Using what you have learned in economics, what explanations can you offer for what happened? Were the problems that arose problems of mismanagement by governments, or were they the result of the way the markets worked (or failed to work)? What lessons have we learned?

2. The GDP of any country can be divided into two kinds of goods: capital goods and consumption goods. The proportion of national output devoted to capital goods determines, to some extent, the nation's growth rate.
   a. Explain how capital accumulation leads to economic growth.

   b. Briefly describe how a market economy determines how much investment will be undertaken each period.
   c. "Consumption versus investment is a more painful conflict to resolve for developing countries." Comment.
   d. If you were the benevolent dictator of a developing country, what plans would you implement to increase per capita GDP?

3. "The main reason developing countries are poor is that they don't have enough capital. If we give them machinery, or build factories for them, we can greatly improve their situation." Comment.

4. "Poor countries are trapped in a vicious circle of poverty. For output to grow, they must accumulate capital. To accumulate capital, they must save (consume less than they produce). But because they are poor, they have little or no extra output available for savings—it must all go to feed and clothe the present generation. Thus they are doomed to stay poor forever." Comment on each step in this argument.

5. If children are an "investment in the future," why do some developing nations offer incentives to

households that limit the size of their families? Why are these incentives often ignored?

6. If you were in charge of economic policy for a developing country and wanted to promote rapid economic growth, would you choose to favor industry over agriculture? What about exports versus import substitution? In each case, briefly explain your reasoning. How do you explain the fact that many countries chose industry and a protectionist import-substitution policy?

7. "All we need to do is to promote rapid growth of per capita incomes in the developing nations and the poverty problems will take care of themselves." Comment.

8. "Famines are acts of God, resulting from bad weather or other natural disasters. There is nothing we can do about them except to send food relief after they occur." Explain why this position is inaccurate. Concentrate on agricultural pricing policies and distributional issues.

ECONOMIES IN TRANSITION AND ALTERNATIVE ECONOMIC SYSTEMS

OR 40 YEARS, BETWEEN THE END OF WORLD WAR II AND THE mid-1980s, a powerful rivalry existed between the Soviet Union and the United States. This "cold war" pitted the two superpowers against each other in a bitter struggle for influence and fueled the nuclear arms race. Indeed, at one time the mutual distrust between the United States and the Soviet Union was so strong that the concept of "mutual assured destruction" became a dominant theme in international relations.

But the world began to change in the mid-1980s as the political and economic structures of the Soviet Union and the Eastern European Communist countries started to crumble. In 1989, relatively peaceful revolutions took place in rapid succession in Poland, Hungary, and Czechoslovakia (now the Czech Republic). A bloody revolution in Romania toppled Nicolae Ceausescu, who had ruled with an iron fist for 24 years. The Berlin Wall, which had separated the two halves of Germany since 1961, was knocked down and the country reunited. Then, in August 1991, after a failed coup attempt by hard-line Communists, the Soviet Union itself began to come apart. By the end of 1991, the Soviet Union had dissolved into 15 independent states, the largest of which is the Russian Republic. Ten of these 15 republics formed the Commonwealth of Independent States (CIS) in December 1991. The Cold War was over.

Why do we reflect on historical political rivalries in an economics text? There are two reasons. First, the 40-year struggle between the United States and the Soviet Union was fundamentally a struggle between two economic systems: market-based capitalism (the U.S. system) and centrally planned socialism (the Soviet system). Second, the Cold War ended so abruptly in the late 1980s because the Soviet and Eastern European economies virtually collapsed during that period. In a sense, one could say that 1991 was the year that the market triumphed.

But what now? The independent states of the former Soviet Union and the other former Communist economies of Eastern Europe are struggling to make the transition from centrally planned socialism to some form of market-based capitalism. In some countries, such as Serbia and Bosnia-Herzegovina, economic reforms have taken a back seat to bitter and violent ethnic and political rivalries that have been simmering for decades. In other countries, like Poland and Russia, the biggest issue continues to be economic transformation.

The success or failure of this transition from centrally planned socialism to market-based capitalism will determine the course of history, yet it has no historical precedent. Although many countries have made the transition from a market-based system to a centrally planned system, the opposite has never occurred. Undoubtedly, the process has been and will continue to be painful and filled with ups and downs. Between 1989 and 1992, industrial production fell more than 40% in countries like the former East Germany, Albania, Poland, and Romania. In Russia, production decreased about 30 percent. In all these nations, fairly prosperous people suddenly found themselves with annual real incomes closer to those of people in developing countries. For many people, the issue became survival: how to get enough food and fuel to get through the winter.

By 1995, things had turned around, and while much uncertainty and many problems remained, output was rising in much of Eastern and Central Europe. A growing sense of optimism seemed to be spreading slowly. The biggest success story was in East Germany, where real output in 1994 grew by over 9%, the fastest growth rate of any region of Europe. A construction boom, rapid development of infrastructure, low inflation, and rising exports all contributed to the region's success. But East Germany's situation is unique because it was absorbed by a prosperous, fully developed, and modern West Germany that has made development in the East its primary goal.

The countries of Central Europe, including Hungary, Poland, the Czech Republic, Bulgaria, and Romania, also achieved basic macroeconomic stability and began to grow in 1993 and 1994. Poland enjoyed the most rapid economic growth in the group (around 4.5%). Fueled by foreign investment, privatization, and entrepreneurship, the Polish private sector by 1992 accounted for well over one third of the nation's total output, although many problems persist. (For more details, see the Global Perspective box titled "The Challenges to Private Enterprise in Poland.") Russia and the former countries of the Soviet Union have achieved less through 1995. Nonetheless, conditions have improved and prospects for success are greater than they were only a few years ago.

In this chapter, we focus on the ongoing debate over economic reform. What can be done to make the transition from socialism to capitalism successful? In what sequence should changes be made? How quickly can market institutions be established? How much help from the United States and the rest of the world will be required?

To understand the transformation process, it is necessary to begin with some history. From what are these countries making a transition? Our chapter starts with

THE CHALLENGES TO PRIVATE ENTERPRISE IN POLAND

Since 1991 the private sectors of most of the countries of the former Soviet Union and the formerly Communist countries of Central and Eastern Europe have expanded dramatically. Outside of East Germany, Poland's private sector has expanded the most, and it now accounts for well over a third of the economy's production.

This private expansion comes from four sources:

■ **FIRST,** thousands of entrepreneurs have started new businesses. It is estimated that more than 2 million Polish entrepreneurs have formed businesses, and small business in Poland is growing at about 10% per year.

■ **SECOND,** foreign investment is flowing into the region, although not at the pace once anticipated.

■ **THIRD,** "spontaneous privatizations," initiated by managers of state-owned enterprises, have converted many firms to private ownership without a great deal of state participation. The earliest forms of spontaneous privatization in Russia took the form of managers setting up parallel private firms opposite or even inside state-owned enterprises. The new private firm would buy the product of the state-owned enterprise at a controlled price and then resell it at the market price.

■ **FOURTH,** most countries have been selling off state-owned private enterprises directly or indirectly to private shareholders.

Because the process of selling off state-owned assets has been slow, much of the economic action has occurred in small entrepreneurial businesses. But as *The Wall Street Journal* has reported, 95% of the new entrepreneurial businesses in Poland are "mom and pop" proprietorships. In

95% OF THE NEW ENTREPRENEURIAL BUSINESSES IN POLAND ARE SMALL "MOM AND POP" PROPRIETORSHIPS.

such businesses, the potential for generating serious job growth or raising the country's standard of living is not great. Even the 5% of larger start-ups face serious difficulties.

KRAKOW, Poland—At first, making money in capitalist Poland was easy: All you did was buy low and sell high.

Qumak International remembers those days fondly. Customers were begging the Krakow company to import computers from Singapore. Its profits were fat. Its revenues quadrupled to $8 million last year [1994] from $2 million in 1990. Its founders expected to "earn a lot of money and build a big and strong company," says Krzysztof Pyzik, its president.

They were in for a surprise. Now struggling to break even amid growing competition, Qumak has eliminated 20 of its 100 jobs. It has left the personal-computer market to focus on potentially more lucrative

business computers. And it says revenue could plunge 25% this year. . . .

Mr. Pyzik's predicament is one facing millions of East European entrepreneurs. After an initial burst of capitalist energy, they are being slowed by cash shortages, high interest rates and foreign competition. They still lack the managerial skills required to turn small trading operations into large, stable, businesses that can make products, create jobs and underpin an entire economy. Often alumni of state companies, they have little experience dealing with inflation, load payments, inventories and accounts receivable.*

Sources: *Dana Milbank, "Polish entrepreneurs Revitalize Economy but Battle Huge Odds," *The Wall Street Journal*, March 31, 1995, p. 1; Olivier Jean Blanchard, Kenneth A Froot, and Jeffrey D. Sachs, eds., *The Transition in Eastern Europe* (Chicago: University of Chicago Press, 1994).

a discussion of alternative economic systems, the vision of communism, and a brief description of the economic structure of the former Soviet Union. We then turn to the current debate over the transition process, focusing on the experiences of Poland and Russia. We end the chapter by examining a different kind of economic transformation that has been ongoing for some time in China and discussing the performance of the Japanese economy since World War II.

POLITICAL SYSTEMS AND ECONOMIC SYSTEMS: SOCIALISM, CAPITALISM, AND COMMUNISM

Every society has both a political system and an economic system. Unfortunately, the political and economic dimensions of a society are often confused.

The terms "democracy" and "dictatorship" refer to *political* systems. A *democracy* is a system of government in which ultimate power rests with the people, who make governmental decisions either directly through voting or indirectly through representatives. A *dictatorship* is a political system in which ultimate power is concentrated either in a small elite group or a single person.

Historically, two major alternative *economic* systems have existed: socialism and capitalism. A **socialist economy** is one in which most capital—factories, equipment, buildings, railroads, and so forth—is owned by the government rather than by private citizens. *Social ownership* is another term that is often used to describe this kind of system. A **capitalist economy** is one in which most capital is privately owned. Beyond these systems is a purely theoretical economic system called *communism*.

Communism is an economic system in which the people control the means of production (land and capital) directly, without the intervention of a government or state. In the world envisioned by communists, the state would wither away and society would plan the economy in much the same way that a collective would. In fact, although some countries still consider themselves communist—including China, North Korea, Cuba, and Tanzania–economic planning is done by the government in all of them. Thus:

> In terms of comparing economies today, the real distinction is between centrally planned socialism and capitalism, not between capitalism and communism.

No pure socialist economies and no pure capitalist economies exist. Even the Soviet Union, which was basically socialist, had a large private sector. Fully one fourth of agricultural output in what was the USSR was legally produced on private plots and sold, and in a large "second economy" private citizens provided goods and services to each other, sometimes in violation of the law. Conversely, the strongly capitalistic United States supports many government enterprises, including the postal system. Nonetheless, public ownership is the exception in the United States and private ownership was the exception in the Soviet Union.

Whether particular kinds of political systems tend to be associated with particular kinds of economic systems is hotly debated. The United States and Japan are examples of countries with essentially capitalist economic systems and essentially democratic political institutions. China and North Korea have basically socialist economies with political power highly concentrated in a single political party. These observations do not imply that all capitalist countries have democratic political institutions, however, or that all socialist countries are subject to totalitarian party rule.

socialist economy *An economy in which most capital is owned by the government rather than by private citizens. Also called social ownership.*

capitalist economy *An economy in which most capital is privately owned.*

communism *An economic system in which the people control the means of production (capital and land) directly, without the intervention of a government or state.*

Many countries—Indonesia and Taiwan, for example–have basically capitalist economies without democratic political systems. Many other countries that are much closer to the socialist end of the economic spectrum also maintain strong democratic traditions. The people of France, for instance, elected the socialist government of François Mitterrand in 1981, and that government promptly nationalized several major industries. Great Britain and Sweden are other examples of democratic countries that support certain strong socialist institutions.

But do certain kinds of economic systems lead to repressive governments? Austrian economist Friedrich Hayek argues that the answer is yes:

> Economic reforms and government coercion are the road to serfdom. . . . Personal and economic freedoms are inseparable. Once you start down the road to government regulation and planning of the economy, the freedom to speak minds and select political leaders will be jeopardized.[1]

The recent events in Eastern Europe and Russia seem to support Hayek's thesis. There, economic and political reforms are proceeding side by side, and the evidence is mounting that the heart of both the market system *and* democracy is individual freedom.

Nonetheless, some counter Hayek's argument by claiming that social reform and active government involvement in the economy are the only ways to prevent the rise of a totalitarian state. They argue that free and unregulated markets lead to inequality and the accumulation of economic power. Accumulated economic power, in turn, leads to political power that is inevitably used in the interests of the wealthy few, not in the interests of all.

CENTRAL PLANNING VERSUS THE MARKET

In addition to the degree to which capital is owned by private citizens rather than the government, economic systems also differ significantly in the extent to which economic decisions are made through central planning rather than through a market system. In some socialist economies, the allocation of resources, the mix of output, and the distribution of output are determined centrally according to a plan. The former Soviet Union, for example, generated one-year and five-year plans laying out specific production targets in virtually every sector of the economy. In market economies, decisions are made independently by buyers and sellers responding to market signals. Producers produce only what they expect to sell. Labor is attracted into and out of various occupations by wages that are determined by the forces of supply and demand.

Just as there are no pure capitalist and no pure socialist economies, there are no pure market economies and no pure planned economies. Even in the former Soviet Union markets existed and determined, to a large extent, the allocation of resources. Production targets in the United States are set by many agencies, including the Pentagon.

Generally, socialist economies favor central planning over market allocation, while capitalist economies rely to a much greater extent on the market. Nonetheless, some variety exists. The former Yugoslavia, for example, was a socialist country that made extensive use of the market. While ownership of capital and land rested with the government, individual firms determined their own output levels and prices and made their own investment plans. Yugoslavian firms borrowed from banks to finance investments and paid interest on their loans. This type of system, which combines government ownership with market allocation, is often referred to as a **market-socialist economy.**

market-socialist economy *An economy that combines government ownership with market allocation.*

---

[1]*Friedrich Hayek,* The Road to Serfdom *(Chicago: University of Chicago Press, 1944).*

THE ECONOMIC THEORIES OF KARL MARX

The conflict between economic systems has taken place on two levels. On one hand, there are alternative economic *theories* that lead to dramatically different conclusions about the relative merits of market-capitalist and planned socialist systems. On the other hand, the actual *performance* of these differently organized economies must be considered.

The events of the early 1990s in Eastern Europe provide strong evidence that central planning has come up a big loser on the basis of performance. Why, then, should we spend time studying the theoretical underpinnings of communism and socialism? There are at least three reasons. First, for over 70 years in the Soviet Union, and for over 40 years in most parts of Eastern Europe and China, socialist ideology was dominant. Until very recently, about one third of the world's population lived in countries whose economies were based on socialist and communist philosophies. Second, even though the economies of the republics of the former Soviet Union and the economies of Eastern Europe are moving rapidly toward a market-based system, a number of other countries remain firmly committed to the ideas of centrally planned socialism. Finally, to understand the capitalist system, one must understand the criticisms that have been leveled against it.

■ **Marxian Economics: An Overview** Perhaps no single modern thinker has had a greater impact on the world in the twentieth century than Karl Marx, whose work is the basis of the communist ideology. Stated simply, Marxian economic analysis concludes that the capitalist system is morally wrong and doomed to ultimate failure.

The most common misconception about Marx's work is that it contains a blueprint for the operation of a socialist or communist economy. In fact, Marx did not write much about socialism; he wrote about capitalism. Published mostly after his death in 1883, his major work, the three-volume *Das Kapital*, is an extensive analysis of how capitalist economies function and how they are likely to develop over time. *The Communist Manifesto* (written with Friedrich Engels and published in 1848) and his other writings contain only a rough sketch of the socialist and communist societies that Marx predicted would ultimately replace capitalism.

Marx's economic theories lie at the root of his interpretation of history. In examining his work, let us begin with what might be called "Marxian microeconomics" and then turn to the macroeconomic conclusions that emerge from it.

■ **The Labor Theory of Value** The centerpiece of Marx's economic theories is the **labor theory of value.** Marx argued that the value of a commodity depends exclusively upon the amount of labor required to produce it. Commodities are thus the physical embodiment of the labor that produced them:

> A commodity has value, because it is a crystallization of social labor. The greatness of its value, of its relative value, depends upon the greater or less amount of that social substance contained in it. . . .The relative values of commodities are, therefore, determined by the respective quantities or amounts of labor, worked up, realized, fixed in them.[2]

The labor theory of value also addresses the nature and uses of capital. As you know, goods can be produced with a variety of combinations of capital and labor. Are goods produced with a lot of capital and little labor worth less than those produced with a lot of labor and little capital? The answer is no. Capital, according to Marx, is the physical embodiment of the *past labor* that was used to produce it. When used in production, capital contributes value by passing that past labor through to the final product. A machine that took 100 hours to build contributes

labor theory of value *Marx's theory that the value of a commodity depends exclusively upon the amount of labor required to produce it. Commodities are the physical embodiment of the labor that produced them, and capital is the physical embodiment of the past labor used to produce it.*

---

[2]*Karl Marx*, Wages, Price and Profit *(Beijing: Foreign Languages Press, 1975), pp. 34–35.*

100 hours of value to final products over its lifetime. The value of a commodity is thus the sum of the values contributed by present labor and past labor (capital).

■ **The Nature of Profit: The Marxian View**   If, as Marx believed, commodity values depend only on labor's contribution, where does profit come in? The answer is simple. Capitalists own the **means of production,** Marx's term for land and capital. They hire individual workers who have no way to make a living except by selling their labor power. Capitalists make a profit by paying workers a daily wage that is less than the value that workers contribute to final products in a day.

The wage rate is the **value of labor power,** and it is determined in the same way as the value of any other commodity. That is, the value of labor power depends on the amount of labor required to "produce" it. To produce and sustain labor power requires food, clothing, shelter, basic education, medical care, and so forth. The value of labor power, then, is determined by the amount of labor it takes to produce those things necessary to sustain a worker and his or her family. In essence, Marx was proposing a *subsistence theory of wages:* Capitalists will pay a wage that is just enough for laborers to live on.

Let's suppose that it takes four hours to produce everything necessary to sustain a worker for a day. Marx would argue in this case that a day's wage paid by capitalists will be the equivalent of four hours' worth of value. If a worker is employed for 12 hours, the capitalist ends up with a final product containing 12 hours of value but needs to give only four hours' worth of value—or wages—to the worker. The difference (eight hours), which Marx called **surplus value,** is profit.

Profit is thus value created by workers but "expropriated" by capitalists. Capitalists are able to expropriate surplus value because they own the means of production and control access to them. Profit is not a reward for any productive activity; it is extracted solely by virtue of ownership. Marx referred to the ratio of surplus value to the value of labor power as the **rate of exploitation.**

■ **The Nature of Profit: The Neoclassical View**   The bulk of this text has presented mainstream, or neoclassical, economic theory, with its deep roots in nineteenth-century philosophy. At this point we should reflect briefly on the nature of profit in that model, because it is so different from the Marxian notion of surplus value.

Neoclassical economics views both capital and labor as productive factors of production. If you have one worker digging a hole and you want a bigger hole faster, you can accomplish your goal by hiring a second worker *or* by giving the first worker a better shovel. Add labor and you get more product; add capital and you also get more product. According to neoclassical theory, every factor of production in a competitive market economy ends up being paid in accordance with the market value of its product. Profit-maximizing firms hire labor and capital as long as both contribute more to the final value of a product than they cost.

In sum:

> Neoclassical theory views profit as the legitimate return to capital. Marx, however, saw profit as value created by labor and unjustly expropriated by nonproductive capitalists, who own the means of production and thus are able to exploit labor.

■ **Marx's Predictions**   The labor theory of value led Marx to conclude that capitalism was doomed. The essence of his argument was that the rate of profit has a natural tendency to fall over time. With the rate of profits falling, capitalists increase the rate of exploitation, pushing workers deeper and deeper into misery. At the same time, the ups and downs of business cycles become more and more extreme. Ultimately, Marx believed, workers would rise up and overthrow the repressive capitalist system.

means of production *Marx's term for land and capital.*

value of labor power *The wage rate, dependent on the amount of clothing, shelter, basic education, medical care, and so on required to produce and sustain labor power.*

surplus value *The profit a capitalist earns by paying workers less than the value of what they produce.*

rate of exploitation *The ratio of surplus value to the value of labor power.*

The theory that capitalism would ultimately collapse under its own weight was part of Marx's longer view of history. Capitalism had emerged naturally from a previous stage (*feudalism*) which had emerged from an even earlier stage (*ancient slavery*), and so forth. In the economic evolutionary process, Marx believed, capitalism would come to be replaced by socialism, which ultimately would be replaced by communism.

At each stage of economic evolution, Marx said, a set of rules called the *social relations of production* defines the economic system. Contradictions and conflicts inevitably arise at each stage, and these problems are ultimately resolved in the establishment of a new set of social relations. The conflicts in capitalism include alienation, increasing exploitation, misery (or, as Marx called it, "emiserization"), and deeper and deeper business cycles.

It is clear that Marx was eager for the demise of capitalism. He advocated strong and powerful labor unions for two reasons. First, unions would push wages above subsistence and transfer some surplus value back to workers. Second, unions were a way of raising the consciousness of workers about their condition. Only through class consciousness, Marx believed, would workers be empowered to throw off the shackles of capitalism.

At the heart of Marx's ideas is the argument that private ownership and profit are unfair and unethical. Even if it could be demonstrated that the incentives provided by the institution of private property result in faster economic growth or improved living standards, anyone who accepts Marx's interpretation has to reject capitalism on moral grounds, on ideological grounds, or on both.

ECONOMIES IN TRANSITION: EXPERIENCES OF RUSSIA AND EASTERN EUROPE

The Eastern European nations' transitions to market systems were in large measure the result of the economic failures of centrally planned socialism, which had ultimately failed to "deliver the goods." To understand the failure of the Eastern European socialist economies and the difficult process of transition that lies ahead for them, students of economics must be aware of these countries' economic histories. In this section, we briefly describe the Soviet system as it existed for nearly 75 years and the changes taking place today. Although the transformation process is well underway, it will be some time before the process of dismantling the old system is complete.

THE SOVIET UNION: HISTORY AND REFORM

Marx believed that socialist revolution would occur in advanced capitalist states where a repressive industrial society would push workers to unite and rise up against their industrialist masters. The Russian nation in 1913 had experienced the beginnings of modern economic growth, but it could hardly have been called an advanced capitalist system. Table 24.1 shows that its relative position in terms of per capita income had improved in the half century prior to 1913, but that it still lagged far behind the other industrial countries of the world.

When the Bolsheviks took power after the October Revolution in 1917, they found themselves without the advanced industrial base that Marx had envisioned and with no real blueprint for running a socialist or communist state. Marx's writings provided only the broadest guidelines. Undaunted, the new government immediately abolished private land ownership and ordered that the land be distributed to those who worked on it. It also established worker control of industry and nationalized the banks. Sweeping nationalization of industry began in June 1918. Money, private trade, and wage differentials were abolished. All decisions were made centrally.

TABLE 24.1		
PER CAPITA INCOME (RUBLES)		
	1861	**1913**
Russia	71	119
U.K.	323	580
France	150	303
Germany	175	374
U.S.	450	1,033
Netherlands	—	366
Norway	166	659
Sweden	112	340
Italy	183	261
Spain	—	199
Austria-Hungary	—	190

Source: Paul Gregory and Robert Stuart, *Soviet Economic Structure and Performance*, 2nd ed. (New York: Harper & Row, 1981), p. 20.

The headlong rush into uncharted waters was too much too soon, and between 1921 and 1928 Soviet leaders retreated from their initial hard line back toward a market orientation. The **New Economic Policy** of the period was characterized by decentralization. Most smaller industrial enterprises were denationalized, although the peasants remained in control of agriculture. State control of production was replaced by market links between consumers and industry and between industry and agriculture.

The relative merits and demerits of these two periods, 1917–1921 and 1921–1928, were debated at length among the Soviet leadership. Finally, in 1928, the Soviet Union settled on an economic structure that lasted into the 1980s: comprehensive central planning and collectivization of agriculture. In 1928, under the leadership of Joseph Stalin, the first of many **five-year plans** was approved. The plan emphasized rapid industrialization and the production of industrial capital; in fact, the plan called for a doubling of the fixed capital stock of the Soviet Union in five years. Consumer goods were to be produced only when all other needs of the new industrial structure had been met.

The industrialization program depended on a steady flow of food and agricultural raw materials from the countryside, and that did not come easily. As a result, Stalin was forced to rely more and more on coercion. In 1929 the land holdings of the peasants were organized into collective farms that were obligated to deliver state-ordered quotas of farm products. Repression was severe, and millions of peasants perished.[3]

No serious debate about economic matters took place in the Soviet Union until after Stalin's death in 1953. In 1965 official reforms were introduced by the government of Alexei Kosygin. More recently, Mikhail Gorbachev announced a series of reforms in 1986 and more dramatic reforms in 1987, but the structure of the economy was not changed fundamentally on either of these occasions.

Since 1991, Boris Yeltsin has been president of the Russian Republic and the champion of reform. Yeltsin has deregulated most prices, begun the privatization process, and attempted to stabilize the macroeconomy. By 1995 progress had been slow but significant. Privatization had made steady progress, reaching a point in 1994 where the private sector was generating 60% of personal income. Inflation was down, and a new "economic constitution" in the form of revised laws to establish property rights and stimulate economic activity went into effect in 1995. But things were not going well across the board. Organized crime was becoming a huge force as privatization and desperation provided a new incentive for criminal activity. In addition, oil production continued to fall, and Russian agriculture produced the smallest harvest since the mid-1980s.

■ **Economic Performance** The Stalinist/Soviet strategy to achieve high rates of growth worked for many years. The highest rates of growth in Soviet GNP were during the 1950s. Official Soviet statistics put the real growth rate during that decade at over 10%, an extraordinary rate at which real output would double every seven years. Even the CIA's more conservative estimates, shown in Table 24.2, estimated the Soviet growth rate at 5.7%, nearly 80% above the U.S. average for the decade.

In 1957, the Soviet Union's GNP stood at about 39% of the United States' GNP. A year later, Soviet GNP had jumped to nearly 44% of U.S. GNP. The rate at which the Soviet Union was catching up was so remarkable that it prompted Soviet Premier Nikita Khrushchev to promise, "We will bury you!" If the Soviet growth rate estimates had been correct, and if both countries had continued to grow at the same rates that they did during the 1950s, Soviet GNP would indeed have surpassed U.S. GNP by 1970.

New Economic Policy *The Soviet economic policy in effect between 1921 and 1928; characterized by decentralization and a retreat to a market orientation.*

five-year plans *Plans developed in the Soviet Union that provided general guidelines and directions for the next five years.*

---

[3]*George Orwell's novel* Animal Farm *is a parable of this period in Soviet history.*

TABLE 24.2	ECONOMIC GROWTH AND INVESTMENT IN THE SOVIET UNION AND THE UNITED STATES, 1950–1990				
	ANNUAL AVERAGE RATE OF GROWTH				
	USSR NET MATERIAL PRODUCT (USSR, OFFICIAL FIGURES)	USSR REAL GNP (CIA)	USA REAL GNP	USSR CAPITAL STOCK	USA CAPITAL STOCK
1950–1960	10.3	5.7	3.2	9.5	3.6
1960–1970	7.1	5.1	4.0	8.0	4.0
1970–1975	5.7	3.7	2.6	7.9	4.0
1975–1980	4.3	2.7	3.7	6.8	3.9
1980–1984	—	2.6	2.7	6.3*	3.6
1984–1987	—	1.8	2.4	NA	NA
1988–1990	—	0.0	2.4	NA	NA

Note: *1980–1983. NA = not available. GDP data not available.

Sources: Abram Bergson, "Gorbachev Calls for Intensive Growth," *Challenge*, November–December 1985. For the United States, *Statistical Abstract of the United States, 1986 and 1990; Historical Statistics of the United States,* and *Economic Report of the President, 1990.*

The primary force behind Soviet growth was capital accumulation. During the 1950s, the capital stock of the USSR grew at 9.5% annually; in the United States, the corresponding figure was only 3.6 percent. Through 1975 Soviet capital stocks grew at twice the rate of capital accumulation in the United States. But these growth rates did not continue, and during the late 1970s they slowed down. Between 1975 and 1985, even the slowly growing U.S. economy outperformed the Soviet Union. In 1975, per capita GNP in the Soviet Union stood at 48.2% of per capita GNP in the United States. In 1985 the figure was 48.1 percent.

■ **Gorbachev and *Perestroika*** In March 1985, Mikhail Gorbachev became general secretary of the Soviet Communist Party and almost immediately began to press for reforms that had an enormous impact on the world. In 1990, Gorbachev won the Nobel Peace Prize for ending the Cold War and was named "Man of the Decade" by *Time* magazine. Yet despite his enormous popularity around the world and his political successes, one prize continued to elude Gorbachev: improved economic performance in the Soviet Union.

Gorbachev's reforms fell into two broad categories: *glasnost* ("openness") and *perestroika* ("restructuring"). *Glasnost* led to the almost completely open discussion of virtually every aspect of political and economic reform in the Soviet Union. It also led to a new set of political institutions, including an end to the power monopoly of the Communist party[4] and more free elections. Glasnost was relatively easy to achieve, but the establishment of new economic structures—the key element of Gorbachev's *perestroika*—proved much more difficult.

---

[4]*For many years, membership in and loyalty to the Communist party were the ticket to the good life in the Soviet Union. Under the* nomenklatura *party patronage system, Communist party leaders received power and privilege in exchange for loyalty to the party. In addition to determining the staffing of government and industrial posts (a practice that led to a good deal of favoritism and nepotism), party members also enjoyed the right to shop at special state-run stores. These stores stocked luxury items that were not available to the general public. Travel privileges, admissions to the best colleges and universities, larger apartments, and bigger cars also went to members of the* nomenklatura. *In 1990, the Central Committee of the Soviet Communist Party approved a proposal by President Gorbachev calling for an end to the party's constitutional guarantee of power and thus an end to the* nomenklatura. *After the failed August 1991 coup, the Communist party was completely dismantled.*

The initial goal of *perestroika* was to increase workers' responsibilities and discipline by attacking corruption and alcoholism. In these arenas, Gorbachev met with some success. Numerous bureau chiefs were replaced, alcoholism was reduced through strict law enforcement, absenteeism declined, and productivity increased. Then, in 1986, the focus of reform shifted to the performance of agriculture. In that year, Gorbachev announced a major restructuring of the agricultural sector that gave local farm units and the peasantry significant new freedoms. Local farm units, for example, were allowed to use the market to dispose of any surplus over five-year plan levels. Payments to state and collective farm workers were tied to productivity and profits, and local directors were given much more authority over management and investment decisions.

But the best was yet to come. In June of 1987, Gorbachev announced yet another series of reforms. The package included some surprising changes. First, price subsidies were to be drastically reduced or eliminated, even on such staple items as meat, bread, dairy products, and housing. Second, all limits on what workers could earn were to be removed, and salaries were to be tied directly to performance. Third, the decision-making authority of the farms and enterprises was to be greatly expanded. Central plans were to contain far less detail than in previous years. At the same time, Gorbachev called for sharp increases in small-scale family farming and for a "competitive atmosphere" among enterprises to ensure that goods were sold to consumers at the lowest possible prices that would still cover costs of production.

Perhaps the most radical of the 1987 reforms, however, was that job security, a sacred tenet of the Soviet system, would be reduced. For the first time, enterprises could actually fire lazy workers, and unproductive enterprises could be shut down.

■ **Economic Crisis and Collapse** Although many of Gorbachev's ideas seemed promising, the situation in the Soviet Union deteriorated sharply after 1987. The attempted transition from central planning to a partly free-market system caused major problems. Growth of output slowed to a crawl in 1989 and 1990, and in 1991 the economic system collapsed. Industrial production dropped sharply, food shortages grew worse, inflation became a serious problem, and external debt increased rapidly.

Gorbachev ran out of time in August of 1991 as the struggle between the hard-liners and the radical reformers came to a head. The hard-liners took Gorbachev prisoner and assumed control of the government. The coup lasted only three days. People took to the streets of Moscow and resisted the tanks, the Soviet army refused to obey orders, and the hard-liners were out.

But the end was near for both Gorbachev and the Soviet Union. In December of 1991, the Soviet Union was dissolved, 10 of the former Soviet republics formed the Commonwealth of Independent States (CIS), and Boris Yeltsin became president of the Russian Republic as Gorbachev became part of history. From the beginning, Yeltsin showed himself to be a reformer committed to converting the Russian economy rapidly into a market system while maintaining hard-won political freedoms for the people. His reform plan called for deregulating prices, privatizing public enterprises, and stabilizing the macroeconomy.

THE TRANSITION TO A MARKET ECONOMY

The reforms underway in the Russian Republic and in the other formerly communist countries of Eastern Europe have taken shape very slowly and amid a great deal of debate about how best to proceed. It is important to remember that there is absolutely no historical precedent to provide lessons. Despite this lack of precedent,

IF THE GOVERNMENT SETS PRICES BELOW MARKET-CLEARING LEVELS, BLACK MARKETS ARE LIKELY TO DE-
VELOP. IN UKRAINE, IT IS SOMETIMES EASIER TO BUY POTS AND PANS ON THE STREET THAN IT IS TO FIND
THEM IN STORES.

however, there is substantial agreement among economists about what needs to be done. Specifically:

> Economists generally agree on six basic requirements for a successful transition from socialism to a market-based system: (1) macroeconomic stabilization; (2) deregulation of prices and liberalization of trade; (3) privatization of state-owned enterprises and development of new private industry; (4) the establishment of market-supporting institutions, such as property and contract laws, accounting systems, and so forth; (5) a social safety net to deal with unemployment and poverty; and (6) external assistance.

We discuss each of these components in the sections that follow. While we focus on the experience of the Russian Republic, keep in mind that these principles apply to all economies in transition.

■ **Macroeconomic Stabilization** Virtually every one of the countries in transition has had a problem with inflation, but nowhere has it been worse than in Russia. As economic conditions worsened, the government found itself with serious budget problems. As revenue flows slowed and expenditure commitments increased, large budget deficits resulted. At the same time, each of the new republics established its own central bank. Each central bank began issuing "ruble credits" to keep important enterprises afloat and to pay the government's bills. The issuance of these credits, which were generally accepted as a means of payment throughout the country, led to a dramatic expansion of the money supply.

Almost from the beginning, the expanded money supply meant that too much money was chasing too few goods. This situation was made worse by government-controlled prices set substantially below market-clearing levels. The combination of monetary expansion and price control was deadly. Government-run shops that sold goods at controlled prices were empty. People waited in line for days and often became violent when their efforts to buy goods at low official prices were thwarted. At the same time, suppliers found that they could charge much higher prices for their products on the black market—which grew bigger by the day, further exacerbating the shortage of goods at government shops. Over time, the ruble became worth less and less as black market prices continued to rise ever more rapidly. As a result, Russia found itself with near hyperinflation in 1992.

To achieve a properly functioning market system, prices must be stabilized. To do so, the government must find a way to move toward a balanced budget and to bring the supply of money under control.

■ **Deregulation of Prices and Liberalization of Trade** To move successfully from central planning to a market system, individual prices must be deregulated. A system of freely moving prices forms the backbone of a market system. When people want more of a good than is currently being produced, its price will rise. This higher price increases producers' profits and provides an incentive for existing firms to expand production and for new firms to enter the industry. Conversely, if an industry is producing a good for which there is no market or a good that people no longer want in the same quantity, the result will be excess supply and the price of that good will fall. This reduces profits or creates losses, providing an incentive for some existing firms to cut back on production and for others to go out of business. In short, an unregulated price mechanism ensures an efficient allocation of resources across industries. Until prices are deregulated, this mechanism cannot function.

Trade barriers must also be removed. To achieve a successful transition, reform-minded countries must be able to import capital, technology, and ideas from abroad. In addition, it makes no sense to continue to subsidize industries that cannot be competitive on world markets. If it is cheaper to buy steel from an efficient West German steel mill than to produce it in a subsidized antiquated Russian mill, the Russian mill should be modernized or shut down. Ultimately, as the theory of comparative advantage suggests, liberalized trade will push each country to produce those products that it produces best.

Deregulating prices and eliminating subsidies can bring serious political problems. Many products in Russia and the rest of the socialist world were priced below market-clearing levels for equity reasons. Housing, food, and clothing were considered by many to be entitlements. Making them more expensive, at least relative to their prices in previous times, is not likely to be popular. In addition, forcing inefficient firms to operate without subsidies will lead many to go out of business, and jobs will be lost. So while price deregulation and trade liberalization are necessary, they are very difficult politically.

■ **Privatization** One problem with a system of central ownership is a lack of accountability. Under a system of private ownership, owners reap the rewards of their successes and suffer the consequences of their failures. Private ownership provides a strong incentive for efficient operation, innovation, and hard work that is lacking when ownership is centralized and profits are distributed to the people.

The classic story used to illustrate this point is called the **tragedy of commons.** Suppose that an agricultural community has 10,000 acres of grazing land. If the land were held in common so that all farmers had unlimited rights to graze their animals, each farmer would have an incentive to overgraze. He or she would reap the full benefits from grazing additional calves while the costs of grazing the calves would be borne collectively. The system provides no incentive to manage the land

tragedy of commons *The idea that collective ownership may not provide the proper private incentives for efficiency because individuals do not bear the full costs of their own decisions but do enjoy the full benefits.*

efficiently. Similarly, if the efficiency and benefits of my hard work and managerial skills accrue to others or to the state, what incentive do I have to work hard or to be efficient?

One solution to the tragedy of commons attempted in eighteenth-century Britain was to divide up the land into private holdings. Today, many economists argue, the solution to the incentive problem encountered in state-owned enterprises is to privatize them and let the owners compete.

In addition to increasing accountability, privatization means creating a climate in which new enterprises can flourish. If there is market demand for a product not currently being produced, individual entrepreneurs should be free to set up a business and make a profit. During the last months of the Soviet Union's existence, private enterprises such as taxi services, car repair services, restaurants, and even hotels began to spring up all over the country.

Like deregulation of prices, privatization is difficult politically. Privatization means that many protected enterprises will go out of business because they cannot compete at world prices. Going out of business means a loss of jobs, at least temporarily.

■ **Market-Supporting Institutions**   Between 1991 and 1995, U.S. firms raced to Eastern Europe in search of markets and investment opportunities and immediately became aware of a major obstacle. The institutions that make the market function relatively smoothly in the United States do not exist in Eastern Europe.

For example, the capital market, which channels private saving into productive capital investment in developed capitalist economies, is made up of hundreds of different institutions. The banking system, venture capital funds, the stock market, the bond market, the commodity exchanges, brokerage houses, investment banks, and the like have all developed in the United States over a period of hundreds of years, and they will not simply be replicated overnight in the formerly communist world.

Many market-supporting institutions are so basic that Americans take them for granted. The institution of private property, for example, is a set of rights that must be protected by laws that the government must be willing to enforce. Suppose that the French hotel chain Novotel decides to build a new hotel in Moscow. Novotel must first acquire land. Then it will construct a building based on the expectation of renting rooms to customers. These investments are made with the expectation that the owner has a right to use them and a right to the profits that they produce. For such investments to be undertaken, these rights must be guaranteed by a set of property laws. This is equally true for large business firms and for Russian entrepreneurs who want to start their own enterprises.

Similarly, the law must provide for the enforcement of contracts. In the United States, a huge body of law determines what happens to you if you break a formal promise made in good faith. Businesses exist on promises to produce and promises to pay. Without recourse to the law when a contract is breached, contracts will not be entered into, goods will not be manufactured, and services will not be provided.

Another seemingly simple matter that turns out to be quite complex is the establishment of a set of accounting principles. In the United States, the rules of the accounting game are embodied in a set of Generally Accepted Accounting Principles (GAAP) that carry the force of law. Companies are required to keep track of their receipts, expenditures, and liabilities so that their performance can be observed and evaluated by shareholders, taxing authorities, and others who have an interest in the company. If you have ever taken a course in accounting, you know how detailed these rules have become. Imagine trying to do business in a country operating under hundreds of different sets of rules and you can imagine what has been happening in Russia.

Another institution worthy of mention is insurance. Whenever a venture undertakes a high-risk activity, it buys insurance to protect itself. Several years ago, Amnesty International (a non-profit organization that works to protect civil liberties around the world) sponsored a worldwide concert tour with a number of well-known rock bands and performers. The most difficult part of organizing the tour was obtaining insurance for the artists and their equipment when they played in the then-communist countries of Eastern Europe.

■ **Social Safety Net** In a centrally planned socialist economy, the labor market does not function freely. Everyone who wants a job is guaranteed one somewhere. The number of jobs is determined by a central plan to match the number of workers. Thus, in centrally planned economies, there is essentially no such thing as unemployment. This, it has been argued, is one of the great advantages of a planned system. In addition, a central planning system provides basic housing, food, and clothing at very affordable levels for all. With no unemployment and necessities available at very low prices, there is no need for unemployment insurance, welfare, or other social programs.

Transition to a free labor market and liberalization of prices means that some workers will end up unemployed and everyone will pay higher prices for necessities. Indeed, during the early phases of the transition process, unemployment will be high. Inefficient state-owned enterprises will go out of business; some sectors will contract while others expand. As more and more people experience unemployment, popular support for reform is likely to drop unless some sort of social safety net is erected to ease the transition. This social safety net might include unemployment insurance, aid for the poor, and food and housing assistance. The experiences of the developed world have shown that such programs are expensive.

■ **External Assistance** Very few believe that the transition to a market system can be achieved without outside support and some outside financing. Knowledge of and experience with capitalist institutions that exist in the United States, Western Europe, and Japan are of vital interest to the Eastern European nations. The basic skills of accounting, management, and enterprise development can be taught to Eastern Europe, and many argue that it is in everyone's best interest to do so. Many also argue that the world's biggest nightmare is an economically weak or desperate Russia armed with nuclear weapons giving up on reform or falling into the hands of a dictator.

There is little agreement about the extent of *financial* support that should be given, however. The United States has pushed for a worldwide effort to provide billions of dollars in aid. This aid, many argue, will help Russia stabilize its macroeconomy and buy desperately needed goods from abroad. However, critics in both the United States and other potential donor countries argue that pouring money into Russia now is like pouring it into a black hole. No matter how much money we donate, they say, it will have little impact on the ultimate success or failure of the reforms.

SHOCK THERAPY OR GRADUALISM?

Although economists generally agree on what the former socialist economies need to do, much debate exists about the sequence and timing of specific reforms.

The popular press describes the debate as one between those who believe in "shock therapy" (sometimes called the "Big Bang" approach) and those who prefer a more gradual approach. Advocates of **shock therapy** believe that the economies in transition should proceed immediately on all fronts. That is, they should stop printing money, deregulate prices and liberalize trade, privatize, develop market

shock therapy *The approach to transition from socialism to market capitalism that advocates rapid deregulation of prices, liberalization of trade, and privatization.*

institutions, build a social safety net, and acquire external aid—all as quickly as possible. The pain will be severe, the argument goes, but in the end it will be forgotten as the transition raises living standards. Advocates of a *gradualist* approach believe the best course of action is to build up market institutions first, gradually decontrol prices, and privatize only the most efficient government enterprises first.

Those who favor moving quickly point to the apparent success of Poland, which moved quite rapidly through the first phases of reform. Russia's experience during the first years of its transition have demonstrated that, at least in that country, change must be to some extent gradual. In theory, stabilization and price liberalization can be achieved instantaneously. But to enjoy the benefits of liberalization, a good deal of privatization must have taken place—and that will take more time. As one analyst has said, privatization means "selling assets with no value to people with no money." Some estimates suggest that as many as half of Russian state-owned enterprises are incapable of making a profit at world prices. Simply cutting them loose would create chaos. In a sense, Russia has no choice but to move slowly.

ALTERNATIVE ECONOMIC SYSTEMS

We now turn to a discussion of two alternative economic systems: that of China and that of Japan.

THE PEOPLE'S REPUBLIC OF CHINA

Continuing around the globe eastward from the Russian Republic lies China, the world's most populous country. With 1.2 billion people, mainland China accounts for one out of every five people in the world.

China remains a country in which political dissent is not tolerated and the economic system remains communist but in which private enterprise is permitted and even encouraged. This seemingly incongruous system is performing, at least for now, as well as any economy in the world. China, like Russia, is an enormously important power in the world, and understanding its history and the nature of its economic institutions is an essential part of understanding economics.

Compared to the United States, the People's Republic of China is very large and very poor. Per capita income in China is about one twentieth of per capita income in the United States. The history of the People's Republic, established after the communist victory in the revolution of 1949, has been marked by wild gyrations of policy and some extraordinary economic experiments.

■ **Socialization under Mao Zedong** Soon after gaining power, the Chinese Communists, under the leadership of Chairman Mao Zedong, became involved in the Korean War and found themselves heavily dependent on the Soviet Union. Not surprisingly, then, the early structure of the Chinese economic system was built on the Soviet-Stalinist model. China's first five-year plan, from 1953 to 1957, focused on developing capital-intensive heavy industries. Agriculture was collectivized, household farming was eliminated, and compulsory output quotas were put in place.

In 1958 China departed sharply from the Soviet model and launched a new economic strategy called the **Great Leap Forward.** The focus of production shifted from large-scale, capital-intensive industry to small-scale, labor-intensive industry scattered across the countryside. In addition, material incentives were reduced and replaced by the motivating power of revolutionary ideology and inspiration. Although initially successful, the strategy ultimately failed. In the early 1960s,

Great Leap Forward *The economic strategy in the People's Republic of China that began in 1958 when it departed from the Soviet model and shifted from large-scale, capital-intensive industry to small-scale, labor-intensive industry scattered across the countryside. Material incentives were reduced and replaced by the motivating power of revolutionary ideology and inspiration.*

output fell below 1958 levels. Between 1961 and 1965, material incentives were restored and a period of relative calm followed.

During the late 1960s and 1970s, economic development in China suffered a heavy blow from the **Great Proletarian Cultural Revolution** which began in 1966. For almost a decade, the rule was ideological purity. The faithful—which included almost everyone—denounced those who favored material incentives and reform, and scientists, engineers, managers, and scholars whose views were out of favor were sent to the countryside to work in the fields. The universities were essentially closed down. Untrained revolutionary *cadres* (small groups of leaders) replaced trained specialists in almost all jobs, and the economy suffered terribly. Most estimates place per capita income and consumption in the late 1970s at levels only slightly above the levels of 1956–1957.[5]

Great Proletarian Cultural Revolution (1966–1976) *A period of ideological purity in the People's Republic of China: Material incentives and reforms were denounced and highly trained specialists were sent to work in the fields. The effect of the Cultural Revolution on the Chinese economy was catastrophic.*

■ **The Reforms of Deng Xiaoping**   When Chairman Mao died in September of 1976, the Cultural Revolution formally ended. In the meantime, China watched as its once poor neighbors—Japan, South Korea, Taiwan, and Singapore—enjoyed extraordinary growth and prosperity.

In December of 1978, the Chinese Central Committee, under the leadership of Deng Xiaoping, announced sweeping reforms. These early reforms focused on agriculture, and they signaled the beginning of profound changes in the Chinese economy that would continue over the next ten years.

Prior to 1978, each agricultural commune had distributed the harvest equally among its members. Incentives were purely collective, with everything done for the glory of the revolution. Because the cadres often overstated harvests, the state raised local delivery quotas, leaving the peasants with barely enough to go around. The new system begun under Deng Xiaoping gave individual families, through a 15-year family contract, formal rights to the land that they worked. Families were also given the rights to dispose of any surpluses and to hire out part of the family labor force to enterprises outside the family plot. Deng gave the Chinese peasants permission to enrich themselves, and they did.

The results were extraordinary. Output of grain and other basic necessities, such as cotton, increased substantially. More importantly, rural industry grew dramatically, employing over 20% of the rural labor force by 1985. From 1978 through 1983, wheat production increased at an annual rate of 8.6%, rice at 4.3%, and cotton at 16.4 percent. From 1981 to 1984, the growth rate of all agricultural output reached 11.0% annually. In 1984 China actually became an exporter of food, despite a population of over one billion. Peasant income more than doubled in less than a decade, and private consumption and housing construction increased sharply.[6]

Similar reforms were implemented in Chinese industry on an experimental basis. Initially, enterprises were able to retain 15% to 25% of any profits over and above those specified by the plan. By 1984, Chinese enterprises across the country were retaining over 85% of increased profits. As with agricultural reform, the goals of industrial reform were to increase the role of the producing unit, to increase individual incentives, and to reduce the role of the state and the central planners.

The most significant element of all these reforms, however, was the movement by the Chinese government to support the expansion of enterprise rights. In the

[5]*See Nicholas Lardy, "Agricultural Reform," Journal of International Affairs, Winter 1986.*
[6]*"China: Economic Performance in 1985, A Report to the Subcommittee on Economic Resources, Competitiveness and Security of the Joint Economic Committee." The Central Intelligence Agency, Washington, D.C.: March 17, 1986 (mimeo), p. 2.*

spirit of the Soviet New Economic Policy of the 1920s, the Chinese are actively encouraging small private trade and manufacturing. Today there is an increasingly important Chinese private sector competing with state stores in style, service, quality, and even price. By 1986, 480,000 "new economic associations" were employing 4.2 million people.[7] China is also now encouraging foreign investment. Initially only joint ventures with the government were permitted, but now foreigners retain 100% ownership in several projects.

■ **China after Tiananmen Square** Despite the economic advances that China has made in the last decades, there is a great deal of political unrest in the country. In May of 1989, thousands of university students openly challenged the authority of the government by occupying Tiananmen Square in Beijing. Many went on hunger strikes to protest China's lack of democracy. The "democracy movement" was crushed on June 3, 1989, when the government cleared the square with troops and tanks as the world watched in horror.

The events of 1989 turned the tide of world opinion against the Chinese and at least temporarily slowed the movement toward economic reform. A number of joint ventures were canceled, and the amount of direct aid flowing into China was reduced. But even before Tiananmen Square, Chinese economic reforms were beginning to encounter difficulty.

In 1988, China experienced serious inflation for the first time. By late 1988, prices were rising in historically unprecedented amounts, nearly 30% per year. In September, the government began implementing an austerity program that included strict price controls, reduced state investment, and reduced imports. The rate of inflation had dropped by 1989, but output of goods and services in China fell in 1989 and grew only slightly in 1990.

The years 1991–1995 saw a dramatic turnaround for China. While the current Communist government has retained power and maintained a hard line on the political front, economic freedoms have been extended into every sphere. Private enterprise continues to be encouraged (see the Global Perspective box on page 581 titled "China: Free Enterprise in a Communist Country"). A stock market was established and stock prices have boomed dramatically. Everyone in China, it seems, wants a piece of the action. In October of 1992, First Boston Corporation, Merrill Lynch and Co., and Salomon Brothers offered five million shares in and raised more than $75 million for the JinBei Vehicle Manufacturing Company in the city of Shenyang. Hundreds of billions of dollars in foreign investment are now flowing into China from the United States, Japan, Singapore, Taiwan, and Korea.

Recent estimates put China's growth rate at more than 10% per year and climbing. There has been a real estate boom in Shanghai, where a middle-class home is now more expensive than a comparable house in the United States. There are even stories of a kind of "capitalist mania" breaking out in a number of locations. Nonetheless, some problems and challenges remain. First, many fear that food shortages are imminent. While the Chinese population has continued to grow, the country's expanding industrial and housing sectors have led to a declining amount of land under cultivation. (In fact, China contains 20% of the world's population but only 7% of the world's arable land.) Second, over 50,000 state-owned enterprises continue to operate, although the process of selling these enterprises to foreign investors and allowing them to go into a form of bankruptcy continues. The third problem is inflation, which at the beginning of 1995 was running at 22% annually, with sharp increase in the price of food leading the way (grain up 60%, vegetables up 49 percent).

---

[7]Beijing Review, *no. 25, June 23, 1986.*

The following excerpt from a recent *New York Times* article summarizes quite nicely what seems to be happening in a rapidly changing China:

QIAOTOU, China—For a glimpse into China's economic revolution, it is useful to stroll down the main street of this humble little town. . . [which] has propelled itself over the last dozen years into the button capital of the world.

Each year, the privately run factories of Qiaotou produce about 12 billion buttons. . . . This button boom, amounting to two buttons annually per inhabitant on earth, has transformed rice paddies into factory districts, and peasants into tycoons.

One of them is Zhan Yusheng, a 27-year-old who began making buttons in his home 10 years ago. Today he owns a button factory with 100 employees, and last year he had sales of nearly $200,000.

"Now we need to upgrade our quality and produce more high-quality buttons," said Chen Jianlin, Qiaotou's Communist Party secretary. "Then we can expand on the international market.". . . Mr. Chen sees his mission primarily as promoting private enterprise.

"My most important job is building up the economy," Mr. Chen said as he sipped tea at the conference table in his office. "People here say: 'If you push the economy along, you're

EACH YEAR, THE PRIVATELY-RUN FACTORIES OF QIAOTOU, CHINA, PRODUCE ABOUT 12 BILLION BUTTONS, PRIMARILY OF THE INEXPENSIVE KIND FOUND ON DISCOUNT-PRICED CLOTHING.

a good leader. Otherwise, you're not.' "

While his salary is only $20 a month, about a third as much as the 20,000 migrant workers employed in Qiaotou's factories,. . . the party covers most of his expenses, supplies him with a house, a chauffered Audi, a phone with international direct dialing, a beeper, and a Mastercard.

"A lot of people here now carry credit cards when they travel," Mr. Chen said, beaming as he passed around his Mastercard for inspection. "Credit cards are very convenient and you don't have to carry so much cash."

Source: Nicholas D. Kristof, "Free Enterprise Encouraged," *The New York Times,* January 18, 1993.

JAPAN

No discussion of alternative economic systems would be complete without a few words on Japan. No country in history has accomplished what the Japanese economy has during the post–World War II period. Japan's economic progress over the last several decades is, with good reason, called the "Japanese economic miracle."

Since 1950 per capita GNP in Japan has grown from less than 20% of U.S. GNP to over 70 percent. Between 1951 and 1973, real GNP in Japan grew at an average annual rate of over 10%—in just over two decades, a seven-and-a-half-fold increase. Since the mid-1970s, economic growth in Japan has slowed, but until very recently the Japanese economy still significantly outperformed the U.S. economy.

What led to the Japanese "miracle"? Was it simply a matter of culture? Japan is a very disciplined society with a strong work ethic and a long tradition of co-operation. But although cultural differences may be part of the story, there is far more to it than that.

Structurally, Japan's is essentially a free-market capitalist economy. No industrialized country in the world has a smaller public sector, and none has a more "pro-business" government. To a very large extent, the private decisions of households and firms produced the miracle.

To explain Japan's success more specifically, analysts point to four major factors: (1) very high rates of saving and investment, (2) a highly trained labor force, (3) rapid absorption and effective utilization of technology, much of it imported, and (4) a pro-growth government policy.[8] Of these, perhaps the single most important cause of Japan's growth has been its incredible rate of investment. Between 1951 and 1973, the capital stock of Japan grew by more than 9% per year, and for a substantial period of time investment approached 40% of GNP. Between 1960 and 1980, the capital stock in the United States increased at about 4% per year, while gross investment fluctuated between 15% and 17% per year. Virtually all of Japan's investment was financed with domestic saving. Japan's rate of saving by households has been the highest in the world.

Until recent years, rates of return on new investment in Japan were high. But today Japan faces a new problem. Its high rates of investment have virtually exhausted the investment opportunities in the nation and pushed rates of return on saving to very low levels. The saving rate has remained high, however, and this has led many Japanese citizens to look abroad for a place to put their savings. A significant part of those savings flowed to the United States during the 1980s. Real interest rates are much higher in the United States than in Japan, and a considerable number of new U.S. government bonds are now being sold to the Japanese. The Japanese are also investing billions of dollars in U.S. common stocks and real estate.

The second factor contributing to Japan's economic success is the quality of the Japanese labor force. As early as 1950, Japan had an education level comparable to that of the United States, despite a much lower level of economic development. Most Japanese workers were employed in jobs that demanded extremely low productivity relative to the education and training of those holding them. As the country's capital stock grew, workers moved easily into higher-productivity jobs.

Japan also consciously adopted the most advanced industrial technologies in the world. Much of the knowledge necessary to do this was available in technical journals or obtainable in U.S. graduate schools, and some came embodied in machinery and equipment imported into Japan. The Japanese were extremely

---

[8]*This discussion owes much to an excellent paper by Hugh Patrick and Henry Rosovsky, "Japan's Economic Performance: An Overview" in* Asia's New Giant, *eds. Hugh Patrick and Henry Rosovsky (The Brookings Institution, 1976).*

effective at improving upon and commercializing what they imported. By importing technology, Japan did not have to develop it on its own; and, until recently, Japan devoted a smaller portion of its GNP to research and development than did the United States.

The role of government in the Japanese economy is certainly different from the role of government in the United States. There is disagreement among economists about the importance of government as an instrument of growth in Japan. It is clear that the main source of growth has been the private sector but that the government has played a supportive role. For example, after World War II, the Japanese government, through the **Ministry of Trade and Industry (MITI)**, used tariffs and quotas to protect and subsidize a number of key industries, including coal, steel, electric power, and shipbuilding. During the 1960s, chemicals and machinery were added to the list. In the mid-1980s, the government and the private sector launched a partnership designed to develop and market the next generation of computers. MITI also helps some sectors of the economy plan orderly reductions in capacity. In short, the Japanese government is actively involved in the allocation process and has much to say about which industries will grow and which will not.

Ministry of Trade and Industry (MITI) *The agency of the Japanese government responsible for industrial policy. It uses tariffs and subsidies to protect and subsidize key industries and helps some sectors plan orderly reductions in capacity.*

■ **Japan in the 1990s** The enormous success of the Japanese economy led to seemingly unbounded optimism at the end of the 1980s. Spurred by the profitability of Japanese firms, the market prices of Japanese stocks raced to unprecedented levels. At the same time, Japanese land values boomed. At one point, land in Tokyo was trading for as much as $6000 per square foot. At that price, a small 100 by 100 foot plot of land (less than a quarter of an acre) was worth $60 million!

Then, in 1992, the bottom fell out of the Japanese stock market and land prices began to fall. For the first time in the history of modern Japan, confidence in the future was shaken. During 1992 and 1993, Japan slipped into a recession, which continued into 1994, and real GDP fell. People in Japan began referring to the 1980s as the period of the "bubble economy." Late 1994 saw a return to growth, but 1995 brought a series of setbacks, including a devastating earthquake in the city of Kobe as well as a tremendous increase in the value of the yen. A more expensive yen made Japanese products look much more expensive to the rest of the world and threatened to choke off demand and plunge the Japanese economy back into recession.

Despite these setbacks, Japan remains an enormous economic power and a vital U.S. trading partner. As the economy becomes even more globalized in the coming years, it will be essential to understand more fully the successes and failures of Japanese industrial policy.

CONCLUSION

This chapter has introduced very briefly the structure, history, and performance of several different economic systems. It has also discussed the enormous problems of transforming a socialist economy into a market-based economy. So brief a description and analysis, we acknowledge, must be somewhat frustrating. After all, many volumes have been written on these topics. But a study of basic economics without such a "tour," however hasty, would be incomplete.

Studying alternative economic systems is a fitting way to conclude an introduction to economics. One of the themes running through this book has been the role of government in a market economy. We have tried to present a balanced description of how economies function, both in theory and in the real world. Throughout, we have focused on the potential benefits and problems associated with public-sector involvement. Eastern Europe, Russia, China, and Japan present very different perspectives on the interaction between the private and public sectors.

Concluding with this chapter is also, we hope, an enticement to further study. This is an exciting time in the world's economic history. Never before have systems changed so dramatically in such a short time. Many believe that the reforms in China, Eastern Europe, and Russia have brought the world much closer together and that the time is ripe for a significant reduction in world political tensions. Others believe that the problems of transition are so difficult that the whole process will disintegrate into chaos. Only time will tell.

SUMMARY

POLITICAL SYSTEMS AND ECONOMIC SYSTEMS: SOCIALISM, CAPITALISM, AND COMMUNISM

1. A *socialist economy* is one in which most capital is owned by the government rather than by private citizens. A *capitalist economy* is one in which most capital is privately owned. *Communism* is a theoretical economic system in which the people directly control the means of production (capital and land) without the intervention of a government or state.

2. Economies differ in the extent to which decisions are made through central planning rather than through a market system. Generally, socialist economies favor central planning over market allocation, and capitalist economies rely to a much greater extent on the market. Nonetheless, there are markets in all societies, and planning takes place in all economies.

THE ECONOMIC THEORIES OF KARL MARX

3. According to Marxian thought, private ownership and profit are both unfair and unethical. Profit is value that is created by labor but expropriated by nonproductive capitalists, who are able to exploit labor by virtue of their ownership of the means of production (land and capital).

4. Marx predicted that falling rates of profit, increasing exploitation, and deeper business cycles would eventually cause capitalism to collapse.

5. Neoclassical economics sees profit as a return to a productive factor (capital) just as wages are the return to another productive factor (labor).

ECONOMIES IN TRANSITION: THE EXPERIENCES OF RUSSIA AND EASTERN EUROPE

6. When the Bolsheviks took power in Russia after the October Revolution in 1917, they found themselves without the advanced industrial base that

Marx had envisioned and with no real blueprint for running a socialist or communist state. Marx had written mainly about capitalism, not socialism.

7. In 1928, the Soviet Union settled into comprehensive central planning and collectivization of agriculture, an economic structure that lasted into the 1980s. Virtually all productive assets, including most land and capital, were publicly owned. There was no formal private business sector, no market for capital goods, and no income from property.

8. The Soviet Union grew rapidly through the mid-1970s. During the late 1950s, the Soviet Union's economy was growing much faster than that of the United States. The key to early Soviet success was rapid planned capital accumulation. The late 1970s saw things begin to deteriorate. Dramatic reforms were finally introduced by Mikhail Gorbachev after his rise to power in 1985. Nonetheless, the Soviet economy collapsed in 1991. The Soviet Union was dissolved, and the new president of the Russian Republic, Boris Yeltsin, was left to start the difficult task of transition to a market system.

9. Economists generally agree on six requirements for a successful transition from socialism to a market-based system: (1) macroeconomic stabilization, (2) deregulation of prices and liberalization of trade, (3) privatization, (4) the establishment of market-supporting institutions, (5) a social safety net, and (6) external assistance.

10. Much debate exists about the sequence and timing of specific reforms. The idea of *shock therapy* is to proceed immediately on all six fronts, including rapid deregulation of prices and privatization. The gradualist approach is to build up market institutions first, gradually decontrol prices, and privatize only the most efficient government enterprises first.

ALTERNATIVE ECONOMIC SYSTEMS

11. China, the largest country in the world, became communist following the revolution of 1949. In its early years under Chairman Mao Zedong, China organized under the Soviet model of central planning and rapid capital accumulation in heavy industry. In 1958, China departed sharply from the Soviet model, shifting instead to emphasis on small-scale, labor-intensive industry scattered around the countryside.

12. In 1978 Deng Xiaoping instituted sweeping reforms in the organization of the Chinese economy, particularly in agriculture. These reforms moved China away from central planning toward a system driven by market incentives.

13. China remains a country in which political dissent is not tolerated and the economic system remains communist, but in which private enterprise is permitted and even encouraged. In the last several years the country has enjoyed rapid growth and substantial outside investment. However, inflation has been a problem, a fear of food shortages remain, and more than 50,000 state-owned enterprises continue to operate.

14. No country in history has accomplished what the Japanese economy has during the post-war period. Analysts point to four major factors to explain Japan's success: (1) a very high rate of saving and investment, (2) a highly trained labor force, (3) rapid absorption and effective utilization of technology, much of it imported, and (4) a pro-growth government policy. Despite some setbacks in the 1990s, Japan remains an important economic power.

REVIEW TERMS AND CONCEPTS

capitalist economy 566

communism 566

five-year plans 571

Great Leap Forward 578

Great Proletarian Cultural Revolution 579

labor theory of value 568

market-socialist economy 567

means of production 569

Ministry of Trade and Industry (MITI) 583

New Economic Policy 571

rate of exploitation 569

shock therapy 577

socialist economy 566

surplus value 569

tragedy of commons 575

value of labor power 569

PROBLEM SET

1. Choose one of the transitional economies of Central Europe (Poland, Hungary, Bulgaria, the Czech Republic, or Romania) or one of the ten countries of the Commonwealth of Independent States (Armenia, Azerbaijan, Ukraine, Uzbekistan, Russia, etc.). Write a brief paper on how the transition to a market economy was proceeding in 1995 and 1996. Has the economy (prices, employment, etc.) stabilized? Has there been economic growth? How far has privatization progressed? What problems have been encountered? (A good source of information would be the chronological index to a publication like *The Economist* or *The New York Times*.)

2. "The difference between the United States and the Soviet Union is that the United States has a capitalist economic system and the Soviet Union had a totalitarian government." Explain how this comparison confuses the economic and political aspects of the two societies. What words describe the former economic system of the Soviet Union?

3. What is the "tragedy of commons"? Suppose that all workers in a factory are paid the same wage and have no chance of being fired. Use the logic of the "tragedy of commons" to predict the result. How would you expect workers to behave?

4. You are assigned the task of debating the strengths of a socialist economy (regardless of your own viewpoint). Outline the points that you would make in the debate. Be sure to define socialism carefully in your presentation.

5. Explain why Karl Marx thought profit was unjustified. Be sure to specifically define the labor theory of value. Contrast the Marxian view with the neoclassical view of profit.

6. Do you agree or disagree with each of the following statements? Explain your answers.

a. Over time, the Chinese have shifted from a decentralized approach to economic development to a more centrally planned system. Since the events of 1989 in Tiananmen Square, there has been a severe crackdown on private businesses.

b. Both Japan and the Soviet Union grew rapidly during the 1950s and 1960s. Growth in the Soviet Union was based on rapid accumulation of capital forced by the central plan under Stalin and Khrushchev. In Japan, the growth was not due to capital accumulation.

c. Although economists generally agree that transition from socialism to a market-based system must proceed rapidly, there is little agreement about what must be done to make the transition successful.

7. The distribution of income in a capitalist economy is likely to be more unequal than it is in a socialist economy. Why is this so? Is there a tension between the goal of limiting inequality and the goal of motivating risk taking and hard work? Explain your answer in detail.

8. "There is no doubt that a centrally planned socialist system has the potential to grow faster than a market-oriented capitalist system." Do you agree or disagree? What are some of the trade-offs facing socialist planners who set target growth rates?

9. In the 1990s the world witnessed the rapid decline of several Eastern European governments (East Germany, Poland, and Romania, to name just a few). Poland immediately began moving its socialist economy toward a capitalist economy. Some of the effects of this transition have been increased unemployment and price inflation. Can you explain why? (*Hint:* Focus on differences between socialist and capitalist systems regarding the determination of prices and production levels.)

THE UNITED STATES AND THE ASIA-PACIFIC ECONOMIC COOPERATION FORUM

ECONOMIC GROWTH IN MANY OF THE ASIAN NATIONS HAS BEEN REMARKABLE IN RECENT YEARS. TWO SIGNS OF THIS GROWTH: *(LEFT)* A VERY ACTIVE STOCK MARKET IN SINGAPORE, WHERE EMPLOYEES WEAR COLOR-CODED JACKETS; *(RIGHT)* THE GINZA, ONE OF TOKYO'S MOST POPULAR SHOPPING DISTRICTS.

Since 1990, an array of international agreements and new international organizations have pushed the world toward closer trading ties and economic cooperation. The most visible of these have been the Maastricht Treaty, which urged the nations of the European Union closer to economic unity; the North American Free Trade Agreement (NAFTA), which created the first free-trade agreement among countries with widely different levels of per capita income; and the World Trade Organization, which investigates complaints of unfair trade practices. Numerous other regional agreements have also been signed or reactivated, particularly in Latin America and Africa.

Many observers, however, feel that economic developments in Asia will be the most important for the United States. This is true for four reasons. First Southeast Asia has been the world's fastest-growing region. Second, Japan and China are two of the world's largest economics. Third, the United States' largest trade deficit is with Japan. Fourth, 18 Asian countries have now banded together to form the Asia-Pacific Economic Cooperation (APEC) forum. APEC's ultimate goal: the creation of a Pacific free-trade zone.

The United States is anxious to be included in APEC. Because many of the Asian economies are more closed than the U.S. economy and tend to enact more protectionist legislation, the United States has also pushed for the inclusion of Chile and Mexico (both more open economies) in APEC, as well as the participation of Australia and New Zealand. The United States is particularly concerned that it will lose its dominance in Asia to a more assertive Japan, which has started to invest heavily in the region to offset the effects of its strengthening currency.

In November of 1994, the 18 APEC leaders met in Indonesia, where they signed an agreement to reduce trade barriers within the group over the next 25 years. Despite U.S. pressure, the statement contained no binding clauses.

Malaysia continued to be a vocal critic of U.S. involvement, arguing that APEC should focus on intra-Asian trade rather than trans-Pacific trade. Nonetheless, APEC aims to reduce not only tariffs but also nontariff barriers to trade by computerizing customs processes to reduce the paperwork involved in developing international industrial standards.

Questions for Analytical Thinking:

1. Opponents of free trade often claim that low-wage countries have an unfair advantage when trading with high-wage countries; this was one of the primary arguments made in the United States against NAFTA. How might this situation affect APEC's members? Consider the case of Thailand, which was a magnet for foreign investment five years ago, but is now investing heavily abroad itself.

2. What difficulties might the creation of a free trade area consisting of both mercantilist (that is, protectionist) closed economies and open economic systems pose? How might they be resolved? Some observers believe that the United States should focus its attention on regions with more similar economies, such as Europe or Latin America, rather than Asia, which offers larger markets and faster growth at present. Do you agree or disagree?

3. The APEC summit in Indonesia brought a number of related issues to the fore: human rights violations in Timor (an Indonesian island); the exclusion of Taiwan—a democratic, open economy—from APEC in deference to China; and legislation to protect labor and the environment. How important do you believe non-economic issues should be in the signing of trade agreements? Should political and social issues be given equal treatment? How might trade help or hurt in reaching those goals?

Sources: Robert Steiner, "Asia's Central Banks Unlading Dollars in Shift Toward Yen as Trade Currency, *The Wall Street Journal,* April 12, 1995; "Indonesia Hosts APEC Summit; Trade Liberalization Pledged," *Facts on File,* November 17, 1994; Nigel Holloway, "Waning Clout: U.S. Ability to Set APEC's Agenda Weakens," *Far Eastern Economic Review,* November 17, 1994; Tai-Ying Liu, "APEC's Missing Man," *Far Eastern Economic Review,* November 17, 1994.

CONCISE DICTIONARY OF ECONOMIC TERMINOLOGY

ability-to-pay principle A theory of taxation which holds that citizens should bear tax burdens in line with their ability to pay taxes.

absolute advantage The advantage in the production of a product enjoyed by one country over another when it uses fewer resources to produce that product than the other country does.

accelerator effect The tendency for investment to increase when aggregate output increases and decrease when aggregate output decreases, thus accelerating the growth or decline of output.

actual investment The actual amount of investment that takes place; it includes items such as unplanned changes in inventories.

adjustment costs The costs that a firm incurs when it changes its production level—for example, the administration costs of laying off employees or the training costs of hiring new workers.

adverse selection An imperfect-information problem that can occur when a buyer or seller enters into an exchange with another party who has more information.

aggregate behavior The behavior of all households and firms taken together.

aggregate demand The total demand for goods and services in the economy.

aggregate demand (AD) curve A curve that shows the negative relationship between aggregate output (income) and the price level. Each point on the AD curve is a point at which both the goods market and the money market are in equilibrium.

aggregate income The total income received by all factors of production in a given period.

aggregate output The total quantity of goods and services produced (or supplied) in an economy in a given period.

aggregate output (income) (Y) A combined term used to remind you of the exact equality between aggregate output and aggregate income.

aggregate production function The mathematical representation of the relationship between inputs and national output, or gross domestic product.

aggregate supply The total supply of all goods and services in an economy.

aggregate supply (AS) curve A graph that shows the relationship between the aggregate quantity of output supplied by all firms in an economy and the overall price level.

American Federation of Labor (AFL) Founded in 1881, the AFL was successfully led by Samuel Gompers from 1886 until 1924. A practical, nonideological union, the AFL existed as a "confederation" of individual craft unions representing skilled workers, each with an independent organization and an exclusive jurisdiction. Now merged with the CIO, the AFL maintains a preeminent position among unions today.

animal spirits of entrepreneurs A phrase coined by Keynes to describe investors' feelings.

Antitrust Division (of the Department of Justice) One of two federal agencies empowered to act against those in violation of antitrust laws. It initiates action against those who violate antitrust laws and decides which cases to prosecute and against whom to bring criminal charges.

appreciation of a currency The rise in value of one currency relative to another.

asymmetric information A situation in which the participants in an economic transaction have different information about the transaction.

automatic destabilizers Revenue and expenditure items in the federal budget that automatically change with the economy in such a way as to destabilize GDP.

automatic stabilizers Revenue and expenditure items in the federal budget that automatically change with the state of the economy in such a way as to stabilize GDP.

autonomous variable A variable that is assumed not to depend on the state of the economy—that is, when it is taken as given.

average fixed cost (AFC) Total fixed cost divided by the number of units of output; a per unit measure of fixed costs.

average product The average amount produced by each unit of a variable factor of production.

average propensity to consume (APC) The proportion of income households spend on consumption. Determined by dividing consumption (C) by income (Y).

average total cost (ATC) Total cost divided by the number of units of output.

average variable cost (AVC) Total variable cost divided by the number of units of output.

average-cost pricing Setting price to cover average cost per unit including a fair return.

Averch-Johnson effect The tendency for regulated monopolies to build more capital than they need. Usually occurs when allowed rates of return are set by a regulatory agency at some percent of fixed capital stocks.

balance of payments The record of a country's transactions in goods, services, and assets with the rest of the world; also the record of a country's sources (supply) and uses (demand) of foreign exchange.

balance of trade A country's merchandise exports minus its merchandise imports. Also called the *merchandise trade balance*.

balance on capital account In the United States, the sum of the following (measured in a given period): the change in private U.S. assets abroad, the change in foreign private assets in the United States, the change in U.S. government assets abroad, and the change in foreign government assets in the United States.

balance on current account The balance of trade plus net exports of services, plus net investment income, plus the category "net transfer payments and other."

balanced-budget multiplier The ratio of change in the equilibrium level of output to a change in government spending where the change in government spending is balanced by a change in taxes so as not to create any deficit. The balanced-budget multiplier is equal to one: The change in Y resulting from the change in G and the equal change in T is exactly the same size as the initial change in G or T itself.

barrier to entry Something that prevents new firms from entering and competing in an industry.

barter The direct exchange of goods and services for other goods and services.

base year In computing an index, the year in which the index is assigned a specified value—usually 1 or 100. In computing a fixed-weight index, the year chosen for the weights.

benefits-received principle A theory of fairness which holds that taxpayers should contribute to government (in the form of taxes) in proportion to the benefits that they receive from public expenditures.

black market A market in which illegal trading takes place at market-determined prices.

brain drain The tendency for talented people from developing countries to become educated in a developed country and remain there after graduation.

breaking even The situation in which a firm is earning exactly a normal profit rate.

budget constraint The limits imposed on household choices by income, wealth, and product prices.

budget deficit The difference between what a government spends and what it collects in taxes in a given period: $G - T$.

business cycle The cycle of short-term ups and downs in the economy.

capital Things that have already been produced that are in turn used to produce other goods and services.

capital flight The tendency for both human capital and financial capital to leave developing countries in search of higher rates of return elsewhere.

capital income Income earned on savings that have been put to use through financial capital markets.

capital market The input/factor market in which households supply their savings, for interest or for claims to future profits, to firms that demand funds in order to buy capital goods.

capital stock   The current market value of a firm's plant, equipment, inventories, and intangible assets.

capital-intensive technology   Technology that relies heavily on capital rather than human labor.

capitalist economy   An economy in which most capital is privately owned.

cartel   A group of firms that gets together and makes joint price and output decisions in order to maximize joint profits.

Celler-Kefauver Act (1950)   Extended the government's authority to ban mergers and prevented firms from acquiring the physical stock of competition.

ceteris paribus   Literally, "all else equal." Used to analyze the relationship between two variables while the values of other variables are held unchanged.

change in business inventories   The amount by which firms' inventories change during a period. Inventories are the goods that firms produce now but intend to sell later.

change in inventory   Production minus sales.

choice set, or opportunity set   The set of options that is defined and limited by a budget constraint.

circular flow   A diagram showing the income received and payments made by each sector of the economy.

Clayton Act   Passed by Congress in 1914 to strengthen the Sherman Act and clarify the rule of reason, the act outlawed specific monopolistic behaviors such as tying contracts, price discrimination, and unlimited mergers.

Coase theorem   Under certain conditions, when externalities are present, private parties can arrive at the efficient solution without government involvement.

collective bargaining   The process by which union leaders bargain with management as the representatives of all union employees.

collusion   The act of working with other producers in an effort to limit competition and increase joint profits.

command economy   An economy in which a central authority or agency draws up a plan that establishes what will be produced and when, sets production goals, and makes rules for distribution.

commodity monies   Items used as money that also have intrinsic value in some other use.

communism   An economic system in which the people control the means of production (capital and land) directly, without the intervention of a government or state.

community rating   A system in which insurance providers must accept all applicants and charge premiums based only on age, location, and perhaps some elements of behavior (such as smoking).

comparative advantage   The advantage in the production of a product enjoyed by one country over another when that product can be produced at lower cost in terms of other goods than it could be in the other country.

compensating differentials   Differences in wages that result from differences in working conditions. Risky jobs usually pay higher wages; highly desirable jobs usually pay lower wages.

compensation of employees   Includes wages, salaries, and various supplements—employer contri-butions to social insurance and pension funds, for example—paid to households by firms and by the government.

complementary inputs   Factors of production that can be used together to enhance each other.

complements, complementary goods   Goods that "go together"; a decrease in the price of one results in an increase in demand for the other, and vice versa.

Congress of Industrial Organizations (CIO)   Founded by John L. Lewis, president of the United Mine Workers, after the AFL rejected his plan to organize the steel, rubber, automobile, and chemical industries in 1935. The CIO was the first union to organize semiskilled laborers in the mass production industries. After 20 years of independence, it merged with the AFL in 1955.

consent decrees   Formal agreements on remedies between all the parties to an antitrust case that must be approved by the courts. Consent decrees can be signed before, during, or after a trial.

constant dollars   Dollars in a given base year. Used under the BEA's old procedure for computing real GDP.

constant returns to scale   An increase in a firm's scale of production has no effect on average costs per unit produced.

constrained supply of labor   The amount a household actually works in a given period at the current wage rate.

consumer goods   Goods produced for present consumption.

consumer price index (CPI)   A price index computed each month by the Bureau of Labor Statistics using a bundle that is meant to represent the "market basket" purchased monthly by the typical urban consumer.

consumer sovereignty   The idea that consumers ultimately dictate what will be produced (or not produced) by choosing what to purchase (and what not to purchase).

consumer surplus   The difference between the maximum amount a person is willing to pay for a good and its current market price.

consumption function   The relationship between consumption and income.

contraction, recession, or slump   The period in the business cycle from a peak down to a

trough, during which output and employment fall.

contractionary fiscal policy   A decrease in government spending or an increase in net taxes aimed at decreasing aggregate output (income) *(Y)*.

contractionary monetary policy   A decrease in the money supply aimed at decreasing aggregate output (income) *(Y)*.

copayment   A fixed amount of money that an insured person pays for each visit to a doctor's office.

Corn Laws   The tariffs, subsidies, and restrictions enacted by the British Parliament in the early nineteenth century to discourage imports and encourage exports of grain.

corporate bonds   Promissory notes issued by corporations when they borrow money.

corporate income taxes   Taxes levied on the net incomes of corporations.

corporate profits   The income of corporate businesses.

corporation   A form of business organization resting on a legal charter that establishes the corporation as an entity separate from its owners. Owners hold shares and are liable for the firm's debts only up to the limit of their investment, or share, in the firm.

cost shock, or supply shock   A change in costs that shifts the aggregate supply *(AS)* curve.

cost-benefit analysis   The formal technique by which the benefits of a public project are weighed against its costs.

cost-of-living adjustments (COLAs)   Contract provisions that tie wages to changes in the cost of living. The greater the inflation rate, the more wages are raised.

cost-push, or supply-side, inflation   Inflation caused by an increase in costs.

Cournot model   A model of a two-firm industry (duopoly) in which a series of output-adjustment decisions leads to a final level of output that is between that which would prevail if the market were organized competitively and that which would be set by a monopoly.

cross-price elasticity of demand   A measure of the response of the quantity of one good demanded to a change in the price of another good.

crowding-out effect   The tendency for increases in government spending to cause reductions in private investment spending.

currency debasement   The decrease in the value of money that occurs when its supply is increased rapidly.

current dollars   The current prices that one pays for goods and services.

cyclical deficit   The deficit that occurs because of a downturn in the business cycle.

cyclical unemployment   The increase in unemployment that occurs during recessions and depressions.

debt rescheduling An agreement between banks and borrowers through which a new schedule of repayments of the debt is negotiated; often some of the debt is written off and the repayment period is extended.

decreasing returns to scale, or diseconomies of scale An increase in a firm's scale of production leads to higher average costs per unit produced.

deductible An annual out-of-pocket expenditure that an insurance policy holder must make before the insurance plan makes any reimbursement.

defensive medicine The practice of ordering medical tests, procedures, or treatments that are not cost-effective to protect oneself from being sued for malpractice later on.

deficit response index (DRI) The amount by which the deficit changes with a one dollar change in GDP.

demand curve A graph illustrating how much of a given product a household would be willing to buy at different prices.

demand determined price The price of a good that is in fixed supply; it is determined exclusively by what firms and households are willing to pay for the good.

demand schedule A table showing how much of a given product a household would be willing to buy at different prices.

demand-pull inflation Inflation that is initiated by an increase in aggregate demand.

dependency theory The theory that the poverty of the developing nations is due to the "dependence" of the developing world on nations that are already developed; it suggests that even after the end of colonialism, this dependence is maintained because developed countries are able to use their economic power to determine to their own advantage (and to the disadvantage of others) the relative prices and conditions under which the international exchange of goods takes place.

depreciation The amount by which an asset's value falls in a given period.

depreciation of a currency The fall in value of one currency relative to another.

depression A prolonged and deep recession. The precise definitions of prolonged and deep are debatable.

derived demand The demand for resources (inputs) that is dependent on the demand for the outputs those resources can be used to produce.

descriptive economics The compilation of data that describe phenomena and facts.

desired, or planned, investment Those additions to capital stock and inventory that are planned by firms.

desired, or optimal, level of inventories The level of inventory at which the extra cost (in lost sales) from lowering inventories by a small amount is just equal to the extra gain (in interest revenue and decreased storage costs).

diamond/water paradox A paradox stating that (1) the things with the greatest value in use frequently have little or no value in exchange, and (2) the things with the greatest value in exchange frequently have little or no value in use.

discount rate Interest rate that banks pay to the Fed to borrow from it.

discouraged-worker effect The decline in the measured unemployment rate that results when people who want to work but cannot find jobs grow discouraged and stop looking, thus dropping out of the ranks of the unemployed and the labor force.

discretionary fiscal policy Changes in taxes or spending that are the result of conscious changes in government policy.

disposable personal income, or after-tax income. Personal income minus personal income taxes. The amount that households have available to spend or save.

dividends The portion of a corporation's profits that the firm pays out each period to shareholders. Also called *distributed profits*.

dominant strategy In game theory, a strategy that is best no matter what the opposition does.

drop-in-the-bucket problem A problem intrinsic to public goods: The good or service is usually so costly that its provision generally does not depend on whether or not any single person pays.

dumping Takes place when a firm or industry sells products on the world market at prices below the cost of production.

durable goods Goods that last a relatively long time, such as cars and household appliances.

easy monetary policy Fed policies that expand the money supply in an effort to stimulate the economy.

economic costs The full costs of production including (1) a normal rate of return on investment and (2) the opportunity cost of each factor of production.

economic growth An increase in the total output of an economy. It occurs when a society acquires new resources or when it learns to produce more using existing resources. Defined by some economists as an increase of real GDP per capita.

economic income The amount of money a household can spend during a given time period without increasing or decreasing its net assets. Wages, salaries, dividends, interest income, transfer payments, rents, and so forth are sources of economic income.

economic integration Occurs when two or more nations join to form a free-trade zone.

economic problem Given scarce resources, how exactly do large, complex societies go about answering the three basic economic questions?

economic profits, or excess profits Profits over and above the normal rate of return on investment.

economic theory A statement or set of related statements about cause and effect, action and reaction.

economics The study of how individuals and societies choose to use the scarce resources that nature and previous generations have provided.

efficiency The condition in which the economy is producing what people what at least possible cost.

efficiency wage theory An explanation for unemployment that holds that the productivity of workers increases with the wage rate. If this is so, firms may have an incentive to pay wages above the market-clearing rate.

efficient market A market in which profit opportunities are eliminated almost instantaneously.

elastic demand A demand relationship in which the percentage change in quantity demanded is larger in absolute value than the percentage change in price (a demand elasticity with an absolute value greater than 1).

elasticity A general concept that can be used to quantify the response in one variable when another variable changes.

elasticity of labor supply A measure of the response of labor supplied to a change in the price of labor. Can be positive or negative.

elasticity of supply A measure of the response of quantity of a good supplied to a change in price of that good. Likely to be positive in output markets.

empirical economics The collection and use of data to test economic theories.

employed Any person 16 years old or older (1) who works for pay, either for someone else or in his or her own business for one or more hours per week, (2) who works without pay for 15 or more hours per week in a family enterprise, or (3) who has a job but has been temporarily absent, with or without pay.

employer mandate A system of health-care insurance provision in which all employers are required to provide health insurance and to pay on average 80% of the community-rated premiums.

entrepreneur A person who organizes, manages, and assumes the risks of a firm, taking a new idea or a new product and turning it into a successful business.

equilibrium The condition that exists when quantity supplied and quantity demanded are equal. At equilibrium, there is no tendency for price to change. In the macroeconomic goods market, equilibrium occurs when planned aggregate expenditure is equal to aggregate output.

equilibrium price level The point at which the aggregate demand and aggregate supply curves intersect.

equity Fairness.

European Union (EU) The European trading bloc composed of Austria, Belgium, Denmark, Finland, France, Germany, Greece, Ireland, Italy, Luxembourg, the Netherlands, Portugal, Spain, Sweden, and the United Kingdom.

excess burden The amount by which the burden of a tax exceeds the total revenue collected. Also called *dead weight losses*.

excess demand The condition that exists when quantity demanded exceeds quantity supplied at the current price.

excess labor, excess capital Labor and capital that are not needed to produce the firm's current level of output.

excess reserves The difference between a bank's actual reserves and its required reserves.

excess supply The condition that exists when quantity supplied exceeds quantity demanded at the current price.

exchange rate The price of one country's currency in terms of another country's currency; the ratio at which two currencies are traded for each other.

excise taxes Taxes on specific commodities.

expansion or boom The period in the business cycle from a trough up to a peak, during which output and employment rise.

expansionary fiscal policy An increase in government spending or a reduction in net taxes aimed at increasing aggregate output (income) *(Y)*.

expansionary monetary policy An increase in the money supply aimed at increasing aggregate output (income) *(Y)*.

expected rate of return The annual rate of return that a firm expects to obtain through a capital investment.

expenditure approach A method of computing GDP that measures the amount spent on all final goods during a given period.

experience rating The insurance-company practice of charging individuals or groups of individuals premiums that are linked to their current state of health or to the probability that they will become sick.

explicit contracts Employment contracts that stipulate workers' wages, usually for a period of one to three years.

export promotion A trade policy designed to encourage exports.

export subsidies Government payments made to domestic firms to encourage exports.

externality A cost or benefit resulting from some activity or transaction that is imposed or bestowed upon parties outside the activity or transaction. Sometimes called *spillovers* or *neighborhood effects*.

factor endowments The quantity and quality of labor, land, and natural resources of a country.

factor substitution effect The tendency of firms to substitute away from a factor whose price has risen and toward a factor whose price has fallen.

factors of production The inputs into the production process. Land, labor, and capital are the three key factors of production.

fallacy of composition The belief that what is true for a part is necessarily true for the whole.

favored customers Those who receive special treatment from dealers during crises.

featherbedding The common union practice of preserving jobs even when it is inefficient to do so.

Federal Open Market Committee (FOMC) A group composed of the seven members of the Fed's Board of Governors, the president of the New York Federal Reserve Bank, and four of the other eleven district bank presidents on a rotating basis; it sets goals regarding the money supply and interest rates and directs the operation of the Open Market Desk in New York.

Federal Reserve System (the Fed) The central bank of the United States.

Federal Trade Commission (FTC) A federal regulatory group created by Congress in 1914 to investigate the structure and behavior of firms engaging in interstate commerce, to determine what constitutes unlawful "unfair" behavior, and to issue cease-and-desist orders to those found in violation of antitrust law.

federal budget The budget of the federal government.

federal debt The total of all accumulated federal deficits minus surpluses over time, or the total amount owed by the federal government.

federal debt held by the public The privately held (non-government-owned) debt of the U.S. government.

federal deficit The difference between what the federal government spends and what it collects in taxes in a given period $(G - T)$.

fee-for-service reimbursement A program in which insurance companies reimburse health-care providers for the services they've rendered.

fertility rate The birth rate. Equal to (the number of births per year divided by the population) × 100.

fiat, or token, money Items designated as money that are intrinsically worthless.

filtering The process wherby the newest and best housing goes to the wealthy, whose former housing passes down to those of middle income, whose former housing passes down to those of low income. Thus housing "filters" down the income-ditribution ladder.

final goods and services Goods and services produced for final use.

financial capital market The complex set of institutions in which suppliers of capital (households that save) and the demand for capital (business firms wanting to invest) interact.

financial intermediaries Banks and other institutions that act as a link between those who have money to lend and those who want to borrow money.

fine tuning The phrase coined by Walter Heller to refer to the government's role in regulating inflation and unemployment.

firm An organization that transforms resources (inputs) into products (outputs). Firms are the primary producing units in a market economy.

fiscal drag The negative effect on the economy that occurs when average tax rates increase because taxpayers have moved into higher income brackets during an expansion.

fiscal policy The spending and taxing policies used by the government to influence the economy.

five-year plans Plans developed in the Soviet Union that provided general guidelines and directions for the next five years.

fixed cost Any cost that a firm bears in the short run that does not depend on its level of output. These costs are incurred even if the firm is producing nothing. There are no fixed costs in the long run.

fixed-weight procedure A procedure for computing an index that uses weights from a given base year.

floating, or market-determined, exchange rates Exchange rates that are determined by the unregulated forces of supply and demand.

food stamps Vouchers that have a face value greater than their cost and that can be used to purchase food at grocery stores.

foreign exchange All currencies other than the domestic currency of a given country.

free entry The condition that exists when there are no barriers to prevent new firms from competing for profits in a profitable industry.

free exit The condition that exists when firms can simply stop producing their product and leave a market. Firms incur no additional costs by exiting the industry.

free-rider problem A problem intrinsic to public goods: Because people can enjoy the benefits of public goods whether they pay for them or not, they are usually unwilling to pay for them.

frictional unemployment The portion of unemployment that is due to the normal working of the labor market; used to denote short-run job/skill matching problems.

full-employment budget What the federal budget would be if the economy were producing at a full-employment level of output.

game theory Analyzes oligopolistic behavior as a complex series of strategic moves and reactive countermoves among rival firms. In game theory, firms are assumed to anticipate rival reactions.

GDP price index A price index for GDP.

General Agreement on Tariffs and Trade (GATT) An international agreement signed by the United States and 22 other countries in 1947 to promote the liberalization of foreign trade.

general equilibrium The condition that exists when all markets in an economy are in simultaneous equilibrium.

ghetto premiums Evidence suggests that during the 1960s and 1970s housing in sections of U.S. cities inhabited predominantly by African–Americans was more expensive than comparable housing in white neighborhoods. The price difference came to be called a ghetto premium.

Gini coefficient A commonly used measure of inequality of income derived from a Lorenz Curve. It can range from zero to a maximum of one.

goods market The market in which goods and services are exchanged and in which the equilibrium level of aggregate output is determined.

government failure Occurs when the governemnt becomes the tool of the rent seeker and the allocation of resources is made even less efficient by the intervention of government.

government franchise A monopoly by virtue of government directive.

government interest payments Cash payments made by the government to those who own government bonds.

government purchases of goods and services (G) Expenditures by federal, state, and local governments for final goods and labor.

government spending multiplier The ratio of the change in the equilibrium level of output to a change in government spending.

government transfer payments Cash payments made by the government directly to households for which no current services are received. They include social security benefits, unemployment compensation, and welfare payments.

Gramm-Rudman-Hollings Bill Passed by the U.S. Congress and signed by President Reagan in 1986, this law set out to reduce the federal deficit by $36 billion per year, with a deficit of zero slated for 1991.

Great Depression The period of severe economic contraction and high unemployment that began in 1929 and continued throughout the 1930s.

Great Leap Forward The economic strategy in the People's Republic of China that began in 1958 when it departed from the Soviet model and shifted from large-scale, capital-intensive industry to small-scale, labor-intensive industry scattered across the countryside. Material incentives were reduced and replaced by the motivating power of revolutionary ideology and inspiration.

Great Proletarian Cultural Revolution (1966–1976) A period of ideological purity in the People's Republic of China: Material incentives and reforms were denounced and highly trained specialists were sent to work in the fields. The effect of the Cultural Revolution on the Chinese economy was catastrophic.

Green Revolution The agricultural breakthroughs of modern science, such as the development of new, high-yield crop varieties.

gross domestic product (GDP) The total market value of all final goods and services produced within a given period by factors of production located within a country.

gross investment The total value of all newly produced capital goods (plant, equipment, housing, and inventory) produced in a given period.

gross national product (GNP) The total market value of all final goods and services produced within a given period by factors of production owned by a country's citizens, regardless of where the output is produced.

gross private investment (I) Total investment in capital—that is, the purchase of new housing, plants, equipment, and inventory by the private (or nongovernment) sector.

Hart-Scott-Rodino Act The 1980 antitrust legislation that extended the antitrust laws to proprietorships and partnerships and requires that all proposed mergers be reported to the Department of Justice.

health maintenance organization (HMO) A health-care plan that provides comprehensive medical services for employees and their families at a flat fee.

Heckscher-Ohlin theorem A theory that explains the existence of a country's comparative advantage by its factor endowments: A country has a comparative advantage in the production of a product if that country is relatively well endowed with inputs used intensively in the production of that product.

Herfindahl-Hirschman Index (HHI) A mathematical calculation that uses market share figures to determine whether or not a proposed merger will be challenged by the government.

homogeneous products Undifferentiated products; products that are identical to, or indistinguishable from, one another.

households The consuming units in an economy.

human capital A form of intangible capital that includes the skills and other knowledge that workers have or acquire through education and training and that yields valuable services to a firm over time.

hyperinflation A period of very rapid increases in the overall price level.

identity Something that is true at all times.

Immigration Act of 1990 Increased the number of legal immigrants allowed into the United States each year by 150,000.

Immigration Reform and Control Act (1986) Granted amnesty to about 3 million illegal aliens and imposed a strong set of employer sanctions designed to slow the flow of immigrants into the United States.

imperfect competition An industry in which single firms have some control over price and competition. Imperfectly competitive industries give rise to an inefficient allocation of resources.

imperfect information The absence of full knowledge regarding product characteristics, available prices, and so forth.

imperfectly competitive industry An industry in which single firms have some control over the price of their output.

implementation lag The time that it takes to put the desired policy into effect once economists and policy makers recognize that the economy is in a boom or a slump.

import substitution An industrial trade strategy that favors developing local industries that can manufacture goods to replace imports.

impossibility theorem A proposition demonstrated by Kenneth Arrow showing that no system of aggregating individual preferences into social decisions will always yield consistent, nonarbitrary results.

income The sum of all a household's wages, salaries, profits, interest payments, rents, and other forms of earnings in a given period of time. It is a flow measure.

income approach A method of computing GDP that measures the income—wages, rents, interest, and profits—received by all factors of production in producing final goods.

income effect of higher wages When wages rise, people are better off. If leisure is a normal good, they may decide to consume more of it and to work less.

income elasticity of demand Measures the responsiveness of demand with respect to changes in income.

incomes policies Direct attempts by the government to control prices and wages.

increasing returns to scale, or economies of scale An increase in a firm's scale of production leads to lower average costs per unit produced.

index A measure of a variable or group of variables.

indirect taxes Taxes like sales taxes, customs duties, and license fees.

inductive reasoning The process of observing regular patterns from raw data and drawing generalizations from them.

Industrial Revolution The period in England during the late eighteenth and early nineteenth centuries in which new manufacturing technologies and improved transportation gave rise to the modern factory system and a massive movement of the population from the countryside to the cities.

industrial policy Government involvement in the allocation of capital across manufacturing sectors.

industry All the firms that produce a similar product. The boundaries of a "product" can be drawn very widely ("agricultural products"), less widely ("dairy products"), or very narrowly ("cheese"). The term *industry* can be used interchangeably with the term *market*.

inelastic demand Demand that responds somewhat, but not a great deal, to changes in price. Inelastic demand always has a numerical value between zero and minus one.

infant industry A young industry which may need temporary protection from competition from the established industries of other countries in order to develop an acquired comparative advantage.

inferior goods Goods for which demand falls when income rises.

inflation An increase in the overall price level.

inflation rate The percentage change in the price level.

injunction A court order forbidding the continuation of behavior that leads to damages.

innovation The use of new knowledge to produce a new product or to produce an existing product more efficiently.

input or factor markets The markets in which the resources used to produce products are exchanged.

inputs The goods and services that firms purchase and turn into output.

intangible capital Nonmaterial things that contribute to the output of future goods and services.

interest The fee that a borrower pays to a lender for the use of his or her funds. Almost always expressed as an annual rate.

interest rate The annual interest payment on a loan expressed as a percentage of the loan. Equal to the amount of interest received per year divided by the amount of the loan.

interest sensitivity or insensitivity of planned investment The responsiveness of planned investment spending to changes in the interest rate. *Interest sensitivity* means that planned investment spending changes a great deal in response to changes in the interest rate; *interest insensitivity* means little or no change in planned investment as a result of changes in the interest rate.

intermediate goods Goods that are produced by one firm for use in further processing by another firm.

International Monetary Fund An international agency whose primary goals are to stabilize international exchange rates and to lend money to countries that have problems financing their international transactions.

international sector From any one country's perspective, the economies of the rest of the world.

Interstate Commerce Commission (ICC) A federal regulatory group created by Congress in 1887 to oversee and correct abuses in the railroad industry.

invention An advance in knowledge.

inventory investment Occurs when a firm produces more output than it sells within a given period.

investment The process of using resources to produce new capital. Although capital is measured at a given point in time (a stock), investment is measured over a period of time (a flow). The flow of investment increases the stock of capital.

J-curve effect Following a currency depreciation, a country's balance of trade may get worse before it gets better. The graph showing this effect is shaped like the letter *J*, hence the name "J-curve effect."

job search The process of gathering information about job availability and job characteristics.

kinked demand curve model A model of oligopoly in which the demand curve facing each individual firm has a "kink" in it. The kink follows from the assumption that competitive firms will follow suit if a single firm cuts price but will not follow suit if a single firm raises price.

Knights of Labor One of the earliest successful labor organizations in the United States, it recruited both skilled and unskilled laborers. Founded in 1869, the power of the Knights declined after the Chicago Haymarket bombing in 1886.

labor demand curve A graph that illustrates the amount of labor that firms want to employ at the particular wage rate.

labor force The number of people employed plus the number of unemployed.

labor market The input/factor market in which households supply work for wages to firms that demand labor.

labor market discrimination Occurs when one group of workers receives inferior treatment from employers because of some characteristic irrelevant to job performance.

labor productivity Output per worker hour; the amount of output produced by an average worker in one hour.

labor supply curve A diagram that shows the quantity of labor supplied as a function of the wage rate. Its shape depends on how households react to changes in the wage rate.

labor theory of value (1) Stated most simply, the theory that the value of a commodity depends only on the amount of labor required to produce it. (2) Marx's theory that the value of a commodity depends exclusively upon the amount of labor required to produce it. Commodities are the physical embodiment of the labor that produced them, and capital is the physical embodiment of the past labor used to produce it.

labor-force participation rate The ratio of the labor force to the total population 16 years old or older

labor-intensive technology Technology that relies heavily on human labor rather than capital.

Laffer Curve The graph, named after Arthur Laffer, with the tax rate measured on the vertical axis and tax revenue measured on the horizontal axis. The Laffer Curve shows that there is some tax rate beyond which the supply response is large enough to lead to a decrease in tax revenue for further increases in the tax rate.

laissez-faire economy Literally from the French: "allow [them] to do." An economy in which individual people and firms pursue their own self-interests without any central direction or regulation.

land market The input/factor market in which households supply land or other real property in exchange for rent.

law of demand The negative relationship between price and quantity demanded: As price rises, quantity demanded decreases. As price falls, quantity demanded increases.

law of diminishing marginal utility The more of any one good consumed in a given period, the less satisfaction (utility) generated by consuming each additional (marginal) unit of the same good.

law of diminishing returns When additional units of a variable input are added to fixed inputs after a certain point, the marginal product of the variable input declines.

law of one price If the costs of transportation are small, the price of the same good in different countries should be roughly the same.

law of supply The positive relationship between price and quantity of a good supplied: An increase in market price will lead to an increase in quantity supplied, and a decrease in market price will lead to a decrease in quantity supplied.

legal tender Money that a government has required to be accepted in settlement of debts.

lender of last resort One of the functions of the Fed: It provides funds to troubled banks that cannot find any other sources of funds.

liability rules Laws that require A to compensate B for damages imposed.

life-cycle theory of consumption A theory of household consumption: Households make lifetime consumption decisions based on their expectations of lifetime income.

liquidity property of money The property of money that makes it a good medium of exchange as well as a store of value: It is portable and readily accepted and thus easily exchanged for goods.

logrolling Occurs when congressional representatives trade votes, agreeing to help each other get certain pieces of legislation passed.

long run That period of time for which there are no fixed factors of production. Firms can increase or decrease scale of operation, and new firms can enter and existing firms can exit the industry.

long-run average cost curve (LRAC) A graph that shows the different scales on which a firm can choose to operate in the long run.

long-run competitive equilibrium When $P = SRMC = SRAC = LRAC$ and economic profits are zero.

Lorenz Curve A widely used graph of the distribution of income, with cumulative percentage of families plotted along the horizontal axis and cumulative percentage of income plotted along the vertical axis.

Lucas supply function The supply function, named after Robert Lucas, that embodies the idea that output (Y) depends on the difference between the actual price level and the expected price level.

M1, or transactions money Money that can be directly used for transactions.

M2, or broad money M1 plus savings accounts, money market accounts, and other near monies.

macroeconomics The branch of economics that deals with the economy as a whole. Macroeconomics focuses on the determinants of total national income, deals with aggregates such as aggregate consumption and investment, and looks at the overall level of prices rather than individual prices.

marginal cost (MC) The increase in total cost that results from producing one more unit of output. Marginal costs reflect changes in variable costs.

marginal damage cost (MDC) The additional harm done by increasing the level of an externality-producing activity by one unit. If producing product X pollutes the water in a river, MDC is the additional cost imposed by the added pollution that results from increasing output by one unit of X per period.

marginal factor cost (MFC) The additional cost of using one more unit of a given factor of production.

marginal private cost (MPC) The amount that a consumer pays to consume an additional unit of a particular good.

marginal product The additional output that can be produced by adding one more unit of a specific input, *ceteris paribus*.

marginal product of labor (MP_L) The additional output produced by one additional unit of labor.

marginal productivity theory of income distribution At equilibrium, all factors of production end up receiving rewards determined by their productivity as measured by marginal revenue product.

marginal propensity to consume (MPC) That fraction of a change in income that is consumed, or spent.

marginal propensity to import (MPM) The change in imports caused by a $1 change in income.

marginal propensity to save (MPS) That fraction of a change in income that is saved.

marginal revenue (MR) The additional revenue that a firm takes in when it increases output by one additional unit. In perfect competition, $P = MR$.

marginal revenue product (MRP) The additional revenue a firm earns by employing one additional unit of input, ceteris paribus.

marginal revenue product of labor (MRP_L) The additional revenue that a firm will take in by hiring one additional unit of labor, *ceteris paribus*. For perfectly competitive firms, the 1 marginal revenue product of labor is equal to the marginal physical product of labor times the price of output.

marginal social cost (MSC) The total cost to society of producing an additional unit of a good or service. MSC is equal to the sum of the marginal costs of producing the product and the correctly measured damage costs involved in the process of production.

marginal utility (MU) The additional satisfaction gained by the consumption or use of *one more* unit of something.

market The institution through which buyers and sellers interact and engage in exchange.

market demand The sum of all the quantities of a good or service demanded per period by all the households buying in the market for that good or service.

market failure Occurs when resources are misallocated, or allocated inefficiently. The result is waste or lost value.

market organization The way an industry is structured. Structure is defined by how many firms there are in an industry, whether products are differentiated or are virtually the same, whether or not firms in the industry can control prices or wages, and whether or not competing firms can enter and leave the industry freely.

market power An imperfectly competitive firm's ability to raise price without losing all demand for its product.

market supply The sum of all that is supplied each period by all producers of a single product.

market-socialist economy An economy that combines government ownership with market allocation.

maximin strategy In game theory, a strategy chosen to maximize the minimum gain that can be earned.

means of production Marx's term for land and capital.

Medicaid and Medicare In-kind government transfer programs that provide health and hospitalization benefits: Medicare to the aged and their survivors and to certain of the disabled, regardless of income, and Medicaid to people with low incomes.

medium of exchange, or means of payment What sellers generally accept and buyers generally use to pay for goods and services.

microeconomic foundations of macroeconomics The under-lying microeconomic principles behind macroeconomic analysis.

microeconomics The branch of economics that deals with the functioning of individual industries and the behavior of individual decision-making units—business firms and households.

midpoint formula A more precise way of calculating percentages using the value halfway between P_1 and P_2 for the base in calculating the percentage change in price, and the value halfway between Q_1 and Q_2 as the base for calculating the percentage change in quantity demanded.

minimum wage The lowest wage that firms are permitted to pay workers.

minimum wage laws Laws that set a floor for wage rates—that is, a minimum hourly rate for any kind of labor.

Ministry of Trade and Industry (MITI) The agency of the Japanese government responsible for industrial policy. It uses tariffs and subsidies to protect and subsidize key industries and helps some sectors plan orderly reductions in capacity.

model A formal statement of a theory. Usually a mathematical statement of a presumed relationship between two or more variables.

modern economic growth The period of rapid and sustained increase in real output per capita that began in the Western World with the Industrial Revolution.

monetary policy The behavior of the Federal Reserve regarding the money supply.

money income The measure of income used by the Census Bureau. Because it excludes noncash transfer payments and capital gains income, it is less inclusive than "economic income."

money market The market in which financial instruments are exchanged and in which the equilibrium level of the interest rate is determined.

money multiplier The multiple by which deposits can increase for every dollar increase in reserves; equal to one divided by the required reserve ratio.

monocentric models Models of residential location that assume central employment. As people move farther from the center, their costs of commuting increase. Equilibrium in the housing market exists only where land prices just offset the lower transport costs closer to the center.

monopolistic competition An industry structure (or market organization) in which many firms compete, producing similar but slightly differentiated products. There are close substitutes for the product of any given firm. Monopolistic competitors have some control over price. Price and quality competition follow from product differentiation. Entry and exit are relatively easy, and success invites new competitors.

monopoly An industry structure (or market organization) in which there is only one large firm that produces a product for which there are no close substitutes. Monopolists can set prices but are subject to market discipline. For a monopoly to continue to exist, something must prevent potential competitors from entering the industry and competing for profits.

monopsony A market in which there is only one buyer for a good or service.

moral hazard Arises when one party to a contract passes the cost of his or her behavior on to the other party to the contract

moral suasion The pressure exerted by the Fed on member banks to discourage them from borrowing heavily from the Fed.

mortality rate The death rate. Equal to (the number of deaths per year divided by the population) × 100.

movement along a demand curve What happens when a change in price causes quantity demanded to change.

multiplier The ratio of the change in the equilibrium level of output to a change in some autonomous variable.

Nash equilibrium In game theory, the result of all players playing their best strategy given what their competitors are doing.

National Labor Relations Board (NLRB) A watchdog board established by the Wagner Act in 1935. Its duties include ensuring that all workers are guaranteed the right to join unions and that firm managers participate fairly in collective bargaining if so requested by a majority of their employees.

national income The total income earned by the factors of production owned by a country's citizens.

national income and product accounts Data collected and published by the government describing the various components of national income and output in the economy.

natural monopoly An industry that realizes such large economies of scale in producing its product that single-firm production of that good or service is most efficient.

natural rate of population increase The difference between the birth rate and the death rate. It does not take migration into account.

natural rate of unemployment The unemployment that occurs as a normal part of the functioning of the economy. Consistent with the notion of a fixed long-run output at potential GDP. Sometimes taken as the sum of frictional unemployment and structural unemployment.

near monies Close substitutes for transactions money, such as savings accounts and money market accounts.

negative demand shock Something that causes a negative shift in consumption or investment schedules or that leads to a decrease in U.S. exports.

net exports (EX − IM) The difference between exports (sales to foreigners of U.S.-produced goods and services) and imports (U.S. purchases of goods and services from abroad). The figure can be positive or negative.

net factor payments to the rest of the world Payments of factor income to the rest of the world minus the receipt of factor income from the rest of the world.

net income The profits of a firm.

net interest The interest paid by business.

net investment Gross investment minus depreciation.

net national product (NNP) Gross national product minus depreciation; a nation's total product minus what is required to maintain the value of its capital stock.

net taxes (T) Taxes paid by firms and households to the government minus transfer payments made to households by the government.

New Economic Policy The Soviet economic policy in effect between 1921 and 1928; characterized by decentralization and a retreat to a market orientation.

nominal GDP Gross domestic product measured in current dollars.

nominal wage rate The wage rate in current dollars.

nondurable goods Goods that are used up fairly quickly, such as food and clothing.

nonexcludable A characteristic of most public goods: Once a good is produced, no one can be excluded from enjoying its benefits.

nonlabor, or nonwage, income Any income that is received from sources other than working—inheritances, interest, dividends, transfer payments, and so on.

nonresidential investment Expenditures by firms for machines, tools, plants, and so on.

nonrival in consumption A characteristic of public goods: One person's enjoyment of the benefits of a public good does not interfere with another's consumption of it.

nonsynchronization of income and spending The mismatch between the timing of money inflow to the household and the timing of money outflow for household expenses.

normal goods Goods for which demand goes up when income is higher and for which demand goes down when income is lower.

normal rate of profit, or normal rate of return A rate of profit that is just sufficient to keep owners and investors satisfied. For relatively risk-free firms, it should be nearly the same as the interest rate on risk-free government bonds.

normative economics An approach to economics that analyzes outcomes of economic behavior, evaluates them as good or bad, and may prescribe courses of action. Also called policy economics.

North American Free-Trade Agreement (NAFTA) An agreement signed by the United States, Mexico, and Canada in which the three countries agreed to establish all of North America as a free-trade zone.

not in the labor force People who are not looking for work, either because they do not want a job or because they have given up looking.

occupational segregation The concentration of men and women in certain occupations. Women are concentrated in administrative support positions; men in executive, administrative, and management positions.

Ockham's razor The principle that irrelevant detail should be cut away.

Okun's Law The theory, put forth by Arthur Okun, that the unemployment rate decreases about one percentage point for every 3% increase in real GDP. Later research and data have shown that the relationship between output and unemployment is not as stable as Okun's "law" predicts.

oligopoly An industry structure (or market organization) with a small number of (usually) large firms producing products that range from highly differentiated (automobiles) to standardized (copper). In general, entry of new firms into an oligopolistic industry is difficult but possible.

on-the-job training The principal form of human capital investment financed primarily by firms.

Open Market Desk The office in the New York Federal Reserve Bank from which government securities are bought and sold by the Fed.

open market operations The purchase and sale by the Fed of government securities in the open market; a tool used to expand or contract the amount of reserves in the system and thus the money supply.

operating profit (or loss) or net operating revenue Total revenue minus total variable cost ($TR - TVC$).

opportunity cost That which we give up, or forgo, when we make a choice or a decision.

optimal level of provision for public goods The level at which resources are drawn from the production of other goods and services only to the extent that people want the public good and are willing to pay for it. At this level, society's willingness to pay per unit is equal to the marginal cost of producing the good.

optimal method of production The production method that minimizes cost.

optimal scale of plant The scale of plant that minimizes cost.

outputs Usable products.

Pareto efficiency or Pareto optimality A condition in which no change is possible that will make some members of society better off without making some other members of society worse off.

partial equilibrium analysis The process of examining the equilibrium conditions in individual markets and for households and firms separately.

partnership A form of business organization in which there is more than one proprietor. The owners are responsible jointly and separately for the firm's obligations.

patent A barrier to entry that grants exclusive use of the patented product or process to the inventor.

per capita GDP or GNP A country's GDP or GNP divided by its population.

per se rule A rule enunciated by the courts declaring a particular action or outcome to be a *per se* (intrinsic) violation of anti-trust law, whether the result is reasonable or not.

perfect competition An industry structure (or market organization) in which there are many firms, each small relative to the industry, producing virtually identical products and in which no firm is large enough to have any control over prices. In perfectly competitive industries, new competitors can freely enter and exit the market.

perfect knowledge The assumption that households possess a knowledge of the qualities and prices of everything available in the market and that firms have all available information regarding wage rates, capital costs, and output prices.

perfect substitutes Identical products.

perfectly contestable market A market in which entry and exit are costless.

perfectly elastic demand Demand in which quantity demanded drops to zero at the slightest increase in price.

perfectly inelastic demand Demand in which quantity demanded does not respond at all to a change in price.

permanent income The average level of one's expected future income stream.

personal consumption expenditures (C) A major component of GDP: expenditures by consumers on goods and services.

personal income The total income of households. Equals (national income) minus (corporate profits minus dividends) minus (social insurance payments) plus (interest income received from the government and households) plus (transfer payments to households). The income received by households after paying social insurance taxes but before paying personal income taxes.

personal saving The amount of disposable income that is left after total personal spending in a given period.

personal saving rate The percentage of disposable personal income that is saved. If the personal saving rate is low, households are spending a large amount relative to their incomes; if it is high, households are spending cautiously.

Phillips Curve A graph showing the relationship between the inflation rate and the unemployment rate.

physical or tangible capital Material things used as inputs in the production of future goods and services. The major categories of physical capital are nonresidential structures, durable equipment, residential structures, and inventories.

planned aggregate expenditure (AE) The total amount the economy plans to spend in a given period. Equal to consumption plus planned investment: $AE \equiv C + I$.

plant-and-equipment investment Purchases by firms of additional machines, factories, or buildings within a given period.

policy mix The combination of monetary and fiscal policies in use at a given time.

positive economics An approach to economics that seeks to understand behavior and the operation of systems without making judgments. It describes what exists and how it works.

post hoc, ergo propter hoc Literally, "after this (in time), therefore because of this." A common error made in thinking about causation: If Event A happens before Event B happens, it is not necessarily true that A caused B.

potential output, or potential GDP The level of aggregate output that can be sustained in the long run without inflation.

poverty line The officially established income level that distinguishes the poor from the non-poor. It is set at three times the cost of the Department of Agriculture's minimum food budget.

preferred provider organization (PPO) A managed health-care plan in which an employer or insurance company establishes a network of doctors and hospitals to provide a broad set of medical services for a flat fee per participant. In return for the lower fee, the doctors and hospital who join the PPO network expect to receive a larger volume of patients.

price The amount that a product sells for per unit. It reflects what society is willing to pay.

price ceiling A maximum price that sellers may charge for a good, usually set by government.

price discrimination Occurs when a firm charges different buyers different prices for the same product. Such strategies are illegal if they drive out competition.

price elasticity of demand The ratio of the percentage change in quantity demanded to the percentage change in price.

price feedback effect The process by which a domestic price increase in one country can "feed back" on itself through export and import prices. An increase in the price level in one country can drive up prices in other countries. This in turn increases the price level in the first country.

price index A measurement showing how the average price of a bundle of goods changes over time.

price leadership A form of oligopoly in which one dominant firm sets prices and all the smaller firms in the industry follow its pricing policy.

price rationing The process by which the market system allocates goods and services to consumers when quantity demanded exceeds quantity supplied.

price surprise The actual price level minus the expected price level.

principle of neutrality All else equal, taxes that are neutral with respect to economic decisions (that is, taxes that do not distort economic decisions) are generally preferable to taxes that distort economic decisions. Taxes that are not neutral impose excess burdens.

principle of second best The fact that a tax distorts an economic decision does not always imply that such a tax imposes an excess burden. If previously existing distortions exist, such a tax may actually improve efficiency.

private good A product produced by firms for sale to individual households. People can be excluded from the benefits of a private good if they do not pay for it.

private sector Includes all independently owned profit-making firms, nonprofit organizations, and households; all the decision-making units in the economy that are not part of the government.

privatization The transfer of government business to the private sector.

produce-marketing boards The channels through which the governments of some developing countries buy domestic farm output and then sell it to urban residents at government-controlled prices.

producer price indexes (PPIs) Measures of prices that producers receive for products at all stages in the production process.

producers Those people or groups of people, whether private or public, who transform resources into usable products.

product or output markets The markets in which goods and services are exchanged.

product differentiation A strategy that firms use to achieve market power. Accomplished by producing products that have distinct positive identities in consumers' minds.

production The process by which resources are transformed into useful forms.

production function or total product function A numerical or mathematical expression of a relationship between inputs and outputs. It shows units of total product as a function of units of inputs.

production possibility frontier (ppf) A graph that shows all the combinations of goods and services that can be produced if all of society's resources are used efficiently.

production technology The relationship between inputs and outputs.

productivity, or labor productivity Output per worker hour; the amount of output produced by an average worker in one hour.

productivity of an input The amount of output produced per unit of an input.

profit The difference between total revenues and total costs.

progressive tax A tax whose burden, expressed as a percentage of income, increases as income increases.

property income Income from the ownership of real property and financial holdings. It takes the form of profits, interest, dividends, and rents.

proportional tax A tax whose burden is the same proportion of income for all households.

proprietors' income The income of unincorporated businesses.

proprietorship A form of business organization in which a person simply sets up to provide goods or services at a profit. In a proprietorship, the proprietor (or owner) is the firm. The assets and liabilities of the firm are the owner's assets and liabilities.

protection The practice of shielding a sector of the economy from foreign competition.

public assistance, or welfare Government transfer programs that provide cash benefits to (1) families with dependent children whose incomes and assets fall below a very low level and (2) the very poor regardless of whether or not they have children.

public choice theory An economic theory that proceeds on the assumption that the public officials who set economic policies and regulate the players act in their own self-interest, just as firms do.

public goods, or social goods Goods or services that bestow collective benefits on members of society; they are, in a sense, collectively consumed. Generally, no one can be excluded from enjoying their benefits. The classic example is national defense.

public sector Includes all agencies at all levels of government—federal, state, and local.

purchasing-power-parity theory A theory of international exchange that holds that exchange rates are set so that the price of similar goods in different countries is the same.

pure monopoly An industry with a single firm that produces a product for which there are no close substitutes and in which significant barriers to entry prevent other firms from entering the industry to compete for profits.

pure rent The return to any factor of production that is in fixed supply.

quantity demanded The amount (number of units) of a product that a household would buy in a given period if it could buy all it wanted at the current market price.

quantity supplied The amount of a particular product that a firm would be willing and able to offer for sale at a particular price during a given time period.

quantity theory of money The theory based on the identity $M \cdot V \equiv P \cdot Y$ and the assumption that the velocity of money (V) is constant (or virtually constant).

queuing A nonprice rationing mechanism that uses waiting in line as a means of distributing goods and services.

quota A limit on the quantity of imports.

racial covenants Provisions spelled out in property deeds that prohibit sale of that property to members of specific racial or ethnic groups.

rate of exploitation The ratio of surplus value to the value of labor power.

ration coupons Tickets or coupons that entitle individual persons to purchase a certain amount of a given product per month.

rational-expectations hypothesis The hypothesis that people know the "true model" of the economy and that they use this model to form their expectations of the future.

Rawlsian justice A theory of distributional justice that concludes that the social contract emerging from the "original position" would call for an income distribution that would maximize the well-being of the worst-off member of society.

real business cycle theory An attempt to explain business-cycle fluctuations under the assumptions of complete price and wage flexibility and rational expectations. It emphasizes shocks to technology and other shocks.

real GDP A measure of GDP that removes the effects of price changes from changes in nominal GDP.

real interest rate The difference between the interest rate on a loan and the inflation rate.

real wage rate The amount that the nominal wage rate can buy in terms of goods and services.

real wealth, or real balance, effect The change in consumption brought about by a change in real wealth that results from a change in the price level.

recession Roughly, a period in which real GDP declines for at least two consecutive quarters. Marked by falling output and rising unemployment.

recognition lag The time it takes for policy makers to recognize the existence of a boom or a slump.

regressive tax A tax whose burden, expressed as a percentage of income, falls as income increases.

relative-wage explanation of unemployment An explanation for sticky wages (and therefore unemployment): If workers are concerned about their wages relative to other workers in other firms and industries, they may be unwilling to accept a wage cut unless they know that all other workers are receiving similar cuts.

rent-seeking behavior Actions taken by households or firms to preserve extranormal profits

rental income The income received by property owners in the form of rent.

required reserve ratio The percentage of its total deposits that a bank must keep as reserves at the Federal Reserve.

reserves The deposits that a bank has at the Federal Reserve bank plus its cash on hand.

residential investment Expenditures by households and firms on new houses and apartment buildings.

resources or inputs Anything provided by nature or previous generations that can be used directly or indirectly to satisfy human wants.

response lag The time that it takes for the economy to adjust to the new conditions after a new policy is implemented; the lag that occurs because of the operation of the economy itself.

retained earnings The profits that a corporation keeps, usually for the purchase of capital assets. Also called *undistributed profits*.

revenue, or total revenue Receipts from the sale of a product ($P \times Q$).

rule of reason The criterion introduced by the Supreme Court in 1911 to determine whether a particular action was illegal ("unreasonable") or legal ("reasonable") within the terms of the Sherman Act.

run on a bank Occurs when many of those who have claims on a bank (deposits) present them at the same time.

saving (S) The part of its income that a household does not consume in a given period. Distinguished from *savings,* which is the current stock of accumulated saving.

services The things we buy that do not involve the production of physical things, such as legal and medical services and education.

shares of stock Financial instruments that give to the holder a share in the firm's ownership and therefore the right to share in the firm's profits.

Sherman Act Passed by Congress in 1890, the act declared every contract or conspiracy to restrain trade among states or nations illegal and declared any attempt at monopoly, successful or not, a misdemeanor. Interpretation of which specific behaviors were illegal fell to the courts.

shift of a demand curve The change that takes place in a demand curve when a new relationship between quantity demanded of a good and the price of that good is brought about by a change in the original conditions.

shock therapy The approach to transition from socialism to market capitalism that advocates rapid deregulation of prices, liberalization of trade, and privatization.

short run The period of time for which two conditions hold: The firm is operating under a fixed scale (fixed factor) of production and firms can neither enter nor exit an industry.

short-run industry supply curve The sum of marginal cost curves (above *AVC*) of all the firms in an industry.

shut-down point The lowest point on the average variable cost curve. When price falls below the minimum point on *AVC*, total revenue is insufficient to cover variable costs and the firm will shut down and bear losses equal to fixed costs.

Smoot-Hawley tariff The U.S. tariff law of the 1930s, which set the highest tariffs in U.S. history (60 percent). It set off an international trade war and caused the decline in trade that is often considered a cause of the worldwide depression of the 1930s.

social capital, or infrastructure Capital that provides services to the public. Most social capital takes the form of public works (roads and bridges) and public services (police and fire protection).

social choice The problem of deciding what society wants. The process of adding up individual preferences to make a choice for society as a whole.

social, or implicit, contracts Unspoken agreements between workers and firms that firms will not cut wages.

social insurance, or payroll, taxes Taxes levied at a flat rate on wages and salaries. Proceeds support various government-administrated social-benefit programs, including the social security system and the unemployment benefits system.

social overhead capital Basic infrastructure projects such as roads, power generation, and irrigation systems.

social security system The federal system of social insurance programs. It includes three separate programs that are financed through separate trust funds: the Old Age and Survivors Insurance program (OASI), the Disability Insurance program (DI), and the Health Insurance program (HI, or Medicare).

socialist economy An economy in which most capital is owned by the government rather than by private citizens. Also called social ownership.

sources side/uses side The impact of a tax may be felt on one or the other or on both sides of the income equation. A tax may cause net income to fall (damage on the sources side), or it may cause prices of goods and services to rise so that income buys less (damage on the uses side).

speculation motive One reason for holding bonds instead of money: Because the market value of interest-bearing bonds is inversely related to the interest rate, investors may wish to hold bonds when interest rates are high with the hope of selling them when interest rates fall.

spreading overhead The process of dividing total fixed costs by more units of output. Average fixed cost declines as *q* rises.

stability A condition in which output is steady or growing, with low inflation and full employment of resources.

stabilization policy A term used to describe both monetary and fiscal policy, the goals of which are to smooth out fluctuations in output and employment and to keep prices as stable as possible.

stabilization program An agreement between a borrower country and the International Monetary Fund in which the country agrees to revamp its economic policies to provide incentives for higher export earnings and lower imports.

stagflation Occurs when the overall price level rises rapidly (inflation) during periods of recession or high and persistent unemployment (stagnation).

sticky prices Prices that do not always adjust rapidly to maintain equality between quantity supplied and quantity demanded.

sticky wages The downward rigidity of wages as an explanation for the existence of unemployment.

store of value An asset that can be used to transport purchasing power from one time period to another.

structural adjustment A series of programs in developing nations designed to (1) reduce the size of their public sectors through privatization and/or expenditure reductions, (2) decrease their budget deficits, (3) control inflation, and (4) encourage private saving and investment through tax reform.

structural deficit The deficit that remains at full employment.

structural unemployment The portion of unemployment that is due to changes in the structure of the economy that result in a significant loss of jobs in certain industries.

subsidies Payments made by the government for which it receives no goods or services in return.

substitutable inputs Factors of production that can be used in place of each other.

substitutes Goods that can serve as replacements for one another; when the price of one increases, demand for the other goes up.

substitution effect of higher wages Consuming an additional hours of leisure means sacrificing the wages that would be earned by working. Thus, when the wage rate rises leisure becomes a more expensive commodity, and households may "buy" less of it. This means working more.

sunk costs Costs that cannot be avoided, regardless of what is done in the future, because they have already been incurred. Another name for fixed costs in the short run because firms have no choice but to pay them.

supply curve A graph illustrating how much of a product a firm will supply at different prices.

supply schedule A table showing how much of a product firms will supply at different prices.

supply-side policies Government policies that focus on aggregate supply and increasing production rather than stimulating aggregate demand.

surplus value The profit a capitalist earns by paying workers less than the value of what they produce.

sustained inflation Occurs when the overall price level continues to rise over some fairly long period of time.

tacit collusion *Collusion* occurs when price- and quantity-fixing agreements among producers are explicit. *Tacit collusion* occurs when such agreements are implicit.

tariff A tax on imports.

tax base The measure or value upon which a tax is levied.

tax incidence The ultimate distribution of tax's burden.

tax multiplier The ratio of change in the equilibrium level of output to a change in taxes.

tax rate structure The percentage of a tax base that must be paid in taxes—25% of income, for example.

tax shifting Occurs when households can alter their behavior and do something to avoid paying a tax.

technological change The introduction of new methods of production or new products intended to increase the productivity of existing inputs or to raise marginal products.

terms of trade The ratio at which a country can trade domestic products for imported products.

theory of comparative advantage Ricardo's theory that specialization and free trade will benefit all trading parties, even those that may be absolutely more efficient producers.

three basic questions The questions that all societies must answer: (1) What will be produced? (2) How will it be produced? (3) Who will get what is produced?

Tiebout hypothesis An efficient mix of public goods is produced when local land/housing prices and taxes come to reflect consumer preferences just as they do in the market for private goods.

tight monetary policy Fed policies that contract the money supply in an effort to restrain the economy.

time lags Delays in the economy's response to stabilization policies.

total cost (*TC*) Fixed costs plus variable costs.

total fixed costs (*TFC*), or overhead The total of all costs that do not change with output, even if output is zero.

total revenue (*TR*) The total amount that a firm takes in from the sale of its product: The price per unit times the *q*uantity of output the firm decides to produce ($P \times q$).

total utility The total amount of satisfaction obtained from consumption of a good or service.

total variable cost (*TVC*) The total of all costs that depend on or vary with output in the short run.

total variable cost curve A graph that shows the relationship between total variable cost and the level of a firm's output.

trade deficit Occurs when a country's exports of goods and services are less than its imports of goods and services in a given period.

trade feedback effect The tendency for an increase in the economic activity of one country to lead to a worldwide increase in economic activity.

trade surplus The situation when a country exports more than it imports.

tragedy of commons The idea that collective ownership may not provide the proper private incentives for efficiency because individuals do not bear the full costs of their own decisions but do enjoy the full benefits.

transaction motive The main reason that people hold money–to buy things.

transfer payments Cash payments made by the government to people who do not supply goods, services, or labor in exchange for these payments. They include social security benefits, veterans' benefits, and welfare payments.

Treasury bonds, notes, and bills Promissory notes issued by the federal government when it borrows money.

trust An arrangement in which shareholders of independent firms agree to give up control of their stock in exchange for trust certificates that entitle them to a share of the trust's common profits. A group of trustees then operates the combined firm as a monopoly, controlling output and setting price.

U.S.-Canadian Free-Trade Agreement An agreement in which the United States and Canada agreed to eliminate all barriers to trade between the two countries by 1998.

unconstrained supply of labor The amount a household would like to work within a given period at the current wage rate if it could find the work.

underground economy The part of the economy in which transactions take place and in which income is generated that is unreported and therefore not counted in GDP.

unemployed A person 16 years old or older who is not working, is available for work, and has made specific efforts to find work during the previous four weeks.

unemployment compensation A state government transfer program that pays cash benefits for a certain period of time to laid-off workers who have worked for a specified period of time for a covered employer.

unemployment rate The ratio of the number of people unemployed to the total number of people in the labor force.

unit of account A standard unit that provides a consistent way of quoting prices.

unitary elasticity A demand relationship in which the percentage change in quantity of a product demanded is the same as the percentage change in price (a demand elasticity of −1).

urban decline The deterioration of the private and social capital stock of a city that results from the lack of investment by both private and public sectors.

urban renewal Government programs designed to confront and correct the problems of urban decay.

utilitarian justice The idea that "a dollar in the hand of a rich person buys less than a dollar in the hand of a poor person." If the marginal utility of income declines with income, transferring income from the rich to the poor will increase total utility.

utility The basis of choice. The satisfaction, or reward, a product yields relative to its alternatives.

utility possibilities frontier A graphical representation of a two-person world that shows all points at which A's utility can be increased only if B's utility is decreased.

value added The difference between the value of goods as they leave a stage of production and the cost of the goods as they entered that stage.

value of labor power The wage rate, dependent on the amount of clothing, shelter, basic education, medical care, and so on required to produce and sustain labor power.

variable A measure that can change from time to time or from observation to observation.

variable cost Any cost that a firm bears that depends on the level of production chosen.

velocity of money The number of times a dollar bill changes hands, on average, during the course of a year; the ratio of nominal GDP to the stock of money.

vicious-circle-of-poverty hypothesis Suggests that poverty is self-perpetuating because poor nations are unable to save and invest enough to accumulate the capital stock that would help them grow.

voting paradox A simple demonstration of how majority-rule voting can lead to seemingly contradictory and inconsistent results. A commonly cited illustration of the kind of inconsistency described in the impossibility theorem.

wealth or net worth The total value of what a household owns minus what it owes. It is a stock measure.

weight The importance attached to an item within a group of items.

Wheeler-Lea Act (1938) Extended the language of the Federal Trade Commission Act to include "deceptive" as well as "unfair" methods of competition.

Willis-Graham Act (1921) Declared the telephone industry a natural monopoly and exempted telephone mergers from review.

World Bank An international agency that lends money to individual countries for projects that promote economic development.

yellow-dog contracts Contracts in which workers agree not to join unions.

SOLUTIONS TO EVEN-NUMBERED PROBLEMS

CHAPTER 1:

2. a, c, and f are examples of positive economics. b, d, and e are examples of normative economics because they make value judgments about the outcomes.

4. Total tax if 200 students are used = 200 students × 10 days × 5 hours per day × $5 per hour = $50,000. This would mean a tax of $5 per person ($50,000 ÷ 10,000 citizens).

  Total tax if 400 students are used = 400 students × 10 days × 5 hours per day × $5 per hour = $100,000. This would mean a tax of $10 per person.

  By paying an additional $5 in tax (i.e., $10 instead of $5), people avoid standing in line for an hour. If time is valued at $10 per hour, every citizen gains value of $5 when the waiting time is eliminated ($10 in benefits from reduced waiting time minus $5 in additional taxes). Moving from 200 to 400 students makes all citizens better off, and since the students are willing to work for $5, no one is worse off! Thus, switching to 400 students from 200 students would be efficient. One could argue that it is also fair because everyone is paying an equal amount, and because everyone gains from the higher tax in proportion to what he or she pays.

6. Equity is "fairness" in distributing burdens and benefits. Building the bridge would certainly be fair if those who used it and gained from its existence also paid the cost of building it.

Appendix:

2. The slopes are as follows:
  a. −2
  b. −4
  c. 6
  d. −1/500 or −.002

CHAPTER 2:

2. Both land and capital are inputs, but capital is something that is produced by human beings. Trees growing wild are like land; they are not produced by human beings. However, an orchard that is planted by human beings can be classified as capital. It took time, labor, and perhaps machinery to plant the orchard and to prune the trees.

4. **a.** A straight-line ppf curve intersecting the Y axis at 1000 units of luxury goods and intersecting the X axis at 500 units of necessity goods. These are the limits of production if all resources are used to produce only one good.

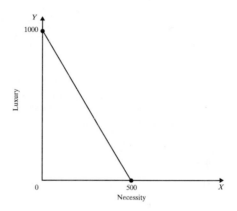

b. Unemployment or underemployment of labor would put the society inside the ppf. Full employment would move the society to some point on the ppf.

c. Answers will vary, but the decision should be based on the relative value of necessities and luxuries, and the degree of concern that all fellow citizens have enough necessities.

d. If left to the free market, prices would (at least ideally) be determined by market forces; incomes would be determined by a combination of ability, effort, and inheritance. It would be up to each individual to find a job and determine how to spend the income.

6. Answers will vary.

CHAPTER 3:

2. **a.** In 1992, there were:
  3,043 counties (7.8% of total)
  19,279 municipal governments (49.4% of total)
  16,656 townships (42.7% of total)
   50 states (.13% of total)
    1 federal government (.002% of total)
  Note: Total percentages do not add to 100 due to rounding.

b. The biggest functions of local government in 1992 were education, police, sewers and sanitation, highways, and fire protection.

c. People in different places may have different preferences or demands for assigning a function to local government as opposed to state or federal government.

4. Unions were the key opponents of GATT, especially unions in industries vulnerable to foreign competition (for example, sugar producers). Export industries, including the National Association of Manufacturers, favored GATT. Their reason: the theory of comparative advantage. (See Chapter 2.)

6. Government expenditure as a percentage of GDP increased from 31.8% in 1980 to 33.5% in 1994 (see Table 3.5). But government employment as a percentage of total employment decreased from 18.0% in 1980 to 16.8% in 1994. Government purchases of goods and services have fallen as a percentage of GDP in the two decades since 1970.

8. Disagree. Change the word *corporations* to *sole proprietorships* and the statement is true (see Table 3.1).

10. No matter how much the firm produces, it is so small relative to the total market that its output has no effect on the market price. Therefore, the firm must be a "price taker"; it accepts the market-determined price charged by all other firms as a given that it cannot influence.

12. Government spending could increase while taxes are decreasing due to deficit spending (borrowing). Government spending could increase while government employment is decreasing if government is purchasing goods and services from the private sector that it formerly produced itself.

CHAPTER 4:

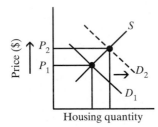

Housing quantity

2. a. A simple demand shift: same diagram for both cities.

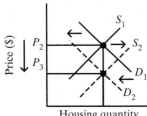

Housing quantity

b. Rightward shift of supply with new development; leftward shift of demand with falling incomes: same diagram for both cities.

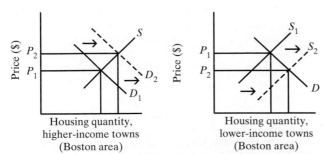

| Housing quantity, higher-income towns (Boston area) | Housing quantity, lower-income towns (Boston area) |

c. Trade-up buyers shift demand in the higher-income towns and supply in the lower-income towns.

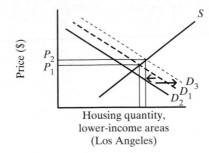

Housing quantity, lower-income areas (Los Angeles)

d. Falling income pushes demand to the left; more households push demand to the right. The rightward shift is stronger.

4. a. This sequence confuses changes in demand (shifts of the demand curve) with changes in quantity demanded (movements along a demand curve). First, a demand *shift* does cause price to rise. As price rises, the *quantity supplied* increases along the supply curve, and the *quantity demanded* declines along the demand curve as the market moves to reestablish equilibrium. Nothing here suggests that demand shifts back down.

b. This sequence confuses a change in price (per unit) with a change in total spending on meat. When price falls, the *quantity demanded* increases along the demand curve. Thus, the total amount spent (price × quantity demanded) depends on whether quantity demanded goes up by more than price per unit falls. Total spending could increase if demand responds strongly to the lower price.

6. If the price of tobacco is supported by limiting land used to grow it, then the supply curve for tobacco shifts to the left. The anti-smoking publicity works to shift the demand curve to the left. Both of these policies work together to reduce consumption of tobacco.

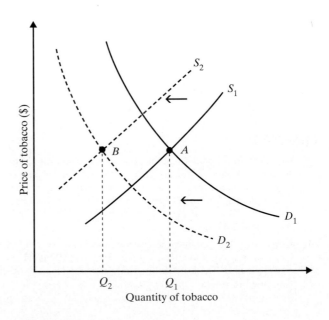

Quantity of tobacco

8. a.

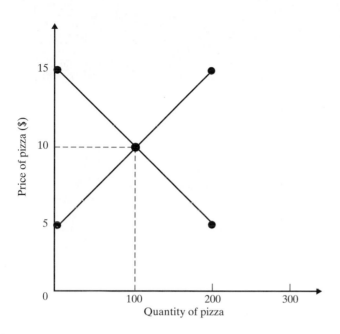

Price of pizza ($) vs Quantity of pizza

b. $Q_d = Q_s \rightarrow 300 - 20P = 20P - 100 \rightarrow P = \$10$. Substitute $P = \$10$ into either the demand or supply equation to get $Q = 100$.

c. With $P = \$15$, producers would want to supply $20(15) - 100 = 200$ pizzas, but consumers would want to buy $300 - 20(15) = 0$ pizzas. There would be an excess supply of pizzas, which would bring the price down. As the price decreased, quantity supplied would decrease while quantity demanded would increase until both were equal at a price of $10 and quantity of 100.

d. The new market demand for pizzas would be $Q_d = 600 - 40P$.

e. $Q_d = Q_s \rightarrow 600 - 40P = 20P - 100 \rightarrow P = 700/60 = \$11.66$. Substitute $P = \$11.67$ into either the demand or supply equation to get $Q = 133.2$.

CHAPTER 5:

2. Answers will vary. But scalping—regardless of its morality—helps to eliminate shortages by creating a "market" where the price can rise to its equilibrium value. Anyone willing to pay the equilibrium price should be able to obtain a ticket. Also, by allowing price rationing to work somewhat, scalping reduces the need for waiting in line, and so results in less wasted time.

4. Absolutely not. This statement confuses a shift of demand with change in quantity demanded along a demand curve. The demand for blue jeans shifted up, causing price to rise.

CHAPTER 6:

2. Answers will vary.

4. This could occur if relatively more blue-collar employees were laid off, so that the proportion of (lower-paid) white-collar em-

ployees in the company's work force actually increased. This example points out how looking only at broad macroeconomic aggregates can be misleading.

6. Wars result in high levels of government spending, which helps to increase total spending in the economy.

*8. When demand shifts to the right in a market, prices tend to rise. Higher interest rates make buying a car or a home more expensive to those who must borrow to finance those items. Thus, high interest rates tend to shift demand curves back to the left, taking pressure off prices.

CHAPTER 7:

2. Every payment made by a buyer becomes income for the seller. Thus, the dollar value of the purchases of new goods and services in a year must be the dollar value of the income generated in that year.

4. a. 1994: 100 1995: 142   percentage change: 42%

b. 1994: 100 1995: 123.89 percentage change: 23.89%

c. 1994: 100 1995: 144   percentage change: 44%

d. 1994: 100 1995: 125.63 percentage change: 25.63%

e. 1994: 100 1995: 132.64 percentage change: 32.64%

f. 1994: 100 1995: 134.50 percentage change: 34.50%

g. With fixed-weight indexes, the percentage change in the index from year to year depends on the weights chosen and thus on the base year. We can see that the answers to (a) and (b) vary widely, as do those to (c) and (d).

There are reasons to feel that the index in (a) overstates the change in real output and that the index in (b) understates it. Goods whose output decreases (or increases slowly) because of slowly- or backward-shifting supply curves will have their relative prices increase (in our example, peaches). If we use the old prices as weights, we will tend to understate the importance of this decrease. Implicitly, we are assuming that all of the peaches given up are valued at the old price, which is not true. Likewise, if we use the new prices as weights, we overstate the importance of the production decline, because this says that all the units of peaches given up were valued at the new high price.

Fixed-weight price indexes that use old quantities as weights are generally taken as overestimates of the increase in the price level, because these indexes ignore consumers' opportunities to find substitutes for goods whose relative prices rise. Those that use current-year quantities as weights are taken to underestimate changes in the price level because they implicitly assume that the substitutes people chose for the goods whose relative prices rose are considered just as good as the "real thing."

The use of fixed-weight indexes poses special problems when used to make measurements over long periods of time, because the use of, say, 1950 weights for 1995's economy is not desirable.

The BEA's new approach does two things: First, it takes the (geometric) average of fixed-weight indexes, to deal with the overestimation and underestimation issues. (We can see that real GDP is between the answers to [a] and [b], and the GDP price index is between [c] and [d].) Second, it "updates" the base years for the fixed-weight indexes every time it makes a new calculation, to ensure that the weights remain appropriate. That is, the indexes whose average it takes are those whose base years are the previous year and the current year.

6. **a.** 1994: 100
   1995: 150
   1996: 163.03
   Percentage change 1994–1995: 50%
   Percentage change 1995–1996: 8.69%
   Percentage change 1994–1996: 63.03%

   b. 1994: 100
   1995: 175
   1996: 218.53
   Percentage change 1994–1995: 75%
   Percentage change 1995–1996: 24.87%
   Percentage change 1994–1996: 118.53%

8. The pizza is entirely consumed in the year it was produced, while the car will last many years. To correct for this, we could count just the value of the services provided by the car *each year*. For example, if the car lasts 5 years, then 20% of its value could be counted in each year's GDP.

10. There is no right or wrong answer here. But counting environmental damage requires a dollar estimate of this damage, about which there will be little consensus.

CHAPTER 8:

2. "Full employment" is another term for the natural rate of unemployment. The idea behind this terminology is that if the only unemployment in the economy is the unemployment that comes about as the result of the normal working of the labor market, then there is no "unnecessary" unemployment. Labor is being "fully" utilized because the only unemployment that exists is the natural consequence of an efficiently-working market. Thus the economy can be at full employment with a 5% unemployment rate, provided that the 5% unemployment is frictional and structural only.

4. This is structural unemployment, which can sometimes exist for long periods, especially when workers must learn new skills to find jobs. The social costs of this unemployment might be greater than the costs of retraining these workers, providing some justification for government assistance.

6. Yes, inflation would still be a problem. There are other costs of inflation besides the redistribution of income that occurs when incomes are not indexed. These include the waste of time and resources spent coping with inflation, and the higher risk on financial assets in an inflationary environment. See the section on "Administrative costs and inefficiencies" under the heading "Costs of inflation."

8. Yes, both statements can be true. The labor force of Tappania may have grown faster than the number of employed, implying an increase in the number who are looking for work but not working, and an increase in the unemployment rate.

CHAPTER 9:

2. Actual investment includes unplanned changes in inventories that occur when sales fall short of firms' expectations.

4. **a.** $MPC = .8$; $MPS = .2$

b.

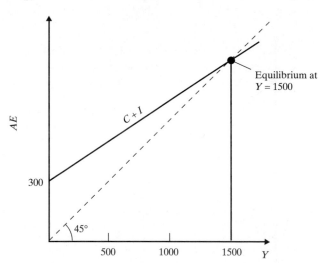

c. $\Delta Y = (1/MPS)\,\Delta I$. Multiplier $= 1/MPS = 1/.2 = 5$. In this case, with the multiplier equal to 5 and an increase in investment of 10, $\Delta Y = (5)(10) = 50$. Equilibrium Y increases from 1500 to 1550.

d. $S = Y - C$
$\quad = Y - (200 + .8Y)$
$\quad = -200 + .2Y$

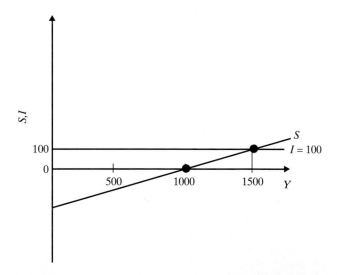

The equilibrium must be the same in both graphs because $Y = C + I$ and $S = I$ are the same condition. To see this, remember that $Y = C + S$ always. Substitute $C + S$ for Y in the equilibrium condition $Y = C + I$ to obtain $C + S = C + I$, which simplifies to $S = I$.

*6. No. *AE* is *planned* aggregate expenditure. If you add unplanned changes in inventory to it, the sum equals aggregate output (income).

CHAPTER 10:

2. a. $Y = 1000$, $Y_d = 800$, $C = 600$, $S = 200$, $I = 100$, $G = 200$. Since total spending $= C + I + G = 600 + 100 + 200 = 900$ is less than total output of 1000, one would predict that inventories will pile up, and firms will decide to reduce output.

b. Y would settle at 600. At this level of output, we would have $C = 300$, $I = 100$, and $G = 200$ so that $Y = C + I + G = 600$.

c. Cutting government purchases would make the fall in output worse! In particular, a cut of 25 would cause equilibrium Y to decline by $25(1/MPS) = (25)(4) = 100$. This would mean Y would decline to 500 instead of 600.

4. a. Equilibrium with government requires that output = spending, or that $Y = C + I + G$. Since we know that $Y = C + S + T$ by definition, then equilibrium also requires that $I + G = S + T$. To see if $Y = 200$ is an equilibrium, add $C + I + G$ to obtain $160 + 30 + 0 = 190$. This is *not* an equilibrium, because spending (190) is less than output (200). Alternatively, saving + taxes $= 40 + 0 = 40$, while investment + government spending $= 30 + 0 = 30$. Thus, $S + T$ is not equal to $I + G$.

In the coming months, we can expect output (Y) to decline and workers to be laid off. Equilibrium $Y = 150$. At $Y = 150$, $C + I + G = 0.8(150) + 30 + 0 = 150$.

b. Set $G = 10$ with taxes $= 0$. In this case, we would have $Y = C + I + G$ or $200 = 160 + 30 + 10$. (Note: There are other combinations of G and T that will bring equilibrium Y to 200, such as $G = 26$ and $T = 20$.)

c. Set $G = 20$ with taxes $= 0$. In this case, we would have $Y = C + I + G$ or $250 = 200 + 30 + 20$. Other combinations that would accomplish the same result include $G = 60$ and $T = 50$ or $G = 44$ and $T = 30$.

d. Yes. $Y = C + I + G$ ($200 = 160 + 40 + 0$). Also, $S + T = I + G$ ($40 + 0 = 40 + 0$).

e. We can get the answer directly from the multiplier:

$\Delta Y = \Delta G(1/MPS)$

$\Delta Y = (30)(5)$

$\Delta Y = 150$

The new level of Y is therefore $200 + 150 = 350$. C will be equal to $(.8)(350) = 280$, while $S = (.2)(350) = 70$.

f. Once again, we can get the answer directly from the tax multiplier:

$\Delta Y = \Delta T(-MPC/MPS)$

$\Delta Y = 30(-4)$

$\Delta Y = -120$. Y falls by 120. The new level of Y is therefore $200 - 120 = 80$. Disposable income is $80 - 30 = 50$, so $C = (.8)50 = 40$, while $S = (.2)50 = 10$. The change in GNP is larger when government spending changes by 30 than when taxes change by 30. This reflects the fact that the government spending multiplier is larger than the tax multiplier. A change in government spending affects ouput directly, while a change in taxes affects output indirectly, by a smaller amount, because households will reduce their spending by only a fraction of the tax change.

6. a. Govt. spending multiplier $= 1/.4 = 2.5$.

b. Govt. spending multiplier $= 1/(1 - .9) = 10$.

c. Govt. spending multiplier $= 1/(1 - .5) = 2$.

d. Tax multiplier $= -.75/(1 - .75) = -3$.

e. Tax multiplier $= -.9/(1 - .9) = -9$.

f. MPC must be .833. Tax multiplier $= -.833/(1 - .833) = -5.0$.

g. MPC must be .666. Government spending multiplier $= 1/(1 - .666) = 3.0$.

h. Output will increase by \$100 billion (use the balanced-budget multiplier, which has a value of 1).

CHAPTER 11:

2. Before the change, the bank is holding \$79.9 billion (10% of demand deposits) in reserve assets against demand deposits. Changing the reserve requirement does not increase or decrease the quantity of reserves. Rather, it changes the volume of deposits that can be held for each dollar of reserves. At an 11% reserve requirement, \$79.9 billion can support only about \$726 billion in demand deposits. Thus, the money supply would have to shrink by \$73 billion (\$799 billion − \$726 billion) to restore banks to compliance with the reserve requirement.

4. $M2$ includes everything in $M1$, plus savings accounts, money market accounts, and some other categories. A shift of funds between, say, savings accounts and checking accounts will affect $M1$ but not $M2$, because both savings accounts and checking accounts are part of $M2$.

*6. a. Money injected through open market operations results in a multiple expansion of the money supply only if it leads to loans, and loans can be made only if the new money ends up in banks as reserves. If the Fed buys a bond from James Q. Public, who immediately deposits the proceeds into a dollar-denominated Swiss bank account, the U.S. money supply won't expand at all. If the money ends up in his pockets or in his mattress, the expansion of the money supply will stop right there. If he had deposited the proceeds in a U.S. bank, excess reserves would have been created, stimulating lending and further money creation.

b. Reserves will increase by \$750 (75% of \$1000) and the multiplier is $1/(\text{required reserve ratio}) = 1/.12 = 8.333$. $\$750(8.333) = \$6,250$. Thus, the money multiplier is reduced to 6.25.

8. In addition to controlling the money supply, the Fed clears interbank payments, is responsible for many of the regulations governing banking practices and standards, and is the lender of last resort for the banking system. It is also responsible for managing exchange rates and the nation's foreign exchange reserves.

Answers to the second part of the question will vary.

CHAPTER 12:

2. If households believe that interest rates will rise, why should they lend money now? They will desire to hold more of their wealth as money for the time being, betting that they can get a higher interest rate if they wait. If they buy bonds now, they risk a capital loss (a decrease in the value of their assets), because bond prices fall when interest rates rise. When households hold money to speculate in this way, we call their motive for holding money the "speculation motive."

4. A recession is a decline in real GDP. When output falls, there is less economic activity and fewer transactions. Fewer transactions means that (*ceteris paribus*) money demand will fall. This will cause a leftward shift in the M^d curve, which results in a lower equilibrium interest rate (assuming that the money supply remains fixed).

6. Increasing T and lowering G would reduce the equilibrium level of Y (real GDP). Thus, Greenspan might have lowered interest rates to stimulate the economy if he wanted to prevent a recession. To lower interest rates, he would have needed to expand the money supply by engaging in open market operations (buying bonds), lowering the discount rate, or reducing the required reserve ratio.

CHAPTER 13:

2. a. The tax cut causes disposable income to rise and C to rise. $C + I + G > Y$, so inventories fall and output (Y) begins to rise. Increasing Y causes money demand to rise, putting upward pressure on r. Since the Fed does not accommodate, we get a higher Y but also a higher r, which causes I to fall, partially offsetting the effect of the tax cut on Y. (Final result: higher Y, higher r.)

b. The tax increase reduced disposable income and thus consumption. $C + I + G < Y$, so inventories build and output falls. A lower Y means lower money demand. At the same time that the Fed is increasing the money supply. Interest rates will fall sharply, causing I to rise, perhaps offsetting the effects of the initial tax increase on Y. (Final result: ambiguous Y, lower r.)

c. Similar to b. The drop in consumption cuts aggregate expenditure: $C + I + G < Y$, so inventories rise and Y falls. As Y falls, money demand drops. If the Fed holds M^s constant, r will fall. Here again, the lower r may stimulate I, causing I to rise and partially offsetting the initial decline in Y. (Final result: lower Y, lower r.)

d. The Fed expands the money supply. $M^s > M^d$, so r falls. Normally, the lower r might be expected to cause I to rise, but gloomy expectations and no need for new plant and equipment keep I low. Thus the link to the goods market is broken, and the monetary policy doesn't have much impact. (Final result: lower r, little or no change in Y.)

4. a. The decline in investment would be a reduction in aggregate expenditure, causing equilibrium output (income) to decrease in the goods market. In the money market, the drop in income would decrease the demand for money (shift the M^d curve to the left), causing the interest rate to fall and investment spending to rise back up somewhat. But the net effect would be a decline in output (income) and the interest rate.

b. Option 3 is the most expansionary, since the increase in the money supply works to offset the crowding-out effect. Option 2 would come next, but would involve some crowding out. Option 1 would be least expansionary, since the tax increase would decrease consumption spending. (Option 1 relies on the balanced-budget multiplier, which has a value of 1. Option 2 relies on the government spending multiplier, which is larger than 1.)

6. The Fed's tight monetary policy would drive up interest rates, discouraging investment and causing aggregate output to fall. The simultaneous expansionary fiscal policy would increase the government spending and consumption components of aggregate output, increasing money demand and driving up interest rates further. The policies have opposing effects on aggregate output, so the ultimate effect on Y depends on which effect is stronger. But both policies drive interest rates higher. (In 1981, as a result of this policy, the prime interest rate rose to 21.5%!)

CHAPTER 14:

2. a.

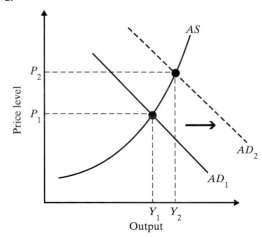

The price level will rise considerably; equilibrium GDP will rise only a little.

b.

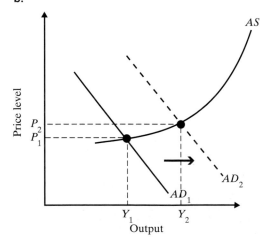

GDP will rise considerably; prices will rise only a little.

c.

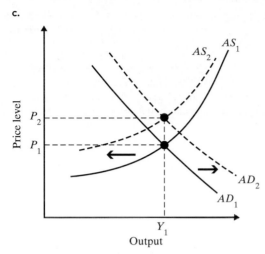

Output

The price level will rise considerably. Equilibrium GDP may fall, but by less than it would if the Fed did not accommodate.

d.

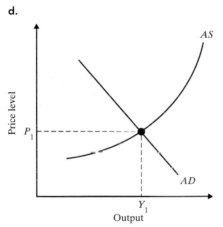

Output

Neither the price level nor output would change. The fiscal and monetary policies have opposing effects on the *AD* curve. If they are of equal strength, there will be no shift in the curve.

4. a.

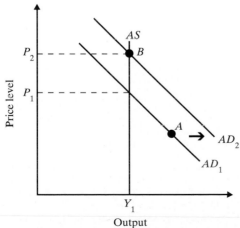

Output

The price level rises, money demand increases, *r* rises, and equilibrium GDP will fall. The expansionary monetary policy reverses the increase in *r* and the decline in Y, but increases the rise in the price level that will occur in the long run as the economy adjusts back to full employment (point *B*).

b.

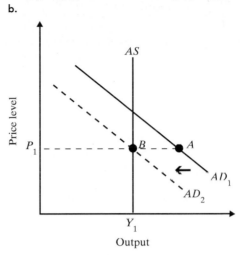

Output

The *AD* curve will shift to the left, and in the long run, GDP will decrease back to its full-employment level. If the shift in *AD* is great enough, the price level will not have to rise during the adjustment process.

c.

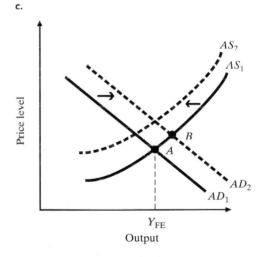

Output

Since the oil price shock is temporary, it will cause the *AS* curve to first shift leftward, and then shift rightward in the long run. The Fed's accommodation will cause a permanent rightward shift in the *AD* curve. The long-run result will be no change in GDP but a higher price level.

6. Expansionary monetary policy is likely to have a greater effect in country B. Because production costs adjust automatically to price increases in country A, the *AS* curve will be vertical. A rightward shift in the *AD* curve would cause an increase in prices without increasing output because costs increase at the same time as prices. In country B, input prices lag behind output prices, so the short-run *AS* curve is not vertical. In the short run, a rightward shift in the *AD* curve will cause an increase in output.

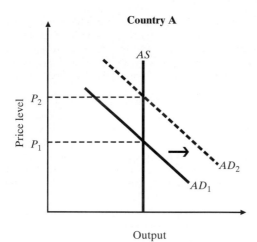

Country A

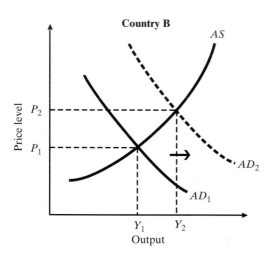

Country B

CHAPTER 15:

2. These factors indicate that Japan probably has a low rate of frictional unemployment. One part of the natural unemployment rate is made up of movers and workers changing jobs.

4. **a.** This policy would decrease frictional unemployment by helping employers and workers find each other. The time spent in job hunting would be reduced.

   b. This policy would decrease structural unemployment by making it profitable to hire workers who would otherwise not be productive enough to employ. (To some extent, however, teenage workers might be substituted for existing workers, thus lessening the impact on unemployment.)

   c. This policy would reduce structural unemployment by providing workers with skills needed in new or expanding industries.

   d. This policy would reduce structural and cyclical unemployment by providing jobs for people who would otherwise be unemployed. The program would cause a direct increase in the demand for labor. A worry might be that to pay them, taxes must be collected, thus reducing demand in the private sector and eliminating some private sector jobs.

   e. Reduces frictional unemployment by aiding workers in their job hunt.

   f. If the President is convincing, wage and price hikes would be moderated. The effect on unemployment would depend on which of the two—wages or prices—is affected more. If wage growth is affected more than price growth, then real labor costs would decrease and the demand for labor would increase, thus reducing unemployment. The reduction would be in all forms of unemployment—structural, cyclical, and frictional.

6. **a.** The effect of a higher wage tax on household labor force behavior is ambiguous. Workers may respond to the decrease in after-tax income by consuming more leisure, which now has a lower opportunity cost, so that labor supply will fall. However, workers are worse off. Since leisure is a normal good, consumption of it might fall and thus labor supply might rise.

   b. Improved child care reduces the opportunity cost of working. It is likely to attract more parents to the work force, increasing the labor force and labor supply. It would also reduce the demand for labor by increasing the full costs of hiring a worker. Over the short run, during which some wage rigidity is likely, the effect of an increase in labor supply and a decrease in labor demand would be an increase in the unemployment rate.

   c. Increased immigration will increase labor supply at a given wage rate without a corresponding increase in jobs. With short-run wage rigidity, unemployment will rise.

   d. Labor supply (and the labor force) should increase as more workers begin to seek even low-paid work to support themselves. With short-run wage rigidity, unemployment will rise.

   e. Increased investment might increase or decrease labor demand, depending on whether the new capital is more complementary or substitutable for labor. There would be no immediate impact on labor supply. The effect on employment and unemployment would be ambiguous.

8. We would not expect any increase in unemployment. The constancy of real wages means that we would move down along a vertical aggregate supply curve. If the prediction of recession causes households to cut back on consumption expenditures and business firms to cut back on investment spending, there will be a leftward shift of the aggregate demand curve. But as long as wages and other input prices fall as fast as prices do, there will be no decline in output or employment.

10. The trade-offs might be different for the two countries because social contracts and long-term explicit and implicit contracts may keep Japanese firms from laying off workers. Because the labor force in the United States is more transient, layoffs may be more likely. In Japan, a given reduction in inflation would probably require a lower increase in unemployment.

CHAPTER 16:

2. a. $Y = C + I + G$
$$= 100 + .8Y_d + 60 + 80$$
$$= 100 + .8[Y - (-150 + .25Y)] + 60 + 80$$
$$= 100 + .8Y + 120 - .2Y + 60 + 80$$
$$= 360 + .6Y$$
$$.4Y = 360$$
$$Y = 360/.4 = 900$$

$$D = G - T$$
$$= 80 - [-150 + .25(900)]$$
$$= 5$$

b. With $G = 75$:
$$Y = C + I + G$$
$$= 100 + .8Y_d + 60 + 75$$
$$= 100 + .8[Y - (-150 + .25Y)] + 60 + 75$$
$$= 100 + .8Y + 120 - .2Y + 60 + 75$$
$$= 355 + .6Y$$
$$.4Y = 355$$
$$Y = 355/.4 = 887.5$$

$$D = G - T$$
$$= 75 - [-150 + .25(887.5)]$$
$$= 3.125$$

The deficit is not zero because the cut in government spending shifts the *AD* curve to the left, decreasing aggregate output and causing a drop in the net tax revenue. Although the original cut in government spending would seem to eliminate the deficit, the resulting drop in GDP tends to raise the deficit, so the net effect is a deficit that is smaller, but not zero.

c. The deficit response index (DRI) is the amount by which the deficit changes in response to a one-dollar change in GDP. In this example, GDP fell by $12.5 billion in response to the decrease in government spending and caused a change in the deficit of $3.1 billion, so the DRI must be $3.1/12.5 = .25$.

To find the required change in G to eliminate the deficit, not that in this example, Δdeficit $= \Delta G - \Delta T = \Delta G - \Delta .25$ (ΔGDP). We also know that ΔGDP $= 2.5(\Delta G)$. Combining these two equations gives us Δ deficit $= \Delta G - .25 (2.5\Delta G) = .375 \Delta G$. We need Δ deficit to equal -5, so $-5 = .375(\Delta G)$ or $\Delta G = (-5/.375) = -13.33$. Government spending must be cut by $13.33 billion.

d. With $I = 55$:
$$Y = C + I + G$$
$$= 100 + .8Y_d + 55 + 80$$
$$= 100 + .8[Y - (-150 + .25Y)] + 55 + 80$$
$$= 100 + .8Y + 120 - .2Y + 55 + 80$$
$$= 355 + .6Y$$
$$.4Y = 355$$
$$Y = 355/.4 = 887.5$$
$$D = G - T$$
$$= 80 - [-150 + .25(887.5)]$$
$$= 8.125$$

Cutting government spending by the required amount (21.666) means that $G = 80 - 21.666 = 58.33$. Solving again for equilibrium GDP:

$$Y = C + I + G$$
$$= 100 + .8Y_d + 55 + 58.33$$
$$= 100 + .8[Y - (-150 + .25Y)] + 55 + 58.33$$
$$= 100 + .8Y + 120 - .2Y + 55 + 58.33$$
$$= 333.33 + .6Y$$
$$.4Y = 333.33$$
$$Y = 333.33/.4 = 833.33$$

4. States that must have balanced budgets are unable to use spending and taxing to offset local economic shocks. Moreover, an adverse shock that sends the state budget into deficit requires the state to raise taxes or cut spending, which will cut local spending and exacerbate the impact of the shock. The effect is therefore destabilizing.

If all states followed this philosophy, the effect would be destabilizing on a national basis. Adverse shocks would send the economy into recession, causing the federal deficit to swell. If states cannot pursue expansionary policies to help a nation out of the recession, then they must rely more heavily on the federal government to do so. Thus, a larger increase in the federal deficit will be necessary to stimulate the economy than would otherwise be the case.

6. Stabilization policy may be difficult to carry out because there are time lags in the economy's response to such policies. Stabilization policies can thus be destabilizing because they may affect the economy much later, when the adjustments are no longer desirable.

8. In all likelihood, the pattern will hold. Labor-market institutions probably explain much of the difference. In Japan, there has been a tradition of "permanent" employment, an understanding that firms do not lay off workers during normal cyclical downturns as they do in the United States and in Europe. In Europe, some claim that generous unemployment compensation and other forms of social welfare expenditures reduce the incentive to work. Others argue that European countries have been running a very tight monetary policy over time. Still others blame the differences on the power of unions in Europe to keep wages higher than equilibrium, creating involuntary unemployment.

CHAPTER 17:

2. When taxes increase (net wages decrease), one of the impacts is a reduction in income. If leisure is a normal good, the decrease in income will lead to less consumption of leisure, and therefore an increase in desired work hours. This serves to counteract the substitution effect of a decrease in wages, which lowers the opportunity cost of leisure and tends to decrease desired work hours.

4. The value of homes is an important component of household wealth. When home prices rise, household wealth rises and consumption tends to increase. When home prices fall, household wealth falls and consumption decreases. Since changes in consumption are changes in aggregate expenditure, they lead to changes in output and employment in the same direction.

6. A given consumption path requires a given amount of lifetime income to pay for it. But, given initial wealth, lifetime income is determined by working hours. This implies that income is not really an "independent" variable in the consumption function. Rather, the desire to consume and the desire to enjoy leisure together will determine how much income one will earn.

8. Expectations of future sales determine how much capital a firm will want to have in place in the future. To have this capital when it is needed, investment spending must take place in earlier periods. Since expectations of future sales are affected by government policy announcements, release of economic data, and "animal spirits"—all of which can change rapidly—the resulting investment spending is quite volatile.

10. Maintaining inventory stocks helps a firm maintain a smooth production level. When sales unexpectedly increase, goods can be sold out of inventory. When sales unexpectedly decrease, goods can be added to inventories. By smoothing production, a firm can save on the adjustment costs associated with frequent changes in capital stock and employment levels. The cost of this policy is the forgone interest from investing funds in inventory stocks instead of lending out the money in financial markets.

CHAPTER 18:

2. **a.** A tax cut of 10% would probably increase consumer spending, increase output, raise the price level, and reduce unemployment. These should push interest rates up, crowding out planned investment spending. The effect on labor supply depends on whether workers respond more strongly to the income effect (and consume more leisure) or to the substitution effect, which focuses on the opportunity cost of leisure (after-tax wages will increase). In general, however, a temporary tax cut is likely to have less impact than a permanent tax cut, so none of the changes will be large.

   b. Same as above, except that all of the effects would be larger.

   c. An expansionary monetary policy will lower interest rates and cause increased planned investment and higher aggregate output, reduced unemployment, and a higher price level. Increased output will drive up wages and increase labor supply (unless the income effect from increased output dominates), and consumers will respond to higher income with increased spending.

   d. An increase in transfer payments will cause an increase in consumption and a decrease in labor supply. The increased consumption will increase aggregate output. Once again, the tight monetary policy combined with a fiscal expansion will drive up interest rates, crowding out private investment.

4. The unemployment rate may have increased because improved job prospects encouraged discouraged workers to reenter the labor force and look for work. It is also possible that real wages rose, leading to an increase in labor supply, but at the same time excess labor prevented firms from doing any new hiring.

CHAPTER 19:

2. **a.** Clinton's tax increases and spending cuts would be fiscal contraction. With no change in Fed policy, output would decrease and unemployment would increase. If the Fed matches the fiscal contraction with a monetary expansion, lowering interest rates to stimulate investment, the decline in output could be avoided.

   b. Monetarists would worry about imperfect policy timing. Fed stimulation might take effect at the wrong time (e.g., after the economy has recovered from the impact of the fiscal contraction). Supply-siders would worry that higher tax rates would decrease the incentive to work and invest. Extreme supply-siders might worry that an increase in tax rates would decrease tax revenue and result in an even larger budget deficit.

   c. To evaluate the supply-side argument, you would need to see what happened to tax revenues and labor supply after the tax-rate increases. An increase in tax revenues, *ceteris paribus,* would contradict the view of extreme supply-siders. If labor supply did not decrease much, general supply-side arguments would be weakened. To evaluate the monetarist argument, you would need to see if investment spending increased as consumption spending declined (proper policy timing), or only after consumption began to recover (poor timing).

4. Nominal income $= M \times V = (\$1000)(5) = \$5000$. If we select the current year as our base year, real income is also $5000. If you are a strict monetarist, you believe V is constant. Therefore, a doubling of the money supply to $2000 will cause a doubling of nominal GDP to $(\$2000)(5) = \$10,000$. If, however, velocity is a function of the interest rate as well as institutional factors, then it cannot be assumed a constant. In this case, an increase in the money supply (which reduces interest rates) would lower velocity, so $M \times V$ would not increase by as great a percentage as M itself increased, and nominal GDP would rise by a smaller percentage than the money supply increased. If the money supply doubles (rises by 100%), nominal GDP will rise by less than 100 percent. (We cannot know how the rise in nominal GDP is apportioned between a rise in P and a rise in real GDP without knowing more about the current state of the economy.)

6. Reagan believed that the lower tax rates would provide incentives for households to work more hours and to save more and for firms to invest more. These actions would expand the supply of goods and services and, thus, expand aggregate income and the tax base. The tax base would rise by so much that tax revenues would actually rise despite the lower tax rates. Bush believed that incentives were important, but that the effects would not be large enough to raise revenues and reduce the deficit.

CHAPTER 20:

2.

TABLE 1

Y/L	GROWTH RATE
4.28	—
4.23	3.7
4.17	3.6
4.12	3.7

TABLE 2

Y/L	GROWTH RATE
4.28	—
4.41	3.9
4.53	3.9
4.66	3.9

TABLE 3

Y/L	GROWTH RATE
4.28	—
4.45	5.0
4.63	5.0
4.81	5.0

In Table 1, L is increasing faster than K and Y, so productivity is falling. In Table 2, K and Y are increasing faster than L, so productivity is growing. The productivity increase is due to more capital per worker. In Table 3, K and L are increasing at the same slow rate, but technology is pushing Y up faster than either is growing.

4. Assuming that the economy stays at full employment, the bill would cause the economy to produce more capital goods and fewer consumption goods. This would lead to a higher growth rate over time. The trade-off is less consumption today. There are also distributional consequences. Capital income earners (who have higher incomes on average) would benefit. The members of the higher-income households (who spend a smaller fraction of their incomes) would bear relatively less of the consumption-tax burden, while the members of the low-income households (who spend a higher fraction of their incomes) would bear relatively more of the consumption-tax burden.

6. High budget deficits are financed with private saving. That saving otherwise would have found its way through financial markets into private capital production. If the deficit is used to finance current expenditures like paying judges and congresspeople, it is not contributing to an expansion of output in the long run. The same is true of a tax cut, which is used to increase current consumption expenditures. But if the government used the money to build capital such as roads and bridges or to increase human capital through better education and job training, it would at least offset part of the reduction in private investment spending. Whether the net result for output growth is positive or negative depends on whether private capital or public capital has a higher rate of return. This is a subject of much debate, and would depend on the specific capital expenditures undertaken by the government.

CHAPTER 21:

2. **a.** Illinois would have an absolute advantage in both wheat and soybeans.

   b. In Illinois, taking one acre out of wheat and moving it into soybeans sacrifices 48 bushels of wheat for 39 bushes of soybeans. This is 48/39 = 1.23 bushels of wheat for each bushel of soybeans. In Kansas, the sacrifice is 40/24 = 1.66 bushels of wheat for each bushel of soybeans.

   c. Based on the calculations in b. above, Kansas has a comparative advantage in wheat, and Illinois has a comparative advantage in soybeans.

   d. Yes, the data are consistent with the conclusions in c. above. Kansas has more acreage devoted to wheat than soybeans, while in Illinois there is more acreage devoted to soybeans than to wheat. Although neither state completely "special-izes," each state seems to be devoting more of its resources to producing the good in which it has a comparative advantage.

4. Answers will vary.

6. **a.** The opportunity cost of a bottle of red wine is 1.5 bottles of white in France and 2 bottles of white in Germany. France, therefore, has a comparative advantage in red wine.

   The opportunity cost of a bottle of white wine is .66 bottles of red in France and .5 bottles of white in Germany. Germany, therefore, has a comparative advantage in white wine.

   b. No. At the current exchange rate, both white and red wine are cheaper in Germany. French citizens will want to import both types of wine from Germany, but Germans will not want to import French wine.

   c. In this situation, we would expect the price of the franc to decrease until French red wine became attractive to Germans while German white wine was still attractive to the French. (An exchange rate between 1.5 and 2 francs per mark would accomplish this.)

   d. In the long run, we would expect exchange rates to adjust until the French are exporting red wine to Germany, and the Germans are exporting white wine to France.

CHAPTER 22:

2. **a.** Answers can include an increase in U.S. incomes, an increase in British interest rates, a decrease in U.S. interest rates, a decrease in the British price level, and an increase in the U.S. price level.

   b. All of the above, except for the increase in U.S. incomes, would also cause the supply curve to shift to the left.

   c. If the exchange rate floats, none of these policies will affect the balance of payments. However, the two changes in interest rates listed in a. and b. above—which would raise the value of the pound without any other simultaneous change in import or export demand—would make British goods relatively more expensive and decrease Britain's trade balance (shrink the surplus, or increase the deficit).

4. **a.** The consumption function does not change, so instead of spending their money on Japanese goods, U.S. citizens will spend it on domestic goods. All else equal, this will stimulate U.S. output and decrease U.S. unemployment, and decrease output and employment in Japan.

   b. If income rises, consumers are likely to buy more imports as well as more domestic goods. Imports from Japan will increase somewhat after the initial decrease.

   c. If imports decrease, then the demand for yen will also decrease because importers will not need as many yen to purchase Japanese goods.

   d. The yen will depreciate and the dollar will appreciate. This gives U.S. consumers more buying power in the market for foreign goods. Consumers will buy more imports, causing a decrease in aggregate expenditure on domestic output. Output and employment in the United States will fall. The current account deficit will rise, but the total balance of payments will still sum to zero.

   e. The quota would have to increase U.S. output and employment, at least in the short run. The increase in the U.S. trade balance increases U.S. output and employment. This causes the dollar to appreciate, which works to decrease output and employment somewhat. But the only reason that the dollar appreciates is because of the improvement in the U.S. trade balance. Thus, it is logically impossible for the dollar to appreciate so much that the trade balance would not improve. And as long as the trade balance improves, U.S. output and employment increase.

6. **a.** $Y = C + I + G + (EX - IM)$
    $= 100 + .8(Y - 40) + 38 + 75 + 25 - .05(Y - 40)$
    $= 238 + .8Y - .8(40) - .05Y + .05(40)$
    $= 208 + .75Y$
    $.25Y = 208$
    $Y = 832$

    Government deficit = $G - T = 75 - 40 = 35$.
    Current account balance = $EX - IM$
    $= 25 - .05(832 - 40)$
    $= -14.6$

    b. The multiplier $= 1/[1 - (MPC - MPM)]$
    $= 1/[1 - (.8 - .05)]$
    $= 4$

    When G increases from 75 to 80, Y will increase by $5(4) = 20$. Imports will rise by $.05(20) = 1$.

    With the quota, the MPM is zero, so the multiplier $= 1/(1 - .8) = 5$. Y will rise by $5(5) = 25$. (This assumes that IM is greater than or equal to 40 without the quota, before the increase in G. Actually it is 39.6, but assuming $MPM = 0$ is a very close approximation.) Imports that rise with income act as a leakage and reduce the size of the multiplier.

    c. With $EX = 25$, we need $IM = .05(Y - 40) = 25$. This implies $Y = 540$. Income is currently 832, so it must be decreased by $832 - 540 = 292$. With a multiplier of 4, this will require a decrease in government spending of $292/4 = 73$.

CHAPTER 23:

2. **a.** Capital increases the productivity of labor. A given-sized labor force can produce more output, and output per capita rises.

    b. In a market economy, individual household savings decisions determine the pool of aggregate savings. Aggregate savings, in turn, is the amount made available for firms to purchase capital. Savings are matched to investment projects in financial markets, where the interest rate adjusts to equate total desired investment with total desired savings.

    c. In developing countries, a greater fraction of output is needed just to ensure the current population's survival. An increase in investment—which requires a decrease in current consumption—cuts dangerously close to this survival level of consumption, and at a minimum causes more discomfort than it would in developed countries.

    d. Answers will vary. Market-oriented economists would stress increased incentives for private investment (political stability, lower government budget deficit, and perhaps loans from abroad). Planning-oriented economists might stress government-directed projects, taxes on luxury goods, and capital controls designed to prevent capital flight to developed countries.

4. It is true that poor countries must accumulate capital in order to grow, but many poor countries do indeed have extra output available for savings. The problem is often that the available savings goes abroad (capital flight). Increased political stability and a more stable investment climate would help investment in the domestic economy. In addition, poor countries can get loans and other assistance from developed countries to help them accumulate capital.

6. A country should work to develop both its agricultural and its industrial sectors. Development of the agricultural sector can have high payoffs because it often requires little capital investment and directly benefits the poorest (rural) segment of society. Experience has shown that import substitution is a poor development policy. Its disadvantages include lessened competition in the domestic market, fewer jobs created, and expensive inputs for domestic industries.

    Many countries favor industry as a more direct route to growth in the capital stock, and also to emulate the production pattern of already developed countries. Import substitution is attractive because it lessens dependence on unstable foreign demand for exports.

8. Many recent famines have resulted from government policies. In some cases, keeping farm prices artificially low has led to a decrease in production. In other cases, a failure to invest in a distributional infrastructure has led to famine in outlying rural areas.

CHAPTER 24:

2. The speaker confuses political systems with economic systems. The Soviet economic system was one of socialism (government ownership of land and capital) and central planning (government direction of resource allocation). Totalitarianism is a political—not an economic—system in which the ruler exercises authoritarian control without the consent of those governed.

4. Socialism is an economic system in which the "means of production" (land and capital) are owned and controlled by government. The possible strengths: rapid growth from planned capital accumulation, internalization of external costs, more fair distribution of income (because no property income).

6. **a.** Disagree. Exactly the opposite has occurred. Since 1958, China has moved toward a decentralized industrial base. Since Tiananmen Square, China has cracked down on political dissent but it has encouraged private enterprise.

    b. The first two sentences are correct, the third is not. Japan's growth was primarily due to very high rates of saving and investment—capital accumulation.

    c. Disagree. The opposite is true. Economists agree about the six components of transition, but disagree about the sequencing and speed.

8. Disagree. While it is true that central planners can command a higher rate of national saving and capital accumulation, central planning requires keen and virtuous planners to ensure that scarce capital flows to where it is needed most. In a capitalist market economy, the self-interest of capital owners steers capital to those sectors where it is needed most—that is, those sectors offering the highest rate of return. Thus, while under central planning there might be more capital accumulation, it will not necessarily be the right kind of capital and will not necessarily find its way to the right places. Empirically, the United States grew faster than the USSR in the 1970s and 1980s.

Gross domestic product (GDP) (*continued*)
    and underground economy, 164–65
    uses of, 61
Gross investment, 149
Gross national product (GNP)
    definition of, 144
    and economic development level, 541
    Japanese, 582
    per capita, 541
    per capita GNP, 165
    relationship to gross domestic product (GDP),
        144–45, 153
    Soviet compared to U.S., 571–72
Gross private investment, 147

H

Hayek, Friedrich, 567
Health care reform, 369–70
Heckscher, Eli, 492
Heckscher-Ohlin theorem, 492
Heller, Walter, 121, 122, 124
History of economics, study of, 10
Homogeneous products, 53
Honda, use of excess labor by, 409
Hong Kong, export promotion by, 549
Hourly compensation, average, 1992–94, 60
Household, as opposed to firm, 74–75
Household consumption, 191–96, 391–402
    average propensity to consume in, 391
    and budget constraints, 399
    consumption function, 192–94, 196
    data on, 400–402
    determinants of, 191
    and employment constraints, 399
    government effects on, 398
    interest rate effects on, 396–98
    Keynesian view of, 391, 393, 400
    life-cycle theory of, 391–93
    marginal propensity to consume, 193
    and nonlabor income, 395–96
    and saving, 191–96
    and tax rate changes, 398
    and transfer payments, 398
    and wage increases, 394–95
    and wealth, 395–96
Household demand, determinants of, 76–84
    expectations, 81–82
    income, 80, 82–84
    price, 77–79, 84
    price of other goods/services, 80–81
    tastes/preferences, 81
    wealth, 80
Household income
    definition of, 80
    and household demand, 80, 82–84
Households. *See also* Household consumption;
        Household demand
    changes over time (1970-1994), 400–402
    and circular flow diagram of economy, 128–30
    definition of, 74
    housing investment by, 300, 401–2
    income calculated from gross domestic prod-
        uct (GDP), 152–54
    labor supply decisions by, 393–96, 398,
        402–3
    tax change effects on, 418
Housing
    interest rates and housing market, 300
    investment in, 300, 401–2

Human capital (human resources)
    development in Third World, 545
    and economic growth, 460–61, 465, 478, 479
    flight from developing nations, 545
    importance of, 27
Humphrey-Hawkins Act, 175
Hyperinflation, 125, 337
    in Germany, 183
    in Russian Republic, 256

I

Identity, definition of, 191
Immigration, and aggregate supply curve, 325
Imperfect information, and unemployment, 350
Implementation lags, 379–80
    definition of, 379
Implicit contracts, 347–48
    definition of, 347
Imports. *See also* Imports and exports
    in circular flow diagram, 130
    in gross domestic product (GDP), 67
    import prices and Phillips curve, 355–56
    import substitution, 548–49
    and multiplier, 430
    nature of, 130
    in planned aggregate expenditure, 228–29
    U.S., types of, 67–69
Imports and exports
    balance of payments, 506–11
    determinants of, 514–17
        of exports, 515
        of imports, 514–15
        price feedback effect, 516–17
        trade feedback effect, 515
    and developing nations, 548–49
        export promotion, 549
        import substitution, 548–49
    and equilibrium output, 511–17
    exchange rate effects on, 525
    in gross domestic product (GDP), 67, 150
    marginal propensity to import, 512
    price, influences on, 516
    price of
        and law of one price, 520–21
        purchasing-power-parity theory on,
            521–23
Import substitution, 548–49
Income. *See also* Aggregate income; Aggregate
        output (income); Equilibrium aggregate
        output (income); Equilibrium output
        (income)
    definition of, 44, 80
    and demand for money, 293
    dependence of tax revenues on, 238–39
    disposable income, 216–17
    in gross domestic product (GDP). *See* Income
        approach
    and household demand, 80, 82–84
    nonlabor income, 395–96, 419–20
    permanent income, 393
    personal income, 152–54
    proprietors' income, 151
    redistribution of, 46
    rental income, 151
Income approach, for calculating gross domestic
    product (GDP), 145–46, 150–52
Income distribution. *See also* Income
        redistribution
    in developing nations, 542

and economic growth, 474
    and inflation, 181–82
Income effect, 80, 82–84
    of interest rate increase, 397–98
    of tax reduction, 419
    of wage changes, 394
Income policies, definition of, 127–28
Income redistribution, 46
Income tax, corporate, 65–66
Income tax, individual, 64, 66
    and budget deficit, 230, 231–32
Income velocity of money, 438
Increasing returns to scale (economies of scale),
    463
Indexes. *See also* Price indexes; Quantity indexes
    base year for, 155
    definition of, 155
    in real GDP calculation, 155–59
    weight concept for, 156
Indirect taxes, components of, 151
Individual income tax. *See* Income tax, individ-
    ual
Inductive reasoning, 11
Industrial organization, study of, 10
Industrial policy, 469–70
    critics of, 470
    definition of, 470, 477
    in East Asia, 477–79
    proponents of, 470
Industrial Revolution, 5, 482
    and economic growth, 456–57
Industrial society, economic growth in, 457
Industry
    barriers to entry into, 55
    definition of, 53
    in developing nations, 547–48
    ease of entry into, 54
    exit from, 54, 55, 56
    infant industry, 500–501
    market organization in, 53–57
Inefficiency. *See also* Efficiency
    in free markets in general, 45–46
    and inflation, 184–85
    on production possibility frontier (ppf),
        34–35, 36
Infant industry, 500–501
    definition of, 500
Inferior goods, 80
Inflation, 178–82, 332–37
    causes of, 332–37
    in China, 580
    cost-push inflation, 334
    costs of, 186–88
    and currency debasement, 244
    definition of, 7, 125, 179, 332
    demand-pull inflation, 332
    and economic growth, 182
    example of 1994 worries over, 182
    and exchange rates, 523
    and expanding economy, 232
    and expectations, 335–36
    and Federal Reserve System, 256, 330, 337,
        361, 374–77
    and German reunification, 256
    global view of, 125, 182–83, 256, 338, 358,
        383, 388, 580
    hyperinflation, 125, 183, 256, 337
    and income distribution, 181–82
    measurement with price indexes, 180
    monetarist view, 440–41
    and money supply, 336–37, 338, 374–75, 441

PHOTO CREDITS

Chapters

Chapter 1, page 6, Kaku Kurith/ Gamma-Liaison, Inc.; page 10, Blake Sell/ Reuters/ Bettmann

Chapter 2, page 40, Greg Girard/ Contact Press Images; page 42, Shepard Sherbell/ Saba Press Photos, Inc.

Chapter 3, page 54, Jim Lott/ Seattle Times; page 60, Stephen Simpson/ FPG International; page 60, Walter Hodges/ Tony Stone Images

Chapter 4, Page 73, Ray NG; page 99, Mitch Kezar/ Tony Stone Images

Chapter 5, page 110, Benali- Swersey/ Gamma-Liaison, Inc.

Chapter 6, page 122, National Archives; page 123, Library of Congress; David Brauchli/ Reuters/ Bettmann

Chapter 7, page 145, Coutesy Honda of America Mfg. Inc.; page 165, Peter Blakely/ Saba Press Photos, Inc.

Chapter 8, page 181, Bettmann; page 181, Robert Cerri/The Stock Market

Chapter 9, page 210, Unilever, PLC, London

Chapter 10, page 228, Leduc/ Monkmeyer Press; page 233, Frank Fournier/ Contact Press Images

Chapter 11, page 244, Jack Fields/ Photo Researchers, Inc.; page 247, John Giordano/ Saba Press Photos, Inc.

Chapter 12, page 276, Michael Krasewitz/ FPG International

Chapter 13, page 300, Grantpix/ Monkmeyer Press

Chapter 14, page 321, Photo Researchers, Inc.; page 330, D. Walker/ Gamma-Liaison, Inc.

Chapter 15, page 346, National Archives; page 358, Andrew Moore/ Katz/ Saba Press Photos, Inc.

Chapter 16, page 370, Cynthia Johnson/ Gamma-Liaison, Inc.

Chapter 17, page 396, Andrew Popper; page 409, Andy Snow/ Saba Press Photos, Inc.

Chapter 18, page 418, Cynthia Johnson/ Gamma-Liaison, Inc.; page 425, Tod Buchanan

Chapter 19, page 442, Andrew Holbrooke/ The Stock Market; page 444, Al Francekevich/ The Stock Market

Chapter 20, page 460, James Marshall/ The Stock Market; page 467, Dennis B. Gray

Chapter 21, page 495, Y. Forestier/ Sygma; page 500, Rory Lysaght. Gamma-Liaison, Inc.

Chapter 22, page 518, Joel Stettenheim/ Saba Press Photos, Inc.; page 526, Patrick Robert/ Sygma

Chapter 23, page 543, Jack Picone Network/ Matrix International; page 556, Jacques Langeuin/ Sygma; page 558, Photo News/ Gamma-Liaison, Inc.

Chapter 24, page 565, D. Aubert/ Sygma; page 574, James Hill/ Colorific; page 581, Teri Stratford

Case Studies

Part 1, page 118, Vince Streano/ The Stock Market; page 133, Joseph Nettis/ Stock Boston

Part 2, page 186, Bob Daemmrich/ Stock Boston

Part 3, page 291, Anerican Numismatic Association

Part 4, page 388, Zigy Kaluzny/ Tony Stone Images; page 388, Peter Menzel/ Stock Boston

Part 7, page 587, Viviane Moos/ Saba Press Photos, Inc.; page 587, Peter Menzel/ Stock Boston